Communications
in Computer and Information Science   483

Shutao Li   Chenglin Liu   Yaonan Wang (Eds.)

Pattern Recognition

6th Chinese Conference, CCPR 2014
Changsha, China, November 17-19, 2014
Proceedings, Part I

 Springer

Volume Editors

Shutao Li
Hunan University, Changsha, China
E-mail: shutao_li@hnu.edu.cn

Chenglin Liu
Chinese Academy of Sciences, Beijing, China
E-mail: liucl@nlpr.ia.ac.cn

Yaonan Wang
Hunan University, Changsha, China
E-mail: yaonan@hnu.edu.cn

ISSN 1865-0929   e-ISSN 1865-0937
ISBN 978-3-662-45645-3   e-ISBN 978-3-662-45646-0
DOI 10.1007/978-3-662-45646-0
Springer Heidelberg New York Dordrecht London

Library of Congress Control Number: 2014954668

Typesetting: Camera-ready by author, data conversion by Scientific Publishing Services, Chennai, India

Printed on acid-free paper

Springer is part of Springer Science+Business Media (www.springer.com)

Message from the Chairs

Welcome to the proceedings of the 2014 Chinese Conference on Pattern Recognition (CCPR 2012) held in Changsha. CCPR 2014 was the sixth in the series, following CCPR 2007 (Beijing), CCPR 2008 (Beijing), CCPR 2009 (Nanjing), CCPR 2010 (Chongqing), and CCPR 2012 (Beijing). From 2012, CCPR is held every other year, to be alternated with the Asian Conference on Pattern Recognition (ACPR), which started in 2011.

In recent years, pattern recognition has increasingly become an enabling technology for many important and often mission-critical applications such as intelligent machines, data mining, business intelligence, Internet content search, public security monitoring, etc. The emergence of big data has triggered enormous demands on pattern recognition technology. The aim of the CCPR conference is to provide a forum for scientific exchange and presentation for pattern recognition researchers in China. CCPR started in 2007 but it can be dated back to the former editions in 1980s. In China, pattern recognition research commenced in the beginning of the 1970s. The China Association for Automation organized seven editions of the National Conference on Pattern Recognition and Machine Intelligence in the 1980s.

As in the previous CCPR events, CCPR 2014 received regular submissions and it invited internationally renowned researchers to give keynote speeches. The proceedings of CCPR 2014 are published by Springer in the *Communications in Computer and Information Science* (CCIS) series. We received 216 full submissions. Each submission was reviewed by three reviewers selected from the Program Committee and other qualified researchers. Based on the reviewers' reports, 112 papers were accepted for presentation at the conference, covering diverse fields, with 14 in pattern recognition fundamentals, 14 in feature extraction and classification, 21 in computer vision, 20 in image processing and analysis, seven in video processing and analysis, ten in biometric and action recognition, seven in biomedical image analysis, nine in document and speech analysis, and ten in pattern recognition applications.

We are grateful to the keynote speakers, Prof. Bo Zhang of Tsinghua University, Prof. Jón Atli Benediktsson of University of Iceland, Prof. Chris H.Q. Ding of the University of Texas at Arlington, and Prof. Zhi-Hua Zhou of Nanjing University. Thanks are due to the authors of all submitted papers, the Program Committee members and the reviewers, and the staff of the Organizing

Committee. Without their contributions, this conference would not have been a success. We are also grateful to Springer for publishing the proceedings, and especially to Ms. Celine (Lanlan) Chang of Springer Asia for her efforts in coordinating the publication.

September 2014   Yaonan Wang
                                                                 Cheng-Lin Liu
                                                                   Shutao Li

Organization

Sponsors

National Laboratory of Pattern Recognition
Hunan University

Co-sponsors

Technical Committee of Pattern Recognition of Chinese Association
for Artificial Intelligence
Hunan Association of Automation

Steering Committee Chair

Tieniu Tan   Institute of Automation of CAS

Steering Committee Members

Cheng-Lin Liu   Institute of Automation of CAS
Yuan-Yan Tang   University of Macau
Hongbin Zha   Peking University
Changshui Zhang   Tsinghua University
Nanning Zheng   Xi'an Jiaotong University

General Chair

Yaonan Wang   Hunan University

Program Chairs

Cheng-Lin Liu   Institute of Automation of CAS
Shutao Li   Hunan University

Organizing Chairs

Changyan Xiao   Hunan University
Xiaogang Zhang   Hunan University
Guocai Liu   Hunan University
Hongshan Yu   Hunan University

Publication Chair

Min Liu   Hunan University

Publicity Chair

Xiaoyan Liu   Hunan University

Organizing Committee

Zhigang Ling   Hunan University
Qiaokang Liang   Hunan University
Huali Li   Hunan University
Zhenjun Zhang   Hunan University
Xiaoqing Lu   Hunan University
Leyuan Fang   Hunan University
Li Zhou   Hunan University
Haiyan Zhang   Hunan University

Technical Program Committee

Xiang Bai   Huazhong University of Science and Technology
Hong Chang   Institute of Computing Technology of CAS
Shengyong Chen   Zhejiang University of Technology
Songcan Chen   Nanjing University of Aeronautics and
                                     Astronautics
Hong Cheng   University of Electronic Science and
                                     Technology of China
Jian Cheng   Institute of Automation of CAS
Dao-Qing Dai   Sun Yat-Sen University
Junyu Dong   Ocean University of China
Leyuan Fang   Hunan University
Jianjiang Feng   Tsinghua University
Jufu Feng   Peking University
Xinbo Gao   Xidian University
Xin Geng   Southeast University
Xiaofei He   Zhejiang University
Zhaoshui He   Zhejiang University
Baogang Hu   Institute of Automation of CAS
Kaizhu Huang   Xi'an Jiaotong-Liverpool University
Yunde Jia   Beijing Institute of Technology
Lianwen Jin   South China University of Technology
Xiaoyuan Jing   Wuhan University
Jun Li   Sun Yat-Sen University
Shutao Li   Hunan University

Wu-Jun Li	Nanjing University
Xuelong Li	Xi'an Institute of Optics and Precision Mechanics of CAS
Cheng-Lin Liu	Institute of Automation of CAS
Guocai Liu	Hunan University
Min Liu	Hunan University
Qingshan Liu	Nanjing University Information Science and Technology
Wenju Liu	Institute of Automation of CAS
Yuehu Liu	Xi'an Jiaotong University
Huchuan Lu	Dalian University of Technology
Jiwen Lu	Advanced Digital Sciences Center, Singapore
Yue Lu	East China Normal University
Bin Luo	Anhui University
Zhenjiang Miao	Beijing Jiaotong University
Yanwei Pang	Tianjin University
Yu Qiao	Shenzhen Institute of Advanced Technology of CAS
He Ran	Institute of Automation of CAS
Nong Sang	Huazhong University of Science and Technology
Huanfeng Shen	Wuhan University
Jun Sun	Fujitsu R&D Center Co., LTD
Xiaoyang Tan	Nanjing University of Aeronautics and Astronautics
Jinhui Tang	Nanjing University of Science and Technology
Dacheng Tao	Hong Kong Polytechnic University
Wenbing Tao	Huazhong University of Science and Technology
Zengfu Wang	University of Science and Technology of China
Hanzi Wang	University of Adelaide
Liang Wang	Institute of Automation of CAS
Liwei Wang	Peking University
Shengjin Wang	Tsinghua University
Yaonan Wang	Hunan University
Yunhong Wang	Peking University
Yihong Wu	Institute of Automation of CAS
Shiming Xiang	Institute of Automation of CAS
Changyan Xiao	Hunan University
Xin Xu	National University of Defense Technology
Pingkun Yan	Philips Research North America
Jian Yang	Nanjing University of Science and Technology
Jian Yu	Beijing Jiaotong University
Yuan Yuan	Xi'an Institute of Optics and Precision Mechanics of CAS

Hongbin Zha   Peking University
Changshui Zhang   Tsinghua University
Daoqiang Zhang   Nanjing University of Aeronautics and
                                 Astronautics
Hongbin Zhang   Beijing University of Technology
Min-Ling Zhang   Southeast University
Jun Zhao   Institute of Automation of CAS
Wenming Zheng   Southeast University
Ping Zhong   National University of Defense Technology
Jie Zhou   Tsinghua University
Zhi-Hua Zhou   Nanjing University
Wangmeng Zuo   Harbin Institute of Technology

Additional Reviewers

Bo Bai	Zhong Ji	Wen Lu
Jiale Cao	Sen Jia	Xiaoqiang Lu
Li Chen	Bo Jiang	Javier López-Fandiño
Mingming Chen	Wei Jiang	Longlong Ma
Pan Chen	Xiaoheng Jiang	Gabriel Martín Herández
Yuxi Chen	Ye Jiang	Liangrui Peng
Zhihui Chen	Mahdi Khodadadzadeh	Antonio Plaza
Zhenchao Cui	Taotao Lai	Javier Plaza
Qing Da	Minxian Li	Lishan Qiao
Qun Dai	Peiqiang Li	Dongwei Ren
Zhijun Dai	Qiming Li	Alim Samat
Cheng Deng	Ying Li	Xiangbo Shu
Hong Deng	Zechao Li	Benqin Song
Xiaoming Deng	Zhaoxin Li	Fengyi Song
Yongsheng Dong	Shan Liang	Yan Song
Fuqing Duan	He Lin	Dengdi Sun
Huixian Duan	Zhigang Ling	Chunna Tian
Bin Fan	Fan Liu	Nicole Tsu
Wei Fan	Lei Liu	Minghua Wan
Jianwu Fang	Li Liu	Bin Wang
Yachuang Feng	Qi Liu	Da-Han Wang
Youji Feng	Qingjie Liu	Faqiang Wang
Lianru Gao	Wei Liu	Jian Wang
Shuhang Gu	Wei Liu	Jun Wang
Lihua Guo	Yi Liu	Liang Wang
Fei He	Yu Liu	Limin Wang
Bo Hu	Luo Longrun	Liuan Wang
Sheng-Jun Huang	Guifu Lu	Peng Wang
Weilin Huang	Shujing Lu	Song Wang

Taiqing Wang
Xg Wang
Xiumei Wang
Ying Wang
Zhe Wang
Ziteng Wang
Chunpeng Wu
Shufu Xie
Yujie Xiong
Guili Xu
Liang Xu
Miao Xu
Xiang Xu
Wei Xue
Zhaohui Xue
Songbai Yan

Yan Yan
Aiping Yang
Wankou Yang
Wei Yang
Xubing Yang
Zhanlei Yang
Cong Yao
Fei Yin
Xiaofang Yuan
Jianlong Zhang
Jiaqi Zhang
Jing Zhang
Mingming Zhang
Shaoquan Zhang
Xin Zhang
Xingyi Zhang

Xu-Yao Zhang
Yanming Zhang
Hao Zheng
Kai Zheng
Liang Zheng
Xiangtao Zheng
Guoqiang Zhong
Xiang-Dong Zhou
Ying Zhou
Yu Zhou
Ximei Zhu
Zhuotun Zhu
Lina Zhuang
Pengcheng Zou

Table of Contents – Part I

Section I: Fundamentals of Pattern Recognition

Section II: Feature Extraction and Classification

Section III: Computer Vision

Table of Contents – Part II

Section IV: Image Processing and Analysis

Section V: Video Processing and Analysis

Section VI: Biometric and Action Recognition

Section VII: Biomedical Image Analysis

Section VIII: Document and Speech Analysis

Section IX: Pattern Recognition Applications

A Nonlinear Classifier
Based on Factorization Machines Model

Xiaolong Liu, Yanming Zhang, and Chenglin Liu

National Laboratory of Pattern Recognition (NLPR)
Institute of Automatic, Chinese Academy of Science
No. 95, Zhongguancun East Road, Beijing, 100190, China
{xiaolong.liu,ymzhang,liucl}@nlpr.ia.ac.cn

Abstract. Polynomial Classifier (PC) is a powerful nonlinear classification method that has been widely used in many pattern recognition problems. Despite its high classification accuracy, its computational cost for both training and testing is polynomial with the dimensionality of input data, which makes it unsuitable for large-scale problems. In this work, based on the idea of factorization machines (FMs), we propose an efficient classification method which approximates PC by performing a low-rank approximation to the coefficient matrix of PC. Our method can largely preserve the accuracy of PC, while has only linear computational complexity with the data dimensionality. We conduct extensive experiments to show the effectiveness of our method.

Keywords: Polynomial Classifier, Factorization Machines model, Low-rank Approximation.

1 Introduction

Classification is one of the most fundamental problems in machine learning, and plays a central role in many applications, such as characters recognition [1], visual object classification [2], and text classification [3]. Actually, classifier design has always been a focus of the machine learning community, and obtained great development in the past decades.

According to the form of the classification function, classification methods can be roughly divided into two categories: linear methods and nonlinear methods. Linear classification methods, such as perceptron [4], linear discriminant analysis (LDA) [5] and linear Support Vector Machines (SVM) [6], are efficient in both training and testing, and thus are ready for large-scale applications which becomes more and more common nowadays. However, due to the limited representation ability of linear functions, these methods are often abused for their low accuracies. On the other hand, nonlinear methods, such as multilayer perceptron (MLP) [7], polynomial classifier (PC) [8], kernel SVM [9], are much more powerful and can always obtain better accuracies than linear methods. However, their computational cost for both training and testing is much higher, and cannot fulfill the requirements of many applications. For example, the cost of kernel SVM is at least $O(n^2)$ for training and $O(n_{sv})$ (n_{sv} is the number of support vectors) for testing.

S. Li et al. (Eds.): CCPR 2014, Part I, CCIS 483, pp. 1–10, 2014.
© Springer-Verlag Berlin Heidelberg 2014

Due to its high performance, PC is a very popular nonlinear classification method in pattern recognition and machine learning. However, for a d-order PC, it has $O(p^d)$ parameters to learn and takes $O(p^d)$ to perform one evaluation operation. Thus, it is slow in both training and testing. In this work, we focus on speeding up PC, while preserving its accuracy as much as possible. Essentially, based on the idea of Factorization Machines (FMs) [10], our approach approximates the coefficient matrix in polynomial function by a low-rank matrix. Using the factorization, our classifier has only $O(kdp)$ parameters (k is the dimensionality of the factorization matrix) and the cost for predicting one sample is also $O(kdp)$.

FMs [10] were originally proposed in the context of Recommender Systems, and have obtained great success in many real-world applications. The current study of FMs is mainly on two aspects: improving the accuracy of FMs by adding specific context-aware information [11, 12], and fast learning algorithms [13]. As far as we know, there is no study about the application of FMs for classifier design.

The paper is organized as follows: Section 2 gives a detailed introduction to the FMs model, including its definition, relationship with PC and the evaluation cost. Section 3 proposes the method for applying the FMs in the classification problem and our learning algorithm. Experiments results are shown in Section 4 to verify the effectiveness of our method.

2   Factorization Machines Model

In this section, we introduce the FMs model in detail and discuss its computational cost for evaluation operation.

2.1   FMs Model [10]

The model equation for a factorization machine of degree $d = 2$ is defined as:

$$\hat{y}(x) = w_0 + \sum_{i=1}^{p} w_i x_i + \sum_{i=1}^{p} \sum_{j=i+1}^{p} \left\langle v_i, v_j \right\rangle x_i x_j \,, \tag{1}$$

where p is the dimensionality of input x, and $\langle \cdot, \cdot \rangle$ denotes the inner product of two vectors. $w_0 \in \mathbb{R}$, $w \in \mathbb{R}^p$, $V \in \mathbb{R}^{p \times k}$ are model parameters which can be estimated from the training set. w_0 is the global bias, w_i is the weight of the feature x_i , and $\hat{w}_{i,j} := \left\langle v_i, v_j \right\rangle$ is the weight of the second-order feature $x_i x_j$.

2.2   Relationship with PC

The decision function of a second-order PC can be written as:

$$\hat{y}(x) = w_0 + w'x + \frac{1}{2} x'Wx \tag{2}$$

where W is a symmetric matrix of size p-by-p. Due to the second-order terms, the evaluation of PC needs $O(p^2)$ operations. On the other hand, it is easy to show the FMs model defined in Eq. (1) can be written as:

$$\hat{y}(x) = w_0 + w'x + \frac{1}{2}x'(VV' - diag(VV'))x \tag{3}$$

where $V = [v_1, v_2, ..., v_p]' \in \mathbb{R}^{p \times k}$, and $diag(VV')$ is a matrix of size p-by-p with its diagonal equals to the diagonal of VV' and all the off-diagonal elements equal to 0.

Thus, from the perspective of matrix approximation, the core idea of FMs is to approximate a symmetric matrix W by $VV' - diag(VV')$. And as we will show immediately, by utilizing this matrix factorization form, a FMs model can be evaluated in $O(kp)$, instead of $O(p^2)$ as in the second-order PC. When the dimensionality of V is low ($k \ll p$), FMs will significantly faster than PC.

2.3   Evaluation Cost

In this section, we show that the evaluation of a FMs model can be done in linear time $O(kp)$, which is the main advantage of our method. We reformulate the third term in Eq. (1) as:

$$\begin{aligned}
&\sum_{i=1}^{p}\sum_{j=i+1}^{p}\langle v_i, v_j \rangle x_i x_j \\
&= \frac{1}{2}\sum_{i=1}^{p}\sum_{j=1}^{p}\langle v_i, v_j \rangle x_i x_j - \frac{1}{2}\sum_{i=1}^{p}\langle v_i, v_j \rangle x_i x_i \\
&= \frac{1}{2}\left(\sum_{i=1}^{p}\sum_{j=1}^{p}\sum_{f=1}^{k} v_{i,f} v_{j,f} x_i x_j - \sum_{i=1}^{p}\sum_{f=1}^{k} v_{i,f} v_{i,f} x_i x_i\right) \\
&= \frac{1}{2}\sum_{f=1}^{k}\left(\left(\sum_{i=1}^{p} v_{i,f} x_i\right)^2 - \sum_{i=1}^{p} v_{i,f}^2 x_i^2\right)
\end{aligned} \tag{4}$$

This equation has only linear complexity for both k and p, thus its computation complexity is $O(kp)$.

2.4   d-way Factorization Machines

The 2-way FMs described above can be smoothly generalized to a d-way FMs:

$$\hat{y}(x) = w_0 + \sum_{i=1}^{p} w_i x_i + \sum_{l=2}^{d}\sum_{i_1=1}^{p}\cdots\sum_{i_l=i_{l-1}+1}^{p}\left(\prod_{j=1}^{l} x_{i_j}\right)\left(\sum_{f=1}^{k_l}\prod_{j=1}^{l} v_{i_j,f}^{(l)}\right) \tag{5}$$

where the weight matrices for the l-order product are factorized by the PARAFAC model [14] with the parameters below $V^{(l)} \in \mathbb{R}^{p \times k_l}, k_l \in \mathbb{N}_0^+$.

The straight forward computation complexity for Eq. (5) is $O(k_d p^d)$. But with the same arguments as in section 2.3, we can show it can be computed in linear $O(k_d d p)$.

3   Training FMs for Classification

In this section, we present how to apply FMs models to classifier design.

3.1   Objective Function

We propose to optimize the following objective function to train a FMs classifier:

$$OPTREG(S, \lambda) = \arg \min_{\Theta} \left(\sum_{(x,y) \in S} l(\hat{y}(x \mid \Theta), y) + \sum_{\theta \in \Theta} \lambda_\theta \theta^2 \right) \tag{6}$$

where $\hat{y}(x \mid \Theta)$ is the FMs classifier, Θ are the classifier parameters, and $l(\hat{y}(x \mid \Theta), y)$ is the loss function that measures the prediction error of the FMs classifier on x. Thus, the first term of the objective function is to minimize the prediction error of the classifier on the training set, and the second term is to regularize the classifier from over-fitting.

For a binary classification problem ($y \in \{-1, 1\}$), we adapt the negative log-likelihood as the loss function, which is defined as:

$$l(\hat{y}(x \mid \Theta), y) = -\ln \sigma(\hat{y}(x \mid \Theta) \cdot y) \tag{7}$$

where $\sigma(x) = \dfrac{1}{1 + e^{-x}}$. For a multi-class problem, we solve it by the standard one-vs-all strategy.

3.2   Learning Algorithm

In this work, we use stochastic gradient descent (SGD) algorithm for training a FMs classifier.

3.3   Stochastic Gradient Descent (SGD)

FMs can be optimized with SGD [10] which has low computation and storage complexity.

The algorithm iterates over all the samples in the training dataset and performs updates on the model parameters.

$$\theta \leftarrow \theta - \eta \left(\frac{\partial}{\partial \theta} l(\hat{y}(x \mid \Theta), y) + 2\lambda_\theta \theta \right) \qquad (8)$$

where $\eta \in \mathbb{R}^+$ is the learning rate for gradient descent. The gradient of the negative log-likelihood loss function is:

$$\frac{\partial}{\partial \theta} l(\hat{y}(x \mid \Theta), y) = \frac{\partial}{\partial \theta} - \ln \sigma(\hat{y}(x \mid \Theta) \cdot y) = (\sigma(\hat{y}(x \mid \Theta) \cdot y) - 1) y \frac{\partial}{\partial \theta} \hat{y}(x \mid \Theta) \qquad (9)$$

3.4   Complexity and Hyper-Parameters

The SGD algorithm for FMs has a linear computational and constant storage complexity. For one iteration over all training cases, the runtime of SGD is $O(knp)$.

For SGD algorithm, there are several critical hyper-parameters.

— Leaning rate η : The convergence of SGD depends largely on η. If η is chosen too big, the SGD doesn't converge, and too small, convergence is slow.
— Regularization parameter λ : The generalization capabilities of FMs depends largely on λ, and in this paper we use grid search to chose the proper λ for SGD algorithm. As there are several regularization parameters, the grid has exponential size and thus this search is very time-consuming. To make the search more feasible, the number of regularization parameters is reduced to only two: λ^w for w_0 and w, and λ^v for factorization matrix V.
— Initialization σ : The model parameters of FMs are initialized with non-constant values which are sampled from a zero-mean normal distribution with standard deviation σ. Typically small values are used for σ.

4   Experiments

To examine the classification performance of FMs model, we compared it with couple of commonly used classifiers on 7 datasets.

4.1   Compared Classifiers

We compare the FMs with PCA-PNC (polynomial network classifier with dimensionality reduction by principal component analysis) [15], linear-SVM, and poly-SVM (SVM with polynomial kernel function).

The PCA-PNC is a subspace-feature-based PNC that can efficiently reduce the computation complexity of PNC and perform fairly well in practice [15]. First, the input feature vector is projected onto an m-dimensional principal subspace ($m < p$); then, the network is computed on the subspace features; finally, the input pattern is classified to the class of maximum output.

For SVM, liblinear [16] and libSVM [17] are used as implementations of linear-SVM and poly-SVM. And the kernel function used for poly-SVM in our experiments is $K(x_i, x_j) = (\gamma x_i 'x_j + r)^d, \gamma > 0$, where $d = 2$.

The linear-SVM and poly-SVM are typical linear and polynomial classifiers on full feature space; comparing with them, we can evaluate the classification capability of FMs. FMs and PCA-PNC have similar structures, so we want to compare the performance of them. Table 1 below lists the training and test computation complexity of them.

Table 1. Training and test computation complextity

Classifier	Training	Test
FMs (bi-class)	$O(knp)$ [10]	$O(kp)$ [10]
PCA-PNC (multi-class)	$O(p^3) + O(m^2n)$	$O(pm) + O(m^2M)$
linear-SVM (bi-class)	$O(pn)$ [6]	$O(p)$ [6]
poly-SVM (bi-class)	$O(pn^2)$ [6]	$O(pn_{sv})$ [6]

Where p is the original dimensionality of feature vectors; n is the sample number of train data subset; M is the number of classes; k is the factorization matrix dimensionality of FMs; m is the subspace dimensionality of PAC-PNC; and n_{sv} is the number of support vectors of SVM.

4.2 Datasets

We select 7 datasets, 5 of them are from the UCI Machine Learning Repository [18] and 2 from LibSVM datasets [19], as summarized in Table 2. We select the multi-class datasets that have at least 10 features.

Most of the data sets have been partitioned into standard training and test subsets. For the others, we arrange the samples in random order and evaluate in 5-fold cross-validation; and we give the average value and standard deviation of the classification accuracy on each of them.

Table 2. Summary of 7 datasets. The right column shows the dimensionality of factorization matrix for FMs or the subspace dimensionality for PCA-PNC (multiple of m_1).

#	Name	#class	#feature	#train	#test	m_1
1	Waveform	3	21	5,000	5-fold	2
2	Vehicle	4	18	846	5-fold	2
3	Segment	7	19	2,100	210	3
4	Letter	26	16	16,000	4,000	3
5	Splice	2	60	1,000	2,175	2
6	Isolet	26	617	6,238	1,559	10
7	Gisette	2	5,000	6,000	1,000	10

4.3 Experiment Design

The PCA-PNC is a network with M output nets, so it can be directly applied to multi-class classification. FMs, linear-SVM and poly-SVM are all bi-class classifiers, and we adopt one-vs-all strategy to make them available for multi-class classification.

For PCA-PNC, we set the dimensionality of subspace as $m = l \cdot m_1$, $l = 1, ..., 5$. m_1 depends on the dataset, and has been listed in the right columns of Table 2. For FMs, we set the dimensionality of factorization matrix as $k = l \cdot m_1$, $l = 1, ..., 5$, corresponding to PCA-PNC. For SVMs, the feature vectors are uniformly scaled.

4.4 Experiments Results

1. FMs and PCA-PNC

The classification accuracy (%) of FMs and PCA-PNC on test subset of the 7 datasets is shown in Table 3. For each dataset, the accuracy of PCA-PNC and FMs on variable dimensionalities is listed in two rows. And we can see, FMs can give test accuracy comparable to PCA-PNC.

Table 3. Test accuracies (%) of FMs and PCA-PNC on 7 dataset

Dataset	PCA= m_1	PCA= $2m_1$	PCA= $3m_1$	PCA= $4m_1$	PCA= $5m_1$
	factor= m_1	factor= $2m_1$	factor= $3m_1$	factor= $4m_1$	factor= $5m_1$
Waveform	63.78	86.40	86.92	**87.12**	86.98
	83.92±1.50	84.36±1.27	85.32±1.01	85.70±0.77	85.90±0.86
Vehicle	53.19	67.38	71.75	76.24	78.37
	78.37±2.91	78.61±2.49	78.85±2.49	79.32±2.89	**80.15±2.88**
Segment	69.14	80.48	83.76	85.86	85.71
	91.10	91.33	92.00	92.29	**92.33**
Letter	26.73	58.73	75.78	84.67	88.20
	78.20	84.33	87.33	89.60	**91.33**
Splice	70.30	77.89	82.94	84.23	84.18
	85.47	85.52	85.56	85.61	**85.66**
Isolet	80.18	91.28	93.52	94.16	95.19
	94.18	94.24	94.78	95.02	**95.45**
Gisette	95.80	97.30	97.60	**98.10**	98.10
	97.10	97.40	97.60	98.00	98.10

For Waveform, when the dimensionality is low, FMs give a higher accuracy than PCA-PNC; when the dimensionality goes up, PCA-PNC surpasses FMs gradually. This can be explained that when the dimensionality is low, the linear terms of FMs with full dimensionality make FMs more expressive; but when the dimensionality goes up, the PCA-PNC shows its power.

On the other datasets, FMs always give higher accuracy than PCA-PNC, especially on lower dimensionality, however, when the dimensionality goes up, the gap is gradually narrowing.

Table 4. Highest accuracier of FMs, PCA-PNC, linear-SVM and poly-SVM

Dataset	FMs	PCA-PNC	linear-SVM	poly-SVM
Waveform	85.90±0.86	**87.12**	86.76	82.37
Vehicle	80.15±2.88	78.37	78.01	**81.21**
Segment	**92.33**	85.86	91.24	92.14
Letter	91.33	88.20	67.50	**94.43**
Splice	85.66	84.18	83.63	**88.32**
Isolet	95.45	95.19	94.61	**96.28**
Gisette	**98.10**	**98.10**	**98.10**	98.75
Average Acc	89.85	88.15	85.69	**90.50**

2.   FMs, PCA-PNC, and SVM

The highest accuracies of FMs, PCA-PNC, linear-SVM and poly-SVM on the 7 datasets are compared in Table 4, and the average classification accuracy of all the classifiers is in the last row.

We can find that in most datasets, the FMs give classification accuracy between linear (linear-SVM) and polynomial (poly-SVM) classifiers. Comparing the accuracy of FMs and PCA-PNC, it is evident that the classification accuracy of FMs is higher than PCA-PNC on most datasets.

4.5   Computation Complexity of FMs

To compare the predict computation complexity of different classifiers, we chose three datasets (Vehicle, Splice, and Isolet) from Table 2, The predict computation time (ms) of FMs ($factor = 5m_1$), PCA-PNC ($m = 5m_1$), linear-SVM and poly-SVM on the test subset is listed in Table 5.

Table 5. The predict computation time of FMs, PCA-PNC, linear-SVM and poly-SVM

Dataset	#test	#dim 5m₁/SVM	FMs	PCA-PNC	linear-SVM	poly-SVM	
		$5m_1$/SVM				#sv	time
Vehicle	169	10/18	4	6	2	667	11
Splice	2175	10/60	67	27	20	481	220
Isolet	1559	50/617	6230	654	800	3106	20410

For all the three datasets, the computation time of FMs and PCA-PNC are much smaller than poly-SVM. This can be explained as the reduced dimensionality of FMs and PCA-PNC speed up the predict operation.

We can find that there is no fixed relationship between the computation time of FMs and PCA-PNC, and this seems contradictory to what we have discussed in Table 1---the computation complexity of FMs is linear, and PCA-PNC is polynomial. We would take a closer look at the computation complexity of FMs and PCA-PNC.

For a dataset whose dimensionality is p and number of classes is M, the computation complexity of the FMs with $factor = k$, is supposed to be $(p + k(2p + 1))M$; and that of the PCA-PNC is $pm + \frac{1}{2}m(m+1) + (m + \frac{1}{2}m(m+1))M$ (where $m = k$). So the practical computation time of FMs and PCA-PNC largely depend on p and M. In most cases, $m \ll p$ is fulfilled, and this makes the practical computation time of FMs comparable, even larger than PCA-PNC when $m = k$.

4.6   Comparison of Classification Performance

To compare the performance of FMs and PCA-PNC, we plot them in Fig. 1, where the horizontal axis is the amount of multiplication calculation for a feature vector, and the vertical axis is the classification accuracy on the test subset.

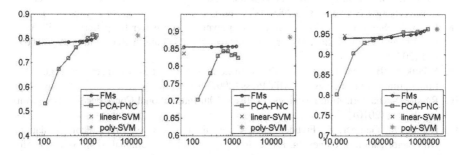

Fig. 1. Performance of FMs and PCA-PNC on Vehicle, Segment, and Isolet

The figures in Fig. 1 from left to right are in turn of Vehicle, Splice, and Isolet datasets. From the figures in Fig. 1, we can conclude that the FMs classifier can give classification accuracy between linear-SVM and poly-SVM. And FMs give much higher classification accuracy than PCA-PNC on low factorization dimensionality; when the dimensionality goes up, they are still comparable.

5   Conclusion

In this paper, we attempt to apply Factorization Machines model to general classifier design. Then we evaluate the classification performance of FMs, PCA-PNC, linear-SVM, and poly-SVM on 7 datasets. And we can now carefully give the following conclusions about FMs and the other three classifiers.

1. FMs can give classification accuracy between linear (linear-SVM) and polynomial (poly-SVM) classifiers, while its computation complexity is linear.

2. FMs can always give higher classification performance than PCA-PNC, especially on low dimensionality, however, when the dimensionality goes up, the gap is gradually narrowing.

References

1. Cheriet, M., Kharm, N., Liu, C.L., et al.: Character recognition systems: A guide for students and practitioners. John Wiley & Sons (2007)
2. Everingham, M., Van Gool, L., Williams, C.K.I., et al.: The pascal visual object classes (voc) challenge. International Journal of Computer Vision 88(2), 303–338 (2010)
3. Joachims, T.: Text categorization with support vector machines: Learning with many relevant features. In: Nédellec, C., Rouveirol, C. (eds.) ECML 1998. LNCS, vol. 1398, pp. 137–142. Springer, Heidelberg (1998)
4. Freund, Y., Schapire, R.E.: Large margin classification using the perceptron algorithm. Machine Learning 37(3), 277–296 (1999)
5. Lzenman, A.J.: Linear Discriminant Analysis. Springer, New York (2008)
6. Burges, C.J.C.: A tutorial on support vector machines for pattern recognition. Data Mining and Knowledge Discovery 2(2) (1998)
7. Pal, S.K., Mitra, S.: Multilayer perceptron, fuzzy sets, and classification. IEEE Transactions on Neural Networks 3(5), 683–697 (1992)
8. Liu, C.L., Sako, H.: Class-specific feature polynomial classifier for pattern classification and its application to handwritten numeral recognition. Pattern Recognition 39(4), 669–681 (2006)
9. Schölkopf, B., Smola, A.J.: Learning with kernels: Support vector machines, regularization, optimization, and beyond. MIT Press (2002)
10. Rendle, S.: Factorization machines. In: IEEE 10th International Conference on Data Mining, ICDM (2010)
11. Rendle, S., Gantner, Z., Freudenthaler, C., et al.: Fast context-aware recommendations with factorization machines. In: Proceedings of the 34th International ACM SIGIR Conference on Research and Development in Information Retrieval (2011)
12. Rendle, S.: Factorization machines with libFM. ACM Transactions on Intelligent Systems and Technology (TIST) 3(3), 57 (2012)
13. Robbins, H., Monro, S.: A stochastic approximation method. The Annals of Mathematical Statistics, 400–407 (1951)
14. Harshman, R.A.: Foundations of the PARAFAC procedure: Models and conditions for an "explanatory" multimodal factor analysis. In: UCLA Working Papers in Phonetics (1970)
15. Liu, C.-L.: Polynomial network classifier with discriminative feature extraction. In: Yeung, D.-Y., Kwok, J.T., Fred, A., Roli, F., de Ridder, D. (eds.) SSPR&SPR 2006. LNCS, vol. 4109, pp. 732–740. Springer, Heidelberg (2006)
16. Fan, R.E., Chang, K.W., Hsieh, C.J., Wang, X.R., Lin, C.J.: LIBLINEAR: A library for large linear classification. The Journal of Machine Learning Research 9, 1871–1874 (2008)
17. Chang, C.C., Li, C.J.: LIBSVM: A library for support vector machines. ACM Transactions on Intelligent Systems and Technology (TIST) 2(3) (2011)
18. UC Irvine Machine Learning Repository, http://archive.ics.uci.edu/ml/ (accessed June 9)
19. LIBSVM Data, http://www.csie.ntu.edu.tw/~cjlin/libsvmtools/datasets/ (accessed June 9)

Training Deep Belief Network
with Sparse Hidden Units

Zhen Hu, Wenzheng Hu, and Changshui Zhang

The State Key Laboratory of Intelligent Technology and Systems,
Tsinghua National Laboratory for Information Science and Technology(TNList)
and the Department of Automation, Tsinghua University, Beijing, China, 100084

Abstract. In this paper, we proposed a framework to train Restricted Boltzmann Machine (RBM) which is the basic block for Deep Belief Network (DBN). By introducing sparsity constraint to the Contrastive Divergence algorithm (CD algorithm), we trained RBMs with better performance than the off-the-shelf model in MNIST handwritten digit data set. The sparse model suffer from saturation slightly, however, by using a trade-off coefficient, the saturation problem can be solved well. To our knowledge, the sparsity constraint was first introduced to the hidden units of RBM.

Keywords: sparsity, DBN, mnist.

1 Introduction

It's well-known that (sigmoid) Neural Network is highly non-convex and thus it's easy to get stuck to a local optima when trained by the widely used Back-propagation algorithm (BP algorithm)[1]. The deeper the neural network is, the more concave and the apter to get stuck. In 1998 Y. Lecun et al. proposed the Convolutional Neural Network model [2] (CNN) and made training deep neural network possible. CNN models are fast because of the parameter-sharing strategy and hence decrease the number of parameters needed. Later in 2006, G. E. Hinton et. al proposed the pre-training strategy to accelerate the training process of deep neural network. Hinton et. al showed that by properly pre-trained, the deep neural network, which was a 9-layer model, converged quickly. And the pre-training strategy made training deep neural network into reality. Since then researchers have found that deep architecture was powerful in feature learning in many areas, such as image recognition proposed in [3], [4] and [5], speech recognition in [6] and [7] and music information retrieval in [8] and [9].

We proposed a new framework to pre-train Restricted Boltzmann Machine (RBM) which is the basic component of a kind of deep neural network named as Deep Belief Network (DBN). In our framework, we modified the contrastive divergence algorithm (CD algorithm) proposed by G. E. Hinton in [10] and [11]. The contrastive divergence algorithm, or CD algorithm, is an asymptotic algorithm to train RBM. As the complexity of the deep network raises the gap between the result of CD algorithm and the true model becomes a key problem.

S. Li et al. (Eds.): CCPR 2014, Part I, CCIS 483, pp. 11–20, 2014.

We can run a longer markov chain to solve the problem to some extend, but we have to spend more time. A large number of experiments showed that neural network in deep architecture was easy to be over-fitting. Some researchers argued that the expressive power of full-linked neural network can be limited by introducing some sort of penalty such as sparsity in [12]. So in our framework we introduced a penalty expression into the optimization formulation for the pre-training and proposed a new pre-training framework for RBM. We found that the penalized model outperformed the original model.

The following paper will be arranged as follows, in section 2 we review Restricted Boltzmann Machine to show how to restrict the hidden units. In section 3 we propose our framework and some necessary analysis.And in section 4 we will make a comment of sparsity and saturation. We show our experiments and results in section 5.

2   Restricted Boltzmann Machine

Restricted Boltzmann Machine is a kind of energy-based neural network as described in [13]. It contains two layers which are visible layer and hidden layer. All connections are inter-layer connection and no connection between two nodes from the same layer. See figure 1 for an example. RBMs are stacked to build

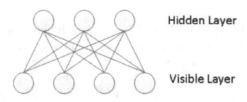

Hidden Layer

Visible Layer

Fig. 1. An example for Restricted Boltzmann Machine

DBN which is a deep neural network.

The energy function for RBM was defined as follows,

$$E(v, h) = -h^T W v - b^T v - C^T h.$$

Where v denotes the value of all visible nodes, and h denotes value of all hidden nodes. The values of all nodes can be either 0 or 1. The probability of state of the network is then defined as follow,

$$P(v, h) = \frac{1}{Z} exp(-E(v, h)).$$

Where Z is a normalization factor.

$$Z = \sum_{v,h} exp(-E(v,h)).$$

Hence the probability for visible nodes should be like this.

$$P(v) = \frac{1}{Z} \sum_{h} exp(-E(v,h)).$$

So the partial derivative of the likelihood function can be written like:

$$\frac{\partial ln P(v)}{\partial \theta} = -\sum_{h} P(h|v)\frac{\partial E(v,h)}{\partial \theta} + \sum_{v,h} P(v,h)\frac{\partial E(v,h)}{\partial \theta} \qquad (1)$$

Where θ indicates the parameters(W_{ij} or b_i).

The conditional probabilistic distribution of h on condition to v was calculated next,

$$\begin{aligned} P(h|v) &= \frac{P(v,h)}{p(v)} \\ &= \frac{exp(h^T W v + b^T v + C^T h)}{\sum_{\hat{h}} exp(-\hat{h}^T W v - b^T v - C^T \hat{h})} \\ &= \Pi_i \frac{exp(h_i(c_i + W_i v))}{\sum_{\hat{h}_i} exp(\hat{h}_i(c_i + W_i v))} \\ &= \Pi_i P(h_i|v) \end{aligned} \qquad (2)$$

It's easy to see that hidden units are conditional independent with each other on condition to visible units. It's straightforward that visible units are independent with each other on condition to hidden units.

$$P(h_i = 1|v) = \frac{e^{c_i + W_i v}}{1 + e^{c_i + W_i v}} = \sigma(c_i + W_i v).$$

$$P(v_i = 1|h) = \frac{e^{b_j + W_{.j}^T h}}{1 + e^{b_j + W_{.j}^T h}} = \sigma(b_j + W_{.j}^T h).$$

Where W_i denotes the i-th row of W and $W_{.j}$ denotes the j-th column of W. It's easy to run a Gibbs sampling process to get a markov chain if time consuming was not a matter. And when the chain reaches the equilibrium distribution both items in equation (1) can be calculated directly. But, unfortunately, time is usually limited in reality. That is the motivation for G. E. Hinton et al. to proposed a fast learning algorithm, CD algorithm, to train RBM in [10] 2006.

In CD algorithm, or specifically speaking CD-n algorithm, the markov chain was not run thoroughly. Instead, a relatively short markov chain was conducted, that is to say the units was updated for n times (here comes the 'n' in 'CD-n') to get v_{rec} and h_{rec}. Hinton et al. reported that CD-n algorithm can get a relatively good result in many practical problem even though theoretically, CD algorithm doesn't equal to the Gibbs sampling algorithm. It's common to set n as 1 when we train RBM and in this paper we also set n as 1 and so did Hinton in [11]. The update equation is also simple:

$$W \leftarrow W + \epsilon(hv^T - P(h = 1|v_{rec})v_{rec});$$
$$b \leftarrow b + \epsilon(h - P(h = 1|v_{rec})); \tag{3}$$
$$c \leftarrow c + \epsilon(v - v_{rec}).$$

Where h is sampled from $P(h|v)$ and $P(h = 1|v_{rec})$ is the probability for h takes the value 1 on condition to v_{rec}.

3   Learning Framework

Let's recall the Gibbs sampling process. If, for every specific input v, the value of hidden units h is determined, we can expect that the states of the network transfer within a certain set of states. Since the number of units is finite, the number of element in the set is finite too. All elements in the set connect to each other in the transmission graph so the chain falls into the equilibrium distribution. We think this is a good result because the output of hidden units is a code for the input and the code is meaningful. Certainly the energy-based model can never be determined since we have to sample the hidden states after all. But if the probability is either close to 1 or close to 0, the state of hidden units is very likely to be a certain state. By choosing proper parameters, this target can be achieved. This is the intuition of our framework.

Our framework can be formulated as follow:

$$\max_{\Theta} L(\Theta) + \lambda P(\Theta). \tag{4}$$

Where Θ denotes the parameters, $L(\Theta) = lnP(v; \Theta)$ is the likelihood function, $P(\Theta)$ is a penalty forcing the hidden units to be determined and λ is the weight for penalty function. So intrinsically we modified the update rule for RBM and in our paper the penalty was elaborately designed so that it works like a sparsity constraint for the hidden units in the model. As the penalty varies the update value for parameters should be divided into two part: one comes from CD algorithm and the other one comes from the negative gradient of penalty w.r.t. the parameters Θ.

As discussed in section 2, the probability of hidden units is:

$$P(h_i = 1|v) = \frac{e^{c_i + W_i v}}{1 + e^{c_i + W_i v}} = \sigma(c_i + W_i v).$$

If $c_i + W_i v$ has a large absolute value the probability can be either close to 1 or close to 0. Inspected by this, we design the penalty part of equation 4 like:

$$P(\Theta) = \sum_i \sigma((c_i + W_i v)^2)$$

By defining the penalty our training algorithm for RBM is easy to generate. The training process was presented in Algorithm 1. We train RBM by this algorithm layer by layer and then stack all RBMs to form a Deep Belief Network. The experiments show that this algorithm reduces the error when applied the network to a dimensionality reducing problem and the hidden units are more determined.

Algorithm 1. RBM Training Algorithm

$[W, b, c] = RBMTraining(v, \epsilon)$
This is the RBM training algorithm
Initialise λ
Input: v and ϵ,
Output: W, b and c defined as follow:
v: a vector of visible units;
ϵ: learning rate;
W: the weight matrix between visible units and hidden units;
b: the biases of visible units;
c: the biases of hidden units.
Randomly guess the value of W, b and c
for all hidden units i **do**
    compute $Q(h_i|v)$. (for binomial hidden units,$\sigma(c_i + W_i v)$)
    sample h from $Q(h_i|v)$
end for
for all visible units j **do**
    compute $P(v_j|h)$. (for binomial hidden units,$\sigma(b_j + W_{.j}^T h)$)
    sample v_{rec} from $P(v_j|h)$
end for
for all hidden units i **do**
    compute $Q(h_i|v_{rec})$. (for binomial hidden units,$\sigma(c_i + W_i v_{rec})$)
end for
$W \leftarrow W + \epsilon(hv^T - Q(h = 1|v_{rec})v_{rec} + \frac{\partial P(\Theta)}{\partial W})$
$b \leftarrow b + \epsilon(h - Q(h = 1|v_{rec}) + \frac{\partial P(\Theta)}{\partial b})$
$c \leftarrow c + \epsilon(v - v_{rec} + \frac{\partial P(\Theta)}{\partial c})$

---

4 Sparsity and Saturation

After the penalized pre-training process, the deep model will be fine-tuned by back-propagation algorithm. From equation 4 we can see that if λ is so large that the likelihood function $L(\Theta)$ can be ignored, the pre-trained model was likely to fall into saturation where the output of the model was constant no matter what the input is. Considering the figure of sigmoid function, if the absolute value of activation is too large, the derivative is small and the training of the model is hard. Saturation doesn't means sparsity. Sparsity means that every input can be transformed into a sparse specific output while saturation means all input are transformed into a same output. So it's very important to avoid to pre-training

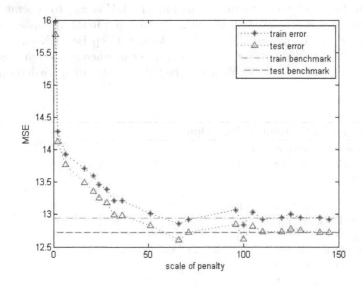

Fig. 2. Relationship between MSE and scale of penalty

a saturated model. If, on the other hand, λ is so small, say 0 as a limit, that the penalty function can be ignored, our pre-training framework degenerate to the original pre-training algorithm which doesn't consider the sparsity of hidden units.

So in reality, a trade-off between sparsity and saturation should be found to balance the model.

5   Experiment and Discussion

In our first experiment, we have trained our framework in the MNIST training dataset.Since we test the property of reconstruction, we measure the square error (MSE). Compared to the off-the-shelf model proposed by G.E.Hinton [11], our framework has a lower error. The MSEs of the training set and the testing set were 12.7272 and 12.5366 respectively, which were approximately 1.5% lower compared with that of G.E.Hinton's experiment where they were 12.9441 and 12.7236 respectively.

In our second experiment, we analyzed the relationship between parameters and the MSE. As shown in figure 2, we showed the relationship between MSE and the strength of penalty. We found that λ should be small and large λ caused large MSE. However λ can not be too small since our result converges to Hinton's when λ approaches to zero. We also found that when λ was less than 1×10^{-4}, MSE varied slightly and our algorithm converged. As shown in figure 3, we analyzed the relationship between MSE and the scale of penalized variables λ.

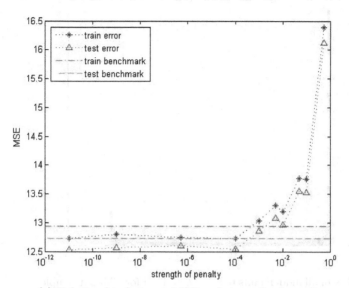

(a) Relationship between MSE and strength of penalty

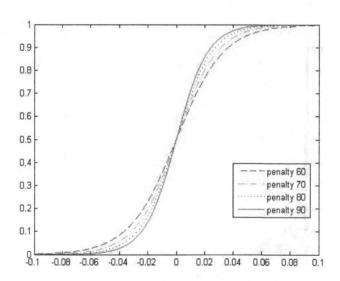

(b) Illustration of the penalty function

Fig. 3. Analysis of the penalty function

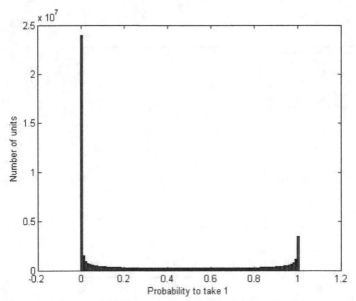

(a) Probability of all hidden units to take the value 1 for all input samples for our model

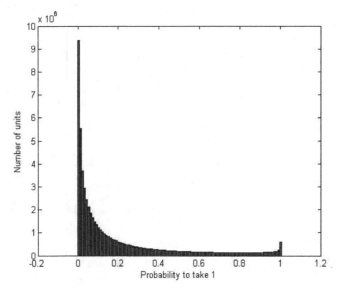

(b) Probability of all hidden units to take the value 1 for all input samples for Hinton's model[11]

Fig. 4. Histogram for probabilities to take 1

As shown in figure 3(a) when λ was large enough, say about 60, MSE changed little since the penalty function was saturated as shown in figure 3(b).

We also investigated the distribution of hidden units on condition to the visible units. We found that on average 3.20% hidden units have the probability less than 1×10^{-4} to take the value 1 and 37.89% hidden units have the probability less than 1×10^{-4} to take the value 0. So in total there 41.09% hidden units are determined. If we don't add the penalty there are 9.07% hidden units to be determined. We drawn the histogram for the probability of all hidden units to take the value 1 for all60, 000 input samples. We drawn the histogram for both our model (shown in 4(a)) and Hinton's model (shown in 4(b)). From these figures we can see that our model push the hidden units to the endpoint indeed.

6   Conclusion

By introducing sparsity constraint, we proposed a framework to train RBM. Results show that we trained RBMs with better performance than the off-the-shelf model. Our model has a smaller reconstructed MSE. Besides, our model is 4.5 times as sparse as Hinton's[11]. Nearly 41.09% of the hidden units have the probability close to 0 or 1, resulting in a better performance in reconstruction. We only test one sparsity constraint, but it is easy to prove that other sparsity constraints have a similar performance in theory.

7   Future Work

We have not applied our model to other problems yet. We believe that the states of most hidden units should be determined leaving just a few to be probabilistic. This intuition matches the reality as we just guess when we are not sure and we can calculate the precise result when we are sure about it. Our experiment shows that the contrast divergence algorithm also get many hidden units to be determined but it's not enough. If we push the probability closer to 0 or 1 we can get a better result. We will do more experiments to verify our model.

We also care about how to design a better penalty. The penalty in this paper is not a well-designed one and we just propose the framework to related researchers for discussion. We also believe that by designing the penalty elaborated we can get a better model which maybe faster and sparser.

Acknowledgments. This work is supported by 973 Program(2013CB329503), NSFC (Grant No. 91120301).

References

1. Rumelhart, D.E., Hinton, G.E., Williams, R.J.: Learning internal representations by error propagation. Technical report, DTIC Document (1985)

2. LeCun, Y., Bottou, L., Bengio, Y., Haffner, P.: Gradient-based learning applied to document recognition. Proceedings of the IEEE 86(11), 2278–2324 (1998)
3. Lee, H., Ekanadham, C., Ng, A.: Sparse deep belief net model for visual area v2. In: Advances in Neural Information Processing Systems, vol. 20, pp. 873–880 (2008)
4. Le, Q., Monga, R., Devin, M., Corrado, G., Chen, K., Ranzato, M., Dean, J., Ng, A.: Building high-level features using large scale unsupervised learning. arXiv preprint arXiv:1112.6209 (2011)
5. Osadchy, M., Cun, Y., Miller, M.: Synergistic face detection and pose estimation with energy-based models. The Journal of Machine Learning Research 8, 1197–1215 (2007)
6. Seide, F., Li, G., Yu, D.: Conversational speech transcription using context-dependent deep neural networks. In: Proc. Interspeech, pp. 437–440 (2011)
7. Hinton, G., Deng, L., Yu, D., Dahl, G., Mohamed, A., Jaitly, N., Senior, A., Vanhoucke, V., Nguyen, P., Sainath, T., et al.: Deep neural networks for acoustic modeling in speech recognition. IEEE Signal Processing Magazine (2012)
8. Lee, H., Largman, Y., Pham, P., Ng, A.: Unsupervised feature learning for audio classification using convolutional deep belief networks. In: Advances in Neural Information Processing Systems, vol. 22, pp. 1096–1104 (2009)
9. Hamel, P., Eck, D.: Learning features from music audio with deep belief networks. In: 11th International Society for Music Information Retrieval Conference, ISMIR 2010 (2010)
10. Hinton, G., Osindero, S., Teh, Y.: A fast learning algorithm for deep belief nets. Neural Computation 18(7), 1527–1554 (2006)
11. Hinton, G., Salakhutdinov, R.: Reducing the dimensionality of data with neural networks. Science 313(5786), 504–507 (2006)
12. Chappell, M., Humphreys, M.S.: An auto-associative neural network for sparse representations: Analysis and application to models of recognition and cued recall. Psychological Review 101(1), 103 (1994)
13. Bengio, Y.: Learning deep architectures for ai. Foundations and Trends® in Machine Learning 2(1), 1–127 (2009)

The Research of Matching Area Selection Criterion for Gravity Gradient Aided Navigation

Kaihan Li[1], Ling Xiong[1], Long Cheng[1], and Jie Ma[2]

[1] School of Information Science and Engineering
Wuhan University of Science and Technology
Wuhan, China
xxling2004@163.com
[2] School of Automation
Huazhong University of Science and Technology
Wuhan, China

Abstract. Matching area selection is the basis of the gravity gradient aided navigation. In this paper, a criterion for gravity gradient matching area selection is proposed based on the gravity gradient tensor matching location, feature extraction and analysis. Matching position experiments on the gravity gradient tensor map are tested by sliding window, and the optimal matching areas on the basis of the gravity gradient tensor maps were found. By means of the gravity gradient feature parameters extraction for the optimal matching areas and analyzing the performance impact of the gravity gradient feature parameters to matching accuracy, a criterion for gravity gradient matching area selection is obtained. Making use of the proposed matching area selection criterion and the average absolute deviation (MAD) matching algorithm, the gravity gradient aided positioning simulation results show that the effect of the matching navigation in the adaptation area is markedly superior to the effect in the non-adaption area, the position error is less than a grid, and matching rate is greater than 90%.

Keywords: Gravity gradient, Matching area selection, Feature extraction, Aided navigation, MAD matching algorithm.

1 Introduction

Gravity gradient aided navigation is a complete high-precision, passive, covert and autonomous navigation [1, 2, 3]. Gravity gradient aided navigation is feasible due to the gradiometer with high precision [4], but the navigation accuracy and rapidity are influenced by many factors, including the gradiometer's precision, the accuracy of the gravity gradient reference map, navigation matching algorithm and matching area and so on.

The features are distinct in the different matching area, so the gravity gradient navigation matching results are bound to be great different in the different matching area. The gravity gradient feature matching results will be better in distinct area, and

S. Li et al. (Eds.): CCPR 2014, Part I, CCIS 483, pp. 21–30, 2014.

mistake matching will be appearing in the non-distinct area. Therefore, the gravity gradient matching area selection is of great significance.

The matching area selection has been becoming an issue of scholars concerned, who are interested in the methods of matching aided navigation. Li Cheng [5] and others give an experimental gravity matching area selection criterion. That is, the local standard deviation and the correlation coefficient of the latitude and longitude direction of the local gravity field are acted as the matching area selection parameter index. Leipin Xi [6] put forward a terrain matching area selection criterion based on terrain entropy. Xiangao Zhou [7] proposed a new method of earth-magnetism navigation matching area selection criterion based on a standard deviation, roughness, entropy and related applications distance on the digital geomagnetic map. In the above methods, the feasibility of the proposed matching area selection criteria are illustrated through simulation experiments, but the proposed matching area selection criteria are guided by practical experiment, and feature information is limited to one or several parameters, lacking of the objective and comprehensive analysis of the actual data and various features [8, 9]. So, in this paper, the gravity gradient matching positioning experiments are tested by sliding windows, the optimal matching area is found based on the gravity gradient tensor chart, and feature parameters in the optimal gravity gradient matching area are extracted. A gravity gradient aided navigation matching area selection criterion is proposed through objective and comprehensive analysis of the impact of the feature parameters on the gravity gradient matching performance.

2 Gravity Gradient Feature Parameters

The gravity gradient data is generally stored in a matrix. Setting an area ,the size of which is M×N grids. $\Gamma(i, j)$ is the gravity gradient value at (i, j). There are some common gravity gradient feature parameters, namely, local standard deviation (σ), local energy (E), local entropy(H), longitude roughness(r_λ), latitude roughness(r_ϕ) , absolute roughness (r), longitude slope (S_λ), latitudinal slope (S_ϕ) , slope(S), longitude correlation coefficient (R_λ) and latitudinal correlation coefficient (R_ϕ). Gravity gradient feature parameters are defined as follows.

- Local standard deviation

$$\sigma = \sqrt{\frac{1}{m(m-n)}\sum_{i=1}^{m}\sum_{j=1}^{n}(\Gamma(i, j)-\overline{\Gamma})^2} \quad , \quad \overline{\Gamma} = \frac{1}{mn}\sum_{i=1}^{m}\sum_{j=1}^{n}\Gamma(i, j) \quad (1)$$

- Local energy

$$E = \sum_{i=1}^{m}\sum_{j=1}^{n}[\Gamma(i, j)]^2 \quad (2)$$

- Local entropy

$$H = \sum_{i=1}^{m} \sum_{j=1}^{n} P_{ij} \log_2 P_{ij} \quad , \quad P_{ij} = \frac{\Gamma(i,j)}{\sum_{i=1}^{m} \sum_{j=1}^{n} \Gamma(i,j)} \tag{3}$$

- Longitude, latitude and absolute roughness

$$r_\lambda = \frac{1}{(m-1)n} \sum_{i=1}^{m-1} \sum_{j=1}^{n} \left| \Gamma(i,j) - \Gamma(i+1,j) \right|, r_\phi = \frac{1}{m(n-1)} \sum_{i=1}^{m} \sum_{j=1}^{n-1} \left| \Gamma(i,j) - \Gamma(i,j+1) \right| \tag{4}$$

$$r = (r_\lambda + r_\phi)/2 \tag{5}$$

- Longitude, latitude slope and slope

$$S_\lambda = \frac{1}{6}[\Gamma(i+1,j+1) + \Gamma(i+1,j) + \Gamma(i+1,j-1) - \Gamma(i-1,j+1) - \Gamma(i-1,j) - \Gamma(i-1,j-1)] \tag{6}$$

$$S_\phi = \frac{1}{6}[\Gamma(i-1,j+1) + \Gamma(i,j+1) + \Gamma(i+1,j+1) - \Gamma(i-1,j-1) - \Gamma(i,j-1) - \Gamma(i+1,j-1)] \tag{7}$$

$$S = \arctan(\sqrt{S_\lambda^2 + S_\phi^2}) \tag{8}$$

- Longitude and latitude correlation coefficient

$$R_\lambda = \frac{1}{(m-1)n\sigma^2} \sum_{i=1}^{m-1} \sum_{j=1}^{n} (\Gamma(i,j) - \bar{\Gamma})(\Gamma(i+1,j) - \bar{\Gamma}) \tag{9}$$

$$R_\phi = \frac{1}{(n-1)m\sigma^2} \sum_{i=1}^{m} \sum_{j=1}^{n-1} (\Gamma(i,j) - \bar{\Gamma})(\Gamma(i,j+1) - \bar{\Gamma}) \tag{10}$$

3   Gravity Gradient Matching Algorithm

According to the relevance principles, there are three procedures in the gravity gradient aided matching navigation.

Firstly, the measured gravity gradient measured values are got at the current time t_s and at the front $(L-1)$ time. The measured values column vectors of the gravity gradient at t_s time, $\Gamma_{ts} : \Gamma_{ts} = (\Gamma_s \quad \Gamma_{s-1} \quad \cdots \quad \Gamma_{s-L+1})^T$, where, L is the gravity gradient matching step. The underwater vehicle line speed is relatively slow, and Marine gravity gradiometer need a longer period of time to get the measured data. It is shown that the size of the matching step L effects the relevant matching, that is, the larger the step length L is, the higher the matching accuracy, after several simulation experiments. But in order to ensure the practicability of correlation matching algorithm, L should be not too big, generally take L = 6 or 10.

Secondly, according to INS indicate the direction and position, the reference gravity gradient vector Γ_{jm} gravity gradient tensor with the same L from the reference image is extracted. The INS pointing direction, location, and the step length L are known, when extracting the gravity gradient vector within the M × N grid area of the reference map. So the reference gravity gradient vectors can be got along the INS direction traversing all the grid area. For example, the current reference gravity gradient vector is $\Gamma_{mj} = (\Gamma_i \quad \Gamma_{i-1} \quad \cdots \quad \Gamma_{i-L+1})^T$, $i = 1,2,3 \cdots S$, when traversing to the i-th cell of the grids. Obviously, S reference gravity gradient vectors are got.

At last, the position of the navigation matching can be determined by making correlation extreme value computing that are between Γ_{ts} and S reference gravity gradient vectors. The average absolute difference (MAD) algorithm is used in this paper. MAD algorithm formula is as shown in formula (11).

$$(\hat{\lambda}, \hat{\phi}) = \min_i \{ \frac{1}{L} \| \Gamma_{ts} - \Gamma_{mi} \|_2 \}, i = 1, 2, ..., S \tag{11}$$

4   Matching Area Selection

4.1   Matching Experiment

There are nine components in a gravity gradient tensor, which are $\Gamma_{xx}, \Gamma_{xy}, \Gamma_{xz}, \Gamma_{yx}, \Gamma_{yy}$, $\Gamma_{yz}, \Gamma_{zx}, \Gamma_{zy}$ and Γ_{zz}. However, in fact, there are only $\Gamma_{xx}, \Gamma_{xy}, \Gamma_{xz}, \Gamma_{yy}, \Gamma_{yz}, \Gamma_{zz}$, which are independent, due to $\Gamma_{xy} = \Gamma_{yx}, \Gamma_{xz} = \Gamma_{zx}, \Gamma_{yz} = \Gamma_{zy}, \Gamma_{xx} + \Gamma_{yy} + \Gamma_{zz} = 0$. And the features of each component of the gravity gradient values are significantly different. Therefore, a different gravity gradient component is chosen that also means to have a different impact on the matching performance.

The component Γ_{xx} map of a gravity gradient tensor is selected as a sample, in order to find the optimal matching area from the gravity gradient tensor reference map. Gravity gradient matching experiment is under way from top to bottom, left to right based on the sliding window in the sample map. The size of Γ_{xx} map is 1024 × 1024 grids, as shown in Figure 1. The matching experimental condition is as follows. Sliding window size is 150 × 150 grids, the size of each grid is 50m × 50m, integral gyro start drift 0.05(°)/h, underwater vehicle do uniform linear motion as a speed of 10m/s along the direction of -45° and gravity gradiometer measurement error is 1.0×10^{-4} E, $1E = 10^{-9}/S^{-2}$. Because the difference of the INS output and real position is small in the whole sliding window, so assuming the two tracks as two lines are available during the experiment.

140 gravity gradient measurement data are recorded during the sliding experiments, interval 7s, in steps of 10 observations. Each experiment carried out 131 consecutive matches as the method in chapter 3. Matching position is considered valid when the position error is less than a grid. Matching rate = 100% × (valid matching points / total matching points).

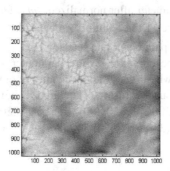

Fig. 1. Γ_{xx} component of a gravity gradient tensor sample

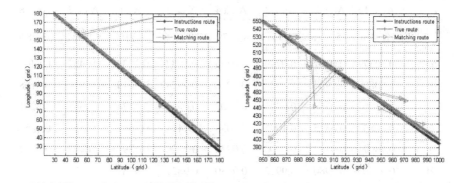

(a) Matching results in area 1(30:180, 30:180)   (b) Matching results in area 8(850:1000, 400:550)

Fig. 2. Matching results

Part (a) and (b) of Figure 2 show the matching results of two different sliding window areas, that are area 1 and area 8, which coordinates are (30:180, 30:180) and(850:1000, 400:550) respectively. Matching rates are 97.1% in area 1 and 59.28% in area 8. In the Fig.2, three different lines, star, cross and triangle, are represented submersible's instructions route, matching route and true route, respectively.

4.2   Feature Parameters Analysis

After the gravity gradient matching experiments, the average values of the feature of different areas are calculated by using the method of moving local window for the gravity gradient feature extraction. By comparison, the features are more obvious when the gravity gradient feature values are extracted from the local window that size is 7×7 grids. In order to eliminate the incomparability among the various feature parameters, the gravity gradient feature parameters are normalized, as the shown in formula (12).

$$y = \frac{x - \min(\omega)}{\max(\omega) - \min(\omega)} \tag{12}$$

Where, y is the feature parameter after normalized, ω is feature parameter data set, $\max(\omega)$ is the maximum value of the feature parameter data set, and $\min(\omega)$ is the minimum value of the feature parameter data set.

The matching rates and the common feature parameter values in different eight areas are shown in Table 1, where the gradient feature parameter values are normalized. Eight areas with various coordinates are area 1: (30:180, 30:180), area 2: (100:250, 800: 950), area 3: (200:350,650:800), area 4: (220:370,620:770) , area 5: (350:500, 10:160), area 6: (360:510, 350:500), area 7: (600:750, 600:750), and area 8: (850:1000, 400:550).

Table 1. Matching rate and   common feature parameter values in different eight areas

	Area 1	Area 2	Area 3	Area 4	Area 5	Area 6	Area 7	Area 8
Matching rate	97.14%	45.71%	75.71%	88.57%	79.29%	90.71%	52.88%	59.28%
σ	0.1237	0.0402	0.0799	0.0759	0.1087	0.1234	0.0452	0.0406
E	0.8089	0.5957	0.7937	0.7946	0.7974	0.8019	0.5957	0.3168
r_λ	0.1111	0.0358	0.0725	0.0702	0.0986	0.1174	0.0391	0.0281
r_ϕ	0.1683	0.0515	0.1075	0.1038	0.1414	0.1607	0.0552	0.0353
r	0.1397	0.0437	0.0900	0.0870	0.1200	0.1391	0.0472	0.0317
H	0.9790	0.9980	0.9922	0.9930	0.9827	0.9789	0.9975	0.9975
S_λ	0.6100	0.6102	0.6106	0.6097	0.6109	0.6106	0.6088	0.6073
S_ϕ	0.4595	0.4604	0.4585	0.4607	0.4615	0.4609	0.4587	0.4606
S	0.6522	0.6527	0.6521	0.6525	0.6534	0.6530	0.6513	0.6513
R_λ	0.7646	0.7581	0.7735	0.7699	0.7690	0.7593	0.7728	0.8294
R_ϕ	0.7526	0.7671	0.7626	0.7589	0.7605	0.7560	0.7850	0.8360

As shown in Table 1, matching rates of area 1 and 6 are greater than 90%, which can be selected as the adaptation areas. The matching rates of area 2, 3, 4, 5, 7, 8 are distributed rang 0% to 89%, which can be considered as non-matching areas. The analysis about the feature parameter values is as following.

The average of standard deviation (σ), gravity gradient mainly reflects the discrete levels and the degree of fluctuation of gravity gradient data component of the local window. The larger the values, the greater the degree of dispersion and fluctuation of the gravity gradient component data, and the more obvious of the gravity gradient feature of the area. As seen from the table 1, the averages of the standard deviation are obviously different in eight different matching areas. The average of standard deviation is larger in the area of higher matching rate. In contrast, it is smaller in the area of lower matching rate.

Local energy (E), the average of the local energy of the gravity gradient component is larger in the area of higher matching rate. In contrast, Local energy is smaller in the area of lower matching rate, which all can also be seen from table 1.

Roughness (r), which reflects the average smoothness of component of the gravity gradient in the window area and can portray finer local ups and downs. It is easily seen from table 1 that roughness (r) is proportional to the matching rate.

The Entropy (H), the longitude correlation coefficient (R_λ) and the latitudinal correlation coefficient (R_φ) of eight matching areas, which are no obvious differences between each other by observing the data of table 1.

Slope(S), which represents the angle between the normal direction and the vertical direction of a point on the surface of the gravity gradient. And it is determined by the slope of the longitude (S_λ) and the latitudinal gradient (S_φ).As seen in table 1, on the one hand, matching rate is relatively high in area 4, but the mean of the standard deviation, the energy, and so on, are not meet the laws between values of these parameters and the matching rate, on the other hand, the change of mean of the slope in the area 8 is not very clear, but it is evident that the slope of area 4 is relatively larger. So It can be concluded that the slope, which although has a certain influence on divided adaptation areas, but not a main factor.

4.3   The Gravity Gradient Matching Area Selecting Criterion

Through the analysis of gravity gradient component data in section 4.2, the matching rate and track features of gravity gradient component parameter values are closely related to the values size. Entropy (H), longitude correlation coefficient (R_λ) , latitudinal correlation coefficient (R_φ) and slope ,the features of which are   not evident .
So they divided little impact on the adaptation area, and cannot be used as parameter indexes to distinguish the adaptation area and the non-adaptation area. But standard deviation (σ), energy (E) and absolute roughness (r) can be used as parameter indexes to distinguish the adaptation area and the non-adaptation area. With the increase of standard deviation, energy, and absolute roughness values, richer information and higher positioning matching rate in the matching of gravity gradient within the sliding window. Thus, the area where the value of standard deviation, energy and absolute roughness is large can be chosen as the matching area, under the premise of 1.0×10^{-4} E measurement error in gravity gradiometer.

After the matching experiments above, as well as the analysis about eight groups regional gravity gradient feature parameter values, it is not difficult to draw that the average value of the standard deviation, the energy and the absolute roughness in the area which matching rate are 90.71% and 97.14% can be used as constraint conditions of gravity gradient matching area directly. Whereas, through experiment simulation, we can find that the proportion of adaption area points accounts for the total matching points is nearly the same when using these two different constraint conditions to mark out adaptation area diagram, the former is 3.1191%, the latter is 3.0134%, and the location of adaptation area is also roughly the same . So the average of the three feature value in the matching rate of 90.71% area is chosen as a constraint condition, then the gravity gradient aided navigation matching area selection criterion is put forward as following.

$$\sigma > 0.1234 \cap E > 0.8019 \cap r > 0.1391 \tag{13}$$

The area satisfied the equation (13) is adapted to adaptive area.

5   Simulations and Results

Gravity gradient aided matching position is simulated on another test gravity gradient tensor map in order to verify the feasibility of the matching area selection criterion proposed in the section 4.3. The component in the xx direction of the test gravity gradient tensor is shown in part (a) of Figure 3.

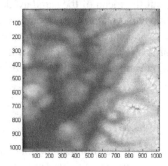 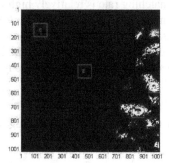

(a) Γ_{xx} component of the test gravity gradient tensor   (b) Adaptive   area

Fig. 3. The test gravity gradient tensor and adaptive area

Using the criterion of formula (13), the adaptive area can be got as shown in the part (b) of Figure 3. Where, the white areas are expressed as adaptation areas; the black areas are expressed as non-adaptation areas.

Simulations did in area A, B, C, D and E respectively.   Area A, B, C, D and E are the square areas circled in the part (b) of Figure 3. Area A, B and D are adaptive areas and area C and E are non-adaptive areas. In order to more accurately verify the accuracy of adaptive and non-adaptive area marked in part (b) of Fig.3, simulation conditions are in the same as the conditions in section 4.1, in addition to the grid window size has been re-specified. The size of sliding window in area A, B, C and E is 100 × 100 grids, area D is 50 × 50 grids. The coordinates of five areas are as follows: area A:(500:600,900:1000),   area B:(670:770,800:900),   area C:(100:200,100:200), area D:(150:200, 950:1000), and area E: (400:500, 400:500). Gravity gradient matching results are as shown in part (a), (b), (c), (d) and (e) of Figure 4.

As shown in part (a), (b), (c), (d) and (e) of Figure 4.   The matching rate of area A, B and D, which are adaptive area, are 91%, 95%, 92%, respectively, which are all greater than 90%. And the matching rate of area C and E, which are non-adaptive area, are 66% and 35%, respectively, which are all smaller than 90%. From the above matching rates, it can be shown that the division of the adaptive area and the non-adaptive area for area A, B, C, D and E according to the proposed matching area selection criterion are correct.

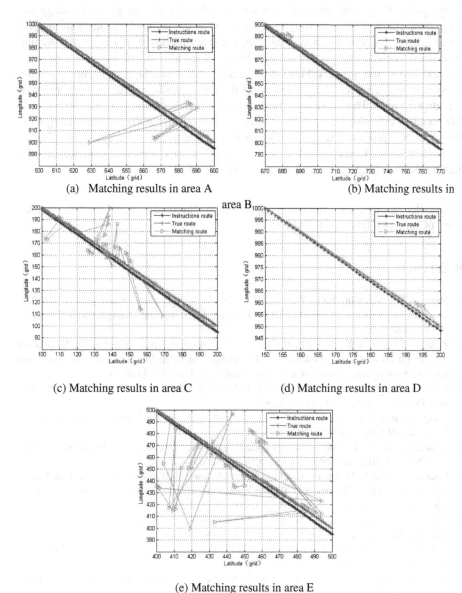

(a)   Matching results in area A   (b) Matching results in area B

(c) Matching results in area C   (d) Matching results in area D

(e) Matching results in area E

Fig. 4. Matching results in five matching areas

6   Conclusions

In this paper, the gravity gradient standard deviation, the gravity gradient energy and the gravity gradient absolute roughness are acted as the parameter indexes of the proposed gravity gradient matching area selection criterion based on a large of matching experiments concerning gravity gradient tensor aided navigation, the feature parameters' extraction and analysis. Simulation results show that a higher matching rate and a less matching error can be got by use of the mean absolute difference algorithm in the adaptive area. The gravity gradient matching area selection criterion proposed in this paper is effective and can be in practice for gravity gradient aided navigation. However, the proposed selection criteria for matching area just based on a single component. In the future we will integrate multiple components into selection criteria, making the matching area selection criteria more perfect.

Acknowledgments. This work was supported by National Natural Science Foundation of China (61104191, 61074156).

References

1. Hays, K.M., Schmidt, R.G., Wilson, W.A., et al.: A Submarine Navigator for the 21st Century. In: Proceeding of IEEE/ION Position Location and Navigation Symposium, pp. 179–188
2. Zhang, F., Chen, X.W., Sun, M., et al.: Simulation Study of Underwater Passive Navigation System Based on Gravity Gradient. In: Proceedings of IEEE International Geoscience and Remote Sensing Symposium, Anchorage, Alaska, pp. 3111–3113 (2004)
3. Guo, Y., Zhong, B.: Earth's Gravity Field to Determine the Gravity Field Matching Navigation. Ocean Mapping 23(5), 61–64 (2003)
4. Yang, T.: Simulation of Underwater Gravity Gradient Based Navigation System. Huazhong University of Science and Technology (2011)
5. Cheng, L., Zhang, Y., Cai, J.: Gravity Aided Navigation Area Matching the Selection Criteria. Chinese Inertial Technology 15(5), 559–564 (2007)
6. Cheng, H., Ma, J., Gong, J.: Matching Selected Based on Least Squares Sup-port Vector Machines for Three-Dimensional Terrain. Huazhong University of Science and Technology (Natural Science Edition) 36(1), 34–37 (2008)
7. Zhou, X., Li, S., Yang, J., Zhang, T.: Geomagnetic Matching Navigation Features in Selected Regions. Chinese Inertial Technology 16(6), 698–703 (2008)
8. Wu, H., Xu, X., Liu, B.: The Research of Matching Area Selection for Gravity. Journal of Surveying and Mapping 37(2), 14–17 (2012)
9. Wang, X., Su, M.: The Matching Adaptation Area Selection of Geomagnetic Navigation. Geodesy and Geodynamics 31(6), 79–83, 88 (2011)

A Manifold Learning Fusion Algorithm
Based on Distance and Angle Preservation

Yanchun Gu[1], Defeng Zhang[1], Zhengming Ma[2], and Guo Niu[2]

[1] School of Electronics and Information Engineering, Foshan University, Foshan, 528000, China
[2] School of Information Science and Technology, Sun Yat-Sen University,
Guangzhou, 510006, China

Abstract. Each manifold learning algorithm has its own advantages and applicable situations. And it is an important question that how to select out the best one as the result. To this end, a manifold learning fusion algorithm is proposed to select out the best one from multiple results yielded by different manifold learning algorithms according to an equation of criterion. Moreover, a kind of local optimal technique is used to optimize the embedded result. By combining the advantages of classical manifold learning algorithms that preserve some properties effectively and the better preservation to distance and angle, our algorithm can yield a more satisfactory result to almost all kind of manifolds. The effectiveness and stability of our algorithm are further confirmed by some experiments.

Keywords: manifold learning, dimensionality reduction, particle swarm optimization, distance and angle.

1   Introduction

Dimensionality reduction occupies a central position in many pattern recognition and machine learning areas. A large number of algorithms have been proposed over the past two decades. Among them, the linear algorithms such as Principal Component Analysis(PCA)[1] and Linear Discriminant Analysis(LDA)[2] have been the two most popular ones because of their simplicity and effectiveness. PCA projects the data set by maximizing the projected variances. LDA maximizes the mean value of Kullback-Leibler divergences between different classes for classification. Recently, from the viewpoint of manifold learning, some new linear methods emerged, including Locality Preserving Projections(LPP)[3], Neighborhood Preserving Embedding(NPE) [4], Orthogonal Neighborhood Preserving Projections(ONPP) [5] and Linear Local Tangent Space Alignment(LLTSA) [6] etc. Linear methods are easy to understand and are very simple to implement, but the linearity assumption is too strict to produce a good result in many real-world applications.

A new line of non-linear dimensionality reduction algorithms came up recently based on the assumption that the input data reside on or close to a low-dimensional

S. Li et al. (Eds.): CCPR 2014, Part I, CCIS 483, pp. 31–43, 2014.

manifold embedded in the ambient space[7-9]. These algorithms focus on constructing some new roles to project the dataset sampled from high-dimensional space into lower-dimensional ones while preserving some native information as much as possible. Though different geometrical properties of the underlying manifold are attempted to preserve in different manifold learning algorithms, most manifold learning algorithms involve distance and angle in some way or another. ISOMAP[10], for example, tries to preserve the geometric distances between data points in low-dimensional space, whereas LLE[11] unfolds the manifold by preserving the local linear reconstruction relationship of each point. LE[12] utilizes spectral graph strategy to preserve proximity relationships to reveal the intrinsic structure of manifold. HLLE[13] employs a quadratic form based on the Hessian instead of the Laplacian to achieve the low-dimensional representation. LTSA[14] exploits the local tangent information as a representation of the local geometry and aligns them to get the global low-dimensional coordinates. Diffusion maps[15] tries to preserve the diffusion distance through computing the transition matrix obtained by random walk on the data. MVU[16] maximizes the dissimilarity distances between distant points and minimizes the similarity distances between neighbors. Conformal Eigenmaps[17] is an angle-preserving embedding method which tries to preserve the similarity of triangles in each neighborhood. Manifold Sculpting[18] discovers manifolds through a process of graduated optimization in which distances in every patches and angles between patches are preserved.

A sharp contrast to the flood of manifold learning algorithms, there is no single kind of algorithm can be suitable for all the manifolds. That is, each manifold learning algorithm has its own advantages and applicable situations. As shown in figure 1, ISOMAP can yield the ideal embedding for intrinsically flat manifolds of zero Gaussian curvature such as "Swiss Roll", but LLE and LE tend to cause a distortion in the low-dimensional space. But to manifold Punctured Sphere, ISOMAP fails to reveal the intrinsic structure whereas LLE and LE yield a more satisfactory result. So it is necessary for us to integrate multiple manifold learning algorithms for dimensionality reduction and select out the best result from them.

To this end, a manifold learning fusion algorithm (MLFA) is proposed. In our algorithm, we first put forward an equation to evaluate the extent of distance and angle preservation and select out the best one from multiple results generated by different manifold learning algorithms as the low-dimensional coordinate. Then, a kind of local optimal technique called Particle Swarm Optimization(PSO)[19] is used to optimize the embedded result. Different from the existing manifold learning algorithms which operate to the data set in high-dimensional space, MLFA does some adjustment and optimization to the low-dimensional coordinates. That is, based on the good preservation to some properties by original manifold learning algorithms, MLFA seeks to find out the better result in which the distance and angle are preserved more faithfully.

The remainder of this paper is organized as follows: In section 2, we give the definitions of distance and angles used in our paper and propose the frame of manifold learning fusion algorithm. A local optimization procedure is also given in this section. Some experiments and analysis are discussed in section 3. Last, we conclude our work in section 4.

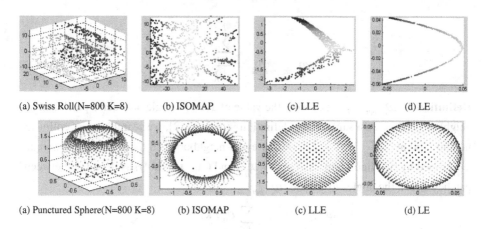

(a) Swiss Roll(N=800 K=8)   (b) ISOMAP   (c) LLE   (d) LE

(a) Punctured Sphere(N=800 K=8)   (b) ISOMAP   (c) LLE   (d) LE

Fig. 1. Different effects with manifold learning algorithms

2   Manifold Learning Fusion Algorithm

We first give the definition of distance and angle used in our algorithm, and then describe how to integrate multiple algorithms and select the result in which the distance and angle are preserved best. Finally, we present an optimization procedure to complete the framework.

2.1   Definitions

Let $X = [x_1, x_2, \cdots x_N]$ be a data matrix, in which each column vector represents a data point in the D-dimensional Euclidean space R^D. For a data point x_i, let $N^i_{D \times k} = [x_{i1}, x_{i2}, \cdots, x_{ik}]$ be its neighborhood matrix where k is the neighborhood size.

Definition 1. $\lambda_{i\_nei\_X}$: denotes the value of average Euclidean distance between points x_i and its neighbors. $\lambda_{i\_nei\_X}$ can be calculated by:

$$\lambda_{i\_nei\_X} = \frac{\sum_{j=1}^{k} \left\| x_i - x_{ij} \right\|}{k} \tag{1}$$

Definition 2. $\omega_{i\_in\_nei\_X}$: denotes the value of average angle in the patch. Connect x_i to its neighbors, we can get k line segments($L_1, L_2, \cdots, L_k$). Then the angles θ_{ij} formed by L_i and L_1 $i = 1, 2, \cdots k$ are computed. Mean the angles we then get the $\omega_{i\_in\_nei\_X}$:

$$\omega_{i\_in\_nei\_X} = \frac{\sum_{j=1}^{k} \theta_{ij}}{k} \qquad (2)$$

Definition 3. $\omega_{i\_bet\_nei\_X}$: denotes the value of average angle between a patch and its neighbor patches. Just same to the definition in paper [12], we search a most collinear neighbor points M_{ij} $j = 1, 2, \cdots k$ for every neighbors, and then calculate the angle ϑ_{ij} formed by two line segments((x_i to x_{ij}) and (x_{ij} to M_{ij})) as the angle between patches. Mean the angles to get the $\omega_{i\_bet\_nei\_X}$:

$$\omega_{i\_bet\_nei\_X} = \sum_{j=1}^{k} \vartheta_{ij} / k \qquad (3)$$

2.2   Framework of Manifold Learning Fusion Algorithm

MLFA aims to select out the result in which the distance and angle can be preserved best from a varieties of manifold learning algorithms. MLFA can be divided into five steps.

Algorithm 1. Framework of Manifold Learning Fusion Algorithm

---

1 Obtain the original low-dimensional coordinates with different manifold learning algorithms, denoted by $Y_{orig} = \{Y_1, Y_2, \cdots, Y_m\}$

2 Normalize the distances to the same sacle, get $Y_{norm} = \{\tilde{Y}_1, \tilde{Y}_2, \cdots, \tilde{Y}_m\}$

3 Compute the deviation error ε_i for each $\tilde{Y}_i$

4 Select out the best result where ε_i is smallest

5 Optimize the result with local optimal method

Step1: Obtain the Original Low-Dimensional Coordinates

The first step of MLFA is applying to different manifold learning algorithms to the data set and getting the original low-dimensional coordinates, which can be denoted by

$$Y_{orig} = \{Y_1, Y_2, \cdots, Y_m\}.$$

Step2: Normalize the Distances to the Same Scale

The second step is to normalize the distances of the original coordinates. As the low-dimensional represents have different scaling levels, which makes the comparison difficult and unfair, we have to zoom the original coordinates to the same scale. We use the average neighborhood distance $\lambda_{ave\_dis\_X}$ and $\lambda_{ave\_dis\_Yi}$ to denote the current scale level of X and Y_i respectively. They can be given by:

$$\lambda_{ave\_dis\_X} = \sum_{j=1}^{N}\left(\frac{\lambda_{j\_nei\_X}}{N}\right)$$

$$\lambda_{ave\_dis\_Yi} = \sum_{j=1}^{N}\left(\frac{\lambda_{j\_nei\_Yi}}{N}\right)$$

(4)

Where $\lambda_{j\_nei\_X}$ and $\lambda_{j\_nei\_Yi}$ can be calculated with eq.(1). Then, we can zoom Y_i to the normalized coordinates $\tilde{Y}_i$ by:

$$\tilde{Y}_i = \frac{\lambda_{ave\_dis\_X}}{\lambda_{ave\_dis\_Yi}}Y_i$$

(5)

Step3: Compute the Deviation Error

Next, we will compute the deviation error ε_i for each normalized coordinates $\tilde{Y}_i$. ε_i is composed of three values: deviation value of average distance in patches, deviation value of average angle in patches and deviation value of average angle between patches. We denote them as ε_{iave_dis}, $\varepsilon_{iave\_ang\_in}$ and $\varepsilon_{iave\_ang\_bet}$ respectively.

ε_{iave_dis} represents the deviation degree of average distance in patches.

$$\varepsilon_{iave\_dis} = \frac{1}{N}\sum_{j=1}^{N}\frac{\left|\lambda_{j\_nei\_X} - \lambda_{j\_nei\_\tilde{Y}i}\right|}{\lambda_{ave\_dis\_X}}$$

(6)

$\varepsilon_{iave\_ang\_in}$ represents the deviation degree of average angle in patches.

$$\varepsilon_{iave\_ang\_in} = \frac{1}{N}\sum_{j=1}^{N}\frac{\left|\omega_{j\_in\_nei\_X} - \omega_{j\_in\_nei\_\tilde{Y}i}\right|}{\omega_{ave\_nei\_X}}$$

(7)

$\varepsilon_{iave\_ang\_bet}$ represents the deviation degree of average angle between patches.

$$\varepsilon_{iave\_ang\_bet} = \frac{1}{N}\sum_{j=1}^{N}\frac{\left|\omega_{j\_bet\_nei\_X} - \omega_{j\_bet\_nei\_\tilde{Y}i}\right|}{\pi} \qquad (8)$$

Then, we can obtain the value of ε_i by:

$$\varepsilon_i = \beta_1\varepsilon_{iave\_dis} + \beta_2\varepsilon_{iave\_ang\_in} + \beta_3\varepsilon_{iave\_ang\_bet} \qquad (9)$$

Where $\beta_i \ \ i=1,2,3$ is the deviation adjustment factor. Of course we can adjust the value of β_i as necessary. But considering from the intuition, the result may be more sensitive to the smaller value. So it is acceptable to get them by:

$$\beta_i = \frac{\eta_i}{\eta_1 + \eta_2 + \eta_3} \qquad (10)$$

Where $i=1,2,3$ and

$$\eta_1 = \frac{\sum_{i=1}^{m}\varepsilon_{iave\_dis} + \sum_{i=1}^{m}\varepsilon_{iave\_ang\_in} + \sum_{i=1}^{m}\varepsilon_{iave\_ang\_bet}}{\sum_{i=1}^{m}\varepsilon_{iave\_dis}}$$

$$\eta_2 = \frac{\sum_{i=1}^{m}\varepsilon_{iave\_dis} + \sum_{i=1}^{m}\varepsilon_{iave\_ang\_in} + \sum_{i=1}^{m}\varepsilon_{iave\_ang\_bet}}{\sum_{i=1}^{m}\varepsilon_{iave\_ang\_in}} \qquad (11)$$

$$\eta_3 = \frac{\sum_{i=1}^{m}\varepsilon_{iave\_dis} + \sum_{i=1}^{m}\varepsilon_{iave\_ang\_in} + \sum_{i=1}^{m}\varepsilon_{iave\_ang\_bet}}{\sum_{i=1}^{m}\varepsilon_{iave\_ang\_bet}}$$

Step4: Select out the Best Result

After we calculate the deviation value of every manifold learning algorithm, we then select out the result which has smallest deviation value as the low-dimensional coordinates. As described previously, different algorithm has different advantages and applicable scope, so the selected algorithm may vary from manifolds.

Step5: Optimize the Result

The last step of our algorithm is to optimize the selected result by some local optimization technique. In our paper, the algorithm Particle Swarm Optimization is chosen.

Let $Y = \tilde{Y}_p$ be the best result. The optimization procedure is listed below. The descriptions to some local variables are also listed.

Algorithm 2. The Optimization Procedure

Input: Yi : a point of Y

Output: $newYi$: the new coordinate of Yi

Procedure:

Initial the part optimization value: POV=error(Y)

Initialize the global optimization value: GOV=error(Y)

Set the initial location: $Li = random(Yi)$, select t locations around Yi

Set the initial velocity: $Vi = \dfrac{mean(Yi)}{\alpha}$

```
for i from 1 to t
    flag=1
    while flag>0
        flag=0
        for j from 1 to d
```

$$Vid = w \times Vid + c_1 \times Rand1 \times (POVd - Yid) + c_2 \times Rand2 \times (PGVd - Yid)$$

```
            Yid=Lid+Vid
            if  newerror(Y)<POV
                flag=1
                    Lid=Yid
            else
                Yid=Yid-2*Vid
                if newerror<POV
                    flag=1
                    Lid=Yid
                else
                    flag=0
                        Yid=Lid+Vid
                endif
            endif
        endfor
        if POV<GOV
            GOV=POV
            newYi=Yi
        endif
    endwhile
endfor
```

In the procedure, POV is the optimal value of current particle, GOV is the optimal value of all the particles, Li denotes the current location, t is the number of particles. And α is factor of step size, d is the number of dimension, w denotes the initial weight, $rand1$ and $rand2$ is a random number between 0 to 1 separately. $c1, c2$ are two learning constants, often be set to 2.

3   Experimental Results

We test our improved dimensionality reduction algorithm with a range of manifolds. As for the parameters, α is set to 10, w is set to 1, $rand1, rand2$ are set to 0.3 and 0.7 respectively. The frequency of our CPU is 1.86GHz, capacity of the memory is 2GB, and the software surrounding is matlab 7.0.

3.1   Test on Mani Data Set

The data sets in Mani program are firstly chosen. The data sets are widely used in manifold learning, and can be conveniently downloaded from [20].

Figure 2 shows the effects of Swiss Roll obtained by MLFA and other classical manifold learning algorithms when the number of original sample points is set by 400 and neighborhood size is 8. The errors of manifold learning algorithms are also listed in table 1. We can see that MLFA can compare and find out the best one from a variety of results and the effect of MLFA has an improvement to the selected algorithm. Concretely, in the four algorithms selected in our experiments, though ISOMAP is not the best one to preserve angles, it has the smallest distance error, so the result of ISOMAP is selected for its smallest overall error. LLE has the best angle error in patches, but it has a so severe distortion to distance in neighborhood. Compare to the selected algorithm, MLFA has a little better in preserving distance, but it makes a significant improvement to the preservation of angles not only in neighborhoods but also between patches.

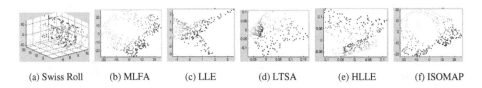

(a) Swiss Roll   (b) MLFA   (c) LLE   (d) LTSA   (e) HLLE   (f) ISOMAP

Fig. 2. Results with different manifold learning algorithms(Swiss Roll, N=400 K=8)

Table 1. Errors of manifold learning algorithms with Swiss Roll(N=400 K=8)

Algorithm	ε_{iave_dis}	$\varepsilon_{iave\_ang\_in}$	$\varepsilon_{iave\_ang\_bet}$	ε_i	Selected
LLE	4.1541	1.2515	0.8331	1.3952	
LTSA	4.0175	1.3064	0.7574	1.3544	
HLLE	3.1156	1.4054	0.8486	1.3209	ISOMAP
ISOMAP	2.3783	1.3993	0.7718	1.1825	
MLFA	2.1082	0.9589	0.5077	0.8601	

The results are not same with the manifold Punctured Sphere. As shown in figure 3 and table 2, the best result is the one obtained by LLE. In this test, though LTSA and ISOMAP have a good preservation to the distance, they cause a relatively larger deviation in angle. LLE, instead, obtain a good preservation both in distance and angle, so the result of LLE is selected in our program.

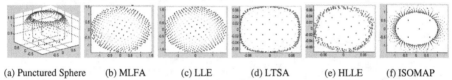

(a) Punctured Sphere   (b) MLFA   (c) LLE   (d) LTSA   (e) HLLE   (f) ISOMAP

Fig. 3. Results with different manifold learning algorithms (Punctured Sphere, N=400 K=8)

Table 2. Errors of manifold learning algorithms with Punctured Sphere (N=400 K=8)

Algorithm	ε_{iave_dis}	$\varepsilon_{iave\_ang\_in}$	$\varepsilon_{iave\_ang\_bet}$	ε_i	Selected
LLE	2.7761	0.9349	0.5132	1.0430	
LTSA	2.6276	2.0051	1.3055	1.7642	
HLLE	3.2288	1.4724	1.0943	1.5875	LLE
ISOMAP	2.2532	1.3046	0.8630	1.2485	
MLFA	2.6368	0.8668	0.5033	0.9916	

As to other manifolds in Mani program, MLFA also offers an advantageous in preserving distance and angle, and the selected algorithm varies with the manifolds.

Table 3. Errors of manifold learning algorithms with other manifolds in Mani program (N=400 K=8)

Manifold	LLE	LTSA	HLLE	ISOMAP	MLFA	Selected
Swiss Hole	1.5491	1.7042	1.6541	1.3900	0.9236	ISOMAP
Twin Peaks	1.4454	0.7309	0.8448	0.9068	0.6637	LTSA
Toroidal Helix	2.3358	1.5541	1.5816	1.2237	0.9160	ISOMAP
Gaussian	0.3425	0.1845	0.1770	0.4090	0.1688	HLLE

3.2   Test on S-Curve Data Set

The "S-Curve" data set are also tested. As shown in figure 4 and table 4, ISOMAP is selected and MLFA is better than other algorithms for its ability to preserve distance and angle more faithfully.

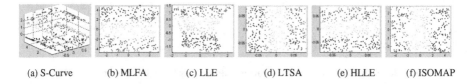

(a) S-Curve   (b) MLFA   (c) LLE   (d) LTSA   (e) HLLE   (f) ISOMAP

Fig. 4. Results with different manifold learning algorithms (S-Curve, N=400 K=8)

Table 4. Errors of manifold learning algorithms with S-Curve (N=400 K=8)

Algorithm	ε_{iave_dis}	$\varepsilon_{iave\_ang\_in}$	$\varepsilon_{iave\_ang\_bet}$	ε_i	Selected
LLE	1.7106	1.1404	0.5512	0.9045	
LTSA	1.4905	0.9894	0.4418	0.7649	
HLLE	1.4888	0.9777	0.4418	0.7618	ISOMAP
ISOMAP	0.9403	0.9319	0.3173	0.5812	
MLFA	0.8755	0.7439	0.2553	0.4877	

3.3   Test on "Frey Face" Data Set

Besides the comparison on simulation data sets, we also test our algorithm on real-world data set such as Frey Face [21]. It contains 1965 images taken from the same person with various facial expressions. From the results we can note our method is also suitable to real-world data set.

Table 5. Errors of manifold learning algorithms with Frey Face

Algorithm	ε_{iave_dis}	$\varepsilon_{iave\_ang\_in}$	$\varepsilon_{iave\_ang\_bet}$	ε_i	Selected
LLE	8.7393	3.4587	1.9630	3.3347	
LTSA	7.8366	2.7376	1.4938	2.7292	HLLE
HLLE	3.7708	1.9954	1.1371	1.7562	
ISOMAP	3.5216	2.1026	1.1577	1.7676	
MLFA	2.5918	1.7023	0.9445	1.4003	

3.4   Comparison of CPU Time

It is notable that, in our algorithm, we must run all the selected algorithms and select out the best one as our initial coordinates and then employ the optimization method to it, all of these inevitably lead to the time complexity of our algorithm is higher that other single algorithm. As listed in table 6, the CPU time demanded by MLFA is longer than other algorithms. But it is also worth while to note with the sample number increases, the running time of MLFA approximately equals to the total time of selected algorithm. This means that the time complexity is mainly embodied in the execution of selected manifold learning algorithms.

Table 6. Comparison of CPU time with different algorithms (s)

Manifold	LLE	LTSA	HLLE	ISOMAP	MLFA
Swiss Roll N=400	0.2095	0.2211	1.2309	3.2454	7.6255
Swiss Roll N=800	0.4988	0.5230	8.4471	25.7366	38.7930
Swiss Roll N=2000	2.3671	2.1055	119.0758	391.7722	531.1877
TwinPeaks N=400	0.1618	0.1981	1.1768	3.1378	7.2284
TwinPeaks N=800	0.3924	0.4438	8.2506	24..8190	36..0695
TwinPeaks N=2000	2.2919	2.0052	117.4560	389.0339	523.9498

4   Conclusions

Nowadays, manifold learning methods has attracted a widespread attention and made a great progress. Since different manifold learning algorithms try to preserve different properties of the original data and distance and angle play a crucial role in describing the intrinsic structure, it is so necessary to select out the result where distance and angle are preserved best from multiple coordinates yielded by different manifold learning algorithms. So, a manifold learning fusion algorithm (MLFA) based on distance and angle is proposed. For the ability of combining the advantages of classical manifold learning algorithms that preserve some properties effectively and the better preservation to distance and angle, our algorithm can yield a more satisfactory result to almost all kind of manifolds. The effectiveness and stability of our algorithm are further confirmed by some experiments.

It is notable that the time complexity of our algorithm is very high. We have pointed out that the time complexity is mainly embodied in the execution of selected manifold learning algorithms. So how to select the proper ones into our fusion algorithm is one of our next works. Another researchable question is how to adjust the parameters such as β, w, c reasonably.

Acknowledgement. This work was partially supported by grant LYM0097.

References

1. Jolliffe, I.T.: Principal Component Analysis. Springer (1986)
2. Fisher, R.A.: The Use of Multiple Measurements in Taxonomic Problems. Annals of Eugenics 7, 179–188 (1936)
3. He, X., Niyogi, P.: Locality Preserving Projections. In: Advances in Neural Information Processing Systems, pp. 37–44. MIT Press, Cambridge (2003)
4. He, X., Cai, D., Yan, S., Zhang, H.: Neighborhood Preserving Embedding. Computer Vision, 1208–1213 (2005)
5. Kokiopoulou, E., Saad, Y.: Orthogonal Neighborhood Preserving Projections: A Projection-Based Dimensionality Reduction Technique. Pattern Analysis and Machine Intelligence 29(12), 2143–2156 (2007)
6. Zhang, T., Yang, J., Zhao, D., Ge, X.: Linear Local Tangent Space Alignment and Application to Face Recognition. Neurocomputing 70, 1547–1553 (2007)
7. Goldberg, Y., Zakai, A., Kushnir, D., Ritov, Y.: Manifold Learning: The Price of Normalization. Machine Learning Research 9, 1909–1939 (2008)
8. Rosman, G., Bronstein, M.M., Bronstein, A.M., Kimmel, R.: Nonlinear Dimensionality Reduction by Topologically Constrained Isometric Embedding. Computer Vision 89, 56–68 (2010)
9. Lin, T., Zha, H.B.: Riemannian Manifold Learning. Pattern Analysis and Machine Intelligence 30(5), 796–809 (2008)
10. Tenenbaum, J.B., De Silva, V., Langford, J.C.: A global Geometric Framework for Nonlinear Dimensionality Reduction. Science 290(5000), 2219–2323 (2000)
11. Roweis, S.T., Saul, L.K.: Nonlinear Dimensionality Reduction by Locally Linear Embedding. Science 290(5000), 2323–2326 (2000)
12. Donoho, D.L., Grimes, C.: Hessian eigenmaps: Locally Linear Embedding Techniques for High-dimensional Data. Proceedings of the National Academy of Sciences 100(10), 5591–5599 (2003)
13. Zhang, Z.Y., Zha, H.Y.: Principal Manifolds and Nonlinear Dimension Reduction via Local Tangent Space Alignment. SLAM Journal of Scientific Computing 26(1), 313–338 (2004)
14. Belkin, M., Niyogi, P.: Laplacian Eigenmaps for Dimensionality Reduction and Data Representation. Neural Computation 15, 1373–1396 (2002)

15. Weinberger, K.Q., Sha, F., Saul, L.K.: Learning a Kernal Matrix for Nonlinear Dimensionality Reduction. In: Proc. 21st ICML, pp. 839–846 (2004)
16. Coifman, R.R., Lafon, S.: Diffusion Maps. Applied and Computational Harmonic Ayalysis 21, 5–30 (2006)
17. Sha, F., Saul, L.K.: Analysis and Extension of Spectral Methods for Nonlinear Dimensionality Reduction. In: Proc. 22nd Int'l Conf. Machine Learning, pp. 785–792 (2005)
18. Gashler, M., Ventura, D., Martinez, T.: Manifold Learning by Graduated Optimization. System, Man, and Cybernetics-Part B: Bybernetics 41(6), 1458–1470 (2011)
19. Kennedy, J., Eberhart, R.: Particle Swarm Optimization. In: Proceedings of IEEE International Conference on Neural Networks, vol. IV, pp. 1942–1948 (2005)
20. Mani Data set, http://www.math.ucla.edu/~wittman/mani/index.html
21. Frey Faces Data Set, http://www.cs.nyu.edu/~roweis/data.html

Application of Modified Teaching-Learning Algorithm in Coordination Optimization of TCSC and SVC

Liwu Xiao, Qianlong Zhu, Canbing Li, Yijia Cao, Yi Tan, and Lijuan Li

College of Electrical and Information Engineering, Hunan University, Changsha, China
licanbing@gmail.com, xlwbeyond@163.com

Abstract. Due to the interaction among FACTS devices, coordination control of multi-FACTS devices is a hot and urgent topic. A multi-objective optimization problem is formulated in this paper. And a modified teaching-learning algorithm (MTLA) is presented to coordinate Thyristor Controlled Series Capacitor (TCSC), Static Var Compensator (SVC) and power angle difference damping characteristics of generators. The optimal parameters of controller are found out to improve the coordination control. Compared with basic-TLA, MTLA applies a new learner phase in order to avoid entrapment into local optima. Then it comes with a locked device phase for the improvement of convergence rate. Meanwhile, several meta-heuristic techniques are utilized to search and save Pareto-optimal solutions of controller parameters. The proposed algorithm is validated and illustrated on IEEE 4-machine 11-bus system.

Keywords: flexible AC transmission system (FACTS), multi-objective optimization, static var compensator (SVC), thyristor controlled series capacitor (TCSC), teaching-learning algorithm (TLA).

1 Introduction

Flexible AC transmission system (FACTS) can play an important role in enhancing system controllability and increasing transmission capacity of modern interconnected system [1]. However, according to some literatures, interactions among FACTS controllers do exist, and negative interactions may lead to the onset of oscillations and directly threaten the security of system operation [2-4]. So the coordinated control of multi-FACTS controllers is necessary.

Many algorithms have been developed to solve this problem. Reference [5] uses a multi-objective honey-bee mating optimization (HBMO) to find optimal location as well as parameters of SVC, TCSC and PSS controllers. References [6, 7] use a multi-objective evolutionary algorithm (MOEA) to solve the coordination design problem of multiple FACTS controllers. However, some algorithm parameters must be determined in advance, such as the inertia weight factor and two acceleration coefficients in PSO, the mutation probability and the crossover probability in GA. Network topology and system parameters, such as power load, are continuously changing during operation. In some cases, considering dynamic adjustable margin, it is difficult to find the global optimal solution.

S. Li et al. (Eds.): CCPR 2014, Part I, CCIS 483, pp. 44–53, 2014.

Teaching-Learning Algorithm (TLA) is a kind of nature-inspired algorithm, firstly presented to solve mechanical design optimization problems [8]. There is no user-defined parameter in this algorithm, which makes it superior than earlier ones [9]. So far, the TLA has been applied to many kinds of power system optimization problems upon conflicting multi-objectives, such as economic emission dispatch, and optimal power flow [10-12]. It's also hopeful for the TLA to play a vital role in static coordination optimization of FACTS devices.

In this paper, a modified TLA, namely MTLA, is proposed to study the coordinated tuning for reducing negative interactions between TCSC and SVC controllers, and multi-objective functions are built for optimization problems. MTLA improves the learner phase and comes with a locked device phase. And several meta-heuristic techniques are applied to perfect the multi-objective optimization method in MTLA. Simulation results show the proposed MTLA is feasible and effective to damp the system oscillations.

2   Optimization Problem and Algorithm

2.1   Problem Description

The MOP can be generally described as follows:

$$
\begin{aligned}
&\text{Minmize } f_i(X), \qquad i = 1, 2, \cdots, N_O; \\
&\text{subject to } g_j(X) \geq 0, \ j = 1, 2, \cdots N_{Eq}; \\
&h_k(X) = 0, \ k = 1, 2, \cdots N_{Ineq};
\end{aligned}
\tag{1}
$$

where N_{Eq} represents number of equality constraints, N_{Ineq} represents number of inequality constraints.

The coordination optimization of SVC and TCSC is regarded as a MOP in this paper. The objective function of coordinated tuning should select some observable state variables in power system, which satisfies the control targets of FACTS devices and exactly reflects transient stability. TCSC can increase power transfer capability, and SVC is connected in parallel for stability enhancement of the transmission voltage, so, here, power difference and voltage difference are considered. Additionally, the integral square-error criterion can be used to indicate the dynamic performance of FACTS device controllers. The relative power-angle damping characteristic, which is a critical factor for the system secure operation, is also considered in this paper.

In this paper, TCSC is a single input single output (SISO) PI-type controller and SVC is a voltage regulator model. X_{TCSC} and B_{SVC} can be described as follows:

$$
\begin{cases}
X_{TCSC} = (K_P + K_I / s)(P_{ref} - P_{TCSC}) \\
\dot{B}_{SVC} = (K_{SVC}(V_{ref} - V_{SVC}) - B_{SVC}) / T_{SVC}
\end{cases}
\tag{2}
$$

where K_P is the proportional constant, K_I is the integral constant, K_{SVC} is the gain constant, T_{SVC} is the time constant.

So the objective functions are defined as follows:

$$
\min \begin{cases} f_1(K_P, K_I, K_{SVC}) = \int_0^{t^{sim}} \left| \Delta V_{SVC} \right| dt \\ f_2(K_P, K_I, K_{SVC}) = \int_0^{t^{sim}} \left| \Delta P_{TCSC} \right| dt \\ f_3(K_P, K_I, K_{SVC}) = \int_0^{t^{sim}} \left(\left| \delta_{12} \right| + \left| \delta_{13} \right| + \left| \delta_{14} \right| \right) dt \end{cases}, \quad \begin{cases} 0 \le K_P \le 20 \\ 0 \le K_I \le 30 \\ 0 \le K_{SVC} \le 150 \end{cases} \quad (3)
$$

2.2 Multi-objective Modified Teaching-Learning Algorithm

The basic-TLA may not obtain a uniformly distributed Pareto-Optimal Front (POF) in some special situations. Particularly, exchanging information only between every two learners is easy to cause local optima and premature convergence. So in this paper, the search mechanism and the search storage are modified.

The Modified Search Mechanism
The process of basic-TLA is divided into two phases: 1) Teacher Phase, 2) Learner Phase. Mimicked as a teacher, the most knowledgeable learner will try to increase the class marks or grades by means of sharing knowledge. In the latter phase, learners exchange their information between every two learners.

In the basic-TLA, the interactions in the learners phase may lead to premature convergence and fail to proceed to the global optimal solution. Therefore, an improved approach is proposed to damp the inappropriate interactions. The learner phase is no longer restricted to two students but combined with a subsidiary phase. And a locked device phase is added to improve convergence rate. Each objective may not conflict with others in special problems. In locked device phase, some certain abilities will be enhanced particularly via locking the parameters, which has close connection with the reconcilable objectives. The process of MTLA is divided into three phases: 1) Teacher Phase, 2) Improved learner phase, 3) Locked Device Phase.

1) Teacher Phase
The optimal solution will be selected as the teacher in the current iteration. And learners will gain part of the knowledge according to the capability of a teacher and the quality of learners at present. This phase uses the mean value to assess the quality of learners in class. The old solution will be modified according to the difference between the existed mean and the teacher's solution. The update will be accepted if the new solution has a better function value than that of the old one. The teacher phase is described as follows:

$$
\begin{cases} X_{i,j}^{new,k} = X_{i,j}^{old,k} + r(X^{teacher,k} - T_f M_j^k) \\ M_j^k = \dfrac{(X_{1,j}^{old,k} + X_{2,j}^{old,k} + \cdots + X_{N_L,j}^{old,k})}{N_L} \end{cases} \quad (4)
$$

where $i=1,2\cdots,N_L$, N_L represents number of learners in the learner repository, $j=1,2\cdots,N_A$, N_A represents number of learners' abilities, $k\in Iter_{max}$, $Iter_{max}$ represents number of maximum iteration, $X_{i,j}^{new,k}$ represents new solution and of jth capability of ith learner in iteration k, $X_{i,j}^{old,k}$ represents old solution and of jth capability of ith learner in iteration k, M_j^k represents mean value of jth capability in iteration k, r represents random number in the range $[0, 1]$, T_f represents either 1 or 2 with equal probability.

2)   Improved Learner Phase

Outstanding learners can help in coordination to improve the knowledge level. The old solution is updated in this phase by exchanging information in a team. But the new solution will be selected with half probability as the member of the next iteration. To ensure the randomness of the searching process, the improved learner phase applies a subsidiary phase to revise the new solution. The learner phase is formulated as follows:

$$X_{i,j}^{new,k} = X_{i,j}^{old,k} + r_1(\frac{X_{i_1,j}^{old,k} + X_{i_2,j}^{old,k}}{2} - X_{i_3,j}^{old,k})$$ (5)

$$\begin{cases} X_{i,j}^{new,k} = X_{i,j}^{new,k} & r_1 \geq 0.5 \\ X_{i,j}^{new,k} = X_{i,j}^{new,k} + r_2(X_{i_2,j}^{old,k} - X_{i_1,j}^{old,k}) & r_1 < 0.5 \end{cases}$$ (6)

where $i\in N_L$, $j\in N_A$, $k\in Iter_{max}$, i_1, i_2 and i_3 are three random learners, and the first learner has the worst marks or grades, r_1 and r_2 represent random number in the range $[0, 1]$.

3)   Locked Device Phase

Locked device phase will optimize partial parameters of FACTS devices with others locked. The locked parameters will remain the same as the present ones in this phase, and the varied parameters will be evolved on their own separate paths. In the locked device searching process, the evolutionary direction is decided by a sign function, and the evolutionary extent is up to the random number r_1. The locked device phase is shown as follows:

$$\begin{cases} X_{i,m}^{new,k} = X_{i,m}^{old,} \\ X_{i,n}^{new,k} = X_{i,n}^{old,k} + r_1 \cdot sign(r_2) \cdot (X_{i_2,n}^{old,k} - X_{i_1,n}^{old,k}) \end{cases}$$ (7)

where $i\in N_L$, $m\in N_{Locked}$, $n\in N_{Varied}$, $k\in Iter_{max}$, i_1 and i_2 are random learners and the former has worse marks or grades, N_{Locked} represents number of locked abilities, N_{Varied} represents number of varied abilities.

Fuzzy-Based Self-Adaptive 'Round Space' Method

The MTLA adopts a dual-population technique. The common archive is called learner repository. And the external archive, named teacher repository, is used to store current

Pareto-optimal solutions. In order to satisfy the default size and get an even distribution in POF, the Fuzzy-based Self-adaptive 'Round Space' method is used to constitute the teacher repository. The process is illustrated in Fig. 1.

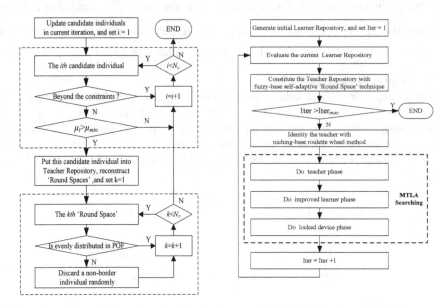

Fig. 1. A flow chart of Fuzzy-based self-adaptive 'Round Space' method

Fig. 2. A flow chart of MTLA

It is worth mentioned that candidate individuals are the newest Pareto-optimal solutions for the current iteration in Fig. 1. The normalized fuzzy membership value is used to recognize the best compromise candidate individual, which is defined in equation (8) and (9) [13].

$$
u_{i,j} = \begin{cases} 1, & f_j(X_i) \le F_j^{\min} \\ \dfrac{F_j^{\max} - f_j(X_i)}{F_j^{\max} - F_j^{\min}}, & F_j^{\min} \le f_j(X_i) \le F_j^{\max} \\ 0, & f_j(X_i) \ge F_j^{\max} \end{cases} \tag{8}
$$

$$
\mu_i = \frac{\sum\limits_{j=1}^{N_F} u_{i,j}}{\sum\limits_{i=1}^{N_C} \sum\limits_{j=1}^{N_F} u_{i,j}} \tag{9}
$$

where $i \in N_C$, N_C represents number of candidate individuals, $j \in N_O$, N_O represents number of objective functions, $F_j^{\max}$ represents maximum value of the jth objective function, F_j^{min} represents minimum value of the jth objective function, $u_{i,j}$ represents fuzzy membership function of the ith objective functions of the jth learner, μ_j represents normalized fuzzy membership value of the jth learner, $f_j(X_i)$ represents the mth objective function value of the ith candidate individual.

Niching-Based Roulette Wheel Method (RMW)

In MTLA, a more excellent teacher can be better in guiding learner repository to find more Pareto-optimal solutions. The niching method based on the fitness sharing is a powerful approach to increase the diversity of the population. The implement of the niching-based RMW to identity a teacher from teacher repository can effectively limit the probability that analogous individuals are selected as a teacher. In this method, the niche count is used to measure the number of analogous individuals in near space. The sharing distance, the sharing fitness function and the niche count can be expressed as follows:

$$d_{i,j} = \sqrt{\sum_{m=1}^{N_O}(f_k(X_i) - f_k(X_j))^2} \tag{10}$$

$$Sh(d_{i,j}) = \begin{cases} 1 - d_{i,j}/\sigma_{share}, & \text{if } d_{i,j} < \sigma_{share} \\ 0, & otherwise \end{cases} \tag{11}$$

$$N(i) = \frac{1}{\sum_{j=1}^{N_T} Sh(d_{i,j})} - 1 \tag{12}$$

where $i, j \in N_T$, $m \in N_o$, σ_{share} represents niche radius, N_T represents number of teachers in the teacher repository, $Sh(d_{i,j})$ represents sharing fitness function value of sharing distance, $N(i)$ represents niche count of the ith teacher for RWM. $d_{i,j}$ represents sharing distance between the ith teacher and the jth teacher.

2.3   Main Procedure of MTLA

The main procedure of MTLA can be illustrated in Fig.2. The termination criterion is set to maximum iteration. The optimization steps will be described as following:

1) Initialize learner groups, according to the space and constrained solutions of controller parameters;
2) Evaluate learner groups using the multi-objective optimization model to solve the objective function of each learner;
3) Build teacher group based on fuzzy-based self-adaptive 'Round Space' method;
4) Select the teacher individual into the teaching search based on niching-based roulette wheel method;
5) MTLA search including teacher search, learner search and locked device search;
6) Return to step 2 until meet the termination conditions.

2.4   The Comparison of Different Algorithms

In order to demonstrate the superiority of the proposed algorithm, evolutionary pro-gramming (EP), basic-TLA and MTLA are compared from the perspective of deter-ministic single-objective optimizations. Fig. 3 shows the convergence performance curve of relative power-angle damping characteristic (3rd objective function). It can be observed that MTLA is superior in searching for the optimal solution than other ones. The mean value, optimal value and worst value of the three algorithms are shown in Tab. 1 respectively, and the improvement of the global searching ability is explored easily through these figures.

Table 1. Comparison among different algorithms

Algorithm	Mean Value	Best Value	Worst Value
EP	7.5499	8.2359	9.1048
TLA	7.4583	7.5889	8.8203
MTLA	7.3630	7.3715	7.3796

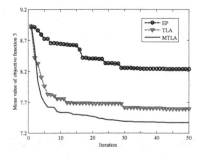 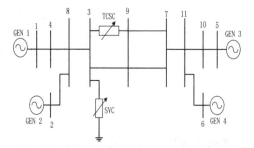

Fig. 3. The curves for single-objective opti-mization by EP, TLA and MTLA

Fig. 4. A single-line diagram of IEEE 11-bus system allocated TCSC and SVC

3   Case Study

3.1   The Simulation System

In this paper, a classical IEEE 4-machine 11-bus system is used, as shown in Fig. 4. TCSC is located at the transmission-line L3-L9. SVC is located at bus 3.

3.2   Interaction Analysis

SVC and TCSC controllers separately designed have good performance when they are individually implemented. However, the combined-operation is unsatisfactory.

Two controllers are designed by the standard controller regulative method in SISO control system. In this method, the parameters are $K_P=0.5$, $K_I=12$, $K_{SVC}=150$

(T_{SVC}=0.05). Fig. 5 shows separated-operation performances of TCSC and SVC in opened-loop control. When the bus with SVC is disturbed at 0.5s, the reference value of node voltage steps from 0.931 to 0.962. When the line with TCSC is disturbed at 0.5s, the reference value of active power in transmission line steps from 0.919 to 0.898. It can be observed that the controller design is successful in separated-operation. But when the combined-operation among FACTS controllers is disturbed at 0.5s, its negative interactions lead to serious oscillation and the oscillation frequency is about 60 Hz in Fig.6.

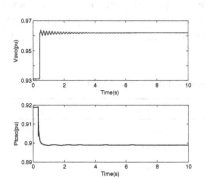

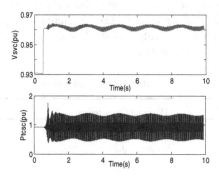

Fig. 5. Separated-operation performances of TCSC and SVC by the standard method

Fig. 6. Combined-operation performances of TCSC and SVC by the standard method

3.3   Coordinated Optimization Control Analysis

The proposed method is implemented to optimize the parameters of the TCSC and SVC controller. In the MTLA, the populations of teacher groups and learner groups are 50 and 100 respectively, and the maximum number of iterations is 50. The obtained POF is shown in Fig. 7. It can be observed that the control target of SVC is not contradictory to relative power-angle damping characteristic in terms of MOP. Therefore, MTLA can improve convergent rate through laying particular stress on locking the parameters of TCSC in the locked device phase.

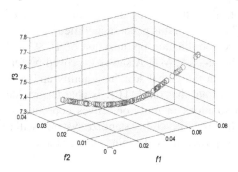

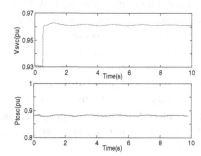

Fig. 7. Pareto-optimal front by MTLA

Fig. 8. Combined-operation perfor-mances of TCSC and SVC by MTLA

Table 2. Controller parameters by standard method and MTLA

Controller Parameter	Standard Method	MTLA
K_P	0.5	0.2417
K_I	12	15.7699
K_{SVC}	150	128.8189

The distinction among different Pareto solutions is manifested as: at least one control target is better while others are worse. Thus, the picked final solution becomes a matter of decision-makers' preference or practical applications. The parameters are given respectively in Tab. 2, which are designed by standard PI-controller regulative method and MTLA.

Table 3. Damping characteristic by standard method and MTLA

Damping Characteristic	Standard Method	MTLA
δ_{12}	1.0798	1.0663
δ_{13}	2.8282	2.7189
δ_{14}	3.7049	3.5854
δ_{sum}	7.6129	7.3706

The implement of the nonlinear time-domain simulations in the system is shown in Fig. 4. And the comparison between Fig. 6 and Fig. 8 shows the difference of two control strategies. The coordinated tuning by MTLA has successfully stabilized the system, especially in damping the high-frequency oscillations. In Tab. 3, the relative power-angle damping characteristic is somewhat satisfied under voltage disturbance through the controller parameters designed by MTLA. By analyzing the statistic, the improvement in inter-area generators is more obvious than that in same area generators.

4   Conclusion

Negative interactions among FACTS controllers, threatening directly the security of system operation, need to be decreased. Therefore, in this paper, a modified teaching-learning algorithm is proposed to solve the coordination optimization of TCSC and SVC controllers. Compared with EP and basic-TLA, MTLA shows improved performance for the single-objective optimization in the global searching ability and convergent rate. And simulation results demonstrate that the MTLA is able to provide high quality and well distributed Pareto solutions in multi-objectives coordination optimization. Moreover, the proposed method is successful to stabilize system oscillations in high-frequency and improve relative power-angle damping characteristic.

Acknowledgements. This work was supported by National Science and technology support program (2011BAA01B02).

References

1. Zhang, X., Rehtanz, C., et al.: Flexible AC Transmission Systems: Modeling and Control. Springer, New York (2006)
2. Li, Y., Rehtanz, C., Ruberg, S., et al.: Assessment and choice of input signals for multiple HVDC and FACTS wide-area damping controllers. IEEE Transmission Power Systems 27(4), 1969–1977 (2012)
3. Wang, H.F.: Design of non-negatively interactive FACTS-based stabilizers in multi-machine power systems. Electric Power Systems Research 50, 169–174 (1999)
4. Gibbard, M.J., Vowles, D.J., Pourbeik, P.: Interactions between and effectiveness of power system stabilizers and FACTS device stabilizers in multimachine systems. IEEE Transmission Power Systems 15(2), 748–755 (2000)
5. Shayeghi, H., Moradzadeh, M., Ghasemi, A., Vandevelde, L.: Simultaneous optimal placement and tuning of SVC, TCSC and PSS parameters using multi objective honey-bee mating optimization. In: Proceedings of the 5th IEEE PES Asia-Pacific Power and Energy Engineering Conference (APPEEC 2013), Hong Kong, China, 5 p. (2013)
6. Zou, Z., Jiang, Q., Zhang, P., et al.: Coordinated design of TCSC and SVC controllers based on multi-objective evolutionary algorithm. Automation of Electric Power Systems 29(6), 60–65 (2005) (in Chinese)
7. Zhang, L., Ye, B., Jiang, Q., Cao, Y.: Application of Multi-Objective Evolutionary Programming in Coordinated Design of FACTS Controllers for Transient Stability Improvement. In: 2006 IEEE PES Power Systems Conference and Exposition, Atlanta, GA, October 29-November 1, pp. 2085–2089 (2006)
8. Rao, R.V., Savsani, V.J., Vakharia, D.P.: Teaching-learning-based optimization: A novel method for constrained mechanical design optimization problems. IEEE Trans. Comput.-Aided Des. 43(3), 303–315 (2011)
9. Rao, R.V., Patel, V.: Multi-objective optimization of two stage thermoelectric cooler using a modified teaching–learning-based optimization algorithm. Electr. Eng. Appl. Artif. Intel. 26, 430–445 (2013)
10. Azizipanah-Abarghooeea, R., Niknama, T., Roostaa, A., et al.: Probabilistic multiobjective wind-thermal economic emission dispatch based on point estimated method. Energy 37(1), 322–355 (2012)
11. Niknam, T., Golestaneh, F., Sadeghi, M.S.: θ-multiobjective teaching–learning-based optimization for dynamic economic emission Dispatch. IEEE Syst. J. 6(2), 341–352 (2012)
12. Nayak, M.R., Nayak, C.K., Rout, P.K.: Application of multi-objective teaching learning based optimization algorithm to optimal power flow problem. In: Proceedings of 2nd International Conference on Communication, Computing & Security, Rourkela, pp. 255–264 (2012)
13. Bui, L.T., Abbass, H., Barlow, M., et al.: Robustness against the decision-maker's attitude to risk in problems with conflicting objectives. IEEE Transactions on Evolutionary Computation 16(1), 1–19 (2012)

Multi-task Sparse Gaussian Processes with Improved Multi-task Sparsity Regularization

Jiang Zhu and Shiliang Sun

Department of Computer Science and Technology
East China Normal University
500 Dongchuan Road, Shanghai 200241, China

Abstract. Gaussian processes are a popular and effective Bayesian method for classification and regression. Generating sparse Gaussian processes is a hot research topic, since Gaussian processes have to face the problem of cubic time complexity with respect to the size of the training set. Inspired by the idea of multi-task learning, we believe that simultaneously selecting subsets of multiple Gaussian processes will be more suitable than selecting them separately. In this paper, we propose an improved multi-task sparsity regularizer which can effectively regularize the subset selection of multiple tasks for multi-task sparse Gaussian processes. In particular, based on the multi-task sparsity regularizer proposed in [12], we perform two improvements: 1) replacing a subset of points with a rough global structure when measuring the global consistency of one point; 2) performing normalization on each dimension of every data set before sparsification. We combine the regularizer with two methods to demonstrate its effectiveness. Experimental results on four real data sets show its superiority.

Keywords: Gaussian processes, multi-task learning, sparse representation, regularization.

1 Introduction

Gaussian processes [1,2] are a popular and powerful non-parametric tool for probabilistic modeling. However, the scaling problem of the cubic time complexity with respect to the training size N limits their widespread use. Lots of efforts [4,5,6,12,13] have been made to overcome the cubic time complexity problem. A common way to solve this is to select a subset of the training set to get a sparse representation of the original Gaussian process, where the subset size d is much smaller than N. The time complexity of the training can be brought down from $O(N^3)$ to $O(d^2 N)$. Various criteria exist for selecting the subset. For example, Lawrence et al. [5] selected the points with the biggest entropy reduction based on information theory. Titsias [6] selected the points with the smallest Kullback-Leibler divergence between the variational distribution and the exact posterior distribution over the latent function value.

S. Li et al. (Eds.): CCPR 2014, Part I, CCIS 483, pp. 54–62, 2014.

Multi-task learning is an active research direction [3,7,8,15]. Simultaneously learning multiple tasks can be more effective than learning them separately because the relationship between tasks can be exploited to benefit learning. In this paper, we focus on multi-task sparse Gaussian processes. Some work [9,10,12] has been done to sparsify multiple Gaussian processes. For example, the multi-task informative vector machine (MTIVM) [9] which is an extension of [5] shares the kernel matrix and the training set among tasks. Then, all the tasks just train one Gaussian process for prediction. Time and memory consumption are much reduced, but the performance of this method could be unsatisfactory when large differences between tasks exist. Based on the idea that global structures of subsets of multiple tasks should be consistent, recently Zhu and Sun[12] proposed a multi-task sparsity regularizer which regularize the subset selection of multiple Gaussian processes.

In this paper, we propose an improved multi-task sparsity regularizer which makes improvements over the above regularizer. It consists of three steps. First, normalization for each data set on each dimension is performed before the subset selection to make them in the same range. Second, it utilizes manifold-preserving graph reduction (MPGR) [12,14] to select one rough global structure for each task. Last, it replaces the already-selected points in the multi-task sparsity regularization formula with the rough global structures when calculating the Euclidean distance of one data point to its k nearest neighbors from other tasks. We integrate the regularizer with MPGR and manifold-preserving graph reduction with outputs (MPGRO) [13] to get IrMTMPGR and IrMTMPGRO, respectively. Here, "I" stands for "improved" to distinguish them from the multi-task Gaussian processes built by the previous multi-task sparsity regularizer, and "r" stands for "relevance" because our method explicitly considers the task relevance. Experimental results show its effectiveness.

A preliminary report [12] has been presented. In this paper, we make significant improvements for the multi-task sparsity regularizer, and conduct more experiments.

The rest of the paper is organized as follows. First we introduce related work with the multi-task sparsity regularizer. After that, we will analyze two shortages of the multi-task sparsity regularizer, propose the improved multi-task sparsity regularizer and apply it to construct multi-task Gaussian processes. We make our conclusion after experiments on four real data sets.

2   Relate Work

In this section, we briefly introduce the multi-task sparsity regularizer[12].

Based on the idea that the global structures of retained points from closely related tasks should be similar and structures from loosely related tasks should be less similar, the multi-task sparsity regularizer is proposed which regularize the subset selection of multiple Gaussian processes.

It is composed of two parts: 1) One to measure the global consistency of two subsets; 2) One to measure the task relevance. For the first part, the authors use the term $\sum_{j=1}^{k} \frac{1}{\|x_{t_n} - x_i^j\|}$ to evaluate, where x_{t_n} is a point considered for selection from task t_n and x_i^j ($j = 1, ..., k$) are k nearest neighbors of x_{t_n} from the already-selected points of another task i. The reciprocal of the Euclidean distance is adopted for the sake of maximizing the regularization formula. For the second part, the authors use the $\frac{1}{\|f_{t_n} - f_i\|}$ to modulate the task relevance, where f_{t_n} is the task-descriptor feature of task t_n. The task-descriptor feature is utilized to describe tasks. Bonilla et al. [11] chose eight crucial points and set the mean of their labels to be the the task-descriptor feature.

The multi-task sparsity regularizer is then reached by combining the two terms mentioned above. The regularization formula is given as

$$Reg(x_{t_n}) = \sum_{i=1, i \neq t_n}^{n_t} \sum_{j=1}^{k} \frac{1}{\| f_{t_n} - f_i \| \| x_{t_n} - x_i^j \|}, \tag{1}$$

where n_t is the total number of tasks. A big value of Reg means that the point to be evaluated is more globally consistent with other tasks for its own task.

In that paper, the authors also integrated the multi-task sparsity regularizer with MPGR to get a multi-task sparse Gaussian process, the relevance multi-task manifold-preserving graph reduction (rMTMPGR). The sparse criterion of rMTMPGR is

$$deg\,(x_{t_n}) + \lambda Reg(x_{t_n}), \tag{2}$$

where $deg\,(x_{t_n}) = \sum_j w(x_{t_n}, j)$, and λ controls the proportion between the MPGR formula and the regularizer.

3 Multi-task Sparse Gaussian Processes with Improved Multi-task Sparsity Regularization

The above multi-task sparsity regularizer seeks to simultaneously construct multiple sparse Gaussian processes utilizing the consistency of global structures of retained points among sparse subsets of different tasks. Although the starting point is reasonable, two shortages still exist.

The first shortage is that the multi-task sparsity regularizer is prone to overfit the initial points. In formula (1), the multi-task sparsity regularizer uses already-selected points of related tasks. This pushes the initial points to a very important position. Many subsequent points would consider the initial points when evaluating their global consistency. Specially before the kth selection, the initial points are used in formula (1) for all the previous iterations. This makes the following selected points prone to be close to the initial points. A straightforward strategy to solve this is to replace the already-selected points with the full data sets. But for every selection, it has to calculate the Euclidean distance from one candidate to all the points in the other tasks. For the efficiency purpose, we replace the already-selected points with a rough global structure. By the rough global structure, we mean that its size should be larger than the targeted sparse number of points d and its points are representative. In this paper, we set the size to $2d$. This can avoid the overfitting shortage, and also improve the generalization ability of the multi-task sparsity regularizer. For the algorithm to select the rough global structure, the MPGR algorithm is suitable because of its superiority on representative-subset selection.

As shown in Fig. 1, we employ the multi-task sparsity regularizer and the improved multi-task sparsity regularizer with the MPGR algorithm, respectively, to choose four points. The top point is set as the initial point. The result demonstrates that the subset selected with the improved multi-task sparsity regularizer is more representative. Fig. 1 is only for illustrative purpose, and more experiments on real data sets will be performed in the next section.

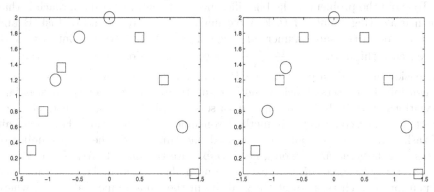

Fig. 1. Different selections by the multi-task sparsity regularizer and the improved multi-task sparsity regularizer. Circle points are already-selected points. Square points are candidate points that have not been selected.

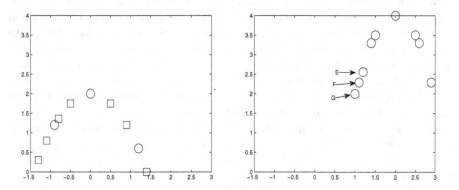

Fig. 2. An illustration of the problem of numerical scale differences that the multi-task sparsity regularizer has to face. Task A (left) is selecting the next point with a related task (right). Points E, F and G will always be the three nearest neighbors of points of task A.

The other shortage is that the multi-task sparsity regularizer disregards the situation that a big difference of the range of input values between tasks exists. Since the Euclidean distance is adopted to reflect similarities in formula

(1), when the ranges of the input values among tasks are very different, the multi-task sparsity regularizer will possibly have a negative effect on the subset selection. See Fig. 2. Suppose tasks A and B are selecting their sparse subsets, and just three nearest neighbors are considered in formula (1). When evaluating the consistency of points in task A at this selection, points E, F and G are counted in because they are closer to points of task A. In addition, these three points would always be the three nearest neighbors of points of task A. This can lead to a critical overfitting problem.

To avoid the problem of the big difference, a straightforward approach is that when evaluating points of task A we make changes to points of task B and let them be in the same numerical range of task A. For every point of task B, we execute this formula $\frac{x^n + m_A^n - m_B^n}{\sigma_B^n / \sigma_A^n}$ for each dimension, where x^n is the nth dimension of one data point in task B, m_A^N and m_B^n are mean values of the nth dimension of data sets of task A and B, respectively, and σ_A^n and σ_B^n are standard deviations of the nth dimension of data sets of task A and B, respectively. The shortage is overcome but this method consumes too much time. For each pair of tasks, the formula would be executed one time. And when the number of tasks is as large as M, it would need to execute the formula $M(M-1)$ times. A better way to solve this is to execute a normalization formula $\frac{x^n - m^n}{\sigma^n}$ for each dimension of each task to let them all be in the same numerical range, where m and σ are the mean value and the standard deviation, respectively. By this method, each task only needs to execute the formula one time, and the formula would be executed M times when the number of tasks is M.

With the two shortages overcome, the obtained method is called the improved multi-task sparsity regularizer. In conclusion, it consists of three steps. First, normalization for each data set on each dimension is performed to make them in the same range. The formula $\frac{x^n - m^n}{\sigma^n}$ is utilized. Second, it utilizes MPGR to select a rough global structure for each task. Last, it replaces the already-selected points with the rough global structures when calculating the distance of a data point to its k nearest neighbors from other tasks. Compared to the previous multi-task sparsity regularizer, it solves the overfitting problem not only to the initial points but also that derived from the big scale difference. At the same time, points that are considered in formula (1) would be more representative. Thus, it improves the generalization ability of the previous regularizer. For comparison, we apply the improved multi-task sparsity regularizer to MPGR and MPGRO to get multi-task sparse Gaussian processes IrMTMPGR and IrMTMPGRO, respectively, in the same way as the previous multi-task sparsity regularizer.

4   Experiments

We evaluate our methods on four real data sets, Landmine, Concrete slump, MONK and Energy efficiency. To demonstrate the generalization ability of our methods, these data sets include problems for binary classification, multi-class classification and regression. All the data sets are public, which can be found from the UCI Machine Learning Repository.

We utilize the GPML toolbox [1] to construct Gaussian processes. All the mean functions, covariance functions, likelihood functions and inference methods are selected by the accuracy of one experiment with the whole training set. We conduct experiments ten times on each data set. The training set and the test set are split randomly. The parameters needed for MPGR and MPGRO are set the same as in [13]. To make λ easy to set, we split it into two parameters, $\lambda = \alpha \times \beta$. First, we use a normalization parameter α which is set to be the ratio of the maximum values of the formula of MPGR or MPGRO and our regularizers, to make them in the same range. Then, we set β to control the relative proportion, which is selected from $\{1/2, 2/3, 1, 3/2, 2\}$. We proceed to choose all the parameters by five-fold cross-validation on the training set. Then we evaluate performance on the test set. We conduct our experiments by a computer with dual 2.53 GHz CPUs and one GB memory.

The error rates and average time are utilized to evaluate the performance of different methods. For classification, the error rate is measured by the rate of misclassification. For regression, the error rate is measured by mean absolute relative error (MARE), which is defined as

$$MARE = \frac{1}{\ell_x} \sum_i \left| \frac{x_i^* - x_i}{x_i} \right|, \qquad (3)$$

where x_i is the real value of the ith point, x_i^* is its predicted value and ℓ_x is the total number of points. The average time is the mean of time on ten experiments, including subset selection and constructing Gaussian processes with the subsets. We choose two kinds of multi-task sparse Gaussian processes as a baseline. As mentioned before, IVM is extended to MTIVM [9] by sharing the kernel parameters and training set among multiple tasks. For comparison purpose in this paper, we develop MPGR algorithm for constructing sparse Gaussian processes to MTMPGR in the same way, which selects the point with the largest degree among points of all the tasks. MPGRO is also extended to MTMPGRO for contrast.

The Landmine data set is collected from a read landmine field. It is a binary classification problem that has 19 related tasks with 9674 data points in total and each point is represented by a nine-dimensional feature vector. Due to the time constraint, we just randomly choose five tasks for experiments, and for each task we randomly choose 320 points as the training data, 80 for test and the subset size is 40. It is necessary to mention that the Landmine data set is an unbalanced data set where the ratio of +1 class is only 6.18% on average. The Concrete slump data set including 103 data points concerns a regression problem. The slump flow of concrete is not only determined by the water content, but also influenced by other concrete ingredients. Seven feature attributes are used to predict three output variables. We apply this multi-output data to multi-task experiments by setting each output as a task. In this setting, from the perspective of inputs, all three tasks are closely consistent both locally and globally. We randomly

---

[1] http://gaussianprocess.org/gpml/

Table 1. Experimental results on the Landmine data set

Method	Error rate (%)	Time (s)
MTMPGR	7.4 ± 2.5	104.9
rMTMPGR	6.9 ± 1.5	105.6
IrMTMPGR	**6.5 ± 1.4**	172.9
MTMPGRO	22.5 ± 7.7	510.4
rMTMPGRO	50.1 ± 8.5	**46.2**
IrMTMPGRO	47.3 ± 10.6	238.7

choose 80 points as the training data, 23 for test, and the subset size is 50. The MONK data set is a famous classification problem which is the basis of

Table 2. Experimental results on the Concrete slump data set

Method	Error rate (%)	Time (s)
MTMPGR	16.5 ± 4.1	**1.3**
rMTMPGR	16.4 ± 2.6	2.3
IrMTMPGR	14.0 ± 1.6	4.9
MTMPGRO	16.4 ± 4.7	2.4
rMTMPGRO	14.5 ± 2.4	1.6
IrMTMPGRO	**13.5 ± 2.5**	7.1

the first international comparison of learning algorithms. It rely on an artificial robot domain, in which robots are described by six different attributes. Three tasks are included, and all their data are randomly selected from 432 robots. They are different in task size, feature setting, misclassification ratio and noise. Their sizes are 124, 169 and 122, respectively. We randomly choose 120 points as the training data, 80 for test, and the subset size is 30. The Energy efficiency

Table 3. Experimental results on MONK

Method	Error rate (%)	Time (s)
MTMPGR	32.1 ± 6	**2.6**
rMTMPGR	**23.0 ± 5.5**	3.0
IrMTMPGR	34.7 ± 4.9	5.1
MTMPGRO	37.6 ± 4.2	3.0
rMTMPGRO	26.4 ± 8.3	2.8
IrMTMPGRO	24.2 ± 7.7	7.5

data set is provided by a study which attempts to assess the heating load and cooling load requirements of buildings (that is, energy efficiency) as a function of building parameters. The data set contains eight features to predict the two responses. It is similar to the concrete slump data set which is also a multi-output regression problem. We randomly choose 300 points as the training data, 100 for test, and the subset size is 50. Tables 1~4 list the experimental results,

Table 4. Experimental results on the Energy efficiency data set

Method	Error rate (%)	Time (s)
MTMPGR	12.7 ± 1.3	14.7
rMTMPGR	23.1 ± 5.4	15.7
lrMTMPGR	14.4 ± 0.4	25.1
MTMPGRO	15.3 ± 2.1	9.4
rMTMPGRO	11.7 ± 1.5	**6.9**
lrMTMPGRO	**11.2 ± 0.1**	27.9

which show the effectiveness of the improved multi-task regularizer. From the overall prediction performance, just like previous informal analysis, the improved multi-task sparsity regularizer is obviously the best among all the methods for constructing multi-task sparse Gaussian processes. From the perspective of error rates, the best learning algorithms associated with the four data sets almost all utilize the improved multi-task sparsity regularizer. As mentioned before, the Landmine data set is an unbalanced data set. Experimental results in Table 1 show that MTMPGRO works badly on this condition, and the results get worse with the regularizer. This unbalanced case is an open problem worth studying in the future.

5   Conclusion

In this paper, we proposed the improved multi-task sparsity regularizer to overcome two shortages of the multi-task sparsity regularizer. We utilized the MPGR algorithm to choose rough global structures and replaced the already-selected points with them in formula (1). Then, we carried out normalization for each data set on each dimension before the subset selection of multiple Gaussian processes. The combined method to get multi-task sparse Gaussian processes is the same as the previous multi-task sparsity regularizer. Experimental results have shown that it indeed improves the performance of the multi-task sparsity regularizer.

As mentioned in the experiment section, the improved multi-task sparsity regularizer combined with MTMPGRO can not perform well on the unbalanced data set. Special considerations on unbalanced data sets will be one of our future research topics. The time consumed by the methods coupled with the improved multitask sparsity regularizer is slightly higher, which will be optimized in the future.

Acknowledgements. This work is supported by the National Natural Science Foundation of China under Project 61370175 and 61075005, and Shanghai Knowledge Service Platform Project (No.ZF1213).

References

1. Rasmussen, C., Williams, C.: Gaussian process for machine learning. MIT Press, Cambridge (2006)
2. Sun, S.: Infinite mixtures of multivariate Gaussian processes. In: Proceedings of the International Conference on Machine Learning and Cybernetics, pp. 1011–1016 (2013)
3. Bonilla, E., Chai, K.M., Williams, C.K.I.: Multi-task Gaussian process prediction. In: Proceedings of the Neural Information Processing Systems, pp. 1–8 (2008)
4. Williams, C., Seeger, M.: Using the Nyström method to speed up kernel machines. In: Advances in Neural Information Processing Systems, vol. 13, pp. 682–688 (2001)
5. Lawrence, N., Seeger, M., Herbrich, R.: Fast sparse Gaussian process methods: The informative vector machine. In: Advances in Neural Information Processing Systems, vol. 15, pp. 609–616 (2002)
6. Titsias, M.: Variational learning of inducing variables in sparse Gaussian processes. In: Proceedings of the 12th International Workshop on Artificial Intelligence and Statistics, pp. 567–574 (2009)
7. Dhillon, P., Foster, D., Ungar, L.: Minimum description length penalization for group and multi-task sparse learning. Journal of Machine Learning Research 12, 525–564 (2011)
8. Jebara, T.: Multitask sparsity via maximum entropy discrimination. Journal of Machine Learning Research 12, 75–110 (2011)
9. Lawrence, N., Platt, J.: Learning to learn with the informative vector machine. In: Proceedings of International Conference on Machine Learning, pp. 1–8 (2004)
10. Wang, Y., Khardon, R.: Sparse gaussian processes for multi-task learning. In: Flach, P.A., De Bie, T., Cristianini, N. (eds.) ECML PKDD 2012, Part I. LNCS, vol. 7523, pp. 711–727. Springer, Heidelberg (2012)
11. Bonilla, E., Agakov, F., Williams, C.: Kernel multi-task learning using task-specific features. In: Proceedings of International Conference on Artificial Intelligence and Statistics, pp. 43–50 (2007)
12. Zhu, J., Sun, S.: Single-task and multitask Gaussian processes. In: Proceedings of the International Conference on Machine Learning and Cybernetics, pp. 1033–1038 (2013)
13. Zhu, J., Sun, S.: Sparse Gaussian processes with manifold-preserving graph reduction. Neurocomputing 138, 99–105 (2014)
14. Sun, S., Hussain, Z., Shawe-Taylor, J.: Manifold-preserving graph reduction for sparse semi-supervised learning. Neurocomputing 124, 13–21 (2014)
15. Sun, S.: Multitask learning for EEG-based biometrics. In: Proceedings of the 19th International Conference on Pattern Recognition, pp. 1–4 (2008)

Short-Term Load Forecasting of LSSVM
Based on Improved PSO Algorithm

Qianhui Gong[1], Wenjun Lu[1], Wenlong Gong[2], and Xueting Wang[1]

[1] College of Electrical and Information Engineering,
Hunan University, Changsha 410082, China
[2] State Grid Chongqing Electric Power CO. Yongchuan Power Supply Company,
Chongqing 400000, China

Abstract. Based on the empirical, the precision of the forecasting will directly affect the reliability, economy and quality of power supply in power system. An improved particle swarm optimizer (IPSO) is proposed to be used on the least squares support vector machine (LSSVM) algorithm, which optimized the initialization parameters and improved the accuracy of short-term load forecasting. This thesis use the historical data of a certain grid to set up the short-term load forecasting model based on the optimization algorithm. While the data had comprehensive consideration the meteorology, weather, date, type and other factors which influencing the load. Compare with the LSSVM algorithm and the standard PSO-LSSVM, the empirical results show that IPSO-LSSVM model is more applicable in terms of convergence effect, accurate prediction and fast speed. The IPSO not only improves the accuracy of load forecasting, but also prevents LSSVM from great reliance on empirical results and random selection.

Keywords: load forecasting, improved particle swarm optimization, least square support vector machine, parameter selection.

1   Introduction

Load forecasting is important to power grid security, economic and high-quality operation. As is known to all, power system is a strong nonlinear system, load forecasting is very complex and need to consider many factors. In order to achieve a higher prediction precision and computational efficiency. The neural network prediction model and the fuzzy system forecasting model have been subjected to intensive studies, which has shown that the generalization ability of this kind of model is often lowly.

The support vector machine (SVM) model has been widely concerned in recent years[1]. This model has gotten the smaller actual risk based on the minimum structure risk principle. Meanwhile, minimize the empirical risk and VC dimension, then it has a better generalization ability for the new sample[2]. While the least squares support vector machine (LSSVM) is an extension of the standard SVM, it use a different loss function from the SVM. The LSSVM use equality constraints instead of inequality constraints so as to minimize square error. In the process of solving linear equations,

S. Li et al. (Eds.): CCPR 2014, Part I, CCIS 483, pp. 63–71, 2014.

the forecasting problem has been simplified and the forecasting efficiency has been obvious improved[3].

The LSSVM have been applied in a number of studies. Literature [4] has put forward a short-term load forecasting model based on the chaotic characteristic of load and LSSVM. Literature [5] has put forward the accounting method of LSSVM short-term load forecasting model, which is combined with rough set theory and genetic algorithm. Literature [6] has put forward a kind of intelligent combination power short-term load forecasting method, which is combined with the gray model and LSSVM regression algorithm. Literature [7] has proposed a method for electric power system short-term load forecasting, which has used the wavelet transform and LSSVM hybrid model. And literature [8] has applied the regression SVM method to power system short-term load forecasting. The above literatures have used LSSVM to overcome the disadvantages of neural network, such as over-fitting, slowly convergence speed, and easy to fall into local extremum, but the prediction accuracy is affected by the parameters. Although it has many advantages, but there is still a weakness need to be improved. That is the select of the parameters will affect the final accuracy. Although the method of determining the parameters has been discussed in the literatures, but these methods are basically based on cross check test heuristics or just by experience, they are certain blindness.

According to optimize the initialization parameters of LSSVM prediction model, a new optimization (IPSO) algorithm has been drawn out. This IPSO algorithm has a quick convergence speed and high robustness, so as to improve the accuracy of load forecasting. Research shows that the IPSO-LSSVM model has more applicable in terms of convergence effect, much more accurate prediction and faster training speed compared with the LSSVM algorithm and the standard PSO-LSSVM algorithm.

2   Improvement of the Standard PSO Algorithm

2.1   The Standard PSO Algorithm

The PSO algorithm is an arithmetic to obtain the optimal solution of particles through the iterative search, which the initial state of particles are random. In the process of iteration, the particles update themself by tracking two extreme value. One is the best solution of the particles themselves, known as the individual extremum p_{ibest}. Another is the optimal solution of entire population, know as the global extremum g_{best} [9-10]. In the standard PSO algorithm, the updating equations of particle's velocity and position are expressed as follows:

$$v_{id}^{t+1} = w^t v_{id}^t + c_1 r_1^t (p_{ibest}^t - x_{id}^t) + c_2 r_2^t (g_{ibest}^t - x_{id}^t) \tag{1}$$

$$x_{id}^{(t+1)} = x_{id}^t + v_{id}^{(t+1)} \tag{2}$$

Where
w is the coefficient of inertia weight, it is able to make the algorithm has the tendency to expand the search space and has the ability to explore new areas,

c_1 and c_2 are the accelerate constants, they represent the weight of accelerating statistical when each particle is pushed to the position of p_{ibest} and g_{best},

r_1 and r_2 are the random number between [0,1],

t is the number of iterations, mean the flight number of particle,

v_{id} is the flight speed of particle and x_{id} is the position of particle.

The standard PSO algorithm is easy to plunge into local extremum points, but the function have more than one local extremum point. The model would failure to get the correct results and resulting in premature convergence.

2.2   IPSO Algorithm

The IPSO algorithm use diversity metrics to describe the population distribution, thus guide the select of initial population on the basis of standard PSO algorithm, in order to avoid premature convergence.

This thesis has put forward the improvement method of PSO algorithm as follows:

(1) Average the particle distance of initial particle swarm

The selection of initial particle swarm is random. In order to increase the searching probability of the global optimal solution in ideal condition, its position should be throughout the whole space. Considering that the number of particle is limited, the solution space is opposite bigger. In order to ensure particles uniform distribution in the whole solution space and avoid local convergence, the concept of average particle distance has been introduced, which is defined as follows:

$$D(t) = \frac{1}{|m||L|} \sum_{i=1}^{|m|} \sqrt{\sum_{j=1}^{n} (p_{ij} - \overline{p_j})^2} \tag{3}$$

Where

m is the population size,

L is the maximum length of the diagonal in search space,

n is the dimension number of the search space,

p_{ij} is the coordinate value in the dimension j of particle i, and $\overline{p_j}$ is the average coordinate value in the dimension j of all particles.

The average particle distance means the discrete degree of particle distribution. It has improved the quality of the forecast and made particles can be searched in the whole search space.

(2) Judge whether premature convergence by fitness

The position of particle would determine its fitness value. And the state of population can be judged according to the overall change of the fitness value of particle. It reflects the aggregation degree of particle population.

Set the fitness value of the ith particle as f_i, and set the current population average fitness value as $\overline{f}$. Then, the variance of the population fitness value can be defined as follows:

$$\overline{f} = \frac{1}{m} \sum_{i=1}^{m} f_i \qquad (4)$$

$$\delta^2 = \sum_{i=1}^{m} (\frac{f_i - \overline{f}}{f})^2 \qquad (5)$$

Where
   m is the particle number,
   f is the normalized factor used to limit the size of δ^2.

The value of f has been determined by the following formula:

$$f = \begin{cases} \max|f_i - \overline{f}|, & \max|f_i - \overline{f}| > 1 \\ 1, & others \end{cases} \qquad (6)$$

The δ^2, means the variance of fitness, reflect the concentration of particles in a population. With the increase of the number of iterations, the fitness value of particles in the population will be closer and closer, and the δ^2 will be smaller and smaller.

The improvement of the standard PSO algorithm can avoid the population fall into a local optimum and the phenomenon of premature convergence.

3   IPSO-LSSVM Forecasting Model

In this thesis, we select λ and δ with the IPSO algorithm. The regularization parameter λ and kernel function's kernel width δ need to be selected after determine the kernel function, when use LSSVM to solve the regression estimation problem.

3.1   The Establishment of the Model

The IPSO algorithm has been used to establishment the LSSVM model, the process is as follows:

(1)Input and process the historical data, form the training sample;
(2)Improve the set of PSO parameters;
(3)Initialize the particle swarm;
(4)Calculate the fitness value of particles, set p_{ibest} and g_{best};

(5)Calculate the average particle distance $D(t)$ and the fitness variance δ^2 in the current;

(6)If ξ is greater than the average particle distance $D(t)$ and β is greater than the fitness variance δ^2 (ξ and β is the threshold given in advance), deem there is a premature convergence, turn to (3), otherwise, turn to (5);

(7)Update each particle's current velocity and position according to the formula (1), (2), and form a new population of $X(t)$;

(8)Calculate each particle's fitness of new species $X(t)$, and compare to the individual extremum and global extremum, if better, replacement, otherwise, remain the same;

(9)Check whether the result meet the end of the optimization conditions (reach T_{max}) or not, if meet, means the result has been reached the end of the optimization, it has already gotten the optimal solution, otherwise, let t=t+1, turn to (4);

(10)Transfer the optimal solution;

(11)To begin load forecasting.

The flow chart of short-term load forecasting based on IPSO-LSSVM model shown in figure 1.

3.2   The Setting of IPSO LSSVM Parameters

Set the search area of the IPSO algorithm for: $\lambda \in [0.1, \ 150]$, $\sigma \in [0.1, \ 10]$. The number of particles can be set up to 20. The distribution of the particle become wider and the scope of search space become bigger when the number of particle become larger, thus easier to find the global optimal solution, and the corresponding running time is longer at the same time.

The maximum number of iteration denoted by T_{max}, which values for 10. And the coefficient of inertia weight denoted by w, it can be linear variation along with the iteration in the process of search, which usually scopes as[0.4,0.9].

Then considering c_1 and c_2. The particles would wander the local scope a lot when the accelerated constant c_1 becomes larger. While the oversize of c_2 would prompt particle premature convergence to local minimum. However, in the research of the short-term load forecasting of IPSO-LSSVM. If the value of c_1 and c_2 is too low, the particles would linger outside the target area before it was back. While the value is too high, the particles would suddenly rush to or over the target area. In order to balance the effect of random factors, c_1 and c_2 both values for 2. The average particle distance threshold denoted by ξ, and the fitness variance threshold denoted by β, respectively: ξ =0.001, β =0.01.

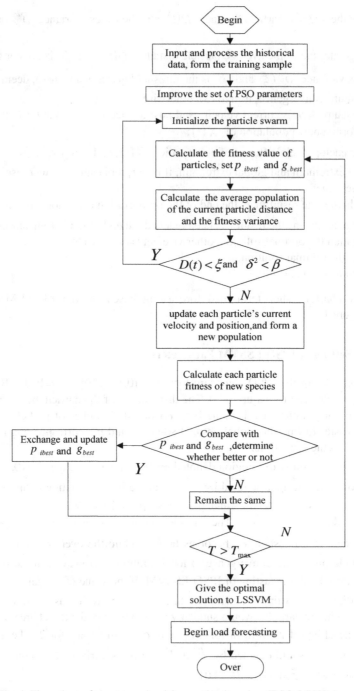

Fig. 1. Flow chart of short-term load forecasting based on IPSO-LSSVM model

4   Calculation and Analysis of Instance Modeling

This thesis has discussed the forecasting model combined with the actual data, in order to verify the effectiveness of the short-term load forecasting model. The data include the daily data and meteorological data of a regional power grid. These data were selected in March, 2009, it include the day type, day load, daily average temperature, daily maximum temperature, daily minimum temperature and daily average humidity.

This thesis select the historical load data as the alternative input variables to do the daily load forecasting. And the select of the historical load data is according to the following twelve characteristic parameters: the historical load, the humidity, day type value, the maximum temperature, the minimum temperature and average temperature in yesterday and two days ago at the same moment. The output of the model is the prediction of the load value.

This research do the modeling calculation and model test on the sample data, with the use of both standard PSO-LSSVM model and IPSO-LSSVM model. Predict and do forecast analysis with the historical data of the last week in march. Comparing with the actual value, the parameters optimization and load forecast errors of the two models have shown in table 1.

Table 1. The parameter optimization and load forecasting error of two models

Date	IPSO-LSSVM			standard PSO-LSSVM		
	λ	σ	ε %	λ	σ	ε %
March 25th	119.53	2.06	1.55	87.38	4.1 1	6.3 1
March 26th	57.0 0	8.99	1.72	94.7 2	2.3 2	2.0 3
March 27th	128.38	2.37	3.46	21.1 2	1.8 3	2.4 3
March 28th	111.74	2.37	2.52	111.76	2.3 7	2.9 6
March 29th	21.1 2	1.83	1.24	128.38	9.2 7	2.0 8
March 30th	94.7 2	2.32	1.39	57.0 0	8.9 9	1.6 8
March 31st	87.3 8	4.11	1.65	122.23	6.5 9	1.7 1

According to table 1, the prediction model based on IPSO-LSSVM has stronger optimal ability and search accuracy. Judging from the comparison results of the average relative error in the seven forecast days, the performance of the IPSO-LSSVM model is much better than the standard PSO-LSSVM model. Among them, the minimum relative error is 1.24%, the maximum relative error is 3.46%, the average relative error is 1.24%. And the average relative error of the standard PSO-LSSVM model is 19.2%.

The figures have shown that the IPSO-LSSVM model have better forecast precision. The experimental results also proved that the performance of the model will be greatly improved, while select an appropriate punishment parameter of kernel function parameters.

The fitting curve of the load forecasting results of two models during march 28th to march 30th in 2009 is shown in figure 2.

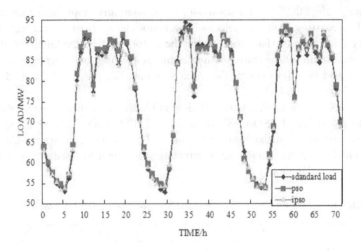

Fig. 2. The actual and forecast load curve

5   Conclusion

The LSSVM model could get the global optimal solution in theory, as for the algorithm transformed the problem which need to be solved into a convex quadratic programming problem. Also, it use the kernel function to solve the nonlinear problem, make the complexity of the algorithm do not affected by the dimension. Therefore the problem become much more simple and speed up the training of the model. According to the limited sample information, compromising between the complexity and learning ability of the model to ensure the better generalization ability.

The IPSO algorithm has selected the initial population and judged the premature convergence of the particles based on the information of species diversity. Essentially, it has introduced a process of rejection after the position of the particle update and attract each other. So as to reach the balance between particles' attraction and rejection, thus avoid the premature convergence. This algorithm update the particle's position when it has trapped in local optimum in the later search. Hence, lead particles jump out of local optimum.

This thesis has optimize selection the parameters of LSSVM through the IPSO algorithm. And it has been verified by experiment that the IPSO-LSSVM prediction model has better convergence effect, better prediction precision and faster training speed.

References

1. Xie, H., Wei, J.-P., Liu, H.-L.: Parameter selection and optimization method of SVM model for Short-term Load Forecasting. Proceedings of the CSEE 26(22), 17–22 (2006)
2. Shevade, S.K., Keerthi, S.S., Bhattacharyy, C., et al.: Improvements to the SMO algorithm for SVM regression. IEEE Trans. on Neural Network 11(5), 1188–1193 (2000)
3. Chen, S., Zhu, J.-N., Pan, J.: Parameters Optimization of LS-SVM and Its Application. Journal of East China University of Science and Technology (Natural Science Edition) 34(2), 278–282 (2008)
4. Wang, D.-Y., Yang, Z., Yang, G.-Q.: Short-Term Load Forecasting Based on Chaotic Characteristic of Loads and Least Squares Support Vector Machines. Power System Technology 32(7), 66–71 (2008) (in Chinese)
5. Cheng, Y., Han, X.-S., Han, L.: Short-Term Load Forecasting Based on Least Squares Support Vector Machines. Power System Technology 32(18), 72–76 (2008)
6. Tang, J.-N., Liu, J.-Y., Yang, K., et al.: Short-Term Load Combination Forecasting by Grey Model and Least Square Support Vector Machine. Power System Technology 33(3), 63–68 (2009)
7. Li, Y., Fang, T., Zhen, G.: Wavelet support vector machines for short-term load forecasting. Journal of university ofscience and technology of China 33(6), 726–732 (2003) (in Chinese)
8. Cherkassky, V., Ma, Y.: Practical selection of SVM parameters and noise estimation for SVM regression. Neural Networks 17(1), 113–126 (2004)
9. Sun, B., Yao, H.-T.: The short-term wind speed forecast analysis based on the PSO-LSSVM predict model. Power System and Control 40(5), 85–89 (2012), (in Chinese)
10. Chen, Z.-M.: Improved PSO and its application to SVM parameter optimization. Computer Engineering and Applications 47(10), 38–40 (2011)

Blob Detection with the Determinant of the Hessian

Xiaopeng Xu

Computer and Information Engineering College, Inner Mongolia Normal University,
Hohhot, 010022, China
xu.xiaopeng@foxmail.com

Abstract. This study detected image blobs and estimated parameters using the determinant of the Hessian operator. To investigate differential detectors quantitatively, a mathematical function was used to represent the blobs and to solve the parameters, including the position, width, length, contrast, offset, and orientation, in a closed form. These proposed parameters are both novel and very accurate. Subpixel localization and interpolation improved the accuracy. Noise is suppressed using the neighbors of the feature. This method was tested with various types of synthesized blobs and real-world images, and it detected fewer duplicated features. Experiments showed that the proposed method outperformed other methods.

Keywords: Blob detection, blob parameter estimation, the determinant of the Hessian, multi-scale, scale-invariance.

1   Introduction

This study investigated blob detection and blob parameter estimation. Estimated blob parameters have many potential applications, such as noise filtering and medical image analysis. Many applications may benefit from these blob parameters, because they produce simpler or more accurate algorithms. Many tasks are difficult using traditional blob detectors for incomplete parameters. Several methods can be used to estimate partial parameters but they have intrinsic problems, such as imprecise localization, duplicated features, or sensitivity to noise. Based on the definition of an ideal blob function, we propose a deterministic method for blob parameter estimation. This method detects features and estimates the parameters directly in the scale-space without further iterative operations. Trilinear interpolation improves the accuracy of the estimated parameters. The method has several important characteristics, i.e., a finite runtime, exceptional accuracy, fewer duplicated features, zero feature losses, and a strong noise filtering capacity.

2   Related Research

Harris considered salient points such as corner features, which are roughly equal to tiny blobs [1]. Detecting blobs at various scales has many applications. Using the

S. Li et al. (Eds.): CCPR 2014, Part I, CCIS 483, pp. 72–80, 2014.

Gaussian distribution function as a convolution kernel, Witkin proposed a scale space [2]. Lindeberg proposed the theory of scale-invariant blob and ridge detection [3]. Brown developed a position localization method [4]. Lowe invented SIFT [5] by integrating many technologies, such as the pyramid algorithm, difference of Gaussian operator, a precise localization method, and a feature descriptor. Mikolajczyk implemented several iterative adaptation methods [6] for estimating blob affine transformation parameters, which roughly equaled the length, width, and orientation parameters.

3   Ideal Blob Detection and Parameter Estimation

Traditional qualitative arguments have difficulty determining the characteristics of blob detectors. Thus, an ideal blob function is needed to investigate these detectors quantitatively, as shown in Eq.1.

$$blob(x, y; a, b, c, d, \theta, x_0, y_0) =$$
$$c \times e^{-\frac{1}{2}(\frac{((x-x_0)cos(\theta)+(y-y_0)sin(\theta))^2}{a^2} + \frac{(-(x-x_0)sin(\theta)+(y-y_0)cos(\theta))^2}{b^2})} + d \tag{1}$$

An ideal blob resembles the Gaussian function, where its (half) width, (half) length, contrast, offset, orientation, and spatial location are denoted by a, b, c, d, θ, x_0, and y_0, respectively. The ideal blob and its parameters are shown in Fig. 1. The orientation of the blob conforms to the direction of the minor semi-axis.

As shown in Eq. 2, a special ideal blob is aligned with the x-y axes, if x_0, y_0, and θ are zero.

$$blob(x, y; a, b, c, d) = c \times e^{-\frac{1}{2}(\frac{x^2}{a^2} + \frac{y^2}{b^2})} + d \tag{2}$$

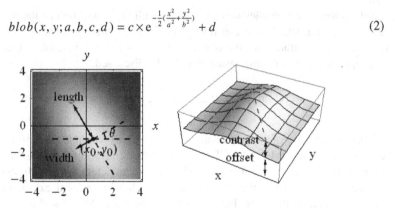

Fig. 1. An ideal blob and its parameters

Like many physical problems, the specific orientation can simplify formula deduction [7]. Using a rotation-invariant differential operator, these parameters will be unrelated to the orientation. Thus, the orientation of the blob can be solved based on the principle directions at the peak. Therefore, the discussion is based mainly on Eq. 2, while Eq. 1 relates to the orientation.

The scale-space of an ideal blob is the convolution of the blob and the Gaussian distribution function, as shown in Eq. 3.

$$L(x, y, \sigma; a, b, c, d) = blob(x, y; a, b, c, d) * \frac{e^{-\frac{x^2+y^2}{2\sigma^2}}}{2\pi\sigma^2} \tag{3}$$

Blob detection using a differential operator in the scale-space yields the differential operator space:

$$doH = \sigma^4 (L_{xx}L_{yy} - L_{xy}L_{xy}) \tag{4}$$

This study uses a doH blob detector. By searching for local extremes in the scale coordinates, the operator can detect the features of some scales. For a round blob, the scale detected is roughly equal to the radius. However, the scale detected cannot depict the length, width, and orientation directly for an elliptical blob.

It is obvious that Gaussian blurring will not change the orientation of an ideal blob while rotating the blob will not change other parameters. Based on these properties, all of the parameters of an ideal blob can be solved.

The value of doH is equal to the product of two eigenvalues (e_1 and e_2) of the Hessian matrix, where the eigenvalues equal two principle curvatures. Without any loss of generalization, the first eigenvalue is assumed to be a larger absolute value. A blob with two large principal curvatures will have a spatial extreme. The doH also has a scale extreme for the ideal blob. Therefore, a local extreme can be found in the doH scale space.

Substituting the variables and parameters with Eq. 5 will reduce the number of variables and parameters so it can reveal relationships among them. x and y are zero. The substitutions transform the operator functions for two variables H and K. Thus, the properties of the operator space can now be discussed.

$$x = 0, y = 0, H = (\frac{a}{\sigma})^2, K = (\frac{b}{a})^2 \tag{5}$$

Let r be the ratio of two eigenvalues and we apply variable substitution to yield a constraint relation for H and K. To obtain another constraint, we substitute the variable of the doH. We assume that the doH operator can detect the ideal blob on a specific scale. In other words, the doH of the ideal blob has a local extremum along the scale coordinate at the peak. For a specific blob, the width (a) and the length (b) are fixed, so K is a constant. According to Eq. 5, H will be a variable because the scale (σ) is a variable. Thus, seeking a local extremum along the scale coordinate becomes seeking a local extremum along the H coordinate for a fixed K. This is the second constraint on K and H. H and K can be solved based on these two constraints, as shown in Eq. 6.

$$\begin{cases} r = \dfrac{e_1}{e_2} = \dfrac{1+HK}{1+H} \\ doH_H = 0 \end{cases} \Rightarrow \begin{cases} H = \dfrac{1}{r} \\ K = r^2 \end{cases} \tag{6}$$

Two Hessian eigenvectors (v_1 and v_2) correspond to two principle directions and they are equal to a blob's orientation. The first and second dimensions of the eigenvectors relate to x and y coordinates. The orientation is then retrieved (Eq. 7). Since we assume that the first eigenvalue (e_1) has a larger absolute value, the corresponding θ_1 is the orientation of the large curvature (minor semi-axis of the ellipse), i.e., the orientation of Fig. 1. In addition to the parameters mentioned above, the contrast and offset can also be estimated, as shown in Eq. 7.

$$\theta = \arctan(\frac{v_1(2)}{v_1(1)})$$

$$a = \frac{\sigma}{\sqrt{r}}$$

$$b = r \times a \tag{7}$$

$$c = \frac{\sqrt{doH^{detected}}(1+r)^2}{r} \times (-1)^{e_2 > 0}$$

$$d = -\frac{c\sqrt{r}}{1+r} + L$$

The threshold of the contrast is used to filter the noise, which has a low contrast. The sign of the contrast is the opposite of the eigenvalues. In the equation, true is evaluated as 1 and false is 0.

The above discussion is based on continuous functions, but the spatial and scale coordinates of the scale-space are located in discrete positions so the parameters estimated are not very precise. Brown et al. proposed a method for accurately localizing extremes in the scale-space. Based on this method, our proposed method detects the extreme in the doH space initially, before refining their locatiosn and using trilinear interpolation to compute the refined values for L_{xx}, L_{yy}, L_{xy}, and L. These interpolated values are used for blob parameter estimation. This procedure greatly improves the accuracy and the relative errors are below one percent in most conditions.

The feature's sub-pixel location has eight direct neighbors in the scale space, which can filter noise, because the doH values of the neighbors are scattered due to noise. A noise is detected when the minimum is far lower than the maximum. A suitable threshold can eliminate noise effectively and maintain the blob features.

4   Experimental

We compared our proposed method with three existing methods, i.e., the Harris-affine, Hessian-affine, and Harris-Hessian-Affine[6], using ideal blobs and synthesized blobs. These other methods share some common problems with iterative approaches, which are lacked from the proposed method. Noisy images of qualitative experiments were added with Gaussian noise with a zero mean and 0.01 variance.

As shown in Fig. 2, several types of blobs were generated using the parameters in Table 1. Post-processing was not performed in the experiment and the estimated windows of the comparison methods were resized in proportion to the proposed method.

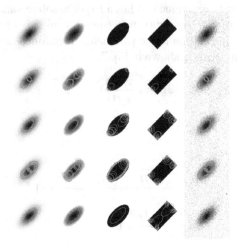

Fig. 2. Results for an ideal blob, parabola blob, elliptical blob, rectangle blob, and noisy ideal blob (from left to right) using the Harris-affine, Hessian-affine, and Harris-Hessian-affine (from up to down), which were introduced by [6]. The first row is the image and the last row is the result using the proposed method.

Table 1. Blob parameters of qualitative experiments

Width	Length	Contrast	Offset	θ	Image size
80	160	-1	1	$\pi/4$	513×513

The ideal blob uses half of the listed width and length

The first column of Fig. 2 shows the detection and estimation results for an ideal blob using the three methods and our proposed method. The ellipse is a blob boundary generated using the length, width, and orientation parameters. Traditional iterative methods tended to detect many redundant features, whereas the proposed method detected fewer redundant features and was more accurate.

Similar conclusion can be drawn based on the other types of synthesized blobs. The second column of Fig. 2 shows typical results with the four methods, which are similar to those in the first column. The third and fourth columns show the results for elliptical and rectangular blobs. The strong variation at the edges affected the iterative methods significantly. The proposed method tended to detect fewer duplicated features. The fourth column shows that, in addition to the rectangular blob, the proposed method also detected corners. It is possible to remove these corners by tuning the implementation. The proposed method is also suitable for noisy images. The results in the fifth column are similar to the noiseless cases. The scale-space based methods are robust to noise and suitable for real-world images. With the proposed method, the noise was removed mainly using the neighbors of the doH values.

After inspecting the estimated and true values, quantitative experiments were conducted to measure the accuracy of the proposed method. Using the ranges listed in Table 2, 1000 ideal blobs were generated randomly for detection and estimation. The resolution of the image was 255×255. The origin point was located at the center and the blob was centered at x_0 and y_0. The gray scale ranged between 0 and 1.

Table 2. Parameter ranges for ideal blobs

Parameter	Minimum	Maximum
θ	$-\pi/2$	$\pi/2$
a	2/3	15
b	2	45
c	-1	1
d	0	1
x_0	-40	40
y_0	-40	40

In most cases, the proposed method detected a single feature. The other methods only detected about one-third of the cases because many features are lost during the iteration process. These types of algorithms search iteratively for the features of the scale and spatial coordinates, which usually detects many features for different parameters close to the true blob locations.

The positional error of a feature was measured based on the distance between the position detected and the peak of the blob. Other parameters were measured based on the relative error of the estimated and true values. The relative error was more reasonable than the absolute error because it eliminated the effect of the absolute value.

Histograms of the positional error and the relative error of the estimated parameters are shown in Fig. 2. The x-axis of the histograms is the (absolute) positional error or the relative error. The y-axis of the histograms reflects the relative frequency or the percentage of errors. With the proposed method, most of the positional errors were below 0.05 pixels and most of the relative errors were below one percent.

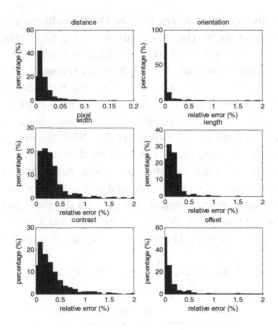

Fig. 3. Positional errors and relative errors of the parameters using the proposed method

Fig. 4 shows the estimation errors with the Hessian-affine detector while the other methods produced similar results.

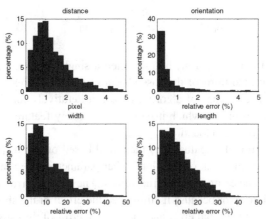

Fig. 4. Positional errors and relative errors of the parameters using the Hessian-affine detector

Table 3. RMSDs of the errors

Parameter	Harris Affine	Hessian Affine	Harris Hessian	The proposed
Distance (pixel)	17.316	1.740	27.709	0.033
Orientation (%)	14.487	10.758	10.951	0.275
Width (%)	21.284	14.758	47.940	0.601
Length (%)	29.710	15.293	62.399	0.321
Contrast (%)	-	-	-	0.712
Offset (%)	-	-	-	3.779

Table 3 shows the RMSDs of the errors with the proposed method and the comparison methods. Positional errors larger than 100 pixels and relative errors larger than 100% were removed as outliers. The proposed method produced lower errors. The high accuracy of the proposed method was attributable largely to the sub-pixel localization and the interpolation in operator spaces. The iterative methods achieve lower accuracies because they deviated from the extreme points.

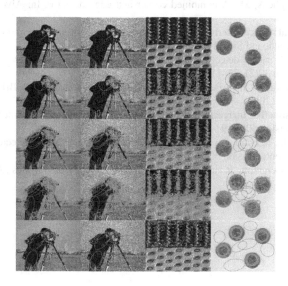

Fig. 5. Results for "cameraman," "noisy cameraman," "bag," and "coins" (from left to right) using the Harris-affine, Hessian-affine, Harris-Hessian-affine, and the proposed method (from top to bottom).

In addition to synthesized images, the proposed method can detect blobs in real-world images. Some of the blobs detected using the other methods formed concentric circles because they were generated by an iterative process. The proposed method detected fewer duplicated features. The proposed method and the other methods were robust to noise (the second column in Fig. 5). The 'bag' image contains blobs with different sizes and shapes. The tiny or background blobs could be filtered using estimated parameters with the proposed method. The last column in Fig. 5 shows a comparison with other methods. The four thick circles were the features with negative contrast and larger widths (greater than 9 pixels).

5   Conclusion

In this study, we developed a deterministic method for detecting blobs and estimating parameters. This method can estimate the parameters of an ideal blob accurately. Initially, the contrast and offset parameters were proposed and estimated, which were more accurate than some traditional methods. The method can detect blobs in synthesized images. Compared with traditional methods, our method detected more features and yielded fewer duplicated features.

References

1. Harris, C., Stephens, M.: A combined corner and edge detector. In: Alvey Vision Conference (1988)
2. Witkin, A.: Scale-space filtering: A new approach to multi-scale description. In: IEEE Conf. Acoustics, Speech, and Signal Processing (1984)
3. Lindeberg, T.: Feature detection with automatic scale selection. International Journal of Computer Vision 30(2), 79–116 (1998)
4. Brown, M., Lowe, D.: Invariant features from interest point groups. In: British Machine Vision Conference (2002)
5. Lowe, D.: Distinctive image features from scale-invariant keypoints. International Journal of Computer Vision 60(2), 91–110 (2004)
6. Mikolajczyk, K., Schmid, C.: Scale & affine invariant interest point detectors. International Journal of Computer Vision 60(1), 63–86 (2004)
7. Feynman, R., Leighton, R., et al.: The Feynman Lectures on Physics. Addison-Wesley, Reading (1964)

A Study on Layer Connection Strategies in Stacked Convolutional Deep Belief Networks

Lei Guo, Shijie Li, Xin Niu, and Yong Dou

National Laboratory for Parallel and Distributed Processing,
National University of Defense Technology, 410073, Changsha, China
{guolei,niuxin,yongdou}@nudt.edu.cn,
13739058625@163.com

Abstract. This paper presents a study on the layer connections in stacked convolutional networks. To this purpose, three layer connection types namely: diverging connection, neighboring connection and full connection have been compared in convolutional deep belief networks (CDBN). The results showed that our proposed full connection could achieve better performance, a lower time and space cost in nearly all conditions compared with the other two strategies. It can be found that full connection strategy combined the features achieved from lower layers well and made a better typical higher layer features.

Keywords: convolutional RBM, convolutional deep belief networks, full connection, diverging connection, neighboring connection, parameters chosen.

1   Introduction

With superior performances in feature extraction and representation, deep learning approaches have been increasingly studied in recent days. In comparison with many traditional learning methods, deep hierarchical model improves the capability to learn complex feature patterns thanks to the unsupervised deep learning schemes, plentiful unlabeled data can be explored, which makes deep learning a promising technology in the age of big data.

In construction of deep learning architectures, one of the most popular unsupervised learning algorithm is Restricted Boltzmann Machine (RBM) [1]. The RBM is a probabilistic model which is comprised by a set of visible variables and a set of hidden variables. In a traditional RBM all visible variables are connected to all hidden variables with independent weights. By stacking multilayer RBMs, a deep belief network (DBN) can be achieved. For training of this deep network, a greedy layer-wise procedure has been proposed by Hinton et al. [2,3]. Although improvement on the performance have been reported in many image classification and pattern recognition applications. One disadvantage, which the number of involved model parameters will expand seriously with the increased image scale, has also been noted. With tremendous training parameters, it becomes difficult to employ a DBN to deal with large images. Moreover, there is no direct way with DBN to exploring spatial relationship within the images.

S. Li et al. (Eds.): CCPR 2014, Part I, CCIS 483, pp. 81–90, 2014.
© Springer-Verlag Berlin Heidelberg 2014

To cope with the explosion of the parameter numbers with large images, a "weight sharing" scheme has been proposed by LeCun et al. [4] and Grosse et al. [5] in their convolutional neural network (CNN). CNN is a special kind of neural network, where the same weights can be shared for the connections between hidden and visible variables at different locations through convolution with sliding kernels. Therefore, the number of connection weights to be learned can be significantly reduced to that of convolutional kernels. Furthermore, with convolution and pooling schemes, CNNs can learn image features with certain spatial invariance. However, CNN applies a supervised learning scheme, where a large number of labeled training data are usually required for a satisfactory application performance.

To explore the unlabeled data through RBM and to reduce the model complexity using convolution scheme, a convolutional RBM (CRBM) has been developed by Lee et al. [6]. CRBM employs a similar convolution and pooling scheme as in CNN to produce features. However, the convolution kernels were trained by contrastive divergence algorithm as in RBM in an unsupervised way. With layer stacked CRBM, a convolutional DBN (CDBN) has been proposed by Norouzi et al. [7]. To make CDBN more statistically analytical, Lee et al. further developed a "probabilistic max-pooling". Such probabilistic max-pooling enables the CDBN performing in max-pooling like behavior, while the probabilistic inference becomes available. Moreover, it introduces more invariant feature learning capabilities in CDBN.

Although there are many studies about CRBM and CDBN [8, 9], few attention has been paid to the formation from CRBM to CDBN, especially the layer connection structures. To this end, a full connection and a diverging connection strategy are proposed in this paper. They have been compared with the neighboring connection which is used in some convolutional neural networks. The major contribution of this paper is to give a comparison among different connection strategies. Configurations of a suitable multilayer CRBM networks was suggested as well.

2   Previous Work

2.1   Restricted Boltzmann Machine

The Restricted Boltzmann Machine (RBM) is a two-layer, undirected graphical model consists of a layer of visible units v and a layer of binary hidden random variables h. A symmetric connections between the two layers is applied, and the weights of connections are represented by a weight matrix W. The probability of a specific status of an RBM is defined by its energy function as follows:

$$P(v,h) = \frac{1}{Z}\exp(-E(v,h)) \tag{1}$$

where v and h denote visible and hidden variables, and Z is the normalization constant.

In a binary RBM where the visible units are binary-valued, the energy function can be defined as:

$$E(v,h) = -\sum_{i,j} v_i W_{ij} h_j - \sum_j b_j h_j - \sum_i c_i v_i \tag{2}$$

where b_j is a hidden unit bias and c_i is a visible unit bias. While in a continuous RBM where visible units are real-valued, the energy function can be defined as:

$$E(v,h) = \frac{1}{2}\sum_i v_i^2 - \sum_{i,j} v_i W_{ij} h_j - \sum_j b_j h_j - \sum_i c_i v_i \tag{3}$$

It can be inferred that in the binary RBM, the conditional probability of a hidden unit is:

$$p(h_j = 1 \mid v) = \sigma(c_j + \sum_i v_i w_{ij}) \tag{4}$$

where $\sigma(x) = 1/(1+e^{-x})$ is the logistic sigmoid function. Units of the binary layer are independent Bernoulli random variables. For the continuous RBM, the conditional distribution of visible units is:

$$p_2(v_i \mid h) = N(b_i + \sum_j w_{ij} h_j, 1) \tag{5}$$

where the visible units are Gaussian with diagonal variance.

2.2 Convolutional RBM

Generally, a CRBM is a kind of RBM with weight sharing scheme through kernel convolution. A traditional CRBM consists of two layers: a visible layer v and a hidden layer h. The hidden units h are divided into K partition $\{h_k\}_{k=1}^K$, each is called a feature map. A unit in a hidden feature map is connected via a filter with size of $N_W \times N_W$ to the covered visible units. Such a filter which represents the connection weights w is shared across all the hidden units within a feature map. As a result, the value of a unit in a feature map gives a measure of such feature at a particular location of an image. Here we define w_k as the parameter of a filter which connects unit h_k and corresponding area of image v. The visible layer consists of an $N_V \times N_V$ array of units. Each feature map is an $N_H \times N_H$ array of binary units, totally $N_H^2 K$ hidden units. And each hidden group has an identical bias b_k and all visible units share a single bias c.

And the joint energy function of hidden and visible variables in a C-RBM is defined as

$$E(v,h) = -\sum_{k=1}^K \sum_{i,j=1}^{N_H} \sum_{r,s=1}^{N_W} h_{ij}^k W_{rs}^k v_{i+r-1,j+s-1} - \sum_{k=1}^K b_k \sum_{i,j=1}^{N_H} h_{ij}^k - c \sum_{i,j=1}^{N_V} v_{ij} \tag{6}$$

Similarly to the sampling process in RBM, a block Gibbs sampling can be performed using the following conditional distributions:

$$p(h_{ij}^k = 1 \mid v) = \sigma((\tilde{W}^k * v)_{ij} + b_k) \tag{7}$$

$$p(v_{ij} = 1 \mid h) = \sigma((\sum_{k=1}^{K} W^k * h^k)_{ij} + c) \tag{8}$$

where σ is the sigmoid function.

3   CDBN

CDBN is a hierarchical generative model which consists of several stacked CRBMs with some pooling operations among the neighboring layers. A connection strategy can define a way of how the output from a lower CRBM layer connects to the input of a higher one. And different connection strategies can therefore define different CDBNs. The focus of this paper is on the influence of the connection strategy to the performance of CDBN. However, there is rarely the descriptions of the connections in previous studies (Norouzi et al. [7] claimed that they had applied a kind of full connection without giving the details. While in some other literatures, only a kind of neighboring connection was often mentioned.). Therefore, we proposed two CDBNs with respectively a kind of full connection and a diverging connection in comparison with the one with neighboring connection.

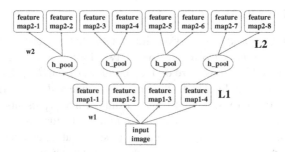

Fig. 1. Diverging connection strategy architecture

3.1   Diverging Connection Strategy

The diverging connection strategy is one of the simplest method in connections between CRBM layers. After pooling process, the pooled feature maps are directly carried to the next layer as the input data. Therefore, when setting k_1 features in layer1 and k_2 features in layer2, at the end of first layer it can get k_1 pooled feature maps. They will become the visible units of layer2. Then, k_1*k_2 feature maps comes out at the end of layer2.

3.2   Neighboring Connection Strategy

Neighboring connection strategy is inspired by 3-D pooling presented by Zeiler et al. [10] in his adaptive deconvolutional networks. A 3-D max-pooling takes operation both within each 2-D feature map and also between adjacent maps, as shown in Fig.2.

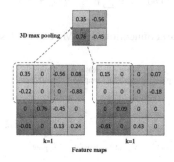

Fig. 2. A 3D max pooling processing

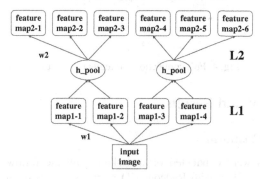

Fig. 3. Neighbor-connect strategy architecture

By applying this method to get the input of the current layer input based on the output of the lower layer, a neighboring connection network is obtained.

3.3   Full Connection Strategy

In our full connection CRBM network, the number of input feature map is not limited. Each output feature map is connected to each input feature map as illustrated in Fig.4. Following the same inference, the energy function of such full connection CRBM with many input feature maps can be defined as:

$$E(v,h) = -\sum_{k=1}^{K}\sum_{i,j=1}^{N_H}\sum_{r,s=1}^{N_W}\sum_{f=1}^{F} h_{ij}^{k}W_{rs}^{kf}v_{i+r-1,j+s-1}^{f} - \sum_{k=1}^{K}b_{k}\sum_{i,j=1}^{N_H}h_{ij}^{k} - \sum_{f=1}^{F}c_{f}\sum_{i,j=1}^{N_V}v_{ij}^{f} \quad (9)$$

Here F is defined as number of input visible feature maps.

And the hidden and visible units have the conditional distributions:

$$p(h_{ij}^k = 1 \mid v) = \sigma((\sum_{f=1}^{F} \tilde{W}^{kf} * v^f)_{ij} + b_k) \qquad (10)$$

$$p(v_{ij}^f = 1 \mid h) = \sigma((\sum_{k=1}^{K} W^{kf} * h^k)_{ij} + c_f) \qquad (11)$$

The architecture of our full connection CRBMs can be described as follows:

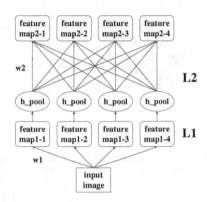

Fig. 4. Full connection strategy architecture

4   Experiment and Results

4.1   Experiment Platform

All the experiments were conducted on a desktop with the following configuration: AMD A-8 APU (3.20GHz) with Radeom HD graphics, 12GB memory size, software platform: Windows 7 ultimate 64-bit service pack 1, MATLAB 2012b. Two datasets MINIST handwritten digits and Coil-100[11] have been chosen in the following comparison.

4.2   Handwritten Digit Classification

It was observed that the error rates among different connect strategies are nearly the same. MINIST handwritten which is a binary value dataset seems too simple for a well-trained CDBN networks. In [7] it was reported that a multilayer CDBN with rbf-SVM can get a 0.67% error rate, while in our experiments an error rate less than 1%(from 0.3% to 0.8%) was also obtained. The difference between three connection strategies is not obvious. Therefore, the detailed comparisons were mainly focused on a more complex dataset Coil-100 which are images captured from real objects.

4.3   COIL-100 Classification

For the classification comparisons, we selected the objects and divided them into 8 classes.

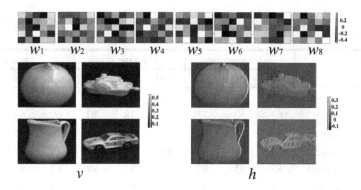

Fig. 5. Convolutional kernels, some visible and hidden layer data

Our CDBN networks contain four layers: the first and third layers are convolutional layers and others are deterministic max-pooling layers. The final subsampled features of the fourth layer were used as the input of a discriminative classifier softmax. During the training, some temporary results were selected and shown in Fig.5. On the top are 8 convolutional kernels, on the bottom left are 4 original images of training data as well as visible layer data. On the bottom right are 4 corresponding feature maps as well as hidden layer data.

4.4   Comparison between 3 Different Connection Strategies

Proper setting of parameters is necessary to get a better result. In our experiment, we tested several selective values for learning rate, train iterations, number of convolutional kernel (w num), size of convolutional kernel (w size) and pooling size. The networks were trained with 400 pieces of 128*128 images.

From table 1 and table 2, it can be found that the train iteration affects the accuracy rate less than other parameters and there is no need to set the iteration too large for this experiment. It can be found that 20 iterations is enough for training layer 2. Pooling size for layer 1 can not be set too big. Otherwise, details of an image will be ignored. While in layer 2, enlarged pooling size is helpful to represent invariant features. Among the 3 different connection strategies, it can be found that diverging connection strategy performs worst. At last a combination of parameters were chosen for each kind of connection strategy for the best performance comparison: learning rate 0.01, w number (8, 16)(which means 8 convolutional kernels for layer 1 and 16 kernels for layer 2), w size (5, 5; 7, 7)(which means the kernel size is 5*5 for layer 1 and that 7*7 for layer 2), pooling size (2 2; 4 4)(which means achieve a maximum value from 2*2 matrix in layer 1 and 4*4 matrix in layer 2) for diverging connection strategy; learning rate 0.005, w number (8, 16), w size (5 5; 9 9), pooling size (2 2; 2 2) for neighboring connection strategy, learning rate 0.001, w number (8, 8), w size (5 5; 5 5), pooling size (2 2; 2 2) for full connection strategy.

Table 1. Accuracy rate comparison among 3 strategies with different learning rate, train iterations and w numbers

accuracy rate (%)		learning rate			train iterations			w num		
		.001	.005	.01	2,10	2,20	2,40	4,2	4,4	4,8
diverge	Layer1	78	80	84	83	87	80	83	83	83
connect	Layer2	63	62	77	75	78	70	68	69	74
neighbor	Layer1	86	89	**84**	89	86	83	79	**86**	86
connect	Layer2	82	**89**	81	**93**	**88**	86	73	85	82
full	Layer1	88	85	80	82	84	**88**	**83**	83	82
connect	Layer2	**91**	86	82	91	83	86	80	82	**86**

Table 2. Accuracy rate comparison among 3 strategies with different w and pooling sizes

accuracy rate (%)		w size					pooling size			
	L 1	5 5	5 5	5 5	7 7	9 9	4 4	2 2	3 3	2 2
	L 2	5 5	7 7	9 9	5 5	5 5	2 2	4 4	3 3	2 2
diverge	Layer1	78	85	85	82	78	83	86	83	78
connect	Layer2	63	79	78	73	84	67	**91**	64	63
neighbor	Layer1	86	87	89	83	87	86	84	84	86
connect	Layer2	82	**90**	**93**	84	87	88	82	**85**	82
full	Layer1	88	82	83	83	84	86	78	79	88
connect	Layer2	**91**	82	91	**87**	**88**	**94**	86	83	**91**

In the following experiments we use those selected best parameters mentioned above as default parameters to train a larger size dataset for comparison (training 1600 images).

It was found, the most important parameters include the number and the size of convolutional kernels. With default parameters frozen, a comparison with a set of different sizes and numbers of convolutional kernels (w num, w size) was conducted for each kind of connection strategy. Constant layer structures with the same number of kernels (4,4) (which means 4 convolutional kernels for layer 1 and 4 kernels for layer 2), (6,6) were compared with the pyramid structure shape (4,2), (6,3) and inverse pyramid shape (4,8), (6,12). Result is shown in Table 3.

From table 3, it can be found that it was better to set number of w in layer 2 no less than that in layer 1. And from the results, full connection strategy showed a best performance in nearly all conditions. Because in a full connection CDBN, simple features from the lower layer can be combined to form a complex feature. While in the diverging connection CDBN, features will be further divided into smaller piece towards higher layers. And in a neighboring connection, only the neighboring features can be used to form a higher level but with the fixed combination weights.

Table 3. Accuracy rate comparison among 3 strategies with different w numbers

accuracy rate (%)		w num					
		4,2	4,4	4,8	6,3	6,6	6,12
diverging	L1	98.8	99	99	99	99	99.2
connect	L2	71	85.6	83.6	74	87	76
neighboring	L1	**99.4**	99.2	99	**99.8**	99	98.8
connect	L2	99.2	**99.8**	98.6	99.6	**99.6**	71
full	L1	98.6	98.8	99	99.4	99.2	**99.4**
connect	L2	99.2	99.2	**99.2**	98	98.6	99.2

4.5   Time and Space Cost Analysis

Despite accuracy rate, the cost in time and space were also analyzed for these connections. And the space cost can be estimated by the formula:

$$s_c = N_{img} \times w_{img} \times h_{img} \times N_{tl} \tag{12}$$

where s_c is total pixels in top feature map layer, it measures the max matrix data in training a certain CDBN, N_{img} is total number of training images, w_{img} and h_{img} are width and height of a training image, N_{tl} is the number of the top hidden layer units. For example, training 1600 pieces images with resolution of 128*128 . The networks takes a (4,8) number of convolutional kernels. 1 pixel is taken as measurement unit. For a diverging connection, the max value of memory usage for layer 2 feature maps would come out to be 1600*128*128*4*8=838860800. If a double float data type is used to store the value of 1 pixel, the memory cost will be 838860800*8 bytes=6.25GB. For a neighboring connect strategy, the cost would be 6.25/2= 3.125GB, and for a full-connect strategy, the cost will decrease to 6.25/4=1.5625GB.

The time cost comparison was carried out with the same parameters of which used to calculate table 3. Results for each strategy are shown in table 4.

Table 4. Time cost comparison among 3 strategies, t means training time, c means classifying time

time cost (s)		w num					
		4,2	4,4	4,8	6,3	6,6	6,12
diverge	train	586	992	1700	1132	1971	3684
connect	classify	32	43	61	55	77	124
neighbor	train	927	1622	2913	1855	3359	6379
connect	classify	28	31	45	45	64	102
full	train	**546**	**836**	**1428**	**966**	**1630**	**3145**
connect	classify	**26**	**27**	**32**	**36**	**42**	**98**

From table 4 it can be observed that with the smaller amount of feature maps, the pooling time will be saved, so the training time of full connection is the shortest. For the same reason, the length of the input data for a softmax classification is much shorter than others in a full connection network. As a result the time of classification is the shortest as well.

5   Conclusion

In this paper, we present a kind of full connection strategy and diverging connection strategy for CRBM to build CDBNs. Comparisons were conducted with these 2 different connection strategies and a neighboring connection. It was observed full connection strategy showed a superior performance in accuracy rate and lower cost in time and space in most of the situations. And when applying CDBN in an image classification like that on COIL-100, an inverse pyramid layer stack structure was found better in comparison with the constant and pyramid structures.

References

1. Rumelhart, D.E., McClelland, J.L.: Parallel distributed processing: Explorations in the microstructure of cognition, vol. 1, 2 (1986)
2. Hinton, G.E., Osindero, S., Teh, Y.-W.: A fast learning algorithm for deep belief nets. Neural Computation 18(7), 1527–1554 (2006)
3. Hinton, G.E., Salakhutdinov, R.R.: Reducing the dimensionality of data with neural networks. Science 313(5786), 504–507 (2006)
4. LeCun, Y., Bottou, L., Bengio, Y., Haffner, P.: Gradient-based learning applied to document recognition. Proceedings of the IEEE 86(11), 2278–2324 (1998)
5. Grosse, R., Raina, R., Kwong, H., Ng, A.Y.: Shift-invariance sparse coding for audio classification. arXiv preprint arXiv:1206.5241 (2012)
6. Lee, H., Grosse, R., Ranganath, R., Ng, A.Y.: Convolutional deep belief networks for scalable unsupervised learning of hierarchical representations. In: Proceedings of the 26th Annual International Conference on Machine Learning, pp. 609–616. ACM (June 2009)
7. Norouzi, M., Ranjbar, M., Mori, G.: Stacks of convolutional restricted Boltzmann machines for shift-invariant feature learning. In: IEEE Conference on Computer Vision and Pattern Recognition, CVPR 2009, pp. 2735–2742. IEEE (2009)
8. Goodfellow, I.J., Le, Q.V., Saxe, A.M., Lee, H., Ng, A.Y.: Measuring Invariances in Deep Networks. In: NIPS, vol. 9, pp. 646–654 (December 2009)
9. Abdel-Hamid, O., Deng, L., Yu, D.: Exploring Convolutional Neural Network Structures and Optimization Techniques for Speech Recognition (2013)
10. Zeiler, M.D., Taylor, G.W., Fergus, R.: Adaptive deconvolutional networks for mid and high level feature learning. In: 2011 IEEE International Conference on Computer Vision (ICCV), pp. 2018–2025. IEEE (November 2011)
11. Columbia university image library (Coil-100), supported on
    http://www.cs.columbia.edu/CAVE/software/
    softlib/coil-100.php

Fault Diagnosis for Distribution Networks Based on Fuzzy Information Fusion

Fangrong Wu[1], Minfang Peng[1], Mingjun Qi[2], Liang Zhu[2],
Hua Leng[2], Yi Su[1], Qiang Zhong[1], and Hu Tan[1]

[1] College of Electrical and Information Engineering,
Hunan University, Changsha 410082, China
wufangrong2006@sohu.com
[2] State Grid Hunan Electric Power Company, Changsha 410007, China
pengminfang@hnu.edu.cn

Abstract. In allusion to realize the fault pattern recognition in distribution network with a low degree of automation, a fault diagnosis method based on the fusion of fuzzy information is presented. For the purpose of improving the efficiency of fault diagnosis on important branch lines, based on the hierarchical model of feeder, the membership function through fusion of equipment alarm information in important branch lines and telephones complain information is improved. Besides, in order to reduce the adverse effects caused by manually setting the threshold too high or too low, the threshold value is partitioned by random sampling on the historical data, then we gets the statistical probability in different sections of threshold. Moreover, the evaluation parameter is defined to revise the fault diagnosis results to make the algorithm owe the ability to diagnosis multiple faults, thus solving the problem that multiple nodes fault is misjudged into fault in their public upstream node. Finally, a distribution line is taken as an example to verify the validity and permissibility of the algorithm in the case of both single failure and multiple failures.

Keywords: Fault pattern identification, Telephones complain, Random sampling, Statistical probability, Multiple faults.

1   Introduction

Fault diagnosis in distribution network is the foundation and precondition of fault isolation, fault recovery and supply restoration, which has important significance for increasing the running efficiency of distribution network, improving the service level, reducing the power outage area.

With the development of economy, the number of network users and the power consumption are increasing rapidly, and coverage area is expanding, thus, probability of failure in distribution network is also increased. Accurate fault location has a great influence on continuous power supply service [1].

S. Li et al. (Eds.): CCPR 2014, Part I, CCIS 483, pp. 91–100, 2014.

Fault diagnosis in distribution network at present can be divided into two types: The feeder terminal unit (FTU) installed on distribution line is mainly used as the detection point in high degree of automation of the region, then fault location can be realized with the help of feeder automation (FA) system, the main methods include time domain numerical analysis [2], artificial neural network [3-4], harmony search algorithm [5] etc. these methods have the disadvantages of relatively fault location complicated model [6] etc. In low degree of automation area, the fault information is usually from complaint telephones accepted by the trouble complaint management (TCM) system, or from a small quantity of alarm equipments received from the dispatching department, according to the topological relationship between power user and network device. The main methods include list analysis method [7], fuzzy set theory [8] and rough set theory [9] etc, but multiple sources fault information are rarely fused in these methods.

In order to further improve the efficiency of fault diagnosis in distribution network with a low degree of automation, in this paper, we are interested in the method that fuses telephones complain information with little alarm information on distribution line. Firstly, according to the flow direction, we stratify all the faulty equipments in distribution network and redefine the membership function, which takes the important load of branch line of alarm information into account. Besides, we calculate the probability within different threshold segments through a random sample of the history fault data in a time frame, and count the fault probability of all equipments based on information from distribution lines, and it will provide the capability of diagnosing multiple faults. Furthermore, we revise the positioning results by defining evaluation parameter according to sources of complain telephones, thus, the method is engaged to solving the problem that multiple sub node failures misjudged into fault in their public upstream node. Based on the above steps, the method proposed in the paper is characterized by easy realization, high efficiency and strong fault tolerance, which are verified by simulation examples.

2   Fuzzy Set Theory

2.1   The Basic Definition of Fuzzy Sets

The fuzzy sets is a standardized tool to get, represent and process fuzziness, and it processes ill-defined problem of category boundaries through continuous generalization of the characteristic function, which can be regarded as a category without clear boundary [14]. The related definitions are given as follows:

For a non empty domain, if μ_A is a mapping from domain U to section [0,1], i.e.,

$$\mu_A : U \to [0,1] , \ x \to \mu_A(x) \tag{1}$$

Where A is the fuzzy sets of domain U, $\mu_A(x)$ is the membership function of fuzzy set A.

2.2   The Related Operation of Fuzzy Sets

The main operations of fuzzy sets include algebra operation and logic operation [15], however, only the elements involved in computing are equal could the fuzzy sets be operated.

2.2.1   Logical Operations of Fuzzy Sets

For $\forall x \in U$ in the universe U, the membership functions $\mu_{A \cap B}$, $\mu_{A \cup B}$ correspond respectively to intersection, union of A and B, μ_{A^c} corresponds to complementary set of A, i.e.,

$$\mu_{A \cap B}(x) = \min \left\{ \mu_A(x), \mu_B(x) \right\} \tag{2}$$

$$\mu_{A \cup B}(x) = \max \left\{ \mu_A(x), \mu_B(x) \right\} \tag{3}$$

$$\mu_{A^c}(x) = 1 - \mu_A(x) \tag{4}$$

2.2.2   Algebraic Operations of Fuzzy Sets

For $\forall x \in U$ in the universe U, the membership functions μ_{A+B}, $\mu_{A \times B}$, $\mu_{A+\wedge B}$ correspond to intersection, union, complementary set of two fuzzy sets A and B, and:

$$\mu_{A+B}(x) = \begin{cases} \mu_A(x) + \mu_B(x) & \mu_A(x) + \mu_B(x) \leq 1 \\ 1 & \mu_A(x) + \mu_B(x) > 1 \end{cases} \tag{5}$$

$$\mu_{A \times B}(x) = \mu_A(x) \times \mu_B(x) \tag{6}$$

$$\mu_{A+\wedge B}(x) = \mu_A(x) + \mu_B(x) - \mu_{A \times B}(x) \tag{7}$$

3   The Mathematical Model and Information Equivalent Treatment

3.1   Membership Function

In the process of knowledge acquisition, we should determine the membership function firstly, and then calculate parameters of membership, which is used to reflect the fuzzy degree [16]. However, the membership function is usually determined by knowledge, experience or statistics in the related field.

To make full use of fault information collected in distribution network, membership function $\mu(x_i)$ is redefined through fusing telephone complaints information with equipments alarm information on distribution line, we use the following formula [8]:

$$\mu(x_i) = \frac{C_i \times i}{\sum\limits_{j=1}^{n} C_j \times j} \tag{8}$$

Where C_i is weighted factor, indicates the failure equipment in layer i corresponding to a complaint telephone, n is fault level. The value of C_i is calculated by the formula (10):

$$C_i = 1.8 \times \phi \times \Delta t + \begin{cases} 0 & i > n \\ 1.3 & i = n, n-1 \\ 1 & i < n-1 \end{cases} \tag{9}$$

In the above equations, if a switch upload alarm information, Δt is equal to 1 in the process of calculating the membership of the corresponding switch, so as to its downstream equipment; otherwise, Δt is 0. ϕ is the accuracy of malfunction reporting from a monitoring device in the lines.

The main difference between membership function in formula (10) and literature [8] is that we take the equipment alarm information into account, and it exists on an important branch of actual distribution lines. However, if the coefficient in the formula is too large, the telephone complaints information will not be used to the full; also, if the coefficient is too small, the positioning time will take too long. A great many of simulations show that if the coefficient is 1.8, the required quantity of complaint telephone can be markedly reduced when the membership of faulty equipment achieving the same value, which means the improving efficiency of fault location. Thus, the fault information of power user is rationally used, and the device alarms in the line are also taken into consideration.

3.2   Statistical Probability of Threshold Segment

In general, the selection of threshold in report investment information systems is usually set subjectively in 0.85~0.95 by the operator. If the threshold setting is inappropriate, false negatives or false positives may generate in system, which will bring many adverse effects.

For the purpose of solving the above problem, we take the probabilistic method and conduct the sample statistics of maximum membership degree of fault equipments in historical records within an allotted time, and then generate the estimated value of threshold probability in the different section according to the statistical results. Considering that the upper bound of threshold probability is 1, we take the lower bound of the probability as 0.80 through symmetrical treatment. The process is shown as follows:

1   Divide interval [0.80,1.00] into ten equal width sections, which are expressed respectively as [0.80,0.82), [0.82,0.84), [0.84,0.86), ...[0.98,1.00), and then recording them respectively as section Q_n, where $n \in \text{int}[1,10]$;

2   Sample the maximum membership of each device in historical records (If the sampling value that is not in section [0.80,1.00) will be abandoned) within an allotted time of fault location, and then estimating the threshold probability in different sections according to the statistical results, which will be respectively recorded as $P_i(n)$ (where i is the equipment number, n is the sector number), and $\sum_{n=1}^{10} P_i(n) = 1$;

3   Calculate the maximum fault membership E of power distribution equipments by using formula (8) according to the telephone complaints information, and we can obtain the fault probability of each device based on the statistical result of threshold segments. Here, the fault probability of a device is the sum of the probability of threshold segment corresponding to the maximum membership and the probability of each section less than the membership. For instance, if the calculation of the maximum membership for device i meets the relation $E \in Q_4$, then its fault probability is $\sum_{n=1}^{4} P_i(n)$.

3.3   Evaluation Parameters

Due to poor maintenance, perennial disrepair, extreme weather and so on, many equipments on the distribution lines have been aging, multiple points of failure will occurs from time to time when encountering emergencies or bad weather. If a fault does not get immediate treatment, the accident is easy to further expand, and then influences the reliability of power supply [18].

When fault occurs simultaneously in different node, if we inverse back the flow direction of the failure nodes, sometimes the fault membership of the public upstream node is greater instead, in this case, the equipment that works normally will be misjudged as failure. Therefore, the evaluation parameter $\rho(K_n)$ is defined to correct preliminary positioning result for equipment K_n in this paper. The specific definition of $\rho(K_n)$ is given as follows:

$$\rho(K_n) = \frac{T_s(K_n)^2}{T_l(K_n)^2} \tag{10}$$

Where $T_s(K_n)$ is the number of supply districts from the downstream of K_n, which exist telephones complain, $T_l(K_n)$ is the actual number of supply districts from the downstream of K_n.

In general, if K_n is faulty equipment, the calculation value of $\rho(K_n)$ will tend to 1, and then the fault probability of K_n will not change too much after correction; however, if K_n is operational equipment, the calculation value of $\rho(K_n)$ will be less than 1, and then the modified probability of K_n will be smaller, thus, we are able to achieve the purpose of eliminating fault positives

4   Example Simulation

In this paper, we use the distribution network model, as shown in Figure 1, for the simulation examples for fault location. It is including substations, circuit breakers, transformers and loads, etc. Due to the important loads exist in $T_3 \sim T_4$, $T_{10} \sim T_{11}$ districts, therefore, the monitoring equipments (such as fault indicators, etc.) are installed on K_8, K_6.

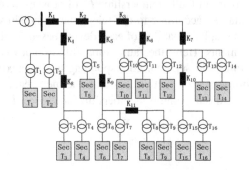

Fig. 1. Structure of the distribution network

4.1   Location of a Single Fault

Suppose the single fault occurs in K_8, meanwhile the master station system receives alarm information from the monitoring device installed on K_8, and the accuracy of fault reporting for this device is 92.15%, the probability of the K_8 in ten threshold segments are respectively: 9.4%, 12.8%, 11.9%, 13.6%, 12.4%, 15.2%, 13.3%, 6.4%, 3.5%, 1.5%. As a contrast, we calculate the fault membership of all equipments on distribution lines with the method in literature [8].

Assuming the first complaint telephone is from the district T_3, then the corresponding equipments are T_3, K_8, K_4, K_1, which are located respectively in the layer 4~1. The results obtained are given as follows: $\mu(T_3) = 0.430$, $\mu(K_8) = 0.322$, $\mu(K_4) = 0.165$, $\mu(K_1) = 0.083$. The second complaint telephone is from the district T_4, then the corresponding equipments are T_4, K_8, K_4, K_1, which are located respectively in the layer 4~1, similarly, we can obtain the calculation as follows: $\mu(T_4) = 0.430$, $\mu(K_8) = 0.322$, $\mu(K_4) = 0.165$, $\mu(K_1) = 0.083$.

For above two complaint telephones, we can preliminarily obtain the fault membership as follows: $\mu(T_3) = \mu(T_4) = 0.430$, $\mu(K_8) = 0.540$, $\mu(K_4) = 0.303$, $\mu(K_1) = 0.159$. The fault membership of K_8 is the largest, however, its value is too small to draw a conclusion, which requires us to wait for more complaint telephones. Suppose we accept a total of eight complaint telephones within a certain period of time, the result of fault location is shown in Table 1.

Table 1. Location results for fault of K_8 without the consideration of alarm information

Times /source	Membership /Number	Fault equipment	Fault probability
1/T3	0.430/T3	--	--
2/T4	0.540/K8	--	--
3/T3	0.688/K8	--	--
4/T4	0.789/K8	--	--
5/T3	0.857/K8	K8	22.2%
6/T3	0.903/K8	K8	67.3%
7/T4	0.934/K8	K8	80.0%
8/T4	0.955/K8	K8	88.9%

According to the improved method in this paper, the fault membership of all equipments are re-calculated by the formula (10), where, Δt is 1, φ is 0.9215. Location result is shown in Table 2.

Table 2. Diagnosis results for fault of K_8 with the consideration of alarm information

Times /source	Membership /Number	Fault equipment	Fault probability
1/T3	0.499/T3	--	--
2/T4	0.608/K8	--	--
3/T3	0.755/K8	--	--
4/T4	0.846/K8	K8	22.2%
5/T3	0.904/K8	K8	67.3%
6/T3	0.940/K8	K8	80.0%
7/T4	0.962/K8	K8	95.3%
8/T4	0.976/K8	K8	95.3%

In Tables 1 and 2, since the power supply districts T_3 and T_4, in the downstream of K_8, both exist complaint telephones, according to the formula (10), the value of $\rho(K_n)$ is 1, thus, the location result of single point of failure after the revision does not change. According to the above location results in two tables, compared with the positioning method in [7-9], the membership function is defined herein based on fusing telephones complaint information and equipments alarm information, and it could reduce the number of telephones to achieve same fault probability exceed 80% for the same equipment, thereby shortening the location time, and it will provide a good basis for the coordination of various departments to complete breakdown rescue and power supply restoration.

To be noted, if K_8 is an operational equipment, the final location result can also exclude the fault positives, since the number of complaint telephones from the downstream of K_8 is little or no.

4.2　Location of Multiple Faults

If K_5 and K_7 broken down simultaneously, according to the network configuration of power distribution shown in Figure 1, the source of complaint telephones will focus on power supply districts $T_5 \sim T_9$, $T_{12} \sim T_{16}$. After receiving multiple complaint telephones from these supply districts within a certain period of time, the result of fault location is shown in Table 3.

Table 3. Diagnosis results for fault of K_5 and K_7

Number	Membership	Initial results	ρ	Corrected result
K1	0.757	0	0.391	0
K2	0.947	88.6%	0.694	61.5%
K3	0.882	47.7%	0.510	24.3%
K4	0	0	0	0
K5	0.940	88.6%	1	88.6%
K6	0	0	0	0
K7	0.974	95.0%	1	95.0%
K8	0	0	0	0
K9	0.879	34.1%	1	34.1%
K10	0.788	0	1	0
K11	0.711	0	1	0
T1	0	0	0	0
T2	0	0	0	0
T3	0	0	0	0
T4	0	0	0	0
T5	0.894	47.7%	1	47.7%
T6	0.599	0	1	0
T7	0.599	0	1	0
T8	0.687	0	1	0
T9	0.321	0	1	0
T10	0	0	0	0
T11	0	0	0	0
T12	0.746	0	1	0
T13	0.599	0	1	0
T14	0.746	0	1	0
T15	0.687	0	1	0
T16	0.539	0	1	0

According to the results shown in Table 3, when multiple faults occur in the distribution network, if we use the method proposed in literature [8-9], it may cause fault information coverage in accordance with fault misjudgment, for instance, the multiple faults of K_5 and K_7 are misclassified as the fault of K_2 in Table 3. In the process of calculation, along with the membership of multiple fault equipments increasing, the membership of non fault equipment in their public upstream node will also increase faster, even more than the actual fault equipments.

Therefore, the evaluation parameter $\rho(K_n)$ is introduced in this paper to solve this problem according to the source of complaint telephones. For example, the equipments with a greater initial fault probability are K_2, K_5, K_7, as shown in the third column of Table 3, however, K_2 is the normal equipment although its fault probability is up to 88.6%, thus the location result is wrong. Then, after the correction calculation of $\rho(K_2)$, the fault probability of K_2 decreases to 61.5% as shown in the fifth column of Table 3, thus we can eliminate the false positives for K_2.

From the above analysis, the function of $\rho(K_n)$ is actually to correct the location results of the multiple faults based on the source of complaint telephones. Because only the telephones information has been collected for the deeper excavation, without the need of additional equipments, therefore, this method proposed in this section has a high value of multiple fault location in distribution network.

5   Conclusion

1. The membership function of fuzzy sets is constructed based on the fusion of complaint telephones information and equipments alarm information, and it could compensate the false positives and false negatives of alarm equipments, while overcoming the drawback of waiting too long time to fault location when only use single telephones complaint information.
2. Dividing the threshold into equal length segments, obtaining the statistical probability in different section by random sampling of historical data, respectively associating the maximum membership value of equipments during a certain time to the appropriate sections of threshold, then come the fault probability of all equipments, thus reducing the adverse effects due to the inappropriate setting of threshold.
3. Defining the evaluation parameters to revise the result of fault location according to the source of complaint telephones, then the problem that the multiple nodes failure is misjudged to the fault of their common upstream node is solved.

Acknowledgements. This work is supported by National Natural Science Foundation of China under Grant No.61173108 and 60973032, and Hunan Provincial Natural Science Foundation of China No.10JJ2045 and 14JJ2150.

References

[1] Borghetti, A., Bosetti, M., Nucci, C.A., et al.: Integrated use of time-frequency wavelet decompositions for fault location in distribution networks: Theory and experimental validation. IEEE Transactions on Power Delivery 25(4), 3139–3146 (2010)

[2] Jamali, S., Talavat, V.: Dynamic fault location method for distribution networks. Electrical Engineering 92(3), 119–127 (2010)

[3] Aslan, Y.: An alternative approach to fault location on power distribution feeders with embedded remote-end power generation using artificial neural networks. Electrical Engineering 94(3), 125–134 (2012)

[4] Shu, H., Dong, J., Duan, R., et al.: The distributed ANN fault location method for radial distribution network based on the natural frequency. Automation of Electric Power Systems 38(5), 83–89 (2014)

[5] Liu, P., Wang, F., Chen, C., et al.: Application of harmony search algorithm for fault location in distribution network containing distributed generation. Transactions of China Electrotechnical Society 28(5), 280–284 (2013)

[6] Guo, Z., Wu, J.: Imitation electromagnetic algorithm for Fault Section Location in distribution network. Proceedings of the CSEE 30(13), 34–40 (2010)

[7] Wen, L.: Diagnosis method for power interruption fault in distribution network based on List method. College of Electrical & Electronic Engineering, Wuhan University (2010)

[8] Shu, H., Ge, Y.: Fault diagnosis method for distribution network based on telephone complaints. Automation of Electric Power Systems 24(11), 39–41 (2000)

[9] Shu, H., Sun, X., Si, D.: Fault location for distribution network with rough set method based on telephone complaints. Power System Technology 28(1), 64–66 (2004)

[10] Meng, W., Qiu, J.: Distribution system reconfiguration based on immune algorithm. Proceedings of the CSEE 26(17), 25–29 (2006)

[11] Xie, K., Li, W.: Incoherent analysis for reliability of distribution network. Proceedings of the CSU-EPSA 23(3), 18–23 (2011)

[12] Guo, M., Yang, G., Huang, J., et al.: Location system for feeder fault section in distribution network. Proceedings of the CSU-EPSA 23(2), 18–23 (2011)

[13] Tu, Q., Liu, W., Guo, Z.: Fault location for distribution network based on fault complain information. Power System Protection and Control 33(24), 24–28 (2006)

[14] Jian, L.: Heterozygous rough set method and its application cater to uncertain decision. Science press (2008)

[15] Wang, R.: Research on the State inspection and fault diagnosis method for Power transformer. College of Electrical & Electronic Engineering, North China Electric Power University, Beijing (2013)

[16] Ma, J., Xu, D., Wang, T., et al.: A new algorithm of wide area multiple fault identification based on fault reliability. Power System Technology 36(12), 88–93 (2012)

[17] Sun, Y., Wang, X., Wang, J., et al.: The fragility curves and its application of Icing flashover trip in regional power grid. Proceedings of the CSEE 32(22), 55–63 (2012)

[18] Zhang, L., Xu, B., Xue, Y., et al.: The transient localization of small ground fault currents based on the line voltage and zero-mode current. Proceedings of the CSEE 32(13), 110–115 (2012)

Kernel-Distance Target Alignment

Peiyan Wang[1,2] and Cai Dongfeng[2]

[1] College of Computer Science and Technology, Nanjing University of Aeronautics
And Astronautics, Jiangsu Nanjing 210016, China
wangpy_kerc@163.com
http://cs.nuaa.edu.cn/
[2] Knowledge Engineering Research Center, Shenyang Aerospace University, Liaoning
Shenyang 110136, China

Abstract. The success of kernel methods are dependent on the kernel, thus a choice of a kernel and proper setting of its parameters are crucial importance. Learning a kernel from the data requires evaluation measures to assess the quality of the kernel. In this paper, we propose a new measure named kernel distance target alignment (KDTA). The measure retains the property of state-of-the-art evaluation measures, kernel target alignment (KTA) and feature space-based kernel matrix evaluation measure (FSM), additionally overcomes the limitation of them. Comparative experiments indicate that the new measure is a good indication of the superiority of a kernel and can get better parameter of RBF kernel.

Keywords: kernel methods, kernel evaluation measure, kernel distance.

1 Introduction

Kernel methods have delivered high performance in a variety of machine learning tasks [14]. The key to success is the incorporation of the kernel trick which amounts to an implicit mapping of data into a feature space (usually higher dimension). The implicit mapping is determined by specifying a kernel function, which calculates the inner product between each pair of examples in the feature space.

$$k(x_1, x_2) = \langle \phi(x_1), \phi(x_2) \rangle \qquad \phi : X \to H \tag{1}$$

Where X is the original data space and H is the feature space. The main advantage of kernel methods is the ability to use linear algorithms in feature space and the nonlinearity is implicitly introduced by the kernel function.

Despite the success of kernel methods, choosing the appropriate kernel function is still crucial importance. In recent years, various evaluation measures of kernel function have been proposed. For classification task, structural risk [6], negative log-posterior [5] and hyperkernels [11] are commonly used measures. These measures do not give a specific value, but only assert certain criteria in form of regularities in certain space, for example, RKHS or hyper RKHS, moreover, they all require the whole learning process for evaluation. Cross-validation

S. Li et al. (Eds.): CCPR 2014, Part I, CCIS 483, pp. 101–110, 2014.

or leave-one-out error also requires the whole learning process and suffers from computational difficulties.

Recently, many efficient kernel evaluation measures have been proposed, *e.g.* kernel target alignment [4], kernel polarization [1,15], kernel class separability [18], feature space-based kernel matrix evaluation measure (FSM) [10], γ [3]. Using the information from the complete training data and efficient computation are the significant properties of these measures. Due to its simplicity, efficiency and theoretical guarantee, kernel target alignment is the most commonly used evaluation measure. There is a large amount of work in the literature for KTA and its application. However, Nguyen and Ho [10] showed that KTA is only a sufficient condition to be a good kernel, but not a necessary condition, since, KTA is not invariant under data translation in the feature space. Then they proposed FSM. FSM is invariant to linear operators in the feature space and retains several properties of KTA, such as efficiency and an error bound guarantee. It has been proofed that FSM is better than KTA in kernel selection. Contrarily, for RBF kernel optimization, FSM tends to prefer small values of the RBF parameter, and the performance is poorer than KTA [3].

In this paper, we propose a new measure which named kernel distance target alignment (KDTA). The measure retains the property of KTA and FSM, and overcome the limitation of them. KDTA is invariant to linear translation in the feature space as FSM and more suitable to RBF kernel optimization than FSM as KTA. We show experimentally that the new measure is more closely correlated to the superiority of the kernel and could get better RBF parameter.

The paper is organized as follows: In section 2 and 3 introduce KTA and FSM respectively and show their limitation. In section 4, the proposed method is presented, and analyzed in section 5. Section 6 presents the experiments. Section 7 the related work. Finally, conclusion and future work are drawn in section 8.

2   Kernel Target Alignment

For binary classification, KTA evaluates how well the kernel matrix K aligns to the ideal target matrix Y. Given n pairs of training examples denoted by $D = \{(x_i, y_i)...(x_n, y_n)\}$, where $x_i \in X \subset R^n$ (The input space) and $y_i \in \{+1, -1\}$, additionally, n_+ examples belong to class 1, n_- examples belong to class -1 and $n_+ + n_- = n$. Each x_i is mapped to $\phi(x_i)$ in feature space by kernel function (Eq. 1). The kernel matrix K for kernel k is defined as :

$$[K]_{i,j} = k(x_i, x_j) \tag{2}$$

The target matrix is defined as :

$$[Y]_{i,j} = y_i \cdot y_j = \begin{cases} 1 & y_i = y_j \\ -1 & y_i \neq y_j \end{cases} \tag{3}$$

The KTA of matrix K is defined as :

$$A(K, Y) = \frac{\langle K, Y \rangle_F}{\sqrt{\langle K, K \rangle_F} \cdot \sqrt{\langle Y, Y \rangle_F}} \tag{4}$$

$\langle \cdot, \cdot \rangle_F$ is the Frobenius inner product. Thus, KTA is the normalized Frobenius inner product between kernel matrix K and target matrix Y.

It has been shown that KTA possesses several convenient theoretical properties [16]. It only uses the training examples and can be efficiently computed in $O(n^2)$. With a simple formula, it could be an objective function in an optimization procedure. Its value is highly concentrated around its expected value. Furthermore, there exists a separation of the data with a low bound on the generalization error, if the expected value of KTA is high.

Due to its properties, KTA is widely used in kernel parameter tuning [2,8], multiple kernel learning [6], spectral kernel learning [7] and feature selection [17,12]. However, Nguyen and Ho [10] showed that KTA is only a sufficient condition to be a good kernel, but not a necessary condition. They mentioned that KTA was not invariant under data translation in feature space and given examples to show that KTA could mistake any kernel to be the best or the worst case.

The Best Case. The kernel maps all examples of class 1 into vector ϕ_+ in feature space and all examples of class -1 into vector ϕ_- in feature space, assume $\langle \phi_+, \phi_+ \rangle = \langle \phi_-, \phi_- \rangle = 1$, $\langle \phi_+, \phi_- \rangle = \alpha$ and $-1 \leq \alpha \leq 1$. For any α, the kernel should be evaluated as optimal. The value of KTA is $A(K,y) = \frac{n_+^2 + n_-^2 - 2n_+ n_- \alpha}{n\sqrt{n_+^2 + n_-^2 + 2n_+ n_- \alpha^2}}$. Alignment values of these kernel matrix change as α varies from 1 to -1, and any value in that range can be the alignment value of a kernel matrix of an optimal feature function. As $\alpha \to 1$, KTA ranges from $(n_+ - n_-)^2/n^2$ to 1 in this case.

The Worst Case. The kernel maps a half of the examples of each class into vector ϕ_+ in feature space and the other half into vector ϕ_- in feature space, assume $\langle \phi_+, \phi_+ \rangle = \langle \phi_-, \phi_- \rangle = 1$, $\langle \phi_+, \phi_- \rangle = \alpha$ and $-1 \leq \alpha \leq 1$. For any α the kernel should be evaluated very low. Once using a linear classifier in feature space, the accuracy should be $1/2$ (Falsely classify half examples of each class). The value of KTA is $A(K,y) = \frac{(n_+ - n_-)^2(1+\alpha)/2}{n^2\sqrt{(1+\alpha^2)/2}}$ As $\alpha \to 1$, KTA ranges from 0 to $(n_+ - n_-)^2/n^2$, which is same as the lower limit of best case. As the best and worst cases cover the whole range of alignment value, any other case would coincide with one of them. Therefore, KTA may mistake any case to be either the best or the worst.

3   Feature Space-Based Kernel Matrix Evaluation Measure

FSM is defined as the ratio of the total within-class standard deviation in the direction between the class centers to the distance between these centers.

$$FSM(K,y) = \frac{std_+ + std_-}{\|\phi(x_+) - \phi(x_-)\|} \qquad (5)$$

Where $\phi(x_+)$ and $\phi(x_-)$ are class centers in the feature space, $\|\phi(x_+) - \phi(x_-)\|$ is the distance between the class centers, std_+ and std_- are standard derivation of the positive and negative class in the direction between the class centers, respectively. The lower the FSM value is, the better the kernel is, and the best value of FSM is 0. There exists a separating hyperplane such that its training error is bounded by:

$$FSMerr = \frac{FSM^2}{1 + FSM^2} \tag{6}$$

FSM can be calculated using the kernel matrix efficiently in $O(n^2)$ time complexity. FSM use kernel distance to measure the similarity between examples in feature space instead of kernel, distance is invariant under translation but inner product is not [13]. Taking the examples in section 2, FSM value of the best case is always 0, and for worst case is always ∞. It has been shown that FSM can overcome the limitation of KTA, and is more capable of kernel selection than KTA.

The drawback of FSM is its tendency to prefer small value of the RBF parameter [3]. The radial basis function (RBF) kernel:

$$k(x_i, x_j) = \exp(-\frac{\|x_i - x_j\|^2}{2\sigma^2}) \tag{7}$$

With $\sigma \to 0$ a kernel matrix of RBF approaches a unit matrix, and auxiliary variables $(a_i, b_i, c_i, d_i, A, B, C$ and $D)$ [3,10] reduce to $A = a_i = \frac{1}{n_+}$, $B = C = b_i = c_i = 0$ and $D = d_i = \frac{1}{n_-}$. It is easy to see that with a unit kernel matrix FSM = 0. With $\sigma \to \infty$ all elements of a kernel matrix of RBF approaches to 1, and auxiliary variables reduce to $a_i = b_i = c_i = d_i = A = B = C = D = 1$. The value of FSM is 0 too. It can be draw from above that FSM not only tends to prefer small value of the RBF parameter but also prefer big value of the RBF parameter. This is clearly not an acceptable property.

When $\sigma \to 0$, the KTA value is $A(K, y) = \frac{1}{\sqrt{n}}$. Its value is related with sampling size n. As $n \to \infty$, $A(K, y) \to 0$ (the worst value of KTA). When $\sigma \to \infty$, the KTA value is $A(K, y) = \frac{(n_+ - n_-)^2}{n^2}$. Its value is related with sampling distribution. When $n_+ = n_- = \frac{n}{2}$, $A(K, y) = 0$. RBF kernel optimization experiment conducted by Chudzian [3] shown KTA is more capable of RBF optimization than FSM.

4   Kernel Distance Target Alignment

In this section, we introduce a new kernel evaluation measure named kernel distance target alignment. We use kernel distance instead of kernel, and evaluate how well the distance kernel matrix aligns to the ideal target matrix. Kernel distance is defined as:

$$\|\phi(x_1) - \phi(x_2)\|^2 = k(x_1, x_1) + k(x_2, x_2) - 2k(x_1, x_2) \tag{8}$$

The kernel distance matrix D for kernel k is defined as :

$$[D]_{i,j} = \|\phi(x_i) - \phi(x_j)\|^2 = k(x_i, x_i) + k(x_j, x_j) - 2k(x_i, x_j) \tag{9}$$

Kernel could be seen as a proximity or similarity measure between two examples in feature space, and the higher the kernel value is the more proximate we get. Contrarily, distance is always seen as a dissimilarity measure [9]. The target matrix should be different from KTA. The target matrix is defined as :

$$[Y]_{i,j} = \begin{cases} 0 & y_i = y_j \\ 1 & y_i \neq y_j \end{cases} \tag{10}$$

The KDTA of matrix D is defined as :

$$A(D,Y) = \frac{\langle D, Y \rangle_F}{\sqrt{\langle D, D \rangle_F} \cdot \sqrt{\langle Y, Y \rangle_F}} \tag{11}$$

KDTA takes the values in range [-1,1]. The higher the KDTA the more aligned both matrices, hence the kernel provides high class separability and good classification result. KDTA can be calculated in $O(n^2)$ time complexity. Thus, it is as efficient as KTA and FSM.

5   Analysis of KDTA

In this section, we analyze the properties of KDTA. KDTA follows the property of invariance as FSM, and could solve the limitation of KTA as FSM does. In the other hand, KDTA follows the property of KTA in RBF kernel optimization, and would be more capable for RBF kernel optimization than FSM.

5.1   Invariance

We take the examples given in section 2 to show this property. For the best case, the value of KDTA is $A(D,Y) = \frac{2 \cdot n_+ n_- \cdot \alpha}{\sqrt{2 \cdot n_+ n_- \cdot \alpha^2} \cdot \sqrt{2 \cdot n_+ n_-}} = 1$. It can be seen that KDTA does not change with the varieties of α and get the theoretical optimal value 1. For the worst case, the KDTA value is $A(D,Y) = \frac{n_+ n_- \cdot \alpha}{\sqrt{\frac{n^2 \cdot \alpha^2}{2}} \cdot \sqrt{2 \cdot n_+ n_-}} = \frac{\sqrt{n_+ n_-}}{n}$. Taking a special case when $n_+ = n_- = n/2$, $A(D,Y)$=1/2. The KDTA is not related with α, but depends on the distribution of the data, and the highest value is the theoretical value 1/2. The examples above show that KDTA is invariant under translation and can accurately evaluate the best case and the worst case. Therefore KDTA can solve the limitation of KTA as well as FSM.

5.2   RBF Optimization

When $\sigma \to \infty$, the KDTA value is $A(D,Y) = \sqrt{\frac{2n_+ n_-}{n(n-1)}}$. Its value is related with sampling distribution. Assume $n_+ = n_- = n/2$, in this case, KDTA value is $A(D,Y) \approx \sqrt{1/2}$. When $\sigma \to 0$, the KDTA value is $A(D,Y) = 0$ (The worst value of KDTA). It can be seen that KDTA follows the property of KTA in RBF kernel optimization. Thus, it would be more capable of RBF kernel optimization than FSM.

As KDTA uses distance directly, it is not suitable to measure sigmoid kernel which is not positive definite [14]. For non-positive definite kernel, the value of Eq. 8 is negative, and does not satisfy the definition of kernel distance. This point is also for FSM.

6   Experiments

This section reports the results of experiments. We use the synthetic data to show the limitations of KTA, and KDTA can overcome it. On eleven UCI datasets, we mimick the model selection process by choosing different kernels, and optimize the parameter of RBF kernel. Classifications are performed using the SVM from the LIBSVM library[1].

6.1   Synthetic Data

We apply the synthetic data mentioned in [10] to show the limitations of KTA, and KDTA can solve this problem as well as FSM. We use 10-fold cross-validation to estimate the error rates and compare the measures to the cross-validation error rates of classification. For presentation purposes, we show the following quantities: 1-KTA, 1-KDTA and FSMerr. These quantities take the values in range $[0, 1]$ and relate to the expected error rates. Synthetic data is in R^2. Linear kernels are used to simulate different data distributions by different kernels in feature space. Two Gaussian distributions are used. Class 1 centres at $\phi_+ = (1, 0) \in R^2$, class -1 centres at $\phi_- = (\cos \beta, \sin \beta) \in R^2$, and the standard derivations are $var_+ = var_- = \|\phi_+ - \phi_-\|/2$. Each class contains 500 examples. For any β, the problems should have the same level of error rates when using linear kernels, i.e. linear kernels should be evaluated at the same level of goodness. We run experiments with different values of 30°, 60°, 90°, 120°, 150° and 180° in turn. The process is repeated 5 times and results are averaged. The results are shown in Figure 1.

From Figure 1, we can see that error is stable across different βs. 1-KDTA and FSMerr are rather stable, varying similarly to error. KTA is quite sensitive to absolute positions of data and changes dramatically. It can be concluded that distance based KDTA can solve the limitations of KTA.

6.2   Benchmark Data

Eleven datasets from UCI repository are applied. Breast Cancer Wisconsin (699 instances; 9 attributes), Pima Indians Diabetes (769; 8), Monks 1 (556; 6) , Monks 2 (601; 6) , Monks 3 (554; 6) and Ionosphere (351; 34) are binary problems. Balance Scale (652; 4), Ecoli (336; 7), Glass (214; 9), Iris (150; 4) and Vehicle (846; 18) consist of observations from 3, 8, 6, 3 and 4 categories. Data is first normalized to $[-1, 1]$. Multi-class datasets are decomposed into binary problems in the one-vs-others scheme. As a result, 30 binary problems are considered during experiments.

---

[1] http://www.csie.ntu.edu.tw/~cjlin/libsvm

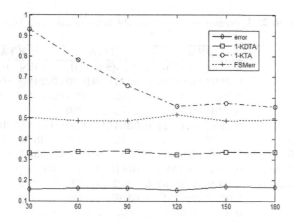

Fig. 1. Results on synthetic data with different β value

Table 1. Ranking the best kernel (in term of error rates) using evaluation measures

Data set	FSM	KDTA	KTA	Data set	FSM	KDTA	KTA
Breast	3	2	1	Ecoli (omL)	2	2	2
Diabetes	2	2	3	Ecoli (pp)	1	1	3
Monks 1	2	2	1	Glass (1)	1	1	3
Monks 2	2	2	2	Glass (2)	1	1	1
Monks 3	2	3	2	Glass (3)	1	1	2
Ionosphere	1	1	1	Glass (5)	1	1	3
Balance Scale (B)	1	1	1	Glass (6)	2	3	2
Balance Scale (L)	3	3	3	Glass (7)	2	3	2
Balance Scale (R)	3	3	3	Iris (setosa)	1	1	1
Ecoli (cp)	1	1	1	Iris (versicolor)	1	1	1
Ecoli (im)	1	1	1	Iris (virginica)	2	1	1
Ecoli (imL)	1	1	1	Vehicle (bus)	2	3	3
Ecoli (imS)	1	1	1	Vehicle (opel)	2	3	3
Ecoli (imU)	1	2	2	Vehicle (saab)	2	3	2
Ecoli (om)	1	1	3	Vehicle (van)	3	2	3
				AVG	1.6333	1.7667	1.9333

Kernel Selection Experiment. We apply the error rates of the cross-validation procedure as the baselines, and monitor KTA, KDTA and FSM, to see how they reflect the baselines. Three types of kernel are chosen for model selection: linear kernels, polynomial kernels (degree 3, gamma 1 and coef0 1)[2] and Gaussian kernels (gamma 1). We collect the rank of the best kernel for each data set. Table 1 presents the rank. On average, FSM ranks the best kernel at 1.6333, KDTA ranks the best kernel at 1.7667, and KTA ranks the best kernel at 1.9333. A

---

[2] Degree, gamma and coef0 are corresponding to the kernel parameter options in LIBSVM.

Table 2. Averaged test error on the benchmark data sets

Data set	FSM	KDTA	KTA
Breast	0.0458(±0.0276)	0.0386(±0.0261)	0.0458(±0.0276)
Diabetes	0.3294(±0.0470)	**0.2421**(±0.0430)	**0.2460**(±0.0399)
Monks 1	0.1653(±0.0486)	**0.0342**(±0.0233)	**0.0359**(±0.0223)
Monks 2	0.1731(±0.0505)	**0.1015**(±0.0460)	0.3429(±0.0655)
Monks 3	0.2400(±0.1072)	**0.0361**(±0.0225)	**0.0361**(±0.0225)
Ionosphere	0.0570(±0.0330)	**0.0512**(±0.0292)	**0.0570**(±0.0269)
Balance Scale (B)	0.4606(±0.0547)	**0.0256**(±0.0173)	**0.0368**(±0.0312)
Balance Scale (L)	0.0784(±0.0306)	0.0784(±0.0306)	0.0784(±0.0306)
Balance Scale (R)	0.4608(±0.0806)	**0.0272**(±0.0227)	**0.0352**(±0.0249)
Ecoli (cp)	0.0297(±0.0284)	0.0326(±0.0298)	0.0267(±0.0299)
Ecoli (im)	0.0807(±0.0536)	0.0807(±0.0536)	0.0836(±0.0512)
Ecoli (imL)	0.0061(±0.0128)	0.0061(±0.0128)	0.0061(±0.0128)
Ecoli (imS)	0.0059(±0.0124)	0.0059(±0.0124)	0.0059(±0.0124)
Ecoli (imU)	**0.0595**(±0.0375)	**0.0626**(±0.0388)	0.1043(±0.0494)
Ecoli (om)	**0.0354**(±0.0551)	**0.0119**(±0.0207)	0.0594(±0.0627)
Ecoli (omL)	0.0000(±0.0000)	0.0147(±0.0250)	0.0147(±0.0250)
Ecoli (pp)	**0.0296**(±0.0312)	**0.0296**(±0.0312)	0.1545(±0.0662)
Glass (1)	**0.2753**(±0.0487)	**0.2331**(±0.0998)	0.3262(±0.0772)
Glass (2)	0.1552(±0.0957)	0.1597(±0.0982)	0.1550(±0.0868)
Glass (3)	0.2673(±0.0973)	0.1959(±0.0660)	0.2006(±0.0672)
Glass (5)	**0.3223**(±0.0921)	**0.2567**(±0.0574)	0.3840(±0.0909)
Glass (6)	0.3701(±0.1168)	**0.2764**(±0.0840)	0.3701(±0.1168)
Glass (7)	0.2675(±0.1296)	0.2656(±0.0876)	0.2561(±0.0903)
Iris (setosa)	0.0000(±0.0000)	0.0000(±0.0000)	0.0000(±0.0000)
Iris (versicolor)	**0.0400**(±0.0344)	**0.0467**(±0.0450)	0.3267(±0.1350)
Iris (virginica)	0.2067(±0.1676)	**0.0400**(±0.0466)	**0.0400**(±0.0466)
Vehicle (bus)	0.2578(±0.0470)	**0.0225**(±0.0162)	0.2567(±0.0490)
Vehicle (opel)	0.2506(±0.0214)	**0.1998**(±0.0391)	**0.2294**(±0.0252)
Vehicle (saab)	0.2564(±0.0552)	**0.2044**(±0.0366)	**0.2091**(±0.0446)
Vehicle (van)	0.2352(±0.0438)	**0.0438**(±0.0202)	0.0768(±0.0344)

t-test (at 95% level of confidence) shows that KDTA and FSM rank the best kernel smaller than KTA.

RBF Kernel Optimization Experiment. For each binary problem and each kernel evaluation measure, optimization is performed using the L-BFGS-B algorithm with the kernel evaluation measure as the objective functions. Values of the RBF kernel parameter $\frac{1}{\sigma^2}$ obtained with the optimization are subsequently used with the SVM algorithm to build the model. Initial value of the RBF kernel parameter is set to 0.1, minimum value is set to 0.0001, and maximum value is set to 1000. 10-fold cross-validation is applied. Table 2 presents the averaged test error on benchmark datasets. The value in blod is significantly better than the others by a *t-test* (at 95% level of confidence). It can be seen that KDTA achieves better result in most of the datasets. KTA is better than FSM in original binary classes datasets such as Diabetes, Monks 1, Monks 2, Monks 3 and Ionosphere. Contrarily, in original multi-class datasets such as Glass and Vehicle, FSM is better than KTA. The reason could be that using one-vs-others scheme makes uneven and multimodal data, KTA can not deal with uneven and multimodal data well but FSM can. KDTA gets stable performance than KTA and FSM.

In summary, we use synthetic data and benchmark datasets to compare evaluation measures against the cross validation error rates. When ranking the best kernel according to the error rates, KDTA shows a lower rank than KTA, on average. However, KDTA is still poor than FSM, it would be our main work in future. In the RBF kernel optimization experiment, KDTA is better than FSM and KTA in most cases. The experiment results confirm the limitations of KTA and FSM, and that KDTA can overcome these limitations.

7 Conclusion

In this study, we introduced a new kernel evaluation measure based on kernel distance called KDTA (Kernel-Distance Target Alignment). Different from kernel target alignment, KDTA uses kernel distance instead of kernel and follows the property of invariance as FSM, and could solve the limitation of KTA as FSM does. In the other hand, KDTA follows the property of KTA in RBF kernel optimization, and would be more capable for RBF kernel optimization than FSM.

Future investigation is need to determine the error bound guarantee of KDTA. In this study, we do not considered the uneven data and multimodal data, it might be the reason that KDTA is worse than FSM in kernel selection, thus, it would be discussed in future work. We use kernel distance instead of kernel in KTA, and how about using kernel distance instead of kernel in other kernel based evaluation measures such as kernel polarization, local kernel polarization and γ. This is an interesting direction to be further investigated. Also, there is a large number of application of this measure on other works, feature selection, multiple kernel learning and kernel optimization.

References

1. Baram, Y.: Learning by kernel polarization. Neural Computation 17, 1264–1275 (2005)
2. Camargo, J.E., González, F.A.: A multi-class kernel alignment method for image collection summarization. In: Bayro-Corrochano, E., Eklundh, J.-O. (eds.) CIARP 2009. LNCS, vol. 5856, pp. 545–552. Springer, Heidelberg (2009)
3. Chudzian, P.: Evaluation measures for kernel optimization. Pattern Recognition Letters 33, 1108–1116 (2012)
4. Cristianini, N., Shawe-Taylor, J., Elisseeff, A., Kandola, J.: On kernel-target alignment. In: Advances in Neural Information Processing Systems, vol. 14, pp. 367–373 (2001)

5. Girolami, M., Rogers, S.: Hierarchic bayesian models for kernel learning. In: Proceedings of the 22nd Internatinoal Conference on Machine Learning, pp. 241–248. Springer, Bonn (2005)
6. Gönen, M., Alpaydin, E.: Multiple kernel learning algorithms. Journal of Machine Learning Research 12, 2211–2268 (2011)
7. Hoi, S.C., Lyu, M.R., Chang, E.Y.: Learning the unified kernel machines for classification. In: Proceedings of the 12th ACM SIGKDD International Conference on Knowledge Discovery and Data Mining, pp. 187–196. Springer, Philadelphia (2006)
8. Igel, C., Glasmachers, T., Mersch, B., Pfeifer, N., Meinicke, P.: Gradient-based optimization of kernel-target aligment for sequence kernels applied to bacterial gene start detections. IEEE Transactions on Computational Biology and Bioinformatics 4(2), 216–226 (2007)
9. Lesot, M.J., Rifqi, M.: Similarity measures for binary and numerical data: A survey. International Journal of Knowledge Engineering and Soft Data Paradigms 1(1), 63–84 (2009)
10. Nguyen, C.H., Ho, T.B.: An efficient kernel matrix evaluation measure. Pattern Recognition 41, 3366–3372 (2008)
11. Ong, C.S., Smola, A.J., Williamson, R.C.: Learning the kernel with hyperkernels. Journal of Machine Learning Research 6, 1043–1071 (2005)
12. Ramona, M., Richard, G., David, B.: Multiclass feature selection with kernel grammatrix-based criteria. IEEE Transactions on Neural Networks and Learning Systems 23(10), 1611–1623 (2012)
13. Schölkopf, B.: The kernel trick for distance. In: Advances in Neural Information Processing Systems, vol. 13, pp. 301–307 (2001)
14. Schölkopf, B., Smola, A.: Learning with Kernels. MIT Press, Cambridge (2002)
15. Wang, T., Tian, S., Huang, H., Deng, D.: Learning by local kernel polarization. Neurocomputing 72, 3077–3084 (2009)
16. Wang, T., Zhao, D., Tian, S.: An overview of kernel alignment and its applications. Artificial Intelligence Review (November 2012)
17. Wong, W.W., Burkowski, F.J.: Using kernel alignment to select features of molecular descriptors in a qsar study. IEEE Transactions on Computational Biology and Bioinformatics 8(5), 1373–1384 (2011)
18. Xiong, H., Swamy, M.N.S., Ahmad, M.O.: Optimizing the kernel in the empirical feature space. IEEE Transactions on Neural Networks 16(3), 461–474 (2005)

A LLE-Based HMM Applied to the Prediction
of Kiln Coal Feeding Trend

Yunlong Liu and Zhang Xiaogang

College of Electrical and Information Engineering, Hunan University, Changsha 410082
liuyunlongdi3@126.com

Abstract. As the data collected in rotary kiln is rather nonlinear , linear transforming such as PCA、ICA and LPP to extract feature is not ideal, while manifold learning performs well in high dimensional nonlinear data transform. A
new Hidden Markov Model (HMM) based method combined with Locally Linear Embedding (LLE) to predict the coal feeding trend is put forward. Firstly,
LLE-HMM conducts nonlinear feature transforms on the sample data by LLE,
then the feature data is quantized into observation symbol and HMM is establish to predict the coal feeding trend finally. Through the simulation of the sample data in rotary kiln production process and compared with PCA-HMM、
ICA-HMM、LPP-HMM, the results of LLE-HMM shows that it has higher
measurement accuracy, better tracking performance, which can satisfy the prediction of coal feeding requirements.

Keywords: Manifold Learning, LLE, HMM, Coal Feeding, ICA, LPP.

1   Introduction

As we known, Rotary kiln is the important equipment during the clinker sintering
which is key process in alumina production. Generally , the coal feeding trend is very
important during the process of clinker sintering, if the wrong operations is occur
during the adjustment, the next steps would deviate from the dissolved rate of normal,
a significant impact on the clinker quality. While the sintering is a continuous、
liquid-solid two phase coexistence of complex industrial process, so it difficult to
predict and control the rotary kiln coal feeding by mechanism analysis and system
identification [1].

In the known literature，there have the research of soft measurement based on the
process flame in the kiln[2], analyze the main parameters of air consumption and
quantity of blending coal on the effect of temperature distribution inside the furnace,
in order to realize the automatic control of rotary kiln[3]. Hidden Markov model is a
double stochastic processes by Markov chains and stochastic process, with its perfect
statistical basis and effective training algorithm，is very suitable for dealing with
time series in dynamic process and very useful for the non-stationary、repeating
poor signal analysis[4]. After years of development, HMM has been widely used in

S. Li et al. (Eds.): CCPR 2014, Part I, CCIS 483, pp. 111–119, 2014.
© Springer-Verlag Berlin Heidelberg 2014

speech recognition[5]、 handwriting recognition[5]、 network intrusion detection [6]
、 biological sequence analysis、 fault diagnosis[8] etc. A large number of industrial
sample data collected provides the condition for the model method with data driven[9]. In this paper, we fully considering the influence of thermal parameters in
rotary kiln sintering process and combining with LLE, the typical method of manifold learning ,using hidden Markov model to predict the trend of coal feeding , in
order to provide operation guide information to the production operation of rotary
kiln.

2   Locally Linear Embedding (LLE)

2.1   Feature Extraction for Time Series Data

Usually the time sequence of the original sample data have a lot of redundancy with
its high dimension, it need extract feature to reduce redundancy and represent the
original characteristics by a low dimension. Feature extraction as a method extracting
some effective features and reducing the dimension , broadly refers to a kind of transformation which was   divided into linear and nonlinear .

2.2   Methods for Linear Feature Transformation

Principal component analysis(PCA) and Independent component analysis(ICA) are
more common linear feature transformation methods, Locality preserserving projections (LPP) is the recent rise method .

Principal component analysis(PCA) is the main idea of the correlation matrix or
covariance matrix of the internal structure of the original variables, comprehensive
variables through an orthogonal transformation of multi-variables into the vast majority of the few can reflect the information of primitive variables .

Independent component analysis(ICA) method is to find a linear transformation[11]as non-Gauss data， the multiple observation signal based on statistical independence principle through the optimization algorithm is decomposed into several
independent components.

Locality Preserving Projections(LPP)[12]algorithm can retain the nonlinear structure of the data within a dimension mapping for high dimensional data to a certain
extent. Although the linear approximation of Laplacian Eigenmaps, but it is a linear
dimensionality reduce method essentially.

2.3   Locally Linear Embedding (LLE)

As the linear transformation is not ideal to extract the feature of the strong nonlinear
data, the nonlinear transformation method is appear. The key objective of the nonlinear transform method is to maintain constant distance, that is to say, when mapping
the data into a low dimensional space, the original close point must be close in the

output space. According to the basic principle of manifold learning[16], manifold learning algorithms can meet this requirement[14]. ISOMAP and LLE are the representative of manifold learning methods at present.

LLE [15] as a nonlinear dimensionality reduction transformation method of manifold learning proposed by Roweis and Saul in 2000, has been widely applied to data dimensionality reduction, feature extraction, clustering and visualization[17].The LLE algorithm are shown as follows:

For the original data set such as $X=\{x_1, x_2, \ldots, x_N\} \subset R^D$, the low dimensional space as $Y=\{y_1, y_2, \ldots, y_N\} \subset R^d$ $(d \ll D)$, LLE uses local linear to approach the global nonlinear.

(1)The Euclidean distance is used to find the K nearest neighborhood for each X_i.

(2)Compute the linear combination of weighted w_{ij} to reconstruct each X_i by solving a constrained least squares problem. The reconstruction error $\mathcal{E}$ is:

$$\mathcal{E}=\sum_{i=1}^{N} \|x_i - \sum_{j=1}^{N} w_{ij} x_{ij}\|^2, \sum_{j=1}^{N} w_{ij} = 1, i = 1, 2, ..., N \tag{1}$$

the weights that out the neighborhood is $w_{ij}=0$, and the constraint is $\sum_{j=1}^{N} w_{ij} = 1$.

(3) In the low dimensional space Y, calculates the best reconstruction weights by minimizing the cost function Φ.

$$\Phi = \sum_{i=1}^{N} \| y_i - \sum_{j=1}^{N} w_{ij} y_j \|^2 \tag{2}$$

Among it, $\sum_{i=1}^{N} y_i = 0, \frac{1}{N} \sum_{i=1}^{N} y_i y_i^T = I$, d minimum non-zero eigenvector of matrix $(I-W)^T(I-W)$ is the cost function solution.

In general, LLE obtain the reconstruction weights of data points by solving a constrained least squares problem firstly, then the reconstruction weights structure for a sparse matrix, finally, the low dimensional embedding of global is acquired by the d minimum non-zero eigenvector of sparse matrix[15].

3   The Hidden Markov Model

3.1   Principle of Hidden Markov Model

A HMM model with N state $\{S_1, S_2, ..., S_N\}$ can be used to describe by π or simple to π. Among them, N is the number of state, M represents each state may estimate value number, three probability parameter defined as π is the meaning of probability distribution, A stand for the state transition probability matrix, B a given state observation distributions of initial state space.

Many papers [5,7,8]have a detailed description of the three basic problems in HMM, and the basic algorithm to solve this three problem: 1). The forward backward algorithm to solve the probabilistic reasoning problems of HMM; 2).The Viterbi algorithm to solve the problem of decoding HMM; 3).The Baum-Welch algorithm to solve the training problem of HMM.

Using HMM to classify different kinds of observation sequence data mainly includes the training and recognition, training stage is to solve the estimation of HMM parameter, in order to get the most likely π, A, B in each model. The recognition stage is the calculation process of probability for each test sample sequence O_i, the forward-backward algorithm is to calculate the output the posterior probability of each training model.

3.2 The Quantization Process of Observation Sequence

HMM is used in this paper to predict coal feeding, it needs to quantize observed sequence into observation symbol before set into the model. The literature [13] introduces some commonly symbolic methods, according to the symbol quantification normalized thought in this paper. For example x is one columns of input sample, taking scaling transformation at first, it can provide consistent form for the symbolization of the feature data.

$$x^{'} = \alpha \cdot x = \frac{k}{x_{max} - x_{min}} \cdot x \tag{3}$$

Then the quantization

$$\overline{x} = \left[\frac{x^{'} - x^{'}_{min}}{x^{'}_{max} - x^{'}_{min}} \cdot D \right] \tag{4}$$

Among them, k is a constant value (this is set to 50), D is quantitative series, symbolic [ ] representation for numerical rounding, $\overline{X}$ is the numerical after quantized.

4　Prediction of Coal Feeding Trend by HMM with LLE

4.1 Select Sample Data and Preprocessing

Through the analysis of the rotary kiln sintering mechanism and the practical experience and the sample data collected in the sintering process. 9 major variables are selected as the initial sample data through the influences on the change of rotary kiln coal feeding. In order to avoid the mistakes that basic trend is extracted, according to the basic trend of increase and reduce to divide the feature points, and the non feature points are removed, then make the feature transformation according to the characteristics of time series [7].

The difference value of the coal feeding is used to search feature points, selection algorithm is following:

$$\Delta = w_{t+1} - w_t \tag{5}$$

Among it, Δ is for change value, w_t for the coal feeding at moment of t, η is the threshold for change, if $\Delta > \eta$, the point is increase trend; if $\Delta < -\eta$, the points is reduce trend.

In PCA transformation, variance contribution rate for more than 85% need 6 principal components , that is the observation sequence length as well. As the dimensions in sample data not high, the focus of this paper lies in the nonlinear feature transform on data , that is to eliminate strong nonlinear objective of the sample data. The number of feature output dimension in LLE transformation select as 6 too, while the number of neighborhood each sample point is chosen as 12, namely d=6, k=12, the numerical symbol after quantized as input of the model.

4.2   The Establishment of LLE-HMM

In the prediction of coal feeding change trend by HMM with LLE, the HMM state number is set to 3 for the actual coal feeding has a smooth trend, the observation sequence length is select as 6, so the number of symbols in observation sequence is 6 as well. The steps of LLE-HMM to predict coal feeding trend are shown as follows:

1) To acquire feature points in the sample data of time series;
2) Use LLE conduct nonlinear transformation for feature extraction;
3) To quantify the feature data, obtain the observation sequence symbol;
4) Establish the respective HMM of different trends by the observation sequence symbols;
5) For sample data of unknown trend, according 1) ~3) to obtain observation sequence symbol;
6) Put the observation sequence symbol into each HMM, acquiring the probability value;
7) Compare the probability values of each model , to get the trend of unknown sample data.

4.3   Validation of LLE-HMM

In order to validate the proposed model, the sample data this paper used is collect from rotary kiln production process in one year of July to August at a branch of Chinese Aluminum Company. The simple data including training and testing, the feature points with 1235 increase feature points and 1211 reduce feature points. From the increase and reduce feature points, each group select 400 points for the model of training and predicting respectively. The training HMM state transition matrix A is shown in Figure 1.

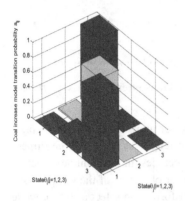 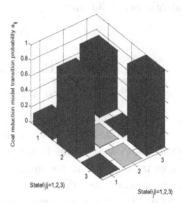

Fig. 1. HMM state transition matrix *A*

From the increase and reduce feature points, select 200 points to predict the trained model respectively, the results of prediction are shown in table 1. We use the root mean square error (RMSE) or the relative root mean square error (RRMSE) to the tracking ability of coal feeding trends, the calculation results are shown in table 2.

Table 1. Comparison of different model with 200 points

Coal feeding	PCA-HMM correct	accurate	ICA-HMM correct	accurate	LPP-HMM correct	accurate	LLE-HMM correct	accurate
Increase	149	74.5%	170	85%	170	85%	174	87%
Reduce	159	79.5%	137	68.5%	168	84%	182	91%
Average		77%		76.75%		84.5%		89%

Table 2. Different models to predict the results of error analysis

	PCA-HMM	ICA-HMM	LPP-HMM	LLE-HMM
RMSE	0.480	0.482	0.394	0.332
RRMSE	24.0%	24.1%	19.7%	16.6%

From table 1 and table 2, we can see that LLE-HMM has a higher accuracy rate than that of PCA-HMM、ICA-HMM、LPP-HMM. Now, Select the points at 6700 – 6900 in sample data, using the above models to predict the coal feeding trend respectively, the results of the simulation are shown in Figure2-5.

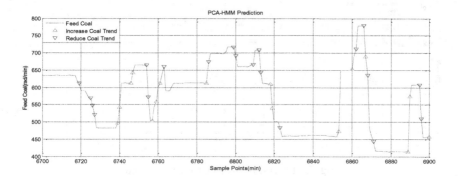

Fig. 2. PCA-HMM Predict coal feeding trend

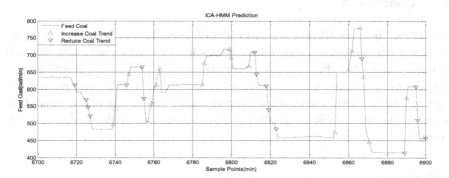

Fig. 3. ICA-HMM Predict coal feeding trend

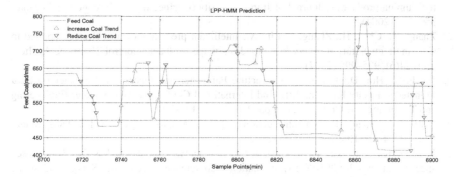

Fig. 4. LPP-HMM Predict coal feeding trend

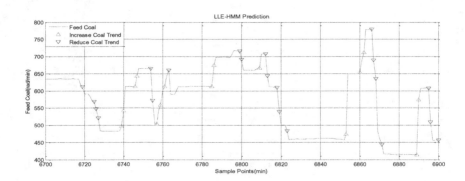

Fig. 5. LLE-HMM Predict coal feeding trend

5   Conclusion

In this paper, by using HMM combined with LLE to predict coal feeding trends of the rotary kiln sintering process，the simulation results of the sample data show that LLE performs better than PCA、ICA、LPP in data preprocessing. Combine with LLE, HMM has a better tracking performance and higher measurement precision, it improves the real-time control of coal feeding clinker sintering process in rotary kiln, improves operating stability、product quality and reduces production energy consumption.

References

1. Zhou, X., Xu, D., Zhang, L., Chai, T.: Integrated automation system of rotary Kiln process for alumina production. Journal of Jilin University (Engineering and Technology Edition), 350–353 (2004)
2. Zhang, X., Chen, H., Zhang, J., Liu, X.: Intelligent predictive control strategy applied to sintering temperature in rotary kiln based on image feedback. Control Theory & Applications 24(6), 995–998 (2007)
3. Jia, F.-R., Hui, D.: Influence of Structure Parameter and Operation Parameter on Heat Transfer in Rotary Kiln. In: 2010 2nd International Conference on Computer Engineering and Technology (ICCET), vol. (5), pp. 276–279. IEEE (2010)
4. Rabiner, L., Juang, B.: An introduction to hidden Markov models. IEEE ASSP Magazine 3(1), 4–16 (1986)
5. Kazumi, K., Nankaku, Y., Tokuda, K.: Factor analyzed voice models for HMM-based speech synthesis. In: 2010 IEEE International Conference on Acoustics Speech and Signal Processing (ICASSP), pp. 4234–4237. IEEE (2010)
6. Dan, S., Yan Ling, S.: Detection of Network Intrusion Based on a HMM Model. In: 2010 Second International Conference on Multimedia and Information Technology (MMIT), vol. 1, pp. 286–289. IEEE (2010)
7. Zhou, Q., Wu, T.: Trend feature extraction method based on important points in time series. Journal of Zhejiang University (Engineering Science) 41(11), 1782–1787 (2007)

8. Ocak, H., Loparo, K.A.: A new bearing fault detection and diagnosis scheme based on hidden Markov modeling of vibration signals. In: Proceedings of the 2001 IEEE International Conference on Acoustics, Speech, and Signal Processing (ICASSP 2001), vol. 5, pp. 3141–3144. IEEE (2001)

9. Lin, B., Jørgensen, S.B.: Soft sensor design by multivariate fusion of image features and process Measurements. Journal of Process Control 21, 547–553 (2011)

10. Gao, Q., Jia, Z.: An application study of the improved PCA method in the TE process fault detection. In: 2010 IEEE International Conference on Intelligent Computing and Intelligent Systems (ICIS), vol. 2, pp. 706–709. IEEE (2010)

11. Hyvärinen, A., Oja, E.: Independent component analysis: algorithms and applications. Neural Networks 13(4), 411–430 (2000)

12. He, X., Niyogi, P.: Locality Preserving Projections. In: Proc. of Advances in Neural Information Processing Systems, pp. 153–160 (2004)

13. Lin, J., Keogh, E., Lonardi, S., Chiu, B.: A symbolic representation of time series, with implications for streaming algorithms. In: Proceedings of the 8th ACM SIGMOD Workshop on Research Issues in Data Mining and Knowledge Discovery, pp. 2–11. ACM (2003)

14. Qiao, H., Zhang, P., Wang, D., Zhang, B.: An Explicit Nonlinear Mapping for Manifold Learning. IEEE Transactions on Cybernetics 43(1), 51–63 (2013)

15. Roweis, S.T., Saul, L.: Nonlinear dimensionality reduction by locally linear embedding. Science 290(5500), 2323–2326 (2000)

16. Silva Vin, D., Tenenbaum, J.B.: Global versus local methods in nonlinear dimensionality reduction. In: Advances in Neural Information Processing Systems, pp. 705–712 (2002)

17. Jiang, Q., Lu, J., Jia, M.: New method of fault feature extraction based on supervised LLE. In: 2010 Chinese Control and Decision Conference, CCDC 2010, pp. 1727–1731. IEEE (2010)

Improved Margin Sampling for Active Learning

Jin Zhou and Shiliang Sun

Department of Computer Science and Technology
East China Normal University
500 Dongchuan Road, Shanghai 200241, China
jinjin.zhou12@gmail.com, slsun@cs.ecnu.edu.cn

Abstract. Active learning is a learning mechanism which can actively query the user for labels. The goal of an active learning algorithm is to build an effective training set by selecting those most informative samples and improve the efficiency of the model within the limited time and resource. In this paper, we mainly focus on a state-of-the-art active learning method, the SVM-based margin sampling. However, margin sampling does not consider the distribution and the structural space connectivity among the unlabeled data when several examples are chosen simultaneously, which may lead to oversampling on dense regions. To overcome this shortcoming, we propose an improved margin sampling method by applying the manifold-preserving graph reduction algorithm to the original margin sampling method. Experimental results on multiple data sets demonstrate that our method obtains better classification performance compared with the original margin sampling.

Keywords: Active learning, Margin sampling, Support vector machine, Manifold-preserving graph reduction.

1 Introduction

In machine learning, supervised models, such as support vector machines (SVMs) are commonly used in classification problems [1,12], owing to their valuable generalization properties and the uniqueness of the solution. However, as any other supervised classifier, SVMs rely on the quality of labeled examples used for training. Therefore, the training examples should completely represent the surface-type statistical properties in order to allow the classifier to find the correct solution. Although people can easily get a large number of unlabeled examples, it usually needs much manual labor to label them, which can be expensive, difficult or time-consuming. Therefore, there is a need for procedures to find a suitable training set automatically, or semi-automatically.

In the machine learning literature, this approach is known as active learning. Active learning is a sampling process by actively selecting and labeling the most informative candidates from a large pool of unlabeled examples. Instead of randomly picking unlabeled examples, active learning selects the examples that are considered the most valuable and informative for human labeling [16]. Through this, a predictor trained on a small set of well-chosen examples can

S. Li et al. (Eds.): CCPR 2014, Part I, CCIS 483, pp. 120–129, 2014.
© Springer-Verlag Berlin Heidelberg 2014

perform as well as a predictor trained on a large number of randomly chosen examples [9,3,18].

There are mainly three classes of methods used in active learning [17]. The first class of active learning methods is large margin-based heuristics, for instance, the margin sampling (MS) strategy which relies on SVM specificities [2,13,10]. MS selects the unlabeled data which lies within the margin of the current SVM since these examples are the most likely to become new support vectors. The second class is committee-based heuristics, for example, entropy query-by-bagging (EQB) [5]. The committee members with different hypotheses about parameters are trained to label the unlabeled data. It tends to select for labeling the unlabeled examples where the disagreement among the classifiers is maximal. The third one relies on the estimation of the posterior probability distribution function of the classes [8]. It selects the examples for manual labeling based on the values of their posterior probabilities. For a binary problem, the selected examples are the ones which give the class membership probability closest to 0.5.

In this paper, we mainly focus on MS which is a state-of-the-art active learning method and has widely applied in many practical issues, such as text mining [14] and remote sensing image retrieval [15]. However, as stated in [17], one of the drawbacks of MS is that the method is optimal only when a single example is chosen each iteration. When several samples are chosen simultaneously, the structural information and distribution in the feature space are not considered. This will lead to a consequence that several samples lying in the same area close to the hyperplane are selected into the training set. However, these points possibly provide the same information, and thus there is no need to select all of them. More importantly, it will cause data redundancy which decreases the classification accuracy. Considering both the distribution structure and uncertainty of the selected examples is an effective way to overcome this shortcoming. Several active learning algorithms have been proposed. For example, Huang et al. [7] presented a principled approach, termed QUIRE, to combine the informativeness and representativeness of an instance and Nguyen [10] proposed a formal model for incorporation of clustering into active learning. In this paper, we propose an improvement of MS by applying an algorithm called manifold-preserving graph reduction (MPGR) [15] beyond the original MS method. MPGR is a simple example sparsification algorithm which takes the space connectivity among samples into account and simultaneously effectively removes outliers and noisy points. By using MPGR, we can construct a subset which represents the global structure of the original distribution of samples. Such a modification of MS can avoid oversampling on dense regions to a large extent. Previously, we have applied MPGR to a different context, that is, active learning with probabilistic models, and got good performance improvements [19].

The remainder of this paper proceeds as follow. In Section 2, we briefly introduce some background about MS. In Section 3, we describe our method which applies MPGR to the original MS method. In Section 4, we show the experimental results on three real data sets to demonstrate the effectiveness of our method. Finally, we provide concluding remarks in Section 5.

2 Background

In this section, we brief reviews some background of margin sampling.

Margin sampling is specific to margin-based active learning algorithm which takes advantage of SVM geometrical properties [13]. An SVM uses a linear optimal hyperplane to discriminate classes, which is induced from the maximum margin principle between two classes [11]. For detailed information about SVM, see [1,12].

As we all know, the distance to the separating hyperplane can straightforwardly estimate the classifier confidence on an unlabeled example. The nearer the distance of an example to the hyperplane is, the lower the classifier confidence on it is. That is to say, the more information the example possesses. Therefore, the points are the most likely to become new support vectors which fall within the margin of the current classifier. Given a labeled training set $L = \{(x_1, y_1), \cdots (x_m, y_m)\}$ $(x_i \in R^d)$ with the corresponding labels $y_i \in \{\pm 1\}$. The goal of MS is to choose the examples with the minimum distance to the decision boundary from a set of n unlabeled examples U $(n \gg m)$.

Consider a binary problem. The distance of a sample to the decision boundary is given by

$$f(q_j) = \sum_{i=1}^{m} \alpha_i y_i K(x_i, q_j) + b, \tag{1}$$

where K is a kernel matrix, which defines the similarity between the candidate q_j and the support vector x_i, α represents the support vector coefficient ($\alpha \neq 0$), and y_i are the labels of the support vectors with the value $\{1, -1\}$. As to multi-class classification, we can just use one-vs-rest to convert the multi-class problem to multiple two-class problems.

Therefore, the candidate selected into the training set is the one respecting the condition

$$x' = \arg\min_{q_j \in U} |f(q_j)|. \tag{2}$$

Then x' and its ture label are is added into L and x' is removed from U simultaneously.

3 Our Proposed Approach

One of the drawbacks of the MS is that the method is optimal only when a single candidate is chosen per iteration. When selecting several examples simultaneously, the problem of oversampling on a small area is unavoidable. In order to remedy the problem, we propose an improvement of MS by considering the space connectivity and the distribution in the feature space of the unlabeled candidates.

3.1 MPGR

In machine learning, manifold assumption is an important assumption which indicates that samples in a small area have similar properties and thus their labels should also be similar. This assumption reflects local smoothness of the decision function which can alleviate the overfitting problems. In addition, sparse manifolds have significant advantages as follows: it can effectively eliminate the influence of noisy points and simultaneously accelerate the evaluation of predictors learned from the manifolds [15].

Manifold-preserving graph reduction (MPGR) is a simple but efficient graph reduction algorithm based on the manifold assumption [15]. For a graph, normally speaking, weights can measure the similarity of linked points. It means that the higher the weight is, the more similar the linked examples are. Here we introduce the definition of degree $d(p)$.

$$d(p) = \sum_{p \sim q} w_{pq} \qquad (3)$$

where $p \sim q$ means that example p is connected with example q (the k-nearest-neighbor rule is used to construct the adjacency graph where k is set to 10 in this paper) and w_{pq} is their corresponding weight. The weight is defined as:

$$W_{pq} = \begin{cases} \exp(-\frac{||x_p - x_q||^2}{t\eta}), & \text{if } x_p, x_q \text{ are neighbors ,} \\ 0, & \text{otherwise .} \end{cases} \qquad (4)$$

Here t is a parameter varying in $\{1,5,10\}$, and η is the mean of all the smallest distances between one point and its neighbors. If two examples are not linked, their weight is regarded as 0. $d(p)$ is generally used as a criterion to construct sparse graphs because of its simplicity. A bigger $d(p)$ means the example p has more information. That is to say, the example p is more likely to be selected into the sparse graphs.

Through the MPGR algorithm, we can construct a manifold-preserving sparse graph, which means that an example outside of the sparse graph has a high space connectivity with an example retained in it. Given a graph composed of all unlabeled examples, the manifold-preserving sparse graph is composed of the candidates which have a high space connectivity with the original unlabeled examples [15]. In other words, the subset constructed by MPGR is high representative and maintains a good global manifold structure of the original data distribution. In addition, when there are noisy examples and outliers in the training data, the MPGR algorithm can remove them effectively.

3.2 Improved Margin Sampling Method

In this section, we introduce our method which applies MPGR to the original MS.

As mentioned above, there are some drawbacks in the traditional MS method, such as not exploiting the space connectivity and not considering the distribution of the examples in the feature space. In order to overcome these shortcomings, we apply the MPGR algorithm to the original MS. We denote the new method as iMS. By exploiting the aforementioned MPGR, iMS tends to select the examples with high space connectivity, that is globally representative examples. As these examples are high representative, we can just use them to represent the whole data set to a large extent. Compared with the original MS, iMS considers the distribution and the manifold structure among the unlabeled data. Moreover, iMS can effectively eliminate the influence of noisy points which will be excluded due to the low space connectivity.

The difference between MS and iMS is on the scale of unlabeled examples needed to be queried. Assuming there are $s1$ unlabeled examples in total and the number of subset is $s2$ ($s1 \geq s2$). MS queries all the $s1$ unlabeled examples, while iMS is just querying $s2$ examples constructed by the MPGR algorithm. Since the subset takes into account the distribution and global structural information of unlabeled examples, it can effectively avoid the aforementioned oversampling in the same region in MS. It is important to notice that if $s1 = s2$, the iMS algorithm is identical to MS.

It can be seen that our method is a refinement of the original MS. Essentially, it consists of two steps. First, we construct a sparse subset by MPGR. Then we use MS to reselect unlabeled points using Eq. 2 from the subset. Thus it can not only reduce the number of unlabeled points to be queried, but also avoid oversampling on dense regions. Moreover it can effectively remove the noisy points and outliers from the candidate points .

4   Experiments

We evaluate our method on three real data sets which are the Ionosphere data set, the Vertebral Column (VC) data set and the Balance Scale (BS) data set. All the three data sets are publicly downloaded from the UCI Machine Learning Repository[1]. To demonstrate the generality of our method, these data sets include both binary classification and multi-class classification tasks.

4.1   Experimental Settings

The optimal parameters $\{C, \sigma\}$ (Gaussian RBF kernel is used) are found by grid search after five-fold cross-validation. C is a parameter which controlls the trade-off between the minimization of the number of misclassified training points and the maximization of the margin [6]. σ is the band-width parameter of Gaussian kernel $k(x, y) = \exp(-\frac{||x-y||^2}{2\sigma^2})$, which is optimized in the range of $\{2^{-3}, 2^{-2}, ...2^0, ...2^3\}$.

For each data set, the algorithms start with a small labeled data set L and select examples iteratively from the candidates set U. We have chosen here to consider the unlabeled set U from the training set ($U = [training\ set] - L$).

---

[1] http://archive.ics.uci.edu/ml/

To show the effectiveness of our method, three methods are compared in this paper: iMS, MS and random selection. During each iteration, we select p points to add into L and accordingly reduce them from U, and then calculate the error rates on the test set T. The difference is that iMS selects the p points from a subset of U (constructed by MPGR), while MS selects them from the whole unlabeled data set U. As a baseline, the method of random selection is randomly picking those points.

In our experiments, we focus on the average error rates and the entire procedure has been repeated 15 times on each data set. In the following experiments, the size of the initial data set L is set to 10. Each algorithm adds five most relevant examples into L per iteration. Note that the size of the subset constructed by MPGR should not be too large. From [15], we can see that the classification accuracy often first increases and then decreases as the proportion of unlabeled examples retained increases.

4.2   Binary Classification

The Ionosphere data set was collected by a system in Goose Bay, Labrador. This system consists of a phased array of 16 high-frequency antennas with a total transmitted power on the order of 6.4 kilowatts. The data set includes 351 examples in total where each data point includes 34 features and an output attribute. It is a binary classification (good/bad) problem. The whole data set of 351 examples are randomly split into a training set (used for both L and U) of 271 examples and a test set T of 80 examples. The size of the subset constructed by MPGR is 100. Fig. 1 shows the performance comparison of iMS with MS and random selection on this data set.

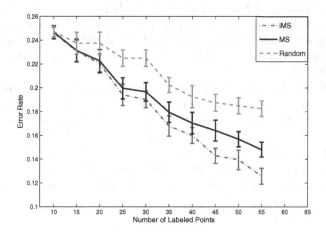

Fig. 1. Performance comparison of iMS, MS and random selection on the Ionosphere data set

The VC data set contains six biomechanical features and an predicted attribute, which is used to classify orthopaedic patients into two classes (normal or abnormal). There are 310 examples in total which are randomly split into a training set of 230 examples and a test set of 80 examples. The subset size is 100. Fig. 2 shows the comparison results of iMS, MS and random selection.

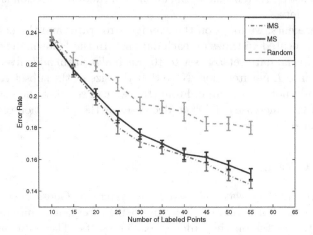

Fig. 2. Performance comparison of iMS, MS and random selection on the VC data set

4.3   Multi-class Classification

The BS data set is generated to model psychological experimental results. Each example is classified as: tip to the left (left), tip to the right (right), or to be balanced (balance). There are 625 examples in which each example contains four feature attributes and an output attribute. It is a multi-class classification problem. We set the subset size to be 150. The 625 examples are randomly split into a training set of 525 examples and a test set of 100 examples. Fig. 3 shows the performance comparison of iMS classification with MS and random selection on the BS data set.

The experimental results on the three data sets, which include binary classification and multi-class classification problems, show that our approach iMS obtains a better performance than MS and random selection. This might be due to the following reasons. Firstly, compared with MS, iMS constructs an important and informative subset which takes into account the global manifold structure and the distribution of the unlabeled examples. Secondly, by using MPGR, the influence of noisy points and outliers can be effectively eliminated.

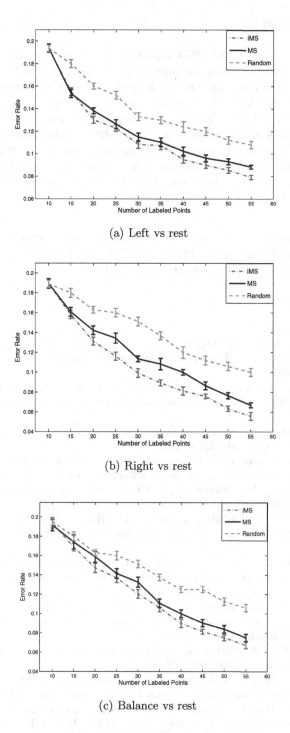

(a) Left vs rest

(b) Right vs rest

(c) Balance vs rest

Fig. 3. Performance comparison of iMS, MS and random selection on the BS data set

5   Conclusions

In this paper, we applied the MPGR algorithm to an active learning method, the SVM-based MS and presented our improved new method iMS. Compared with the original MS, iMS is a refinement making use of the MPGR algorithm, which takes the distribution in the feature space and the structural space connectivity of the unlabeled candidates into account. Especially when there are noisy examples and outliers in the training data, the MPGR algorithm can effectively remove them. Consequently, oversampling on dense regions is avoided. Experimental results on multiple data sets show that our new method iMS outperforms MS and random selection. Extensions of the MPGR algorithm to other learning contexts will be interesting future research.

Acknowledgements. This work is supported by the National Natural Science Foundation of China under Projects 61370175 and 61075005, and Shanghai Knowledge Service Platform Project (No. ZF1213).

References

1. Boser, B.E., Guyou, I.M., Vapnik, V.N.: A training algorithm for optimal margin classifiers. In: 5th Workshop on Computational Learning Theory, Pittsburgh, pp. 144–152 (1992)
2. Campbell, C., Cristianini, N., Smola, A.: Query learning with large margin classifiers. In: 17th International Conference on Machine Learning, Stanford, pp. 111–118 (2000)
3. Cohn, D., Atlas, L., Ladner, R.: Improving generalization with active learning. Machine Learning 15, 201–221 (1994)
4. Ferecatu, M., Boujemaa, N.: Interactive remote-sensing image retrieval image retrieval. IEEE Transactions on Geoscience Remote Sensing 45, 818–826 (2007)
5. Freund, Y., Seung, H.S., Shamir, E., Tishby, N.: Selective sampling using the query by committee algorithm. Machine Learning 28, 133–168 (1997)
6. Hernández, E.P., Ambroladze, A., Taylor, J.S., Sun, S.: PAC-Bayes bounds with data dependent priors. The Journal of Machine Learning Research 13, 3507–3531 (2012)
7. Huang, S., Jin, R., Zhou, Z.: Active learning by querying informative and representative examples. In: 24th Annual Conference on Neural Information Processing Systems, Vancouver, pp. 892–900 (2010)
8. Kapoor, A., Grauman, K., Urtasun, R., Darrell, T.: Active learning with Gaussian processed for object categorization. In: 11th International Conference on Computer Vision, Rio de Janeiro, pp. 1–8 (2007)
9. Mackay, D.J.C.: Information-based objective functions for active data selection. Neural Computation 4, 590–604 (1992)
10. Nguyen, H.T., Smeulders, A.: Active learning using pre-clustering. In: 21st International Conference on Machine Learning, Banff, Canada, pp. 623–630 (2004)
11. Oskoei, M.A., Hu, H.: Support vector machine-based classification scheme for myoelectric control applied to upper limb. IEEE Transactions on Biomedical Engineering 55, 1956–1965 (2008)

12. Schölkopf, B., Smola, A.J.: Learning with Kernels. MIT press, Cambridge (2002)
13. Schohn, G., Cohn, D.: Less is more: Active learning with support vectors machines. In: 17th International Conference on Machine Learning, Stanford, pp. 839–846 (2000)
14. Silva, C., Ribeiro, B.: Margin-based active learning and background knowledge in text mining. In: 4th International Conference on Hybird Intelligent Systems, Washington, pp. 8–13 (2004)
15. Sun, S., Hussain, Z., Taylor, J.S.: Manifold-preserving graph reduction for sparse semi-supervised learning. Neurocomputing 124, 13–21 (2013)
16. Sun, S., Hardoon, D.: Active learning with extremely sparse labeled examples. Neurocomputing 73, 2980–2988 (2010)
17. Tuia, D., Ratle, F., Pacifici, F., Kanevski, M.F., Emery, W.J.: Active learning methods for remote sensing image classification. IEEE Transactions on Geoscience Remote Sensing 47, 2218–2232 (2009)
18. Zhang, Q., Sun, S.: Multiple-view multiple-learner active learning. Pattern Recognition 43, 3113–3119 (2010)
19. Zhou, J., Sun, S.: Active learning of Gaussian processes with manifold-preserving graph reduction. Neural Computing & Applications (2014), doi:10.1007/s00521-014-1643-8

Research on the Ant Colony Optimization Fuzzy Neural Network Control Algorithm for ABS

Changping Wang[1,2,*] and Ling Wang[1]

[1] College of Electrical and Information Engineering,
Hunan University, Changsha 410082, China
[2] No.95333 Troops of PLA, Hunan Changsha, 410111, China
pcwtsz100@163.com

Abstract. As the convergence rate of the conventional fuzzy neural network control (FNC) algorithm for a vehicle anti-lock braking system is slow, an improved ant colony optimization fuzzy neural network control (ACO-FNC) algorithm for ABS is proposed, and the control object of ACO-FNC is slip rate. The simulation model of single-wheel ABS is established. According to the comparison of the results of the conventional FNC algorithm and ACO-FNC algorithm, the performance of ACO-FNC algorithm in convergence speed, slip ratio control quality and braking distance is better than FNC algorithm.

Keywords: Ant Colony Optimization(ACO), fuzzy neural network, control, Anti-locked Braking System(ABS), slip rate.

1   Introduction

The ABS(Anti-locked Braking System, ABS) is an integrated electrical and mechanical system built on the basis of the traditional braking system by using the electronic control technology, to prevent wheel lock when braking. It is composed of three parts which are controller, electromagnetic valve and wheel speed sensor[1]. ABS system can effectively enhance the vehicle braking stability in the process, reduce the braking distance, and play an important role in improving the driving safety coefficient. When the bus is driving, the driving environment of the vehicle is complicated, and there are various of disturbance, therefore the ABS system is a system with serious nonlinear, time-varying, complexity characteristics, it is difficult to use an accurate mathematical model to describe the ABS system [2]. At present, fuzzy control algorithm with the characteristics of strong robustness and independent with accurate mathematical model, the algorithm has been widely used in the ABS system. The fuzzy PID control method for the ABS system is proposed by APAROW V R [3][4] , but for the traditional fuzzy control method, online self-learning ability is weak, difficult to follow the change of the controlled object in time, thus the control effect is not ideal. In order to improve the adaptability of fuzzy control algorithm, an algorithm combined artificial neural networks and fuzzy control fuzzy neural network (Fuzzy Neural Network, FNN) is proposed in the literature [5,6]. The algorithm has a strong

---

* Corresponding author.

S. Li et al. (Eds.): CCPR 2014, Part I, CCIS 483, pp. 130–139, 2014.

self-learning and self-tuning function. As the BP algorithm is adopted in the neural network parameters learning. Therefore, it has the shortcoming of slow convergence speed, and is difficult to achieve satisfactory control effect [7]. In view of the above situation, an improved ABS system control algorithm is presented in this paper, using ant colony optimization algorithm to optimize the parameters of the fuzzy controller, to improve the performance of the fuzzy neural network controller. Simulation results show that the algorithm improves the control algorithm convergence speed effectively, and the problems of slow convergence speed of BP network is solved, moreover, the braking distance is shortened, the braking performance of ABS system is improved.

2   Principle of the ABS

The braking performance of the vehicle is decided by the wheel longitudinal adhesion, and the operating performance of the vehicle is determined by the wheel lateral adhesion, the size of the two kinds of adhesive force is decided by their attachment coefficient and vertical load, what is more, sliding rate is closely related to adhesion coefficient.

The wheel slip is defined as:

$$\lambda = \frac{v_x - v_\omega}{v_x} \times 100\% \tag{1}$$

Where λ, v_x and v_ω are the wheel slip, the vehicle forward velocity and the wheel speed.

According to the analysis above, in normal driving conditions, $v_x = v_\omega$, therefore $\lambda = 0$. In severe braking, it is common to have $v_\omega = 0$, therefore $\lambda = 100\%$. When there are both rolling motion and sliding motion of the wheels, $v_x > v_\omega$, therefore $0 < \lambda < 100\%$.

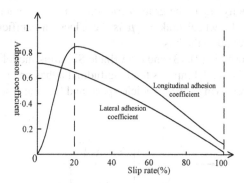

Fig. 1. The relationship between adhesion coefficient of the wheel and sliding rate

According to the relationship curve of figure 1, with the increase of slip rate, the size of the longitudinal adhesion coefficient presented first increases and then decreases, the longitudinal adhesion coefficient in obtain the maximum value when the slip rate is about 20%, while the vehicle lateral adhesion coefficient decreases continuously. When the wheel lock, slip rate is 100%, the wheel lateral adhesion will become very small, the vehicle will be lost to the outside world lateral force resistance ability, the direction of the vehicle will lose stability and steering control ability, easy to skid the risk of out of control. So comprehensive analysis of the longitudinal adhesion coefficient and lateral adhesion coefficient changes, the best control effect will be got when the vehicle brake to control the slip rate is about 20% , then can ensure the quickness of braking can both stability and maneuverability of the vehicle.

The working principle of the ABS system is as follow: first the wheel speed sensor detects wheel speed signal, then the signal after dealing with the electronic control unit, by adjusting the brake pressure to adjust the speed of vehicles, by keeping the slip rate near the optimal slip ratio to get the best braking effect.

3   The Establishment of the ABS System Simulation Model

3.1   Vehicle Dynamics Model

Because this article mainly studies the ABS control algorithm, in order to simplify the research problems, a single wheel vehicle model is used in the paper. When braking wheel force as shown in figure 2, analysis shows equation of motion of the vehicle and the wheel can be expressed as:

$$M\dot{v} = -F_s \tag{2}$$

$$I\dot{\omega} = F_s R - T_b \tag{3}$$

$$F_s = N\mu \tag{4}$$

Where M is1/4 vehicle quality, v is the vehicle speed, R is the effective rolling radius, ω is the angular velocity, F_s is the ground friction, I is the moment of inertia, T_b is the torque applied to the wheel braking, μ is the adhesion coefficient, and N is the support force from ground to the bus.

According to the formula (2), (3) and (4) vehicle Simulink model could be establish as shown in figure3.The model input is the longitudinal adhesion coefficient and brake torque, output is the revolving speed, vehicle speed and braking distance.

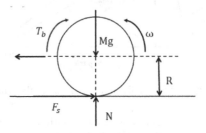

Fig. 2. The diagram of the force on the wheel

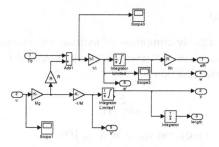

Fig. 3. The vehicle dynamics model

3.2   Model of the Tire

Because of the tire model mainly describe the longitudinal adhesion coefficient in the function of slip ratio, therefore the Timothy tire model for studying the simulation is put forward.

$$\mu(\lambda) = C_1 \left[C_2 \left(1 - e^{-C_3\lambda} \right) - C_4\lambda \right] \tag{5}$$

Where C_1, C_2, C_3, C_4 is the reference coefficient of road surface. Reference coefficient values of Different road are shown in table 1.

Table 1. The referee coefficient of various kinds of road surface

Road Surface	C_1	C_2	C_3	C_4
Dry	0.90	1.07	17.73	0.026
Wet	0.47	1.07	77.30	0.006
Ice	0.17	1.07	38.0	0.003

According to the formula (5), tire Simulink simulation model is set up as shown in figure 4.

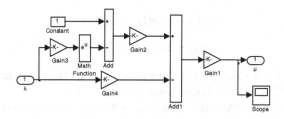

Fig. 4. The tire model

3.3   Arrester Model

The arrester model is mainly composed of hydraulic transmission system and brake torque. In order to carry out the research, the hydraulic drive system is simplified appropriately, its transfer function is:

$$\frac{K}{\lambda(\lambda T+1)} \tag{6}$$

Where the value of T is 0.01, the value of K is 100.
The arrester braking torque is expressed as:

$$T_b = K_p \cdot P \tag{7}$$

Where K_p and P denote the braking efficiency factor and brake pressure.
According to the formula (6), (7) brake simulation model is set up as shown in figure 5.

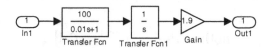

Fig. 5. The vehicle arrester model

4   Fuzzy Neural Network ABS Controller Design

The purpose of ABS system is to assure that the slip rate control near the optimal slip ratio, and to obtain good braking force and lateral adhesion, so that the braking performance and stability of the vehicle at the same time is good.. In this article, the fuzzy controller is designed based on slip ratio control, namely by tracking the reference slip rate to change the size of the brake pressure, so as to adjust   the speed of the wheel, the actual slip rate of the wheel following the change of settings value.

In this paper, the designed controller has two inputs and one output structure, input parameters of the controller e is the difference between actual slip ratio and the reference slip ratio, the other input parameters ec is the change rate of the difference, the output parameter u is the pressure.

$$e(i) = GE[r(i) - y(i)] \tag{8}$$

$$ec(i) = GEC \cdot EC(i) \tag{9}$$

Where $r(i)$ is a given value, $y(i)$ is the output value, $EC(i)$ is the difference rate of change, $GE 、 GEC$ is the quantitative parameters of $e 、 ec$.

NB, NM, NS, ZO, PS, PM, PB is used to show 7 fuzzy subset of the input parameters of e and ec respectively. Their membership functions can be described by Gaussian function.

$$u_{Aij}(x_i) = exp\left[-\frac{(x_i - m_{ij})^2}{\sigma_{ij}^2}\right] \tag{10}$$

Where x_i is the input variable, σ_{ij} is the width of the membership function, m_{ij} is the member ship function center.

The fuzzy inference can express by a set of fuzzy rules, the u, e, ec fuzzy subset can be expressed by U_k, A_{1i}, A_{2j}.

The controller output variables u membership function is a single point fuzzy.

$$u_{U_k}(u) = \begin{cases} 1 & u = \omega_k \\ 0 & u \neq \omega_k \end{cases} \tag{11}$$

The sum-product method is used for fuzzy reasoning, and using the weighted average method for solving fuzzy operation. The system output

$$u = \sum_{k=1}^{49} \omega_k \frac{\alpha_k}{\sum_{m=1}^{49} \alpha_m} = \sum_{k=1}^{49} \omega_k \overline{\alpha_k} \tag{12}$$

$$\alpha_k = u_{A_{1k}}(x_1) \cdot u_{A_{2k}}(x_2) \tag{13}$$

Where α_k is the rule's activate degrees.

According to the above content, the controller designed in the paper should include input unit, membership function units, rules, and output unit four parts, so the controller can be done using a four layer neural network, structure of the neural network is 2-14-49-1, its structure is shown in figure 6. The network layer 1 to 3 are used for the realization of the fuzzy rules, 3~4 layers are used to implement to blur. The fuzzy neural network is different from general neural network, the network parameter is not reflected on the connection weights but in join point. The input and output of every node in the network's is expressed by I_i^k and O_i^k respectively.

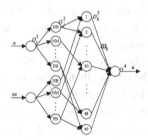

Fig. 6. The structure of fuzzy neural network controller

The first layer is input layer. The layer 2 nodes represent the two input signals of the controller.

$$I_i^1 = x_i, O_i^1 = x_i, i = 1,2$$

$$x_1 = e, x_2 = ec \tag{14}$$

The second layer is blurred layer. This layer has total of 14 nodes, each node of output membership function value for it.

$$I_j^3 = \frac{-(x_i - m_{ij})^2}{\sigma_{ij}^2} \quad O_j^2 = exp\,(I_j^2)$$

$$i = 1,2 \quad j = 1,2,\dots,7 \tag{15}$$

The third layer for fuzzy control rules. This layer has a total of 49 nodes.

$$I_k^3 = x_{k1}^3 x_{k2}^3 \quad O_k^3 = I_k^3$$

$$k_1, k_2 = 1,2,\dots,7 \quad k = 1,2,\dots,49 \tag{16}$$

The fourth layer is the blurred layer. This layer is only one output node.

$$I^4 = \sum_{k=1}^{49} \omega_k O_k^3 \quad u = O^4 = \frac{I^4}{\sum_{k=1}^{49} O^3}$$

$$k=1,2,\dots,49 \tag{17}$$

Where ω_k is the connective weight between 3, 4 layers.

In this fuzzy neural network, the adjustable parameters are all the nodes' membership function parameters m_{ij} and σ_{ij}, and the weights C between 3 and 4 layers.

5   The Ant Colony Optimization to Optimize Fuzzy Neural Network Controller Parameters

Algorithm proposed in this paper it is using the ACO algorithm to optimize fuzzy neural network controller parameters, such as GE, GEC, ω_k, σ_{ij}, m_{ij} and so on. In order to describe conveniently, we take the number of the parameters as M. The basic process of the ACO algorithm is as follows: we record the parameters on the training network, which need to be optimize as $p_i(1 \leq i \leq M)$. Every possible value of each parameter p_i can form the set I_{p_i}, then release proper number of ants from their nests to start looking for food. Each ant start from I_{p_i}, and according to the size of the various element's pheromone in I_{p_i} and rules formula (18), select an element from the collection A randomly. Then adjust the size of the pheromone of each element in I_{p_i} collection according to the formula (19). When all the ants released are in the set A and the unique elements are determined, then all the ant colony had found the food, and began to press the way back to the nest and end an optimization process.

This process is repeated continuously until all the ants are belong to the same path, find the optimal solution, or when the evolution trend is not obvious, the search is quitted for the iterations reaching the maximum number, the whole optimization process is completed.

$$P\big[\tau_j^k(I_{pi})\big] = \frac{\tau_j(I_{pi})}{\sum_{j=1}^N \tau_j(I_{pi})} \tag{18}$$

$$\tau_j(I_{pi})(t+n) = (1-\rho)\tau_j(I_{pi})(t) + \Delta\tau_j(I_{pi}) \tag{19}$$

$$\Delta\tau_j(I_{pi}) = \sum_{k=1}^{K} \Delta\tau_j^k(I_{pi}) \tag{20}$$

$$\Delta\tau_j^k(I_{pi}) = \begin{cases} \frac{Q}{e^k}, & \text{select } j \\ 0, & \text{else} \end{cases} \tag{21}$$

Where $\rho(0 \le \rho < 1)$ is the pheromone volatilization coefficient, $\Delta\tau_j^k(I_{pi})$ is the pheromone ant k left the on element, Q is a constant, which express the size of the pheromone adjustment speed. e^k is the maximum output error, when the neural network weight is the ant colony optimization selected. And e^k on the formula (21) defined as:

$$e^k = \max_{n=1}^{h} |o_n - o_q| \tag{22}$$

Where h is the Sample size. O_n, O_q is the fuzzy neural network's actual output and desired output.

According to the algorithm processes, by using fuzzy neural network controller optimized by the ant colony algorithm of this paper, when take the elements selected by ant as the weights of neural network, and the output of the system error e^k reduce, corresponding elements of the pheromone selected by ant colony will increase. Under the elements selecting rules of the ant colony (that is, the formula of 18), the greater the Pheromones, the greater the elements selected by the ants in the next choice, and the probability of corresponding element pheromone will quickly accumulated quickly , after optimization process again, the output of the system error will be smaller. Thus forming a positive feedback process in the system, the shortest path the ant colony optimization found is the optimal solution, the speed of the algorithm convergence rate is improved. So when the ABS system based on slip ratio control controller is optimized using ant colony algorithm, the slip rate control system can be quickly into a stable state, which greatly improved the stability of the vehicle when braking.

6   Simulation Analysis

For validation based on ant colony optimization the superiority of the fuzzy neural network control, the author use MATLAB language, combined with MATLAB neural network toolbox, the simulation model of the ABS system is established. And for the ant colony optimization fuzzy neural network control of ABS system and conventional fuzzy neural network control of the ABS system, experiment with two algorithms is carried out under the same parameter settings, specific experimental parameters are shown in table 2.

Table 2. Experiment parameter of the vehicle

Parameter	Value	Parameter	Value
The total mass of the vehicle M/kg	1850	The gravitational acceleration $g/(m/s^2)$	9.8
The normal force of the car on the ground F/N	18125	The wheel rolling radius R/m	0.52
The rotational inertia of the vehicle $J/(kg \cdot m^2)$	20	The initial speed the vehicle $v/(m/s)$	25
The range of the brake pressure p/kPa	0~700	The brake force factor $C/(N \cdot m/kPa)$	21

Figure7 is two algorithm slip rate step response. Figure8 is regular as FNC control of ABS system simulation diagram. Figure9 is the simulation graph of the ABS system based on ACO-FNC control.

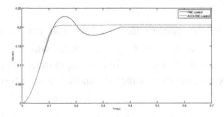

Fig. 7. The result of sliding rate by simulation

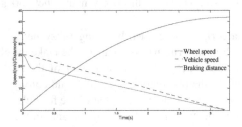

Fig. 8. The result of the conventional FNC control of ABS system by simulation

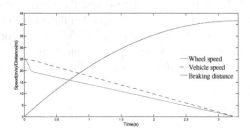

Fig. 9. The result of the ACO-FNC control of ABS system by simulation

Based on the analysis comparison of conventional FNC control and ACO-FNC control ABS system simulation curve we can know: using the ACO optimized, the step response time of sliding rate is shorter, overshoot is smaller, and the result can quickly reach the steady state response, slip rate can quickly held steady at around 20%, slip rate control quality is better. And according to the results of the experiment data shows that the ACO-FNC algorithm braking distance is 41.82m, and the conventional FNC algorithm 42.80m, 2.34% shorter, and the safety of the vehicle braking performance be improved.

7   Conclusion

Aiming at the shortcomings of ABS system of fuzzy neural network control algorithm such as slow convergence speed, this paper presents an algorithm by applying ant colony optimization algorithm in improvement of parameters optimization of fuzzy neural network controller, for the advantages of ant colony optimization algorithm such as optimization ability, convergence speed. And a contrast experiment is been done between this control algorithm and the conventional fuzzy neural network control algorithm, the experimental results show that: the convergence rate of Fuzzy neural network control based on ant colony optimization algorithm is increased significantly, effectively improved the conventional fuzzy neural network control shortcomings of slow convergence speed. The vehicle brake wheel slip rate controlling in the process of quality is improved, and the vehicle braking distance is further shortened, the safety of the vehicle braking performance is improved. Experiments prove that the improved algorithm is effective and feasible.

References

1. Li, G.: Vehicle anti-lock brake control theory and application, pp. 1–2. National Defense Industry Press, Beijing (2009)
2. Sanchez–Torres, J.D., Loukianov, A.G., Galicia, M.I., et al.: Robust nested sliding mode integral control for anti–lock brake system. International Journal of Vehicle Design 62(2), 188–205 (2013)
3. Yan, W.G., Li, G., Yu, D.T., et al.: Study on Fuzzy PID Control Algorithm for Antilock Brake System. Journal of Highway and Transportation Research and Development 7, 032 (2004)
4. Aparow, V.R., Ahmad, F., Hudha, K., et al.: Modelling and PID control of antilock braking system with wheel slip reduction to improve braking performance. International Journal of Vehicle Safety 6(3), 265–296 (2013)
5. Johansen, T.A., Petersen, I., Kalkkuhi, J., et al.: Gain-scheduled wheel slip control in automotive brake systems. IEEE Transactions on Control Systems Technology 11(6), 799–811 (2003)
6. Topalov, A.V., Oniz, Y., Kayacan, E., et al.: Neuro-fuzzy control of antilock braking system using sliding mode incremental learning algorithm. Neuro Computing 74(11), 1883–1893 (2011)
7. Schinkel, M., Hunt, K.: Anti-lock braking control using a sliding mode like. In: American Control Conference, USA, pp. 1376–1381 (2002)

Schatten p-Norm Based Matrix Regression Model for Image Classification

Lei Luo, Jian Yang, Jinhui Chen, and Yicheng Gao

School of Computer Science and Engineering
Nanjing University of Science and Technology,
Nanjing 210094, China
zzdxpyy3001@163.com, csjyang@njust.edu.cn,
{tangxinhao,csycgao}@gmail.com

Abstract. Nuclear norm minimization problems for finding the minimum rank matrix have been well studied in many areas. Schatten p-norm is an extension of nuclear norm and the rank function. Different p provides flexible choices for suiting for different applications. Differing from the viewpoint of rank, we will use Schatten p-norm to characterize the error matrix between the occluded face image and its ground truth. Thus, a Schatten p-norm based matrix regression model is presented and a general framework for solving Schatten p-norm minimization problem with an added l_q regularization is solved by alternating direction method of multipliers (ADMM). The experiments for image classification and face reconstruction show that our algorithm is more effective and efficient, and thus can act as a fast solver for matrix regression problem.

Keywords: Schatten p-norm, ADMM, face recognition, face reconstruction.

1 Introduction

In many applications, notions such as order, complexity, or dimension of a model or design can often be expressed by means of the rank of an appropriate matrix. If the set of feasible models or designs is described by convex constraints, one of the most natural assumptions is that the matrix has a low-rank or approximately low-rank. For example, minimal order system realization, reduced order controller design, low dimensional Euclidean embedding and interference with partial information etc [1, 2].

Minimizing the nuclear norm (sum of singular values) is a popular convex heuristic for low rank matrix approximation, which is first proposed in [3]. Recent research efforts also provided theoretical analysis and conditions for exact recovery of low-rank matrices via nuclear norm optimization [4, 5, 6, 7].

However, the above studies for nuclear norm are from the viewpoint of rank. It's well-known that the characterization of the residual term between the occluded face image and its ground truth plays a key role in regression model based face recognition methods, including LRC [8], SRC [9], CRC [10], etc. Especially, SRC and CRC use l_1 and l_2 (or Schatten 2-norm) to characterize the residual term, respectively. Similar to l_1 -norm, Schatten 2-norm is only based on pixel-level from the statistical significance

S. Li et al. (Eds.): CCPR 2014, Part I, CCIS 483, pp. 140–150, 2014.
© Springer-Verlag Berlin Heidelberg 2014

and ignores the connection between pixels, which can't preserve the spatial informa-tion of an error matrix. As we know, when $p \to 0$, the Schatten p-norm of $\mathbf{X}$ be-comes rank function of $\mathbf{X}$ under $0^0 = 0$. That is to say, when $p < 2$, according to the structural significance of rank function, Schatten p-norm seems to include more struc-tural information than Schatten 2-norm, Thus, from the viewpoint of regression, Yang et al. [11] used nuclear norm to describe the residual term and proposed a nuclear norm based matrix regression (NMR) model. It has been shown that NMR is robust to face recognition with occlusion and illumination changes.

Motivated by the work of Yang et al. [11], Nie et al. [12] and Li et al. [13 14 15], we propose a Schatten p-norm based matrix regression (SMR) model, which genera-lizes CRC and NMR. In order to gain some meaningful properties (e.g. sparsity) of regression coefficients, we add a l_q regularization term in the model. Our model is based on matrix image directly, thus, it preserves the spatial structure information of each image sample. What is more, we provide the general framework for minimizing Schatten p-norm with l_q regularization problem for all $p, q \geq 0$. For the general cases, we bring in an auxiliary variable, which results in a closed form solution for each iteration. The experiments for face recognition and image reconstruction show that our algorithm is more effective than some state of the art methods.

The rest of the paper is organized as follows. In Section 2, we present a matrix re-gression model based on Schatten p-norm and an algorithm to solve such a problem by virtue of ADMM. In Section 3, we design the SMR based classifier. In Section 4, we present the experiments with a series of face reconstruction and recognition prob-lems to demonstrate the robustness and effectiveness of the proposed algorithm. In Section 5, we conclude the paper with a brief conclusion.

2   Matrix Regression Based on Schatten p-Norm

In this section, we first introduce notations that are used throughout the paper. Then we formulate the matrix regression problem based on Schatten p-norm. Lastly we establish a general framework for solving Schatten p-norm minimization with l_q regu-larization problem by using the ADMM.

2.1   Notations

In this paper, the extended Schatten p-norm ($0 < p < \infty$) of a matrix $\mathbf{Y} \in R^{n \times m}$ is de-fined as $\|\mathbf{Y}\|_{S_p} = \left(\sum_{i=1}^{\min\{n,m\}} \sigma_i^{\ p} \right)^{\frac{1}{p}}$, where σ_i is the i-th singular value of $\mathbf{Y}$. The Schatten p-norm of a matrix $\mathbf{Y} \in R^{n \times m}$ to the power p is $\|\mathbf{Y}\|_{S_p}^p = \sum_{i=1}^{\min\{n,m\}} \sigma_i^{\ p}$. If $p=1$ and 2, the Schatten p-norm becomes nuclear norm and Frobenius norm, respectively. l_q-norm ($0 < q < \infty$) of a vector $\mathbf{x} \in R^{n \times 1}$ is denoted by $\|\mathbf{x}\|_q = \left(\sum_{i=1}^n |x_i|^q \right)^{\frac{1}{q}}$, where x_i is the i-th element of the vector $\mathbf{x}$. The l_q-norm of a vector $\mathbf{x} \in R^{n \times 1}$ to the power q is $\|\mathbf{x}\|_q^q = \sum_{i=1}^n |x_i|^q$.

2.2   Problem Formulation

Given a set of n matrices $A_1, \cdots, A_n \in R^{p \times q}$ and a matrix $B \in R^{p \times q}$, let us represent B linearly using $A_1, \cdots, A_n$, i.e., $B = x_1 A_1 + x_2 A_2 +, \cdots, + x_n A_n + E$, where $x_1, x_2, \cdots, x_n$ is a set of representation coefficients, and E is the representation residual. Let us denote the following linear mapping from R^n to $R^{p \times q}$: $A(x) = x_1 A_1 + x_2 A_2 +, \cdots, + x_n A_n$. Then, we can obtain that $B = A(x) + E$. Zhang et al. [9] have shown that it is the collaborative representation (CR) but not the l_1-norm sparse constraint that truly improves the FR performance, thus, for the low computational burden, they proposed to use the regularized least square method, i.e.,

$$\min_x \| A(x) - B \|_F^2 + \tfrac{1}{2} \lambda \| x \|_2^2 . \tag{1}$$

Subsequently, in order to preserve the structural information of the error matrix, Yang et al. [9] presented nuclear norm based matrix regression (NMR) model,

$$\min_x \| A(x) - B \|_* + \tfrac{1}{2} \lambda \| x \|_2^2 , \tag{2}$$

In this paper, we will consider an extensive form for (1) and (2):

$$\min \| Y \|_{S_p}^p + \tfrac{1}{2} \lambda \| x \|_q^q \quad \text{subject to} \quad A(x) - B = Y. \tag{3}$$

It is easy to see that our model can be considered as a Schatten p-norm based matrix regression (SMR) model with l_q regularization. And model (1) and (2) can be considered as a special case of the model (3), respectively. We will provide a general framework for solving model (3) in the following subsection.

2.3   Proposed Algorithm

The alternating direction method of multipliers (ADMM) was proposed originally in [16, 17]. Recently, ADMM has been applied extensively to the nuclear norm optimization problems [18, 19], which updates the variables alternately by minimizing the augmented Lagrangian function with respect to the variables in a Gauss-Seidel manner. Here, we provide the process of using ADMM to solve the problem (3). We first convert (3) to the following equivalent problem:

$$\min \| Y \|_{S_p}^p + \tfrac{1}{2} \lambda \| u \|_q^q \quad \text{subject to} \quad A(u) - B = Y, x = u. \tag{4}$$

As in the method of multipliers, we form the augmented Lagrangian function

$$L_\mu(Y, x, u, Z) = \| Y \|_{S_p}^p + \tfrac{1}{2} \lambda \| u \|_q^q + \text{Tr} \left(Z_1^T (A(x) - Y - B) \right) + z_2^T (x - u) + \tfrac{\mu}{2} (\| A(x) - Y - B \|_F^2 + \| x - u \|_2^2).$$

According to ADMM, we mainly solve the following two key sub-problems

$$u = \arg\min_u L_\mu(Y, x, u, Z) = \arg\min_x \left(\tfrac{1}{2} \| u - (x + \tfrac{1}{\mu} z_2) \|_2^2 + \tfrac{\lambda}{2\mu} \| u \|_q^q \right); \tag{5}$$

$$Y = \arg\min_{Y} L_{\mu}(Y,x,u,Z) = \arg\min_{Y}\left(\| Y \|_{S_p}^{p} + \tfrac{\mu}{2}\| A(x) - (B + Y - \tfrac{1}{\mu}Z) \|_{F}^{2}\right). \tag{6}$$

(I) Solving sub-problem (5): We can convert (5) to the following form:

$$u = \arg\min_{u}\left(\tfrac{\beta}{2}\| u - j \|_{2}^{2} + \| u \|_{q}^{q}\right), \quad \text{where} \ \ \beta = \tfrac{2\mu}{\lambda}, \ j = x + \tfrac{1}{\mu}z_{2}. \tag{7}$$

In fact, the above problem (7) is the same as the problem (5) in [20]. Thus, we can obtain the optimal solution to sub-problem (7) by D. Krishnan and R. Fergus's [20] approach. Although they obtain two analysis solutions for the cases $q=1/2$, and $2/3$, D. Krishnan and R. Fergus's approach can't solve problem (7) completely for all cases. In order to unify the algorithms to solve sub-problem (5) and (6), we introduce the following techniques.

(a) When $q \le 1$, the sub-problem (5) can be converted to

$$u = \arg\min_{u}\left(\tfrac{1}{2}\| u - j \|_{F}^{2} + \rho \| u \|_{q}^{q}\right), \quad \text{where} \ \ \rho = \tfrac{\lambda}{2\mu}. \tag{8}$$

By the structure of $\| u \|_{q}^{q}$, problem (8) can be decomposed into multiple small problems between corresponding elements of u and j. That is, we only need to solve the following problem:

$$\min_{\eta} \tfrac{1}{2}(\eta - a)^{2} + \rho |\eta|^{q}. \tag{9}$$

Let $h(\eta) = \tfrac{1}{2}(\eta - a)^{2} + \rho |\eta|^{q}$, we can see that the gradient of $h(\eta)$ is

$$g(\eta) = h'(\eta) = \eta - a + \rho q |\eta|^{q-1} \operatorname{sgn}(\eta). \tag{10}$$

Denote a constant $v = (\rho q(1-q))^{\frac{1}{2-q}}$, the optimal solution to problem (9) can be obtained by

$$\eta^{*} = \begin{cases} \arg\min_{\eta \in \{0,\eta_1\}} h(\eta), & \text{when } g(v) < 0 \\ \arg\min_{\eta \in \{0,\eta_2\}} h(\eta), & \text{when } g(-v) > 0, \\ 0, & \text{when } g(v) \ge 0, g(-v) \le 0, \end{cases} \tag{11}$$

where η_1 and η_2 are the roots of $g(\eta) = 0$ at $v < x < a$ and $-a < x < v$, which can be easily obtained with Newton method initialized at a.

(b) When $p \ge 1$, we can use the following Theorem 1 to solve problem (8).

Theorem 1. [21] Let $q \ge 1$, $\rho \ge 0$, then the optimal solution to the problem (9) is $\eta^{*} = \operatorname{sign}(a)\sigma$, where σ is the unique solution in $[0, +\infty]$ to the equation:

$$\sigma + q\rho\sigma^{q-1} = |a|. \tag{12}$$

In particular, the solutions of the problem (8) has the following closed-form expressions

If $q = 4/3$, $\eta = a + \tfrac{4\rho}{3\cdot2^{1/3}}\left((b-a)^{1/3} - (b+a)^{1/3}\right)$, where $b = \sqrt{a^{2} + 256\rho^{3}/729}$;

If $q = 3/2$, $\eta = a + 9\rho^2 sign(a)(1 - \sqrt{1 + 16|a|/(9\rho^2)})/8$;

If $q = 3$, $\eta = sign(a)\left(\sqrt{1 + 12\rho|a|} - 1\right)/(6\rho)$;

If $q = 4$, $\eta = \left((b + a)/8\rho\right)^{1/3} - \left((b - a)/8\rho\right)^{1/3}$, where $b = \sqrt{a^2 + 1/(27\rho)}$.

(II) Solving sub-problem (6): The Schatten p-norm of a diagonal matrix is the l_p -norm of the vector formed by its diagonal elements: $\|diag(\mathbf{u})\|_{S_p} = \|\mathbf{u}\|_p$ for a vector $\mathbf{u}$. The role of the Schatten p-norm in convex heuristics for rank minimization therefore parallels the use of the l_q -norm in sparse approximation or cardinality minimization. Thus, we can solve sub-problem (5) by the corresponding techniques in Subsection (I).

Let $\mathbf{A}(\mathbf{x}) - \mathbf{B} + \frac{1}{\mu}\mathbf{Z} = \mathbf{G}$, the sub-problem (6) can be expressed as

$$\mathbf{Y} = \arg\min_{\mathbf{Y}} L_\mu(\mathbf{Y}, \mathbf{x}, \mathbf{Z}) = \arg\min_{\mathbf{Y}}\left(\frac{1}{\mu}\|\mathbf{Y}\|_{S_p}^p + \frac{1}{2}\|\mathbf{Y} - \mathbf{G}\|_F^2\right). \tag{13}$$

Thus, we only need to consider the problem:

$$\min_{\mathbf{Y}}\left(\rho\|\mathbf{Y}\|_{S_p}^p + \frac{1}{2}\|\mathbf{Y} - \mathbf{G}\|_F^2\right), \text{ where } \rho = \frac{1}{\mu}. \tag{14}$$

Theorem 2 [12, 22] The optimal solution $\mathbf{Y}$ to problem (14) is $\mathbf{Y} = \mathbf{U}\Sigma\mathbf{V}^\mathrm{T}$, where $\mathbf{U}$ and $\mathbf{V}$ are the left and right singular vector matrices of $\mathbf{G}$, respectively. Moreover, if a_i is the i-th singular value of $\mathbf{G}$, the i-th diagonal element δ_i of the diagonal matrix Σ is given by the optimal solution to the following problem

$$\min_{\delta_i \geq 0}\frac{1}{2}(\delta_i - a_i)^2 + \rho\delta_i^p. \tag{15}$$

(a) When $p \leq 1$, we can solve the problem (15) by Theorem 2. If we consider q in (13) as p, then the optimal solution to problem (15) can be obtained similarly by

$$\eta^* = \begin{cases} 0, & when\ g(v) \geq 0, \\ \arg\min_{\eta \in \{0, \eta_1\}} h(\eta), & when\ g(v) < 0, \end{cases} \tag{16}$$

Remark 1. When $q = 1$ and $p = 1$, the derived solution (11) and (16) is the same as a soft- thresholding operator in [19] and a singular value shrinkage operator in [23], respectively. Thus, Theorem 2 provides a more concise proof for singular value shrinkage operator.

(b) When $p \geq 1$, we solve the problem (15) by Theorem 1 easily. And when $q \in \{1, 4/3, 3/2, 2, 3, 4\}$, we also have similar closed-form expressions.

The detailed algorithm for solving Schatten p-norm based matrix regression model (3) (SMR) is summarized in Algorithm 1.

Algorithm 1: (SMR Algorithm via ADMM)

Input: A set of matrices $\mathbf{A}_1, \cdots, \mathbf{A}_n$ and a matrix $\mathbf{B} \in R^{p \times q}$, the model parameters λ and μ, the termination condition parameters ε.

1. Set $t = 0$. Initialize $\mathbf{Y} = \mathbf{Z}_1 = \mathbf{0}, \mathbf{x} = \mathbf{z}_2 = \mathbf{0}$;

2. Update $\mathbf{u}$ by the optimal solution to the problem (7);

3. Update $\mathbf{x}$ by

$\mathbf{x} = (\mathbf{M}^T \mathbf{M} + \mathbf{I}) \backslash (\mathbf{M}^T \mathrm{Vec}(\mathbf{B} + \mathbf{Y} - \frac{1}{t}\mathbf{Z}_1) + \mathbf{u} - \frac{1}{t}\mathbf{z}_2)$, where $\mathbf{M} = [\mathrm{Vec}(\mathbf{A}_1), \cdots, \mathrm{Vec}(\mathbf{A}_n)]$;

4. Update $\mathbf{Y}$ by the optimal solution to problem (14);

5. Update $\mathbf{Z}_1$ and $\mathbf{z}_2$ by $\mathbf{Z}_1 = \mathbf{Z}_1 + \mu(A(\mathbf{x}) - \mathbf{Y} - \mathbf{B})$ and $\mathbf{z}_2 = \mathbf{z}_2 + \mu(\mathbf{x} - \mathbf{u})$, respectively.

Remark 2. If $q = 2$, we can consider model (3) directly and don't need to bring in an auxiliary variable. Thus, the step 2 and 3 in Algorithm 1 can be simplified to: $\mathbf{x} = \left(\frac{\lambda}{\mu}\mathbf{I} + \mathbf{M}^T \mathbf{M}\right)^{-1} \mathbf{M}^T \mathrm{Vec}(\mathbf{B} + \mathbf{Y} - \frac{1}{\mu}\mathbf{Z})$, where $\mathbf{Z}$ is the unique Lagrange multiplier.

In this paper, we will use the following termination criterion:

$$\|A(\mathbf{x}) - \mathbf{B} - \mathbf{E}\|_\infty \leq \varepsilon \text{ and } \|\mathbf{x} - \mathbf{u}\|_\infty \leq \varepsilon. \tag{17}$$

3   The Design of the Classifier

In this paper, we will use Schatten p-norm to characterize the distance between the test sample and the class training samples. We first use Algorithm 1 to obtain the optimal representation coefficients $\mathbf{x}^*$ for a test image $\mathbf{B}$, then use the reconstruction image $A(\mathbf{x}^*)$ of all training images as the new reference image of classification, which will be more reasonable for recognition because of its closeness to clear face. In addition, let $\sigma_i : R^n \rightarrow R^n$ be the characteristic function that selects the coefficients associated with the i-th class. For $\mathbf{x} \in R^n$, $\sigma_i(\mathbf{x})$ is a vector whose only nonzero entries are the entries in $\mathbf{x}$ that are associated with class i. Using the coefficients associated with the i-th class, one can get the reconstruction of $\mathbf{B}$ in Class i as $\hat{\mathbf{B}}_i = A(\sigma_i(\mathbf{x}^*))$. Finally, the Schatten p-norm of the representation residual is used to characterize the distance between reconstruction image and classes, i.e., $r_i(\mathbf{B}) = \|A(\mathbf{x}^*) - A(\sigma_i(\mathbf{x}^*))\|_{S_p}$ for

$i = 1, \cdots k$. Thus, the class which $\mathbf{B}$ belongs to can be determined by $\mathrm{identity}(\mathbf{B}) = \arg\min_i r_i(\mathbf{B})$. The designed classifier is named SMR based classifier

(SMRC). It is worth noting that our classifier is different from SRC. Firstly, our regard reconstruction image as the test image; secondly, we use Schatten p-norm as a (quasi) metric.

4   Experiment and Analysis

In this section, we conduct numerical experiments to test the performance of proposed algorithm in Section 2 by applying them to face recognition and image reconstruction on two well-known face image databases (AR and Yale B). The AR database was employed to test the performance of the system under different occlusions and different parameter p. And we compare face image reconstruction performance of our method with other methods. The Yale B database is used to evaluate the performance of SMR Algorithm as on AR database. We can choose the optimal parameter $\lambda \in [0.005, 1]$, $\mu = 1$ and $\varepsilon = 10^{-4}$ for all experiments. For the sake of clarity, we will set $p = q$ in model (3) for the following experiments.

4.1   Experiment Using the AR Database

The AR face database [24] contains over 4,000 color face images of 126 people (70 men and 56 women), including frontal views of faces with different facial expressions, lighting conditions and occlusions. The pictures of most persons were taken in two sessions (separated by two weeks). Each section contains 13 color images and 120 individuals (65 men and 55 women) participated in both sessions. The images of these 120 individuals were selected and used in our experiment. We manually cropped the face portion of the image and then normalized it to 50×40 pixels [25, 26].

(1) **Recognition of Clear Images:** Fourteen face images without occlusions (clear case) of these 120 individuals are selected and used in our experiment. These images vary as follows: (a) neutral expression, (b) smiling, (c) angry, (d) screaming, (e)-(h) are taken under the same conditions; And (i) right light on (j) left light on (k) all sides light, (l)-(n) are taken under the same conditions. Images from (a)–(h) are used for training, and images from (i)–(n) are used for testing.

(2) **Recognition of Images with Glasses:** In this experiment, the training images are the same as (1), but we choose the other seven images with dark glasses as the testing images: (i) wearing sun glasses (j) wearing sun glasses and left light on (k) wearing sun glasses and right light on, and (l)-(n) are taken under the same conditions as (i)–(k).

(3) **Recognition of Images with Scarf:** In this experiment, the training images are the same as f in (1), but we choose the other six images with the scarf as the testing images: (i) wearing scarf (j) wearing scarf and left light on (k) wearing scarf and right light on, and (l)-(n) are taken under the same conditions as (i)–(k).

In all experiments mentioned above, SRC (using sparse representation algorithm: BPDN_homotopy_function [27]), LRC (linear regression classifier), CRC (collaborative representation classifier), RSC [28] and the SMRC (SMR based classifier) proposed in this paper are, respectively, used for image classification. For comparing the influence of different metric to recognition performance, we choose Schatten 0.5-quasi norm (r=0.5), Schatten 1-norm (r=1) and 2-norm (r=2) to characterize the distance between reconstruction image and classes, respectively. The maximal recognition rate of each method is compared in Table 1, from which we can find that the when p=1 or 4/3, our method performs better than CRC, SRC, LRC and RSC. Especially, for the scarf case, our maximal recognition rates is 11.3 percent higher than SRC, which reflects fully the advantage of Schatten p-norm for recognition with real face disguise.

Table 1. The maximal recognition rates of SMRC, SRC, LRC and CRC

Experiment		SMRC					CRC	SRC	RSC	LRC
		p=0.3	p=0.5	p=0.8	p=1	p=4/3				
Clear	r=0.5	95.8	96.7	99.0	99.9	99.6				
	r=1	93.5	95.3	98.6	99.9	99.6	98.9	99.2	99.0	86.8
	r=2	90.7	93.3	98.1	99.9	99.9				
Glasses	r=0.5	85.7	88.6	95.1	97.6	97.4				
	r=1	83.2	86.4	94.4	97.1	97.8	92.9	95.1	96.7	93.2
	r=2	80.0	83.8	93.5	97.5	97.8				
Scarf	r=0.5	58.2	61.1	69.4	77.5	76.5				
	r=1	54.9	58.9	66.2	76.1	74.7	63.7	66.2	64.3	30 .7
	r=2	51.0	52.9	63.3	74.6	71.4				

Additionally, it noted that we only choose Schatten 0.5-quasi norm as a metric in $[0,1]$. This is because that, when $p \in [0,1]$, $p=0.5$ is a key point for the change of recognition performance. In Table 2, we chose $p=1$ and $p=4/3$ for model (3), and compared the performance of different Schatten r- (quasi) norm as a metric for recognition of images with scarf, which is varying in the range of $\{0.1, 0.2, \cdots, 1, 4/3, 3/2, 2\}$.

Table 2. Image classification performance of SMRC with different r

r \ p	0.1	0.2	0.3	0.4	0.5	0.6	0.7	0.8	0.9	1	4/3	3/2	2
1	73.3	75.1	76.1	76.4	77.5	77.5	77.5	77.2	76.8	76.0	75.1	75.0	74.6
4/3	72.6	74.0	74.9	75.8	76.2	76.2	76.2	75.7	75.1	74.4	72.8	72.4	70.8

(4) Face Image Reconstruction: To evaluate the method proposed in this paper, we experiment on the AR database with artificial occlusion. Specifically, given fourteen face images selected from the AR face database, as shown in the first line for Fig. 1, which are used for training. We choose the first image as the original image from training images. The original image with white block is denoted by **B** as the testing image. A comparison of our method, RSC, CRC, LRC is shown in the second line for Fig.1. From Fig.1, we can find that the reconstruction performance of SMR Algorithm ($p = 4/3$) is superior to the other methods.

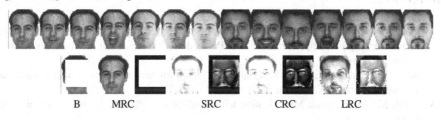

B   MRC   SRC   CRC   LRC

Fig. 1. The first line is the fourteen samples of cropped images of one person for training on AR database; the second line is the comparison of our method, SRC, CRC and LRC based on face reconstruction for artificial occlusion image B

4.2   Experiment Using the Extended Yale B Database

The extended Yale B face database contains 38 human subjects under nine poses and 64 illumination conditions the light source direction and the camera axis. The 64 images of a subject in a particular pose are acquired at camera frame rate of 30 frames/s, so there is only small change in head pose and facial expression for those 64 images. All frontal-face images marked with P00 are used, and each image is resized to 42×48 pixels in our experiment. We use the first16 images per subject for training, and the remaining images for testing [25, 27].

A detail comparison of maximal recognition rate with some latest approaches is shown in Table 2. We can find that the proposed SMRC outperforms evidently the SRC, CRC and LRC, RSC for face recognition with illumination.

Table 3. The maximal recognition rates of SMRC, SRC, CRC and LRC

Experiment	SMRC					CRC	SRC	RSC	LRC
	p=0.3	p =0.5	p =0.8	p =1	p=4/3				
r=0.5	91.7	94.0	96.7	97.6	97.1				
r=1	89.1	91.5	95.3	97.2	96.5	81.9	94.0	94.2	94.3
r=2	86.2	89.2	93.4	96.5	95.9				

5   Conclusion

This paper presented matrix regression model based on Schatten p-norm and a general framework for minimizing Schatten p-norm with l_q regularization problem for all $p, q \geq 0$. Our model was based on 2D image matrices, which didn't damage the spatial structure information of each sample, and connected the structural information of error and the sparsity of coefficient. We investigated the optimal solutions of two key sub-problems under different cases and solved such a problem by using alternating direction method of multipliers (ADMM). Numerical experiments for image classification and face reconstruction also showed that our algorithm was more efficient than other algorithms such as CRC, SRC, RSC, LRC. It should be noted that the method presented in this paper could be applied to other fields.

References

1. Fazel, M., Hindi, H., Boyd, S.P.: A rank minimization heuristic with application to minimum order system approximation. In: Proceedings of American Control Conference, vol. 6, pp. 4734–4739 (2001)
2. Recht, B., Fazel, M., Parrilo, P.: Guaranteed minimum rank solutions of matrix equations via nuclear norm minimization. arxiv:0706.4138 (2007)
3. Fazel, M.: Matrix Rank Minimization with Applications. PhD thesis, Stanford University (2002)
4. Recht, B., Xu, W., Hassibi, B.: Necessary and sufficient conditions for success of the nuclear norm heuristic for rank minimization. In: Proceedings of the 47th IEEE Conference on Decision and Control, pp. 3065–3070 (2008)

5. Candés, E.J., Recht, B.: Exact matrix completion via convex optimization. Foundations of Computational Mathematics (2009)

6. Liu, Z., Vandenberghe, L.: Interior-Point Method for Nuclear Norm Approximation with Application to System Identification. SIAM Journal on Matrix Analysis and Applications 31(3), 1235–1256 (2009)

7. Hansson, A., Liu, Z., Vandenberghe, L.: Subspace system identification via weighted nuclear norm optimization. In: Proceedings of the IEEE 51st Annual Conference on Decision and Control, pp. 3439–3444 (2012)

8. Naseem, I., Togneri, R., Bennamoun, M.: Linear regression for face recognition. IEEE Trans. Patt. Anal. Mach. Intell. 32(11), 2106–2112 (2010)

9. Wright, J., Yang, A.Y., Ganesh, A., Sastry, S.S., Ma, Y.: Robust face recognition via sparse representation. IEEE Transactions on Pattern Analysis and Machine Intelligence 31(2), 210–227 (2009)

10. Zhang, L., Yang, M., Feng, X.C.: Sparse representation or collaborative representation: Which helps face recognition? In: 2011 IEEE International Conference on Computer Vision (ICCV), pp. 471–478 (2011)

11. Yang, J., Qian, J., Luo, L., Zhang, F., Gao, Y.: Nuclear Norm based Matrix Regression with Applications to Face Recognition with Occlusion and Illumination Changes, arXiv:1405.1207 (2014)

12. Nie, F., Huang, H., Ding, C.: Low–Rank Matrix Recovery via Efficient Schatten p–Norm Minimization. In: Proc. AAAI 2012 (2012)

13. Li, Z., Liu, J., Yang, Y., Zhou, X., Lu, H.: Clustering-Guided Sparse Structural Learning for Unsupervised Feature Selection (2013)

14. Li, Z., Liu, J., Zhu, X., Liu, T., Lu, H.: Image annotation using multi-correlation probabilistic matrix factorization. In: Proceedings of the International Conference on Multimedia, pp. 1187–1190. ACM (2010)

15. Li, Z., Yang, Y., Liu, J., et al.: Unsupervised Feature Selection Using Nonnegative Spectral Analysis. In: Proc. AAAI (2012)

16. Gabay, D., Mercier, B.: A dual algorithm for the solution of nonlinear variational problems via finite element approximations. Comput. Math. Appl. 2, 17–40 (1976)

17. Gabay, D.: Applications of the method of multipliers to variational inequalities. In: Fortin, M., Glowinski, R. (eds.) Augmented Lagrangian Methods: Applications to the Numerical Solution of Boundary-Value Problems, pp. 299–331. North-Holland, Amsterdam (1983)

18. Boyd, S., Parikh, N., Chu, E., Peleato, B., Eckstein, J.: Distributed optimization and statistical learning via the alternating direction method of multipliers. Foundations and Trends in Machine Learning 3, 1–122 (2011)

19. Lin, Z., Chen, M., Ma, Y.: The Augmented Lagrange Multiplier Method for Exact Recovery of Corrupted Low-Rank Matrices. arXiv preprint arXiv:1009.5055 (2010)

20. Krishnan, D., Fergus, R.: Fast Image Deconvolution using Hyper-Laplacian Priors. In: Advances in Neural Information Processing (2009)

21. Chaux, C., Combettes, P., Pesquet, J.C., Wajs, V.: A variational formulation for frame-based inverse problems. Inverse Probl. 23(4), 1495–1518 (2007)

22. Yu, Y., Schuurmans, D.: Rank/norm regularization with closed-form solutions: Application to subspace clustering. Arxiv preprint arXiv:1202.3772 (2012)

23. Cai, J.F., Candès, E.J., Shen, Z.: A singular value thresholding algorithm for matrix completion. SIAM Journal on Optimization (2010)

24. Martinez, A.M., Benavente, R.: The AR Face Database. CVC Technical Report (1998)

25. Yang, J., Zhang, D., Frangi, A.F., Yang, J.Y.: Two-Dimensional PCA: A New Approach to Appearance-Based Face Representation and Recognition. IEEE Transactions on Pattern Analysis and Machine Intelligence 26(1), 131–137 (2004)
26. Yang, J., Zhang, L., Xu, Y., Yang, J.: Sparse Representation Classifier Steered Discriminative Projection With Applications to Face Recognition. IEEE Transactions on Neural Networks and Learning Systems (2012)
27. Asif, M.S.: Primal Dual Pursuit: A homotopy based algorithm for the Dantzig selector. Master's thesis, Georgia Institute of Technology (2008)
28. Yang, M., Zhang, L., Yang, J., Zhang, D.: Robust sparse coding for face recognition. In: CVPR (2011)

Hyperspectral Image Classification by Exploiting the Spectral-Spatial Correlations in the Sparse Coefficients

Dan Liu, Shutao Li, and Leyuan Fang

College of Electrical and Information Engineering,
Hunan University, Changsha, 410012, China
{liudan1,shutao_li,leyuan_fang}@hnu.edu.cn

Abstract. This paper proposes a novel hyperspectral image (HSI) classification method based on sparse model, which incorporates the spectral and spatial information of the sparse coefficient. Firstly, a sparse dictionary is built by using the training samples and the sparse coefficient is obtained through the sparse representation method. Secondly, a probability map for each class is established by summing the sparse coefficients of each class. Thirdly, the mean filtering is applied on each probability map to exploit the spatial information. Finally, we compare the probability map to find the maximum probability for each pixel and then determine the class label of each pixel. Experimental results demonstrate the effectiveness of the proposed method.

Keywords: Hyperspectral image classification, sparse representation, spectral-spatial information, mean filter.

1 Introduction

Hyperspectral image (HSI) is formed by tens to hundreds of continuous and subdivided spectral bands while reflecting interested target areas simultaneously. In HSI, different materials have different spectral information, which can be used for classification.

Many multispectral image classification methods, such as support vector machines (SVMs) [1], [2], neural network [3], and adaptive artificial immune network [4], have been applied to HSI classification. Generally, these methods have obtained good performance.

Researchers show that HSI contains rich spatial information and the pixels in a small neighborhood have similar spectral characteristics. If the pixels are in a small neighbor, they should belong to the same material. Therefore, Some methods [5], [6], [7] have combined spectral information and spatial information, and the classification accuracy has been improved. In particular, the segmentation based method [8] first segment the HSI into many local region with similar spectral characteristics and then classify each region. After using the spatial information, the classifiers can obtain improved performance.

Recently, sparse representation has become a powerful tool to solve some problems, such as face recognition [9], target detection [10], [11], remote sensing image

S. Li et al. (Eds.): CCPR 2014, Part I, CCIS 483, pp. 151–158, 2014.
© Springer-Verlag Berlin Heidelberg 2014

fusion [12] and medical image reconstruction [13], [14]. Recently, the sparse representation method has also been extended to HSI classification [7], [15], [16]. Basically, the previous sparse representation based HSI classification methods utilize the reconstruction error for the classification. In this paper, we propose a novel method that can combines the spatial information and spectral information in the sparse coefficients for the classification. Firstly, we use the training samples to construct the training dictionary and then utilize the simultaneous orthogonal matching pursuit (SOMP) to obtain the sparse coefficient of each spectral pixel. Differ from other sparse representation based methods which uses the residual to determine the pixel's class, the proposed method first employs the coefficients to construct several probability maps. Subsequently, we exploit the spatial information by filtering every map and gain a probability map for each class. Finally, we can determine the pixel's class by comparing the probability maps.

The rest of this paper is constructed as follows. Section 2 introduces the proposed classification method. Section 3 shows the experimental results and conclusions are given in the section 4.

2   The Proposed Classification Method

Fig. 1 shows the schematic of the proposed classification method. It is constructed by four steps: Firstly, the sparse representation method is adopted to obtain the sparse coefficients. Then, the coefficients belonging to each class are summed to obtain probability map for each pixel. Subsequently, a mean filtering is conducted on each probability map to exploit the spatial information. Finally, classification is accomplished by comparing the maps. The details of each step are illustrated in the follows.

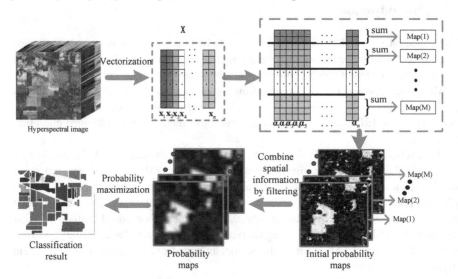

Fig. 1. The scheme of the proposed classification method

Step 1: In HSI, every spectral pixel can be regarded as a vector $\mathbf{x}_i$ and the training pixels construct a matrix $\mathbf{D} = [\mathbf{d}_1, \mathbf{d}_2, ..., \mathbf{d}_n]$ which is called dictionary. Every pixel can be represented by the dictionary.

$$\mathbf{x}_i = \mathbf{d}_1\alpha_i^1 + \mathbf{d}_2\alpha_i^2 + ... + \mathbf{d}_n\alpha_i^n = \mathbf{D}\alpha_i \tag{1}$$

In the equation (1), $\mathbf{d}_1, \mathbf{d}_2, ..., \mathbf{d}_n$ is called atom and $\alpha_i = [\alpha_i^1, \alpha_i^2, ..., \alpha_i^n]$ is called sparse coefficient vector. The sparse coefficient vector can be obtained by solving the optimization problem.

$$\hat{\alpha}_i = \arg\min \|\mathbf{x}_i - \mathbf{A}\alpha_i\|_2 \text{ subject to } \|\alpha_i\|_0 \leq K_0 \tag{2}$$

where K_0 is the maximum value of the sparsity level. This optimization problem is a NP-hard and cannot be solved directly. However, it can be solved by greedy algorithms approximately, such as subspace pursuit (SP) [17], orthogonal matching pursuit (OMP) [18] and Simultaneous OMP (SOMP) [7]. In this paper, the SOMP is adopted to obtain the sparse coefficient vector $\hat{\alpha}_i$ for each spectral pixel $\mathbf{x}_i$.

Step 2: In the sparse coefficient vector $\hat{\alpha}_i$, there are only a few nonzero sparse coefficients. The larger the nonzero coefficients values in one specific class, the more probability the test pixel belongs to this class. We denote the nonzero coefficients in one class as the $\alpha_{i,m}$, where $m \in \{1, 2, ..., M\}$, and M is the total number of classes. Then, we sum the nonzero coefficients $\alpha_{i,m}$ for each class of each spectral pixel,

$$\alpha_{i,m}^{sum} = \text{sum}(\alpha_{i,m}), \quad m \in \{1, 2, ..., M\}, \text{and } i \in \{1, 2, ..., N\} \tag{3}$$

where N is the total number of spectral pixels in the HSI. In each class, the summed coefficients $\alpha_{i,m}^{sum}$ for all the spectral pixels in the HSI can construct one probability map z_m.

Step 3: As discussed above, one coefficient in a class probability map z_m can be regarded as the likelihood for the corresponding pixel belonging to this class. If the probability map z_m is directly used for determining the class of each pixel, the spatial information in the probability map is not exploited. To exploit the spatial information, a mean filtering operation is conducted on each z_m,

$$z_m^{meanf} = \text{meanfiltering}(z_m), \quad m \in \{1, 2, ..., M\} \tag{4}$$

where the window for mean operation is selected to 3×3.

Step 4: the class label of each pixel $\mathbf{x}_i$ is obtained by comparing the coefficients in the filtered probability maps,

$$\hat{m}_i = \max_{m=1,...,M} z_{m,i}^{meanf}(\mathbf{x}_i), \quad i \in \{1, 2, ..., N\} \tag{5}$$

where max is the operation to compute the max coefficient among different maps.

3   Experimental Results

This section tests the effectiveness of the proposed classification method on two real HSIs (Indian pines and Salinas scene). The classification results of the proposed method are compared with those obtained by SVM [19], SVM-CK [20], OMP [7] and SOMP [7]. SVM [19] is designed for the classification of the spectral pixel without utilizing the spatial information. SVM-CK [20] is a method that incorporates spatial information via a composite kernel. OMP and SOMP are two sparse representation based methods.

In our first experiment, we used Airborne Visible/Infrared Imaging Spectrometer (AVIRIS) image Indian pines as testing HSI. This image is a widely used data set and was taken over Indiana's Indian Pine test site in June 1992. The Indian Pines has a size of $145 \times 145 \times 220$, with 220 spectral bands. Because 20 bands is water absorption, these bands are removed. There are 16 ground-truth classes and the size is from 20 to 2455 pixels (the total pixels are 10249).

We chose 10% of the samples for each class as training sample and the remainder as testing samples. For each method, we did five experiments and averaged the results. The number of the training sample and the testing sample is presented in Table 1.In this table, we can see the overall accuracy (OA), average accuracy (AA) and the kappa coefficient by using different methods (the SOMP-P is denoted as our method).

Table 1. Training sets, testing sets and classification accuracy (%) obtained from different methods for the Indian Pines image

Class	Train	Test	SVM	SVM-CK	OMP	SOMP	SOMP-P
Alfalfa	6	40	77.73	91.25	55.12	92.26	**95.04**
Corn-N	144	1284	77.35	92.79	61.60	93.46	**97.77**
Corn-M	84	746	78.56	93.98	58.62	90.22	**97.40**
Corn	24	213	68.75	87.28	42.21	87.32	**95.11**
Grass-M	50	433	88.87	94.90	87.29	**95.20**	94.04
Grass-T	75	655	89.12	**99.51**	95.30	96.12	96.57
Grass-P	3	25	95.37	85.20	85.20	87.10	**87.14**
Hay-W	49	429	95.09	99.91	96.44	99.10	**99.87**
Oats	2	18	67.65	**83.33**	36.67	55.78	0
Soybean-N	97	875	78.64	90.33	71.10	93.45	**93.47**
Soybean-M	247	2208	81.19	96.25	74.11	95.10	**99.20**
Soybean-C	62	531	79.74	89.04	51.05	87.49	**97.61**
Wheat	22	183	92.26	**99.07**	96.85	88.20	97.76
Woods	130	1135	92.72	98.63	91.85	99.00	**100**
Buildings	38	348	69.79	92.64	41.67	83.05	**97.72**
stone	10	83	97.96	90.24	91.90	91.51	**99.35**
OA	-	-	82.91	94.82	73.38	93.66	**97.49**
AA	-	-	83.17	**92.77**	71.06	89.83	91.01
k	-	-	0.805	0.941	0.696	0.931	**0.971**

The Table 1 shows the training sets, testing sets and classification maps obtained by SVM, SVM-CK, OMP, SOMP and SOMP-P and the result is the average of five experiments. From the Table 1, we can see that our algorithm has the best performance in terms of overall accuracy and kappa coefficient. As for its average accuracy, it is only a little worse than the classifier SVM-CK.

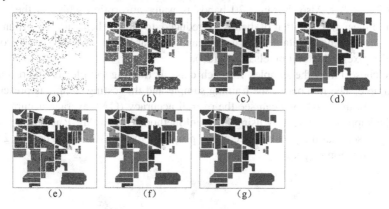

(a)   (b)   (c)   (d)

(e)   (f)   (g)

Fig. 2. Indian Pines: (a) Train samples, (b)Test samples, and the classification results obtained by (c) SVM, (d) SVM-CK, (e) OMP, (f) SOMP, (g) SOMP-P

Table 2. Training sets, testing sets and classification accuracy (%)obtained from different methods for the Salinas scene image

Class	Train	Test	SVM	OMP	SOMP	SOMP-P
Weed_1	20	1989	99.88	98.68	**100**	**100**
Weed_2	37	3689	98.52	98.78	99.72	**99.95**
Fallow	20	1956	92.48	94.55	**98.70**	98.41
Fallow plow	14	1380	97.46	99.35	96.93	**99.69**
Fallow smooth	27	2651	97.19	93.26	97.45	**99.24**
Stubble	40	3919	99.98	99.72	99.97	**100**
Celery	36	3543	98.14	99.40	99.55	**100**
Grapes	113	11158	76.11	72.83	84.50	**94.12**
Soil	62	6141	98.63	97.41	99.37	**100**
Corn	33	3245	89.29	88.14	95.24	**98.04**
Lettuce 4wk	11	1057	92.82	96.18	99.26	**100**
Lettuce 5wk	19	1908	96.16	**99.77**	96.73	99.73
Lettuce 6wk	9	907	94.99	98.05	92.53	**99.15**
Lettuce 7wk	11	1059	94.85	90.87	97.40	**99.43**
Vineyard untrained	73	7195	71.90	57.77	**85.24**	83.15
Vineyard trellis	18	1789	98.87	95.06	98.91	**98.92**
OA	-	-	89.16	86.48	93.47	**96.21**
AA	-	-	93.59	92.53	96.13	**98.11**
k	-	-	0.890	0.849	0.9274	**0.958**

In the Fig. 3, (a) and (b) are an example of the training and testing samples. (c) is the classification map obtained from SVM, similarly, (d), (e), (f) are the classification maps of SVM-CK, OMP, SOMP and SOMP-P respectively.

In our second experiment, we use the HSI Salinas scene which was collected by 224-band over Salinas Valley and California. The size of the Salinas image is $512 \times 217 \times 224$. Also, because 20 bands is water absorption which is the same as Indian Pines, the number of bands is reduced to 204. There are 16 ground-truth classes containing vegetables, bare soils, and vineyard fields and the size is from 916 to11271 pixels (the total pixels are 54129).

We chose 1% of the samples for each class as training sample and the rest as testing sample. The number of the training sample and the testing sample is presented in Table 2. In this table, we can see the overall accuracy (OA), average accuracy (AA) and the kappa coefficient by using different methods (the SOMP-P is our method). It is easy to see that the performance of the proposed methods is fine. The Fig. 2 shows the classification maps.

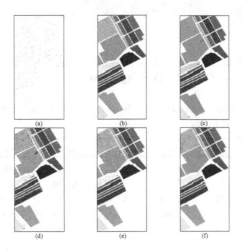

Fig. 3. Salinas scene: (a) Train samples, (b) Test samples, and the classification results obtained by(c) SVM, (d) OMP, (e) SOMP, (f) SOMP-P

4   Conclusions

In this paper, we have proposed a novel HSI classification method base on sparse representation. Differ from other traditional sparse classification technologies which exploit the sparse coefficient and residual to classify directly, this method uses the sparse coefficient to construct probability maps and then exploits the spatial information in the maps for classification. Experimental results show that the proposed method has better performance than several well-known classifiers.

Acknowledgement. This work was supported in part by the National Natural Science Foundation of China under Grant No. 61172161, the National Natural Science Foundation for Distinguished Young scholars of China under Grant No. 61325007.

References

1. Gualtieri, J.A., Cromp, R.F.: Support Vector Machines for Hyperspectral Remote Sensing Classification. In: Proc. SPIE, vol. 3584, pp. 221–232 (1998)
2. Melgani, F., Bruzzone, L.: Classification of Hyperspectral Remote Sensing Image with Support Vector Machines. IEEE. Trans. Geosci. Remote Sens. 42(8), 1778–1790 (2004)
3. Ratle, F., Camps, G.V., Weston, J.: Semisupervised Neural Networks for Efficient Hyperspectral Image Classification. IEEE Trans. Geosci. Remote Sens. 48(5), 2271–2282 (2010)
4. Zhong, Y., Zhang, L.: An Adaptive Artificial Immune Network for Supervised Classification of Multi-/Hyperspectral Remote Sensing Imagery. IEEE Trans. Geosci. Remote Sens. 50(3), 894–909 (2012)
5. Rand, R.S., Keenan, D.M.: Spatially smooth partitioning of hyperspectral imagery using spectral/spatial measures of disparity. IEEE Trans. Geosci. Remote Sens. 41(6), 1479–1490 (2003)
6. Kang, X., Li, S., Fang, L.: Extended Random Walker-Based Classification of Hyperspectral Images. IEEE Trans. Geosci. Remote Sens., 1–10 (May 2014)
7. Chen, Y., Nasrabadi, N.M., Tran, T.D.: Hyperspectral Image Classification Using Dictionary-Based sparse Representation. IEEE Trans. Geosci. Remote Sens. 49(10), 3973–3985 (2011)
8. Driesen, J., Thoonen, G., Scheunders, P.: Spatial Hyperspectral Image Classification by Prior Segmentation. In: IEEE Geosci. Remote Sens. Symp., vol. 3, pp. 709–712 (2009)
9. John, W., Yang, A.Y., Arvind, G., Sastry, S.S., Ma, Y.: Robust Face Recognition via Sparse Representation. IEEE Trans. Pattern Anal. 31(2), 210–227 (2009)
10. Chen, Y., Nasrabadi, N.M., Tran, T.D.: Sparse Representation for Target Detection in Hyperspectral Imagery. IEEE Journal of Selected Topics in Signal Processing 5(3), 629–640 (2011)
11. Fang, L., Li, S., Hu, J.: Multitemporal image change detection with compressed sparse representation. IEEE Image Processing, 2673–2676 (2011)
12. Li, S., Yin, H., Fang, L.: Remote Sensing Image Fusion via Sparse Representations Over Learned Dictionaries. IEEE Trans. Geosci. Remote Sens. 51(9), 4779–4789 (2013)
13. Fang, L., Li, S., Kang, X., Benediktsson, J.A.: Spectral-Spatial Hyperspectral Image Classification via Multiscale Adaptive Sparse Representation. IEEE Trans. Geosci. Remote Sens., 1–12 (2014)
14. Fang, L., Li, S., Ryan, M., Qing, N., Anthony, K.: Fast Acquisition and Reconstruction of Optical Coherence Tomography Image via Sparse Representation. IEEE Trans. Med. Imag. 32(11), 2034–2049 (2013)
15. Fang, L., Li, S., Kang, X., Benediktsson, J.: Spectral-Spatial Hyperspectral Image Classification via Multiscale Adaptive Sparse Representation. IEEE Trans. Geosci. Remote Sens., 1–12 (2014)
16. Fang, L., Li, S., Kang, X.: Spectral-Spatial Hyperspectral Image Classification via Multiscale Adaptive Sparse Representation. IEEE Trans. Geosci. Remote Sens. 52(12), 7738–7749 (2014)
17. Dai, W., Milenkovic, O.: Subspace Pursuit for Compressive Sensing Signal Reconstruction. IEEE Trans. Inf. Theory 55(5), 2230–2249 (2009)

18. Tropp, J., Gilbert, A.: Signal recovery from random measurements via orthogonal matching pursuit. IEEE Trans. Inf. Theory 53(12), 4655–4666 (2007)
19. Gualtieri, J.A., Cromp, R.F.: Support Vector machines for Hyperspectral Remote Sensing Classification. In: Proc. SPIE, vol. 3584, pp. 221–232 (1998)
20. Fauvel, M., Chanussot, J., Benediktsson, J.A.: Adaptive Pixel Neighborhood Definition for the Classification of Hyperspectral Images with Support Vector Machines and Composite Kernel. In: Proc. IEEE Int. Conf. Image Process., pp. 1884–1887 (2008)

Spectral-Spatial Hyperspectral Image Classification Using Superpixel and Extreme Learning Machines

Wuhui Duan, Shutao Li, and Leyuan Fang

College of Electrical and Information Engineering, Hunan University,
Changsha, China, 410082
3960277010qq.com, shutao_li@hnu.edu.cn, fangleyuan@gmail.com

Abstract. We propose an efficient framework for hyperspectral image
(HSI) classification based on superpixel and extreme learning machines
(ELMs). One superpixel can be regarded as a small region consisting
of a number of pixels with similar spectral characteristics. The novel
framework utilizes superpixel to exploit spatial information which can
improve classification accuracy. Specifically, we first adopt an efficient
segmentation algorithm to divide the HSI into many superpixels. Then,
spatial features of superpixels are extracted by computing the mean of
the spectral pixels within each superpixel. The mean feature can combine
the spatial and spectral information of each superpixel. Finally, ELMs
is used for the classification of each mean feature to determine the class
label of each superpixel. Experiments on two real HSIs demonstrate the
outstanding performance of the proposed method in terms of classification accuracies and high computational efficiency.

Keywords: Hyperspectral image, superpixel, extreme learning
machines, spectral-spatial classification.

1 Introduction

With the development of the remote sensor technology, hyperspectral images
(HSI) have been widely used in different applications[1]. The spectral information with hundreds of spectral wavelengths for each image pixel allows the
classification of landcovers with improved accuracy. So, a lot of works have been
done to build accurate pixel-wise classifiers using the spectral vectors for HSI, including neural networks[2], AdaBoost[3], multinomial logistic regression[4], and
support vector machines (SVMs)[5] which have shown good performance in accuracy. However, due to the high dimensionality in spectral domain of HSI, finding
optimal parameters for the supervised classifiers is time-consuming.

To improve the accuracy further, many spectral-spatial classification methods
in HSI have been proposed recently, such as spatial feature extraction[6], probabilistic modeling based methods[7], sparse representation[8,9]and segmentation
[10]. Spatial feature extraction method[6] defines an adaptive neighborhood for
each pixel by using the extended morphological profiles filter operations so that

S. Li et al. (Eds.): CCPR 2014, Part I, CCIS 483, pp. 159–167, 2014.
© Springer-Verlag Berlin Heidelberg 2014

the local neighborhood information could be preserved in the resulting features. Probabilistic method[7] aims at refining the probability maps obtained by pixel-wise classification. Segmentation based method[10] incorporates the spatial information derived from segmentation map in spatial-spectral classification. Experimental results proved that combining spatial and spectral information can result in better accuracy than pixel-wise classification.

In this paper, a novel spectral-spatial classification method based on super-pixels and extreme learning machines (ELMs)[11] is proposed. This method is designed for the classification of superpixels rather than the single spectral pixel. The extracted mean spectral vectors in each superpixel can combine both spatial and spectral information. Our work can achieve very high efficiency and accuracy compared to other classification methods.

The remainder of the paper is organized as follows. Section 2 introduces the proposed framework. Section 3 gives the experiment results. Finally, conclusions are given.

2   The Proposed Approach

In this section, we introduce the framework by combining superpixels and ELMs classification. The schematic of the proposed method is shown in Fig. 1. To make full use of the spatial-spectral information, we utilize superpixel-level classification instead of pixel-level which can greatly improve the classification accuracy.

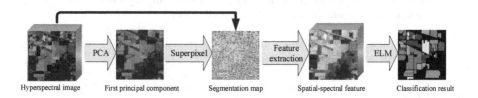

Fig. 1. A schematic of proposed framework

The proposed approach consists of three steps: First, entropy rate superpixel method is used to segment the principal component image into many superpixels. Then,the the spatial feature of the superpixel is extracted by computing the mean of the spectral pixels within each superpixel. Finally, ELMs[11] is applied to classify each feature to determine the class label of each superpixel.

Notations that will be adopted in this paper are defined as follows. $x = (x_1, \ldots, x_h) \in \mathbb{R}^{d \times h}$ is the hyperspectral image made up of a set of d-dimensional spectral vectors. $\{1, \ldots, P\}$ is a set of P labels. $y = \{y_1, \ldots, y_h \mid y_i \in \mathbb{R}\}$ denote an image of labels.

2.1 Superpixel Segmentation Algorithm

Superpixel segmentation[12] segments the HSI into many non-overlapping homogeneous regions which are treated as a basic unit. After evaluating several superpixel algorithms, including ERS[12], TP09[13], NC05[14] and SLIC[15], we finally adopt entropy rate superpixel segmentation (ERS)[12] since it can well preserve the object boundaries.

Pixels in HSI have high-dimensional spectral information. In order to efficiently apply ERS for superpixel segmentation, the principle component analysis (PCA) is adopted to reduce the spectral dimension. The PCA is conducted on x which gives an optimal representation of the hyperspectral image. Since the first principal component (PC) contains most information of HSI, we use the first PC to construct superpixel map with the ERS.

The ERS is a graph-based segmentation method. Firstly, a weighted graph $G = (V, E)$ is constructed with the first PC where V is the vertex set and E is the edge set. Vertices refer to the pixels of the first principal component and edges refer to the links between two adjacent pixels. The similarity between vertices is given by weight function: $\omega_{i,j} = exp\left(-\frac{d(v_i,v_j)^2}{2\sigma^2}\right)$ where $d(v_i, v_j)$ is defined as the intensity difference multiplied by spatial distance.

Then, the graph is partitioned into K superpixels $S_{N_A} = \{S_1, S_1, \cdots, S_k\}$ by selecting a subset of edges $A \in E$, i.e., maximizing an objective function which consists of an entropy rate $H(A)$ term and a clustering distribution balancing term $B(A)$, the resulting graph consists of K connected subgraphs.

$$\max_{A} \quad H(A) + \lambda B(A)$$
$$subject\ to\ a \subseteq E\ and\ N_A \geq K \tag{1}$$

where $\lambda \geq 0$ is the weight of the balancing term, K is the number of superpixels. The approach for optimizing the object function is a greedy algorithm[16] which is much more efficient than other graph based methods. The detailed solution can be found in[12].

2.2 Feature Extraction

A labeled segmentation map is achieved by superpixel algorithm in 2.1. Pixels within each superpixel have similar characteristics and can be given with the same class label and feature. The number of pixels in each superpixel S_i is denoted as n_i. Then, the feature of each superpixel is extracted by conducting the mean operation on the pixels in each superpixel [17],

$$m_i = \frac{\sum_{n_i} x_{n_i}}{n_i} \tag{2}$$

where x_{n_i} denote the set of spectral vectors between the superpixel S_i, m_i denote the mean vector of S_i. Every image pixels share the same feature which is the mean of pixels in corresponding superpixels.

2.3   Classification Using ELM

ELM is an efficient learning algorithm for single layer feedback networks (SLFNs) [18]. Given a training set with N samples $D_N = \{(m_1, y_1), \ldots, (m_N, y_N) \mid m_i \in \mathbb{R}^d, y_i \in \mathbb{R}, i = 1, \cdots, N\}$, activation function $g(x)$, and hidden node number L. The model of a single hidden layer neural network can be expressed as

$$\sum_{j=1}^{L} \beta_j \cdot g(\langle \omega_j, m_i \rangle + b_j) = y_i, \quad i = 1, \cdots, N. \tag{3}$$

where ω_j and β_j denote the weight vectors from inputs to hidden layer and from hidden layer to output layer, respectively, b_j is the bias of jth hidden neuron. The above N equations can be written concisely as

$$H \cdot \beta = Y \tag{4}$$

where H is the hidden layer output matrix of SLFNs and β is the output weight matrix. Here are learning methods of ELM:

Step1: Randomly assign input weight $W = [\omega_1, \omega_2, \ldots, \omega_L]^{\mathrm{T}}$ and bias $B = [b_1, b_2, \ldots, b_L]^{\mathrm{T}}$, T represents matrix transpose operation.

Step2: Calculate the hidden layer output matrix H.

Step3: Calculate the output weight $\beta = H^{\dagger}Y$, where $Y = [y_1, \ldots, y_N]$, $H^{\dagger}$ is the Moore-Penrose generalized inverse of matrix H.

After the learning process, the mean features $M_U = \{m_1, \ldots, m_k \mid m_i \in \mathbb{R}^d, i = 1, \ldots, k\}$ are classified into P class $y_i \in \{1, \ldots, P\}$. The classification steps are:

Step1: Calculate the hidden layer output matrix of new instances $M_U : H_U = g(W \cdot M_U + B)$.

Step2: Get the labels of new instances: $Y_U = H_U \cdot \beta$.

Finally, the class label of each mean feature can be assigned to the corresponding superpixel.

3   Experimental Results

3.1   Experiments with AVIRIS Indian Pines Data Set

In this section, we evaluate the proposed framework using the Indian Pines data set. The Indian Pines image was acquired by the Airborne Visible/Infrared Imaging Spectrometer (AVIRIS) sensor in 1992. The image has 220 bands of size 145×145 with a spatial resolution of 20 m per pixel and a spectral coverage ranging from 0.4 to 2.5 μm (20 water absorption bands no. 104-108, 150-163, and 220 were removed before experiments). The Indian Pines image contains 16 classes. The Indian Pines image and ground truth data are shown in Fig. 2.

In this experiment, segmentation map were obtained by ERS ($k = 400$). In the classification process, 10% training samples are randomly selected from the labeled pixels while the rest 90% are used to test the classifiers. The ELMs input hidden neurons is set $N = 950$, which similar to the number of training samples.

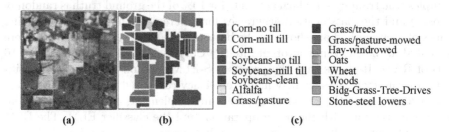

Corn-no till
Corn-mill till
Corn
Soybeans-no till
Soybeans-mill till
Soybeans-clean
Alfalfa
Grass/pasture

Grass/trees
Grass/pasture-mowed
Hay-windrowed
Oats
Wheat
Woods
Bldg-Grass-Tree-Drives
Stone-steel lowers

(a)   (b)   (c)

Fig. 2. Indian Pines data set(a) three-band color composite of the Indian Pines image. (b) and (c) ground truth data of the Indian Pines image.

We evaluate classification accuracy and computing time with the Indian Pines image using different classification methods. Three widely used methods including pixel-wise SVM [5], the EMP with SVM [6] and LORSAL-MLL approaches [7]. The pixel-wise SVM algorithm is implemented in the LIBSVM library [19] with Gaussian kernel. The parameters were obtained by five-fold cross validation. The EMP with SVM method exploits the spatial information by extracting extended morphological profile. LORSAL-MLL also utilizes spatial information modeled by means of an MLL prior [20]. The parameters for the EMP and LORSAL-MLL were set to the default values reported in [6,7]. For simplicity, S-ELM denotes the superpixel and ELM based classification method proposed in this paper in the tables. Three widely used quality indexes are adopted to evaluate the performance of the proposed method. The overall accuracy (OA) is the percentage of correctly classified pixels. The average accuracy (AA) is the mean of the percentage of correctly classified pixels for each class. The kappa coefficient gives the percentage of correctly classified pixels corrected by the number of agreements that would be expected purely by chance.

For illustrative purpose, Fig. 3 shows the classification maps obtained by four different methods.

It can be seen that some noisy pixels are obvious in (a) and (b). The proposed method (S-ELM) can greatly increases the OA compared to the pixel-wise classification method (SVM). Table 1 presents the number of training set and test

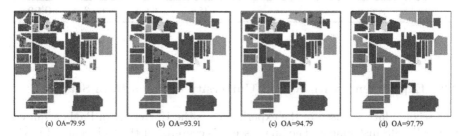

(a) OA=79.95   (b) OA=93.91   (c) OA=94.79   (d) OA=97.79

Fig. 3. Classification maps and overall accuracies for the AVIRIS Indian Pines image. (a) SVM method (b) EMP method (c) LORSAL-MLL method (d) superpixel and ELM based method.

samples (the training set which accounts for 10% of the ground truth is randomly chosen) and the classification accuracies for different methods. The computing times of each method are shown in the bottom of Table 1. All the programs were executed in the environment of an Intel(R) Core i7-3720 CPU 2.60 GHz and 16 GB of RAM. It shows that the proposed S-ELM method gives higher classification accuracy with extremely higher efficiency compared with other methods. The reason is that the proposed method only implements PCA decomposition, feature extraction with the mean operation, and the classifier ELM. The ELM is computationally efficient since the learning speed is extremely fast.

Table 1. OAs, AAs, individual classification accuracies (in percent) and the run time (second) for the AVIRIS Indian Pines image in different method with 10% training set

Class	Train	Test	SVM	EMP	LORSAL-MLL	S-ELM
Alfalfa	5	41	60.60	98.13	64.63	**100.00**
Corn-no till	143	1285	71.89	92.50	95.25	**97.50**
Corn-min till	83	747	73.23	87.08	93.40	**97.72**
Corn	24	213	60.89	83.61	91.31	**99.81**
Grass/Pasture	48	435	87.51	93.09	93.53	**97.48**
Grass/Trees	73	657	89.03	97.40	**99.46**	98.89
Grass/Pasture-mowed	3	25	87.65	86.55	79.50	**100.00**
Hay-windrowed	48	430	90.94	**100.00**	99.91	**100.00**
Oats	2	18	69.01	**96.44**	52.77	79.08
Soybeans-no till	97	875	75.45	92.41	90.55	**96.78**
Soybeans-min	246	2209	79.26	93.10	96.17	**97.48**
Soybean-clean	59	534	71.20	87.88	97.35	**98.80**
Wheat	21	184	89.67	99.35	**99.59**	99.34
Woods	127	1138	91.71	**99.18**	97.89	99.14
Building-Grass-Trees-Drives	39	347	72.60	**98.71**	88.54	92.70
Stone-steel Towers	9	84	98.62	98.19	77.38	**98.93**
OA	-	-	79.98	93.63	95.08	**97.78**
AA	-	-	77.09	93.98	88.58	**97.10**
Kappa	-	-	0.79	0.93	0.88	**0.97**
Time(seconds)	-	-	158.1	64.2	69.3	**0.99**

3.2   Experiments with ROSIS University of Pavia Data Set

The second data set used in the experiments is the University of Pavia acquired by the ROSIS instrument. The image scene is centered at the University of Pavia with size of 610 × 340 pixels. It comprises 103 spectral channels after removing 12 bands due to noise and water absorption and 9 ground truth classes. In the experiment, we randomly select 300 pixels from each class for training and the

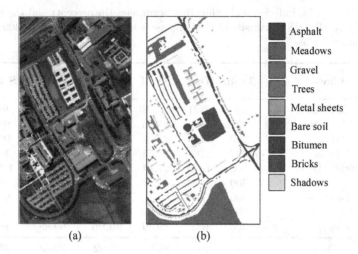

Fig. 4. University of Pavia data set. (a) three-band color composite of the University of Pavia image. (b) and (c) ground truth data of the University of Pavia image.

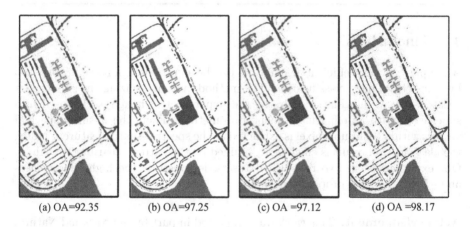

(a) OA=92.35   (b) OA=97.25   (c) OA =97.12   (d) OA =98.17

Fig. 5. Classification maps and overall accuracies for the ROSIS University of Pavia image (a) SVM method (b) EMP method (c) LORSAL-MLL method (d) superpixel and ELM based method (S-ELM)

rest are used as the test set. The University of Pavia image and ground truth data are shown in Fig. 4. The University of Pavia image is segmented into 1500 superpixels by ERS. The ELM parameter N is set to 2000 which still relate to the training set. Fig. 5 shows the classification maps obtained by four different methods. Table 2 presents the classification results and computing times with several methods. As can be observed, the proposed framework outperforms the compared methods while is still very fast.

Table 2. OAs, AAs, individual classification accuracies (in percent) and the run time (second) for the ROSIS University of Pavia image in different method with 300 training samples for each class

Class	Train	Test	SVM	EMP	LORSAL-MLL	S-ELM
Asphalt	300	6331	96.78	**98.88**	95.17	98.53
Meadows	300	18349	97.83	99.03	98.92	**99.47**
Gravel	300	1799	77.78	94.50	87.82	**99.10**
Trees	300	2764	87.74	97.04	**98.55**	90.76
Metal sheets	300	1045	97.94	98.52	99.86	**100.00**
Bare soil	300	4729	81.48	88.04	**99.93**	98.51
Bitumen	300	1030	69.12	89.60	98.37	**99.07**
Bricks	300	3382	86.94	**98.57**	93.99	95.77
Shadows	300	647	99.89	**99.96**	99.88	95.72
OA	-	-	91.80	96.92	97.53	**98.17**
AA	-	-	88.39	96.02	96.94	**97.46**
Kappa	-	-	0.90	0.96	0.97	**0.98**
Time(seconds)	-	-	213.1	141.3	526.7	**14.54**

4   Conclusions

A simple but very efficient framework has been proposed for spectral-spatial hyperspectral image classification. The method aims at utilizing the superpixels spectral-spatial information. Firstly, the hyperspectral image is clustered into superpixels with an efficient segmentation method. Then, the mean of spectral vectors within each superpixel is extracted as the spectral-spatial feature. Finally, the classification result is efficiently obtained by the extreme learning machines. Our experiments on two real HSI datasets demonstrate the high effectiveness and efficiency of the proposed method.

Acknowledgement. This work was supported in part by the National Natural Science Foundation of China under Grant (No. 61172161), the National Natural Science Foundation for Distinguished Young Scholars of China under Grant (No. 61325007).

References

1. Plaza, A., Benediktsson, J.A., Boardman, J.W., Brazile, J., Bruzzone, L., Camps-Valls, G., Chanussot, J., Fauvel, M., Gamba, P., Gualtieri, A., Marconcini, M., Tilton, J.C., Trianni, G.: Recent advances in techniques for hyperspectral image processing. Remote Sens. Environ. 113(suppl. 1), 110–122 (2009)
2. Ratle, F., Camps-Valls, G., Weston, J.: Semisupervised neural networks for efficient hyperspectral image classification. IEEE Trans. Geosci. Remote Sens. 48(5), 2271–2282 (2010)

3. Kawaguchi, S., Nishii, R.: Hyperspectral image classification by bootstrap AdaBoost with random decision stumps. IEEE Trans. Geosci. Remote Sens. 45(11), 3845–3851 (2007)
4. Li, J., Bioucas-Dias, J., Plaza, A.: Semi-supervised hyperspectral image segmentation using multinomial logistic regression with active learning. IEEE Trans. Geosci. Remote Sens. 48(11), 4085–4098 (2010)
5. Melgani, F., Bruzzone, L.: Classification of hyperspectral remote sensing images with support vector machines. IEEE Trans. Geosci. Remote Sens. 42(8), 1778–1790 (2004)
6. Benediktsson, J.A., Palmason, J.A., Sveinsson, J.R.: Classification of hyperspectral data from urban areas based on extended morphological profiles. IEEE Trans. Geosci. Remote Sens. 43(3), 480–491 (2005)
7. Li, J., Bioucas-Dias, J.M., Plaza, A.: Hyperspectral image segmentation using a new Bayesian approach with active learning. IEEE Trans. Geosci. Remote Sens. 49(10), 3947–3960 (2011)
8. Li, S., Yin, H., Fang, L.: Remote sensing image fusion via sparse representations over learned dictionaries. IEEE Trans. Geosci. Remote Sens. 51(9), 4779–4789 (2013)
9. Fang, L., Li, S., Hu, J.: Multitemporal image change detection with compressed sparse representation. In: IEEE Conf. on Image Processing, pp. 2673–2676 (2011)
10. Fauvel, M., Tarabalka, Y., Benediktsson, J.A., Chanussot, J., Tilton, J.C.: Advances in spectral-spatial classification of hyperspectral images. Proc. IEEE 101(3), 652–675 (2013)
11. Huang, G.B., Zhu, Q.Y., Siew, C.K.: Extreme learning machine: theory and applications. Neurocomputing 70, 489–501 (2006)
12. Liu, M.Y., Tuzel, O., Ramalingam, S., Chellappa, R.: Entropy Rate Superpixel Segmentation. In: Proc. IEEE Conf. Computer Vision and Pattern Recognition, pp. 2097–2104 (2011)
13. Levinshtein, A., Stere, A., Kutulakos, K., Fleet, D., Dickinson, S., Siddiqi, K.: Turbopixels: Fast superpixels using geometric flows. IEEE Trans. Pattern Anal. Machine Intell. 31(12), 2290–2297 (2009)
14. Shi, J., Malik, J.: Normalized cuts and image segmentation. IEEE Trans. Pattern Anal. Machine Intell. 22(8), 888–905 (2000)
15. Achanta, R., Shaji, A., Smith, K., Lucchi, A., Fua, P., Susstrunk, S.: SLIC superpixels compared to state-of-the-art superpixel methods. IEEE Trans. Pattern Anal. Machine Intell. 34(11), 2274–2281 (2012)
16. Nemhauser, G.L., Wolsey, L.A., Fisher, M.L.: An analysis of the approximations for maximizing submodular set functions. Mathematical Programming, 265–294 (1978)
17. Camps-Valls, G., Gomez-Chova, L., Muñoz-Marí, J., Vila-Francés, J., Calpe-Maravilla, J.: Composite kernels for hyperspectral image classification. IEEE Geosci. Remote Sens. Lett. 3(1), 93–97 (2006)
18. Heras, D.B., Argüello, F., Quesada-Barriuso, P.: Exploring ELM-based spatial-spectral classification of hyperspectral images. Int. J. Remote Sens. 35(2), 401–423 (2014)
19. Chang, C.C., Lin, C.J.: LIBSVM: A library for support vector machines. ACM Trans. Intell. Systems Technology 2(3), 27:1–27:27 (2011)
20. Fang, L., Li, S., Kang, X., Benediktsson, J.A.: Spectral-spatial hyperspectral image classification via multiscale adaptive sparse representation. IEEE Trans. Geosci. Remote Sens. 52(12), 7738–7749 (2014)

Visual Tracking with Weighted Online Feature Selection

Yu Tang[1], Zhigang Ling[1], Jiancheng Li[2], and Lu Bai[2]

[1] Electrical and Information Engineering Institution of Hunan University, Changsha, China
[2] China Highway Engineering Consulting Group Co, Ltd, Beijing, China

Abstract. Most tracking-by-detection algorithms adopt an online learning classifier to separate targets from their surrounding background. These methods set a sliding window to extract some candidate samples from the local regions surrounding the former object location at current frame. The trained classifier is then applied to these samples, which sample with the maximum classifier score is considered as the new object location. However, in classifier training procedure, noisy samples may often be included when they are not *correct* enough, thereby causing visual drift. Online discriminative feature selection (ODFS) method has been recently introduced into the tracking algorithms, which can alleviate drift to some extent. However, the ODFS tracker may detect the candidate sample that is less accurate because it does not discriminatively take the sample importance into consideration during the feature selection procedure. In this paper, we present a novel weighted online discriminative feature selection (WODFS) tracker, which integrates the sample's contribution into the optimization procedure when selecting features, the proposed method optimizes the objective function in the steepest ascent direction with respect to the weighted positive samples while in the steepest descent direction with respect to the negative. Therefore, the selected features directly couple their scores with the contribution of samples which result in a more robust and stable tracker. Numerous experiments on challenging sequences demonstrate the superiority of the proposed algorithm.

Keywords: visual tracking, feature selection, online learning, tracking by detection.

1   Introduction

Recently, Visual tracking has become a very hot research topic in the field of computer vision because of its wide applications, e.g. video indexing, traffic monitoring, and human computer interaction [1] etc. Numerous methods have been proposed in the past decades [2-10]. However, it is still a challenging task to develop a robust tracking algorithm that works universally for diverse application, because tracker often suffer from some factors such as appearance changes, pose variations, partial or full

S. Li et al. (Eds.): CCPR 2014, Part I, CCIS 483, pp. 168–182, 2014.
© Springer-Verlag Berlin Heidelberg 2014

occlusions and illumination changes. Therefore designing a robust appearance model [21] that can adapt to these factors becomes a main task in most recently proposed algorithms [1-9]. According to different appearance model, the recently proposed tracking algorithms can be classified into two classes based on their difference representation scheme: generative models[2,3,4,22]and discriminative models[5,6,7,8,9].

Generative models typically learn an appearance model to represent the target, and then search for the target region with minimal error [20]. For example, Black *et al.* [3] learned an offline subspace appearance model to represent object, however, the offline learned appearance model is hard to deal with the appearance changes. To deal with this problem, some online learning models have been proposed such as the WLS tracker [11] and IVT [2] tracker. Adam *et al* [12] utilized multiple instances to update an appearance model which is robust to partial occlusions. Those generative models require numerous samples to learn appearance feature, which will greatly increase the complexity. Furthermore, these models do not take background information [10] into account in which some useful information can help to visual tracking.

Discriminative models regard visual tracking as a classification task [13] in which a classifier is trained to separate targets from their surrounding background within a local region [20]. The *ll* tracker [10] was firstly proposed while many norm-related minimization problems need to be solved. Despite some advanced methods are proposed, it is still far away from being real-time. Boosting [6, 14] method has been introduced to object tracking in which weak classifiers with pixel-based features are combined. Collins *et.al* [13] demonstrated that discriminative features selection online can improve tracking performance. For example: Grabner *et al.* [6] proposed an online boosting feature selection method for object tracking. However, these above-mentioned discriminative algorithms [5-9] merely utilize one positive sample (the tracking result at the fore-frame) and multiple negative samples to update classifier. If the object location at previous frame is not precise, the positive sample will be noised and result in a sub optimal classifier update. Consequently, errors will be accumulated to cause tracking drift or failure [7]. In Ref [9], the MIL (multiple instance learning) model [7] is adopted to select features in a supervised learning model for object tracking, but, it has a great computational complexity. Recently, many improved tracking algorithms that based the MIL framework [7, 8, 9, 15, 16, 18] have been developed. For example: Zhang *et al.* proposed an ODFS tracker [16], which adopts a new strategy to select discriminative features and improved the performance to some extent. However, the classifier may inaccurate because it does not take the importance of positive samples into consideration during the feature selection strategy, moreover, this method only adopts the reverse gradient of sole *correct* positive sample to replace the average of whole positive samples during the objective function optimization, which may lead to less discriminative features to be selected.

In this paper, based on the ODFS tracker's framework, we proposed a weighted online discriminative feature selection tracker that integrates the sample's contribution into feature selection strategy. A new probability function integrating the weight of instances is present and then an efficient method is adopted to approximately optimize the objective function. Experimental results on challenging video sequences demonstrate the superior performance of our method in robustness and precision to some state-of-the-art tracking methods.

The paper is organized as follows: In Section 2, we firstly introduces the framework [7, 8, 9, 15, 16] of this proposed tracking algorithm and explains some related works, Section 3 gives the principle of our method and analysis its advantages over other methods in details. Section 4 presents the detailed experiment setup and demonstration of our tracking performance. Finally, a conclusion is given in Selection5.

2   Tracking by Detection and Related Works

2.1   System Overview

Let $l_t(\mathbf{x}) \in R^2$ denotes the location of sample $\mathbf{x}$ at tth frame. The basic flow of tracking by detection is described as follow: based on the tracking result $l_{t-1}(\mathbf{x}_0)$ at t-$1th$ frame, when tth frame is coming, the tracker firstly crops some candidate samples [25] from set $X^\gamma = \{x \| l_t(\mathbf{x}) - l_{t-1}(\mathbf{x}_0)| < \gamma\}$ with a relativity large radius γ surrounding the tracking result $l_{t-1}(\mathbf{x}_0)$; then the coped samples are classified and a sample (location $l_t(\mathbf{x}_0)$) with the maximum confidence is assume to be the new object at tth frame; finally, the classifier is updated by the positive and negative samples which cropped from region $X^\alpha = \{\mathbf{x} \| l_t(\mathbf{x}) - l_t(\mathbf{x}_0)| < \alpha\}$ and $X^{\xi,\beta} = \{\mathbf{x} | \xi < l_t(\mathbf{x}) - l_t(\mathbf{x}_0)| < \beta\}$ respectively. Based on the object location $l_t(\mathbf{\hat{x}})$ at tth frame, the tracking system is running by repeating the above-mentioned procedures.

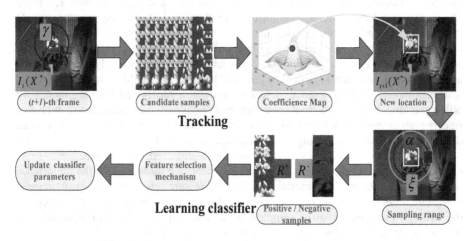

Fig. 1. The basic flow of tracking by detection algorithm

Algorithm 1. Tracking by detection

Input: tth video frame

1. Get a set of candidate image samples: $X^\gamma = \{x \| l_t(\mathbf{x}) - l_{t-1}(\mathbf{x}_0) \| < \gamma\}$, where $l_{t-1}(\mathbf{x}_0)$ is the target location at t-1th frame, and extract features $\{f_k(\mathbf{x})\}_{k=1}^{K}$ for each image samples.

2. Apply classifier in (2) to each candidate samples and find the sample location $l_t(\mathbf{x}_0)$ with the maximum confidence.

3. Get two sets of image samples $X^\alpha = \{\mathbf{x} \| l_t(\mathbf{x}) - l_t(\mathbf{x}_0) \| < \alpha\}$ and $X^{\xi,\beta} = \{\mathbf{x} | \xi < l_t(\mathbf{x}) - l_t(\mathbf{x}_0) \| < \beta\}$ for positive samples and negative respectively.

4. Select features by the proposed feature selection strategy and update the classifier parameters according to (3) and (4).

Output: tracking location $l_t(\mathbf{x}_0)$ and classifier parameters.

2.2 Classification

In the tracking by detection algorithm, classifier [16] estimates the confidence of each sample via it's posterior probability function:

$$c(\mathbf{x}) = p(y = 1 | \mathbf{x}) = \sigma(\mathbf{h}_K(\mathbf{x})) \tag{1}$$

where $\mathbf{x}$ is a sample and $y \in \{0,1\}$ is a binary variable that represents the sample as positive or negative, $\sigma(z) = 1/(1+e^{-z})$ is a sigmoid function and the classifier h_K is a liner combination of weak classifiers. Then the appearance model based on classifier $h_K(x)$ is defined as

$$h_K(\mathbf{x}) = \log\left(\frac{\prod_{k=1}^{K} p(f_k(\mathbf{x}) | y=1) P(y=1)}{\prod_{k=1}^{K} p(f_k(\mathbf{x}) | y=0) P(y=0)} \right) = \sum_{k=1}^{K} \phi_k(\mathbf{x}) \tag{2}$$

where function $\phi_k(\mathbf{x}) = \log\left(\frac{p(f_k(\mathbf{x}) | y=1)}{p(f_k(\mathbf{x}) | y=0)} \right)$ is a weak classifier, $f(\mathbf{x}) = (f_1(\mathbf{x}), ..., f_K(\mathbf{x}))^T$ is a haar-like feature vector [7,16,17,18] for sample $\mathbf{x}$ and K is the number of features to be selected.

2.3 Classifier Construction and Update

The location distribution $p(f_k | y=1)$ and $p(f_k | y=0)$ in the classifier $h_K(\bullet)$ are assumed to be Gaussian distributed like the CT tracker [18] method with four parameters $(\mu_k^+, \sigma_k^+, \mu_k^-, \sigma_k^-)$ and they are defined as follows :

$$p(f_k | y=1) \sim N(\mu_k^+, \sigma_k^+), \ p(f_k | y=0) \sim N(\mu_k^-, \sigma_k^-) \tag{3}$$

.

The parameters $(\mu_k^+, \sigma_k^+, \mu_k^-, \sigma_k^-)$ in (3) are incrementally updated as follows

$$\mu_k^+ \leftarrow \eta\mu_k^+ + (1-\eta)\mu^+$$
$$\sigma_k^+ \leftarrow \sqrt{\eta(\sigma_k^+)^2 + (1-\eta)(\sigma_k^+)^2 + \eta(1-\eta)(\mu_k^+ - \mu^+)^2} \tag{4}$$

where $\sigma^+ = \sqrt{\frac{1}{N}\sum_{i=0|y=1}^{N-1}(f_k(\mathbf{x}_i) - u^+)^2}$, $\mu^+ = \frac{1}{N}\sum_{i=0|y=1}^{N-1} f_k(\mathbf{x}_i)$ and N is the number of positive samples. Similarly, the tracker updates the parameters (μ_k^-, σ_k^-). The above-mentioned (3) and (4) can be easily deduced by maximum likelihood function and η is a learning rate to adjust the effect between the previous frames and the current one.

A feature pool with M ($M>K$) features is maintained during learning procedure. As demonstrated in Ref [5], online selection of the discriminative features between object and background can improve the tracking performance significantly. Tracking task is to detect the sample that with the maximum confidence based on the selected features.

2.4   Related Works on Feature Selection Strategy

Recently, Zhang et al. [16] has proposed an online discriminative feature selection technique to improve the tracking performance to some extent. The ODFS tracker selects a subset of weak classifier to maximizes the average confidence of positive samples while suppressing the average confidence of negative samples. However, Zhang et al [16] made a rough simplification by representing the average gradient of all positive samples with the reverse gradient of classifier score of object location at previous frame, which may lead the ODFS tracker easily select less effective features. Moreover, the appearance model does not consider the different contributions of the positive samples into the feature selection procedure, which may cause drafting when the target location is not precise at previous frame. In the next section, we proposed an efficient online feature selection method which is a sequential forward selection method [17] where the number of feature combination is MK, thereby facilitating real-time processing.

3   Weighted Online Discriminative Feature Selection

3.1   Principle of Our Method

Similarly, the proposed feature selection strategy selects a subset of weak classifiers $\{\phi_k\}_{k=1}^{K}$ that have highest classification score between positive and negative samples from the feature pool Φ. These positive samples have different distance to the fore-tracking result and they also make different contributions to the objective function, so we assure that samples near the *correct* sample contribute more to the objective function than those far from it. Therefore, unlike the Noisy-OR model [16] adopted by

ODFS tracker, our method naturally integrates the sample importance into feature selection strategy and define the sample importance as follows

$$w_{i0} = \frac{1}{c} e^{-\|l(x_i)-l(x_0)\|}$$ (5)

where $l(\bullet) \in R$ indicates the location and c is a normalization constant. Simply, negative samples are considered as making the same contribution to the objective function because all of the negative samples are far away from the center of *correct* sample. Finally, we define a margin as the difference of the total confidence of weighted positive samples minus the total confidence of negative samples. Then the objective function can be formed as follows

$$E_{margin} = \frac{1}{N}\sum_{i=0}^{N-1} w_{i0}\sigma(\sum_{k=1}^{K}\phi_k(\mathbf{x}_i)) - \frac{1}{L}\sum_{i=N}^{N+L-1}\sigma(\sum_{k=1}^{K}\phi_k(\mathbf{x}_i))$$
$$\approx \frac{1}{N}(\sum_{i=0}^{N-1} w_{i0}\sigma(\sum_{k=1}^{K}\phi_k(\mathbf{x}_i)) - \sum_{i=N}^{N+L-1}\sigma(\sum_{k=1}^{K}\phi_k(\mathbf{x}_i)))$$ (6)

where N and L is the number of positive samples and negative samples respectively, $\sigma(z)=1/(1+e^{-z})$ is a sigmoid function. Each selected feature must maximize the margin function, thus the weak classifier can be selected as follows

$$\phi_k = \arg\max_{\phi \in \Phi}(\sum_{i=0}^{N-1} w_{i0}\sigma(h_{k-1}(\mathbf{x}_i)+\phi(\mathbf{x}_i)) - \sum_{i=N}^{N+L-1}\sigma(h_{k-1}(\mathbf{x}_i)+\phi(\mathbf{x}_i)))$$ (7)

where h_{k-1} is a liner combination of previous *k-1* weak classifiers. We define $g_{k-1}(x)$ is the inverse gradient (the steepest descent direction) of the posterior probability function $\sigma(h_{k-1})$ with respect to classifier h_{k-1}. We introduced the gradient into objective function in a way that similar to the method in Ref [19], then the objective function can be translated into follows

$$\phi_k = \arg\max_{\phi \in \Phi}(\sum_{i=0}^{N-1} w_{i0}(g_{k-1}(\mathbf{x}_i)-\phi(\mathbf{x}_i))^2 + \sum_{i=N}^{N+L-1}(-g_{k-1}(\mathbf{x}_i)-\phi(\mathbf{x}_i))^2$$ (8)

where the gradient function $g_{k-1}(x)$ is defined as

$$g_{k-1}(\mathbf{x}) = -\frac{\partial\sigma(h_{k-1}(\mathbf{x}))}{\partial h_{k-1}} = -\sigma(h_{k-1}(\mathbf{x}))(1-\sigma(h_{k-1}(\mathbf{x})))$$ (9)

However, the constraint between the selected ϕ_k and the inverse gradient direction g_{k-1} is very strong because ϕ_k is limited to the classifier pool Φ, which will bring huge computation. To alleviate these problems, we proposed a multiple grades strategy which divides the positive samples into three different grades. Within the radius of cropping positive samples, we set three different crop grades to get variety of positive samples. The radius difference between each grade is two pixels. Sample that near closest to the fore-tracking location center is adopt to replace the samples of corresponding grade for inverse gradient calculation. The weight of each grade can be calculated by the distance between the tracking location and sample that near closest to the tracking location in corresponding class. So the objective function can be formulated into

$$
\phi_k = \arg\max_{\phi \in \Phi} \left(\sum_{i=0}^{N_1-1} w_{i0}(g_{k-1}(\mathbf{x}_i) - \phi(\mathbf{x}_i))^2 + \sum_{i=N_1}^{N_2-1} w_{i0}(g_{k-1}(\mathbf{x}_i) - \phi(\mathbf{x}_i))^2 \right.
$$
$$
\left. + \sum_{i=N_2}^{N-1} w_{i0}(g_{k-1}(\mathbf{x}_i) - \phi(\mathbf{x}_i))^2 + L(\overline{g}_{k-1} - \overline{\phi})^2 \right) \tag{10}
$$

where $\overline{g}_{k-1} = \frac{1}{L} \sum_{i=N}^{N+L-1} g_{k-1}(\mathbf{x}_i)$ indicates the average inverse gradient of classification score of fore-combined k-1 classifiers, $\overline{\phi} = \frac{1}{L} \sum_{i=N}^{N+L-1} \phi(\mathbf{x}_i)$ indicates the average classifier score of all negative samples. Then we take a simplification strategy into the optimization: average the inverse gradient of fore k-1 classifications by replacing $\sum_{i=0}^{N_1-1} w_{i0}g_{k-1}(\mathbf{x}_i)$, $\sum_{i=N_1}^{N_2-1} w_{N_10}g_{k-1}(\mathbf{x}_{N_1})$ and $\sum_{i=N_2}^{N-1} w_{N_20}g_{k-1}(\mathbf{x}_{N_2})$ with $w_{00}g_{k-1}(\mathbf{x}_{00})$, $w_{N_10}g_{k-1}(\mathbf{x}_{N_10})$, and $w_{N_20}g_{k-1}(\mathbf{x}_{N_20})$ respectively, then only the current classifier should be applied to all of the positive samples and the feature selection criterion becomes:

$$
\phi_k = \arg\max_{\phi \in \Phi} \left(E_{WODFS}(\phi) = w_{00}(N_1 g_{k-1}(\mathbf{x}_0) - \sum_{i=0}^{N_1} \phi(\mathbf{x}_i))^2 + w_{N_10}((N_2 - N_1)g_{k-1}(\mathbf{x}_{N_1}) - \sum_{i=N_1-1}^{N_2} \phi(\mathbf{x}_i))^2 \right.
$$
$$
\left. + w_{N_20}((N - N_2)g_{k-1}(\mathbf{x}_{N_2}) - \sum_{i=N_2-1}^{N} \phi(\mathbf{x}_i))^2 + L(-\overline{g}_{k-1} - \overline{\phi})^2 \right) \tag{11}
$$

where $\mathbf{x}_{00}, \mathbf{x}_{N_10}, \mathbf{x}_{N_20}$ is the representative sample of different classes, $\mathbf{x}_{00}$ is the *correct* sample indeed , $\mathbf{x}_{N_10}, \mathbf{x}_{N_20}$ are the samples that near closest to the tracking location in grade 2 and grade 3 respectively.

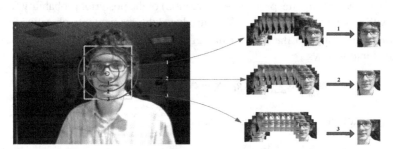

Fig. 2. The multiple grades strategy of positive samples

It is worth noting that the classifier must be applied to all weighted positive samples and negative samples when selecting current feature and the hierarchical strategy only used for the inverse gradient of the former k-1 features. Moreover, the average strategy of each grade samples is adopted to reduce computation. In addition, the weighted gradient of the most *correct* sample in different grades helps to select effective features which can reduce sample ambiguity errors. When a new frame arrives, we update all the weak classifiers in the pool Φ in parallel, and select K weak classifiers sequentially based on the strategy in (11). The main steps of the proposed feature selection algorithm are summarized in Algorithm 2.

Algorithm2. Advanced Online Discriminative Feature Selection

Input: Samples $\{\mathbf{x}_i, y_i\}_{i=0}^{N+L-1}$ where $y_i \in \{0,1\}$

    1. Update the weak classifier pool $\Phi = \{\phi_m\}_{m=1}^{M}$ with samples $\{\mathbf{x}_i, y_i\}_{i=0}^{N+L-1}$.

    2. Update the weighted weak classifier outputs $\sum_{i=0}^{N-1} \phi(\mathbf{x}_i)$ and $\bar{\phi}_m^{-}$, $m=1,...,M$.

    3. Update weight for each positive samples by (5)

    4. Initialize $h_0(\mathbf{x}_i)=0$

    5. **for** $k=1$ to K **do**

    6. Update $g_{k-1}(\mathbf{x}_i)$

    7.   **for** $m=1$ to M **do.**

    8.

$$\phi_k = \arg\max_{\phi \in \Phi} (E_{WODFS}(\phi) = w_{00}(N_1 g_{k-1}(\mathbf{x}_0) - \sum_{i=0}^{N_1} \phi(\mathbf{x}_i))^2 + w_{N_1 0}((N_2 - N_1)g_{k-1}(\mathbf{x}_{N_1}) - \sum_{i=N_1}^{N_2}$$

$$+ w_{N_2 0}((N-N_2)g_{k-1}(\mathbf{x}_{N_2}) - \sum_{i=N_2-1}^{N} \phi(\mathbf{x}_i))^2 + L(-\bar{g}_{k-1} - \bar{\phi}^{-})^2)$$

    9.   **end for**

    10. $m^* = \arg\max_m (E_m)$.

    11. $\phi_k \leftarrow \phi_{m^*}$.

    12. $h_k(\mathbf{x}_i) \leftarrow \sum_{j=1}^{k} \phi_j(\mathbf{x}_i), h_k(\mathbf{x}) \leftarrow h_k(\mathbf{x}) / \sum_{j=1}^{k} |\phi_j(\mathbf{x})|$

    13. **end for**

Output: Strong classifier $h_K(\mathbf{x}) = \sum_{k=1}^{K} \phi_k(\mathbf{x})$ and confidence function $P(y=1|\mathbf{x}) = \sigma(h_K(\mathbf{x}))$.

3.2   Discussion

In this selection, we discuss the advantages of our method over other methods.

A . *Equal and Different Weight.* In (11), we give the sample that near the tracking location at current frame a larger weight based on the assumption that the tracking location at current frame is the most *correct* positive sample. This assumption is adopted in most generative models[2,3,4] and some discriminative models[5,6,7,8,9]. In fact, it is impossible to ensure a complete drift free tracker without any prior models and learning classifier online. However, the proposed tracker can deal with the drift problem based on a weighted feature selection strategy which maximizes the total classification confidence of weighted positive samples while suppressing the total classify confidence of negative ones. If different positive samples are given the same weight, the classifier can become confused that it cannot select discriminative features because each positive samples contributes equally to the objective function.

B . *Sample Ambiguity Problem.* Babenko.*et al.* [7] recently demonstrated that the location ambiguity problem can be alleviated with online multiple instance learning, but MIL tracking is still not stable in some challenging tracking tasks. There may be several factors. Firstly, the Noisy-OR model [16] adopted in ODFS tracker could not eliminate error that brought in by uncertainty samples, and may select less effective features; secondly, the classifier is only trained by the binary labels without considering the different contributions of these samples. On the contrary, the feature selection criterion in our method explicitly relates the classifier score with the importance of samples. Therefore, the ambiguity problem can be better deal with.

C . *Advantages of Our Method over ODFS Tracker.* The ODFS tracker adopts a rough simplification that only using the sole *correct* sample to represent the average of whole positive samples while some noise may included when drafting. Our method divides the positive samples into three classes and weights the contribution of positive samples to reduce error. Thus the proposed method can select more effective feature than ODFS tracker, especially in case of drastic illumination variation and pose changes.

4   Experimental Results

In this section, we use a radius (6 pixels) to crop positive samples. A small α can generates incorrect samples when drafting while a large α can make positive samples much more variety which are sufficient to avoid noise. The inner and outer radius for the set $X^{\xi,\beta}$ that generates negative samples are set as $\xi=12$ $\beta=48$ respectively. Then we randomly select a set of 50 negative samples from the set $X^{\xi,\beta}$. The radius for searching new target location in the next frame is set as 25 which can fully include all candidate targets because the target motion between two consecutive frames is often smooth. We set K ,M and c as 15,50 and 4 respectively. A small learning rate can make the tracker quickly adopts to the fast appearance changing while a large learning rate can reduce the likelihood that the tracker drifts off the target. The best learning rate can be set as $\eta=0.80$ in experiments. For other competing algorithms, we use the original source codes or binary codes released by the authors. Our tracker is implemented in MATLAB and runs at 25 fps on Intel Dual-Core 1.7GHz CPU with 2.0 GB RAM. The videos used in the experiments can be found at http://youtube/3UobcBa-V1Q.

4.1   Quantitative Evaluation

To evaluate the performance of the algorithm, two performance indexes--*center location error* and *success rate* [18] are adopted to evaluate the proposed method with other 5 trackers [7,15,16,18,23]. The *center location error* is measured as the Euclidean distance between the center location of the tracked target and ground truth. *Success rate* indicates the percentage of successful frames whose overlap score is larger than the half of $|r_g|$. The overlap score is defined as $OS=\frac{|r_t \cap r_g|}{|r_t \cup r_g|}$, where r_t indicates the tracked bounding box, r_g represents the ground truth bounding box, $\cap$ and $\cup$ represent the intersection and union of two regions, and $|\bullet|$ denotes the number of pixels in the region. We draw *center location error* plots and present average *center location error* and *success rate* in tabular form to show super performance over other methods. Overall, our method favorably performs against other trackers.

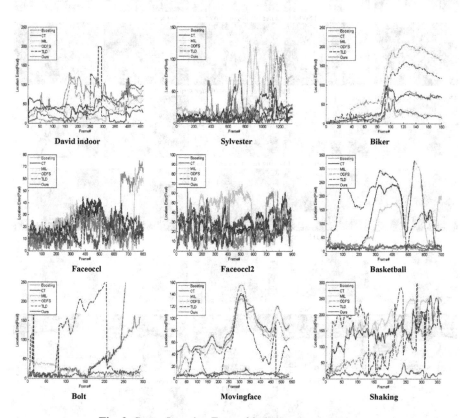

Fig. 3. Center Location Error of 9 challenging sequences

(a) Some tracking results of *David indoor* sequence

(b) Some tracking results of *Sylvester* sequence

(c) Some tracking results of *Biker* sequence

(d) Some tracking results of *Faceoccl* sequence

(e) Some tracking results of *Faceoccl2* sequence

(f) Some tracking results of *Basketball* sequence

(g) Some tracking results of *Bolt* sequence

(h) Some tracking results of *Movingface* sequence

(i) Some tracking results of *Shaking* sequence

Boosting ——— CT ——— MIL ······· ODFS ······· TLD ——— Ours

Fig. 4. Some tracking results in 9 challenging sequences

Table 1. Average Center Location Error (ACLE)

Video	Boosting	CT	MIL	ODFS	TLD	Ours
David indoor	67	54	25	47	44	**19**
Sylvester	16	22	46	22	9	**8**
Biker	45	44	18	109	72	**17**
Faceoccl	23	22	20	**15**	20	15
Faceoccl2	24	24	37	**22**	26	24
Basketball	18	115	103	14	165	**12**
Bolt	42	73	17	74	89	**10**
Moving face	**7**	80	76	72	43	7
Shaking	106	145	169	91	147	**14**
Average ACLE	38	64	56	51	68	**14**
Average fps	8	**33**	10	30	9	25

The **Bold** fonts indicate the best performance in this test.

Table 2. Average Success Rate (ASR) (%)

Video	Boosting	CT	MIL	ODFS	TLD	Ours
David indoor	32	64	71	68	47	**81**
Sylvester	80	83	53	94	81	**99**
Biker	66	74	**75**	35	30	73
Faceoccl	82	76	**94**	94	87	90
Faceoccl2	80	77	82	**90**	82	90
Basketball	71	35	4	69	0	**87**
Bolt	15	45	90	48	14	**92**
Moving face	**78**	47	27	24	25	78
Shaking	0	25	1	73	0	**74**
Average ASR	56	58	56	66	40	**84**

The **Bold** fonts indicate the best performance in this test.

4.2 Qualitative Evaluation

Scale and Pose Change: Although our tracker only estimates the transnational motion similar to most state-of-art algorithms (Boosting, MIL, CT), it can also handle scale and orientation changes because of the compressed Haar-like features [18]. In the *David indoor* sequence, the target has big scale and pose changes and illumination variation, it is noting that the MIL,CT and ODFS trackers perform well in some extent on this sequence while the Boosting, TLD tracker drift. The compressed feature enable MIL and our tracker to handle the scale and pose changes well, and our tracker yields more accurate results (frame#150, #200, #300) than the ODFS tracker because it can select more informative features to separate target from background by eliminating errors.

The CT tracker suffers some drifts because it does not select features online. The TLD tracker fails to track the object mainly because it relies heavily on the visual information in the first frame to re-detect the object. Moreover our method performs well on the *Sylvester* and *Biker* sequence in which the targets undergo significant pose changes.

Background Clutter and Pose Variation: For the sequence (*Bolt, Basketball*) shown in Fig4(f,g), the pose of the object change gradually and background are full of clutter. Only MIL and our tracker perform well on the video *Bolt* (frame#150, #200, #250), to deal with cluttered background, the MIL tracker set some instances from positive and negative instance bags respectively to learn the classifier to resist background interference; the boosting tracker is a generative model that does not take the background information into consideration and it drifts to the background. The features maintained in CT and ODFS may be contaminated by clutter background, which will result in the tracking failure. In *Basketball,* the Boosting, ODFS and our tracker perform well because they select discriminative feature for object representation which can well handle pose variation and shape deformation. The MIL, CT and TLD trackers do not perform well as generative models are less effective to account for appearance change caused by large shape and pose variation, thereby making the method drift away to similar objects.

Occlusion and Rotation: The target object in sequences *Faceoccl* and *Faceoccl2* undergoes large pose variation and heavy occlusion. In test video *Faceoccl*, the ODFS and our tracker perform well (frame#193, #282, #387) due to their efficient online feature selection strategy. The CT and MIL tracker extract some positive and negative samples to update classifier while they do not take informative features into consideration. In *Faceoccl2*, the ODFS and our tracker can handle rotation well (frame#200, #346, #648) because the tracker can also extract informative features to update classifier when target rotated while the other trackers drift seriously on this sequence.

Large Illumination Change and Pose Variation: For the *shaking* sequence shown in Fig4(i), the illumination and pose of the object both change gradually. The appearance of the singer's head in the *shaking* sequence changes significantly due to large variation of illumination and head pose. The CT and TLD tracker fails (frame#15) to track the head when the stage light drastically changes, whereas our tracker can accurately locate the target. The Boosting and ODFS tracker drift when the heavy illumination change and pose variation as shown in frame#50, #100, MIL tracker fails to track the object when heavy illumination change at frame #50 while our tracker is able to adjust the classifier quickly to appearance change and thus the proposed method performs well when illumination change and pose variation.

5   Conclusion

In this paper, a robust tracker based on an online updating appearance is proposed, which naturally integrate the positive sample importance into learning procedure.

The proposed method assumes the object location at current frame is the *correct* sample with which to make each sample contribute differently to the learning strategy: the closer the sample is to the center of *correct* sample, the more it contributes to the objective function. Experiments demonstrate that the classifier learned by the approach adopted in this paper is much more stable and robust than those in ODFS algorithm. The proposed method performs well on challenging sequences indicate the superiority over other state-of-the art algorithms in terms of accuracy and robust.

Acknowledgments. This research work was supported by the National 863 Program (No. 2012AA112312), National Nature Science Foundation of China (No.61175075) and Doctoral Program Foundation of Institutions of Higher Education of China, (No.20110161120006).

References

[1] Yilmaz, A., Javed, O., Shah, M.: Object tracking: A survey. ACM Computing Survey 38 (2006)

[2] Ross, D., Lim, J., Lin, R., Yang, M.: Incremental learning for robust visual tracking. International Journal of Computer Vision 77(1), 125–141 (2008), 1, 2, 7, 8

[3] Jepson, A., Fleet, D., EI-Maraghi, T.: Robust online appearance model for visual tracking. IEEE Transactions on Pattern Analysis and Machine Intelligence 25, 1296–1311 (2003)

[4] Mei, X., Ling, H.: Robust visual tracking using l1 minimization. In: International Conference on Computer Vision, pp. 1436–1443 (2009)

[5] Collins, R., Liu, Y., Leordeanu, M.: Online selection of discriminative tracking features. IEEE Transactions on Pattern Analysis and Machine Intelligence 27, 1631–1643 (2005)

[6] Grabner, H., Grabner, M., Bischof, H.: Real-time tracking via online boosting. In: British Machine Vision Conference, pp. 47–56 (2006)

[7] Babenko, B., Yang, M., Belongie, S.: Robust object tracking with online multiple instance learning. IEEE Transaction on Pattern Analysis and Machine Intelligence 33, 1619–1632 (2011)

[8] Li, H., Shen, C., Shi, Q.: Real-time visual tracking using compressive sensing. In: Proceeding of IEEE Conference on Computer Vision and Pattern Recognition, pp. 1305–1312 (2011)

[9] Zhang, K., Song, H.: Real-time visual tracking via online weighted multiple instance learning. Pattern Recognition 46(1), 397–411 (2013)

[10] Zhong, W., Lu, H., Yang, M.: Robust object tracking via sparsity based collaborative model. In: Proceedings of IEEE Conference on Computer Vision and Pattern Recognition, pp. 1838–1845 (2012)

[11] Jepson, A., Fleet, D., EI-Maraghi, T.: Robust online appearance models for visual tracking. IEEE Transaction on Pattern Analysis and Machine Intelligence 25, 1296–1311 (2003)

[12] Adam, A., Rivlin, E., Shimshoni, I.: Robust fragments-based tracking using the integral histogram. In: IEEE Conference on Computer Vision and Pattern Recognition, pp. 798–805 (2006)

[13] Avidan, S.: Support vector tracking. IEEE Transactions on Pattern Analysis and Machine Intelligence 26, 1064–1072 (2004)

[14] Avidan, S.: Ensemble tracking. IEEE Transaction on Pattern Analysis and Machine Intelligence 29, 261–271 (2007)

[15] Grabner, H., Leistner, C., Bischof, H.: Semi-supervised on-line boosting for robust tracking. In: Forsyth, D., Torr, P., Zisserman, A. (eds.) ECCV 2008, Part I. LNCS, vol. 5302, pp. 234–247. Springer, Heidelberg (2008)

[16] Zhang, K., Zhang, L.: Real-tine object tracking via online discriminative feature selection. IEEE Transaction on Image Processing, 4664–4677 (2013)

[17] Dollar, P., Tu, Z., Tao, H., Belongie, S.: Feature mining for image classification. In: IEEE Conference on Computer Vision and Pattern Recognition, pp. 1–8 (2007)

[18] Zhang, K., Zhang, L., Yang, M.-H.: Real-time compressive tracking. In: Fitzgibbon, A., Lazebnik, S., Perona, P., Sato, Y., Schmid, C. (eds.) ECCV 2012, Part III. LNCS, vol. 7574, pp. 864–877. Springer, Heidelberg (2012)

[19] Friedman, J.: Greedy function approximation: A gradient boosting machine. The Annas of Statistics 29, 1189–1232

[20] Wu, Y., Lim, J., Yang, M.-H.: Online object tracking: A benchmark. In: CVPR (2013)

[21] Salti, S., Cavallaro, A., Di Stefano, L.: Adaptive appearance modeling for video tracking: Survey and evaluation. IEEE Transaction on Image Processing 21(10), 4311–4348 (2012)

[22] Wang, S., Lu, H., Yang, F., Yang, M.: Superpixel tracking. In: Proceedings of the IEEE International Conference on Computer Vision, pp. 1323–1330 (2011)

[23] Kalal, Z., Matas, J., Mikolajczyk, K.: Pn learning: Bootstrapping binary classifiers by structural constraints. In: Proceedings of IEEE Conference on Computer Vision and Pattern Recognition, pp. 49–56 (2010)

[24] Wright, J., Yang, A., Ganesh, A., Sastry, S., Ma, Y.: Robust face recognition via spare representation. IEEE Transaction on Pattern Analysis and Machine Intelligence 31(2), 210–227 (2009)

[25] Liu, L., Fieguth, P.: Texture classification from random features. IEEE Transaction on Pattern Analysis and Machine Intelligence 34(3), 574–586 (2012)

A System of Image Aesthetic Classification and Evaluation Using Cloud Computing

Weining Wang, Jiancong Liu, Weijian Zhao, and Jiachang Li

School of Electronic and Information, South China of University of Technology, 510640, China
wnwang@scut.edu.cn, {598905380,564676319}@qq.com,
walsonory@gmail.com

Abstract. Image aesthetic analysis is a new direction of computer vision, whose purpose is to simulate the visual perception and aesthetic criterion of human being to assess aesthetic value of a given image. Nowadays, due to the popularization of smart phones with built-in cameras, functions like automatic image management and aesthetic guidance in mobile devices are valuable and in great demand. In order to remedy the gap between the large amount of computation and the hardware limitation of mobile devices, an image aesthetic classification and evaluation system using cloud computing is built in this paper. The time consuming parts such as feature extraction and machine learning algorithms are deployed on the virtual machine in the cloud server, while the simple part such as user interface is left for client. In addition, to make full use of the cloud server, a parallel-processing strategy of feature extraction is put to use in the system The result shows that our approach achieves a promising accuracy and is well correlated with the subjective aesthetics evaluation of human. And the system is more efficient and easier to be used in mobile devices with the help of cloud computing.

Keywords: Image aesthetics, Feature extraction, Cloud computing, Aesthetic classification, Aesthetic evaluation.

1   Introduction

Aesthetics has been discussed in the world of philosophy for ages. With the rapid development of computer vision technology, researches on computational aesthetics of image has attracted much attention in recent years.[1-7] Visual aesthetics exists widely in human daily life. People always unconsciously estimate the aesthetics of visual information. Although there is slight difference in aesthetic ideas among different groups of people, most of the aesthetic standards are in common. Because of the explosive growth of digital images on internet and in mobile devices, we hope computers can help us to make some aesthetic decision. For example, we hope the system can pick out images with high-aesthetic value in image retrieval. We hope the photographic device can help us to get more beautiful photos after shooting. And we

S. Li et al. (Eds.): CCPR 2014, Part I, CCIS 483, pp. 183–195, 2014.

need an auto-selection strategy to delete images with low-aesthetics when storing a large amount of photos. In a word, the research on computational image aesthetics aims to simulate aesthetic processing of human beings to assess image aesthetics automatically.

The image aesthetic computing includes image classification and evaluation, which means getting the aesthetic ranking and aesthetic score of images. Due to its subjectivity and complexity, computational aesthetics is a highly challenging task. Many researchers have attempted to solve these problems[2,4,5]. The framework of computational visual aesthetics usually comprises two stages. First, they extract features on the basis of certain theories and assumptions about aesthetics. Second, they combine the features to build models of classification and regression pattern. Wang et.al.[5] selected 15 effective features including brightness, color distribution, wavelet transform, depth of field of an image, subsequently they used SVM to get a aesthetic model to classify and evaluate the aesthetic quality of an image. Although the correct rate was not very high, it showed the feasibility of image aesthetic analysis. Wong[8] applied the visual attention model to extracting regional features and finally achieved a better classification result. Li[2] used SVM and Adaboost to classify paintings in aesthetics by extracting its artistic features. We[12] also developed a system of aesthetic classification and evaluation based on features of different levels and SVM algorithm. The results are acceptable compared with other works. Generally, the process of aesthetic analysis is quite complicated and costs a lot of time, however, the existing works haven't make any use of cloud computing to improve the efficiency. Therefore, we try to combine our previous work with cloud computing.

Nowadays, due to the popularization of smart phones with built-in cameras, people can take pictures and store large amount of images more conveniently. Functions of automatic image selection and aesthetic guidance in mobile devices are valuable and in great demand. However, most of existing models are only implemented on PCs. The algorithms need a large amount of calculation and cost time. It is not feasible to run on mobile devices.

The development of cloud computing provides us a good opportunity to solve the existing problems. Cloud computing is a kind of internet service which provides amount of dynamically-scalable and virtual resources In recent years, cloud computing has been widely used in image processing and pattern recognition [9, 10]. By using cloud service, users can easily access the strong computing capability through internet anytime and anywhere. All kinds of complicated algorithms can be accomplished on the server side. Therefore, cloud computing can largely save calculation time and simplify the work on the client side.

In the services offered by the cloud computing provider, IaaS (Infrastructure as a Service) is suitable for the applications of image aesthetics assessment. Provider of IaaS offers virtual hardware resources to software developers as services (such as virtual server, storage and database management). Service provider is responsible for all the actual construction and maintenance of the equipment. Software development users do not need to purchase the actual equipment. They can simply accompolish their development work on the cloud platform by connecting to the Internet. If the application or software is deployed on the cloud server, it is no longer limited by the terminal's hardware. The complicated computation can be finished in the cloud server.

Therefore, in this paper we develop a system of image aesthetic classification and evaluation using cloud computing. By moving some high-complexity computation parts of the algorithms such as feature extraction to cloud server, a complex system can be accessed effectively in a simple client such as portable device. A user only needs to take a picture with his handhold device and then uploads it to the server in the backend cloud, where the picture will be processed and eventually the result will be sent back to the client side. With the help of cloud computing, aesthetic classification and evaluation could be widely used in daily life.

The remainder of the paper is organized as follows. In section 2, we will present an overview of the framework of our image aesthetics classification and evaluation system. In section 3, we will describe the deployment of this system on cloud computing, including both the client and server side. The paralleled processing will be also introduced in this section. Conclusions on our work and an outlook of future research are given in section 4.

2   Image Aesthetic Classification and Evaluation

We had developed an image aesthetic classification and evaluation system on computer previously [12]. The system was comprised of two parts, namely, image aesthetic classification model and aesthetic evaluation model. The first one was an support vector machine(SVM) classifier, which could estimate whether an image is high or low in aesthetics. The latter one was a score prediction model using support vector regression (SVR) method, which could give an aesthetic score to an image. To

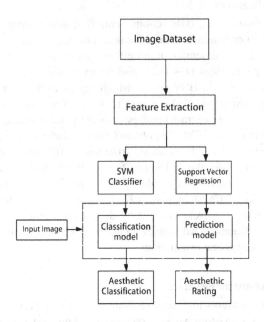

Fig. 1. The framework of our aesthetic system

construct the classifier and the score prediction model, a group of aesthetic related image features were firstly extracted, including low-level visual features, high-level aesthetic features and regional features. Then these image features were combined with image aesthetic labels given by human beings in our database to train the classifier and the score prediction model by using SVM and SVR methods. As a result, the aesthetic category (high-aesthetic VS. low-aesthetic), as well as the aesthetic score, of an image can be obtained automatically through our models. We compared the results of automatic assessment with subjective aesthetics evaluation from human. The results showed that our models achieved a promising accuracy and were well correlated with the subjective labels. The framework of this system is shown in Fig. 1.

2.1   Feature Extractions

In order to cover most possible relation of image features to human's subjective perception on image aesthetics, we extracted diverse features from different aesthetic perspectives. Some of the features were selected because they had been widely used and verified by previous studies. Other features are derived from prior knowledge under certain disciplines i.e. photography, art, psychology etc. In addition, we made several improvements on some proposed features of existing work to enhance the performance of our model. These features mainly include low-level visual features (227-dimension), high-level aesthetic features (24-dimension) and regional features (10-dimension). The detailed expression of these features can be found in [12].

1) Level Visual Features

Low-level visual features are basic components that depict images in an objective manner, including color features, texture features and shape features. To indicate color features, we made a 128-dimension non-uniform quantized histogram of HSV space from an image to get features f1 ~ f128, and we extracted the first 3 orders of color moments for each channel in HSV space, which represent the average, variance and skewness of color respectively. As a result, we obtained features f129~f137. To indicate texture features, we extract features such as Gabor wavelet, Tamura, and gray level co-ocurrence matrix(GLCM). We obtain Gabor features f138~f185 by calculating averages and variances of results obtained from Gabor filtering in 6 directions and 4 scales. Moreover, we apply the 6 Tamura features(f186~f191), namely, roughness, contrast, linelikeness, coarseness, regularity and directionality corresponding to the visual perception. In GLCM features (f192~f211) we select 5 properties including energy, contrast, entropy, correlation, inverse difference moment in four orientations. To indicate shape features, we obtain features f212~f227 from a 16-dimension histogram of Sobel edges and orientations.

2) High-Level Aesthetic Features

High-level aesthetic features are more relevant to human's preference for an image. With the conclusion of existing works, psychological knowledge and common rules in photography, we detailed high-level aesthetic features as image complexity features, color balance features, energy features and field of depth. Aesthetic visual features are the core part of aesthetic research.

(1) Complexity Features

Complexity of an image is considered to be a highly accuracy-correlated measurement in image aesthetics. Machado et al. [13] concluded that images that are easy to process (means low processing complexity)   but visually complex (means high image complexity) are of higher aesthetic value. IC (image complexity) can be presented as the ratio between the error and compressibility of a JPEG image, and PC (processing complexity) can be presented as the compressibility of fractal images. In feature extraction, PC includes order complexity and entropy complexity (f228~f229). IC includes color complexity (f230~f232) and texture complexity (f233).

(2) Color Balance

A balanced distribution of colors brings higher aesthetic value. We used two measurements to access the color balance of an image. They are the distribution of color entropy(MS) and color visual balance(EMD_LUV and EMD_RGB). Color visual balance can be measured by the earth-movers-distance(EMD) between the primary image and an ideal color-balanced image. So we obtained f234~f336 in this part.

(3) Image Energy

Image energy indicates the richness of information in an image. Moreover, it is closely associated with the image aesthetic value. The image energy concentrates on low frequency component. We performed the 3-layer Daubchies wavelet transform upon a single-channel image, and figure out the sum of low frequency energy of each layer as the wavelet energy of an image. Finally, we obtained f237~f248.

(4) Depth of Field

Depth of field(DOF) is the distance between the nearest and farthest objects in a scene that appear acceptably sharp in an image.. If the DOF is small enough, it can make the object clearer and prominent, and enhance the aesthetic value of an image.

Fig. 2. The region numbers and central region used to computing DOF

As shown in Fig. 2, firstly, we split the image into a 4*4 blocks equally M1~M16. After that, we obtain the 3rd Daubchies wavelet bands with three coefficients, and figure out the energy of the 3 coefficients to represent the DOF. So we obtained f249~f251 for each channel in HSV.

3) Regional Features

Generally, people always pay more attention to the salient region containing abundant information in an image. So the salient region plays a more important role in aesthetics than other regions. In this paper, we used an efficient method combining image segmentation with gradient information to extract the salient region to help compute regional features. We figure out the color moments(f252~f260) and shape ratio (f261) of the salient region as regional features. f252~f260 are the first, second and third moments of 3 channels in HSV, and f261 is the ratio between the sums of pixels of the salient region and the whole image.

2.2   Aesthetic Classification and Evaluation

To classify images in accordance with people's aesthetic feelings, efficient machine learning algorithm are important for trainings. SVM has been widely used in image analysises and recognitions. Some relevant studies[2,5] have proved its efficiency and feasibility in image aesthetics computing. The basic idea of SVM is to construct an optimal separating hyperplane to maximize the interval between different classes. It solved the problem of underfitting and overfitting existing in neural network algorithm and avoided the curse of dimensionality. Therefore, we trained image features with SVM algorithm to obtain the aesthetic classifier, which could classify images into high-aesthetic and low-aesthetic ones. Grid search method was used to found the optimums of parameter C and γ in kernel function RBF of SVM model. In the established model, 256 was set to C and 0.5 was set to γ. Classification accuracy were computed and shown as the confusion matrix to measure the performance of classification in Table 1.

Moreover, SVR algorithm was used to train the image aesthetic evaluation model. The aesthetic score assessed by this model were compared with the subjective score given by human on correlation, RMSE, and other three error measurement in Table 2.

The images we used in our system need to be attached with aesthetic scores made by subjects, so the suitable databases are not easy to attain. We used the database provided in paper[5] to train and test our models. The images in this database were collected from photo.net, a professional image website. Each image had been evaluated by at least 10 subjects for its aesthetic score ranging between 0 and 7. There are in a total of 3140 images in the database. Referring to the existing work[5], we set the images whose score is higher than 5.8 as high-aesthetic ones, lower than 4.2 as low-aesthetic ones. Then we got 750 images in high-aesthetic class and 644 ones in low-aesthetic class. The classification accuracies were shown in Table 1. HA is short for high-aesthetics, and LA is for low-aesthetics. The classification model achieved a 75.37% accuracy on image aesthetics.

In addition, in order to verify the effectiveness of different image features, we also gave the accuracies of the models under training of different feature groups in Table 1.

It is shown that the correct rate of classification with low-level features is 72.21%, and it ascends to 75.37% after considering the high-level features and regional features.

Table 1. The comparison of image aesthetic classification accuracy

%	Low-level		Low-level+high-level		All features	
	HA	LA	HA	LA	HA	LA
HA	**75.33**	24.67	**77.47**	22.53	**77.60**	22.40
LA	30.91	**69.09**	28.57	**71.43**	26.86	**73.14**
Average accuracy	72.21		74.45		75.37	

Table 2. The performance of score prediction

%	correlation	RMSE	Average absolute error	Average relative error	Standard residual deviation
Low-level	0.753	0.257	0.489	0.097	0.577
Low &high-level	0.773	0.249	0.476	0.094	0.561
All features	**0.790**	**0.244**	0.467	0.093	0.548

6.12   6.05   5.88

High-aesthetics

4.10   3.95   3.62

Low-aesthetics

Fig. 3. Image samples with aesthetic class labels and prediction scores

The comparison of the aesthetic score results of machine and human are displayed in Table 2. The experiment results demonstrate that our aesthetic score prediction model got a correlation coefficient of 0.79 and RMSE of 0.244 on images aesthetic score between automatic assessment and subjective aesthetics evaluation of human.

The results above show that our image aesthetic classification and evaluation models achieved a promising accuracy and were well correlated with the subjective scores. Some image samples with their aesthetic classes and scores assessed by machine are shown in Fig. 3.

3   Aesthetic Classification and Evaluation Using Cloud Computing

We have developed a system of image aesthetic classification and evaluation in Section 2 who worked well in computer. However, the system responded very slow and halted sometimes after it was transplanted in to a handhold device. This is mainly because of the heavy computation requirement of the algorithms. In order to reduce the computing burden of terminal devices, we distributed the main algorithms including feature extractions, classification and evaluation to the virtual machine created in a cloud platform.

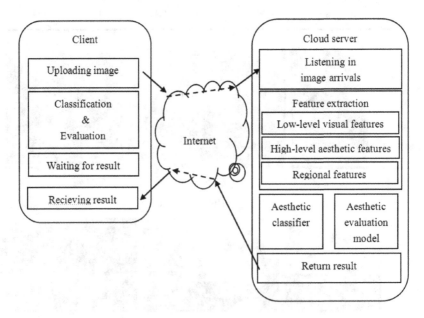

Fig. 4. The frame of aesthetic classification and evaluation system based on cloud computing

The framework of image aesthetic classification and evaluation system using cloud computing is divided into 2 parts: client side and cloud server side. As shown in Fig. 4, the client side is only responsible for collecting images and transmitting them to the cloud server, and subsequently waiting for the result to return from the server side. The system on cloud server side is responsible for most of the computing work, including extracting the features, classifying or evaluating according to users' requests and response to the client with results.

3.1   Client Side and   Communication Modules

The client only needs to collect images and send them to the server, then waits for the result from the server. So the development of client is simple. The client side can work on various operating systems, including Windows, Android, Mac OS and so on. We have deployed the client on Windows and Android 4.2, as shown in Fig. 5. Android 4.2 is one of the most popular mobile platforms in the world. Since our main algorithms are implemented in C++, it is required to use Android Native Development Kit(NDK) to compile our codes so as to be compatible with the framework of Android. In Windows platform, we implemented our application in a MFC framework.

Fig. 5. The clients on Windows and Android

For Android client, the main modules include Send/Recieve and ImageView, as shown in Fig.6. Send/Recieve is used to initiate a client request to server side and then transmit selected photos to it. ImageView allows users to select the service they want (classification or evaluation) and shows the score received from the server side.

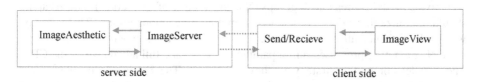

Fig. 6. Core modules of android client and server side

Fig.6 also illustrates the core modules of the server side. ImageServer is responsible for waitng for requests from clients. When a request comes it will store the received image in a specific path as the input of ImageAesthetic. Then ImageAesthetic will implement the aesthetic classification and evaluation. The communication module is developed on the following platform: a smart phone, with Android OS 4.2 and Java Development Kit in Eclipse.

3.2   Cloud Server Side

In the system of image aesthetic classification and evaluation using cloud computing, the server side is in charge of image feature extraction, implementing classification and evaluation algorithms and returning the results to the client. It can be realized on a virtual machine created in cloud severs.

It is highly customizable and secure if we build a cloud platform by ourselves with connecting several computers. However, compared with the public cloud service offered by cloud computing suppliers, the maintenance of the platform is quite difficult and is a great cost. Therefore, we chose an IaaS offered by Aliyun for the deployment of our system.

The elastic computing services (ECS) provided by Aliyun, integrate basic resources of computing and storage, and offer computing services on Web, with functions like self management, data security, automatic fault recovery and protection against network attacks, which can help users to simplify the development and deployment process, reduce operation and maintenance costs, and construct application frameworks.

After creating a virtual machine in the cloud platform, we deploy the server part of our system on it. A request-listener is set in the system. When a request from client arrives, the system accepts it and begins to work, and responds with the result finally. In order to test the performance of our system, we created virtual machines elastically with different capability of computing, and ran our system on them respectively.

In order to make full use of the virtual machine of cloud service, we employed a parallel processing for our algorithms. After the analysis on the algorithms in time consuming, we found that feature extraction cost most of the time. So we design the parallel strategy specially for this part, in which time consumption of each feature and the number of CPU cores of the virtue machine should be considered.

Firstly we calculate the average computing time of all the features respectively, and then divide these features into N groups (N is the number of CPU cores). The grouping should minimize the variance of feature-computing time among groups. That is to say, we should distribute all the calculations to N cores equally as much as possible to let these N computing processes run in parallel, so as to take full advantage of the CPU. The parallel computing strategy is shown in Fig.7. The bands of different colors correspond to extraction process of different feature. The length of a band represents its time-consumption. Serial computing is as shown on the left, and parallel computing is on the right. It is clear that the processing time is greatly shortened using parallel computing.

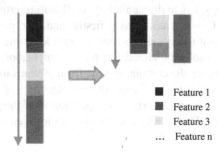

Fig. 7. The parallel computing strategy of feature-extraction

Table 3. The average computing time in different strategy of parallelization

		Time of computing Gabor features (ms)	Time of computing all features T (ms)
Serial computing		3242	**3996**
2-core	Strategy 1	3287	3287
	Speed-up ratio	0.99	1.22
	Strategy 2	1636	**2346**
	Speed-up ratio	1.98	1.70
4-core	Strategy 1	3235	3235
	Speed-up ratio	1.00	1.24
	Strategy 2	999	**1687**
	Speed-up ratio	3.25	2.37
8-core	Strategy 1	3222	3222
	Speed-up ratio	1.01	1.24
	Strategy 2	928	**1582**
	Speed-up ratio	3.49	2.53

In addition, we found that Gabor features extracting took up more than 80% of the time. We could also do some work on parallelizing the Gabor features extraction algorithm by distributing more cores to it, and distribute less cores to other features extraction process.

We use OpenMP to complete the parallel computing and run it on Aliyun cloud servers with 2, 4 and 8 cores respectively. We use 100 color images whose average size is about 633*538 to test the performance of parallelization. The results are shown in Table 3.

In Table 3, Strategy 1 is to do paralleling to all feature groups. Strategy 2 is that we split the process of Gabor feature group firstly, and then parallelize them with other groups. It indicates that the system consumes much less time after parallel computing. Because strategy 2 also parallelized the process of Gabor features, it has a better performance by reducing the computing time from 3996ms to1582 ms in average than Strategy 1. But according to the Gabor filtering algorithm, the paralleled parts of this algorithm is limited in 4 which restricts the promotion of the paralleling process when involving more cores. That is why the speed-up ratio in an 8-core server is not much higher than that in a 4-core server.

4   Summary and Future Work

Image aesthetic analysis is a challenging and promising topic in the field of computer vision. In this paper, we develop an image aesthetic classification and evaluation system, and make it run smoothly on mobile device by using cloud computing. Parallel processing strategies to the system are designed to make full use of the cloud sever. This system resolves the conflict between the large amount of calculation of the algorithm and the hardware limitation of mobile devices.

In the future, we will continue to work on the following aspects: first, we will explore MapReduce based on SVM to shorten the training time, and try to use MapReduce programming model to feature extraction algorithm, due to the limitation of our parallelizing strategy. Second, we hope to expand our system with a multiple-client access. We will compose a Hadoop cluster server to settle our aesthetic system, which helps shorten the delay time when large amount of clients are waiting for service.

Acknowledgements. We gratefully acknowledge the support from NSFC (No.61171142), the Fundamental Research Funds for the Central Universities (No.2014ZZ0036), and the Science and Technology Planning project of Guangdong Province (No.2011A010801005).

References

1. Wu, Y., Bauckhage, C., Thurau, C.: The good, the bad, and the ugly: Predicting aesthetic image labels. In: Proceedings of 2010 20th International Conference on Pattern Recognition, Istanbul, Turkey, pp. 1586–1589 (2010)
2. Li, C.C., Tsuhan, C.: Aesthetic visual quality assessment of paintings. IEEE Journal of Selected Topics in Signal Processing 3(2), 236–252 (2009)
3. Subhabrata, B., Rahul, S., Mubarak, S.: A framework for photo quality assessment and enhancement based on visual aesthetics. In: Proceedings of the ACM Multimedia 2010 International Conference, Firenze, Italy, pp. 271–280 (2010)
4. Amirshahi, S.A., Koch, M., Denzler, J., et al.: PHOG analysis of self-similarity in aesthetic images. In: Proceedings of SPIE - The International Society for Optical Engineering, Burlingame, US, p. 8291 (2012)

5. Datta, R., Wang, J.Z.: ACQUINE: Aesthetic quality inference engine real-time automatic rating of photo aesthetics. In: Proceedings of the ACM SIGMM International Conference on Multimedia Information Retrieval, New York, pp. 421–424 (2010)
6. Joshi, D., Datta, R., Fedorovskaya, E., et al.: Aesthetics and emotions in images: A computational perspective. IEEE Signal Processing Magazine 28(5), 94–115 (2011)
7. Wang, W.-N., Yi, J.-J.: Review for computational image aesthetics. Journal of Image and Graphics, 17(8), 893–901 (2012) (in Chinese)
8. Wong, L.K., Low, K.L.: Saliency-enhanced image aesthetics class prediction. In: Proceedings of 2009 IEEE International Conference on Image, Los Alamitos, pp. 997–1000 (2009)
9. Gao, Y., Jin, L., He, C.: Handwriting Character Recognition as a Service: A New Handwriting Recognition System based on Cloud Computing. In: International Conference on Document Analysis and Recognition, ICDAR 2011, pp. 885–889 (2011)
10. He, C., Jin, L., Zhou, G.: Handwriting recognition system based on cloud computing platform. Telecommunications Science, 84–89 (September 2010) (in Chinese)
11. Duan, P., Wang, W., et al.: Food Image Recognition Using Pervasive Cloud Computing. In: International Conference on Green Computing and Communications and IEEE Internet of Things and IEEE Cyber, Physical and Social Computing, Beijing, China, August 20-23, pp. 1631–1637 (2013)
12. Wang, W., Yi, J., Xu, X., Wang, L.: Computational Aesthetics of Image Classification and Evaluation. Accepted by Journal of Computer-Aided Design & Computer Graphics (in Chinese)
13. Machado, P., Cardoso, A.: Computing aesthetics. In: de Oliveira, F.M. (ed.) SBIA 1998. LNCS (LNAI), vol. 1515, pp. 219–228. Springer, Heidelberg (1998)

Image Feature Extraction via Graph Embedding Regularized Projective Non-negative Matrix Factorization

Haishun Du, Qingpu Hu, Xudong Zhang, and Yandong Hou

Institute of Image Processing and Pattern Recognition, Henan University,
Kaifeng 475004, China
{jddhs,hydong}@henu.edu.cn, huqingpu_henu@126.com,
xudong2366@163.com

Abstract. Non-negative matrix factorization (NMF) has been widely used in image processing and pattern recognition fields. Unfortunately, NMF does not consider the geometrical structure and the discriminative information of data, which might make it unsuitable for classification tasks. In addition, NMF only calculates the coefficient matrix of the training data and how to yields the coefficient vector of a new test data is still obscure. In this paper, we propose a novel graph embedding regularized projective non-negative matrix factorization (GEPNMF) method to address the aforementioned problems. By introducing a graph embedding regularization term, the learned subspace can preserve the local geometrical structure of data while maximizing the margins of different classes. We deduce a multiplicative update rule (MUR) to iteratively solve the objective function of GEPNMF and prove its convergence in theory. Experimental results on ORL and CMU PIE databases suggest the effectiveness of GEPNMF.

Keywords: Graph embedding, Non-negative matrix factorization, Feature extraction, Face recognition.

1   Introduction

Recently, non-negative matrix factorization (NMF) [1] [2] has been widely used in image processing and pattern recognition fields. NMF aims at finding two non-negative matrices whose product can approximate the original data matrix. The non-negative constrains lead to a parts-based representation because they only permit non-subtractive combinations of non-negative basis vectors to approximate the original data. Lee and Seung [1] performed NMF on ORL database had shown that NMF's basis matrix consists of basis vectors that represent eyes, noses, mouths, etc., respectively. This property is consistent with the psychological and physical interpretation of the parts-based representation in human brain [3]. Even so, there is no explicit guarantee in NMF to support this property besides non-negativity constrains. Several works, such as

S. Li et al. (Eds.): CCPR 2014, Part I, CCIS 483, pp. 196–209, 2014.

local NMF (LNMF) [4] and non-negative sparse coding (NSC) [5], were proposed to ensure the learned basis vectors to be parts-based.

In many practical applications, data are usually drawn from a low-dimensional manifold embedding in a high-dimensional ambient space. It is necessary to consider the local geometrical structure of data for classification tasks. Unfortunately, NMF does not discover the local geometrical structure of data. To solve this issue, Cai *et al.* [6] proposed a graph-regularized NMF (GNMF), in which the local geometrical structure of data is encoded by a nearest-neighbor (NN) graph. Guan *et al.* [7] presented a manifold regularized discriminative NMF (MD_NMF) by incorporating a manifold regularization term into NMF.

Moreover, NMF and its variants mentioned above only calculate the coefficient matrix of training data. How to yields the coefficient vector of a new test data is still obscure. To solve this problem, Yang *et al.* [8] proposed a projective NMF (PNMF), which can obtain a non-negative projective subspace by slightly advising the cost function of NMF. Similar to NMF, PNMF also does not consider the local geometrical structure of data. In this paper, we propose a graph embedding regularized projective non-negative matrix factorization (GEPNMF) method to learn a discriminative subspace that can preserve the local geometrical structure of data. In GEPNMF, we first construct two adjacent graphs to respectively encode the local geometrical structure and the discriminative information of data. Based on the two adjacent graphs, we give a graph embedding regularization term that preserves the local geometrical structure of data while maximizing the margins between different classes. By incorporating the graph embedding regularization term with the objective function of PNMF, we present the objective function of GEPNMF. Finally, we deduce a multiplicative update rule (MUR) to iteratively solve the objective function and prove its convergence in theory.

The rest of this paper is organized as follows. Section 2 briefly reviews the PNMF method. Section 3 presents our proposed GEPNMF in detail. Section 4 shows the experimental results on two benchmark face image databases. We conclude this paper in Section 5.

2   Outline of PNMF

Given a non-negative data matrix $X = [x_1, \cdots, x_n] \in \mathbb{R}_+^{m \times n}$, each column of X is a data vector. NMF finds two low-rank non-negative matrices $W \in \mathbb{R}_+^{m \times r}$ and $H \in \mathbb{R}_+^{r \times n}$, with $r < \min\{m, n\}$, whose product can approximate the original matrix, i.e. $X \approx WH$ .NMF uses the K-L divergence to measure the error between X and the approximation WH .

Since NMF lacks of theoretical foundation when one directly uses the basis matrix W to deal with a new test data, it is strictly not a subspace learning method. To solve this issue, Yang *et al.* [8] proposed a projective NMF (PNMF), which tries to find a non-negative projective matrix $P \in \mathbb{R}_+^{m \times n}$ to satisfy $X \approx PX$. Specifically, PNMF calculates the factorization $P = WW^T$ with $W \in \mathbb{R}_+^{m \times r}$. Compared with NMF in which $X \approx WH$, PNMF only replaces the coefficient matrix H with $W^T X$. This makes PNMF become a subspace learning method that close to non-negative PCA. Projected a new test data onto the spanned subspace of the basis matrix W, one can obtain its low-dimensional representation. Similarly, PNMF also uses the K-L divergence to measure the quality of the approximation $X \approx PX$. The objective function is formulated as follows:

$$\min_{W,H} D\left(X \| WW^T X\right) =$$

$$\min_{W,H} \sum_{i,j} \left(X_{ij} \log \frac{X_{ij}}{\left(WW^T X\right)_{ij}} - X_{ij} + \left(WW^T X\right)_{ij} \right) \tag{1}$$

$$\text{s.t. } W \geq 0$$

Yang $et.al$ [8] presented the MUR of W:

$$W_{ik} \leftarrow W_{ik} \frac{\left(ZX^T W\right)_{ik} + \left(XZ^T W\right)_{ik}}{\sum_j \left(W^T X\right)_{kj} + \left(\sum_j X_{ij}\right)\left(\sum_a W_{ak}\right)} \tag{2}$$

3   Graph Embedding Projective NMF

As a subspace learning method, PNMF can directly project a novel test data onto the spanned subspace of the basis matrix W to obtain its low-dimensional features. However, PNMF does not take into account the local geometrical structure and the discriminative information of data, which is essential to cope with the real-world classification problems. In this section, we propose a graph embedding regularized projective non-negative matrix factorization (GEPNMF) method to address this problem by considering the local geometrical structure and the discriminative information of data.

3.1   Objective Function

Suppose $X = [x_1, \cdots, x_n] \in \mathbb{R}_+^{m \times n}$ is sampled from a low-dimensional manifold that embeds in an ambient space. The class label of the sample x_i is denoted by $c_i \in \{1, 2, \cdots, N_c\}$, in which N_c is the amount of classes. Let π_c denote the subset of samples from the cth class and n_c denote the amount of the samples belonging to the cth class.

To encode the local geometrical structure of data, we construct an undirected weighted graph $G^p = \{X, S_p\}$, in which a data pair is connected if one data is among the k_1 nearest neighbors of the other and they belong to the same class. The edge weight S_{ij}^p is defined as follow:

$$S_{ij}^p = \begin{cases} 1, & \text{if } x_i \in N_{k_1}^+(x_j) \\ & \text{or } x_j \in N_{k_1}^+(x_i) \\ 0, & \text{otherwise} \end{cases} \tag{3}$$

Where $N_{k_1}^+(x_i)$ denotes the set of the k_1 nearest neighbors of the sample x_i in same class. We minimize $\operatorname{tr}(HL_pH^T)$ to maintain the local geometrical structure of data, in which $L_p = D_p - S_p$ is the graph Laplacian matrix, and the i th element of the diagonal matrix D_p is $D_{ii}^p = \sum_j S_{ij}$.

To encode the discriminative information of data, we construct another undirected weighted graph $G^c = \{X, S_c\}$. In graph G^c, k_2 nearest sample pairs for each class, in which one data is in-class and the other is out-of-class, are connected. The edge weight S_{ij}^c is calculated as follows:

$$
S_{ij}^c = \begin{cases} 1, & \text{if } (x_i, x_j) \in P_{k_2}(c_i) \\ & \quad \text{or } (x_i, x_j) \in P_{k_2}(c_j) \\ 0, & \text{otherwise} \end{cases} \tag{4}
$$

Where $P_{k_2}(c_i)$ is a set of data pairs that are the k_2 nearest pairs among the set $\{(x_i, x_j) \mid x_i \in \pi_{c_i}, x_j \notin \pi_{c_i}\}$. We maximize $\operatorname{tr}(HL_cH^T)$ to ensure the data in different classes separated, in which $L_c = D_c - S_c$ is graph Laplacian matrix, and the i th element of the diagonal matrix D_c is $D_{ii}^c = \sum_j S_{ij}$.

Motived by [7], we give a graph embedding regularization term:

$$
\operatorname{tr}(H(L_c^{-1/2})^T L_p L_c^{-1/2} H^T) \tag{5}
$$

Since L_c is not always positive definite, it may be invertible. Following the work of [9], we add a tiny perturbation to the diagonal of the graph Laplacian matrix L_c, i.e., $\tilde{L}_c = L_c + \zeta I$, to ensure that it is invertible all the time. In this paper, we empirically set ζ as $10^{-4}\operatorname{tr}(L_c)$. For convenience of description, we still let L_c denote the perturbed matrix $\tilde{L}_c$ in the rest of this paper.

By incorporating (5) with PNMF, and letting $H = W^T X$, we can obtain:

$$
\min_W D(X \| WW^T X) +
$$

$$
\frac{\beta}{2}\operatorname{tr}(W^T X (L_c^{-1/2})^T L_p L_c^{-1/2} X^T W) \tag{6}
$$

$$
\text{s.t. } W \geq 0
$$

Where β is the balance parameter.

To ensure the learned basis vectors to be parts-based, we introduce an orthogonal regularization term [10]:

$$
\sum_{i \neq j} w_i^T w_j = \operatorname{tr}(WEW^T) \tag{7}
$$

Where E is the matrix whose diagonal elements are zero and the other elements are all one. Combining (6) with (7), we present the objective function of GEPNMF:

$$J_D(W) = D\left(X \parallel WW^T X\right) + \frac{\alpha}{2} \mathrm{tr}\left(WEW^T\right)$$

$$+ \frac{\beta}{2} \mathrm{tr}\left(W^T X \left(L_c^{-1/2}\right)^T L_p L_c^{-1/2} X^T W\right)$$

(8)

where α is the balance parameter of the orthogonality.

3.2   Multiplicative Update Rule

To obtain the basis matrix W that minimizes the objective function (10), we first derive the MUR of W. The objective function (10) can be rewritten as $J_D(W) = J_{D1}(W) + J_{D2}(W) + J_{D3}(W)$, in which

$$J_{D1}(W) = D\left(X \parallel WW^T X\right)$$

$$= \sum_{i,j} \left[X_{ij} \log X_{ij} - X_{ij} \log \left(WW^T X\right)_{ij} \right.$$

$$\left. - X_{ij} + \left(WW^T X\right)_{ij} \right]$$

(9)

$$J_{D2}(W) = \frac{\alpha}{2} \mathrm{tr}\left(WEW^T\right)$$

(10)

$$J_{D3}(W) =$$

$$\frac{\beta}{2} \mathrm{tr}\left(W^T X \left(L_c^{-1/2}\right)^T L_p L_c^{-1/2} X^T W\right)$$

(11)

We denote $D \triangleq \left(L_c^{-1/2}\right)^T D_p L_c^{-1/2}$ and $S \triangleq \left(L_c^{-1/2}\right)^T S_p L_c^{-1/2}$. It is easy to prove that both D and S is non-negative [7]. We also denote $L \triangleq \left(L_c^{-1/2}\right)^T L_p L_c^{-1/2} = D - S$.

The first-order partial derivatives of $J_{D1}(W)$, $J_{D2}(W)$ and $J_{D3}(W)$ with respect to W_{ab} are

$$\frac{\partial J_{D1}(W)}{\partial W_{ab}} = -\left(ZX^T W\right)_{ab} - \left(XZ^T W\right)_{ab}$$

$$+ \sum_j \left(\left(W^T X\right)_{bj} + \sum_i W_{ib} X_{aj} \right)$$

(12)

where $Z_{ij} = X_{ij} / \left(WW^T X\right)_{ij}$.

$$\frac{\partial J_{D2}(W)}{\partial W_{ab}} = \alpha (WE)_{ab} \tag{13}$$

$$\frac{\partial J_{D3}(W)}{\partial W_{ab}} = \beta \left(XLX^T W \right)_{ab} \tag{14}$$

According to (12), (13) and (14), we have the gradient of $J_D(W)$ with respect to W_{ab}:

$$\begin{aligned}
\nabla_{W_{ab}} = &-\left(ZX^T W \right)_{ab} - \left(XZ^T W \right)_{ab} \\
&+ \sum_j \left(\left(W^T X \right)_{bj} + \sum_i W_{ib} X_{aj} \right) \\
&+ \alpha (WE)_{ab} + \beta \left(XLX^T W \right)_{ab}
\end{aligned} \tag{15}$$

By some simple algebra, we separate the gradient (15) into positive and negative parts as follows:

$$\nabla_{W_{ab}} = \nabla^+_{W_{ab}} - \nabla^-_{W_{ab}} \tag{16}$$

where,

$$\begin{aligned}
\nabla^+_{W_{ab}} = &\sum_j \left(\left(W^T X \right)_{bj} + \sum_i W_{ib} X_{aj} \right) \\
&+ \alpha (WE)_{ab} + \beta \left(XDX^T W \right)_{ab}
\end{aligned} \tag{17}$$

$$\begin{aligned}
\nabla^-_{W_{ab}} = &\left(ZX^T W \right)_{ab} + \left(XZ^T W \right)_{ab} \\
&+ \beta \left(XSX^T W \right)_{ab}
\end{aligned} \tag{18}$$

According to (16), we update W in the negative gradient direction at each iteration step t:

$$W_{ab}^{t+1} = W_{ab}^t - \eta_{ab}^t \left(\nabla^+_{W_{ab}^t} - \nabla^-_{W_{ab}^t} \right) \tag{19}$$

To ensure the non-negativity of W at each iteration, we choose:

$$\eta_{ab}^t = \frac{W_{ab}^t}{\nabla^+_{W_{ab}^t}} \tag{20}$$

And then,

$$W_{ab}^{t+1} = W_{ab}^t \frac{\nabla_{W_{ab}^t}^-}{\nabla_{W_{ab}^t}^+} \qquad (21)$$

Finally we can obtain the MUR of W:

$$W_{ab}^{t+1} = W_{ab}^t \frac{\left(Z'X^TW'\right)_{ab} + \left(XZ'^TW'\right)_{ab} + \beta\left(XSX^TW'\right)_{ab}}{\sum_j\left(W'^TX\right)_{bj} + \left(\sum_j X_{aj}\right)\left(\sum_i W_{ib}^t\right) + \alpha\left(W'E\right)_{ab} + \beta\left(XDX^TW'\right)_{ab}} \qquad (22)$$

3.3   Convergence Analysis

To prove the convergence of MUR for GEPNMF, we first give a definition and some lemmas as follows:

Definition 1 [2]: $G(x,x')$ is an auxiliary function for $J(x)$ if the conditions $G(x,x') \geq J(x)$, $G(x,x) = J(x)$ are satisfied.

Lemma 1 [2]: if $G(x,x')$ is an auxiliary function of $J(x)$, then $J(x)$ is non-increasing under the update:

$$x^{t+1} = \arg\min_x G(x,x') \qquad (23)$$

Lemma 2 [11]: For any matrices $X \in \mathbb{R}_+^{m\times n}, W \in \mathbb{R}_+^{m\times r}$ $W' \in \mathbb{R}_+^{m\times r}$ and $H \in \mathbb{R}_+^{r\times n}$, it holds:

$$-\sum_{i,j} X_{ij} \log(WH)_{ij}$$
$$\leq -\sum_{i,j} X_{ij} \sum_k \alpha_{ijk}\left(\log W_{ik}H_{kj} - \log\alpha_{ijk}\right), \qquad (24)$$
$$\alpha_{ijk} = \frac{W_{ik}^t H_{kj}}{\sum_l W_{il}^t H_{lj}}$$

Lemma 3 [11]: For any matrices $A \in \mathbb{R}_+^{m\times r}, W \in \mathbb{R}_+^{m\times r}$ and $W' \in \mathbb{R}_+^{m\times r}$, it holds:

$$\sum_{i,j} A_{ij}W_{ij} - \sum_{ij} A_{ij}W_{ij}' - \sum_{ij} A_{ij}W_{ij}' \log\frac{W_{ij}}{W_{ij}^t} \geq 0 \qquad (25)$$

Lemma 4 [11]: For any matrices $B \in \mathbb{R}_+^{m\times m}, W \in \mathbb{R}_+^{m\times r}$ and $W' \in \mathbb{R}_+^{m\times r}$, it holds:

$$\text{tr}(WW^TB) \geq \sum_{i,j,k} B_{kl}W_{ij}'W_{kj}'\left(1 + \log\frac{W_{ij}W_{kj}}{W_{ij}'W_{kj}'}\right) \qquad (26)$$

For the update rule, we have the following theorem:

Theorem 1: The objective function $J_D(W)$ is non-increasing under the MUR (22).
Proof: Firstly, we rewrite the objective function (8) as follows:

$$J_D(W,H) = D\left(X \| WW^T X\right) + \frac{\alpha}{2}\mathrm{tr}\left(WEW^T\right)$$
$$+ \frac{\beta}{2}\mathrm{tr}\left(HDH^T\right) - \frac{\beta}{2}\mathrm{tr}\left(W^T XSX^T W\right) \qquad (27)$$
$$s.t. \quad H = W^T X$$

By introducing Lagrangian multiplier $\{\varphi_{ij}\}$, the general Lagrangian function of the objective function (27) is formulated as follows:

$$L_D(W) \equiv \tilde{J}_D(W,H) =$$

$$D\left(X \| WW^T X\right) + \frac{\alpha}{2}\mathrm{tr}\left(WEW^T\right)$$

$$+ \frac{\beta}{2}\mathrm{tr}\left(HDH^T\right) - \frac{\beta}{2}\mathrm{tr}\left(W^T XSX^T W\right)$$

$$+ \mathrm{tr}\left(\psi^T\left(H - W^T X\right)\right)$$

$$= \sum_{i,j}(WH)_{ij} + \sum_{i,j}\left(X_{ij}\log(WH)_{ij} - X_{ij}\right)$$

$$- \sum_{i,j}X_{ij}\log(WH)_{ij} \qquad (28)$$

$$+0 \qquad (29)$$

$$+ \frac{\alpha}{2}\mathrm{tr}\left(WEW^T\right) \qquad (30)$$

$$+ \frac{\beta}{2}\mathrm{tr}\left(HDH^T\right)$$

$$- \frac{\beta}{2}\mathrm{tr}\left(W^T XSX^T W\right) \qquad (31)$$

$$+ \mathrm{tr}\left(\psi^T H\right) - \mathrm{tr}\left(\psi^T W^T X\right)$$

Construct a function as follows:

$$G_D\left(W,W'\right) =$$

$$\sum_{i,j}(WH)_{ij} + \sum_{i,j}\left(X_{ij}\log(WH)_{ij} - X_{ij}\right)$$

$$- \sum_{i,j}X_{ij}\sum_k \frac{W'_{ik}H_{kj}}{\sum_l W'_{il}H_{lj}}\left(\log W_{ik}H_{kj} - \log\frac{W'_{ik}H_{kj}}{\sum_l W'_{il}H_{lj}}\right) \qquad (32)$$

$$+ \sum_{i,j}A_{ij}W_{ij} - \sum_{i,j}A_{ij}W'_{ij} - \sum_{i,j}A_{ij}W'_{ij}\log\frac{W_{ij}}{W'_{ij}} \qquad (33)$$

$$+\alpha\left(W^{t}E\right)_{ij}\left(W_{ij}-W_{ij}^{t}\right)+C \tag{34}$$

$$+\frac{\beta}{2}\operatorname{tr}\left(HDH^{T}\right)$$

$$-\frac{\beta}{2}\sum_{i,j,k}\left(XSX^{T}\right)_{ki}W_{ij}^{t}W_{kj}^{t}\left(1+\log\frac{W_{ij}W_{kj}}{W_{ij}^{t}W_{kj}^{t}}\right) \tag{35}$$

$$+\operatorname{tr}\left(\psi^{T}H\right)-\operatorname{tr}\left(\psi^{T}W^{T}X\right)$$

Here we denote $A \triangleq XZ^{tT}W^{t}$ for notational brevity, where $Z_{ij}^{t}=X_{ij}\big/\left(W^{t}H\right)_{ij}$.

According to Lemma 2, 3, and 4, we know Eq. (28) ≤ Eq.(32), Eq. (29) ≤ Eq.(33), and Eq. (31) ≤ Eq. (35). Eq. (34) is the Taylor expansion of Eq. (30) at W_{ij}^{t}, where C is a positive scalar. It is also easy to prove $G_{D}\left(W,W\right)=L_{D}(W)$. So $G_{D}\left(W,W^{t}\right)$ is an auxiliary function of $L_{D}(W)$.

Given $\partial G_{D}\left(W,W^{t}\right)\big/\partial W_{ab}=0$, we get

$$\sum_{j}H_{bj}-\frac{W_{ab}^{t}}{W_{ab}}\left(Z^{t}X^{T}W^{t}\right)_{ab}-\left(X\psi^{T}\right)_{ab}$$

$$+A_{ab}-\frac{W_{ab}^{t}}{W_{ab}}A_{ab}+\alpha\left(W^{t}E\right)_{ab} \tag{36}$$

$$-\beta\frac{W_{ab}^{t}}{W_{ab}}\left(XSX^{T}W^{t}\right)_{ab}=0$$

Moreover, we can obtain W_{ab} that minimizes $G_{D}\left(W,W^{t}\right)$:

$$W_{ab}=W_{ab}^{t}\frac{\left(Z^{t}X^{T}W^{t}\right)_{ab}+A_{ab}+\beta\left(XSX^{T}W^{t}\right)_{ab}}{\sum_{j}H_{bj}-\left(X\psi^{T}\right)_{ab}+A_{ab}+\alpha\left(W^{t}E\right)_{ab}} \tag{37}$$

The Lagrangian multipliers can be determined by using KKT conditions. According to:

$$\frac{\partial\tilde{J}_{D}(W^{t},H)}{\partial H_{ab}}=$$

$$\sum_{i}W_{ia}^{t}-\left(W^{tT}Z^{t}\right)_{ab}+\Psi_{ab}+\beta\left(HD\right)_{ab}=0$$

We can obtain

$$\boldsymbol{\Psi}_{ab} = \left(\boldsymbol{W}^{tT}\boldsymbol{Z}^t\right)_{ab} - \sum_i \boldsymbol{W}_{ia}^t - \beta\left(\boldsymbol{HD}\right)_{ab}$$

$$\left(\boldsymbol{X\Psi}^T\right)_{ab} = \\ \left(\boldsymbol{XZ}^{tT}\boldsymbol{W}^t\right)_{ab} - \left(\sum_j \boldsymbol{X}_{aj}\right)\left(\sum_i \boldsymbol{W}_{ib}^t\right) - \beta\left(\boldsymbol{XDH}^T\right)_{ab} \tag{38}$$

Setting $\boldsymbol{H} = \boldsymbol{W}^{tT}\boldsymbol{X}$, and Substituting (38) into (37), one can get:

$$\boldsymbol{W}_{ab} = \boldsymbol{W}_{ab}^t \frac{\left(\boldsymbol{Z}^t\boldsymbol{X}^T\boldsymbol{W}^t\right)_{ab} + \left(\boldsymbol{XZ}^{tT}\boldsymbol{W}^t\right)_{ab} + \beta\left(\boldsymbol{XSX}^T\boldsymbol{W}^t\right)_{ab}}{\sum_j \left(\boldsymbol{W}^t\boldsymbol{X}\right)_{bj} + \left(\sum_j \boldsymbol{X}_{aj}\right)\left(\sum_i \boldsymbol{W}_{ib}^t\right) + \alpha\left(\boldsymbol{W}^t\boldsymbol{E}\right)_{ab} + \beta\left(\boldsymbol{XDX}^T\boldsymbol{W}^t\right)_{ab}} \tag{39}$$

Now according to Lemma 1, let $\boldsymbol{W}_{ab}^{t+1} = \boldsymbol{W}_{ab}$, we can obtain the update rule (22).

3.4 Feature Extraction

Have obtained the basis matrix $\boldsymbol{W}$, we can represent $\boldsymbol{x} \in \mathbb{R}^m$ as $\boldsymbol{y} \in \mathbb{R}^r$ in the spanned subspace of $\boldsymbol{W}$, i.e. $\boldsymbol{x} \approx \boldsymbol{Wy}$. So, given a new data $\boldsymbol{x} \in \mathbb{R}^m$ in original data space, we can obtain its low-dimensional feature $\boldsymbol{y}$ as follows:

$$\boldsymbol{y} = \boldsymbol{W}^\dagger \boldsymbol{x} \tag{40}$$

where $\boldsymbol{W}^\dagger = \left(\boldsymbol{W}^T\boldsymbol{W}\right)^{-1}\boldsymbol{W}^T$ is the pseudo-inverse of $\boldsymbol{W}$.

4 Experiments

In this section, we perform experiments on ORL [12] and CMU PIE [13] databases to evaluate the performance of our proposed GEPNMF. We compare our proposed method with some representative methods, including NMF[1][2], LNMF[4], PNMF[8], GNMF[6] and MD_NMF[7]. Noted that Nearest Neighbor classifier is used as classifier in all the methods.

4.1 ORL Database

The ORL face database [12] consists of 400 images of 40 individuals. There are 10 images each individual, with varying the lighting, facial expressions (open/closed eyes, smiling/not smiling) and facial details (glasses/no glasses). The images were acquired with a tolerance for some tilting and rotation of the face up to 20°. The original images have size 112×92 with 256 gray levels. In our experiments, all images are manually cropped and resized to be 32×32 pixels. A random subset with l (=3, 5, 7) images each individual is selected for training, and the rest for testing. For each given l, all the methods are independently run five times, and the average recognition rates are reported.

Figure 1 shows the curves of recognition rate versus feature dimension of all the methods. Table 1 gives the best recognition rates of all the methods. From Figure 1, one can see that GEPNMF outperforms the other methods in most of feature dimensions under different training sets on ORL database. From Table 1, one can also find that GEPNMF method has highest recognition rate under different training sets on ORL database.

Table 1. The best recognition rates (%) of all the methods on ORL database

method	3	5	7
NMF	76.71	89.30	92.17
LNMF	78.36	89.10	91.00
PNMF	75.36	86.50	89.00
GNMF	80.86	91.20	93.50
MD_NMF	79.29	90.70	90.17
GEPNMF	**82.79**	**93.20**	**95.33**

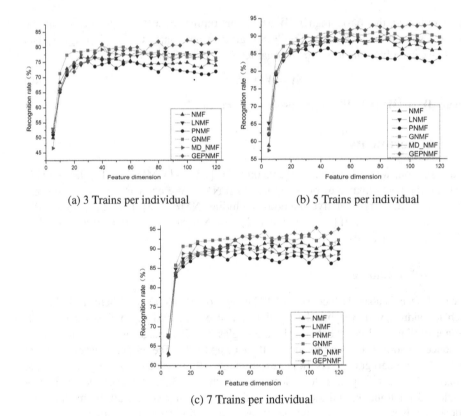

(a) 3 Trains per individual   (b) 5 Trains per individual

(c) 7 Trains per individual

Fig. 1. Recognition rate versus feature dimension of all the methods on ORL database

4.2   CMU PIE Database

The CMU PIE database [13] contains more than 40,000 face images of 68 individuals. The images were acquired across 13 poses, under 43 illumination conditions, and with 4 facial expressions. Here we use a near frontal pose subset, namely C07, for experiments, and thus, each individual has 21 images. In our experiments, each image is also cropped and resized to 32×32 pixels. l (=5, 10, 15 respectively) images each individual are randomly selected for training, and the rest for testing. For each given l, all the methods are performed independently five times, and the average recognition rates are reported.

Table 2. The best recognition rates (%) of all the methods on CMU PIE database

method	5	10	15
NMF	83.94	91.04	97.31
LNMF	75.22	78.95	84.91
PNMF	81.81	90.35	97.45
GNMF	82.26	88.93	96.48
MD_NMF	81.53	83.48	89.56
GEPNMF	**87.49**	**95.80**	**98.58**

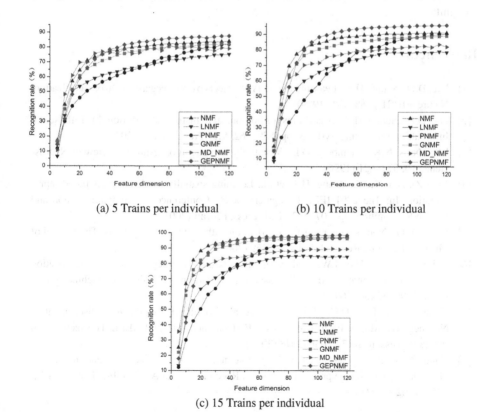

(a) 5 Trains per individual   (b) 10 Trains per individual

(c) 15 Trains per individual

Fig. 2. Recognition rate curves versus the feature dimensions of all the methods on CMU PIE database

The curves of recognition rate versus feature dimension of all the methods are presented in Figure 2. The best recognition rates of all the methods are shown in Table 2. From Figure 2 and Table 2, one can clearly see that GEPNMF outperforms the other methods under different training sets on CMU PIE database.

5   Conclusion

In this paper, we proposed a feature extraction method, namely GEPNMF, which incorporates both the local geometrical structure and the discriminative information of data into the learned subspace. According to the data label information, we first constructed two adjacent graphs that are used to create a graph regularization term. By introducing the graph embedding regularization term, the learned GEPNMF subspace can preserve the local geometrical structure of data while maximizing the margins of different classes. Experimental results on ORL and CMU PIE databases show that GEPNMF exceeds other NMF-based methods in term of recognition accuracy in face recognition.

References

[1] Lee, D.D., Seung, H.S.: Learning the parts of objects by non-negative matrix factorization. Nature 401(21), 788–791 (1999)

[2] Lee, D.D., Seung, H.S.: Algorithms for non-negative matrix factorization. In: 13th Neural Information Processing Systems, pp. 556–562. MIT Press, Denver (2001)

[3] Logothetis, N.K., Sheinberg, D.L.: Visual object recognition. Annual Review of Neuroscience 19, 577–621 (1996)

[4] Li, S.Z., Hou, X.W., Zhang, H.J., et al.: Learning spatially localized, parts-based representation. In: The 2001 IEEE Computer Society Conference on Computer Vision and Pattern Recognition, pp. 207–212. IEEE Press, Hawaii (2001)

[5] Hoyer, P.O.: Non-negative matrix factorization with sparseness constrains. The Journal of Machine Learning Research 5, 1457–1469 (2004)

[6] Cai, D., He, X.F., Han, J.W., et al.: Graph Regularized Non-negative Matrix Factorization for Data Representation. IEEE Transactions on Pattern Analysis and Machine Intelligence 33(8), 1548–1560 (2011)

[7] Guan, N.Y., Tao, D.C., Luo, Z.G., et al.: Manifold Regularized Discriminative Non-negative Matrix Factorization with Fast Gradient Descent. IEEE Transactions on Image Processing 20(7), 2030–2048 (2011)

[8] Yang, Z., Yuan, Z., Laaksonen, J.: Projective non-negative matrix factorization with application to facial image processing. Pattern Recognition and Artifical Intelligence 21(8), 1353–1362 (2007)

[9] Belkin, M.: Problems of learning on manifolds, PH.D. Dissertation, Dept. Math., University of Chicago, Chicago, IL (2003)

[10] Ding, C., Li, T., Peng, W., et al.: Orthogonal non-negative matrix tri-factorizations for clustering. In: 12th ACM SIGKDD International Conference on Knowledge discovery and Data Mining, pp. 126–135. ACM Press, New York (2006)

[11] Yang, Z., Oja, E.: Linear and nonlinear projective non-negative matrix factorization. IEEE Transactions on Neural Networks 21(6), 734–749 (2010)

[12] Samaria, F., Harter, A.: Parameterization of a stochastic model for human face identification. In: The 2nd IEEE Workshop on Applications of Computer Vision, pp. 138–142. IEEE Press, Sarasota (1994)

[13] Sim, T., Baker, S., Bsat, M.: The CMU pose, illumination, and exprssion database. IEEE Transactions on Pattern Analysis and Machine Intelligence 25(12), 1615–1618 (2003)

Sparse Manifold Preserving for Hyperspectral Image Classification

Hong Huang[1], Fulin Luo[1], Jiamin Liu[1], and Zezhong Ma[2]

[1] Key Laboratory of Optoelectronic Technology and Systems of the Education
Ministry of China, Chongqing University, Chongqing 400044, China
[2] Chongqing Institute of Surveying and Planning for Land, Chongqing 400020, China

Abstract. The graph embedding (GE) algorithms have been widely
applied for dimensionality reduction (DR) of hyperspectral image (HSI).
However, a major challenge of GE is unclear how to select the neighborhood size and define the affinity weight. In this paper, we propose
a new sparse manifold learning method, called sparse manifold preserving (SMP), for HSI classification. It constructs the affinity weight using
the sparse coefficients which reserves the global sparsity and manifold
structure of HSI data, while it doesn't need to choose any model parameters for the similarity graph. Experiments on PaviaU HSI data set
demonstrate the effectiveness of the presented SMP algorithm.

Keywords: Hyperspectral image classification, dimensionality reduction, graph embedding, sparse representation, manifold learning.

1 Introduction

Hyperspectral imagery (HSI) contains rich spectral information and has proven
to be very effective for discriminating the subtle differences in ground objects
[1]. However, classification of HSI still faces some challenges. A major one is
the curse of dimensionality, which reduces the predictive power as the dimension
increases in a fixed number of training samples [2]. Therefore the most important
and urgent issue is how to reduce the number of those bands largely with little
loss of information or classification accuracy [3].

In recent years, Yan et al. [4] proposed a graph embedding (GE) framework for
DR. In this framework, the essential issue is the way to compute the similarity
matrix of the graph and select the constraint matrix. The traditional way uses
k-nearest neighbor or ϵ-radius ball to capture the similarity matrix and the
constraint matrix. However, it is unclear how to select the neighborhood size
and define the affinity weight matrix [5,6].

Recently, some new methods were proposed for DR based sparse representation (SR) [7,8] . The representative algorithms include sparse principal component analysis (SPCA) [9], sparsity preserving projections (SPP) [10]. With
regard to SPP, it can also be unified under the GE, which need to construct
a specific graph with SR called ℓ_1-graph. The SR has the natural discriminating power, for it contains the natural discriminating information in the graph.

S. Li et al. (Eds.): CCPR 2014, Part I, CCIS 483, pp. 210–218, 2014.

Furthermore, SPP does not have to encounter model parameters such as the neighborhood size and heat kernel width incurred in LPP, NPE, etc.

In this paper, according to GE and SR, we propose a novel method named sparse manifold preserving (SMP) to obtain the similarity matrix and the constraint matrix for DR. The method inherits many merits of sparse reconstruction and constructs an adapting graph without any model parameters. It not only preserves the sparse structure relations, but also effectively extracts the discriminant feature of the data. As a result, the discriminating power of SMP is further improved than SPP and LPP.

2   Related Works

For convenience, we first give some notations used in this article. Let $\mathbf{X} = \{\mathbf{x}_1, \mathbf{x}_2, \cdots, \mathbf{x}_N\}$ be a set of N points in a high-dimensional data space $\Re^D$. The corresponding set of N points is denoted in the embedding space $\Re^d$ by $\mathbf{Y} = \{\mathbf{y}_1, \mathbf{y}_2, \cdots, \mathbf{y}_N\}$, typically $d \ll D$.

2.1   Graph Embedding

The GE framework [4] provides a unified perspective to understand most traditional DR algorithms. In GE, it needs to construct an intrinsic graph that characterizes certain statistical or geometrical properties of data. The intrinsic graph $\mathbf{G} = \{\mathbf{X}, \mathbf{W}\}$ is an undirected weighted graph with vertex set $\mathbf{X}$ and similarity matrix $\mathbf{W} \in \Re^{N \times N}$. Let $\mathbf{W} = [w_{ij}]_{N \times N}$ be a symmetric matrix, where w_{ij} is the weight measuring the similarity of the edge joining vertices i and j .

The purpose of GE is to map each vertex of the graph into a low dimensional space that preserves similarities between the vertex pairs. Then the optimal low dimensional vectors are given by the graph preserving criterion of GE as follows:

$$\mathbf{y} = \arg \min_{\mathbf{y}^T \mathbf{B} \mathbf{y} = c} \sum_{i \neq j} \|\mathbf{y}_i - \mathbf{y}_j\|^2 w_{ij} = \arg \min_{\mathbf{y}^T \mathbf{B} \mathbf{y} = c} \mathbf{y}^T \mathbf{L} \mathbf{y} \qquad (1)$$

where c is a constant, $\mathbf{B}$ is the constraint matrix defined to avoid a trivial solution of the objective function, and $\mathbf{L}$ is the Laplacian matrix of Graph $\mathbf{G}$. Typically, $\mathbf{B}$ is a diagonal matrix for scale normalization, and the Laplacian matrix $\mathbf{L}$ is difined as

$$\mathbf{L} = \mathbf{D} - \mathbf{W}, \quad \mathbf{D}_{ii} = \sum_{j \neq i} w_{ij}, \forall_i. \qquad (2)$$

2.2   Sparse Representation

In recent years, SR [11] gives rise to the attention of many researchers, which accounts for most or all information of a signal with a linear combination of a small number of elementary signals in an over-complete dictionary.

SR has compact mathematical expression. Given a signal $\mathbf{x}_i \in \Re^D$ and a matrix $\mathbf{X} = [\mathbf{x}_1, \mathbf{x}_2, \cdots, \mathbf{x}_N] \in \Re^{D \times N}$ containing the elements of an over-complete dictionary in its columns. The purpose of SR is to represent $\mathbf{x}_i$ using as few entries of $\mathbf{X}$ as possible. The objective function can be expressed as follows:

$$\min_{\mathbf{s}_i} \ \|\mathbf{s}_i\|_0$$
$$s.t. \ \ \|\mathbf{x}_i - \mathbf{X}\mathbf{s}_i\| < \varepsilon \tag{3}$$

where ε can be seen as an error tolerance, $\|\cdot\|$ represents the ℓ_2-norm operation, and $\|\mathbf{s}_i\|_0$ denotes the ℓ_0-norm of $\mathbf{s}_i$ which is equal to the number of non-zero components in $\mathbf{s}_i$.

3   Sparse Manifold Preserving

In the GE framework, k-nearest neighbor or ϵ-radius ball is mainly used to capture the similarity matrix of the graph and the constraint matrix. However, it is very difficult to select the parameters k or ϵ and define the affinity weight matrix. At the same time, SR has the merits of discovering the local relationship from the global structure of the data, the natural discriminating power and the function of selecting neighborhood automatically.

In this paper, we propose a new method, called sparse manifold preserving or SMP for short, to define the similarity matrix of the graph and the constraint matrix. The SMP algorithm constructs the sparse relationship graph and computes the similarity of among the vertices of the graph with the sparse representation coefficients. As a result, it doesn't need any model parameters for graph construction and preserves the sparse structure relationship of the data.

At first, we uses sparse representation to compute the similarity matrix of the graph. The solution of Eq. (3) is a NP-hard which can be solve using ℓ_1 instead of ℓ_0. In order to avoid the sparse coefficients to be negative, an additional condition is added in the Eq. (3), which is $\mathbf{s}_i \geq 0$. Therefore, we adopt non-negative sparse representation to solve the sparse coefficients. The objective function is formulated as follows:

$$\min_{\mathbf{s}_i} \|\mathbf{s}_i\|_1$$
$$s.t. \ \ \|\mathbf{x}_i - \mathbf{X}\mathbf{s}_i\| < \varepsilon, \ \mathbf{s}_i \geq 0 \tag{4}$$

where ε can be seen as an error tolerance.

According to the sparse coefficients matrix $\mathbf{S}$, we construct the graph $\mathbf{G}_s$ with the criterion that the vertices i and j are connected with an edge if the sparse coefficient $s_{ij} \neq 0$. The similarity weight w_{ij} is set as the value of the sparse coefficient s_{ij}. In order to preserve the sparse character in the embedding space, the objective function can be defined as follows:

$$\min \sum_{i,j=1}^{N} \left\| \mathbf{V}^T \mathbf{x}_i - \mathbf{V}^T \mathbf{x}_j \right\|^2 w_{ij} \tag{5}$$

where the similarity weight can be defined as

$$w_{ij} = \begin{cases} s_{ij}, & s_{ij} \neq 0 \\ 0, & others \end{cases} \tag{6}$$

With some simple algebraic formulations, the objective function can be reduced as

$$
\begin{aligned}
&\sum_{i,j=1}^{N} \left\| \mathbf{V}^T \mathbf{x}_i - \mathbf{V}^T \mathbf{x}_j \right\|^2 w_{ij} \\
&= \sum_{i,j=1}^{N} \mathbf{V}^T (\mathbf{x}_i w_{ij} \mathbf{x}_i^T - \mathbf{x}_i w_{ij} \mathbf{x}_j^T + \mathbf{x}_j w_{ij} \mathbf{x}_j^T - \mathbf{x}_j w_{ij} \mathbf{x}_i^T) \mathbf{V} \\
&= \sum_{i,j=1}^{N} \mathbf{V}^T (\mathbf{x}_i w_{ij} \mathbf{x}_i^T - \mathbf{x}_i w_{ij} \mathbf{x}_j^T) \mathbf{V} \\
&= 2tr(\mathbf{V}^T \mathbf{X} (\mathbf{D}_s - \mathbf{W}_s) \mathbf{X}^T \mathbf{V}) \\
&= 2tr(\mathbf{V}^T \mathbf{X} \mathbf{L}_s \mathbf{X}^T \mathbf{V})
\end{aligned} \tag{7}
$$

where $tr(\cdot)$ denotes the trace of matrix, $\mathbf{D}_s$ is a diagonal matrix with $\mathbf{D}_{ii} = \sum_{j=1}^{N} w_{ij}$, and $\mathbf{L}_s = \mathbf{D}_s - \mathbf{W}_s$ is the Laplacian matrix, $\mathbf{W}_s = [w_{ij}]_{N \times N}$ is symmetric matrix.

To remove an arbitrary scaling factor in the embedding, a constraint is imposed as follows:

$$\mathbf{V}^T \mathbf{X} \mathbf{D}_s \mathbf{X}^T \mathbf{V} = \mathbf{I} \tag{8}$$

The objective function can be recast as the following optimization problem:

$$
\begin{aligned}
&\arg \min_{\mathbf{V}} tr(\mathbf{V}^T \mathbf{X} \mathbf{L}_s \mathbf{X}^T \mathbf{V}) \\
&s.t. \mathbf{V}^T \mathbf{X} \mathbf{D}_s \mathbf{X}^T \mathbf{V} = \mathbf{I}
\end{aligned} \tag{9}
$$

With the method of Lagrangian multiplier, the optimization problem is formulated as

$$\frac{\partial}{\partial \mathbf{V}} tr \left[\mathbf{V}^T \mathbf{X} \mathbf{L}_s \mathbf{X}^T \mathbf{V} - \lambda_i (\mathbf{V}^T \mathbf{X} \mathbf{D}_s \mathbf{X}^T \mathbf{V} - \mathbf{I}) \right] = 0 \tag{10}$$

where λ_i is the Lagrangian multiplier. Then, we can get

$$\mathbf{X} \mathbf{L}_s \mathbf{X}^T \mathbf{v}_i = \lambda_i \mathbf{X} \mathbf{D}_s \mathbf{X}^T \mathbf{v}_i \tag{11}$$

where $\mathbf{v}_i$ is the generalized eigenvector. So, we can get the transformation matrix $\mathbf{V} = [\mathbf{v}_1, \mathbf{v}_2, \cdots, \mathbf{v}_d]$.

4 Experiments and Discussion

In this section, we conducted a set of experiments to evaluate the effectiveness of SMP for HSI classification.

4.1 PaviaU HSI Data Set

The PaviaU HSI data set was acquired by the ROSIS sensor during a flight campaign over Pavia University, nothern Italy, in 2002. The size of it is 610×340 pixels after removing some of the samples without information. Some channels have been removed due to noise. The remaining number of spectral bands is 103 and the geometric resolution is 1.3 meters. The image is available at http://tlclab.unipv.it. The hyperspectral image in false color and its corresponding ground truth are shown in Fig. 1(a) and Fig. 1(b) respectively.

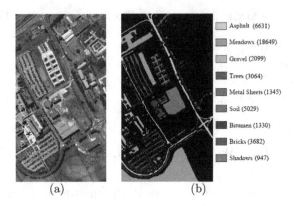

      (a)   (b)

Fig. 1. (a) The PaviaU HSI in false color. (b) Corresponding ground truth. Note that the number of samples for each class is shown in the brackets.

4.2 Experimental Setup

In the experiments, after removing noise and water absorption phenomena spectral bands of each sample, the other bands are combined into a high-dimensional vector. Then, each sample is normalized to have zero mean and unit variance.

To test every method, we adopt the the nearest neighborhood classifier (1-NN), the support vector machine classifier (SVM) and the sparse representation classifier (SRC) for classification. We use the overall classification accuracy (OA), and kappa coefficient (κ) to evaluate the classification results. To robustly evaluate the performance of different algorithms in different training and testing conditions, we selected samples randomly and repeated the experiment 20 times in each condition. The mean and standard deviation of each evaluation method is given as the final results.

In all experiments, SMP is compared with several representative DR algorithms such as PCA, LDA, MFA, NPE, LPP and SPP. In order to avoid the selection of kernel parameters, the line kernel function in Matlab Toolbox, LSSVM [13], is applied for SVM. And the penalty factor C is obtained by cross-validation. Empirically, the number of nearest neighbors k is set as 6 for MFA, NPE and LPP, and the heat kernel parameter is equal to the variance of each sample for LPP. For the error tolerance ε of sparse representation, it is optimistically set to be 0.00001 for SPP and SRC and 0.99 for SMP with the experiments in the HSI data sets.The embedding dimension of LDA is c-1 where c is the number of classes, and 40 for the other methods in the experiments.

4.3   Experiments on the PaviaU Data Set

In this subsection, classification experiments are conducted on the PaviaU data set to evaluate the performance of different methods. In the experiments, the number of training samples n_i is randomly selected from each class, and the other samples are used for testing. Table 1 shows the OA and its corresponding standard deviations (std) in the brackets for different DR algorithms and different classifiers with different n_i values.

Table 1. The OAs (in percent) of different methods and training samples on the PaviaU HSI data set

classifier	DR	$n_i = 100$	$n_i = 150$	$n_i = 200$	$n_i = 250$
	PCA	69.39(0.91)	71.14(1.06)	72.20(0.76)	73.32(0.52)
	LDA	71.15(4.10)	**75.31**(2.17)	**75.54**(2.61)	**76.53**(1.96)
	MFA	62.22(1.58)	63.69(1.31)	64.57(1.42)	65.31(1.14)
1-NN	NPE	67.92(1.12)	70.09(1.23)	71.11(1.12)	72.18(1.01)
	LPP	69.56(1.24)	72.20(1.07)	73.90(1.02)	74.81(0.74)
	SPP	66.35(1.37)	68.23(1.32)	69.65(0.87)	70.06(0.75)
	SMP	**72.05**(0.94)	74.23(0.86)	**75.10**(0.64)	**75.87**(0.70)
	PCA	**73.29**(1.62)	75.06(1.17)	75.52(1.24)	75.53(1.19)
	LDA	66.85(2.11)	68.83(1.77)	69.16(1.89)	69.46(1.15)
	MFA	66.74(1.98)	68.06(1.90)	68.19(1.77)	68.68(1.81)
SVM	NPE	70.98(2.02)	73.11(1.18)	74.05(1.39)	74.58(1.18)
	LPP	70.22(1.98)	73.11(1.17)	73.86(1.20)	74.87(1.11)
	SPP	67.89(2.14)	70.04(1.51)	70.66(1.53)	71.49(1.29)
	SMP	**72.89**(2.21)	**75.29**(1.46)	**75.73**(1.42)	**76.01**(1.39)
	PCA	69.37(0.91)	71.11(1.06)	72.18(0.76)	73.29(0.51)
	LDA	68.72(4.04)	73.11(1.88)	73.03(2.69)	73.93(2.42)
	MFA	62.90(1.63)	64.09(1.08)	64.93(1.59)	65.72(1.29)
SRC	NPE	67.84(1.12)	70.07(1.23)	71.08(1.12)	72.16(1.01)
	LPP	68.98(1.22)	71.75(1.18)	73.45(1.07)	74.39(0.83)
	SPP	66.33(1.40)	68.11(1.35)	69.54(0.84)	69.90(0.76)
	SMP	**72.57**(0.96)	**74.72**(0.90)	**75.61**(0.61)	**76.41**(0.71)

As can be seen from Table 1, for all methods, the overall classification accuracy improves with the increase of training samples. Clearly, SMP outperforms other DR methods with SVM and SRC in various number of training samples, which indicates that SMP based on graph embedding and sparse representation can preferably extract discriminative features giving benefits to HSI classification. It is also worth noting that LDA is superior to other methods in the 1-NN classifier, but LDA is a supervised methods which has a large cost to obtain the class information of training samples. Meanwhile the results of SMP is almost similar to LDA.

In order to show the classification performance of SMP for each class, we evaluate the classification accuracy of the proposed method with 250 samples per class for training, and all samples are used for testing. In the experiment, SRC are used to classify the class of test samples for all the methods. Table 2 shows the classification accuracy of each class with different DR methods using the SRC classifier, and Fig. 2 gives the classification maps of different DR methods with SRC.

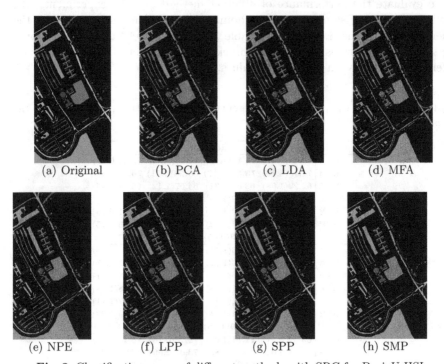

| (a) Original | (b) PCA | (c) LDA | (d) MFA |

| (e) NPE | (f) LPP | (g) SPP | (h) SMP |

Fig. 2. Classification maps of different methods with SRC for PaviaU HSI

As shown in Table 2, The SMP with SRC method gives the best results than other methods with SRC, which indicates that SMP is more effective for HSI data classification. It is important that SMP contains the sparsity and intrinsic manifold structure of data, which can obtain a good discriminant feature. In order to visualize the classification results, classification maps is given in Fig. 2, in which the result of SMP is smother compared with other methods.

4.4   Discussion

The experiments on the PaviaU HSI data set have revealed some interesting points.

Table 2. The classification results of each class using different methods with SRC on the PaviaU HSI data set

Algorithms	DR+SRC (%)						
	PCA	LDA	MFA	NPE	LPP	SPP	SMP
C1	49.98	60.01	33.33	49.65	**54.53**	52.95	53.70
C2	81.54	65.93	76.28	78.11	81.36	75.12	**85.98**
C3	79.80	73.42	54.31	76.51	79.37	73.65	**81.85**
C4	90.86	90.73	**93.11**	90.08	91.61	89.33	92.20
C5	99.63	99.48	99.85	99.55	99.55	99.78	**99.93**
C6	69.20	62.68	64.59	67.15	70.53	63.49	**73.06**
C7	75.34	**85.86**	48.80	74.96	80.75	72.78	75.56
C8	61.41	62.74	42.78	62.06	**67.93**	60.78	58.15
C9	**98.94**	98.42	97.99	99.26	99.05	99.16	98.84
OA(%)	74.81	68.89	65.86	72.85	76.35	71.26	**77.70**
κ	0.6735	0.6096	0.5622	0.6504	0.6941	0.6316	**0.7092**

- The proposed SMP method consistently outperforms PCA, LDA, MFA, NPE, LPP and SPP in most experiments on the PaviaU HSI data set. The reason is that SMP is a sparse manifold learning method, which preserve the global sparsity and the manifold structure of data. That is to say, our proposed method captures more intrinsic information hidden in the training set than other methods.
- As shown in Table 2, SMP with SRC achieves the best performance for the classification of HSI. The extracted feature obtained by SMP is more appropriate to the classification of SRC, which can truly reveal the intrinsic manifold structure of HSI. Then SMP achieve more accurate for HSI classification without choice of parameters to construct graph.

5 Conclusion

In the paper, a new method called sparse manifold preserving is proposed, based on sparse representation and graph embedding, for dimensionality reduction of hyperspectral image. The SMP method reserves the global sparsity and the manifold structure of HSI data, which can obtain more discriminative features for HSI classification. Experiment on PaviaU data set show SMP provides significantly better than PCA, LDA, MFA, NPE, LPP and SPP. How to extend the proposed SMP method to discover the multiple manifolds in HSI data appears to be another interesting direction of future work.

Acknowledgments. This work is supported by National Science Foundation of China (61101168, 41371338), the Basic and Frontier Research Programs of Chongqing (cstc2013jcyj A40005), China Postdoctoral Science Foundation (2012M511906, 2013T60837, XM2012001), the Science and Technology Project from the Land Resource and Housing Management Bureau of Chongqing (CQGT-KJ-2012028),and the Fundamental Research Funds for the Central Universities of China (1061120131204, 1061120131207, 106112013CDJZR125501).

References

1. Chen, Y., Nasrabadi, N., Tran, T.: Hyperspectral image classification via kernel sparse representation. IEEE Transactions on Geoscience and Remote Sensing 51(1), 217–231 (2013)
2. Plaza, A., Martinez, P., Plaza, J., Perez, R.: Dimensionality reduction and classification of hyperspectral image data using sequences of extended morphological transformations. IEEE Transactions on Geoscience and Remote Sensing 43(3), 466–479 (2005)
3. Huang, H., Huang, Y.: Improved discriminant sparsity neighborhood preserving embedding for hyperspectral image classification. Neurocomputing 136, 224–234 (2014)
4. Yan, S., Xu, D., Zhang, B.: Graph embedding and extensions: a general framework for dimensionality reduction. IEEE Transactions on Pattern Analysis and Machine Intelligence 29(1), 40–51 (2007)
5. Huang, H.: Classification of hyperspectral remote-sensing images based on sparse manifold learning. Journal of Applied Remote Sensing 7(1), 073464 (2013)
6. Chen, H., Chang, H., Liu, T.: Local discriminant embedding and its variants. In: IEEE Computer Society Conference on Computer Vision and Pattern Recognition, vol. 2, pp. 846–853 (2005)
7. Wright, J., Yang, A., Ganesh, A., Sastry, S., Yi, M.: Robust face recognition via sparse representation. IEEE Transactions on Pattern Analysis and Machine Intelligence 31(2), 210–227 (2009)
8. Sun, X., Wang, J., Mary, F., Kong, L.: Scale invariant texture classification via sparse representation. Neurocomputing 122, 338–348 (2013)
9. Zou, H., Hastie, T., Tibshirani, R.: Sparse principal component analysis. Journal of Computational and Graphical Statistics 15(2), 265–286 (2006)
10. Qiao, L., Chen, S., Tan, X.: Sparsity preserving projections with applications to face recognition. Pattern Recognition 43(1), 331–341 (2010)
11. Gui, J., Sun, Z., Jia, W.: Discriminant sparse neighborhood preserving embedding for face recognition. Pattern Recognition 45(8), 2884–2893 (2012)
12. Fauvel, M., Benediktsson, J., Chanussot, J., Sveinsson, J.: Spectral and spatial classification of hyperspectral data using svms and morphological profiles. IEEE Transactions on Geoscience and Remote Sensing 46(11), 3804–3814 (2008)
13. Suykens, J.A.K., Vandewalle, J.: Least squares support vector machine classifiers. Neural Processing Letters 9(3), 293–300 (1999)

Hyperspectral Image Classification Using Local Collaborative Representation

Yishu Peng [1], Yunhui Yan[1], Wenjie Zhu[2], and Jiuliang Zhao[1]

[1] School of Mechanical Engineering & Automation,
Northeastern University, Shenyang, 110819, China
[2] School of Electronic Engineering, Xidian University, Xi'an 710071, China
{yishu_peng,yunhui_yan,wenjie_zh,jiuliang_zhao}@126.com

Abstract. In this paper, a new local collaborative representation-based method is proposed for the hyperspectral image classification. First, some significant atoms are selected to represent the neighbors of the pixels based on the collaborative representation algorithm via replacing L1 with L2 to reduce the representation cost. Then, the query pixel is considered as a linear combination of these selected active atoms belong to different classes, and the ultimate classification is carried out based on the contribution of each class to the query pixel and its local neighbors. Experimental results on the real hyperspectral image confirm the effectiveness, accuracy of the method proposed.

Keywords: Hyperspectral image classification, local collaborative representation, atoms selection.

1 Introduction

Hyperspectral image (HSI) technique advances more and more rapidly, and it has many applications, such as target detection and land cover investigation [1-2]. HSI is captured by the remote sensors in hundreds of narrow spectral bands spanning the visible to infrared spectrum [3]. The bands information of a pixel in the HSI is expressed as a vector. As one of the most important application, supervised HSI classification task seeks the right class from some labeled pixels. Various techniques have been developed for HSI classification, including dimension reduction [4], support vector machines (SVMs) [5-6], fusion decision [7], and sparse representation based methods [8].

However, dimension reduction methods perform poor due to the feature extraction problem, and it is hard to make sure a proper dimension for classification task. Fusion decision accounts for too many features, and the performance depends on the decision in a big degree. As for SVMs, once the number of training samples is great, the parameters training process has a high cost. Hence, a high accuracy and effective process should be carried out for the HSI classification task.

Sparse representation based classification (SRC) has been proposed in [9]. With the assumption that the testing sample can be well represented by the training samples

S. Li et al. (Eds.): CCPR 2014, Part I, CCIS 483, pp. 219–228, 2014.
© Springer-Verlag Berlin Heidelberg 2014

from the same class, SRC fulfills the classification task with a sparse representation problem. However, [10] presents that sparsity is not the key in classification task but the collaborative representation. With a least square regularized, collaborative representation based classification (CRC) performs well. Based on the same dictionary and classifier, the only difference is that SRC selects only a few active atoms from the over-completed dictionary and CRC does not select any atoms. Hence, SRC is supervised in active atoms selection compared with CRC.

Combined with the advantages from the two dictionary-based methods, this work addresses a new solution to perform the HSI classification task based on local collaborative representation.

2   Proposed Method

2.1   Brief Review From SRC to CRC

SRC is proposed in [9], it assumes that the samples belonging to the same class lie in a low-dimension space. Hence, given a sample set $Y=[y_1, y_2, ..., y_n]$ from the same class ci, one sample of the set $y_i \in R^d$ can be well represented by the remains in the same class but other classes,

$$yi{=}j{=}1,j{\neq}inajyj{+}c{=}1,c{\neq}ci,kj{=}1nbjzj \tag{1}$$

Where the value of $\sum_{j=1,j\neq i}^{n}|a_j|$ is much bigger than that of $\sum_{c=1,c\neq c_i}^{k}\sum_{j=1}^{n}|b_j|$, k is the number of the class, and there are n samples in each class. The first term indicates the sample represented by the same class, while the second term is the representation via the samples from other $k - 1$ classes. Since the samples in each class lie in a low-dimension space, it is no doubt that all the training samples set D across k classes can represent the testing sample with a sparse coefficient:

$$y_{test} = D\alpha \tag{2}$$

Since the coefficient is sparse based on the analysis above, it solves the problem via the following optimization:

$$\tilde{\alpha} = arg \min_{\alpha}\|\alpha\|_1, \quad s.t. \ y_{test} = D\alpha \tag{3}$$

where $\|\cdot\|_1$ denotes L1 replaces   L0 indicates the number of the nonzero elements of the given vector for a low computation cost.

The class of the test sample is determined via:

$$\hat{c} = arg \min_{c}\|y_{test} - D\delta_c(\tilde{\alpha})\|_2^2 \tag{4}$$

In Eq. (4), $\delta_c(\cdot)$ is an indicator function that only keeps the elements corresponding to the i th class while setting all others to be zero.

SRC has been widely used for face recognition [11], and HSI classification task [8]. While the importance of sparsity is much emphasized in SRC and many related works, [10] devotes to analyze the working mechanism of SRC, and indicates that it is the collaborative representation but not the L0 that makes SRC powerful for classification. Hence, it solves the classification task with least square:

$$\tilde{\alpha} = arg \min_\alpha \|y_{test} - D\alpha\|_2^2 + \mu\|\alpha\|_2^2 \tag{5}$$

Where μ is the parameter, the second term is weaker than L1 in sparsity, however, it has a lower cost on solving the coefficient compared with L1, and performs well due to the first term, collaborative representation. The coefficient can be obtained easily via

$$\tilde{\alpha} = (D^T D + \mu I)^{-1} D^T y_{test} \tag{6}$$

$(\cdot)^T$ and $(\cdot)^{-1}$ denotes the transpose and inverse of a matrix, respectively. I is a unit matrix.

From SRC to CRC, the dictionary based method reduces the requirement for the representation. SRC searches for the sparsest coefficient while has a high cost on looking for the nonzero entries, and CRC pursues a low cost and remains the key term. However, it can be seen that in the final representation, SRC keeps only s(s is much smaller than the whole number of the training samples) atoms, while CRC obtain the representation across the whole training samples. It is no doubt that CRC has a low cost; the problem is that the atoms selection which SRC does while CRC not is helpful to the classification task?

2.2   Local Collaborative Representation for HSI Classification

As discussed above, SRC is too strict in solving the coefficient and has a high cost, while CRC lacks of selecting active atoms from the dictionary. It should be noted that atoms selection is important to the classification task. Atoms selection can select active training samples that helpful for classifying and decrease the impact of the negative ones. Hence, in the HSI classification task, we can select some active representation for classification with the representation obtained from collaborative representation. In this way, both the problem of computation cost of SRC and negative atoms involved in CRC can be solved in the classification task.

Local collaborative representation (LCR) means not all the training samples (atoms) are used in the final collaborative representation, preventing from the problem of   L0, and employing a least square as regularity. Diverse from CRC, with the representation derived from (6), LCR selects a few atoms to represent the testing sample for classification. Hence, with a sharper distribution than CRC that uses all the training samples to represent the testing sample, the method in [12] is appreciated in classification.

As for HSI classification, it's well known that pixels in a small spatial neighbor share the common material. For each pixel (or testing sample), the neighbors can help it select active atoms. Given a samples set consists of the testing sample and its neighbors $T = [y_{test} \ Ny]$, where the neighbors of the testing sample $Ny = [y_{test}^1, y_{test}^1, ..., y_{test}^M]$, and M is the number of the neighbors. As CRC says, we can derive the representation via:

$$\tilde{\beta} = arg \ min_\beta \|T - D\beta\|_2^2 + \mu\|\beta\|_2^2 \tag{7}$$

Similar with the solution to Eq. (5):

$$\tilde{\beta} = (D^T D + \mu I)^{-1} D^T T \tag{8}$$

It's known that rows of the coefficient are corresponding to the atoms from the dictionary that consists of different classes, and represents the contribution to the test sample. Hence, this work selects some active atoms and then computes a new representation based on them. For example, $d_l(l = 1,2, ..., N)$ is the atoms selected from the dictionary that have great contribution in representing the testing sample. We can change D into the sub-dictionary D_s that consists of the atoms selected already, and obtain the new coefficient $A = (D_s^T D_s + \mu I)^{-1} D_s^t y_{test}$.

With the new coefficient and dictionary,

$$y_{test} \approx \underbrace{A_1 d_1 + A_2 d_2}_{C_1} + \cdots \underbrace{A_l d_l + A_N d_N}_{C_k} \tag{9}$$

The class where the testing sample belongs can be determined via computing the sum of the reconstructed parts from the same class C_j. Hence, minimize the residual error $\|y_{test} - C_j\|_2$ to determine the class where the testing sample belongs.

3   Experiment Results and Analysis

3.1   Databases in the Experiment

Indiana Pines is gathered by AVIRIS sensor over the Indian Pines test site in Northwestern Indiana and consists of 145 by 145 pixels and 224 spectral reflectance bands. We have reduced the number of bands to 200 by removing bands covering the region of water absorption. As for the experiment, 9 classes of the sub-dataset are considered, with a half number of training and test samples for each class. Training samples have been randomly chosen from the reference data.

University of Pavia is of an urban area, acquired by the ROSIS sensor. It is of 610 by 340 pixels, with 103 spectral channels. The reference data contain nine classes of interest. There are 9 classes of interest in the region. 10% numbers of the training samples are randomly chosen from the reference data.

KSC is gathered by the AVIRIS sensor in the Kennedy Space Center. The original image is of 512 by 614 pixels, with 224 spectral channels, reducing the number of bands to 176 by removing bands covering the region of water absorption. In this experiment, the sub image of the original one with 512 by 455 pixels is processed. In the dataset, there are 13 classes of interest in the region. As for the number of training samples and testing samples, we select 10% of the samples as the training samples, and the rest ones are testing samples.

3.2   Experiments

3.2.1   Experiments on Performance of Atoms Selection

We make comparative experiment on the coefficient that a testing sample represented via the dictionary. First, we present the collaborative representation (global version without atoms selection) of the testing sample in Fig.1 (blue rectangle). The absolute value of the coefficient indicates the relative degree between the testing sample and the training samples.

In the nature of things the more atoms with bigger value exist in the first class the better classification result can be obtained. Fig.1 (red rectangle) presents the local collaborative representation that selects the active atoms according to the collaborative representation and represents the testing sample again.

It's well known that classification task is carried out via the linear correlation of the testing sample and the training samples in different classes. Enhancing the linear correlation of the testing sample and the training samples in the same class and repressing the linear correlation of the testing sample and the training samples in other classes can effectively guide the correct classification. Hence, we just have a check that whether active collaborative representation does this critical step.

In this experiment, 10 samples in 3 classes on Indiana Pines are selected as the training samples and a testing sample from the first class is represented via the training samples. It can be seen in Fig.1 that the LRC keeps the active atoms remain in the next step for classification and makes the active value bigger than that in collaborative representation. Besides, active collaborative representation represses the other atoms' value that may fail to have a correct classification.

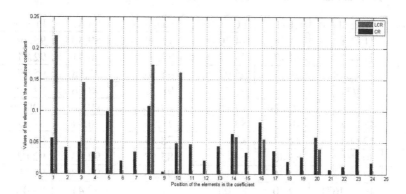

Fig. 1. Local collaborative representation (red rectangle) and collaborative representation (blue rectangle) of the testing sample selected in the simulation experiment

3.2.2 Diverse Methods on the Datasets

In the experiment, we verify the performance of the proposed method compared with the state-of-the-art methods SVM, CRC, PCA, and LDA. SVM performs well in hyperspectral image classification, and CRC has been proved parallel with SRC and easy in computing in [10].

As for the proposed method local collaborative representation, the parameter μ is set to 0.01, and the number of neighbors is 8. As two of the popular transformed methods, PCA and LDA are compared with the proposed method. With the methods of PCA and LDA that extract the feature of the samples, the nearest neighbor classifier is employed to finish the classification task.

The experimental results on the three databases are presented in Table I. It can be seen that the proposed method gets better classification accuracy than the compared methods on the Indiana Pines dataset and KSC. Among the compared methods, SVM gets the best result; however, the proposed method improves 9% at least than SVM on the Indiana Pines database, and 2% on the KSC database. As for the University of Pavia dataset, the image with many divided small regions, the proposed method performs worse than SVM due to the fact that the neighbors may come from different classes, however, better than other compared methods.

Table 1. The classification results of different methods on three databases

Methods	Indiana Pines	University of Pavia	KSC
CRC	79.30%	75.23%	70.13%
PCA+NN	84.05%	86.47%	70.32%
LDA+NN	84.14%	87.18%	75.61%
SVM	93.41%	**88.38%**	74.29%
Proposed	**94.46%**	87.77%	**76.52%**

Table 2. Classification accuracy(%) for each class on Indiana Pines dataset

class	Train/Test	CRC	PCA+NN	LDA+NN	SVM	Proposed
1	717/717	88.28	74.20	76.99	89.40	**95.40**
2	417417	40.77	73.62	72.42	90.41	**92.81**
3	249/248	81.45	95.97	95.56	**97.58**	95.97
4	374/373	96.78	97.86	98.12	**98.66**	97.59
5	245/244	**100.00**	99.18	99.18	99.18	**100.00**
6	484/484	49.38	83.68	72.93	**90.91**	87.81
7	1234/1234	82.17	80.88	78.85	91.17	**92.38**
8	307/307	65.80	66.45	85.67	**92.83**	**92.83**
9	647/647	98.76	98.15	99.23	99.38	**99.69**
all	4674/4671	79.30	84.05	84.14	93.41	**94.46**

Table 3. Classification accuracy(%) for each class on KSC dataset

class	Train/Test	CRC	PCA+NN	LDA+NN	SVM	Proposed
1	76/685	75.18	87.45	63.36	**94.45**	93.72
2	24/219	56.62	36.99	**66.67**	41.10	65.75
3	26/230	55.65	59.13	49.13	73.48	**86.52**
4	25/227	29.96	26.87	31.28	**34.36**	32.16
5	16/145	**60.00**	38.62	39.31	35.86	27.59
6	23/206	52.43	34.95	**67.48**	33.50	37.38
7	11/94	**94.68**	61.70	82.98	71.28	77.68
8	43/388	27.84	38.66	61.60	48.71	**79.38**
9	52/468	**91.45**	67.95	76.92	80.77	90.81
10	40/364	76.92	84.89	92.03	88.19	**93.68**
11	42/377	89.39	98.94	**99.20**	94.69	62.60
12	50/453	50.33	59.82	**84.99**	55.85	43.49
13	93/834	94.60	97.60	97.72	97.60	**100.00**
all	521/4890	70.13	70.32	75.61	74.29	**76.52**

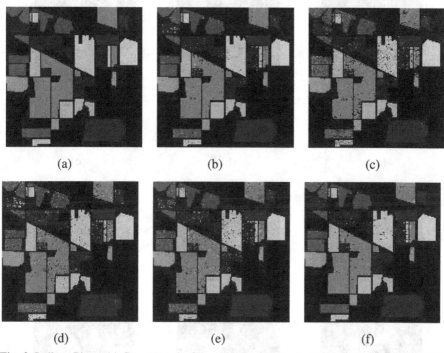

(a)   (b)   (c)

(d)   (e)   (f)

Fig. 2. Indiana Pines: (a) Ground truth. Classification results via (b) SVM, (c) CRC, (d) PCA, (e) LDA, and (f) the proposed method.

The classification results of different classes on Indiana Pines and KSC datasets are presented in Table 2 and Table 3, respectively. As for the result for each class of Indiana Pines presented in Table 2, SVM and the proposed method have an obviously better performance than others. More precisely, the proposed method outperforms SVM. As for KSC in Table 3, it can be seen that the dictionary based methods get a better result than SVM on the most of classes, however, the proposed method get the best overall result. Indiana Pines has a relatively bigger number of training samples than KSC. Hence, the projection based methods seem more active than SVM. The visual results of different methods on the three datasets are presented in Fig. 2, Fig.3, and Fig.4, respectively. In Fig. 2-4, (a) is the ground truth of the scene classification result, and the different label information is painted with different colors. From (b) to (f) are SVM, PCA, LDA, and the proposed method, respectively. It is obvious to observe the performance of the different methods used for comparison.

As the results of simulation experiment and the real hyperspectral image classification presented, the proposed method that uses the local training samples to collaboratively represent the testing samples can make the testing sample discriminative for classification task.

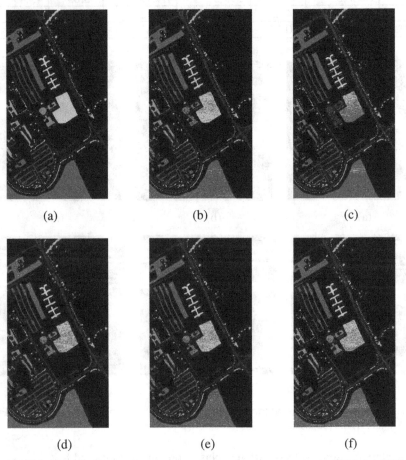

Fig. 3. University of Pavia: (a) Ground truth. Classification results via (b) SVM, (c) CRC, (d) PCA, (e) LDA, and (f) the proposed method.

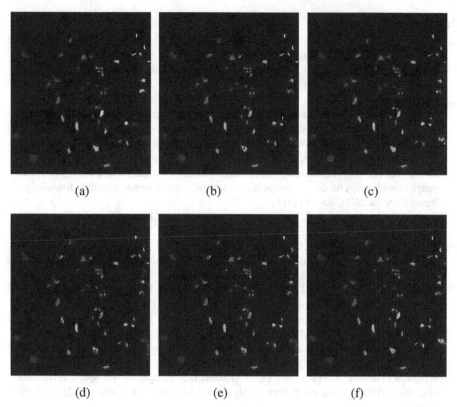

Fig. 4. KSC: (a) Ground truth. Classification results via (b) SVM, (c) CRC, (d) PCA, (e) LDA, and (f) the proposed method.

4   Conclusions

A novel local collaborative representation of the testing sample approach for HSI classification has been proposed in this paper. The method selects the active atoms that benefits for representing the discriminative feature via the primal collaborative representation. The proposed method prevents from the non-convex problem solution while keeping the active key in the sparse dictionary based methods. Simulation experimental result conducts that the collaborative representation leads to a better classification performance, and experimental result on the real hyperspectral image datasets improve the accuracy.

Acknowledgement. This project is supported by NSF of China (60703109) and Fundamental Research Funds for Central Universities (K50510020023).

References

1. Patel, N.K., Patnaik, C., Dutta, S., Shekh, A.M., Dave, A.J.: Study of crop growth parameters using airborne imaging spectrometer data. International Journal of Remote Sensing 22(12), 2401–2411 (2001)
2. Datt, B., McVicar, T.R., Van Niel, T.G., Jupp, D.L.B., Pearlman, J.S.: Preprocessing EO-1 hyperion hyperspectral data to support the application of agricultural indexes. IEEE Trans. Geoscience and Remote Sensing 41(6), 1246–1259 (2003)
3. Borengasser, M., Hungate, W.S., Watkins, R.: Hyperspectral Remote Sensing—Principles and Applications. CRC Press, Boca Raton (2008)
4. Li, S., Wu, H., Wan, D., Zhu, J.: An effective feature selection method for hyperspectral image classification based on genetic algorithm and support vector machine. Knowledge–Based Systems 24(1), 40–48 (2011)
5. Gualtieri, J.A., Cromp, R.F.: Support vector machines for hyperspectral remote sensing classification. In: Proc. SPIE, vol. 3584, pp. 221–232 (1998)
6. Melgani, F., Bruzzone, L.: Classification of hyperspectral remote sensing images with support vector machines. IEEE Trans. Geoscience and Remote Sensing 42(8), 1778–1790 (2004)
7. Zhang, L., Zhang, L., Tao, D., Huang, X.: On Combining Multiple Features for Hyperspectral Remote Sensing Image Classification. IEEE Trans. Geoscience and Remote Sensing 50(3), 879–893 (2012)
8. Chen, Y., Nasrabadi, N.M., Tran, T.D.: Hyperspectral Image Classification Using Dictionary-Based Sparse Representation. IEEE Trans. Geoscience and Remote Sensing 49(10), 3973–3985 (2011)
9. Wright, J., Ganesh, A., Yang, A., Yi, M.: Robust face recognition via sparse representation. IEEE Transactions on Pattern Analysis and Machine Intelligence 31(2), 210–227 (2009)
10. Zhang, L., Yang, M., Feng, X.C.: Sparse representation or collaborative representation: which helps face recognition? In: ICCV (2011)
11. Yang, J., Wang, J., Huang, T.: Learning the sparse representation for classification. In: ICME (2011)
12. Xu, Y., Zhang, D., Yang, J., Yang, J.: A Two-Phase Test Sample Sparse Representation Method for Use with Face Recognition. IEEE Trans. Circuits and Systems for Video Technology 21(9), 1255–1262 (2011)

Simplified Constraints Rank-SVM
for Multi-label Classification

Jiarong Wang[1], Jun Feng[1], Xia Sun[1,2], Su-Shing Chen[2], and Bo Chen[1]

[1] Information Science and Technology College, Northwest University, Xi'an 710127
[2] Computer Information Science and Engineering Department,
University of Florida, Gainesville, FL 32611
`jiarongrongg@gmail.com`

Abstract. In this paper, we propose a Simplified Constraints Rank-SVM (SCRank-SVM) for multi-label classification based on well established Rank-SVM algorithm. Based on the features of the application, we remove the bias term b and modify the decision boundary. Due to the absence of term b, SCRank-SVM has milder optimization constraints. Therefore, SCRank-SVM achieves better solution space compared with Rank-SVM. Experimental results on five datasets show that the proposed algorithm is a powerful candidate for multi-label classification, compared with four existing state of the art multi-label algorithms according to four indicative measures.

Keywords : Rank-SVM, multi-label classification, bias b.

1   Introduction

Traditional supervised learning investigates problems in which each instance is only associated with a single class label and these class labels are mutually exclusive. However, in many real-world applications, one instance might be complicated and possibly belongs to several labels simultaneously. For instance, in functional genomics, each gene may have multiple functions, such as metabolism, transcription and protein synthesis, yielding multiple labels. Such classification setting is referred to multi-label classification.

Nowadays, two distinct strategies are proposed for multi-label classification: problem transformation and algorithm adaptation [1].

Problem transformation tackles multi-label classification problem by transforming it into either one or more single-label sub-problems, and solves these sub-problems. Furthermore, it constructs sub-classifier using well-established learning technique, and then assembles sub-classifiers into an entire multi-label classifier [2]. The representative algorithms include Binary Relevance [3] and Label Powerset [4].

Different from problem transformation, algorithm adaptation extends some specific multi-class classification algorithm to deal with multi-label data directly. Multi-label k Nearest Neighbor (ML-kNN) [5] algorithm is one of algorithm adaptation, which is

S. Li et al. (Eds.): CCPR 2014, Part I, CCIS 483, pp. 229–236, 2014.

derived from the traditional k Nearest Neighbor (kNN) algorithm. What's more, multi-label BP neural network (BP-MLL) [6] and Multi-label Support Vector Machine (Rank-SVM) [7] are also typical algorithm adaptation method.

Focusing on both the computational cost reducing and the classification performance improvement, in this paper, we propose a Simplified Constraints Rank-SVM (SCRank-SVM) for multi-label classification. We find that, for some kinds of data, the parameter b in SVM classifier can be simplified, and the theoretic proving further confirms the conclusion. To consummate this classification framework, firstly, the decision boundary and separating margin of multi-label classification system without bias b is defined, and then the separating margin is maximized, while keeping minimization of the Ranking loss function. Afterwards, the multi-label model is built by solving a quadratic optimization problem. Eventually, the corresponding label sets for the unseen instances are predicted by the threshold function which is estimated by linear regression. Experimental results on five datasets show that SCRank-SVM achieves rather competitive performance, compared with four existing state of the art multi-label algorithms according to four indicative measures.

The rest of this paper is organized as follows. Rank-SVM algorithm is summarized in Section 2. Our algorithm is proposed in Section 3. Section 4 is devoted to experiments with five datasets. And this paper ends with conclusions in Section 5.

2   Rank-SVM for Multi-label Classification

Rank-SVM [7] adapts maximum margin strategy to solve multi-label problem, and meanwhile a set of linear classifiers are optimized to minimize the empirical ranking loss and enabled to handle nonlinear cases with kernel tricks. Here, we summarize Rank-SVM algorithm briefly.

Denote a training set of size m by $D = \{(x_i, Y_i) | 1 \leq i \leq m\}$, where $x_i \in R^d$ is a d-dimension feature vector and $Y_i \subseteq \mathcal{Y}, \mathcal{Y} = \{y_1, y_2, \ldots, y_q\}$, x_i and Y_i represent the ith instance and its relevant label sets respectively. In the same time, the complement of Y_i, i.e. $\bar{Y}_i = \mathcal{Y} \setminus Y_i$, is called as the irrelevant set of labels.

Discrimination boundary is defined as $\langle w_k - w_l, x \rangle + b_k - b_l = 0$, here $w_k, w_l \in R^d$ and $b_k, b_l \in R$ is the weight vectors and bias terms respectively. Correspondingly, the classification system's margin on (x_i, Y_i) is defined. It is reasonable that the labels belonging to an instance should be ranked higher than those not belonging to that instance.

$$\min_{(y_k, y_l) \in Y_i \times \bar{Y}_i} \frac{\langle w_k - w_l, x_i \rangle + b_k - b_l}{w_k - w_l} \tag{1}$$

After that, maximize the classification system's margin in the whole training set D and meanwhile a slack variable is incorporated by considering real-world situation. Therefore, we can get:

$$\max_{w_j,\,j=1,\ldots,q} \;\min_{(x_i,Y_i)\in D} \;\min_{(y_k,y_l)\in Y_i\times\overline{Y}_i} \frac{1}{\left\|w_k - w_l\right\|^2} \tag{2}$$

Subject to: $\left\langle w_k - w_l, x_i \right\rangle + b_k - b_l \geq 1 - \xi_{ikl}\,,\;\; \xi_{ikl} \geq 0\left(1 \leq i \leq m, \left(y_k, y_l\right) \in Y_i \times \overline{Y}_i\right)$

Accordingly, an approximate ranking loss function can be expressed as:

$$\text{Ranking loss} \approx \frac{1}{m}\sum_{i=1}^{m}\frac{1}{\left|Y_i\right|\left|\overline{Y}_i\right|}\sum_{(y_k,y_l)\in Y_i\times\overline{Y}_i}\xi_{ikl} \tag{3}$$

The Ranking loss is utilized as an empirical loss function after $1/m$ is omitted.

The original optimization problem of Rank-SVM is formulated as:

$$\min_{w_j,\,j=1,\ldots,q}\sum_{k=1}^{q}\left\|w_k\right\|^2 + C\sum_{i=1}^{m}\frac{1}{\left|Y_i\right|\left|\overline{Y}_i\right|}\sum_{(y_k,y_l)\in Y_i\times\overline{Y}_i}\xi_{ikl} \tag{4}$$

Subject to: $\left\langle w_k - w_l, x_i \right\rangle + b_k - b_l \geq 1 - \xi_{ikl}\,,\;\; \xi_{ikl} \geq 0\left(1 \leq i \leq m, \left(y_k, y_l\right) \in Y_i \times \overline{Y}_i\right)$

Where C represents the regularization constant.

Using the standard Lagrangian technique, the dual version of (4) is derived by:

$$\min_{\alpha_{ikl}}\frac{1}{2}\sum_{k=1}^{q}\sum_{h,i=1}^{m}\eta_{kh}\eta_{ki}\left\langle x_h, x_i \right\rangle - \sum_{i=1}^{m}\sum_{(y_k,y_l)\in Y_i\times\overline{Y}_i}\alpha_{ikl} \tag{5}$$

Subject to: $\displaystyle\sum_{i=1}^{m}\sum_{(y_j,y_l)\in Y_i\times\overline{Y}_i}c_{ijl}\alpha_{ijl} = 0\;\;,0 \leq \alpha_{ikl} \leq C_i = \frac{C}{\left|Y_i\right|\left|\overline{Y}_i\right|}$

with $c_{ijl} = \begin{cases} 0,\; j \neq k,\, l \neq k \\ +1,\; j = k \\ -1,\; l = k \end{cases}$ and $\eta_{ki} = \displaystyle\sum_{(y_j,y_l)\in Y_i\times\overline{Y}_i}c_{ijl}\alpha_{ijl}$

Here, the dot product between two vectors in (5) can be replaced by various kernels.

Additionally, an optimal threshold is determined via the following formulation:

$$t(x_i) = \arg\min_t \left| \left\{ y_k \in Y \text{ s.t.} f_k(x_i) \leq t \right\} \right| + \left| \left\{ y_k \in \overline{Y} \text{ s.t.} f_k(x_i) \geq t \right\} \right| \tag{6}$$

where $f_k(x_i) = \langle w_k, x_i \rangle + b_k$. Finally, this threshold form is to predict the relevant labels in the testing phase by (7):

$$Y = \left\{ y_k | f_k(x) > t(x), 1 \leq k \leq q \right\} \tag{7}$$

3   Simplified Constraints Rank-SVM

Support Vector Machine (SVM) is originated from Support Vector Networks. Based on neural networks, Cortes [8] proposed the concept of Support Vector Networks. However, Cortes made no mention of the significance of bias term b, and whether the bias term b is always needed or not.

Poggio [9] has testified that the bias term b is not essential when the kernel function is positive definite. Furthermore, in application domains, Extreme Learning Machine [10] and Selective Recursive Kernel Learning [11] have achieved competitive performance in the situation which has not the bias term b. On the other hand, through XOR classification experiments, Ding [12] has proved that origin SVM tends to find a solution which is sub-optimal to SVM without bias term b, and SVM without bias term b obtains better generalization performance and lower computational complexity than origin SVM.

According to the above theory, we propose Simplified Constraints Rank-SVM (SCRank-SVM) multi-label classification algorithm. First, we redefine the decision boundary of the Rank-SVM, yielding the hyperplanes:

$$\langle w_k - w_l, x \rangle = 0 \tag{8}$$

The classification system's margin on the whole training set D is written as:

$$\min_{(x_i, Y_i) \in D} \min_{(y_k, y_l) \in Y_i \times \overline{Y}_i} \frac{\langle w_k - w_l, x_i \rangle}{\|w_k - w_l\|} \tag{9}$$

The original optimization problem of SCRank-SVM is constructed as:

$$\min_{w_j, j=1,\ldots,q} \sum_{k=1}^{q} \|w_k\|^2 + C \sum_{i=1}^{m} \frac{1}{|Y_i||\overline{Y}_i|} \sum_{(y_k, y_l) \in Y_i \times \overline{Y}_i} \xi_{ikl} \tag{10}$$

Subject to: $\langle w_k - w_l, x_i \rangle \geq 1 - \xi_{ikl}$, $\xi_{ikl} \geq 0 \left(1 \leq i \leq m, (y_k, y_l) \in Y_i \times \overline{Y}_i \right)$

Here C is a user-specified parameter to provide a trade-off between the separating margin and the ranking loss.

Using the standard Lagrangian technique, we derive the dual version of (10) as:

$$\min_{\alpha_{ikl}} \frac{1}{2} \sum_{k=1}^{q} \sum_{h,i=1}^{m} \eta_{kh} \eta_{ki} \langle x_h, x_i \rangle - \sum_{i=1}^{m} \sum_{(y_k, y_l) \in Y_i \times \overline{Y}_i} \alpha_{ikl} \tag{11}$$

$$\text{Subject to: } 0 \leq \alpha_{ikl} \leq C_i = \frac{C}{|Y_i||\overline{Y}_i|} \text{ with } \eta_{ki} = \sum_{(y_j, y_l) \in Y_i \times \overline{Y}_i} c_{ijl} \alpha_{ijl}$$

Similarly, our SCRank-SVM can also be kernelized by various kernels satisfying Mercer theorem. Additionally, SCRank-SVM also needs a threshold function, which is estimated using the same method as in Rank-SVM.

From the dual version of Rank-SVM and SCRank-SVM, i.e. formulation (5) and (11), it is found that, Rank-SVM and SCRank-SVM have similar optimization objective functions, while different from the Rank-SVM, SCRank-SVM only needs to satisfy the condition $0 \leq \alpha_{ikl} \leq C_i$ and has not equality constraint. Since, SCRank-SVM has milder optimization constraints, thus, Rank-SVM obviously tends to find a solution which is sub-optimal to SCRank-SVM's solution.

Furthermore, Rank-SVM always searches for the optimal solution in the hyperplane $\sum_m \sum c_{ijl} \alpha_{ijl} = 0$ within the cube $[0, C_i]^m$. It means that Rank-SVM's search area depends more on the target labels instead of the combination of (x_i, Y_i). If the instances of two different training sets are irrelevant while the label sets associated with the instances are similar to each other, the Rank-SVM may search optimal solution in the similar areas of the cube $[0, C_i]^m$ for two different cases, which actually implies that the bias b should not be required.

4   Experiments

4.1   Comparing Algorithms , Datasets and Evaluation Metrics

In this paper, we selected four existing multi-label classification methods for performance comparison: Rank-SVM [7], BP-MLL [6], MLNB [13] and ML-kNN [5]. We accept their recommended parameter settings in [6] [13] [5].

To compare the proposed SCRank-SVM with the above mentioned four classification methods, we collect five open datasets: Genbase, Emotions, Yeast, Scene and Enron. Table 1 shows some useful statistics of these datasets, such as, the number of instances in the training and testing sets, the number of attributes, the number of labels, and the average labels. These datasets cover four different domains, i.e. biology, music, scene and text.

Table 1. Statistics for our five datasets in the experiment

Dataset	Domain	Instances		Attributes	Labels	Average
		Train	Test			labels
Genbase	Biology	463	199	1185	27	1.35
Yeast	Biology	1500	917	103	14	4.24
Emotions	Music	391	202	72	6	1.87
Scene	Scene	1211	1196	294	6	1.07
Enron	Text	1123	579	1001	53	3.38

Four popular metrics are adopted in our experiment, i.e. one error, coverage, ranking loss and average precision [1]. Multi-label algorithm should achieve a larger value for the average precision, and smaller values for the other three metrics.

4.2   Experimental Results

In our work, the Gaussian kernel $k(x_i, x_j) = e^{(\gamma \|x_i - x_j\|_2^2)}$ is employed for the SCRank-SVM and Rank-SVM. Besides, there are five parameters: $\gamma, C, M, \lambda, \alpha$ in both SCRank-SVM and Rank-SVM. To reduce the search space of possible parameter combinations, we set $M = 50$, $\lambda = 10^{-6}$ and $\alpha = 10^{-3}$. Therefore, two parameter γ and M need to be tuned based on testing data. In table 2, the optimal γ and M values and corresponding Average Precision criterions are shown on the five datasets. The other experimental results are presented in Tables 3-5 according to other three various measures. Furthermore, the best performance among the five comparing algorithms is highlighted in boldface.

Table 2. The optimal (γ, C) and corresponding Average Precision on five datasets

Datasets	Algorithm						
	SCRank-SVM		Rank-SVM		ML-kNN	BP-MLL	MLNB
Genbase	$(2^1, 2^1)$	**0.9954**	$(2^{-2}, 2^3)$	0.9937	0.9914	0.9914	0.0568
Emotions	$(2^1, 2^2)$	**0.8149**	$(2^{-1}, 2^0)$	0.7958	0.7907	0.7757	0.7696
Yeast	$(2^3, 2^3)$	**0.7708**	$(2^0, 2^2)$	0.7668	0.7585	0.7504	0.7461
Scene	$(2^{-2}, 2^2)$	0.8763	$(2^{-4}, 2^3)$	**0.8814**	0.8512	0.4532	0.8167
Enron	$(2^{-5}, 2^6)$	**0.6953**	$(2^{-6}, 2^2)$	0.6718	0.6234	0.6926	0.2203

Table 3. Coverage from five methods on five datasets

datasets	Algorithm				
	SCRank-SVM	Rank-SVM	ML-kNN	BP-MLL	MLNB
Genbase	**0.4472**	0.4472	0.5779	0.6030	21.1307
Emotions	**1.7970**	1.8267	1.8762	1.9703	2.0644
Yeast	**6.0981**	6.4427	6.4144	6.4242	6.5889
Scene	**0.4423**	0.4540	0.5686	2.1798	0.6530
Enron	11.7927	11.8290	13.1226	**11.4301**	20.6874

As shown in Table 2, SCRank-SVM and Rank-SVM achieve four and one best Average Precision values respectively, obviously, SCRank-SVM is superior to Rank-SVM and other four methods. In Table 3 and Table 5, SCRank- SVM and BP-MLL work the best on four datasets and one dataset. Furthermore, SCRank-SVM performs better than the remained four methods. In table 4 of one error, SCRank-SVM and Rank-SVM work the best on two datasets respectively. Additionally, SCRank-SVM is superior to Rank-SVM on Enron dataset. Therefore, SCRank-SVM further obtains the best performance. It is surprised that MLNB fails on Genbase dataset because of its unacceptable metric values.

Table 4. One error from five methods on five datasets

Datasets	Algorithm				
	SCRank-SVM	Rank-SVM	ML-kNN	BP-MLL	MLNB
Genbase	0	0.0050	0.0050	0	1
Emotions	**0.2772**	0.3069	0.3020	0.3069	0.3218
Yeast	0.2268	**0.2236**	0.2345	0.2366	0.2519
Scene	0.2082	**0.1923**	0.2425	0.8269	0.3010
Enron	0.240069	0.248705	0.3040	**0.2332**	0.4836

Table 5. Ranking loss from five methods on five datasets

Datasets	Algorithm				
	SCRank-SVM	Rank-SVM	ML-kNN	BP-MLL	MLNB
Genbase	**0.0037**	0.0038	0.0064	0.0077	0
Emotions	**0.1515**	0.1586	0.1615	0.1826	0.1883
Yeast	**0.1598**	0.1681	0.1715	0.1751	0.1792
Scene	**0.0681**	0.0693	0.0931	0.4179	0.1118
Enron	0.0764	0.080025	0.0933	**0.0739**	0.1586

According to the above experiments and analysis, it can be demonstrated that our SCRank-SVM is the strongest method compared with four state of the art multi-label methods.

5   Conclusion

In this paper, we propose a Simplified Constraints Rank-SVM (SCRank-SVM) for multi-label classification. From the point of Poggio, the bias b is not necessary. Hence, the bias term b is simplified and the decision boundary is recast to obtain lower computational cost and better classification performance. Experimental results on five datasets demonstrate that SCRank-SVM achieves rather competitive performance, compared with four existing state of the art multi-label classification algorithms according to four indicative measures. In future, we will further research the validity of SVM-type algorithm without term b.

References

1. Zhang, M., Zhou, Z.: A Review on Multi-Label Learning Algorithms. IEEE Transactions on Knowledge and Data Engineering (2013)
2. Xu, J.-H.: An efficient multi-label support vector machine with a zero label. Expert Systems with Applications 39(5), 4796–4804 (2012)
3. Boutell, M.R., Luo, J., Shen, X., et al.: Learning multi-label scene classification. Pattern Recognition 37(9), 1757–1771 (2004)
4. Li, S.-N., Li, N., Li, Z.-H.: Multi-label Data Mining: A Survey. Computer Science 40(4), 14–21 (2013) (李思思,李宁,李战怀. 多标签数据挖掘技术：研究综述. 计算机科学 40(4), 14–21 (2013))
5. Zhang, M.-L., Zhou, Z.-H.: ML-kNN: A lazy learning approach to multi-label learning. Pattern Recognition 40(7), 2038–2048 (2007)
6. Zhang, M.-L., Zhou, Z.-H.: Multi-label neural networks with applications to functional genomics and text categorization. IEEE Transactions on Knowledge and Data Engineering 18(10), 1338–1351 (2006)
7. Elisseeff, A., Weston, J.: A kernel method for multi-labeled classification. In: NIPS, vol. 14, pp. 681–687 (2001)
8. Cortes, C., Vapnik, V.: Support vector networks. Machine Learning 20(3), 273–297 (1995)
9. Poggio, T., Mukherjee, S., Rifkin, R., et al.: Technical Report A.I.Memo.No.2001-011, Artificial Intelligence Laboratory, Massachusetts Institute of Technology, USA (2001)
10. Huang, G.B., Ding, X., Zhou, H.: Optimization method based extreme learning machine for classification. Neurocomputing 74(1), 155–163 (2010)
11. Liu, Y., Wang, H., Yu, J., et al.: Selective recursive kernel learning for online identification of nonlinear systems with NARX form. Journal of Process Control 20(2), 181–194 (2010)
12. Ding, X.-J., Zhao, Y.-L.: Influence of Bias b on Generalization Ability of SVM for classification. Acta Automatica Sinica 37(9), 1105–1113 (2011) (丁晓剑,赵银亮. 偏置b 对支持向量机分类问题泛化性能的影响. 自动化学报 37(9), 1105–1113 (2011))
13. Zhang, M.-L., Peña, J.M., Robles, V.: Feature selection for multi-label naive bayes classification. Information Sciences 179(19), 3218–3229 (2009)

Semi-supervised Image Classification Learning Based on Random Feature Subspace

Liu Li[1,2], Zhang Huaxiang[1,2], Hu Xiaojun[1,2], and Sun Feifei[1,2]

[1] School of Information Science and Engineering, Shandong Normal University, Jinan 250014
[2] Shandong Provincial Key Laboratory for Novel Distributed Computer Software Technology, Jinan 250014

Abstract. Image classification is a well-known classical problem in multimedia content analysis. In this paper a framework of semi-supervised image classification method is presented based on random feature subspace. Firstly, color spatial distribution entropy is introduced to represent the color spatial information, and texture feature are extracted by using Gabor filter. Then random subspaces of the feature vector are dynamically generated from mixed feature vector as different views. Finally, three classifiers are trained by the classified images and tri-training algorithm is applied to classify sample images. Experimental results strongly demonstrate the effectiveness and robustness of the proposed system.

Keywords: semi-supervised learning, feature extraction, random subspace, tri-training.

1 Introduction

Image classification is one of the fundamental problems in computer vision and plays a critical role in many applications [1-4]. Although supervised learning methods [5-8] have been widely employed and proven effective in image classification, they normally depend on a large amount of classified data, which usually involves high cost in labor and time. To overcome this problem, various semi-supervised learning methods are proposed to effectively utilize a small scale of classified images along with a larger amount of unclassified images.

However, most of existing semi-supervised learning methods seldom consider a more common case where class distribution is imbalanced. If there are not enough training images from image classes, it will be difficult to get good image classification results. In fact, semi-supervised learning on imbalanced classification is rather challenging, so imbalanced classification requires specifically-designed classification algorithm. Although many methods [9-13] have been proposed to solve this issue, it is still difficult to select suitable method to handle the imbalanced problem in image classification.

To deal with the imbalanced problem in image classification, we utilize the classified images fully from initial training images and combine them to form new initial training sets. Accordingly, a semi-supervised tri-training method can be used to classify unclassified images. Besides, to get better classification results, color spatial

S. Li et al. (Eds.): CCPR 2014, Part I, CCIS 483, pp. 237–242, 2014.

distribution entropy for each color channel is introduced and texture feature are extracted by using Gabor filter.

The remainder of this paper is organized as follows. Section 2 introduces the color and texture feature extraction. In Section 3, the image classified method is described. Section 4 presents the experimental results. Finally, conclusions are given in Section 5.

2   Color and Texture Feature Extraction

The feature extraction plays an important role in image classification. The color and texture are important features for image representation which are widely used.

2.1   Color Feature

For given image $I(x,y)$ with size $P \times Q$, the color of a certain color channel is divided into N blocks $B_1, B_2, ..., B_N$ uniformly. Set the image center C as the center of circles, then the image is segmented to some ring areas by concentric circles. The segmentation radius of the $i-th$ ring area is defined as follows

$$R_i = \frac{kr^q}{M}, 1 \leq k \leq M \tag{1}$$

where r is the basic radius, and M is a positive integer. The tags of the inner ring and outer ring are 1 and K respectively.

After the image is segmented into some ring areas, we obtain the spatial distribution density of color block B_i in the $j-th$ ring area

$$P_{ij} = |R_{ij}| / |R_i| \tag{2}$$

where $|R_i|$ denotes the number of pixels whose color is in color block B_i, and $|R_{ij}|$ represents the number of pixels whose color is in color block B_i of the $j-th$ ring.

The distribution of pixels in the same color block is more concentrated, the human visual simulation of color is stronger. So weight function $f(j)$ is utilized to express the contribution of human visual stimulation due to the different position of ring area. The spatial distribution entropy of the color block B_i is defined as follows

$$E_i = -\sum_{j=1}^{K} f(j) P_{ij} \log_2 P_{ij} = -\sum_{j=1}^{K} e^{-r^j} P_{ij} \log_2 P_{ij} \tag{3}$$

The other two color channels are processed as above, and then the color feature can be extracted to express the color distribution.

2.2   Texture Feature

Gabor filters are a group of wavelets, with each wavelet capturing energy at a specific frequency and a specific direction. The scale and orientation tunable property of Gabor filter make it especially useful for texture analysis.

For a given image $I(x,y)$ with size $P \times Q$, its discrete Gabor wavelet transform is given by a convolution

$$G_{mn}(x, y) = \sum_{s} \sum_{t} I(x-s, y-t) \psi_{mn}^{*}(s,t)$$

(4)

where s and t are filter mask size variables, and ψ_{mn}^{*} is the complex conjugate of which is a class of self-similar functions generated from dilation and rotation of the following mother wavelet.

The self-similar Gabor wavelets are obtained through the generating function

$$\psi_{mn}(x, y) = a^{-m} \psi(\tilde{x}, \tilde{y})$$

(5)

where m and n specify the scale and orientation of the wavelet respectively, with $m = 0,1,...,M-1$, $n = 0,1,..., N-1$, and

$$\tilde{x} = a^{-m}(x\cos\theta + y\sin\theta)$$
$$\tilde{y} = a^{-m}(-x\sin\theta + y\cos\theta), (a>1, \theta = n\pi / N)$$

(6)

After applying Gabor filter on the image with different orientation at different scale, we obtain an array of magnitudes

$$E(m, n) = \sum_{x} \sum_{y} |G_{mn}(x, y)|$$

(7)

These magnitudes represent the energy content at different scale and orientation of the image. The mean μ_{mn} and standard deviation σ_{mn} of the transformed coefficients are used to represent the feature

$$\mu_{mn} = \frac{E(m,n)}{P \times Q}$$

$$\sigma_{mn} = \frac{\sqrt{\sum_{x} \sum_{y} (|G_{mn}(x, y)| - \mu_{mn}|)^2}}{P \times Q}$$

(8)

A feature vector is created using μ_{mn} and σ_{mn} as the feature components.

3   Semi-supervised Learning for Image Classification

This paper employs the tri-training technique in semi-supervised learning for image classification. In particular, different views are generated from random feature subspaces.

3.1   Random Subspace Generation

Assume $x = (x_1, x_2,..., x_n)$ the training data and x_i a m-dimensional vector $X_i = (x_{i1}, x_{i2},..., x_{im})$. Random subspace generation method randomly selects $r(r < m)$ features and thus obtains r-dimensional random subspace from the original m-dimensional feature vector. In this way, a modified training set $X^s = (X_1^s, X_2^s, ..., X_n^s)$ consisting of r-dimensional samples $X_i^s = (x_{i1}^s, x_{i2}^s, ..., x_{in}^s)(i=1,...,r)$ is generated. Normally, multiple classifiers can be first constructed in random subspaces using modified training sets.

In this study, the m-dimensional feature vector combined with color feature and color feature is divided into different feature subspaces randomly. The dimension numbers of the three random subspaces are m_1, m_2 and $m_3 (m_1 + m_2 + m_3 = m)$ respectively, and the positions are selected randomly to generate the feature subspace vectors. In our implementation, we use the three subspace vectors to train different classifiers.

3.2   Semi-supervised Learning

Given the classified images, random subspace generation can naturally be applied to generate three subspace classifiers in tri-training. To fully utilize the training images, we iteratively perform image classification until the new classified image set remains unchanged. As a result, the unclassified images are divided into two parts: classified data set and unclassified data set.

Input: Classified images set L, unclassified images set U
Output: Automatically classified image set A
Procedure:
Step 1: Generate random three subspaces respectively from the m-dimensional feature space.

Step 2: Utilize the relevant subspaces of the initial classified training images to train three different classifiers H_1, H_2, H_3.

Step 3: Initialize $A = L$, and for $\forall x \in U$:

Step 3.1: if the classified result $H_2(x) = H_3(x)$, put x into the training set of classifier H_1 and renew the training set $S_1 = L \cup \{x | x \in U, H_2(x) = H_3(x)\}$

Step 3.2: Update training set S_2 and S_3 of classifiers H_2 and H_3 similarly

Step 3.3: Repeat Step 3.1 and 3.2 to train the three classifiers until S_1, S_2 and S_3 are unchanged.

Step 4: Construct the new classified image set $A = S_1 \cup S_2 \cup S_3$.

The sample images in set $B = A - L$ are classified according to the classifiers in tri-training, but the rest images in set $U - B$ are still unclassified. So majority voting method is adopted to integrate the classified results from three classifiers to classify the images in set $U - B$.

4   Experimental Results

A series experiments are constructed and their results are discussed in three approaches. A single SIFT feature with static semi-supervised learning is adopted in the first method, and combined feature proposed in this paper with static semi-supervised learning is used in the second method. Here, the third method is our proposed method.

The dimension numbers of color and texture feature are 60 and 56, so the combination feature vector is 116 dimensions. The feature vectors of the three methods have similar dimension numbers.

We adopt three datasets in the experiments, and select about different percent training images per class and test on the remaining. The three datasets are Caltech-101, UIUC-Sport and Scene 15. Caltech-101 contains 9144 images from 101 object categories including animals, flowers, faces and a background category, and each category has 31–800 images with significant variance in shape and color. UIUC-Sport dataset contains images collected from 8 kinds of different sports scene. There are 1792 images in all, and the number of images ranges from 137 to 250 per category. Scene 15 is a dataset containing 15 scene categories. It contains 4485 images, which are divided into15 categories. Each category contains about 200–400 images.

Table 1. Classification results of three methods with 8 percent training images per class

Method	Accuracy (%)		
	Caltech-101	UIUC-Sport	Scene 15
SIFT feature using static strategy	66.12	74.22	72.65
Color and texture feature using static strategy	78.63	80.01	79.81
Color and texture feature using dynamic strategy	81.51	83.11	81.64

Table 2. Classification results of three methods with 15 percent training images per class

Method	Accuracy (%)		
	Caltech-101	UIUC-Sport	Scene 15
SIFT feature using static strategy	80.03	83.63	81.72
Color and texture feature using static strategy	82.20	85.41	83.26
Color and texture feature using dynamic strategy	86.23	88.86	86.12

Table 3. Classification results of three methods with 25 percent training images per class

Method	Accuracy (%)		
	Caltech-101	UIUC-Sport	Scene 15
SIFT feature using static strategy	83.39	86.50	86.07
Color and texture feature using static strategy	87.34	88.98	87.32
Color and texture feature using dynamic strategy	88.27	90.12	89.86

Table 1, 2 and 3 show the classification results of three classified methods with different numbers of training images. As can be observed, classification results are affected by the feature extraction and training images. These results suggest that the mixed color and texture feature is better than single feature. Besides, we can see that if the number of training images is too small, enough training information can not been extracted. The dynamic strategy makes the involved subspace classifiers quite different from each other even when the training images become similar after some iterations, so we can get more training information.

5   Conclusion

In this paper, we address semi-supervised learning for image classification. We first extract combined features according to spatial distribution and Gabor filter respectively, and then a semi-supervised learning method based on dynamic subspace generation to guarantee enough variation among the involved classifiers. Evaluation shows that our method can successfully make use of the classified images and significantly outperforms traditional static subspace generation.

Acknowledgements. The work described in this paper is supported by the National Science Foundation of China (No.61170145), the Specialized Research Fund for the Doctoral Program of Higher Education of China (No.20113704110001), the Natural Science Foundation of Shandong (No.ZR2010FM021), the Technology and Development Project of Shandong (No.2013GGX10125) and the Taishan Scholar Project of Shandong, China.

References

1. Park, D.C.: Multiple feature-based classifier and its application to image classification. In: Proceedings of IEEE International Conference on Data Mining Workshops, pp. 65–71. IEEE Computer Society, Sydney (2010)
2. Promdaen, S., Wattuya, P., Sanevas, N.: Automated microalgae image classification. Procedia Computer Science 29, 1981–1992 (2014)
3. Zhang, L., Ma, C.: Low-rank decomposition and Laplacian group sparse coding for image classification. Neurocomputing 135, 339–347 (2014)
4. Rigamonti, R., Lepetit, V.: On the relevance of sparsity for image classification. Computer Vision and Image Understanding 125, 115–127 (2014)
5. Yang, J., Yu, K., Huang, T.: Supervised translation-invariant sparse coding. In: IEEE Conference on Computer Vision and Pattern Recognition, pp. 3517–3524 (2010)
6. Olshausen, B.A., et al.: Emergence of simple-cell receptive field properties by learning a sparse code for natural images. Computer Vision and Image Understanding, 607–609 (1996)
7. Ando, R.K., Zhang, T.: A framework for learning predictive structures from multiple tasks and unlabeled data. The Journal of Machine Learning Research 6, 1817–1853 (2005)
8. Hofmann, T.: Unsupervised learning by probabilistic latent semantic analysis. Machine Learning 42(2), 177–196 (2001)
9. Zhu, X., Ghahramani, Z., Lafferty, J.: Semi-supervised learning using gaussian fields and harmonic functions. In: Proc. of the IEEE Conference on Machine Learning, Washington, USA, pp. 912–919 (2003)
10. Li, D.-X., Peng, J.-Y., Li, Z., Bu, Q.: LSA based multi-instance learning algorithm for image retrieval. Signal Process. 91(8), 1993–2000 (2001)
11. Zhou, Z.-H., Zhang, M.-L.: Multi-instance multi-label learning with application to scene classification. Advances in Neural Information Processing Systems 19, 1609–1616 (2007)
12. Zhou, Z.-H., Xu, J.-M.: On the relation between multi-instance learning and semi-supervised learning. In: Proceedings of the 24th ICML, Corvalis, Oregon, pp. 1167–1174 (June 2007)
13. Li, H., Wei, Y., Li, L., Yuan, Y.: Similarity learning for object recognition based on derived kernel. Neurocomputing 83, 110–120 (2012)

An Improved Multi-label Classification Ensemble Learning Algorithm

Zhongliang Fu, Lili Wang, and Danpu Zhang

Chengdu Inst. of Computer Application, Chinese Academy of Sci., Sichuan Chengdu China
fzliang@netease.com, wanglili8773@163.com, linda_zdp@126.com

Abstract. This paper proposes an improved algorithm based on minimizing the weighted error of mistake labels and miss labels in multi-label classification ensemble learning algorithm. The new algorithm aims to avoid local optimum by redefining weak classifiers. This algorithm considers the correlations of labels under the precondition of ensuring the error drops with the number of weak classifiers increasing. This paper proposes two improved approaches; one introduces combinational coefficients when combining weak classifiers, another smooth the weak classifier's output to avoid local optimum. We discuss the basis of these modifications, and verify the effectiveness of these algorithms. The experimental results show that all the improved algorithms are effective, and less prone to over fitting.

Keywords: multi-label classification problem, statistical learning, ensemble learning, AdaBoost algorithm, confidence.

1 Introduction

Both binary classification and multi-class classification problem belong to single label classification problem, multi-label classification problem is introduced and discussed when an instance belongs to multiple classes simultaneously, single label classification is a special case of multi-label classification problem. So, the research on multi-label classification learning algorithm is universal and meaningful.

At present, there are many methods to solve multi-label classification problems, which could be divided into two categories: problem transformation and algorithm adaptation [1, 2, 3]. The problem transformation is a common method which using the existing single label classification algorithms to solve the multi-label classification problems, such as power set method [4], MSSBoost [5], one-to-many decomposition strategy [6], classifier chains method [7] and ML-LOC method [8], and all these methods transfer the multi-label classification problem into single label classification problem through modifying the data, and then use single label classification algorithms to solve the problem; The representations of algorithm adaptation include ML-kNN [9], Rank-SVM [10], AdaBoost.MH [11, 12, 13], BoosTexter [14] and maximum entropy multi-label algorithm (MLME) [17], which modify the existing single label classification learning algorithm to adapt multi-label classification. Focus of the multi-label classification algorithm is considering the correlations of labels, and therefore, the latter method is generally better than the former.

S. Li et al. (Eds.): CCPR 2014, Part I, CCIS 483, pp. 243–252, 2014.

Ensemble learning algorithm improves classification accuracy by integrating simple weak classifiers, and receives considerable attention [15, 16]. Typical algorithms include AdaBoost.MH [11, 12, 13] and BoosTexter [14]. Based on the idea of Boosting, literature [18, 19] give several multi-label real AdaBoost algorithms which give each label a confidence, and output the label corresponding to the maximal confidence.

The multi-label classification problem can be transformed to binary classification problem, we can construct multi-label classification ensemble learning algorithm similar to literature [18, 19]. This algorithm combines weak classifiers depending on the ratio of probabilities containing and not containing each label, however, this ratio may cover the real probabilities, and this approach maybe lead learning results drop into local optimum, not global optimum.

The above two problems are analyzed in this paper, and two improved methods have been proposed for multi-label classification ensemble learning algorithm. The improved algorithm can ensure that learning error gradually reduces as the number of the weak classifiers increases, and take more consideration of the correlations between labels by redefining the weak classifier's output. Finally, the experimental results show that the performance of the improved methods is obviously promoted.

2   Multi-label Classification Ensemble Learning Algorithm

2.1   Construction of Multi-label Classification Ensemble Learning Algorithm

Let X be an instance space, $S = \{(x_1, Y_1),...,(x_m, Y_m)\}$ be a set of training examples, $Y_i \subseteq L$ be label set, $L = \{1, 2,..., K\}$, $i = 1,..., m$. Let $h_t(x, l)$ be the confidence of weak classifier $h_t(x)$ $(t = 1,..., T)$ corresponding to label l. The output label set of weak classifier $h_t(x)$ is $\{h_t(x)\} = \{k : h_t(x, k) \geq 0\}$. $f(x, l) = \sum_{t=1}^{T} h_t(x, l)$ is combination classifier, which output label set $\{f(x)\} = \{k : f(x, k) \geq 0\}$, $(x, Y) \in S$ shorthand be $x \in S$, Y is the label set of x.

Define $\{f(x)\} - Y$ as mistake labels set and $Y - \{f(x)\}$ as miss labels set. The ideal multi-label classifier should neither mistake nor miss labels, and then use the weighted sum of mistake rate and miss rate to define the loss, so get the loss function

$$\varepsilon = E_{x \in X}\left[c_{over} \left| \{f(x)\} - Y \right| + c_{def} \left| Y - \{f(x)\} \right| \right] \tag{1}$$

where c_{def}, c_{over} are weighted coefficients, which satisfy $1 \geq c_{def} \geq 0$ and $c_{over} = 1 - c_{def}$. The average error rate corresponding to the instance space is

$$\varepsilon = \sum_{i=1}^{m} \left(\omega_i \left(c_{over} \left| \{f(x_i)\} - Y_i \right| + c_{def} \left| Y_i - \{f(x_i)\} \right| \right) \right) \tag{2}$$

where $\omega_i = 1/(mK)$, so $0 \leq \varepsilon \leq 1$.

Let $c_0(i,l) = [\![l \notin Y_i]\!]$,that is, $c_0(i,l) = 1$ when $l \notin Y_i$, otherwise $c_0(i,l) = 1$,and $c_1(i,l) = 1 - c_0(i,l)$, $i = 1,...,m$, $l = 1,...,K$. Therefore,

$$
\begin{aligned}
\varepsilon &= \sum_{i=1}^{m}\sum_{l=1}^{K}\left(\omega_i c_0(i,l)c_{over}[\![f(x_i,l) \geq 0]\!] + \omega_i c_1(i,l)c_{def}[\![f(x_i,l) < 0]\!]\right) \leq \\
&\sum_{i=1}^{m}\sum_{l=1}^{K}\left(\omega_i c_0(i,l)c_{over}\exp(f(x_i,l)) + \omega_i c_1(i,l)c_{def}\exp(-f(x_i,l))\right) = \\
&Z_0 \sum_{i=1}^{m}\sum_{l=1}^{K}\left(\omega_{i,l}^{1,1}\prod_{t=1}^{T}\exp(h_t(x_i,l)) + \omega_{i,l}^{1,2}\prod_{t=1}^{T}\exp(-h_t(x_i,l))\right)
\end{aligned}
\tag{3}
$$

where

$\omega_{i,l}^{1,1} = \omega_i c_0(i,l)c_{over}/Z_0$, $\omega_{i,l}^{1,2} = \omega_i c_1(i,l)c_{def}/Z_0$, $Z_0 = \sum_{i=1}^{m}\sum_{l=1}^{K}\left(\omega_i c_0(i,l)c_{over} + \omega_i c_1(i,l)c_{def}\right)$ is the normalization factor of $\omega_{i,l}^{1,1} + \omega_{i,l}^{1,2}$. Extract the terms containing $h_1(x)$ from Eqs.(3) and let

$$
Z_1 = \sum_{i=1}^{m}\sum_{l=1}^{K}\left(\omega_{i,l}^{1,1}\exp(h_1(x_i,l)) + \omega_{i,l}^{1,2}\exp(-h_1(x_i,l))\right)
\tag{4}
$$

$$
\omega_{i,l}^{2,1} = \frac{\omega_{i,l}^{1,1}}{Z_1}\exp(h_1(x_i,l))
\tag{5}
$$

$$
\omega_{i,l}^{2,2} = \frac{\omega_{i,l}^{1,2}}{Z_1}\exp(-h_1(x_i,l))
\tag{6}
$$

Eqs.(3) becomes

$$
Z_0 Z_1 \sum_{i=1}^{m}\sum_{l=1}^{K}\left(\omega_{i,l}^{2,1}\prod_{t=2}^{T}\exp(h_t(x_i,l)) + \omega_{i,l}^{2,2}\prod_{t=2}^{T}\exp(-h_t(x_i,l))\right)
\tag{7}
$$

So we can minimize Z_1 to construct $h_1(x)$. Because Eqs.(7) is similar to Eqs.(3), we can construct recursive algorithm. Generally, we can minimize Z_t to define $h_t(x)$,

$$
Z_t = \sum_{i=1}^{m}\sum_{l=1}^{K}\left(\omega_{i,l}^{t,1}\exp(h_t(x_i,l)) + \omega_{i,l}^{t,2}\exp(-h_t(x_i,l))\right)
\tag{8}
$$

Assume $h_t(x)$ divide the instance space X into n_t parts. The instances in the same partition have the same confidence, this partition in S can be expressed as $S = S_1^t \cup \cdots \cup S_{n_t}^t$, $S_i^t \cap S_j^t = \varnothing$, $(i \neq j)$. For $x_i \in S_j^t$, $h_t(x_i,l)$ is written as $\alpha_t^{j,l}$, $j = 1,...,n_t$. Merge the same terms in the partition and denote $p_t^{j,l} = \sum_{i:(x_i \in S_j^t)}\omega_{i,l}^{t,1}$, $q_t^{j,l} = \sum_{i:(x_i \in S_j^t)}\omega_{i,l}^{t,2}$, then Eqs.(8) becomes

$$Z_t = \sum_{j=1}^{n_t}\sum_{l=1}^{K}\left(p_t^{j,l}\exp\left(\alpha_t^{j,l}\right)+q_t^{j,l}\exp\left(-\alpha_t^{j,l}\right)\right) \tag{9}$$

When $\alpha_t^{j,l}=0.5\ln\left(q_t^{j,l}/p_t^{j,l}\right)$, formula $p_t^{j,l}\exp\left(\alpha_t^{j,l}\right)+q_t^{j,l}\exp\left(-\alpha_t^{j,l}\right)$ reaches its mini-

mum $Z_t = 2\sum_{j=1}^{n_t}\sum_{l=1}^{K}\sqrt{p_t^{j,l}q_t^{j,l}}$ .Then we get the multi-label classification ensemble

learning algorithm as follows:

Algorithm 1. Multi-label Classification Ensemble Learning Algorithm

Input: $S=\{(x_1,Y_1),...,(x_m,Y_m)\}$, $x_i\in X$, $Y_i\subseteq L$, $L=\{1,2,...,K\}$;

Initialize distribution: $\omega_{i,l}^{1,1}=\omega_i c_0(i,l)c_{over}/Z_0$, $\omega_{i,l}^{1,2}=\omega_i c_1(i,l)c_{def}/Z_0$, Z_0 is a normali-

zation factor of $\omega_{i,l}^{1,1}+\omega_{i,l}^{1,2}$, $\omega_i = 1/(mK)$, $i=1,...,m$, $l=1,...,K$;

For $t=1,...,T$ **do**

  Train weak classifiers :

    Partition S into n_t disjoint blocks: $S=S_1^t\cup\cdots\cup S_{n_t}^t$;

    Calculate $p_t^{j,l},q_t^{j,l}$: $p_t^{j,l}=\sum_{i:(x_i\in S_j^t)}\omega_{i,l}^{t,1}$, $q_t^{j,l}=\sum_{i:(x_i\in S_j^t)}\omega_{i,l}^{t,2}$, $j=1,...,n_t$;

    Define $h_t(x)$: $\forall x\in S_j^t$, $h_t(x,l)=0.5\ln\left(q_t^{j,l}/p_t^{j,l}\right)$;

    Choose $h_t(x)$: Choose $h_t(x)$ to minimize $Z_t = 2\sum_{j=1}^{n_t}\sum_{l=1}^{K}\sqrt{p_t^{j,l}q_t^{j,l}}$;

  Update weights:

    $\omega_{i,l}^{t+1,1}=\left(\omega_{i,l}^{t,1}/Z_t\right)\exp\left(h_t(x_i,l)\right)$;

    $\omega_{i,l}^{t+1,2}=\left(\omega_{i,l}^{t,2}/Z_t\right)\exp\left(-h_t(x_i,l)\right)$;

End for

Output: $\{k:f(x,k)\geq 0\}$, where $f(x,l)=\sum_{t=1}^{T}h_t(x,l)$.

According to the derivation above, we can get the upper bound of the learning error
rate:

$$\varepsilon\leq\prod_{t=0}^{T}Z_t \tag{10}$$

where $Z_t\leq\sum_{j=1}^{n_t}\sum_{l=1}^{K}\left(p_t^{j,l}+q_t^{j,l}\right)=\sum_{i=1}^{m}\sum_{l=1}^{K}\left(\omega_{i,l}^{t,1}+\omega_{i,l}^{t,2}\right)=1$, for all $j\in\{1,...,n_t\}$ and

$l\in\{1,...,K\}$, if $p_t^{j,l}=q_t^{j,l}$, we get $Z_t=1$. So the training error rate of Algorithm 1 de-

creases as T increasing.

2.2   Analysis of Multi-label Classification Ensemble Learning Algorithm

According to the definition, $h_t(x)$ output label l when $h_t(x,l)\geq 0$, equivalent to

$p_t^{j,l}\leq q_t^{j,l}$. The essence of Algorithm 1 is to output label l according to value $q_t^{j,l}/p_t^{j,l}$,

that is probability containing and not containing label l in the same partition.

Specially, when $K = 2$ and $c_{def} = c_{over} = 0.5$, we can simple Algorithm 1 as real AdaBoost [12], and the estimate error of Eqs.(10) is the same as the literature [12]. When $c_{def} = c_{over} = 0.5$, Algorithm 1 is equal to the algorithm Real AdaBoost.MH [12].

3   Improved Multi-label Classification Ensemble Learning Algorithm

3.1   The Improve thought of Multi-label Classification Ensemble Learning Algorithm

In order to let ε reach the minimum, $h_t(x)$ in Algorithm 1 always let Z_t reach the minimum according to the derivation process. $h_t(x)$ is got one by one, Z_t reaches its minimum but it can't ensure $\prod_{t=0}^{T} Z_t$ reach the minimum, because Z_{t+1} will be affected by $h_t(x)$. In other words, learning result could fall into local optimal value rather than global optimal value, the pursuit of a single Z_t minimization may not be the most ideal, therefore, it is necessary to improve Algorithm 1.

The classification error of combination classifier drops with the number of weak classifier increasing only if "$Z_t \le 1$ and generally $Z_t < 1$", therefore, all the improvements of Algorithm 1 need to ensure "$Z_t \le 1$ and generally $Z_t < 1$" in condition that not change algorithm process to guarantee condition (10), therefore, improvements should focus more on the weak classifier. Considering the possible correlation of labels, we need consider the affection of other labels when adjusting weak classifier.

3.2   Improved Multi-label Classification Ensemble Learning Algorithm (1)

For weak classifier $h_t(x)$, whether output label l is depend on $h_t(x,l) = 0.5\ln\left(q_t^{j,l}/p_t^{j,l}\right)$. It is reasonable for single weak classifier. However, the combination classifier, that is $f(x,l) = \sum_{t=1}^{T} h_t(x,l)$, lead to comparability problem of weak classifiers.

Classifier $h_t(x)$ output label l according to the comparison of $q_t^{j,l}$ and $p_t^{j,l}$, ignoring the values $q_t^{j,l}$ and $p_t^{j,l}$.

We introduce combination coefficients into weak classifier $h_t(x)$:

$$h_t(x,l) = 0.5\sum_{k=1}^{K}\left(q_t^{j,k} + p_t^{j,k}\right)\ln\left(q_t^{j,l}/p_t^{j,l}\right) \tag{11}$$

The $h_t(x,l)$ in Eqs. (11) is related to $q_t^{j,l}$, $p_t^{j,l}$ and $q_t^{j,l}/p_t^{j,l}$, it seems more reasonable. It is needed to prove whether the weak classifier given by Eqs. (11) satisfies condition that "$Z_t \le 1$ and generally $Z_t < 1$".

Let $C_t^j = 0.5\sum_{k=1}^{K}\left(q_t^{j,k} + p_t^{j,k}\right)$, put Eqs. (11) into Eqs. (9), we get

$$Z_t = \sum_{j=1}^{n_t}\sum_{l=1}^{K}\left(\left(p_t^{j,l}\right)^{1-C_t^j}\left(q_t^{j,l}\right)^{C_t^j} + \left(p_t^{j,l}\right)^{C_t^j}\left(q_t^{j,l}\right)^{1-C_t^j}\right) \leq$$

$$\sum_{j=1}^{n_t}\sum_{l=1}^{K}\left(\left(1-C_t^j\right)p_t^{j,l} + C_t^j q_t^{j,l} + C_t^j p_t^{j,l} + \left(1-C_t^j\right)q_t^{j,l}\right) =$$

$$\sum_{j=1}^{n_t}\left(\sum_{l=1}^{K}q_t^{j,l} + \sum_{l=1}^{K}p_t^{j,l}\right) = 1 \qquad (12)$$

If and only if $p_t^{j,l} = q_t^{j,l}$ hold for all $j \in \{1,...,n_t\}$ and $l \in \{1,...,K\}$, equation $Z_t = 1$ is established, therefore the improved algorithm satisfies condition that "$Z_t \leq 1$ and generally $Z_t < 1$".

3.3   Improved Multi-label Classification Ensemble Learning Algorithm (2)

The $f(x,l)$ in Algorithm 1 output label l when $0.5\ln\left(\prod_{t=1}^{T}q_t^{j,l}\big/\prod_{t=1}^{T}p_t^{j,l}\right) > 0$. However, if $q_t^{j,l}/p_t^{j,l}$ is too large or too small for some weak classifier, and some instances in the same partition are misclassified (frequently happen, or completely classified correctly), the learning result will fall into local optimum instead of global optimum.

So, we need to smooth the comparison. Modify $h_t(x)$ as follows without affecting the order of $q_t^{j,l}$ and $p_t^{j,l}$:

$$h_t(x,l) = 0.5\ln\left(\left(\frac{1}{2K}\sum_{k=1}^{K}(q_t^{j,k}+p_t^{j,k})+q_t^{j,l}\right)\right) - 0.5\ln\left(\left(\frac{1}{2K}\sum_{k=1}^{K}(q_t^{j,k}+p_t^{j,k})+p_t^{j,l}\right)\right) \quad (13)$$

or

$$h_t(x,l) = 0.5\ln\left(\left((q_t^{j,l}+p_t^{j,l})/2+q_t^{j,l}\right)\right) - 0.5\ln\left(\left((q_t^{j,l}+p_t^{j,l})/2+p_t^{j,l}\right)\right) \qquad (14)$$

Both classifiers weaken the difference between $q_t^{j,l}$ and $p_t^{j,l}$ without affecting their order, avoid learning result falling into local optimum. Besides, the classifier defined by Eqs. (13) concerned more about the correlation between labels.

We will prove that the classifiers defined by Eqs. (13) and Eqs. (14) satisfy "$Z_t \leq 1$ and generally $Z_t < 1$" as follows:

Let $\alpha_t^{j,l} = 0.5\ln\left(\left(C_t^j + q_t^{j,l}\right)\big/\left(C_t^j + p_t^{j,l}\right)\right)$, where $C_t^j = \sum_{k=1}^{K}\left(q_t^{j,k}+p_t^{j,k}\right)\big/2K$ in Eqs. (13),

and $C_t^j = \left(q_t^{j,k}+p_t^{j,k}\right)\big/2$ in Eqs. (14), put $\alpha_t^{j,l}$ it into Eqs. (9), we get

$$Z_t = \sum_{j=1}^{n_t}\sum_{l=1}^{K}\left(p_t^{j,l}\left(\left(C_t^j+q_t^{j,l}\right)\big/\left(C_t^j+p_t^{j,l}\right)\right)^{1/2} + q_t^{j,l}\left(\left(C_t^j+p_t^{j,l}\right)\big/\left(C_t^j+q_t^{j,l}\right)\right)^{1/2}\right) \qquad (15)$$

Because $p_t^{j,l}\left(\left(C_t^j+q_t^{j,l}\right)\big/\left(C_t^j+p_t^{j,l}\right)\right)^{1/2}+q_t^{j,l}\left(\left(C_t^j+p_t^{j,l}\right)\big/\left(C_t^j+q_t^{j,l}\right)\right)^{1/2}\;\leq p_t^{j,l}+q_t^{j,l}$

when $C_t^j\geq 0$, therefore $Z_t\leq\sum_{j=1}^{n_t}\sum_{k=1}^{K}\left(q_t^{j,k}+p_t^{j,k}\right)=1$, and $Z_t=1$ is established   if

and only if $p_t^{j,l}=q_t^{j,l}$ for all $j\in\{1,...,n_t\}$ and $l\in\{1,...,K\}$. So both   classifiers de-

fined by Eqs. (13) and Eqs. (14) satisfy " $Z_t\leq 1$ and generally $Z_t<1$ ", ensuring that

classification error of combination classifier drops with the number of weak classifier

increasing, and avoiding over fitting.

4   Experiment and Analysis

4.1   Experimental Methods and Data

We compare these four algorithms on data sets available, the Yeast, Emotions and
Scene are from Mulan (http://mulan.sourceforge.net/datasets.html), and Image is
available in http://cse.seu.edu.cn/people/zhangml/Resources.htm#data, detailed in
table 1. We take 60% of data as training data set randomly, the others as test data set
and rerun 20 times for each algorithm.

Table 1. The experimental data set

Name	instances	numeric	labels	cardinality	density
Yeast	2417	103	14	4.237	0.303
Emotions	593	72	6	1.869	0.311
Scene	2407	294	6	1.074	0.179
Image	2000	294	5	1.236	0.2472

Weak classifier is constructed based on single attribute, dividing samples into 4
partitions. We note MLPBoost, MLPBoost-IMP1, MLPBoost-IMP2, MLPBoost-
IMP3 as Algorithm 1, and three improved algorithm given by Eqs. (11), Eqs. (13),
Eqs. (14) respectively.

4.2   Experimental Results and Analysis

Fig. 1 - Fig. 3 illustrate experimental results on Emotions, Hamming Loss, One-error
and Ranking Loss are defined in [20], detailed in table 2. (T represents the number of
weak classifier).   Fig. 4 - Fig. 6 illustrate the Hamming Loss performant on Yeast,
Scene, Image respectively, detailed in table 3. The experimental results show that
Algorithm 1 and three improved algorithms decrease with the number of weak classifier increasing, the performance of three improved algorithms is apparently better
than Algorithm 1, and there is no need to worry about over fitting. Besides, the performance of MLPBoost-IMP1 is better than MLPBoost-IMP2 and MLPBoost-IMP3,
namely, the performance of improved algorithm through introducing combination
coefficient into weak classifier is better than improved algorithm through smoothing
weak classifier's output.

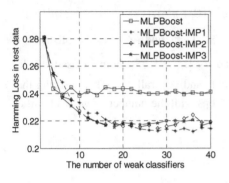

Fig. 1. The Hamming Loss on Emotions

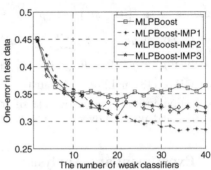

Fig. 2. The One Error on Emotions

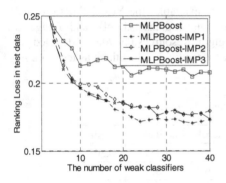

Fig. 3. The Ranking Loss on Emotions

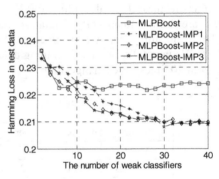

Fig. 4. The Hamming Loss on Yeast

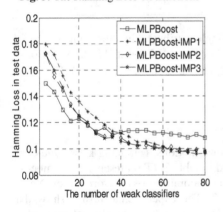

Fig. 5. The Hamming Loss on Scene

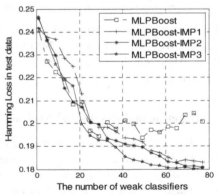

Fig. 6. The Hamming Loss on Image

Table 2. The experimental results on Emotions(T=40)

	MLPBoost	MLPBoost-IMP1	MLPBoost-IMP2	MLPBoost-IMP3
Hamming-Loss	0.2414	0.2133	0.2185	0.2180
One-error	0.3703	0.2827	0.3291	0.3165
Ranking Loss	0.2083	0.1711	0.1783	0.1735

Table 3. The Hamming Loss on data sets

	MLPBoost	MLPBoost-IMP1	MLPBoost-IMP2	MLPBoost-IMP3
Emotions(T=40)	0.2415	0.2133	0.2185	0.2180
Yeast(T=40)	0.2248	0.2096	0.2097	0.2095
Scene(T=80)	0.1099	0.0957	0.0964	0.0989
Image(T=80)	0.2053	0.1810	0.1763	0.1825

5   Conclusions

This paper proposes an improved multi-label classification ensemble learning algorithm, which promotes learning performance through redefining weak classifier's output, considering the correlation of labels. The improved algorithm can ensure that the learning error drops with the number of weak classifier increasing. An improved algorithm introduce combination coefficient which depends on sample size in the same partition into weak classifier. Another algorithm smooth weak classifier's output, so that it is not easy to fall into local optimum, and avoids over fitting. Theoretical analysis and experimental results indicate that the algorithm is reasonable and effective.

References

1. Tsoumakas, G., Katakis, I.: Multi-label classification: an overview. International Journal of Data Warehousing and Mining 3(3), 1–13 (2007)
2. Zhou, Z.H., Zhang, M.L., Huang, S.J., Li, Y.F.: Multi-instance multi-label learning. Artificial Intelligence 176(1), 2291–2320 (2012)
3. Wu, F., Han, Y., Tian, Q., Zhuang, Y.: Multi-label boosting for image annotation by structural grouping sparsity. In: Proceedings of the 18th ACM International Conference on Multimedia, Firenze, Italy, pp. 15–24 (2010)
4. Trohidis, K., Tsoumakas, G., Kalliris, G., Vlahavas, I.: Multi-label classification of music into emotions. In: 9th International Conference on Music Information Retrieval, ISMIR, Philadelphia, pp. 325–330 (2008)
5. Yan, R., Tesic, J., Smith, J.R.: Model-shared subspace boosting for multi-label classification. In: Proceedings of the 13th ACM SIGKDD Conference on Knowledge Discovery and Data Mining, CA, San Jose, pp. 834–843 (2007)
6. Boutell, M.R., Luo, J., Shen, X.P., Christopher, C.M., Brown, M.: Learning multi-label scene classification. Pattern Recognition 37(9), 1757–1771 (2004)

7. Read, J., Pfahringer, B., Holmes, G., Frank, E.: Classifier chains for multi-label classification. Machine Learning 85(3), 333–359 (2011)

8. Huang, S.J., Zhou, Z.H.: Multi-label learning by exploiting label correlations locally. In: Proceedings of the 26th AAAI Conference on Artificial Intelligence (AAAI 2012), pp. 949–959 (2012)

9. Zhang, M.L., Zhou, Z.H.: A k-nearest neighbor based algorithm for multi-label classification. In: Proceedings of the IEEE International Conference on Granular Computing, pp. 718–721. Springer, Heidelberg (2004)

10. Elisseeff, A., Weston, J.: A kernel method for multi-labeled classification. In: Proceedings of Advances in Neural Information, pp. 681–687. BIO wulf Technologies, New York (2003)

11. Benbouzid, D., Busa-Fekete, R., Casagrande, N., et al.: MultiBoost: A multi-purpose boosting package. Journal of Machine Learning Research 13, 549–553 (2012)

12. Schapire, R.E., Singer, Y.: Improved boosting algorithms using confidence-rated predictions. Machine Learning 37(3), 297–336 (1999)

13. Zhu, J., Rosset, S., Zou, H., et al.: Multi-class AdaBoost. Statistics and Its Interface 2, 349–360 (2009)

14. Schapire, R.E., Singer, Y.: Boostexter: a boosting based system for text catego-rization. Machine Learning 39(2/3), 135–168 (2000)

15. Shi, C., Kong, X., Yu, P.S., Wang, B.: Multi-label ensemble learning. In: Gunopulos, D., Hofmann, T., Malerba, D., Vazirgiannis, M. (eds.) ECML PKDD 2011, Part III. LNCS, vol. 6913, pp. 223–239. Springer, Heidelberg (2011)

16. Tahir, M.A., Kittler, J., Mikolajczyk, K., Yan, F.: Improving multilabel classification performance by using ensemble of multi-label classifiers. In: El Gayar, N., Kittler, J., Roli, F. (eds.) MCS 2010. LNCS, vol. 5997, pp. 11–21. Springer, Heidelberg (2010)

17. Zhu, S.H., Ji, X., Xu, W., et al.: Multi-labeled classification using maximum entropy method. In: Proceedings of the 28th Annual International ACM SIGIR Conference on Research and Development, pp. 274–281. ACM, Salvador (2004)

18. Fu, Z.L.: An ensemble learning algorithm for direction prediction. Shanghai Jiaotong University. Science Edition 46(2), 250–258 (2012)

19. Fu, Z.L.: Cost-Sensitive AdaBoost Algorithm for Multi-class Classification Problems. Acta Automatica Sinica 37(8), 973–983 (2011)

20. Tsoumakas, G., Katakis, I., Vlahavas, I.: Mining Multilabel data. In: Data Mining and Knowledge Discovery Handbook (2010)

An Improved Sparse Representation De-noising for Keeping Structural Features

Zhi Cui[*]

School of Communication and Electronic Engineering,
Hunan City University, Hunan Yiyang 413000, China
zhicui@yeah.net

Abstract. Considering the current image de-noising methods may lose some structural features, this paper proposes an improved sparse representation based method by adopting the histogram structural similarity. When the initial over-complete dictionary was applied in the sparse decomposition, similarity factor could replace the reconstruction error as the factor of fidelity. The orthogonal matching pursuit algorithm(OMP) is used to reconstruct the denoised image. The experimental results show that the proposed method could provide better PSNR and HSSIM results compared with the wavelet transformation, the K-SVD algorithm and the method presented in [10], meanwhile, and the structural features can be reserved effectively by the proposed method.

Keywords: Structural feature, Similarity factor, Sparse representation, Image de-noising.

1   Introduction

Image is the visual basis of the people to know the world, and is also the important carrier of getting and transferring information. However, in the actual environment, the light sources, the imaging system and the transmission processes may reduce the quality of the image and cause some mistakes in the information communication. Image de-noising is a hotspot of the image processing to improve the quality of image. At present, the main image de-noising methods are based on the transform domain. These methods usually try to find the rules of spectral distribution and separate the detailed features and the noise in the transform domain, such as the wavelet transformation [1,2].The transform domain   methods are based on the knowledge that the noise in the image mainly existed in the high-frequency part, and the detailed features existed in the low-frequency part [3,4]. However, the experiments have confirmed that the high-frequency part included the detailed features, and the low-frequency part also had the noise [5]. The above denoising methods in the

---

[*] Corresponding author.

S. Li et al. (Eds.): CCPR 2014, Part I, CCIS 483, pp. 253–262, 2014.

transform domain may eliminate part of the detailed features while low-frequency part can't be well de-noised [6].

The sparse representation as the newly emerged theory of signal analysis and processing has attracted much attention in these years. The basic idea of this method is to adopt the redundant basis of the over-completed dictionary to represent the orthogonal basis of the domain transformation [7]. Recently, various approaches have been proposed to address the problem of image de-noising. The main steps of the existing methods are as follows. First, the sparse decomposition of the signal selects the best portfolio from the over-completed dictionary, then it distinguishes the information and the noise according to that if the data has the sparse representation in the dictionary, so that the de-noising can be completed [8]. For example, Dong, Li, Zang and Shi proposed a method for denoising the high resolution remote sensing images by combining sparse repersentation and dictionary learning [9]. In [9], a dictionary which has an efficient description remote sensing image content is obtained based on K-SVD algorithm, meanwhile, denoising is realized by using sparse representation. Wang and Jean proposed a remote sensing image denoising method based on K-SVD and residual ratio iteration termination [10]. With the characteristics of the added noise of remote sensing images, the residual ratio is used as the iteration termination of OMP algorithm to remove the noise.

From the research course of the image de-noising based on the sparse representing, it is known that most of the current de-noising methods consider the reconstruction error of the images before and after de-noising as the fidelity, which means the image's structural similarity isn't considered enough. In order to keep the structural features information as much as possible when the image is effectively de-noised, this paper introduces the image quality evaluation index of histogram structural similarity (HSSIM) into the sparse representation, and proposes an improved sparse representation de-noising algorithm which considers the HSSIM as the fidelity. The experiments have shown that, compared with the wavelet transformation, the K-SVD algorithm and the method presented in [10], the proposed method could acquire better PSNR and HSSIM values, and it is consistent with the subjective visual effect.

The rest of this paper is organized as follows. In Section II, the theory of sparse representation is briefly reviewed. The proposed method is presented in Section III. The experimental results and comparisons are given in Section IV. The conclusions are drawn in Section V.

2   De-noising Method Based on Sparse Representation

A. Sparse Representing De-noising Model

In the two-dimensional space, an observed image with fixed displacement can be modeled as follows:

$$F = G + E \tag{1}$$

where F, G and E are the observed image, the clear image and the noise. The aim of de-noising is to eliminate or reduce the the noise from the observed image so that the difference between the observed image f and the clear image g is minimized.

Any ideal image can be described by the model of $g \in R^{n \times n}$ in which the image is devided into $\sqrt{n} \times \sqrt{n}$ parts. According to the sparse representation, a dictionary martic $D \in R^{n \times m}$ $(n < m)$ is defined to represent all the image parts as follows [11]:

$$\hat{a} = \arg\min\|a\|_0 \quad s.t. \quad \|Da - F\|_2^2 \le \varepsilon \tag{2}$$

where $a \in R^m$ is the sparse representation, $\|a\|_0$ is the number of the non-zero values and it means the sparsity of a, D is the dictionary.

Assuming the white noise has been added into the image F, the de-noising result of F is the solution of the following model [12]:

$$\hat{a} = \arg\min\|a\|_0 \quad s.t. \quad \|Da - F\|_2^2 \le T \tag{3}$$

where T is determined by ε and σ, σ is the variations of noise. The de-noised image can be described by $G = D\hat{a}$.

Transform the constraint to the penalty term. According to the regularization optimization, the equation (3) can be changed into [13]:

$$\hat{a} = \arg\min\|Da - F\|_2^2 + u\|a\|_0 \tag{4}$$

where u is the regularization parameter. When an appropriate value is assigned to u, the equation (3) is equivalent to equation (4).

B. K-SVD Algorithm

K-SVD algorithm is an iteration algorithm which alternates the sparse coding and the dictionary. Considering an ideal image of $\sqrt{n} \times \sqrt{n}$ parts, the model of K-SVD algorithm is [14]:

$$\{\hat{a}_{ij}, \hat{G}\} = \arg\min_{a_{ij}, g} \lambda \|G - F\|_2^2 + \sum_{i,j} u_{ij} \|a_{ij}\|_0 + \sum_{i,j} \|Da_{ij} - R_{ij}G\|_2^2 \tag{5}$$

where λ is the Lagrange multiplier, u_{ij} is a coefficient, the first component represents the integral similarity between the noised image and the clear image, and it should be less than the convolution of $C * \sigma^2$ (C is a constant). The second one is the sparse constraint. R_{ij} is the $n \times N$ matrix to extract the image block in (i, j) from the image of $\sqrt{n} \times \sqrt{n}$. D is the over-completed dictionary. For each image block, The OMP algorithm can solve the following model to acquire the optimal $\hat{a}_{ij}$:

$$\hat{a}_{ij} = \mathrm{argmin}_{a_{ij}} u_{ij} \|a_{ij}\|_0 + \|Da_{ij} - R_{ij}G\|_2^2 \tag{6}$$

The iteration ends when the error satisfies $\|Da_{ij} - R_{ij}G\|_2^2 < T$. After all the blocks are sparsely decomposed, the denoised image G is updated by

$$\hat{G} = \mathrm{argmin}_g \lambda \|G - F\|_2^2 + \sum_{i,j} \|Da_{ij} - R_{ij}G\|_2^2 \tag{7}$$

3   De-nosing Algorithm to Keep the Structural Features

From the analysis from equation (5) to (7), K-SVD algorithm takes the reconstruction error as the fidelity. This method minimizes the error through an appropriate setting of the threshold T, but don't consider the structural features information. To keep more feature information of the image, this paper proposes an improved sparse representation de-noising algorithm to get better de-noising and visual result.

A. Histogram Structural Similarity

The histogram structural similarity is a method to evaluate the image quality and comes from the analysis of the human's visual system. Assume x and y represent the clear and the observed images respectively, the histogram structural similarity $HSSIM(x, y)$ is calculated as follows [15]:

$$HSSIM(x, y) = [l(y, y)]^\alpha \cdot [c(x, y)]^\beta \cdot [h(x, y)]^\gamma \tag{8}$$

where $l(x, y)$, $c(x, y)$ and $h(x, y)$ are the intensity correlation function, contrast correlation function and ambiguity correlation function of the two images. Let α , β , γ be 1, the Structural Similarity can be expressed as follows:

$$HSSIM(x, y) = \frac{(2\mu_x\mu_y + c_1)(2\sigma_x\sigma_y + c_2)(2s_xs_y + c_3)}{(\mu_x^2 + \mu_y^2 + c_1)(\sigma_x^2 + \sigma_y^2 + c_2)(s_x^2 + s_y^2 + c_3)} \tag{9}$$

The value of $HSSIM$ is between 0 and 1. When it is close to 1, which means the two images are similar in structure, and vice versa. In equation (9), μ_x and μ_y are the means of the two images, σ_x and σ_y are the variations, c_1, c_2 and c_3 are the minimal positive constants in the values of the pixel, s_x and s_y are the ambiguity and are determined as follows:

$$s = \sum_{x_i=0}^{255} p(x_i) \Delta(x_i) \qquad (10)$$

$$\Delta(x_i) = \begin{cases} \dfrac{x_i}{\overline{x}} & x_i < \overline{x} \\ \dfrac{255 - x_i}{255 - \overline{x}} & x_i \geq \overline{x} \end{cases} \qquad (11)$$

where x_i is the gray level, $\overline{x}$ is the mean of the Grey levels, $\Delta(x_i)$ is the weight, $p(x_i)$ is the possibility of x_i in the image.

B. The Proposed Algorithm

This paper introduces the histogram structural similarity into the K-SVD algorithm, and proposes an improved sparse representation based de-noising model, i.e:

$$\{\hat{a}_{ij}, \hat{G}\} = \operatorname{argmin}_{a_{ij},g} \lambda \|G - F\|_2^2 + \sum_{i,j} u_{ij} \|a_{ij}\|_0 + \sum_{i,j} (1 - HSSIM \ (Da_{ij}, R_{ij}G)) \ (12)$$

where $\hat{a}_{ij}$ is the coefficient of the sparse representation, λ is the Lagrange multiplier. The first and the second parts on the right side are the constraints, and the third one is the similarity factor which replaces the reconstruction error of K-SVD as the new computational fidelity.

Assume that D is a given over-complete dictionary, and the initial condition is $G = F$. The sparse coefficient of each image patch is calculated by:

$$\hat{a}_{ij} = \operatorname{argmin}_{a_{ij}} u_{ij} \|a_{ij}\|_0 + (1 - HSSIM \ (Da_{ij}, R_{ij}G)) \qquad (13)$$

Assuming $1 - HSSIM \ (Da_{ij}, R_{ij}G) < T$ where T is between 0 and 1, the result of de-noising can be acquired by solving the G partial derivatives of equation (14):

$$\hat{G} = \lambda I + \sum_{i,j} R_{ij}^T R_{ij}^{-1} (\lambda F + \sum_{i,j} R_{ij}^T D \hat{a}_{ij}) \qquad (14)$$

where I is the unit matrix.

From the above analysis, the procedure of the algorithm is summarized as follows:

(1)The initial stage

The completed DCT dictionary is adopted as the initial dictionary, satisfying $G = F$.

(2)The stage of sparse coding

According to the proposed model, the histogram structural similarity is incorporated into the OMP algorithm, and each image patch is sparsely decomposed. In the process, the iteration condition is modified to $1 - HSSIM(Da_{ij}, R_{ij}G) < T$ (T is the hard threshold).

(3)The stage of updating dictionary

The error matrix is defined as $E_k = G - \sum d_j a_j^T$,where d_j is the first column of dictionary atom, and a_j^T is the first column of the sparse coefficient matrix. The atom used for the sparse separation in the dictionary is defined as $\omega_i = \{i | 1 \le i \le k, a_j^T(i) \neq 0\}$. The dictionary updating problem is switched to the following problem:

$$\min_{d_j, c_j} (1 - HSSIM(G, \sum_{j \neq k} d_j a_j^T)) \quad s.t. \quad c_j^T \subseteq \omega_i \tag{15}$$

The equation (15) can be solved by the SVD decomposition of E_k and the fist-order approaching:

$$E_k = U\Delta V^T \tag{16}$$

The first column of updated dictionary atom is the first one of U, and the first column of the updated sparse coefficient matrix is the first one of the result of $\Delta(1,1)$ multiplied by V^T.

Repeat the stage (3) until the stop criterion.

(4)The stage of outputting result

Through the equation (14) to solve $\hat{G}$, then output the de-noised image.

4   Experimental Results and Analyses

In order to test the performance of the algorithm, the white noises with the variations of $\sigma = 5, 10, 15, 25$ were added to the images of Mandi、 Concordorthophoto and Lena. The proposed algorithm is compared with the wavelet transformation where the db2 wavelet basis, the soft threshold and decomposition level 3 were applied, the K-SVD algorithm and the method [10] in the de-noising experiment. All the experiments were done in the same environment. Considering the objectivity of the effect evaluation,

PSNR and HSSIM were adopted as the objective indices to evaluate the quality of denoised images.

The results of PSNR (Peak Signal to Noise Ratio) and HSSIM have been listed in Table 1 after the images were dealt by the above methods. In Table 1, it can be found that when the variations of the noise are same, the result of proposed method is better than the other methods. The reason includes two aspects: First, the wavelet transformation needs to choose the wavelet basis and the optimal decomposition level. Different choices significantly affect the de-noising result. The sparse representation based methods don't pay much attention on this problem. Meanwhile, the sparse representation definitely separates the available information and the noise, which can extract the useful information from the image with noise and reconstruct the image with high quality. The sparse representation based methods are better than the wavelet transformation. Second, the proposed method makes use of the structural similarity as the fidelity. Compared with the K-SVD algorithm and the method [10], the proposed method have some advantages to keep the feature information in images, which is suitable for the characteristics of the human's visual system and has better de-noising effect.

Table 1. The comparison between the three de-noising methods

Image	Noise variance	PSNR/dB				HSSIM			
		Wavelet	K-SVD	Method [10]	Proposed	Wavelet	K-SVD	Method [10]	Proposed
Mandi	5	29.743	33.398	33.410	33.794	0.936	0.946	0.952	0.977
	10	28.350	32.219	32.235	32.611	0.882	0.933	0.941	0.954
	15	25.667	30.772	30.781	31.065	0.834	0.905	0.913	0.927
	25	20.074	28.946	29.128	29.653	0.795	0.852	0.880	0.906
Concordor	5	27.927	33.547	33.821	34.114	0.874	0.949	0.955	0.971
	10	25.672	32.455	32.517	32.883	0.712	0.931	0.937	0.963
	15	24.804	31.761	31.967	32.025	0.605	0.903	0.912	0.947
	25	22.213	30.458	30.472	31.383	0.591	0.875	0.884	0.903
Lena	5	29.517	35.605	35.697	35.831	0.877	0.945	0.953	0.966
	10	26.372	33.914	34.006	34.902	0.785	0.917	0.932	0.951
	15	24.425	32.775	32.863	33.058	0.724	0.904	0.916	0.933
	25	23.590	31.163	31.205	31.913	0.661	0.837	0.865	0.913

The Gaussian white noise with variation $\sigma = 15$ is added to the three images. The de-noised effects by four methods are shown in Figure 1 to Figure 3. From the aspect of the subjective visual effect, the proposed method is better than the other methods.

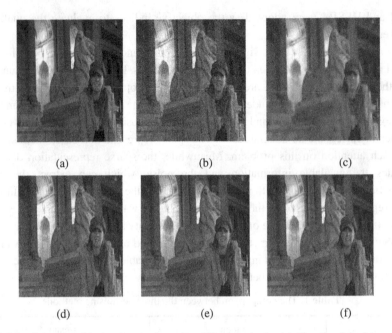

Fig. 1. Mandi image with the denoised results of four methods. (a) Mandi original image. (b) Noisy image($\sigma = 15$). (c) Wavelet. (d) K-SVD. (e) Method [10]. (f) Proposed.

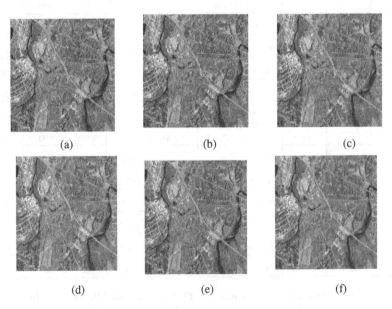

Fig. 2. Concordor image with the denoised results of three methods. (a) Concordor original image. (b) Noisy image($\sigma = 15$).(c) Wavelet. (d) K-SVD. (e) Method [10]. (f) Proposed.

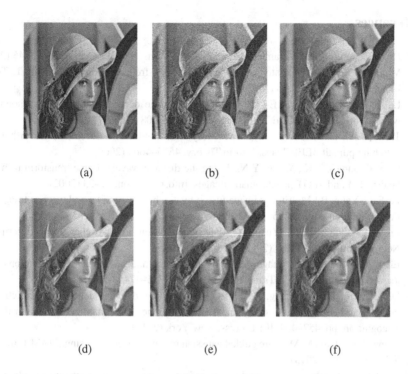

(a)   (b)   (c)

(d)   (e)   (f)

Fig. 3. Lena image with the denoised results of three methods. (a) Lena original image. (b) Noisy image($\sigma = 15$).(c) Wavelet. (d) K-SVD. (e) Method [10]. (f) Proposed.

5   Conclusions

The traditional de-noising algorithms based on the sparse representation make use of the initial completed dictionary and OMP algorithm to achieve the sparse separation, and take the reconstruction error as the fidelity, which doesn't consider the image's structural features. This paper proposed a new algorithm which replaces the structural similarity factor with the sum of the squares of the reconstruction error as the fidelity. The PSNR and HSSIM were selected to evaluate the performances of tested methods. Experimental results show that the proposed method can provide better results than the existing methods, such as the wavelet transformation, the K-SVD algorithm and the method [10]. The work can be further extended by improving the dictionary learning method.

Acknowledgment. This paper was supported by scientific research found of hunan provincial education department (13C122). The author would like to thank Prof. Shutao Li for his insightful comments and suggestions, which have greatly improved this paper. The author would also like to thank the reviewers for their helpful comments and Dr. Y. Tan for modify the syntax error which led improvement in quality of this paper.

References

[1] Do, M.N., Vetterli, M.: Framing pyramids. IEEE Trans. Signal Proces., 3736–3745 (2003)

[2] Mallat, S., Zhang, Z.: Matching pursuits with time-frequency dictionarys. IEEE Trans. Image Proces., 3397–3415 (1993)

[3] Luisier, F., Blu, T.: SURE-LET multichannel image denoising: Interscale orthonormal wavelet thresholding. IEEE Trans. Image Proces. (2008), 1057-7149

[4] Tropp, J.A., Gllbert, A.C.: Signal recovery from random measurements via orthogonal matching pursuit. IEEE Trans. Inform Theory, 4655–4665 (2007)

[5] Li, S.T., James, T.K., Wang, Y.N.: Using the discrete wavelet frame transform to merge landsat TM and SPOT panchromatic images. Inform. Fusion, 17–23 (2002)

[6] Li, S.T., Yang, B.: Multifocus image fusion by combining curvelet and wavelet transform. Pattern Recogn. Lett., 1295–1301 (2008)

[7] Li, S.T., Gong, D.Y., Yuan, Y.: Face recognition using weber local descriptors. Neurocomputing, 272–283 (2013)

[8] Elad, M., Aharon, M.: Image denoising via sparse and redundant representations over learned dictionaries. IEEE Trans. Image Proces., 3736–3745 (2006)

[9] Dong, W.S., Li, X., Zhang, L., Shi, G.: Sparsity-based image denoising via dictionary learning and structural clustering. In: IEEE Conference on Computer Vision and Pattern Recognition, pp. 457–464. IEEE Press, New York (2011)

[10] Wang, Y.Q., Jean, M.M.: Sure guided gaussian mixture image denoising. SIAM J. Imaging Sci., 1936–1954 (2013)

[11] Needell, D., Vershynin, R.: Signal recovery from incomplete and inaccurate measurements via regularized orthogonal matching pursuit. IEEE J. STSP, 310–316 (2010)

[12] Li, S.T., Kang, X.D., Hu, J.W.: Image fusion with guided filtering. IEEE Trans. Image Proces., 2864–2875 (2013)

[13] Li, S.T., Yin, H.T., Fang, L.Y.: Remote sensing image fusion via sparse representations over learned dictionaries. IEEE Trans. Geosci. Remote., 4779–4789 (2013)

[14] Aharon, M., Elad, M.: B.: K-SVD: An algorithm for designing overcomplete dictionaries for sparse representation. IEEE Trans. Image Proces., 4311–4322 (2006)

[15] Wang, Z., Bovic, A.C.: Mean square error: Love it or leave it? A new look at signal fidelity measures. IEEE Signal Proc. Mag., 98–117 (2009)

A SVM Method Trained by Improved Particle Swarm Optimization for Image Classification

Qifeng Qian, Hao Gao, and Baoyun Wang

College of Automation, Nanjing University of Posts and Telecommunications,
Jiang Su 210023, China
bywang@njupt.edu.cn

Abstract. As an important classification method, SVM has been widely used in different fields. But it is still a problem how to choose the favorable parameters of SVM. For optimizing the parameters and increasing the accuracy of SVM, this paper proposed an improved quantum behaved particle swarm algorithm based on a mutation operator (MQPSO). The new operator is used for enhancing the global search ability of particle. We test SVM based on MPSO method on solving the problem of image classification. Result shows our algorithm is quite stable and gets higher accuracy.

Keywords: PSO, SVM, Global search ability, Parameter optimization, Image classification.

1   Introduction

SVM is one of the most effective classifier, which was proposed by Vladimir N.Vapnik and improved by Vapnik and Corinna Cortes in 1995 [1]. But in practice, the parameters of SVM are quite difficult to choose, which directly affect the accuracy of classification. To design a SVM, we should determine a soft margin constant C and the kernel function parameter. In addition, the weight parameter has a great impact on unbalance dataset. Recently, as a popular optimization method, particle swarm optimization has been widely developed for solving optimization problems in power systems, fuzzy system control, and others.

Particle swarm optimization (PSO) is an evolutionary computation technique developed by Kennedy and Eberhart [2]. Compared to other optimization algorithm, the PSO has a faster and stable convergence rate. Then, by applying PSO algorithm in training the parameters of SVM, we should get better accuracy parameters. In this paper, we apply an improved QPSO algorithm in training SVM, which reduce the probability of falling local optima. Compared with the traditional PSO, QPSO shows power global search ability and is easier to control for it only has one parameter. For further enhancing its exploration ability, we introduce a mutation method into the original QPSO. At each iteration, particles may jump out of the local optimum by a certain probability.

S. Li et al. (Eds.): CCPR 2014, Part I, CCIS 483, pp. 263–272, 2014.
© Springer-Verlag Berlin Heidelberg 2014

Image classification has attracted more attention in the computer vision community in last decade. The task includes such as object recognition [3, 4] and scene classification [5, 6]. There are several methods used for image classification. Because of its high generalization ability, Support vector machines (SVM) are one of the most useful methods for data classification. After getting the trained parameters of SVM by using the improved QPSO, we use this model to classify the images. Since many tested datasets in this paper are unbalanced, we not only optimize the penalty parameter but also optimize the weight parameter, which set the weight of penalty parameter of certain class. In that case, we can get more precise model and better predicted accuracy.

2   Weighted-SVM

Support vector machines are the leading techniques used in classification. The interested property of SVM is that it is an approximate implementation of the structural risk minimization principle in statistical learning theory rather than the empirical risk minimization method.

The main idea behind SVM technique is to derive a unique separating hyper-plane (i.e. the optimal margin hyper-plane) that maximizes the margin between the two classes.

Given a set of instance label pairs (x_i, y_i), i=1,2...l, SVM require the solution of the following constrained optimization problem:

$$Minimize\ \Phi(\omega) = \frac{1}{2}\omega^T\omega + C\sum_{i=1}^{l}\xi_i \tag{1}$$

St: $y_i(\langle\omega, \phi(x_i) + b\rangle) \geq 1 - \xi_i, i = 1,...,l$ $\xi \geq 0, i = 1,...,l$

where ξ_i is a loss function, and C>0 is a penalty parameter. Here, we mapped sample x_i from the low-dimensional space into high-dimensional space by the kernel function ϕ, which can be linear function, Gaussian function, histogram intersection function, etc. The corresponding decision function is obtained by

$$f(x) = sign(\langle\omega_0, \phi(x_i) + b_0\rangle)$$
$$= sign(\sum_{i=0}^{l} a_i y_i K(x, x_i) + b_0) \tag{2}$$

But there still has a problem, if the given dataset is unbalanced, the optimal decision boundary will be pushed to the side of more samples. The results are shown on Fig 1.

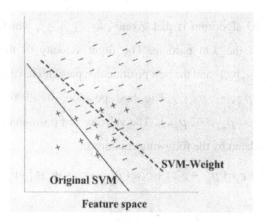

Fig. 1. The optimal decision boundary of unbalanced data

In Fig 1, to predict 4 data of minority class correctly, SVM misclassify 14 samples of majority class. To solve this problem, Weighted-SVM [7] was proposed. Its main idea is that we set different penalty parameter C for different class.

$$C_i = weight_i * C, i = 1, 2, ..., 1 \tag{3}$$

For example, $C_i = weight_i * C$ is the penalty parameter of class one. Weight-SVM has been proved to be an efficient way to solve multiclass and unbalance data,

With the optimal weights for each class, the objective of multiclass SVM in Formula (1) can be rewritten as

$$\min_W \frac{1}{2} \|W\|^2 + C \sum_{i=1}^{n} \omega_{y_i} \cdot \xi_i \tag{4}$$

We set different values for the penalty parameter of each class before training. Usually, larger value is set for majority class and smaller for the minority class [7]. Although appropriate weight parameter can perform very well on the problem mentioned above, the parameter ω_{y_i} is very hard to choose by the common approach (e. g., gradient descent method) as the objective function is nonlinear and non-convex function. Then we introduce an improved particle swam optimization algorithm.

3   An Improved Quantum Particle Swarm Optimization

3.1   Particle Swarm Optimization

Particle swarm optimization (PSO) [2] is a population-based stochastic optimization algorithm, which is inspired by bird flocking and fish schooling. Compared with other Evolutionary Algorithm, PSO shows fast convergence rate. Then, it is quite fit to find the best parameters of SVM fast.

The standard PSO algorithm is that given $z_i = (z_{i1}, z_{i2}, \cdots z_{iD})$, which represent the D dimension vector of the i th particle. The flight velocity of the i th particle is $V_i = (V_{i1}, V_{i2}, \cdots, V_{id}, \cdots, V_{iD})$ and the best position that particles have searched by now is $P_i = (p_{i1}, p_{i2}, \cdots, p_{id}, \cdots, p_{iD})$. The best position of all the particle swarm is $P_g = (P_{g1}, P_{g2}, \cdots, P_{gd}, \cdots, P_{gD})$. The velocity and position of particle i at (k + 1)th iteration are updated by the following equations:

$$V_{id}^{k+1} = wV_{id}^{k+1} + c_1 r_1 (p_{id} - z_{id}^k) + c_2 r_2 (p_{gd} - z_{id}^k) \ V_{id} \in [-v_{max}, v_{max}] \quad (5)$$

$$z_{id}^{k+1} = z_{id}^k + v_{id}^{k+1} \quad (6)$$

where w is the inertia weight, which plays a role in balancing the ability of searching global optimum and local optimum. c_1, c_2 represent the learning factors.

3.2   Quantum Particle Swarm Optimization and Its Improvement

The main disadvantage of PSO is that global convergence cannot be guaranteed (Bergh, 2001) [9]. When the particles fall in local optimum, they don't have the ability to jump out of the local point. To conquer the premature of the original PSO algorithm, QPSO was proposed by Shuyuan Yang [10], Sun, Feng, & Xu [11] .

The main difference between QPSO and PSO is that the particles updating equation is quantum which is similar to the wave function. Following is the equation how the particles move.

$$Z_{k+1} = P_i - \beta * (mBest - Z_k) * \ln(1/u) \text{ if } k \geq 0.5$$
$$Z_{k+1} = P_i + \beta * (mBest - Z_k) * \ln(1/u) \text{ if } k < 0.5 \quad (7)$$

where $P_i = \varphi * pBest_i + (1-\varphi) * gBest_i$ and $mBest = \dfrac{1}{N} \sum_{i=1}^{N} pBest_i$.

Compared with the traditional PSO algorithm, the introduced exponential distribution of positions makes QPSO have more global search ability. But the difference of particles becomes smaller especially in the later stage of iteration, then the particles of QPSO have less opportunity to jump out of the local optimum. Then, we introduce a mutation operator (**MQPSO**) to enhance the particles' capacity of jumping out of local optimum. The particle's position is updated with a certain probability by using the following formula, which enables the particle to jump out of the poor local optimum.

$$Z'_{k+1,j} = \begin{cases} (z\max - z\min) * \text{rand}() + z\min \\ \quad\quad\quad\quad , \text{if RandInt}()=j \\ Z_{k+1,j} \quad\quad\quad , other \end{cases} \quad (8)$$

where RandInt() function generate a random integer from 1 to the number of particle swarm at a certain probability(we set the probability to 50%).

At each iteration, particles will update positions. After calculating Z_{k+1} by equation (7), we begin to mutate. If RandInt() function generates an integer equal to j, then the jth particle will mutate position to random number from $z\min$ to $z\max$. In other words, we force the particles to fly to the new position which follows the uniform distribution. If RandInt() function generates an integer not equal to j, particles don't mutate. MQPSO algorithm not only remains the original particle swarm's intelligence, but also improves the individuality of each particle, which makes the particle jump out of the local attractor point.

Due to the advantage of the MQPSO, it can be applied to finding the proper parameters of the weighted SVM. We use the cross validation to calculate the accuracy of SVM, which represents by the fitness of the improved QPSO. The SVM's parameters are represented by the particle's position. The specific experiment is introduced in the following section.

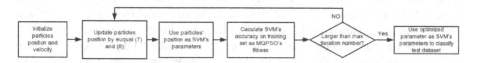

Fig. 2. Flow diagram using MQPOS to optimize SVM's parameters

4   Experimental Results

4.1   Performance on Small Scale Dataset

To verify our method on choosing SVM's parameters, firstly we test it on Heart dataset, which is a small scale dataset and commonly used in classification.

We divide the dataset into two parts, one for training and the other for testing. By using MQPSO algorithm to train SVM, we utilize the cross validation to calculate the MQPSO's fitness and then we will get the optimized parameters for SVM in this dataset. After that, we take the trained SVM model to classify the image dataset.

In our experiment, we repeat 200 times trials for the procedure mentioned above to reduce its occasionality.

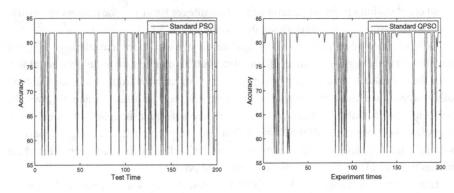

Fig. 3. Best accuracy of 200 trials using standard PSO   **Fig. 4.** Best accuracy of 200 trials using standard QPSO

In Fig 2, 3and 4,the vertical coordinate means the best accuracy of SVM using the optimal parameters searched by PSO algorithm, which also can represents the fitness value of PSO. The horizontal ordinate represents the number of trials. From these three figs, we can see standard PSO and QPSO will fall in local optimum very often and QPSO is better than PSO because of fewer times and a little bit higher accuracy when fall in local optimum. On the other hand, MQPSO algorithm is quite stable and almost every trial converges to the best accuracy among 200 times repetitions.

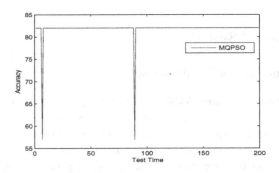

Fig. 5. Best accuracy of 200 repeated trials using random mutation QPSO

We also calculate the mean fitness value in 200 runs and the max iteration of each run is set as 500 in PSO algorithms. Then results of the mean value in 200 runs for 500 iterators are shown in Fig 5. As the results shown in Fig. 5, our algorithm gets the best results among the compared algorithms. It shows that MQPSO gets the fastest convergence rate and best accuracy than the other algorithms. Fig 6 shows MQPSO gets the minimum standard deviation, which proves MQPSO is quite stable.

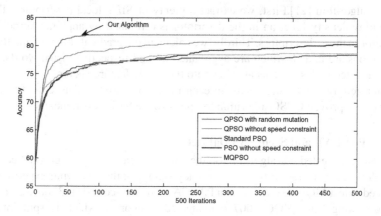

Fig. 6. Mean fitness curve of 200 times repeated experiment on various PSO

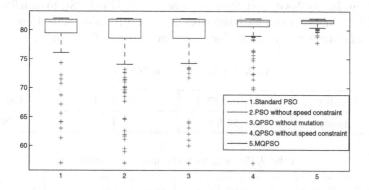

Fig. 7. STD of 200 times repeated experiment on various PSO

4.2   Image Classification

4.2.1   SVM in Image Classification

Since SVM is an effective tool of classifier, it has been applied into the image classification [12]. Accordingly, the linear SVM's computational complexity is $O(n)$ in the training phase, where n is the training size. Generally, the accuracy of linear SVM is lower than that of nonlinear SVM. But in image classification, dimension of image feature are very high and usually larger than several thousand. In practice, the accuracy of linear SVM is almost similar with that of nonlinear SVM in image classification.

As the results shown in the previous section, we can see our algorithm gets more accuracy andstable performance. So we apply our algorithm to train the parameter of SVM, then introduce the hybrid method into the images classification. We refer to

ScSPM algorithm [21].First, we extract a plenty of SIFT local descriptors. Then the probability density function in the descriptor is estimated by applying kernel density estimator to those descriptors. Thirdly, we calculate the gradients on p.d.f and then their orientations are coded, which are aggregated around respective visual words. Finally the aggregated codes are concatenated into the image feature vector.

After getting the feature vector in each image, we use SVM to classify them and apply our improved QPSO algorithm to optimize the SVM's parameters .

4.2.2   PASCAL and Scence-15 Dataset

Since we have tested our algorithm on the dataset "heart", it has been verified that our algorithm can converge to the best accuracy stably. In the following experiments, we just need to test MQPSO only once in PASCAL [3] and Scene-15[13] dataset for saving the computing time. VOC 2007 contains 20 categories, which is spilt into 5,011 training images and 4,952 test images. Scene 15 is a dataset of 15natural scene categories that expands on the 13category dataset released by Fei-Fei Li[26].

Jianchao Yang uses linear spatial pyramid matching method based on sparse coding (ScSPM) to classify this dataset. We base on ScSPM and use MPSO to train SVM, then to classify the images. Compared with other image classification method, our algorithm gets more favorable performance. The results are shown in Table1and 2.

Table 1. Performance on VOC 2007

Algorithm	ScSPM [21]	BoF [20]	**Ours**
Accuracy	54.6	61	**75**

Table 2. Performance on Scence-15 dataset[13]

Algorithm	Lazebnik et al.[13]	Yand and Newsam[14]	Dixit et al.[15]	Huang et al.[16]	Liu et al.[17]	Boureau et al.[18]	Fisher kernel [19]	BoF (256 words) [20]	ours
Accuracy	81.40 ±0.50	82.51 ±0.43	85.4	82.55 ±0.41	83.76 ±0.59	84.3 ±0.5	82.94 ±0.78	85.63 ±0.67	87

4.2.3   Caltech 101 Dataset

We also test our algorithm on Caltech 101 Dataset which contains pictures of objects belonging to 101 categories (including faces, airplanes, motorbikes, car, etc.), about 40 to 800 images per category. Most categories have about 50 images. The size of each image is roughly 300 x 200 pixels.

Takumi proposed a p.d.f gradients method for image classification. This is a novel feature extraction for image classification. In the framework of BoF [20] which extracts a plenty of local descriptors from an image, the proposed method is built upon the probability density estimator to those local descriptor. The last step is also using SVM to classify the feature vector. So our algorithm is still suitable for this method. As the results shown in Table 3, the bigger values of accuracy are, the better the algorithm. Then we can find that our algorithm gets better result than Takumi.

Table 3. Performance on Caltech 101

Algorithms	Zhang et al[22]	KSPM [5]	NBNN [23]	ML+CORR [24]	KC [25]	ScSPM [21]	BOF [20]	Ours
Accuracy	66.2	64.4	70	69.6	64.1	73.2	70.8	**82**

5   Conclusion and Further Work

In this paper, we proposed a random mutation quantum particle swarm algorithm and use it to train SVM to seek the best parameters. Compared to other algorithms, our algorithm shows more stable and favorable results. We also apply the hybrid method into image classification. Result shows our algorithm can obtain higher classification accuracy.

In future, we make effort to apply the hybrid algorithm to solve more complex problems and find more favorable results.

References

[1] Vapnik, V.: The nature of statistical learning theory. Springer (2000)
[2] Kennedy, J., Eberhart, R.: Particle swarm optimization. In: Proceedings of IEEE International Conference on Neural Networks, vol. 4(2), pp. 1942–1948 (1995)
[3] Everingham, M., Van Gool, L., Williams, C.K.I., et al.: The pascal visual object classes (voc) challenge. International Journal of Computer Vision 88(2), 303–338 (2010)
[4] Griffin, G., Holub, A., Perona, P.: Caltech-256 object category dataset (2007)
[5] Lazebnik, S., Schmid, C., Ponce, J.: Beyond bags of features: Spatial pyramid matching for recognizing natural scene categories. In: IEEE Computer Society Conference on Computer Vision and Pattern Recognition, vol. 2, pp. 2169–2178. IEEE (2006)
[6] Li, L.J., Fei-Fei, L.: What, where and who? classifying events by scene and object recognition. In: IEEE 11th International Conference on Computer Vision, ICCV 2007, pp. 1–8. IEEE (2007)
[7] Tang, Y., Zhang, Y.Q., Chawla, N.V., et al.: SVMs modeling for highly imbalanced classification. IEEE Transactions on Systems, Man, and Cybernetics, Part B: Cybernetics 39(1), 281–288 (2009)
[8] Zhou, Z.H., Liu, X.Y.: On Multi-Class Cost-Sensitive Learning. Computational Intelligence 26(3), 232–257 (2010)
[9] Van Den Bergh, F., Engelbrecht, A.P.: Training product unit networks using cooperative particle swarm optimisers. In: Proceedings of the International Joint Conference on Neural Networks, IJCNN 2001, vol. 1, pp. 126–131. IEEE (2001)
[10] Yang, S., Wang, M., Jiao, L.: A quantum particle swarm optimization. In: Congress on Evolutionary Computation, CEC 2004, vol. 1, pp. 320–324. IEEE (2004)

[11] Sun, J., Xu, W., Feng, B.: Adaptive parameter control for quantum-behaved particle swarm optimization on individual level. In: 2005 IEEE International Conference on Systems, Man and Cybernetics, vol. 4, pp. 3049–3054. IEEE (2005)

[12] Chapelle, O., Haffner, P., Vapnik, V.N.: Support vector machines for histogram-based image classification. IEEE Transactions on Neural Networks 10(5), 1055–1064 (1999)

[13] Lazebnik, S., Schmid, C., Ponce, J.: Beyond bags of features: Spatial pyramid matching for recognizing natural scene categories. In: 2006 IEEE Computer Society Conference on Computer Vision and Pattern Recognition, vol. 2, pp. 2169–2178. IEEE (2006)

[14] Yang, Y., Newsam, S.: Spatial pyramid co-occurrence for image classification. In: 2011 IEEE International Conference on Computer Vision (ICCV), pp. 1465–1472. IEEE (2011)

[15] Dixit, M., Rasiwasia, N., Vasconcelos, N.: Adapted gaussian models for image classification. In: 2011 IEEE Conference on Computer Vision and Pattern Recognition (CVPR), pp. 937–943. IEEE (2011)

[16] Huang, Y., Huang, K., Yu, Y., et al.: Salient coding for image classification. In: 2011 IEEE Conference on Computer Vision and Pattern Recognition (CVPR), pp. 1753–1760. IEEE (2011)

[17] Liu, L., Wang, L., Liu, X.: In defense of soft-assignment coding. In: 2011 IEEE International Conference on Computer Vision (ICCV), pp. 2486–2493. IEEE (2011)

[18] Boureau, Y.L., Bach, F., LeCun, Y., et al.: Learning mid-level features for recognition. In: 2010 IEEE Conference on Computer Vision and Pattern Recognition (CVPR), pp. 2559–2566. IEEE (2010)

[19] Perronnin, F., Dance, C.: Fisher kernels on visual vocabularies for image categorization. In: IEEE Conference on Computer Vision and Pattern Recognition, CVPR 2007, pp. 1–8. IEEE (2007)

[20] Kobayashi, T.: BFO Meets HOG: Feature Extraction Based on Histograms of Oriented pdf Gradients for Image Classification. In: 2013 IEEE Conference on Computer Vision and Pattern Recognition (CVPR), pp. 747–754. IEEE (2013)

[21] Yang, J., Yu, K., Gong, Y., et al.: Linear spatial pyramid matching using sparse coding for image classification. In: IEEE Conference on Computer Vision and Pattern Recognition, CVPR 2009, pp. 1794–1801. IEEE (2009)

[22] Zhang, H., Berg, A.C., Maire, M., et al.: SVM-KNN: Discriminative nearest neighbor classification for visual category recognition. In: 2006 IEEE Computer Society Conference on Computer Vision and Pattern Recognition, vol. 2, pp. 2126–2136. IEEE (2006)

[23] Lazebnik, S., Schmid, C., Ponce, J.: Beyond bags of features: Spatial pyramid matching for recognizing natural scene categories. In: 2006 IEEE Computer Society Conference on Computer Vision and Pattern Recognition, vol. 2, pp. 2169–2178. IEEE (2006)

[24] Jain, P., Kulis, B., Grauman, K.: Fast image search for learned metrics. In: IEEE Conference on Computer Vision and Pattern Recognition, CVPR 2008, pp. 1–8. IEEE (2008)

[25] van Gemert, J.C., Geusebroek, J.-M., Veenman, C.J., Smeulders, A.W.M.: Kernel codebooks for scene categorization. In: Forsyth, D., Torr, P., Zisserman, A. (eds.) ECCV 2008, Part III. LNCS, vol. 5304, pp. 696–709. Springer, Heidelberg (2008)

[26] Fei-Fei, L., Perona, P.: A bayesian hierarchical model for learning natural scene categories. In: IEEE Computer Society Conference on Computer Vision and Pattern Recognition, CVPR 2005, vol. 2, pp. 524–531. IEEE (2005)

Sparsity Based Feature Extraction
for Kernel Minimum Squared Error

Jiang Jiang[1], Xi Chen[2], Haitao Gan[3], and Nong Sang[1]

[1] Science and Technology on Multi-spectral Information Processing Laboratory,
School of Automation, Huazhong University of Science and Technology,
Wuhan 430074, China
nsang@hust.edu.cn
[2] Information and Telecommunication Branch of Hainan Power Grid,
Hainan 570203, China
[3] School of Automation, Hangzhou Dianzi University, Hangzhou 310018, China

Abstract. Kernel minimum squared error(KMSE) is well-known for its effectiveness and simplicity, yet it suffers from the drawback of efficiency when the size of training examples is large. Besides, most of the previous fast algorithms based on KMSE only consider classification problems with balanced data, when in real world imbalanced data are common. In this paper, we propose a weighted model based on sparsity for feature selection in kernel minimum squared error(KMSE). With our model, the computational burden of feature extraction is largely alleviated. Moreover, this model can cope with the class imbalance problem. Experimental results conducted on several benchmark datasets indicate the effectivity and efficiency of our method.

Keywords: Pattern classification, Kernel MSE, sparsity, weighted, feature extraction.

1 Introduction

Kernel-based methods have been popular in regression and classification fields because of their excellent performance in solving nonlinear problems[13]. The main motivation of kernel-based methods is that nonlinear problems involving linearly inseparable data can be transformed into linear separable problems by mapping the data into a new higher-dimensional feature space. By exploiting the kernel trick, the exact form of the mapping functions need not to be revealed, which enormously encourages the pervasion of such methods. There are several well-known kernel-based methods, such as support vector machine(SVM)[4,2], kernel principle component analysis(KPCA)[16], kernel Fisher discriminant analysis(KFDA)[12] and kernel minimum squared error(KMSE)[20].

KMSE has attracted much attention in the field of pattern recognition mostly due to its simplicity. For other kernel-based methods, SVM's primary difficulty is to solve a quadratic optimization problem and KFDA involves calculating the eigenvectors. However, KMSE needs only to solve a group of linear equation, which is much simpler than the above two problems. Moreover, it has been

S. Li et al. (Eds.): CCPR 2014, Part I, CCIS 483, pp. 273–282, 2014.

proved[20] that by properly choosing the output coding schemes and regularization terms, KMSE is a unified framework for kernel Fisher discriminant(KFD), least square version for support vector machine(LS-SVM)[17] and kernel ridge regression(KRR)[15].

However, despite the good properties mentioned above, KMSE suffers from the drawback in efficiency when the size of training examples are large. According to KMSE algorithm, for any new coming test example, we have to compute the kernel functions between this example and all of the training examples. In other words, the efficiency of KMSE decreases as the number of the training examples increases. This has been a huge limitation for using KMSE in real world applications. Hence, it is of great necessity and importance to develop a fast method for KMSE. Methods have been proposed to accelerate the feature extraction procedure of KMSE. Basically, the parsimonious principle is employed by selecting only a small subset of the original training set to linearly express the feature extractor. This portion of training examples is often referred as significant nodes[21,23]. By establishing a certain criterion to choose significant nodes, consequently, in the feature extraction procedure, the number of kernel functions needed to be calculated reduces to the number of significant nodes. Thus, the computational burden has been largely eased. Following this thought, Xu et al.[21] propose a fast kernel-based nonlinear method(FKNM) which uses forward algorithm to perform subset selection. In[24], Zhu et al. introduce a simplified KMSE by establishing an integrated criterion to select the significant nodes. Later, Zhu[23] presents to use the backward greedy algorithm to construct a reformative nonlinear feature extraction method for selecting significant nodes according to the absolute value of the combination coefficients. Zhao et al.[22] propose to employ sequential forward greedy learning algorithm for subset selection. In [19], a significant nodes selection method based on the contribution of the nodes to the class decision function is proposed. Jiang et al.[11] propose a sparsity based model for feature extraction. However, in spite of designing different approaches to decide the significant nodes, the above mentioned methods haven't formulated any explicit model for this subset selecting problem except of [11]. Besides, except for [21], these methods are designed only for two-class problem. Xu et al.[21] simply extend the method of two-class classification to multi-class situation by one-against-one or one-against-the-rest approach and omit the sample imbalance problem which commonly occurs in one-against-the-rest strategy. Their results suggest that one-against-the-rest is superior to one-against-one.

In this paper, we propose an explicit model, namely weighted sparsity based KMSE (WSKMSE), for significant nodes selection. By introducing a sparsity shrinkage term and a weight matrix, the subset selection procedure for balanced and imbalanced datasets discussed above can be formulated as a sparsity regularized optimization problem. The nodes corresponding to the nonzero coefficients are naturally chosen to be the significant nodes. Using these small amount of nodes, the computational burden of feature extraction is alleviated. For multi-class classification, our model can overcome the imbalance problem while adopting one-against-the-rest strategy.

The rest of the paper is organized as follows. The naive KMSE is briefly reviewed in Section 2. In Section 3, we describe our algorithm in detail. Experimental results on several real world datasets are discussed in Section 4. We conclude our paper in Section 5.

2   Naive KMSE Model

For the classification problem of two classes, $Tr = \{(x_1, y_1), (x_2, y_2), \ldots, (x_l, y_l)\}$ is a training set of size l, where $x_i \in \mathbb{R}^m$, $y_i = 1$ if x_i belongs to class c_1 or $y_i = -1$ if x_i belongs to class c_2. By a nonlinear mapping ϕ, the original feature space is transformed into a new feature space, which means the training feature examples $x_1, x_2, \ldots, x_l$ become $\phi(x_1), \phi(x_2), \ldots, \phi(x_l)$. The task of KMSE is to build a linear model in the new feature space so that the projective values of the training examples mapping from this model are equal to their labels. The model is expressed as following

$$\Phi B = Y \tag{1}$$

where

$$\Phi = \begin{bmatrix} 1 & 1 & \ldots & 1 \\ \phi(x_1) & \phi(x_2) & \ldots & \phi(x_l) \end{bmatrix}^T, B = \begin{bmatrix} \alpha_0 & b^T \end{bmatrix}^T, \quad \text{and} \quad Y = [y_1, y_2, \ldots, y_l]^T$$

According to the theory of reproducing kernels[12,14], b can be represented as

$$b = \sum_{i=1}^{l} \alpha_i \phi(x_i) \tag{2}$$

Assuming k is a Mercer kernel that $k(x_i, x_j) = \phi^T(x_i)\phi(x_j)$, substituting Eq.(2) into Eq.(1), we obtain

$$K\alpha = Y \tag{3}$$

where

$$K = \begin{bmatrix} 1 & k(x_1, x_1) & \ldots & k(x_1, x_l) \\ 1 & k(x_2, x_1) & \ldots & k(x_2, x_l) \\ \vdots & \vdots & \ddots & \vdots \\ 1 & k(x_l, x_1) & \ldots & k(x_l, x_l) \end{bmatrix} \quad \text{and} \quad \alpha = \begin{bmatrix} \alpha_0 \\ \alpha_1 \\ \vdots \\ \alpha_l \end{bmatrix}$$

For KSME, in order to avoid an ill-posed problem, the objective function is as following in a regularized least squares form

$$\hat{\alpha} = \arg \min_{\alpha} \|Y - K\alpha\|_2^2 + \mu \alpha^T \alpha \tag{4}$$

where μ is the coefficient of the regularization term. The solution is

$$\hat{\alpha} = (K^T K + \mu I)^{-1} K^T Y \tag{5}$$

where I is an identity matrix of size $(l+1) \times (l+1)$.
Then the class of a test data x can be calculated as

$$f(x) = \hat{\alpha}_0 + \sum_{i=1}^{l} \hat{\alpha}_i k(x, x_i) \qquad (6)$$

If $f(x) > 0$ then x belongs to class c_1 and if $f(x) < 0$ then x belongs to class c_2.

3   WSKMSE Model

From Eq.(6), we can see that to decide the class label for a given test example, as much as l kernel functions require to be calculated. For a large l, this process is undoubtedly time consuming. In this section, we introduce a weighted sparsity based model to deal with this drawback of naive KMSE. Since the second term in Eq.(4) is just to avoid illness, the subset selecting problem can be formulated as

$$(Q_0): \qquad \hat{\alpha} = \arg\min_{\alpha} \|Y - K\alpha\|_2^2 + \lambda\|\alpha\|_0 \qquad (7)$$

where $\|\cdot\|_0$ denotes l^0 norm, which counts the number of nonzero entries in a vector, and $\lambda > 0$ is a parameter controls the balance between fidelity and sparsity. The solution of Eq.(7) naturally selects important training nodes for classification. However, the l^0 problem is NP-hard and the procedure of finding the sparsest solution cannot be done in polynomial time. Fortunately, under the condition that the solution of α is sparse enough, which can be confirmed by experimental results discussed in section 4 , the solution of l^0-minimization problem(7) can be relaxed to the following l^1-minimization problem[5]:

$$(Q_1): \qquad \hat{\alpha} = \arg\min_{\alpha} \|Y - K\alpha\|_2^2 + \lambda\|\alpha\|_1 \qquad (8)$$

where $\|\cdot\|_1$ denotes the l^1 norm. Here lies an assumption that each data samples are equally punished when they are classified into the wrong class. However, there exists in real world that some class should cost more than others when they are misclassified. For instance, suppose there is a rare disease which only a few people around the world have got, that is, the samples from this sick class is very limited. In diagnosis we would rather suspect that one person is sick than claim a sick one being healthy. In order to deal with data with imbalanced distribution and significance, furthermore, we incorporate the above Q_1 model with a misclassification cost matrix. Without loss of generality, here we use data distribution imbalance to illustrate our model. Suppose that the number of examples in class c_1 and c_2 are respectively l_1 and l_2, than we formulate our model as

$$\hat{\alpha} = \arg\min_{\alpha} \|W(Y - K\alpha)\|_2^2 + \lambda\|\alpha\|_1 \qquad (9)$$

where

$$W = diag([w_1 \quad w_2 \quad \ldots \quad w_l]) \qquad (10)$$

where

$$w_j = \begin{cases} \gamma \cdot \frac{l_2}{l_1} \; if \; y_j = +1 \\ 1 \qquad if \; y_j = -1 \end{cases} \tag{11}$$

where γ is a factor that tunes the misclassification cost and decided by cross validation. In this case, different misclassification costs are assigned to different classes. It is natural to increase the cost of the minority class. By substituting WY as $\tilde{Y}$ and WK as $\tilde{K}$ in Eq.(9), our model becomes

$$\hat{\alpha} = \arg\min_{\alpha} \|\tilde{Y} - \tilde{K}\alpha\|_2^2 + \lambda\|\alpha\|_1 \tag{12}$$

This convex optimization problem is known as Least Absolute Shrinkage and Selection Operator(LASSO)[18] in statistics and Basis Pursuit(BP)[3] in signal and image processing. It has been proved that solving l^1 not only provides a way to get regression, but it also selects a small subset of features, known as model selection[7]. Several off-the-shelf methods can efficiently solve this problem, such as Least Angle Regression Stagewise(LARS)[6], Coordinate Descent[8], Bregman Iteration[10], Nesterov's method[1], et al. By tuning λ, different subset of α are chosen to be nonzero and considered as candidates of important nodes in our algorithm. Here we use LARS to solve our subset selecting problem but not to estimate the coefficients[11]. Algorithm 1 summarizes our classification procedure.

Algorithm 1. Weighted Sparsity based KMSE(WSKMSE)

Input: Label vector for training examples $Y = [y_1, y_2, \ldots, y_l]^T, y_i \in \{-1, +1\}$, kernel matrix $K \in \mathbb{R}^{l \times (l+1)}$, weight matrix W, parameter $\lambda > 0$, $\gamma > 0$.
1: Assigning $\tilde{Y} = WY$, $\tilde{k} = WK$.
2: Using LARS to solve Eq.(12) and get the active subset of coefficients $\mathcal{A}$ which correspond to the selected nodes of training examples.
3: Using only the selected subset of training nodes to solve the original KMSE problem:

$$\hat{\alpha}^{\mathcal{A}} = \arg\min_{\alpha^{\mathcal{A}}} \|\tilde{Y} - \tilde{K}_{\mathcal{A}}\alpha^{\mathcal{A}}\| + \mu(\alpha^{\mathcal{A}})^T\alpha^{\mathcal{A}} \tag{13}$$

where $\tilde{K}_{\mathcal{A}} = [\mathbb{1} \; \tilde{K}_1 \; \ldots \; \tilde{K}_{|\mathcal{A}|}]$, in which $\mathbb{1}$ is a column vector whose entries are all 1's and $\tilde{K}_i = [w_1k(x_1, x_{\mathcal{A}_i}) \; \ldots \; w_lk(x_l, x_{\mathcal{A}_i})]^T$ for $i = 1, \ldots, |\mathcal{A}|$. The solution to Eq.(13) is

$$\hat{\alpha}^{\mathcal{A}} = (\tilde{K}_{\mathcal{A}}^T\tilde{K}_{\mathcal{A}} + \mu I)^{-1}\tilde{K}_{\mathcal{A}}^T\tilde{Y} \tag{14}$$

4: The class of any new test example x is decided by

$$f(x) = \hat{\alpha}_0^{\mathcal{A}} + \sum_{i=1}^{|\mathcal{A}|} \hat{\alpha}_i^{\mathcal{A}} k(x, x_{\mathcal{A}_i}) \tag{15}$$

If $f(x) > 0$ then the label of x is 1 and if $f(x) < 0$ then the label of x is -1.

Using Eq.(15) instead of Eq.(6) to determine the label of a test example, the kernel functions to be calculated decrease from l to $|\mathcal{A}|$. While $|\mathcal{A}| \ll l$, the computational efficiency is largely increased.

4   Experimental Results

In this section, a series of experiments are conducted to evaluate the performance of our algorithm. First we conduct experiments on balanced two-class case to prove our ability on selecting proper significant nodes, then we evaluate our model with toy experiments for imbalanced two-class classification problem and multi-class face recognition task under one-against-the-rest configuration to verify the classification capability on imbalanced data. We compare WSKMSE with RKMSE[23], IKMSE[22] and FKNM[21] in both experiments. Five real-world datasets chosen from the well-known UCI machine learning repository[1] and LIBSVM data[2] are used for balanced data experiment. For two-class imbalanced classification, we randomly generate 500 two dimensional points of two classes with Gaussian distribution, and choose different portion of points from these two classes for training. Three publicly available datasets are used for multi-class face recognition: the Olivetti Research Lab(ORL) database[3] the Yale database[4] and the Extended Yale B[9]. The results for any dataset presented in this section are the average taken through 10 random partitions of this dataset. Gaussian kernel $k(x_i, x_j) = \exp \frac{(-\|x_i - x_j\|_2^2)}{(2\sigma^2)}$ is chosen as the kernel function in our algorithm except for the toy experiments. Linear kernel $k(x_i, x_j) = x_i^T x_j$ is used for the toy experiments for better illustration. The kernel parameter σ is determined by cross-validation. For fair comparison, the same kernel is extended to other algorithms. We use SN as the abbreviation for "significant nodes" in this section.

The configurations of all the real world datasets are described in Table 1. Figure 1 shows some sample images from the face recognition databases. The results for balanced data on training and testing set are shown in Table 2 and 3 respectively. Figure 2 shows the results on toy experiments. The experimental results on face recognition are shown in Table 4, 5 and 6. The misclassification cost factor γ is set to 1 in balanced data experiments and set to different values in imbalanced data experiments which is given besides the accuracies of WSKMSE in 5 and 6.

From Table 2 and Table 3 we have two observations. First, with much less nodes than naive KMSE, all of the four fast methods designed for feature extraction can achieve fairly good results. It can be concluded that the strategy of selecting significant nodes not only accelerates the feature extraction speed, but also preserves as much information as needed for classification task. And

---

[1] http://archive.ics.uci.edu/ml/

[2] http://www.csie.ntu.edu.tw/ cjlin/libsvmtools/datasets/

[3] http://www.cl.cam.ac.uk/research/dtg/attarchive/facedatabase.html

[4] http://cvc.yale.edu/projects/yalefaces/yalefaces.html

Table 1. Description of the experimental datasets

Dataset	#Features	#Classes	#Training examples	#Testing examples
Breast	10	2	479	204
Diabetes	8	2	538	230
Liver	6	2	242	103
Heart	13	2	189	81
German	24	2	700	300
ORL	1024	40	200	200
Yale	1024	15	90	75
Yale B	1024	38	491	1923

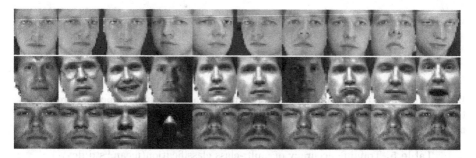

Fig. 1. Some face images from ORL(top), Yale(middle) and Extended Yale B(bottom)

Table 2. Training accuracy of balanced two-class classification(mean±std-dev%)

Dataset	number of SN	KMSE	RKMSE	IKMSE	FKNM	WSKMSE
Breast	120	97.06±0.47	97.06±0.49	97.06±0.49	97.22±0.50	**97.22±0.47**
Diabetes	108	77.21±0.88	77.21±0.85	77.21±0.85	77.19±0.91	**77.22±0.89**
Liver	61	**69.55±1.74**	69.21±1.90	69.17±1.82	66.90±2.08	69.47±1.91
Heart	38	**86.30±1.26**	86.03±1.25	86.08±1.30	85.56±1.48	85.71±1.27
German	203	**83.40±0.87**	83.13±0.82	83.03±0.91	80.91±0.74	83.09±0.77

Table 3. Testing accuracy of balanced two-class classification(mean±std-dev%)

Dataset	number of SN	KMSE	RKMSE	IKMSE	FKNM	WSKMSE
Breast	120	96.67±0.83	96.67±0.83	96.67±0.83	96.52±0.78	**96.72±0.70**
Diabetes	108	**78.22±1.74**	78.17±1.83	78.17±1.83	78.13±1.82	78.19±1.76
Liver	61	66.89±5.13	**67.09±5.33**	66.99±5.16	63.30±3.51	66.93±3.88
Heart	38	83.95±2.91	84.32±3.03	84.32±3.03	84.69±2.74	**84.81±3.03**
German	203	**76.40±0.72**	76.23±0.83	76.17±0.89	75.70±0.99	76.30±1.04

Table 4. Average number(rounded up) of significant nodes used in multi-class classification

Dataset	RKMSE	IKMSE	FKNM	WSKMSE
ORL	49	52	55	**47**
Yale	26	26	28	**25**
Yale B	128	130	137	**122**

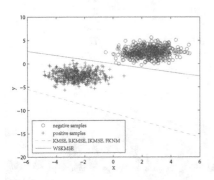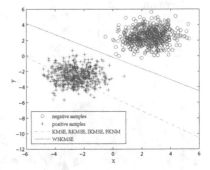

Fig. 2. Results of toy experiments, the number of chosen points for positive and negative classes are 5:500(left) and 10:500(right). For all of the fast methods, 3 significant nodes are chosen.

Table 5. Training accuracy of multi-class classification(mean±std-dev%)

Dataset	KMSE	RKMSE	IKMSE	FKNM	WSKMSE(γ)
ORL	100	100	100	100	100(0.5)
Yale	100	100	100	95.56±1.92	100(0.9)
Yale B	100	100	100	98.10±0.24	100(0.2)

Table 6. Testing accuracy of multi-class classification(mean±std-dev%)

Dataset	KMSE	RKMSE	IKMSE	FKNM	WSKMSE(γ)
ORL	92.00±1.26	91.67±1.76	91.83±1.26	88.00±2.25	**94.17±0.29**(0.5)
Yale	86.67±1.63	84.44±3.85	83.56±4.07	72.44±3.08	**87.26±2.78**(0.9)
Yale B	90.08±2.13	89.36±1.22	89.10±0.89	81.31±0.86	**91.94±1.03**(0.2)

our method although is not the best in some of the datasets, the gap between the results of naive KMSE and ours are really small. Moreover, our algorithm outperforms the naive KMSE on the Breast Cancer and Heart datasets. This interesting observation reveals that keeping all the features may not be better than finding the most representative ones when dealing with classification problems.

In imbalanced data case, Figure 2 shows that our method can find the best classification plane with the same amount of significant nodes. The reason is that the positive samples are always sacrificed while there are much more negative samples. Moreover, we can see from Table 4, 5 and 6 that our method achieves the best recognition accuracies with the fewest significant nodes on all three datasets. And the gap between our method and others are bigger in ORL and Extended Yale B datasets with respectively 40 and 38 classes than in Yale dataset with only 15 classes, which means the higher the imbalance rate is, the more beneficial our method is. Another observation is that when the imbalance rate is high, such as in ORL and Extended Yale B datasets, the best misclassification factor γ is small. This is probably because when the number of minority class examples is too few to represent the distribution of this class, merely increasing the misclassification cost of them will cause over-fitting. Results on the three datasets demonstrate that our improved model for imbalanced data classification task is superior than other methods.

5   Conclusion

In this paper, we introduce a weighted sparsity based feature extraction model, namely WSKMSE, for fast and effective kernel minimum squared error(KMSE). The method incorporates the sparsity shrinkage and a misclassification weight matrix in the objective function of KMSE. By solving a standard LASSO or BP problem, the most representative features are selected to form the kernel matrix. With much less nodes used, the computational burden of KMSE is largely alleviated. Our model can also deal with multi-class classification and other class imbalance problems. A series of experiments are conducted on both artificial and real-world datasets. The results show that our algorithm can obtain satisfactory performance in both balanced and imbalanced problem. Our future work will concentrate on the analysis of the connection between regression error and classification performance.

References

1. Becker, S., Bobin, J., Candès, E.J.: Nesta: a fast and accurate first-order method for sparse recovery. SIAM Journal on Imaging Sciences 4(1), 1–39 (2011)
2. Burges, C.J.: A tutorial on support vector machines for pattern recognition. Data Mining and Knowledge Discovery 2(2), 121–167 (1998)
3. Chen, S.S., Donoho, D.L., Saunders, M.A.: Atomic decomposition by basis pursuit. SIAM Journal on Scientific Computing 20(1), 33–61 (1998)
4. Cortes, C., Vapnik, V.: Support-vector networks. Machine Learning 20(3), 273–297 (1995)
5. Donoho, D.L.: For most large underdetermined systems of linear equations the minimal l1-norm solution is also the sparsest solution (English summary). Comm. Pure Appl. Math. 59(6), 797–829 (2006)
6. Efron, B., Hastie, T., Johnstone, I., Tibshirani, R.: Least angle regression. The Annals of Statistics 32(2), 407–499 (2004)
7. Elad, M.: Sparse and redundant representations: from theory to applications in signal and image processing. Springer (2010)
8. Friedman, J., Hastie, T., Höfling, H., Tibshirani, R.: Pathwise coordinate optimization. The Annals of Applied Statistics 1(2), 302–332 (2007)

9. Georghiades, A., Belhumeur, P., Kriegman, D.: From few to many: Illumination cone models for face recognition under variable lighting and pose. IEEE Trans. Pattern Anal. Mach. Intelligence 23(6), 643–660 (2001)
10. Goldstein, T., Osher, S.: The split bregman method for l1-regularized problems. SIAM Journal on Imaging Sciences 2(2), 323–343 (2009)
11. Jiang, J., Chen, X., Gan, H.T.: Feature extraction for kernel minimum squared error by sparsity shrinkage. Applied Mechanics and Materials 536, 450–453 (2014)
12. Mika, S., Ratsch, G., Weston, J., Scholkopf, B., Mullers, K.: Fisher discriminant analysis with kernels. In: Neural Networks for Signal Processing IX, Proceedings of the 1999 IEEE Signal Processing Society Workshop, pp. 41–48. IEEE (1999)
13. Muller, K.R., Mika, S., Ratsch, G., Tsuda, K., Scholkopf, B.: An introduction to kernel-based learning algorithms. IEEE Transactions on Neural Networks 12(2), 181–201 (2001)
14. Saitō, S.: Integral transforms, reproducing kernels and their applications, vol. 369. CRC Press (1997)
15. Saunders, C., Gammerman, A., Vovk, V.: Ridge regression learning algorithm in dual variables. In: (ICML 1998) Proceedings of the 15th International Conference on Machine Learning, pp. 515–521. Morgan Kaufmann (1998)
16. Schölkopf, B., Smola, A., Müller, K.R.: Kernel principal component analysis. In: Gerstner, W., Hasler, M., Germond, A., Nicoud, J.-D. (eds.) ICANN 1997. LNCS, vol. 1327, pp. 583–588. Springer, Heidelberg (1997)
17. Suykens, J.A., Vandewalle, J.: Least squares support vector machine classifiers. Neural Processing Letters 9(3), 293–300 (1999)
18. Tibshirani, R.: Regression shrinkage and selection via the lasso. Journal of the Royal Statistical Society. Series B (Methodological), 267–288 (1996)
19. Wang, J., Wang, P., Li, Q., You, J.: Improvement of the kernel minimum squared error model for fast feature extraction. Neural Computing and Applications, 1–7
20. Xu, J., Zhang, X., Li, Y.: Kernel mse algorithm: a unified framework for kfd, ls-svm and krr. In: Proceedings of the International Joint Conference on Neural Networks, IJCNN 2001, vol. 2, pp. 1486–1491. IEEE (2001)
21. Xu, Y., Zhang, D., Jin, Z., Li, M., Yang, J.Y.: A fast kernel-based nonlinear discriminant analysis for multi-class problems. Pattern Recognition 39(6), 1026–1033 (2006)
22. Zhao, Y.P., Du, Z.H., Zhang, Z.A., Zhang, H.B.: A fast method of feature extraction for kernel mse. Neurocomputing 74(10), 1654–1663 (2011)
23. Zhu, Q.: Reformative nonlinear feature extraction using kernel mse. Neurocomputing 73(16), 3334–3337 (2010)
24. Zhu, Q., Xu, Y., Cui, J., Chen, C.F., Wang, J., Wu, X., Zhao, Y.: A method for constructing simplified kernel model based on kernel-mse. In: Asia-Pacific Conference on Computational Intelligence and Industrial Applications, PACIIA 2009, vol. 1, pp. 237–240. IEEE (2009)

Saliency Detection Based on Spread Pattern and Manifold Ranking

Yan Huang[1], Keren Fu[1], Lixiu Yao[1], Qiang Wu[2], and Jie Yang[1]

[1]Institute of Image Processing and Pattern Recognition,
Shanghai Jiao Tong University, China
[2]University of Technology, Sydney, Australia

Abstract. In this paper, we propose a novel approach to detect visual saliency based on spread pattern and manifold ranking. We firstly construct a close-loop graph model with image superpixels as nodes. The saliency of each node is defined by its relevance to given queries according to graph-based manifold ranking technique. Unlike existing methods which choose a few background and foreground queries in a two-stage scheme, we propose to treat each node as a potential foreground query by assigning to it an initial ranking score based on its spread pattern property. The new concept *spread pattern* represents how the ranking score of one node is propagated to the whole graph. An accurate query map is generated accordingly, which is then used to produce the final saliency map with manifold ranking. Our method is computationally efficient and outperforms the state-of-the-art methods.

Keywords: saliency detection, graph model, spread pattern, manifold ranking.

1 Introduction

Saliency detection refers to the ability of a vision system to select informative subsets in an image for further processing. It can be applied to a number of vision tasks, e.g. image retrieval [1], image compression [2], object recognition and detection [3, 4]. Generally, saliency detection methods can be divided into bottom-up [5–10] and top-down [11] approaches. Bottom-up methods are data driven and use low-level information such as color, intensity, edge and textures, while the top-down ones are task-driven and require high-level information. In the past few years, great effort has been put into developing saliency detection algorithms, and remarkable results have been made.

Recently, saliency detection methods using boundary priors have achieved satisfactory results. Boundary priors were first proposed in [9], indicating that image boundaries are mostly backgrounds. One recent saliency detection method based on graph model, boundary priors and manifold ranking achieved significant progress [10]. In [10], image is represented as a close-loop graph with superpixels as nodes. The saliency of each node is defined by its relevance to given queries. A two-stage ranking process is used to compute pixel saliency. In the first stage,

S. Li et al. (Eds.): CCPR 2014, Part I, CCIS 483, pp. 283–292, 2014.

boundary priors are exploited by using the nodes on each side of the image as background queries. Four saliency maps corresponding to four sides of the image are computed and then integrated as the saliency map of the first stage. In the second stage, foreground queries are generated by applying binary segmentation to the resulted saliency map from the first stage. The saliency of each node is then computed based on its relevance to these foreground queries for the final saliency map.

In the work of [10], background queries are used to activate the whole process, and a second stage is required to generate foreground queries. However, background queries generated using boundary priors provide only limited query information, since non-salient regions are not necessarily constrained to the image boundaries. Furthermore, confidence of query is not used in [10] in which the initial ranking scores of all queries are uniformly set to 1.

In this paper, we seek another way to generate query information for ranking process. Different from [10] which uses background and foreground queries in two stages, we propose to use only foreground queries in a one-stage scheme. More specifically, we treat each node as a potential foreground query by assigning to each node an initial ranking score. A new concept termed as *spread pattern* is presented, based on which the initial ranking scores can be generated. We define how the ranking score of one node is spread to the whole graph as spread pattern. Generally, nodes inside compact object regions have very different spread patterns with nodes inside large homogenous background regions. With each node in the graph be assigned an initial ranking score, an query map is produced. We then use ranking process and the query map to get the final saliency result. The framework of our method is shown in Fig. 1(a).

The rest of the paper is organized as follows. Graph construction and manifold ranking are described in Section 2. Spread pattern analysis and saliency map generation are shown in Section 3. Experiments and conclusion are given in Section 4 and Section 5.

2   Graph Construction and Manifold Ranking

We adopt the graph construction method in [10] with an adjustment on the definition of edge weight. A graph $G = (V, E)$ is constructed using image superpixels as nodes, where V is the set of nodes and E is the set of edges. Each node is connected with the nodes adjacent to it (termed as the first-layer neighbors), and also the nodes that encircle the first-layer neighbors (termed as the second-layer neighbors). The nodes on the four boundaries of the image are all mutually connected, resulting in a close-loop graph (see Fig. 1(b)). The weight between two nodes is redefined as

$$\omega_{ij} = \lambda e^{-\frac{\|c_i - c_j\|}{\sigma^2}} \tag{1}$$

in our work, where c_i and c_j denote the mean CIE LAB color value of the nodes, and σ is the constant to control the strength of the weight. We add a parameter λ to decrease the weights between a node and its second-layer neighbors to better depict the spatial relationship in the double-layer connection

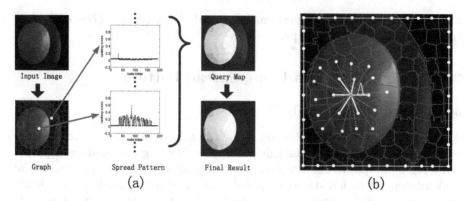

Fig. 1. (a) Framework of our approach. (b) Graph model construction. White solid lines along the image boundaries indicate that all boundary nodes are mutually connected. For node 'A', the white solid lines indicate the first-layer connections, green dashed lines indicate the second-layer connections.

mode. Given G, the affinity matrix is $W = [\omega_{ij}]_{n \times n}$, and the degree matrix is $D = diag\{d_{11}, \ldots, d_{nn}\}$, where $d_{ii} = \sum_j \omega_{ij}$.

The graph-based manifold ranking algorithm aims at exploiting the intrinsic manifold structure of data. All nodes spread their initial ranking scores to their neighbors via the graph repeatedly until a stable state is reached [13]. Given a node set $X = \{x_1, x_2, \ldots, x_n\} \in \Re^{m \times n}$, some nodes are labelled as queries and the rest can be ranked according to their relevances to the queries. Let $f : X \rightarrow \Re^n$ denote a ranking function which assigns to each node x_i a ranking value f_i. We can view f as a vector $f = [f_1, \ldots, f_i, \ldots, f_n]^T$. The optimal ranking of data is computed by solving the optimization problem described as

$$f^* = \arg\min_f \frac{1}{2} \left(\sum_{i,j=1}^{n} \omega_{ij} \| \frac{f_i}{\sqrt{d_{ii}}} - \frac{f_j}{\sqrt{d_{jj}}} \|^2 + \mu \sum_{i=1}^{n} \|f_i - y_i\|^2 \right), \qquad (2)$$

where μ is the parameter to control the balance between smoothness and fitting constraint, and $y = [y_1, \ldots, y_i, \ldots, y_n]^T$ is the vector to store the initial ranking scores of the nodes, termed as query information. In the work of [10], elements in y corresponding to queries are set to 1 and the others are set to 0. We adopt weighted queries by assigning different initial ranking scores to the nodes. The details will be given in Section 3.1. The close-form ranking function can be written as:

$$f^* = (I - \alpha S)^{-1} y, \qquad (3)$$

where I is an identity matrix, $\alpha = \frac{1}{1+\mu}$, and $S = D^{\frac{-1}{2}} W D^{\frac{-1}{2}}$ is the normalized Laplacian matrix. By using the unnormalized Laplacian matrix, another ranking function can be formed:

$$f^* = (D - \alpha W)^{-1} y = Ay, \qquad (4)$$

which proves to have better performance in [10]. We term $A = (D - \alpha W)^{-1}$ as the ranking matrix in this paper.

3   Saliency Detection Using Spread Pattern

3.1   Spread Pattern Analysis

A major issue of saliency detection using graph-based manifold ranking is the selection of queries. We bypass this problem by treating each node as a potential foreground query. The problem then turns into how to compute an initial ranking score for each node. As proposed in [9], most image patches in the background can be easily connected to each other in a piecewise manner, known as the connectivity prior. This reminds us of another prior used in saliency detection called shape prior [12], which means that salient objects tend to have well-defined boundaries. These priors indicate different connectivity properties between background regions and salient object regions. Because backgrounds tend to be homogeneous and widespread, while objects are more likely to be locally compact, we observe that there exist obvious differences between using a background node and an object node as query in ranking process.

In this section, we investigate how exactly the ranking score of one node is spread to the rest of the graph. We pick one node to serve as query each time by setting the corresponding element of the selected query in y to 1 and setting the rest elements to 0. Then we use eq.(4) to get the ranking scores for all the nodes. Some examples are given in Fig. 2. The gray images are visualized results of the ranking scores. Bright regions correspond to high ranking scores and the brightest node in each gray image represents the query. Note that the gray images are normalized for display clarity. Ranking scores are shown in the plots in corresponding columns, in which the red dots are the ranking scores of the queries. As shown in Fig. 2(b) and Fig. 2(c), when a node that belongs

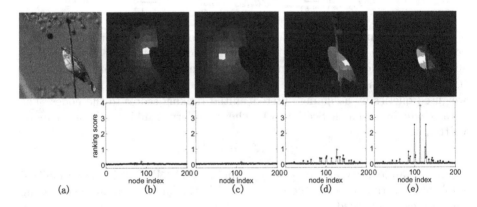

Fig. 2. Spread pattern demonstrations. (a) Input image. (b)-(e) Spread pattern of one selected node.

to the background is chosen as query, the resulted ranking scores of all nodes are uniformly low. When a node that locates inside a relatively compact object region is chosen, the query and its neighboring nodes within this region have much larger ranking scores than the other nodes in the graph, as shown in Fig. 2(d) and Fig. 2(e).

We rewrite the ranking matrix A as $A = [\phi_1, \phi_2, \ldots, \phi_n]$. Each column vector ϕ_i can actually be viewed as the ranking scores with the ith node set as query. From another perspective, ϕ_i can also be understood as the final state of spreading the query score of the ith node to the whole graph. According to the observations in Fig. 2, the different spread patterns between nodes in background regions and object regions motivate a novel way for initializing y in eq.(4).

Since we treat each node as a potential foreground query, nodes inside object regions should have larger initial ranking scores than nodes inside background regions. According to the analysis above, we propose to set the initial ranking score of each node to be the sum of the elements in the corresponding column in A. Since A is symmetric, this can be done efficiently using the following equation:

$$y^{init} = A^{\mathrm{T}} * s_0 = A * s_0, \tag{5}$$

where s_0 is a column vector whose elements are all set to 1. We normalize y^{init} to the range of $[0, 1]$. With each node of the graph be assigned an initial ranking score, an initial saliency map (query map) is produced with eq.(5).

We make some adjustments on the ranking matrix A before calculating the initial saliency map. According to [13], all nodes except query nodes are ranked according to their final ranking scores, which means that the ranking scores of the query nodes are meaningless. It can also be noticed from the plots in Fig. 2 that the ranking score of the query is much larger than the ranking scores of its neighbors, while we can observe from the color image in Fig. 2(a) that the visual appearances of the corresponding query of each plot and its neighboring nodes are not necessarily much different. As a result, we set the diagonal elements of A to 0, just as what is done in [10]. We also notice in experiment that the ranking scores of small isolated regions can be extremely large sometimes. Because we apply a normalization process to y^{init}, this abnormally large scores suppress the scores of other nodes inside salient regions, as shown in the 'N' columns in Fig. 3. Generally, large values in A correspond to nodes that have strong color contrast

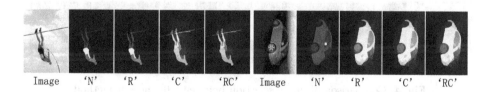

Image   'N'   'R'   'C'   'RC'   Image   'N'   'R'   'C'   'RC'

Fig. 3. Query maps generated with different adjustments. For clarity, 'N' indicates no adjustment is made, 'R' refers to resetting the diagonal elements of A, 'C' refers to filtering process and 'RC' refers to the combination of 'R' and 'C'.

with neighbors and small region sizes. To ensure uniformity within object regions, we empirically select a threshold $T_A = 1$ to filter the elements in A. Any element in A larger than this threshold is set to T_A. The threshold is chosen according to the observation that values beyond this threshold mostly correspond to salient regions.

We test this query map generation method on the MSRA-1000 dataset to verify its generality. The effects of resetting the diagonal elements in A and filtering process are also evaluated. From Fig. 3, it is noted that the query maps are satisfactory, and the salient regions are more uniform with the aforementioned adjustments.

3.2   Final Saliency Map Generation

With query information y initialized by eq.(5), we can generate the final saliency map with eq.(4). We rewrite it as follows:

$$f^* = A * y^{init} = \sum_{i=1}^{n} \phi_i * y_i^{init}. \tag{6}$$

The query map represented by y^{init} provides extensive, weighted and accurate query information when compared with boundary constrained, binary and imprecise query info used in [10], as demonstrated in Fig. 4. Compared with the two-stage scheme in [10] which involves four background query maps (Fig. 4(b)) and one foreground query map (Fig. 4(d)), our method uses only one query map (Fig. 4(f)), thus is more efficient. It can be noticed in Fig. 4(d) that the foreground queries generated in [10] cover many background nodes, and the head and neck parts of the bird are missed. Our query map (Fig. 4(f)) effectively highlights the salient regions and suppresses the background areas, and generates better final saliency result(Fig. 4(g)).

From eq.(6), we can see that the final ranking scores can be viewed as the weighted sum of the ranking results with one node set as query each time. According to the analysis in Section 3.1, the column vectors in A for background nodes have uniformly low values, thus the values in y^{init} for background nodes are also relatively low. While for salient nodes, the corresponding values in y^{init} are much larger. This means that background nodes have much lower contribution to the final saliency assignment than the salient nodes. As a result, salient

(a) Image   (b) Background_query   (c) Stage_1   (d) Foreground_query   (e) Stage_2[10]   (f) Our_query   (g) Our_Result

Fig. 4. Comparison of query selection between [10] and our method

regions are highlighted. To better suppress the background, we take a truncation procedure on y^{init}. Elements in y^{init} that are below threshold T_y are set to 0.

4   Experimental Results

We evaluate the proposed method on the MSRA-1000 dataset which contains 1,000 test images with human labelled masks for salient objects [6]. In all the experiments, each image is segmented into $N = 200$ superpixels. σ is set to $\sigma^2 = 0.1$; λ is set to 0.5 for the second-layer edges and set to 1 for the first-layer edges; α is set to 0.99 and T_y is set to 0.2. Similar as previous works, we use precision-recall curve and F-measure as quantitative evaluations. Averaged precision-recall curve is computed by binarizing the saliency map using thresholds ranging from 0 to 255. The F-Measure is computed by eq.(7) in which $\beta^2 = 0.3$.

$$F_\beta = \frac{(1 + \beta^2)Precision \times Recall}{\beta^2 Precision + Recall} \tag{7}$$

4.1   Graph Model Configuration for Query Map Generation

We firstly evaluate how the close-loop constraint on graph model affects the query map generation stage. Two sets of query maps are generated using graph model constructed with and without the close-loop constraint. Fig. 5(b) demonstrates that the performance of the query map is significantly better with close-loop graph model. In Fig. 5(a), the 1st row shows that when the background is globally homogenous, query map generated without close-loop constraint is comparable to the query map generated with the constraint. When the background is cluttered, query maps computed with the constraint are much better, as shown in the 2nd and 3rd rows. The reason is that the close-loop constraint enables non-adjacent similar background nodes to be connected to form large background regions. Otherwise, these nodes will be locally compact and possess the spread patterns of salient object nodes. This phenomenon is demonstrated

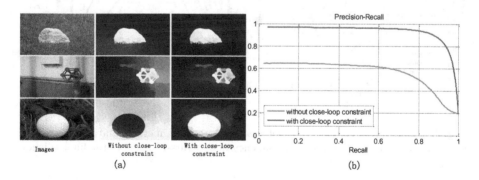

Fig. 5. Query map generated with different graph model configurations

in Fig. 6. To sum up, the close-loop graph model configuration is fundamental for using spread pattern for query map generation.

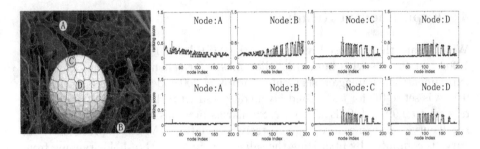

Fig. 6. The effect of close-loop constraint on spread pattern. 1st row: spread pattern without close-loop constraint. 2nd row: spread pattern with close-loop constraint.

4.2   Evaluation of Our Approach

We compare our method with seven existing saliency detection methods: IT [5], FT [6], HC [7], RC [7], SF [8], GS [9] and MR [10]. Fig. 7 presents the precision-recall curses and the F-measure results. From Fig. 7(a), it can be noticed that our proposed method outperforms all the rest. It is even more noticeable that the result of the initial saliency map is quite competitive, better than six of the seven methods in comparison. In Fig. 7(b), it can be seen that our method generates comparable result to the others.

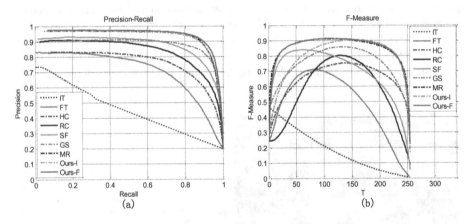

Fig. 7. Quantitative comparisons between the proposed method and seven existing methods. 'Ours-I' refers to the initial saliency map. 'Ours-F' refers to the final saliency map.

Visual comparisons between our method and seven other existing approaches are given in Fig. 8, where the last column marked as 'GT' column shows the ground truth of salient regions. As shown in the column marked as 'Ours-init', the initial saliency map generation stage produces accurate query maps, which alone can be used as a method to detect visual saliency. Background can be further suppressed with ranking process, as shown in the second-last column. Compared with [10], our method retains salient regions that are missed in [10], as shown in the 1st and 2nd rows. Recently, dataset bias is gaining increasing attention [14]. Note the ground truth in the 3rd and 4th row are not convincible according to human perception. Our method successfully detects the intuitively salient parts in these images. The last two rows demonstrate the effectiveness of background suppression of our method. Compared with the other methods, our method generalizes better across different situations and highlights the salient regions more uniformly.

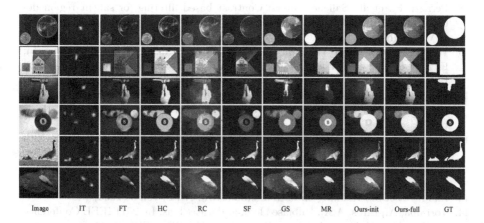

Image   IT   FT   HC   RC   SF   GS   MR   Ours-init   Ours-full   GT

Fig. 8. Visual comparisons between our method and previous approaches

5   Conclusion

We present a novel concept termed as spread pattern in this paper, based on which accurate query information can be efficiently generated for saliency detection using graph-based manifold ranking technique. Our method implicitly treats each node as a potential foreground query instead of selecting imprecise queries using boundary priors and foreground cues in a two-stage scheme. The evaluation on one large dataset demonstrates favorable results of our approach when against seven existing methods. Our future work will focus on incorporating high-level knowledge into the framework.

References

1. Chen, T., et al.: Sketch2Photo: internet image montage. ACM Transactions on Graphics (TOG) 28(5) (2009)
2. Itti, L.: Automatic foveation for video compression using a neurobiological model of visual attention. IEEE Transactions on Image Processing 13(10), 1304–1318 (2004)

3. Walther, D., Koch, C.: Modeling attention to salient proto-objects. Neural Networks 19(9), 1395–1407 (2006)
4. Kanan, C., Cottrell, G.: Robust classification of objects, faces, and flowers using natural image statistics. In: 2010 IEEE Conference on Computer Vision and Pattern Recognition (CVPR). IEEE (2010)
5. Itti, L., Koch, C., Niebur, E.: A model of saliency-based visual attention for rapid scene analysis. IEEE Transactions on Pattern Analysis and Machine Intelligence 20(11), 1254–1259 (1998)
6. Achanta, R., et al.: Frequency-tuned salient region detection. In: IEEE Conference on Computer Vision and Pattern Recognition, CVPR 2009. IEEE (2009)
7. Cheng, M.-M., et al.: Global contrast based salient region detection. In: 2011 IEEE Conference on Computer Vision and Pattern Recognition (CVPR). IEEE (2011)
8. Perazzi, F., et al.: Saliency filters: Contrast based filtering for salient region detection. In: 2012 IEEE Conference on Computer Vision and Pattern Recognition (CVPR). IEEE (2012)
9. Wei, Y., Wen, F., Zhu, W., Sun, J.: Geodesic saliency using background priors. In: Fitzgibbon, A., Lazebnik, S., Perona, P., Sato, Y., Schmid, C. (eds.) ECCV 2012, Part III. LNCS, vol. 7574, pp. 29–42. Springer, Heidelberg (2012)
10. Yang, C., et al.: Saliency detection via graph-based manifold ranking. In: 2013 IEEE Conference on Computer Vision and Pattern Recognition (CVPR). IEEE (2013)
11. Judd, T., et al.: Learning to predict where humans look. In: 2009 IEEE 12th International Conference on Computer Vision. IEEE (2009)
12. Jiang, H., et al.: Automatic salient object segmentation based on context and shape prior. BMVC 3(4) (2011)
13. Zhou, D., et al.: Ranking on data manifolds. In: NIPS, vol. 3 (2003)
14. Torralba, A., Efros, A.A.: Unbiased look at dataset bias. In: 2011 IEEE Conference on Computer Vision and Pattern Recognition (CVPR). IEEE (2011)

A Structural Constraint Based Dual Camera Model

Xinzhao Li, Yuehu Liu, Shaozhuo Zhai, and Zhichao Cui

Institute of Artificial Intelligence and Robotics, Xi'an Jiaotong University, China
{mjperhaps,liuyh,shaozhuozhai,cui.zhichao}@stu.xjtu.edu.cn

Abstract. The combination of fixed camera and PTZ (Pan Tilt Zoom) camera is a technical for picking up high-definition target images in large-scale scene. The challenge of dual camera model is to calculate the PTZ parameters. In this paper, a structural constraint based dual camera model is proposed, which can simplify the calculation of PTZ parameters (pan angle, tilt angle and zoom ratio). The advantage of the proposed approach is that the model parameters are off-line computed just once and cameras don't require recalibration when they are working. Furthermore, a focusable dual camera system has been developed to track interested targets on-line and acquire their high definition images. The proposed approach has been compared with other three typical algorithms, and the implemented dual-camera system is applied to make pedestrian detection in natural scene and obtain their high-definition images. The simulation test and real-scene experiment prove the effectiveness of proposed approach, and the developed system achieves the desired effect.

Keywords: Dual camera model, PTZ parameters, Fixed camera, View field cooperation, Structural constraint.

1 Introduction

In fixed-focus camera, imaging pixel area of targets decreases with increasing target depth (Table 1). Fig.1 shows as the target depth of face and plate increases, their effective pixels will rapidly decrease in the image. So face or plate recognition of target in the image become impossible when depth is beyond 10 meters. This issue is the key problem encountered in monitoring field.

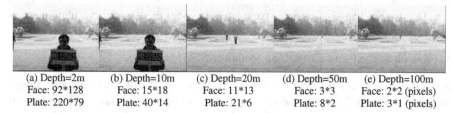

(a) Depth=2m	(b) Depth=10m	(c) Depth=20m	(d) Depth=50m	(e) Depth=100m
Face: 92*128	Face: 15*18	Face: 11*13	Face: 3*3	Face: 2*2 (pixels)
Plate: 220*79	Plate: 40*14	Plate: 21*6	Plate: 8*2	Plate: 3*1 (pixels)

Fig. 1. Imaging area of target (face and plate) decreases with the target depth increasing. In view field of the fixed camera, face and license plate recognition will become impossible when target depth is more 10 meters. The fixed camera resolution is 768*576.

S. Li et al. (Eds.): CCPR 2014, Part I, CCIS 483, pp. 293–304, 2014.
© Springer-Verlag Berlin Heidelberg 2014

PTZ (Pan Tilt Zoom) camera has the capabilities of zoom and rotation which can be used to track interested targets and record their high-definition images. So a dual camera system composed by fixed camera and PTZ camera is able to both ensure continuous monitoring of large scenes and track interested targets automatically.

The bottleneck of this dual camera combination is view field cooperation of cameras, namely enable PTZ camera to effectively track moving targets and obtain high-definition images following the current target region in fixed camera. Difficulty of calculating PTZ parameters on-line leis on the lack of target depth, so there isn't one-to-one correspondence between imaging coordinates of fixed camera and PTZ parameters. PTZ camera's intrinsic and extrinsic parameters changes in real-time zoom process which leads to the change of focus and imaging scale.

In this paper, we propose a simplified approach of dual-camera model by structural constraint of two cameras, which is novel calculation method for PTZ parameters. Advantage of the approach is that it only requires calculation of model parameters off-line once and no need to accurately calibrate external parameters and PTZ intrinsic parameters, enabling implemented dual-camera system used without recalibration.

2   Related Work

As the key technology of dual camera system, many experts had put forward their own PTZ parameter calculation method. Existing dual-camera view field cooperation models can be categorized into three types by realized strategies:

A. Completed Calibrated Method(CCM)

Completed calibrated method was realized under the premise of the completed calibration of the intrinsic and extrinsic parameters of dual cameras. Through the image feature correspondence we could estimate object's space coordinates, which could be used to calculate the PTZ parameters by geometrical relationship. If dual cameras were described by small hole imaging model, the CCM could transform to classic binocular stereo model [1-3]. Many traditional matching methods such as color histogram matching, SIFT matching were used. What's more, Radu[4] and Ankur[5] respectively proposed complicated PTZ rotation model that PTZ camera's optical center misalignment with its rotation center. Limitation of this type of approach is that directly calculation of the object depth is an ill-conditioned problem which needs extra data. Due to the change of intrinsic parameters in zoom process, the calculation errors based on the depth are large.

B. Known Scene Feature Matching Method(KSFMM)

Scene matching method calculated the homographic matrix of dual cameras' image using known image feature in the scene, got the corresponding relationship of several important parameters of cameras view field cooperation model, so as to estimate the PTZ parameters. One kind of this approach obtained the matching relationship between different perspectives cameras using homographic matrix induced by ground plane [6-8]. Another kind used pre-determined figures as a reference image and realized cameras view field cooperation through the matching between the reference image and real-time image[9-10]. This type of approach requires re-calculation of the homography matrix when scene changes. It's over-dependent on scene.

Table 1. The characteristic and performance of proposed approach and other main models

Method	Depth range	Pre-calib complexity	Re-Calib.	zoom	Device complexity	Computational complexity	Calculation accuracy
CCM							
Marchesotti,2005[1]	> 30m	**	Yes	—	**	*	**
Xu,2010[2]	>30m	**	Yes	Dynamic	**	**	**
Hampapur,2003[3]	<10m	***	Yes	Dynamic	***	**	***
Horaud,2006[4]	< 20m	****	Yes	Dynamic	—	**	****
Jain ,2006[5]	< 5m	***	No	Dynamic	**	**	***
KSFMM							
Bodor,2004[6]	5-50m	****	Yes	Dynamic	**	***	*
Wheeler,2010[7]	<50m	***	Yes	Dynamic	**	***	**
Senior,2005[8]	>30m	****	Yes	Dynamic	**	**	**
Del,2010[9]	>30m	****	Yes	Dynamic	**	***	***
Lin,2013[10]	20-50m	****	Yes	Dynamic	**	***	***
SCBM							
Choi,2011[11]	6- 12m	*****	No	Dynamic	*****	***	****
Sun,2013[12]	< 30m	***	Yes	Dynamic	**	***	***
Zhou,2003[13]	20-50m	***	Yes	Dynamic	**	***	***
Liao,2010[14]	> 50m	**	Yes	Fixed	**	**	**
Wan,2008[15]	> 50m	***	Yes	Fixed	**	*****	***
Proposed	2-100m	***	No	Dynamic	***	***	****

C. Structural Constraint Based Method(SCBM)

Structural Constraint Based Method simplified view cooperation calculation using structural constraints of dual-camera and calculated the PTZ parameters by formula directly. The essence of this method was the narrow baseline of dual cameras system, under this condition the binocular imaging principle had been simplified. Choi[11] proposed a coaxial-concentric camera configuration with zero baseline constraint of dual cameras' location. Sun[12] and Zhou[13] proposed a model with one-to-one correspondence between static camera image coordinates and PTZ rotation angles. Liao[14] invented a Hawkeye dual camera system using the PTZ self-calibration approach to calculate the camera parameters. Wan[15] proposed a calculation model based on the spherical coordinates. Such models adopt a variety of simplified model to achieve direct calculation of PTZ parameters. The proposed method belongs to this category.

Table 1 summarizes the main characteristics and performance of existing dual camera models. Our approach adopts structural constraints to achieve a low computational complexity approach without re-calibration.

3   View Field Cooperation Model of Dual Cameras

Before the view field cooperation of dual cameras we should get the interested targets in the scene. Firstly we used Gaussian Mixed Model to segment foreground in the fixed camera. Secondly, morphological filtering was applied on the foregrounds to get blob of targets. Thirdly, through a vote competition process we selected the interested target to track and center on. Subsequently, the dual cameras view field cooperation principle will be elaborated in this section.

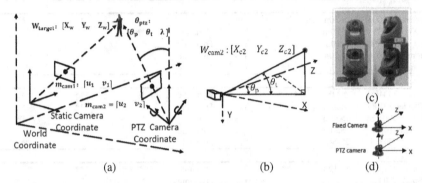

Fig. 2. (a): The dual camera model;   (b): PTZ rotation parameters model;   (c): Physical structural constraints metal holder;   (d): Geometry relationship of structural constraint model

3.1   Problem Formulation

Fig.2(a) shows the dual-camera view field cooperation model. In world coordinate system, $\mathbf{W}_{target}$ denotes target P, corresponding coordinates in different camera coordinate are $\mathbf{W}_{cam1}$ and $\mathbf{W}_{cam2}$ respectively, and camera image coordinates of P are $\mathbf{m}_{cam1} = [u_1 \quad v_1]$ and $\mathbf{m}_{cam2}$. θ_{ptz} denotes the rotation angle of PTZ camera.

PTZ original orientation is defined as reference coordinate system, corresponding to $[\theta_p \quad \theta_t \quad \lambda] = [0, 0, 1]$. When PTZ camera centered on an object as shown in Fig.2(b), rotation angles can be calculated by geometric relationship:

$$\tan \theta_p = \frac{X_{c2}}{Z_{c2}}, \quad \tan \theta_t = \frac{-Y_{c2}}{\sqrt{X_{c2}^2 + Z_{c2}^2}} \tag{1}$$

According to pinhole imaging principle, the relation exists:

$$Z_{ci}\begin{bmatrix} u_i \\ v_i \\ 1 \end{bmatrix} = \mathbf{K}_i \begin{bmatrix} X_{ci} \\ Y_{ci} \\ Z_{ci} \end{bmatrix}, \mathbf{K}_i = \begin{bmatrix} f_{xi} & 0 & c_{xi} \\ 0 & f_{yi} & c_{yi} \\ 0 & 0 & 1 \end{bmatrix} \quad i=1, 2 \tag{2}$$

$\mathbf{K}_1, \mathbf{K}_2$ are respectively the intrinsic parameter matrix of fixed camera and PTZ camera. Using equation 1-2, rotational angle can be calculated by equation 3-4.

$$\theta_p = \tan^{-1}\left(\frac{u_2 - c_{x2}}{f_{x2}}\right) \tag{3}$$

$$\theta_t = \tan^{-1}\left(\frac{-\frac{1}{f_{y2}}(v_2-c_{y2})}{\sqrt{1+\left(\frac{u_2-c_{x2}}{f_{x2}}\right)^2}}\right) = \tan^{-1}\left(\frac{-\frac{1}{f_{y2}}(v_2-c_{y2})}{\sqrt{1+(\tan\theta_p)^2}}\right) \tag{4}$$

3.2   Model Simplification

In practice, PTZ image coordinates of target $\mathbf{m}_{cam2}$ is unknown, therefore, $\mathbf{m}_{cam2}$ should be converted into $\mathbf{m}_{cam1}$. The relationship of extrinsic parameters transformation can be simplified in equation 5 and 6.

$$\mathbf{R}_c = \mathbf{R}_2\mathbf{R}_1^{-1} \tag{5}$$

$$\mathbf{T}_c = -\mathbf{R}_2\mathbf{R}_1^{-1}\mathbf{T}_1 + \mathbf{T}_2 \tag{6}$$

$\mathbf{R}_c$ and $\mathbf{T}_c$ have 6 degrees of freedom which makes the substitution incalculable. So we simplified the dual camera model to avoid the dual-camera parameters calibration. Suppose: (1) define the fixed camera coordinate system as the world coordinate system; (2) the initial optical axis of the two cameras is parallel. In this case $\mathbf{R}_c = \mathbf{I}$ and $\mathbf{T}_2 = [t_{cx}\quad t_{cy}\quad t_{cz}]$. Thus, equation 3 and 4 can be substituted as follow. From equation 7 and 8, it is observed that although the view cooperation relationship has been simplified, PTZ parameters are still affected by target depth Z_{c1}.

$$\theta_p = \tan^{-1}\left(\frac{Z_{c1}}{Z_{c1}+t_{cz}}\frac{u_1-c_{x1}}{f_{x1}} + \frac{t_{cx}}{Z_{c1}+t_{cz}}\right) \tag{7}$$

$$\theta_t = \tan^{-1}\left(\frac{-\frac{1}{f_{y1}}(v_1-c_{y1})+\frac{t_{cy}}{Z_{c1}}}{\sqrt{1+(\tan\theta_p)^2}}\right) \tag{8}$$

So we proposed a structural constraint model to reduce the impact of target depth on the PTZ parameters. The structural constraint was realized by a metal holder (Fig. 2(c)) which make sure that the initial optical axis of two cameras are parallel and two cameras' relative optical center position are fixed on the same vertical axis. The geometry relationship of structural constraint based dual camera model is shown in (Fig. 2(d)), so $\mathbf{T}_2 = [0\quad t_{cy}\quad 0]$. Hence Eq. 7-8 can be simplified to Eq. 9-10. It can be found that θ_p is determined by u_1 only, while θ_t is still affected by Z_{c1} and v_1. From Table 1 we know the function range of cooperation model is beyond 5m. In our model $Z_{c1} \gg 5000mm$ and $t_{cy} = 100mm$. Taking $\frac{t_{cy}}{Z_{c1}} \ll 0.02 \rightarrow 0$ into account, this effect of Z_{c1} can be ignored except that θ_p is extremely small.

$$\tan\theta_p = \frac{u_1-c_{x1}}{f_{x1}} = w_1u_1 + w_2 \tag{9}$$

$$\sqrt{1+(\tan\theta_p)^2}\tan\theta_t = -\frac{1}{f_{y1}}(v_1-c_{y1}) + \frac{t_{cy}}{Z_{c1}} \cong w_3v_1 + w_4 \tag{10}$$

Zoom ratio of PTZ camera is computed by the view size of fixed camera as well as image size of target object, which is defined by Eq. 11. $[W_s \quad H_s]$ is fixed camera's pixel resolution (768,576), and $[w \quad h]$ is the size of bounding box of target in fixed camera. $[f_{u,s} \quad f_{v,s}]$ and $[f_{u,m} \quad f_{v,m}]$ are focal length of fixed camera and PTZ camera respectively.

$$\lambda = \min \left(\frac{W_s}{w} * \frac{f_{u,m}}{f_{u,s}}, \frac{H_s}{h} * \frac{f_{v,m}}{f_{v,s}} \right) \tag{11}$$

3.3   Approach Description

It can be seen from Eq. 9 and 10 that $\mathbf{m}_{cam1}$ and the tangent (variation) of $\boldsymbol{\theta}_{ptz}$ shows linear relationship. So the calculating steps of PTZ parameters descripted as Table 2.

Table 2. Approach description

Step1: Select 20 targets randomly with the depth increasing in the view field of fixed camera;
Step2: Record targets image coordinates of fixed camera $[u_1, v_1]$, while manually adjusting PTZ camera to center on the target, record the rotation angle $[\theta_p \quad \theta_t]$.
Step3: Record 20 groups of data $(\mathbf{m}_{cam1}, \boldsymbol{\theta}_{ptz})$ and use least square approach to compute w_1, w_2, w_3, w_4;
Step4: Compute θ_p by taking u_1 acquired in Eq. 9;
Step5: Compute θ_t by taking $\tan \theta_p$ and v_1 in Eq. 10;
Step6: Compute zoom ratio λ by Eq. 11

4   Experimental Results and Comparison

Three experiments were conducted as follow to evaluate the accuracy and performance of our approach and the compared it with other typical models.

4.1   Digital Simulation Comparison

We design a digital simulation experiment to compare the accuracy of different cooperation methods to our approach. The targets in the digital simulation test are distributed on 912 intersection point of 48 circles and 19 rays which are shown in Fig. 3(a). The circle centers fall on fixed camera focal center within the interval of 2m from 6m to 100m of depth. The rays start from circle center within the interval of 3.5 ° from -35 ° to +35 ° view angle of fixed camera.

Three typical models Choi[11], Liao[14], Bodor[6] and proposed model are listed in the test. The accuracy of different approaches is evaluated by target depth, field angle as independent variable. The evaluation metric are absolute error (AE) and relative error (RE) of PTZ parameters. The intrinsic parameters of fixed camera and PTZ camera have been pre-calibrated by [16] and [17]. The structural constraints (extrinsic parameters) of dual cameras are shown in Fig. 3(b).

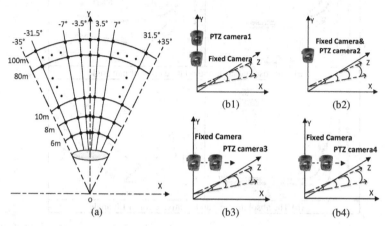

Fig. 3. (a) 912 targets position distribution of simulation scenario (b)Structural constraints of four methods. (b1)Proposed; (b2)Choi's; (b3)Liao's; (b4) Bodor's.

A. Accuracy Comparison with Target Depth Change

Obtained test results of accuracy comparison with target depth change are shown in Fig 4. Both AE and RE of pan and tilt angle calculation accuracy of our approach is better than the others.

In terms of pan angle, Fig. 4(a) shows that convergence errors of the different approaches are all about 0.7 °. But our approach is the fastest to convergence and its relative error can be reduced to about 5% at 10m. Liao[14] and Bodor[6] can only converge to 10% at 30m. The Choi's pan angle relative error is lower than our approach beyond 25m, but its strict concentric structure of two centers is hard to achieve in reality. In terms of tilt angle, Fig. 4(b) shows that as the target depth increases, absolute error of all three approaches gradually converges to about 0.5 °, while our algorithm is smaller. It can be inferred that the farther the target depth the smaller the tilt angle. Due to the fact that longitudinal distance of dual camera is not great, when the target object is far away enough from the camera, tilt angle will be infinitely close to 0, which resulted in divergence of relative error in Fig. 4(b). However, within a limited distance (100m), our approach has less calculation error.

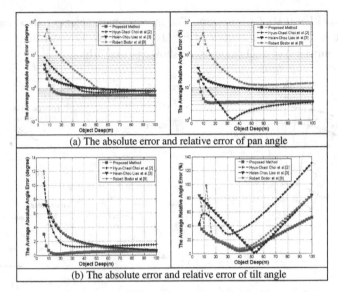

(a) The absolute error and relative error of pan angle

(b) The absolute error and relative error of tilt angle

Fig. 4. The precision comparison of different approach with the changes of target depth (from 6m to 100m)

B. Accuracy Comparison with View Field Angle Change

When targets are of the same depth, the obtained test results of accuracy comparison with changing view angle are shown in Fig. 5.

In terms of the pan angle, Fig. 5(a) shows that as the target field angle changes our approach always obtains smaller absolute error. Bodor's approach shows larger absolute error on pan angle accuracy because it maps the image points of fixed camera to ground plane. Using linear mapping to fit the nonlinear mapping will inevitably lead to the increase of calculation error. The average relative error of tilt angle obtained by our approach is not affected by which verifies the previous model derivation (Fig. 5(b)). Changes in the field angle and maintains at the lower level.

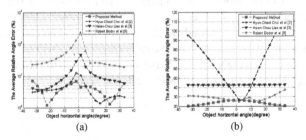

(a)   (b)

Fig. 5. The relative error comparison of different approaches with view angle change of targets(from -35° to 35°)

4.2   Scenario Experiment

A focusable dual camera system was implemented using SonyEVI-D70P camera with resolution of 768 * 576. One of them is PTZ camera and another acts as fixed camera. The system is able to detect pedestrian, automatically drive PTZ camera to track and capture high-definition image of appointed pedestrians.

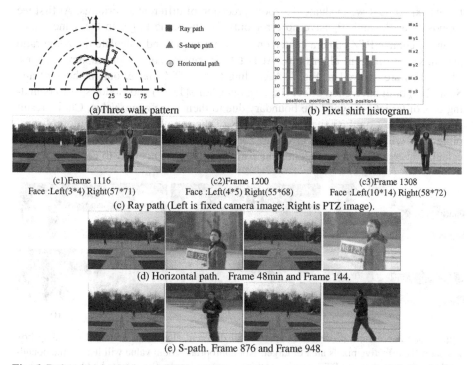

(a)Three walk pattern

(b) Pixel shift histogram.

(c1)Frame 1116
Face :Left(3*4) Right(57*71)

(c2)Frame 1200
Face :Left(4*5) Right(55*68)

(c3)Frame 1308
Face :Left(10*14) Right(58*72)

(c) Ray path (Left is fixed camera image; Right is PTZ image).

(d) Horizontal path.   Frame 48min and Frame 144.

(e) S-path. Frame 876 and Frame 948.

Fig. 6. Pedestrian detection and PTZ tracking result images in natural scene (Left is fixed camera image; Right is PTZ image)

To verify the dual-camera system, different pedestrian walking pattern including horizontal path, S-shaped, circular, diagonal and ray path have been tested. Detailed analysis of ray path, horizontal path and S-shaped path are illustrated in Fig.6.

In field experiment, the pedestrian path was recorded in Fig. 6(a). Fig. 6(c) shows fixed camera image and corresponding high-definition image acquired by PTZ camera in 3 positions. Though in fixed camera image the image region of pedestrian alters as its distance changes, the effective pixels of face remains at the range of 55*65 pixels in PTZ image, which meets the requirements of face recognition. Histogram records the pixels shift between target gravity and image center of PTZ image in Fig. 6(b). Due to the limitation of target detection and PTZ camera hardware, pixels shift is inevitable in reality. From the results, proposed approach can real-time track of dynamic targets under different motion patterns and keep the pixel shift within 100 pixels. The performance proved the robustness of proposed approach.

The result of horizontal and s-shape paths are shown in Fig. 6(d) and Fig. 6(e) respectively. The result indicates that implemented system can keep target's clear imaging near the center of the image when pedestrians walk randomly in the field.

4.3   Accuracy Comparison Test of Zoom Ratio

In this experiment we evaluate the zoom precision of different algorithms. At first we suppose that θ_p and θ_t have no error only for the same target in the same scene. Then we control PTZ camera center on the same target and calculate the zoom ratio parameter by different algorithms. At last PTZ camera zooms and captures images. The results are showed in Fig 7. According to the PTZ image, our method (c) and Sun[13](f) both have good effect (Fig. 7), but Choi's[11](d) and Bodor's[6](e) bounding box of target is beyond the boundary due to their large zoom value. Choi's result is too dependent on the experimental results of the sampling data. Deviation of sampling data will lead to large errors in zoom ratio calculation. Bodor's results have calculation error due to the fact that the parameter γ_{max} is not easy to get.

(a)   (b)   (c)   (d)   (e)   (f)

Fig. 7. The zoom ratio precision comparison of different algorithms. The red bounding box indicates the effective pixels area of target. Not appropriate zoom value will lead to the bounding box of target beyond PTZ images. (a)Fixed camera image, (b) enlarged pedestrian image, (c-f) pedestrian image captured by our method, Choi's, Brdor's and Sun's.

5   Conclusion

This paper presents a structural constraint based dual camera cooperation model, which is a simplified approach to calculate PTZ parameters (pan angle, tilt angle and zoom ratio). The proposed approach provides an effective solution to realize the view field cooperation of dual camera model. It combines the fixed camera and PTZ camera and enables them to real-time track moving targets and obtain high-definition image suitable for further processing.

The novelty of proposed approach is reflected in several aspects: (1) Needless to recalibration in processing because the cameras are fixed by structural constraint. (2) The parameters of dual camera cooperation model are off-line calculated just once and are not needed to recalculate when the system is moved to another scene. (3) Irrelevant with intrinsic parameters of PTZ camera. (4) The extrinsic parameters are not likely to change as the focusable dual camera system is installed on a mechanical structure which guarantees calculation accuracy. The simulation test and field experiment prove the high accuracy of our approach and the effectiveness and availability of our focusable dual camera system.

Acknowledgment. This work is supported by National Natural Science Foundation of China (NSFC) under Grant No.91120009 and Grant No.61328303.

References

1. Marchesotti, L., Piva, S., Turolla, A., et al.: Cooperative multisensor system for real-time face detection and tracking in uncontrolled conditions. In: Conference on Image and Video Communications and Processing, vol. 5685, pp. 100–114 (2005)
2. Xu, Y., Song, D.: Systems and algorithms for autonomous and scalable crowd surveillance using robotic PTZ cameras assisted by a wide-angle camera. Autonomous Robots 29(1), 53–66 (2010)
3. Hampapur, A., Pankanti, S., Senior, A., et al.: Face cataloger: Multi-scale imaging for relating identity to location. In: IEEE Conference on Advanced Video and Signal Based Surveillance, pp. 13–20. IEEE (2003)
4. Horaud, R., Knossow, D., Michaelis, M.: Camera cooperation for achieving visual attention. Machine Vision and Applications 16(6), 1–2 (2006)
5. Jain, A., Kopell, D., Kakligian, K., et al.: Using stationary-dynamic camera assemblies for wide-area video surveillance and selective attention. In: 2006 IEEE Computer Society Conference on Computer Vision and Pattern Recognition, vol. 1, pp. 537–544 (2006)
6. Bodor, R., Morlok, R., Papanikolopoulos, N.: Dual-camera system for multi-level activity recognition. Intelligent Robots and Systems (IROS) 1, 643–648 (2004)
7. Wheeler, F.W., Weiss, R.L., Tu, P.H.: Face recognition at a distance system for surveillance applications. In: Biometrics: Theory Applications and Systems (BTAS), pp. 1–8 (2010)
8. Senior, A.W., Hampapur, A., Lu, M.: Acquiring multi-scale images by pan-tilt-zoom control and automatic multi-camera calibration. In: Application of Computer Vision, WACV/MOTIONS 2005, vol. 1, pp. 433–438 (2005)
9. Bimbo, A.D., Dini, F., Lisanti, G., et al.: Exploiting distinctive visual landmark maps in pan–tilt–zoom camera networks. Computer Vision and Image Understanding 114(6), 611–623 (2010)
10. Lin, C.W., Hung, Y.P., Hsu, W.K., et al.: The construction of a high-resolution visual monitoring for hazard analysis. Natural Hazards 65(3), 1285–1292 (2013)
11. Choi, H.C., Park, U., Jain, A.K., et al.: Face Tracking and Recognition at a Distance: A coaxial & concentric PTZ Camera System. IEEE TCSVT 8(10), 1665–1677 (2011)
12. Hu, J., Hu, S., Sun, Z.: A real time dual-camera surveillance system based on tracking-learning-detection algorithm. In: 2013 25th Chinese Control and Decision Conference (CCDC), pp. 886–891. IEEE (2013)
13. Zhou, X., Collins, R.T., Kanade, T., et al.: A master-slave system to acquire biometric imagery of humans at distance. In: First ACM SIGMM International Workshop on Video Surveillance, pp. 113–120. ACM (2003)

304   X. Li et al.

14. Liao, H.C., Chen, W.Y.: Eagle-Eye: A dual-PTZ-Camera system for target tracking in a large open area. Information Technology and Control 39(3), 227–235 (2010)
15. Wan, D., Zhou, J.: Stereo vision using two PTZ cameras. Computer Vision and Image Understanding 112(2), 184–194 (2008)
16. Zhang, Z.: Flexible camera calibration by viewing a plane from unknown orientations. In: The Proceedings of the Seventh IEEE International Conference on Computer Vision, vol. 1, pp. 666–673. IEEE (1999)
17. Wu, Z., Radke, R.: Keeping a Pan-Tilt-Zoom Camera Calibrated. IEEE Transactions on Pattern Analysis and Machine Intelligence 35(8), 1994–2007 (2013)

Hough Voting with Distinctive Mid-Level Parts
for Object Detection

Xiaoqin Kuang, Nong Sang*, Feifei Chen, Runmin Wang, and Changxin Gao

Science and Technology on Multi-spectral Information Processing Laboratory,
School of Automation, Huazhong University of Science and Technology,
Wuhan, China, 430074
{kxqkuang,nsang,ffchen,runminwang,cgao}@hust.edu.cn

Abstract. This paper presents an efficient method for object detection in natural scenes. It is accomplished via generalized Hough transform of distinctive mid-level parts. These parts are more meaningful than low-level patches such as lines or corners and would be able to cover the key structures of object. We collect the initial sets of parts by clustering with k-means in WHO space and train LDA model for every cluster. The codebooks are generated by applying the trained detectors to discover parts in whole positive training images and storing their spatial distribution relative to object center. When detecting in a new image, the energy map is formed by the voting from every entry in codebook and is used to predict the location of object. Experiment result shows the effectiveness of the proposed scheme.

Keywords: Object detection, Hough Voting, Mid-level Parts, LDA.

1 Introduction

The detection task aims at locating the same object as the given training images in natural scenes. Due to the large intra-class variations in structure or viewpoint and appearance, a single linear classifier over HOG feature vectors can hardly perform well for generic object detection.

In order to handle the large intra-class variation, exemplar-svm [1] uses multiple components instead of single monolithic detector. However, this method has a huge computational complexity to training a separate SVM for each positive example. Method based on parts can solve the problem to a certain extend since parts are easier to compute than whole object and additionally, they can be shared in different instances which would decrease the complexity. Part-based methods [2, 3, 4, 8, 10, 11, 12, 13] become popular in the field in recent years. It is also robust to solve the partial occlusions in detection.

The work in [2] discovers parts with partial correspondence by annotating important matching points between instances of a category. They use the sematic graph to propagate the correspondence and augment part in learning procedure as well.

---

* Corresponding author.

S. Li et al. (Eds.): CCPR 2014, Part I, CCIS 483, pp. 305–313, 2014.

However, the annotation work is time-consuming and hard to do when facing more new categories. Finding parts automatically is important.

The implicit shape model(ISM) in [3] generates codebooks by clustering patches of interest point. The location of patches occurring in object is stored to reflect the spatial distribution of codebook entries. However, this method uses low-level patches as codebook; plenty patches would be found and some of them with little structure information are ineffective to vote.

In method of Hough Forest [4, 5], patches were sampled with uniform probabilities from positive and negative training images. They construct a random forest and each node stores the statistics of class and spatial information. Every leaf node plays the role of codebook to cast probability vote for position for test images. The more densely they are sampled, the more accurate the detection is. But among the sampled patches, many are slightly different or not distinctive enough to vote efficiently.

We intend to find a way of collecting fewer patches but with more information which is typical to reflect the appearance of object class. Mid-level parts have the advantage to be informative. And with the Hough voting method the individual parts are integrated to estimate position of the entire object for detection.

We follow the training method in [6] with iterative algorithm but use LDA model as in [7] instead of SVM to train classifiers of distinctive parts. The authors in [8] propose that a discriminative part should occur frequently from the category it is learnt but rarely from others. They use the Entropy-Rank Curves to measure the discriminative ability. We adopt this idea to select parts in training as well.

Once the collection of part detectors are trained, we apply them to training positive set and get complete parts as codebook for each detector stored with a set of scores and offsets respect to the object centroid.

The experiment result by the proposed scheme achieves good detection results in UIUC-car data sets. The block diagram of the proposed system is shown in Fig. 1.

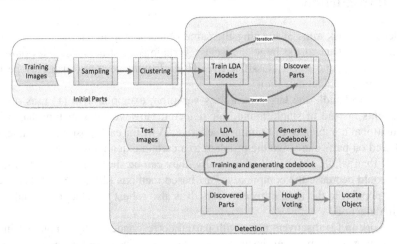

Fig. 1. Block diagram of our method

2   Learning Distinctive Parts

In this section, we describe the procedure of how to find the distinctive parts for codebook. A codebook is a vocabulary of local appearances that are characteristic to
reflect the structure or viewpoint of the known object. It is impossible to annotate all
distinguished parts manually additionally which is time-consuming and hard to label
the same structure exactly for all training images.

2.1   Initial Parts

The ISM [3] uses interest point detectors such as Harris to find interest patches initially and clusters them to generate codebook. However, the low-level patches are easy to
repeat like corners or lines. It needs plenty patches to provide a dense cover of an
object and perform effectively.

In order to use fewer patches but informative to represent the object appearance,
we use mid-level parts to generate codebook. The parts are densely sampled from
training images and the ones with low gradient are leaved out. For the object with
multiple viewpoints or positions, the parts harvested would cover the different status.

We use clustering method to obtain initial part clusters. The k-means algorithm[9]
is employed because of its computational simplicity. Naturally, the clusters are rough
and impure due to this unsupervised clustering. So the training scheme is followed
which uses the initial clusters to train models for every cluster. It aims at collecting
patches purer and more consistent.

2.2   Training

Every training image is equally containing distinctive parts, so we sample densely to
get all possible sub-windows and collect hundreds of thousands of parts. We use the
augmented HOG feature with gradient orientations of dimensionality $d = 31$ as in
[10]. The dimensionality of feature vector is Nd for the part with N cells.

We cluster the collected patches with k-means in whitened histograms of orientations (WHO) space[7]. The feature vector x is transformed to $\hat{x} = \Sigma^{-1/2}(x - \mu_0)$
in which Σ ($Nd \times Nd$ matrix) and μ_0 (Nd dimensinal) are covariance and mean
according to all background features. Clustering with whitening feature can remove
the correlations common in natural images and leave behind only discriminative gradients. Each cluster is the initial group for training by LDA. The LDA model is a
linear classifier over x with weights given by $\omega = \Sigma^{-1}(x_{mean} - \mu_0)$ and x_{mean} is
the mean feature of each cluster.

So as to improve the consistency of each model, we use the cross-validation training scheme. The training set is divided into two set as train-set and validation-set.
Firstly clustering in train-set and training each cluster with LDA model to get the
initial classifiers, and then using the classifiers to detect in validation-set to find the
corresponding parts. Iterate the process until converge (the clusters stay the same) or
the iteration comes to the set maximum. The clusters with small number of parts are

eliminated since they occur rarely to characterize the appearance of object. Thus we obtain the part classifier for every cluster and these classifiers will serve as part detectors at runtime.

2.3   Codebook Generation

When the classifiers have been trained, we use them to detect in the whole positive training set to generate the codebook. A codebook is a vocabulary which collects the parts with the same local appearance of one part in an object and repeatedly occurs in training images. Parts of all codebooks can cover entirely the characteristic of the object.

We have obtain M detectors $\{D_m\}_{m=1}^M$, in which $D_m = (w_m, b_m)$ and w, b are the learned parameters with LDA model in the training procedure. Each detector finds a set of instances $\{P_n = (f_n, d_n, s_n)\}_{n=1}^N$ similar to it in positive training images with scores to reflect the similarity between them. Here, f is the feature vector, $d = (d_x, d_y)$ is the offset respect to object and s is the score of every entry with $s = w^T * f + b$ corresponding to a detector. Hence, one detector and one group of parts detected by it construct a codebook $C_m = (D_m, \{P_{m,n}\}_{n=1}^{N_m})$. The detectors have different abilities to discover parts in image so each part group has different number N_m. Fig. 2 shows an example of procedure of generating the codebook. The parts selected are discriminative structures reflect key properties of cars.

Mid-level parts are highly characteristic structures which are more complicate than the low-level patches. They repeat less frequently than patches with just lines or corners in low level. In one training image there are just a few parts that are very similar to the detector. So when collecting parts for codebook, every training image needs to store only several parts with high scores. Pool all parts found in the whole training set, sort them with scores and store a certain amount of parts with high scores.

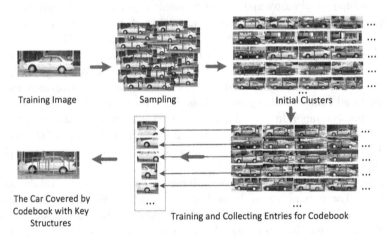

Training Image   Sampling   Initial Clusters

The Car Covered by
Codebook with Key
Structures   Training and Collecting Entries for Codebook

Fig. 2. The procedure of generating the codebook. Training images are densely sampled and clustered. Initial clusters are trained with LDA model. The codebooks store spatial distribution and scores of parts collected from whole training images by trained models.

3   Detection with Hough Voting

Codebooks are used to locate the boundary box of one class object by Hough transform in test image. Each entry in the codebook will vote with its score to predict the position respect to the position of one detected part by one classifier.

Given a test image, we apply the trained classifiers to find parts in every location. Apparently, parts with low scores do not match the model well and parts with the high scores are more confident to be valuable for voting. The advantage of mid-level parts is that it can use fewer numbers of patches to detect, so a small percentage of high score parts are kept.

Let f_m be the feature vector of one part extracted by detector D_m from location $\ell_m = (x_{0m}, y_{0m})$, we obtain a score $sc(D_m|f_m, \ell_m)$ and the learned spatial distribution $sp(x, y|C_m)$ predicting the position (x, y) by codebook C_m. Then the votes from all parts and entries from codebooks are summed up to form an energy map, the scores of each point (x, y) in map can be expressed as:

$$e(x, y|f_m, \ell_m) = sc(D_m|f_m, \ell_m) \, sp(x, y|C_m, \ell_m) \tag{1}$$

The first term is the score that the part detected by a detector which is independent to the location. The second term is the learned spatial distribution and there are n parts expressed as $\{P_{m,n}\}$ existing in codebook C_m. Thus the equation is written as:

$$e(x, y|f_{m,}, \ell_m) = sc(D_m|f_m) sp(x, y|C_m, \ell_m) \tag{2}$$

$$sp(x, y|C_m, \ell_m) = \sum_n sp(x, y|P_{m,n}, \ell_m) \tag{3}$$

However, in order to adapt to the shape deformation and be robust to structure variation, we use the Parzen-window estimate to obtain continuous voting space. Then the equation above is:

$$sp(x, y|C_m, \ell_m) = \sum_n sp(x, y|P_{m,n}, \ell_m) * \frac{1}{2\pi\sigma_x^2\sigma_y^2} \exp\left(\frac{(x-x_0-d_{xn})^2}{-2h\sigma_x^2} + \frac{(y-y_0-d_{yn})^2}{-2h\sigma_y^2}\right) \tag{4}$$

Here, (σ_x, σ_y) is the variance of the predicting position (d_x, d_y) of all entries saved in one codebook. The parameter h is relative to voting contribution of every point. The smaller it is, the clearer is to observe the every voting contribution. In order to reduce the fluctuation of voting points, we set $h = 1$ to obtain a more smooth distribution.

Each detector discovers a set of parts as $\{f_{m,i}\}_{i=1}^{m_i}$, then all parts from the complete detectors will form the final energy map as:

$$E(x, y) = \sum_m \sum_i e(x, y|f_{m,i}, \ell_{m,i}) \tag{5}$$

Fig. 3 presents the procedure of detection using codebook and Hough transform. Parts are firstly discovered by LDA model (Fig.3-A), and then the entries in codebook corresponding to each part cast votes to the location of object center (Fig.3-B). All the votes are summed up to form an energy map reflecting the hypothesis (Fig.3-C), and the objects are located in peaks of map (Fig.3-D). There may be multiple overlapping detections on the same object, so we use non-maximum suppression to keep one hypothesis for every instance.

A: Detecting with part models in test image   B: Voting with every part   C: Energy map by all parts   D: Locating peaks

Fig. 3. The example of detection procedure

4   Experiments

In order to evaluate the performance of the Hough voting with mid-level parts, we apply the method on open dataset UIUC Cars and compare the result with the similar approaches.

The UIUC Cars single-scale test set contains 170 images with 200 side views of cars of approximately the same scale. The images are low contrast with some cars partially occluded and multiple objects would occur. The training set contains 550 training cars of size 100×40 and 500 negative training examples of the same size.

We adhered to the experimental evaluation criteria based on bounding box overlap as previous works. The hypothesis with center (x, y) will be accepted if it is in the ellipse of the annotation center coordinate (x_0, y_0) with size (w, h) that:

$$\frac{|x-x_0|^2}{(0.25w)^2} + \frac{|y-y_0|^2}{(0.25h)^2} \leq 1 \tag{6}$$

We accept one hypothesis as correct detection for every instance and treat others as false positive.

In the experiment, each part extracts a 1116D HOG feature vector by concatenating the 31D vector of 6×6 cells. We have trained 53 detectors using 6 scales parts with size of 26×26, 24×48, 24×96, 32×48, 32×96, 35×35. The car can be covered entirely by detected parts as shown in Fig. 2. Applying the trained detectors to discover parts from test image and forming an energy map of voting. The peaks in the map are hypothesis of object.

Table 1. Comparison of our results on the UIUC-Single car database with other methods

Methods	ISM. No MDL	ISM +MDL	Hough Forest	HF Weaker supervision	Our approach
PR-EER	91%	97.5%	98.5%	94.4%	99.5%

Fig. 4. Examples of detection results. The top row is the location of peaks in energy map of the down row. Objects with some occlusions or multiple instances are detected correctly.

Table 1 shows the result comparison of several similar Hough voting algorithms with recall-precision equal error rate (EER). Our method achieves an impressive 99.5% EER (corresponding to 200 out of 202 detections with 2 false positives) for UIUC-Single database. Fig. 4 is examples of some detection results.

The methods of ISM with MDL verification and Hough Forest (HF) have comparable performances with ours. However, the former one needs segment annotation additionally which is consuming labor; the accuracy of HF interrelated to the sample density so that it needs a large number of patches. Our codebooks generated using trained models are more accurate than clustered only in ISM. What's more, they are discriminative and more informative than patches in HF so that fewer parts are needed to vote for predicting.

As a method based on parts, the size of parts have an impact to the detection performance. We analyze the impact of different scale part and the combination of multiple parts. Result is shown in Fig. 5. The case of two scales has parts with size 24×48 and 32×48, the case of three scales has parts with size 24×48, 32×48 and 35×35, the case of six scales has all scales as presented above.

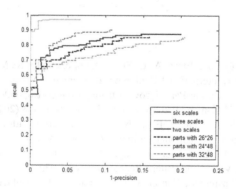

Fig. 5. The impact of different scales of parts to the recall-precision equal error rate (EER) of our method on UIUC-Single dataset

We can infer that the codebook with parts too small or too large will both not perform well. A small part contains less distinctive structures so that the smaller a part is, the more similar parts will be discovered by detectors and more noise interference will be produced from negative objects. On the other side, codebook with large size parts would obtain fewer but more informative parts. However, if the size is too large, then very few parts will be found in image so that the number cannot support a reliable vote.

There is a tradeoff between the distinctive and the number of parts according to the size. Codebook of parts with 32×48 would generate more informative patches to vote while codebook of parts with 26×26 would generate more number patches to vote, so both of them perform better than codebook of parts with 24×48. But the results of all of them are not quite well though.

A solve of this is to use multiple scales to compensate the impact of the two factors. We can observe from Fig. 5 that the performance by codebook of parts with six scales is better than codebook of parts with three scales, and much better than codebook of parts with fewer scales.

5   Conclusion

We proposed a Hough voting method based on codebook of distinctive mid-level parts for object detection. The codebook is generated via LDA training after clustering with kmeans in WHO space. This scheme helps to gain more accurate and consistent structure entries for every codebook. The energy map is formed by voting from the codebook. Experiment results show the effectiveness of our method compared to several similar algorithms.

Acknowledgement . This research is supported by the Natural Science Foundation of China (No.61105014, No.61302137, No.61401170), and the Natural Science Foundation of Hubei Province (2013CFB403).

References

1. Malisiewicz, T., Gupta, A., Efros, A.A.: Ensemble of exemplar-SVMs for object detection and beyond. In: IEEE International Conference on Computer Vision, pp. 89–96 (2011)
2. Maji, S., Shakhnarovich, G.: Part discovery from partial correspondence. In: IEEE Conference on Computer Vision and Pattern Recognition, pp. 931–938 (2013)
3. Leibe, B., Leonardis, A., Schiele, B.: Robust object detection with interleaved categorization and segmentation. International Journal of Computer Vision 77(1-3), 259–289 (2008)
4. Gall, J., Lempitsky, V.: Class-specific hough forests for object detection. In: IEEE Conference on Computer Vision and Pattern Recognition, pp. 1022–1029 (2009)
5. Gall, J., Yao, A., Razavi, N., Van Gool, L.: Hough forests for object detection, tracking, and action recognitions. IEEE Transactions on Pattern Analysis and Machine Intelligence 33(11), 2188–2202 (2011)
6. Singh, S., Gupta, A., Efros, A.A.: Unsupervised Discovery of Mid-Level Discriminative Patches. In: Fitzgibbon, A., Lazebnik, S., Perona, P., Sato, Y., Schmid, C. (eds.) ECCV 2012, Part II. LNCS, vol. 7573, pp. 73–86. Springer, Heidelberg (2012)
7. Hariharan, B., Malik, J., Ramanan, D.: Discriminative Decorrelation for clustering and classification. In: Fitzgibbon, A., Lazebnik, S., Perona, P., Sato, Y., Schmid, C. (eds.) ECCV 2012, Part IV. LNCS, vol. 7575, pp. 459–472. Springer, Heidelberg (2012)

8. Juneja, M., Vedaldi, A., Jawahar, C.V., Zisserman, A.: Blocks that shout: Distinctive parts for scene classification. In: IEEE Conference on Computer Vision and Pattern Recognition, pp. 923–930 (2013)
9. MacQueen, J.: Some methods for classification and analysis of multivariate observations. In: Proceedings of the 5th Berkeley Symposium on Mathematical Statistics and Probability, pp. 281–297 (1967)
10. Felzenszwalb, P.F., Girshick, R.B., McAllester, D., Ramanan, D.: Object detection with discriminatively trained part based models. IEEE Transactions on Pattern Analysis and Machine Intelligence, 1627–1645 (2010)
11. Yao, C., Bai, X., Liu, W., Latecki, L.J.: Human Detection using Learned Part Alphabet and Pose Dictionary. In: Fleet, D., Pajdla, T., Schiele, B., Tuytelaars, T. (eds.) ECCV 2014, Part V. LNCS, vol. 8693, pp. 251–266. Springer, Heidelberg (2014)
12. Wang, X.G., Wang, B.Y., Bai, X., Liu, W.Y., Tu, Z.W.: Max-Margin Multiple Instance Dictionary Learning. In: Proceedings of the 30th International Conference on Machine Learning, pp. 846–854 (2013)
13. Dollár, P., Babenko, B., Belongie, S., Perona, P., Tu, Z.: Multiple component learning for object detection. In: Forsyth, D., Torr, P., Zisserman, A. (eds.) ECCV 2008, Part II. LNCS, vol. 5303, pp. 211–224. Springer, Heidelberg (2008)

A Segmentation Based Change Detection Method for High Resolution Remote Sensing Image

Lin Wu, Zhaoxiang Zhang, Yunhong Wang, and Qingjie Liu

State Key Laboratory of Virtual Reality Technology and Systems,
School of Computer Science and Engineering,
Beihang University, Beijing 100191, China
zxzhang@buaa.edu.cn

Abstract. This paper proposes a segmentation based change detection method for high resolution remote sensing images. Firstly, one of the multi-temporal images is segmented by a new image segmentation algorithm, in which, the particle swarm optimization algorithm (PSO) is adopted to obtain the optimal segmentation results. Secondly, the same segmentation mask is used to extract image regions from the other temporal image. Thirdly, the spectral, shape, texture and vegetation index features are extracted from image regions to identify the changed image regions. The performance of the proposed change detection method is assessed by comparing with 4 other widely used change detection methods on two data sets of multi-temporal ZiYuan-3 (ZY-3) high resolution remote sensing images. Experimental results show that accurate image regions and satisfied changed areas can be acquired by our proposed method.

Keywords: High resolution remote sensing image, Image segmentation, Particle swarm optimization (PSO), Change detection, ZiYuan-3 (ZY-3).

1   Introduction

Change detection could be defined formally as a clustering process that classifies input pixels into changed or unchanged categories when given two multi-temporal remote sensing images of the same geographical area. In the past three decades, a variety of change detection methods have been proposed. These methods could be categorized as either supervised or unsupervised according to the nature of data processing [1]. The former is not widely used because of the absence of ground reference; the latter is the focus of change detection study. The widely used unsupervised change detection methods include image differencing, image rationing, image regression, change vector analysis (CVA), multi-scale analysis, MRF-based and principal component analysis (PCA), etc. [2, 3].

Nowadays, with the increasing availability of high resolution remote sensing images, it is possible to identify detailed changes occurring at the ground. Compared with low or moderate resolution remote sensing images, high resolution remote sensing images contain more detailed information, such as shape, texture, etc.

S. Li et al. (Eds.): CCPR 2014, Part I, CCIS 483, pp. 314–324, 2014.

The research on change detection for high resolution remote sensing images will become the mainstream.

However, the development of high resolution earth observation techniques pose challenges to the aforementioned traditional change detection methods. These change detection methods become ineffective on high resolution remote sensing images due to the following facts. Firstly, they only take single pixel into account and rarely consider the spatial relationships of adjacent pixels, thus easily lead to a large number of spatial data redundancies, waste of resources and are sensitive to noise. Secondly, they are subject to a large number of false alarms and missed alarms when applied to high resolution remote sensing images, due to the effects of scene illumination, sensor view angles and the residual misregistration between multi-temporal remote sensing images [4]. There is a strong need for an effective change detection method, which could effectively use the shape, texture information and be insensitive to noise for high resolution remote sensing images.

Li et al. [5] applied image segmentation technique to high resolution remote sensing image classification and obtained more satisfactory results. In [5], all the features are extracted from image regions instead of single pixels, the spatial information of high resolution remote sensing images is adequately used, such as the geometric structure and texture data, so this method is insensitive to noise. Inspired by this idea, we propose a segmentation based change detection method for high resolution remote sensing images in this paper. The contributions of this study are shown as follows.

(1) A fast region growing image segmentation algorithm is proposed based on heterogeneity minimization. According to our algorithm, only one of the multi-temporal images is segmented. Image regions of the same location and scope are extracted from the other temporal image. In this way, the segments in different temporal images can match one to one and the precision of the other temporal image segmentation can be increased.

(2) The particle swarm optimization (PSO) is used to optimize the segmentation parameters so as to obtain the optimal segmentation results. PSO method is an effective parameter selection method and segmentation based on PSO can obtain satisfactory image segmentation results.

The rest of this paper is organized as follows. The key techniques and the details of the proposed approach are described in Section 2. The experimental results and analysis are shown in Section 3. Finally, the conclusions are given in Section 4.

2   Key Techniques and Methodology

In this section, we first present two techniques including fast region growing image segmentation algorithm, which is based on heterogeneity minimization, as well as segmentation parameter optimization, which is based on PSO. Afterwards, a segmentation based change detection method will be given.

2.1   Fast Region Growing Based on Heterogeneity Minimization

The objective of image segmentation is to divide image into spatially continuous and homogeneous regions [6]. Based on the characteristics of high resolution remote sensing images and traditional region growing image segmentation algorithm [7], we propose a fast region growing algorithm based on heterogeneity minimization to solve high resolution remote sensing image segmentation in this paper. This algorithm is faster than the one in [7] because no seeds are needed before merging and each adjacent pixel couples based on 4-connexity of the image is traversed only once. The key steps of this algorithm are shown as follows.

Segmentation Initialization. Firstly, the values of segmentation parameters are initialized, including the scale T, the weight of spectral heterogeneity $w_{spectrum}$ and the weight of compactness $w_{compact}$. The scale is a measure of the maximum size of regions in segmented images (i.e., the larger the scale value is, the bigger the segments are).

Pixel Couples Sequence Construction. In each spectral band, compute the pairwise similarity $s(p_i, p_j)$ based on 4-connexity according to Equation (1). Then construct the set of adjacent pixel couples in increasing order of $s(p_i, p_j)$ and obtain pixel couples sequence P.

$$s(p_i, p_j) = \max_k \left| p_{ki} - p_{kj} \right| \tag{1}$$

where p_{ki} and p_{kj} are the spectral values of pixel p_i and p_j in the kth spectral band. The smaller the $s(p_i, p_j)$ is, the higher the similarity between p_i and p_j is.

Merging Criterion Definition. The merging criterion is defined in Equation (2).

$$Merging(R_1, R_2) = \begin{cases} true, & if\ f_{heter} < T \\ false, & otherwise \end{cases} \tag{2}$$

where $Merging(R_1, R_2)$ is used to determine whether two adjacent image regions can be merged; f_{heter} is the heterogeneity of newly generated image region which is a merger of adjacent image regions R_1 and R_2. The heterogeneity which can be expressed in Equation (3) shows differences between two adjacent regions and is composed of both shape heterogeneity and spectral heterogeneity [8].

$$f_{heter} = w_{spectrum} h_{spectrum} + (1 - w_{spectrum}) h_{shape} \tag{3}$$

where $0 \le w_{spectrum} \le 1$. Furthermore, $h_{spectrum}$ and h_{shape} are spectral heterogeneity and shape heterogeneity, respectively. They can be expressed as follows [8]:

$$h_{spectrum} = \sum_k N\sigma_k - (N_1\sigma_{k1} + N_2\sigma_{k2}) \tag{4}$$

$$h_{compact} = N\frac{E}{\sqrt{N}} - (N_1\frac{E_1}{\sqrt{N_1}} + N_2\frac{E_2}{\sqrt{N_2}}) \tag{5}$$

$$h_{smooth} = N\frac{E}{L} - (N_1\frac{E_1}{L_1} + N_2\frac{E_2}{L_2}) \tag{6}$$

$$h_{shape} = w_{compact}h_{compact} + (1 - w_{compact})h_{smooth} \tag{7}$$

where $0 \le w_{compact} \le 1$. N and σ_k are pixel number and standard deviation of newly generated region in the kth spectral band. N_1, N_2 and σ_{k1}, σ_{k2} are pixel number and standard deviation of image regions R_1 and R_2 in the kth spectral band, respectively. E and L are boundary length and external rectangular boundary length of newly generated region. E_1, E_2 and L_1, L_2 are boundary length and external rectangular boundary length of image regions R_1 and R_2, respectively.

Region Growing. Traverse the pixel couples sequence P in order, for the current couple of pixels (p_i, p_j), $p_i \in R_i$, $p_j \in R_j$, if R_i, R_j are different image regions and $Merging(R_i, R_j)$ is true, merge the two regions. Then move to the next couple until all the couples of pixels in P are visited. The image will be finally partitioned into regions.

An overview of the proposed image segmentation method is shown in Algorithm 1.

Algorithm 1. *Fast Region Growing Based on Heterogeneity Minimization*

Input: *Image* {with size of $H \times W$ pixels}
Output: *Segments* {also called as image regions}
  1: Initialize *scale*, $w_{spectrum}$ and $w_{compact}$
  2: Initialize *Segments* $= \{x(k, l) | 1 \le k \le H, 1 \le l \le W, \forall\, x(k, l)$ is a positive inte-
       ger and it represents the number of a region, $x(k, l) \ne x(m, n)$ if $k \ne m, l \ne n\}$
  3: **for** each adjacent pixel couple (p_i, p_j) in *Image* **do**
  4:      Calculate the pixel-wise similarity $s(p_i, p_j)$ by Equation (1)
  5: **end for**
  6: Construct the pixel couples sequence P in increasing order of $s(p_i, p_j)$
  7: **for** each pixel couple (p_i, p_j) in P, $p_i \in$ image region R_i, $p_j \in$ image region R_j **do**
  8:      **if** R_i is different from R_j **then**
  9:         Calculate $Merging(R_i, R_j)$ by Equations (3)-(7)
10:          **if** $Merging(R_i, R_j)$ is true **then**
11:            Merge R_i and R_j, i.e. $x(k, l) = x(m, n), \forall(k, l) \in R_i, \forall(m, n) \in R_j$
12:          **end if**
13:      **else**
14:          Move to the next pixel couple
15:      **end if**
16: **end for**
17: **return** *Segments* $= \{x(k, l) | 1 \le k \le H, 1 \le l \le W\}$

The time complexity of the traditional region growing image segmentation algorithm [7] is $O((HW)^2)$, but it is reduced to $O(HW)$ in the proposed algorithm. So the proposed algorithm is faster than the one in [7].

2.2   Segmentation Parameters Optimization Based on PSO

The results of aforementioned image segmentation algorithm are affected by several parameters and there are no clear suggestions for the selection of these parameters. In fact the selection of segmentation parameters is a parameter optimization problem in essence and it has become a key challenge in image segmentation [5]. In this paper, the PSO is employed to find the optimum image segmentation parameters which provide the minimum cost. The detailed explanation of PSO can be found in [9]. Each particle has a cost value (also called as fitness value) which is defined as follows:

$$Fit_i = f(scale, w_{spectrum}, w_{compact}) = \frac{1}{R_{all}} \sum_{n=1}^{T} R_n \left(\sum_{k=1}^{B} \frac{1}{R_{n,neighbors}} \sum_{j=1}^{J} R_{nj} |G_{nk} - G_{njk}| \right) \quad (8)$$

where Fit_i is the fitness value of the ith particle; the segmentation parameters ($scale$, $w_{spectrum}$, $w_{compact}$) described in Section 2.1 represent the position of the ith particle; T is the total number of image regions after segmentation; B is total number of image spectral bands; J is the total number of neighbors of the nth region; R_{all} is the total area of regions after segmentation; R_n is the area of the nth region; $R_{n,neighbors}$ is the total area of all neighbors of the nth region; R_{nj} is the area of the jth adjacent region of the nth region; G_{nk} is the average gray value of the nth region in the kth spectral band; G_{njk} is the average gray value of the jth adjacent object of the nth object in the kth spectral band. The fitness value of each particle can assess the image segmentation quality. The larger the fitness value is, the better the image segmentation quality is.

2.3   The Proposed Segmentation Based Change Detection Method

The flowchart of the proposed segmentation based change detection method is shown in Fig.1 and the key steps of this method are summarized as follows.

(1) Generate the initial particle swarm randomly, the segmentation parameters vector ($scale$, $w_{spectrum}$, $w_{compact}$) is actually the position of the ith particle.

(2) Segment the second-temporal image (of course, we can also segment the first-temporal image firstly) into regions using the proposed image segmentation method.

(3) Compute the fitness value using Equation (8).

(4) Update the position and velocity of the particle swarm.

(5) Exit the loop if the stop criterion is satisfied, and the optimal segmentation results denoted as R_{second} are obtained. Otherwise, go to step (2).

(6) Based on R_{second}, image regions of the same location and scope denoted as R_{first} are extracted from the first-temporal image.

(7) Extract features from R_{first} and R_{second}, which are denoted as F_{first} and F_{second}.

(8) Compute the Euclidian distance between F_{first} and F_{second}. The changed areas will be identified using K-means clustering ($K = 2$).

The feature extraction and K-means clustering are important for the proposed change detection method, and they will be introduced as follows.

Feature Extraction. Feature is the most important criterion to judge whether an image region is changed. In this paper, the spectral, shape, texture, and vegetation index are used for change detection.

(1) Spectral Feature. In this paper, the spectral features are mean and standard deviation of an image region. It is well known that RGB color space can't sufficiently or effectively distinguish the difference of the color separation degree. Lab color space is a kind of uniform color space which is defined by CIE. Lab color space makes up the shortage of RGB color space and colors in nature can be well reflected in this space. So the spectral features are extracted in Lab not in RGB color space in order to improve the change detection accuracy. In this paper, the red, green, and blue spectral bands of remote sensing images are used to construct the Lab color space.

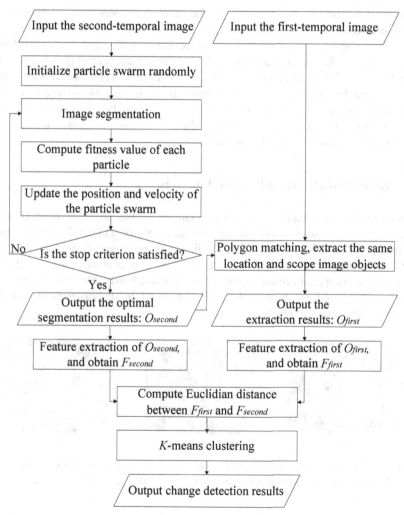

Fig. 1. Flowchart of the proposed segmentation based change detection method

(2) Shape Feature. In this paper, the edge gradient direction histogram of an image region is referred as shape feature. Firstly, the canny operator is used to compute the edges of image regions. Secondly, the gradient direction of each pixel which locates at the edge is computed. The bin size is 5 or 10 degrees in this paper.

(3) Texture Feature. The texture features are often described with gray level co-occurrence matrix (GLCM) [10]. In this paper, four statistics are selected, i.e., contrast, correlation, entropy and inverse difference moment, to characterize the texture features of an image region.

(4) Vegetation Index. The vegetation index is a dimensionless radiation measure and reflects the situation of plant's growth. In this paper, two vegetation indexes are selected, i.e., normalized differential vegetation index (NDVI) and ratio vegetation index (RVI), to characterize the situation of plant's growth of an image region.

K-means Clustering. In this paper, the above features are combined into multidimensional feature vectors one after another, which are denoted as F_{first} and F_{second}. Then the Euclidian distances computed between F_{first} and F_{second} are divided into two disjoint classes, changed (labeled with C_1) and unchanged (labeled with C_2), using K-means clustering algorithm with $K = 2$. Then compute the cluster average values M_1 and M_2 for classes C_1 and C_2, respectively. In fact, when there is a change between two image regions, the Euclidian distance is higher than the value in the regions with no change. Using this strategy, the cluster which has lower average value is assigned as C_2, and the other is assigned as C_1.

3   Experimental Results and Analysis

In order to test the effectiveness and adaptability of the proposed method in this paper, experiments are carried out on two data sets of ZiYuan-3 (ZY-3) remote sensing images. ZY-3 is China's first civilian high resolution cartographic satellite which was launched in Jan. 9, 2012. The ZY-3 images contain four spectral bands with a 5.8 meters spatial resolution and a panchromatic band with a 2.1 meters spatial resolution. It should be noticed that, the data used in the experiments are pan-sharpened multi-spectral images.

| (a) | (b) | (c) |

Fig. 2. The first data set and segmentation results of (b). (a) First-temporal image; (b) Second-temporal image; (c) Segmentation results of (b), *scale* = 4100, $w_{spectrum}$ = 0.6, $w_{compact}$ = 0.05.

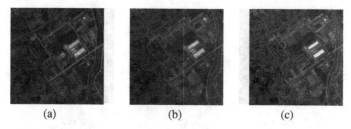

(a)	(b)	(c)

Fig. 3. The second data set and segmentation results of (b). (a) First-temporal image; (b) Second-temporal image; (c) Segmentation results of (b), $scale = 3900$, $w_{spectrum} = 0.65$, $w_{compact} = 0.2$.

The first data set is shown in Fig. 2, which is a sub-region of Guiyang China with size of 400×498 pixels. One was acquired on Feb. 5, 2013 (see Fig. 2(a)), the other was acquired on Apr. 15, 2013 (see Fig. 2(b)). The second data set is shown in Fig. 3, which is a sub-region of Ya'an China with size of 200×200 pixels. One was acquired on Mar. 31, 2012 (see Fig. 3(a)), the other was acquired on Mar. 30, 2013 (see Fig. 3(b)). Multi-spectral image pan-sharpening, registration are conducted on ENVI 4.7.

The second-temporal images in the two data sets are firstly segmented in our experiment. Fig. 2(c) and Fig. 3(c) show the segmentation results of Fig. 2(b) and Fig. 3(b) by using the proposed method, respectively. The size of the particle swarm and the maximum iterations are 20, 30. Human eye is still a strong and experienced source for evaluation of image segmentation [8]. It can be noticed that the images are reasonably segmented. Although there are some over segmentation, they have trivial effects on the performance of change detection.

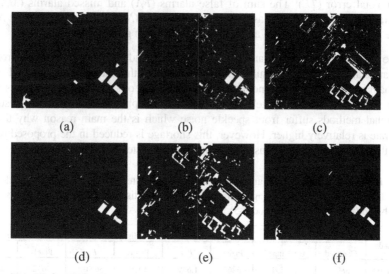

Fig. 4. Change detection results on the first data set. (a) Ground truth; (b) Image differencing; (c) Multiscale-based; (d) PCA-based; (e) MRF-based; (f) Proposed method.

The change detection results obtained from different methods for the first and second data set are shown in Fig. 4 and Fig. 5. The following defined quantities are computed for comparing the change detection results against the ground truth.

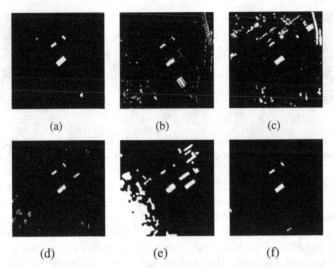

(a)   (b)   (c)

(d)   (e)   (f)

Fig. 5. Change detection results on the second data set. (a) Ground truth; (b) Image differencing; (c) Multiscale-based; (d) PCA-based; (e) MRF-based; (f) Proposed method.

(1) False alarms (FA): The number of unchanged pixels that were incorrectly detected as changed, and the false alarm rate is defined as: $P_{FA} = (FA / N_1) \times 100$.

(2) Missed alarms (MA): The number of changed pixels that were incorrectly detected as unchanged, and the missed alarm rate is defined as: $P_{MA} = (MA / N_0) \times 100$.

(3) Total error (TE): The sum of false alarms (FA) and missed alarms (MA), and the total error rate is defined as: $P_{TE} = ((FA + MA) / (N_0 + N_1)) \times 100$. Where N_0 and N_1 are the number of changed and unchanged pixels in ground truth.

The quantity assessments are listed in Table 1 and Table 2. It is clear from the qualitative and quantitative results on the two data sets that the proposed method obtains the change detection results more accurately than the other traditional methods which obtain many false alarm pixels and missed alarm pixels. The detection results of traditional methods suffer from speckle noise which is the main reason why the total error rate is relatively higher. However, this shortage is reduced in the proposed method since the change detection is based on image regions instead of single pixels.

Table 1. False alarms, missed alarms, and total errors resulted from different change detection methods on the first data set. Image differencing (#1), Multiscale-based (#2), PCA-based (#3), MRF-based (#4), Proposed method (#5).

Methods	Total Pixels		False Alarms		Missed Alarms		Total Errors	
	Changed	Unchanged	Pixels	P_{FA}	Pixels	P_{MA}	Pixels	P_{TE}
#1	3809	195391	3263	1.67%	1379	36.20%	4642	2.33%
#2	3809	195391	12222	6.26%	1202	31.56%	13424	6.74%
#3	3809	195391	497	0.25%	1549	40.67%	2046	1.03%
#4	3809	195391	19794	10.13%	1005	26.38%	20799	10.44%
#5	3809	195391	**464**	**0.24%**	**778**	**20.43%**	**1242**	**0.62%**

Table 2. False alarms, missed alarms, and total errors resulted from different change detection methods on the second data set. Image differencing (#1), Multiscale-based (#2), PCA-based (#3), MRF-based (#4), Proposed method (#5).

Methods	Total Pixels		False Alarms		Missed Alarms		Total Errors	
	Changed	Unchanged	Pixels	P_{FA}	Pixels	P_{MA}	Pixels	P_{TE}
#1	326	38286	803	2.10%	53	16.26%	856	2.22%
#2	326	38286	2039	5.33%	51	15.64%	2090	5.41%
#3	326	38286	222	0.58%	**49**	**15.03%**	271	0.71%
#4	326	38286	6849	17.89%	76	23.31%	6925	17.93%
#5	326	38286	**48**	**0.13%**	58	17.79%	**106**	**0.27%**

4   Conclusion

In this paper, a segmentation based change detection method for high resolution remote sensing image is proposed. We use a fast region growing image segmentation method in which no seeds are required to obtain image homogeneous blocks. Then spectral, shape, texture and vegetation indexes are used as features to identify changed areas. Experimental results show that the proposed change detection method consistently exhibits satisfactory performance on both data sets. It is promising and better than that of the traditional methods. Our future work will pay more attention on high resolution remote sensing images of different sensors.

Acknowledgement. This work is funded by the National Basic Research Program of China (No. 2010CB327902), the National Natural Science Foundation of China (No. 61375036, 61005016), the Beijing Natural Science Foundation (No. 4132064), the Program for New Century Excellent Talents in University, the Beijing Higher Education Young Elite Teacher Project, and the Fundamental Research Funds for the Central Universities. Zhaoxiang Zhang is the corresponding author of this paper.

Reference

1. Lu, D., Mausel, P., Brondizio, E., Moran, E.: Change detection techniques. International Journal of Remote Sensing 25(12), 2365–2401 (2004)
2. Bruzzone, L., Prieto, D.F.: Automatic analysis of the difference image for unsupervised change detection. IEEE Transactions on Geoscience and Remote Sensing 38(3), 1171–1182 (2000)
3. Celik, T.: Multiscale change detection in multitemporal satellite images. Geoscience and Remote Sensing Letters 6(4), 820–824 (2009)
4. Huang, X., Zhang, L.P., Zhu, T.T.: Building Change Detection From Multitemporal High-Resolution Remotely Sensed Images Based on a Morphological Building Index. Selected Topics in Applied Earth Observations and Remote Sensing 7(1), 105–115 (2014)
5. Li, Y., Wu, H., Li, Y., Ye, L.P., Cheng, Z.P., Xu, C.C., Zhao, X.J.: A comparision of high resolution satellite imagery classification between object-oriented and pixel-based method. In: Software Engineering and Service Science, Beijing, China, pp. 1002–1005 (May 2013)

6. Schiewe, J.: Segmentation of high-resolution remotely sensed data-concepts, applications and problems. International Archives of Photogrammetry Remote Sensing and Spatial Information Sciences 34(4), 380–385 (2002)

7. Chen, Z., Zhao, Z.M.: A multi-scale remote sensing image segmentation algorithm based on region growing. Computer Engineering and Applications 41(35), 7–9 (2006)

8. Baatz, M., Schape, A.: Multiresolution Segmentation: An optimization approach for high quality multi-scale image segmentation. Angewandte Geographische Informationsverarbeitung XII, 12–23 (2000)

9. Kennedy, J., Eberhart, R.: Particle swarm optimization. In: IEEE International Conference on Neural Networks, vol. 4(2), pp. 1942–1948 (1995)

10. Haralick, R.M., Shanmugam, K., Dinstein, I.H.: Textural features for image classification. IEEE Transactions on Systems, Man and Cybernetics (6), 610–621 (1973)

Eye Localization Based on Multi-Channel Correlation Filter Bank

Rui Yang[1,2,3], Shiming Ge[1,2,*], Kaixuan Xie[1,2,3], and Shuixian Chen[1,2]

[1]State Key Laboratory of Information Security, IIE, CAS, China
[2]Beijing Key Laboratory of IOT Information Security Technology, IIE, CAS, China
[3]University of Chinese Academy of Sciences
{yangrui,geshiming,xiekaixuan,chenshuixian}@iie.ac.cn

Abstract. Accurate eye localization plays a key role in many face analysis related applications. In this paper, we propose a novel eye localization framework with a group of trained filter arrays called multi-channel correlation filter bank (MCCFB). Each filter array in the bank suits to a different face condition, thus combining these filter array can locate eyes more precisely for variable poses, appearances and illuminations when comparing to single filter/filter array. To demonstrate the performance of our strategy, MCCFB is compared to other eye localization methods, experimental results show superiority of our method in detection ratio, localization accuracy and robustness.

Keywords: Eye localization, Correlation Filter, Filter Bank, Multi-channel, Regression, Biometric Security.

1 Introduction

Eyes are one of the most important features for face analysis. Accurately locating eyes plays a key role in many face related applications such as face recognition, face detection, biometric security etc., thus has received much attention in both the academic and industrial communities recent years.

There are many approaches to locate eyes, however, most of them are conducted in spatial domain. That means such eye detector needs to scan all the possible position of the image to get an optimal result, which makes the locating progress less efficient. Instead, correlation filter based method trains template in the frequency domain. Taking advantage of fast Fourier transform (FFT), correlation/convolution could be efficiently calculated in the frequency domain, which keeps correlation filter superior to other methods in computational cost. Besides, eye localization needs algorithms to estimate eye coordinates in pixel or sub-pixel accuracy. By designing a proper output of the filtering operation,

* Corresponding author. This work is supported in part by the Strategic Priority Research Program(No. XDA06040101), the Special Program for Outstanding Young Talents (No. 1102008202) and the National Key Technology R&D Program (No. 2012BAH20B03).

correlation filter could give locating result in exact pixel. These advantages make correlation filter very suitable for eye localization task.

Although many variants of correlation filter have been proposed, most of them are constituted by a single filter, which can hardly handle face variation in different environments. In this paper, we propose a multi-channel correlation filter bank based method to address eye localization task under diverse conditions. The MCCFB is constructed by a group of filter arrays, each filter array suits better to a certain environment than the others, which increases the adaptability of the whole filter bank compare to a single filter. We formulate eye localization problem as an optimization problem with a well-defined cost function based on MCCFB. The MCCFB is gained with an EM-like adaptive clustering approach and contains several discriminative filters. We evaluated our method with several other eye localization methods, the results shows advantages of our method in both localization performances and robustness.

2   Related Works

According to the information used for building eye detector, the existing eye localization techniques can be classified into three categories: characteristics based methods, hybrid methods and statistics based methods.

Characteristics based methods perform eye localization by measuring eye inhere features such as shape, contrast and context. In [1], Zhou et al. used projection function to locate the x-coordinate of the eye corners and the y-coordinate of the eyelids. These techniques have limitations under the complex or uncontrolled conditions due to unreliable measuring of characteristics.

Hybrid methods integrate structural information into statistical appearance model to improve eye localization. These methods combine the eye characteristics and the appearance under the same framework. The typical methods include enhanced pictorial structure model (EPS) [2], active shape model (ASM) [3], active appearance model (AAM) [4], and so on. Hybrid methods usually localize multiple features simultaneously, and provide a good mechanism to infer the location of an object by estimate the locations of its parts.

In this paper, we focus on statistics based methods. Statistics based methods learn statistical appearance model from a set of training images to extract useful visual features. These methods aim to find a function to discriminate eye and non-eye classes directly. In this way, the problem of eye localization is transformed to a binary classification issue, which aims to train an eye classifier. A well-known classifier is proposed in [5], which uses Haar cascade classifier for face recognition [6] to locate the eyes. However, these classifier are set to optimize the classification accuracy rather than localization accuracy, thus the trained classifier may not give the maximal response at the right object location. One way to tackle this problem is to formulate localization task as a regression rather than a classification problem by incorporating the positions of the eyes. In this setting, given a set of input images with the corresponding eye positions, the training goal is to learn a regressor that maps from the input image to the predicted eye position. In [7], Sun et al. performed facial point detection with deep convolutional neural network. They carefully designed three-level convolutional networks which provides multi-level regression. The convolutional framework learns filters to optimize for minimizing reconstruction error of image patches instead of pattern localization. In [8], Bolme et al. performed regression by constructing a correlation filter that exactly transforms each training image to its correlation image, then simply average all of these exact correlation filters to obtain the final learned filter called average synthetic exact filter (ASEF). As an extension, in [9], Bolme et al. proposed a minimum output sum of squared error (MOSSE) filter, which can get better outcome with fewer training samples. In [10], Hefin et al. adopted a similar method to perform eye localization task by first warping the face image through the candidate response pair and then selecting the one leading to face image with best quality. In [11], Boddeti et al. proposed a vector correlation filter (VCF), which train multi-channel descriptors for car landmark detection. In [12], Galoogahi et al. introduced a similar method called multi-channel correlation filters (MCCF), which saved the computational cost of VCF and was used into eye localization task. The crucial step in correlation filter based methods is filter construction. When the filter fits test samples, good outcome could be expected. However, one single correlation filter or filter array could hardly fit all the testing face images due to huge appearance variations of face in lighting, expression, pose and so on.

3   Proposed Approach

In this section, we present the fundamentals of correlation filter and the proposed method for the task of eye localization. We only conduct localization on the left eye as the situation for the right eye is similar.

Notation: The training set is constituted by n face images $\{f_1, f_2, \ldots, f_n\}$ and the corresponding eye coordinate $\{(x_1, y_1), (x_2, y_2), \ldots, (x_n, y_n)\}$. Matrices are presented in bold (e.g. h). The symbol $\wedge$ applied on any matrix denotes the 2D Discrete Fourier Transform (DFT) of it. Complex conjugate and complex transpose are indicated by $*$ and $\dagger$ respectively. One of the most advantage of DFT lies in its ability to represent convolution/correlation in spatial domain as a Hadamard product in the Fourier domain. The symbol $\odot$ denotes the correlation operation, Hadamard product is represented as the $\circ$ operator.

3.1   Correlation Filter

Correlation filter is a spatial-frequency matrix that is trained for representing a particular pattern. In the task of localization, patterns of interest are searched by cross correlating the query image with the filter, then possible correlation peak is examined as the pattern location across the correlation output. Ideally, the correlation operation would generate the desired output which has a sharp peak at center of the target and (near) zero value for elsewhere. In order to approximate such filter, many approaches have been proposed.

For a single input image f_i and the corresponding output g_i, the exact correlation filter h_i is obtained in frequency domain as $\hat{h}_i^* = \hat{g}_i/\hat{f}_i$, where $\hat{h}_i^*$, $\hat{g}_i$, and $\hat{f}_i$ are the 2D Fourier Transform of the exact filter h_i, the desired output of the i-th image g_i and the i-th training image f_i respectively. ASEF [8] is constructed by averaging all the exact filters:

$$\hat{h} = \sum_{i=1}^{n} \hat{h}_i \tag{1}$$

MOSSE filter [9], as an extension of ASEF, is proposed to get improved performance with fewer training images. Compared to ASEF filter, MOSSE filter has a more reasonable way of combining all the training images and desired output. The main idea is to minimize the sum of average mean square error (MSE) between the actual cross-correlation output and the ideal desired output during training. This can be presented as an optimization problem, i.e.

$$\min_{\hat{h}} \frac{1}{n} \sum_{i=1}^{n} \left\| \hat{f}_i \circ \hat{h}^* - \hat{g}_i \right\|_2^2 + \lambda \left\| \hat{h} \right\|_2^2 \tag{2}$$

where $\hat{h}$ is the 2D Fourier Transform of the filter template h and λ is the regularization parameter.

Boddeti et.al. proposed VCF which can be directly used with vector features besides scalar features(most commonly pixel values). VCF is a filter array, which consists of one correlation filter per feature channel, it can be trained by minimize the sum of average MSE between the ideal output and the joint output of all the feature filters, i.e.

$$\min_{\hat{h}^1, \hat{h}^2, \dots, \hat{h}^k} \frac{1}{n} \sum_{i=1}^{n} \left\| \sum_{j=1}^{k} \hat{f}_i^j \circ (\hat{h}^j)^* - \hat{g}_i \right\|_2^2 + \lambda \sum_{j=1}^{k} \left\| \hat{h}^j \right\|_2^2 \tag{3}$$

where $\hat{h}^j$ is the filter of the j-th channel in the filter array, k is the number of feature channels and $\hat{f}_i^j$ is the 2D Fourier transform of the j-th channel of f_i. During test stage, the query image is first processed to get all feature channels, then all the feature channels are correlated with its corresponding feature channel filters, the final output is then generated by aggregating the outputs of the feature channels.

3.2   Multi-Channel Correlation Filter Bank

VCF, which takes advantage of vector feature channels, gets better outcome than single scalar feature channel. However, training all images to get one single correlation filter array can hardly handle the huge variance among images, which leads to the trained filter array works less well in complicate situations.

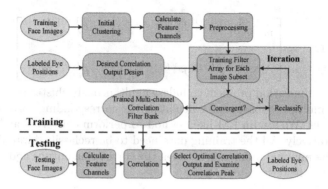

Fig. 1. The procedure of eye localization based on MCCFB

In order to address this problem, we propose a framework with a set of trained discriminative filter arrays called MCCFB which could adaptively handle localization under different face conditions. The whole localization procedure is shown in Fig. 1.

At training stage, the central goal is to learn a group of filter arrays that adaptively suit to face conditions differ from one another. Inspired by VCF, constructing MCCFB can be posed as an optimization problem, i.e.

$$\min_{\boldsymbol{H}^{(l)}} \sum_{l=1}^{M} \left(\frac{1}{n_l} \sum_{i=1}^{n_l} \left\| \sum_{j=1}^{k} \boldsymbol{f}_i^{j,(l)} \odot \boldsymbol{h}^{j,(l)} - \boldsymbol{g}_i^{(l)} \right\|^2 + \lambda \sum_{j=1}^{k} \left\| \boldsymbol{h}^{j,(l)} \right\|^2 \right) \tag{4}$$

where $\boldsymbol{H}^{(l)}$ is the l-th filter array in the bank, M is the number of vector correlation filter in the bank, n_l is the number of training images in the l-th subset and $n = \sum_{l=1}^{M} n_l$. The optimization problem can be solved efficiently in frequency domain where the objective function has the following closed form expression similar with [11],

$$\min_{\hat{\boldsymbol{H}}^{(l)}} \sum_{l=1}^{M} E\left(\hat{\boldsymbol{H}}^{(l)}, C^{(l)} \right) \tag{5}$$

where total energy in Eq. 5 involves all the energy associated with each training subset. $E\left(\hat{\boldsymbol{H}}^{(l)}, C^{(l)} \right)$ is the energy associate with the l-th training subset $C^{(l)}$. Due to energy independence among the training subsets, the solution has the following closed form expression for MCCFB,

$$\hat{\boldsymbol{H}}^{(l)} = \begin{bmatrix} \hat{\boldsymbol{h}}^{1,(l)} \\ \vdots \\ \hat{\boldsymbol{h}}^{k,(l)} \end{bmatrix} = \left[\lambda \mathbf{I} + \hat{\boldsymbol{D}}^{(l)} \right]^{-1} \begin{bmatrix} \frac{1}{n_l} \sum_{i=1}^{n_l} \hat{\boldsymbol{F}}_i^{1,(l)\dagger} \hat{\boldsymbol{g}}_i^{(l)} \\ \vdots \\ \frac{1}{n_l} \sum_{i=1}^{n_l} \hat{\boldsymbol{F}}_i^{k,(l)\dagger} \hat{\boldsymbol{g}}_i^{(l)} \end{bmatrix} \tag{6}$$

where

$$\hat{D}^{(l)} = \begin{bmatrix} \frac{1}{n_l}\sum_{i=1}^{n_l} \hat{F}_i^{1,(l)\dagger} \hat{F}_i^{1,(l)} & \cdots & \frac{1}{n}\sum_{i=1}^{n_l} \hat{F}_i^{1,(l)\dagger} \hat{F}_i^{k,(l)} \\ \vdots & \ddots & \vdots \\ \frac{1}{n_l}\sum_{i=1}^{n_l} \hat{F}_i^{k,(l)\dagger} \hat{F}_i^{1,(l)} & \cdots & \frac{1}{n}\sum_{i=1}^{n_l} \hat{F}_i^{k,(l)\dagger} \hat{F}_i^{k,(l)} \end{bmatrix} \qquad (7)$$

Solving the optimization problem includes simultaneously clustering the training images into multiple subsets and calculating the corresponding correlation filter for each subset. We use an EM-like method to perform clustering and filter calculating iteratively. All the training data need to be reclassified into the subset, which has the minimal difference between the correlation output and the desired output, in the clustering step,

$$l_{best} = \arg\min_{l} \left\| \sum_{j=1}^{k} \hat{f}^j \hat{h}^{j,(l)} - \hat{g} \right\|^2 \qquad (8)$$

The algorithm process is as blow:

Algorithm 1. Training MCCFB

Input:
   Training face images $\{f_1, f_2, \ldots, f_n\}$;
   Labeled eye positions $\{(x_1, y_1), (x_2, y_2), \ldots, (x_n, y_n)\}$;
   The number of filter arrays in MCCFB M;
   The maximal iteration time T;
Output:
   Trained MCCFB $\{\hat{H}^{(l)}\}$;
Training:
1: Initially cluster all training data into M subsets;
2: Calculate k image channels;
3: E step: calculate $\{\hat{H}^{(l)}\}$ with Eq. 6 according to the current clustered subsets;
4: M step: reclassify all the training data with Eq. 8;
5: Check the convergence condition: if reaching the maximal iteration time, finish training and export current $\{\hat{H}^{(l)}\}$ as the final MCCFB , otherwise, go back to step 2.

Using method similar to [12], computational cost of training filter for each subset is reduced to $O(dk^3 + ndk^2)$, where d is product of image width and length. For further improvement, parallel processing can be adopted to speed up the training step.

At testing stage, given the query image, all the k feature channels that used for filter training need to be calculated, then each filter array in the MCCFB is correlated with array of these channels to get M correlation outputs. The optimal correlation output is selected as the one whose peak value holds the greatest share of the output energy, i.e.

$$g^{(o)} = \max_{g^{(l)}} \frac{g_{max}^{(l)}}{\left\| g^{(l)} \right\|_2^2} \qquad (9)$$

where $g_{max}^{(l)}$ denotes the peak value in $\boldsymbol{g}^{(l)}$. Then, the final coordinate is selected as the position of the peak in the optimal correlation output $\boldsymbol{g}^{(o)}$.

4   Experiments

4.1   Database

We conduct our proposed approach on the BioID [13] database, which contains 1521 images, each image shows a frontal view of face with various facial expressions captured in a lab. The database is randomly partitioned into two sets. One set for training with 1000 images and another for testing with 521 images. We use manual annotation of this database from FGnet [14]. All the face extracted from the database are resized to 64×64 pixels. To enlarge the database and improve the robustness, a random similarity transform is operated. The similarity transform contains rotation up to $\pm 15°$, scaling up to 1.0 ± 0.1 and shifting up to ± 4 pixels. Each training image is randomly perturbed 16 times which results in 16,000 training examples.

4.2   Training

Before training, image feature channels need to be calculated. In our experiments, we use two channels, grey-scale intensity and magnitude of gradient. Then a preprocessing step is conducted. All the feature channels of the training samples are first took the log operation and then normalized to make the mean and energy of the pixel values equal 0.0 and 1.0 respectively. To reduce the frequency effect in Fast Fourier Transform (FFT) operation, a cosine window is applied to the image.

The desired outputs are designed as a 2D Gaussian function according to associated position of the target,

$$g_i(x, y) = e^{-[(x-x_i)^2 + (y-y_i)^2]/\sigma^2} \tag{10}$$

where σ is scale parameter for controlling the sharpness of correlation output, (x_i, y_i) is the location of the target, i.e. left eye in our experiments.

The initial clustering step is performed by cropping an 11×15 path centered at the left eye from the training images, then k-means clustering is conducted with these pathes. Afterward, the training set is divided into several subsets according to the results of clustering.

The parameters are set as $M = 3$, $T = 20$ and $\sigma = 1$ respectively in the experiments. Fig. 2(a) gives the total energy defined in Eq. 5 alongside the iteration times. It shows that the total energy is reducing and converging when iteration time grows. The trained MCCFB includes 3 filter arrays, each array has 2 feature channels. Fig. 2(b) shows the 3 filter arrays with their corresponding examples.

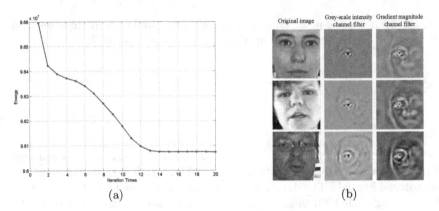

(a)   (b)

Fig. 2. (a) Energy cost against iteration times and (b) the trained MCCFB

4.3   Evaluation

In order to evaluate the performance of the proposed approach, we compare our MCCFB method with other methods including ASEF filter method [8], MOSSE filter method [9], EPS method [2] and VCF filter method [11]. All experiments are exactly managed in the same environment.

In the case of left eye, the accuracy of localization is typically measured by the left eye normalized shifting distance.

$$D_l = \|P_l - L_l\| / \|L_l - L_r\| \tag{11}$$

where P_l is the predicted eye location estimating by the algorithm, L_l and L_r are the real labeled location of the left and right eye. To be counted as a success, normalized shifting distance must within a certain threshold τ, detection ratio is then the percentage of successful localizations. The accuracy and the robustness of the localization algorithm is evaluated by the mean and the standard deviation of the normalized shifting distance respectively.

Table 1. Performance comparisons of five methods

Method	Detection Ratio	Mean	Standard Deviation
ASEF[8]	93.33%	0.0800	0.2472
MOSSE[9]	93.76%	0.0781	0.2346
EPS[2]	96.34%	0.0494	0.1349
VCF[11]	97.85%	0.0306	0.0595
MCCFB	**99.57%**	**0.0279**	**0.0183**

Table 1 gives the results when $\tau = 0.1$, which is usually considered as a reasonable successful detection threshold. It can be seen that our method outperforms the others not only in detection ratio, but also in mean of D_l, which means a better localization accuracy. In addition, the standard deviation of D_l of MC-CFB is extremely low, that means our method is very robust in eye localization task. In order to verify the effectiveness and necessity of the filter choosing step, each filter array in MCCFB is separately used to locate eye. The results are shown in Table 2. We can see that the result of a single filter array is not so promising, that's because each filter array is trained to fit a particular environment. Through a rational selection procedure, MCCFB significantly improved the detection ratio by choosing the right filter array.

Table 2. Localization results using single filter array

Fliter Array	1st	2nd	3rd	ALL
Detection Ratio	91.18%	85.81%	83.23%	99.57%

Fig. 3(a) gives some samples of localization using different methods. Besides the experiments on BioID database, to check the robustness of our algorithm, we run extra experiments on LFW [15] database, which contains more pose changes. The results are quite promising. Fig. 3(b) shows some visual examples of the localization results.

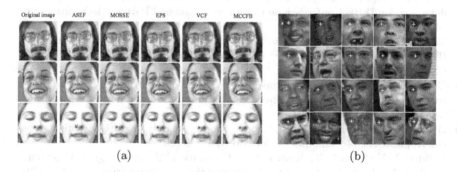

(a)   (b)

Fig. 3. Localization results on (a) BioID and (b) LFW

5   Conclusion

This paper proposed an eye localization framework with an adaptive way to construct a set of multi-channel filter arrays called MCCFB. The trained filter arrays in the bank are discriminative to suit different kinds of conditions. Experiments on eye localization show superiority of our method both in detection ratio, localization accuracy and robustness.

In the future, we want to extend our work to more complicated environments and locate more points on the face, which can incorporate the structure information into our MCCFB method. We also believe our framework will perform well on many other similar tasks, exploiting it into some other fields such as object alignment, object detection, tracking and biometric security will be considered afterwards.

References

1. Zhou, Z.H., Geng, X.: Projection functions for eye detection. Pattern Recognition 37(5), 1049–1056 (2004)
2. Tan, X., Song, F., Zhou, Z., Chen, S.: Enhanced pictorial structures for precise eye localization under uncontrolled conditions. In: IEEE Conference on Computer Vision and Pattern Recognition, pp. 1621–1628 (2009)
3. Cao, X., Wei, Y., Wen, F., Sun, J.: Face Alignment by Explicit Shape Regression. In: IEEE Conference on Computer Vision and Pattern Recognition, pp. 2887–2894 (2012)
4. Matthews, I., Baker, S.: Active appearance models revisited. International Journal of Computer Vision 60, 135–164 (2004)
5. Castrillón-Santana, M., Lorenzo-Navarro, J., Déniz-Suárez, O., Isern-González, J., Falcón-Martel, A.: Multiple face detection at different resolutions for perceptual user interfaces. In: Marques, J.S., Pérez de la Blanca, N., Pina, P. (eds.) IbPRIA 2005. LNCS, vol. 3522, pp. 445–452. Springer, Heidelberg (2005)
6. Viola, P., Jones, M.J.: Robust real-time face detection. International Journal of Computer Vision 57, 137–154 (2004)
7. Sun, Y., Wang, X., Tang, X.: Deep convolutional network cascade for facial point detection. In: IEEE Conference on Computer Vision and Pattern Recognition, pp. 3476–3483 (2013)
8. Bolme, D.S., Draper, B.A., Beveridge, J.R.: Average of synthetic exact filters. In: IEEE Conference on Computer Vision and Pattern Recognition, pp. 2105–2112 (2009)
9. Bolme, D.S., Beveridge, J.R., Draper, B.A.: Visual object tracking using adaptive correlation filtersc. In: IEEE Conference on Computer Vision and Pattern Recognition, pp. 2544–2550 (2010)
10. Heflin, B., Scheirerc, W., Boult, T.E.: For your eyes only. In: IEEE Workshop on the Applications of Computer Vision, pp. 193–200 (2012)
11. Boddeti, V.N., Kanade, T., Kumar, B.V.: Correlation Filters for Object Alignment. In: IEEE Conference on Computer Vision and Pattern Recognition, pp. 2291–2298 (2013)
12. Galoogahi, H.K., Sim, T., Lucey, S.: Multi-channel Correlation Filters. In: IEEE International Conference on Computer Vision, pp. 3072–3079 (2013)
13. Jesorsky, O., Kirchberg, K.J., Frischholz, R.W.: Robust Face Detection Using the Hausdorff Distance. In: Bigun, J., Smeraldi, F. (eds.) AVBPA 2001. LNCS, vol. 2091, pp. 90–95. Springer, Heidelberg (2001)
14. FGNET Annotation of BioID Dataset, http://www-prima.inrialpes.fr/FGnet/data/11-BioID/bioid_points.html (accessed May 21, 2014)
15. Huang, G.B., Mattar, M., Berg, T., Learned-Miller, E.: Labeled faces in the wild: A database for studying face recognition in unconstrained environments. Technical Report, University of Massachusetts, Amherst (2007)

Person Re-identification
by Cascade-Iterative Ranking

Xiangyu Wang, Feng Chen, and Yu Liu

Department of Automation, Tsinghua University,
100084 Beijing, China
{w-xy12,liu-yu12}@mails.tsinghua.edu.cn,
chenfeng@mail.tsinghua.edu.cn

Abstract. State-of-the-art methods on person re-identification usually match the probe set against the candidates in gallery set without the reversed matching process. The one-way methods may not obtain the correct corresponding result by using the limited information in gallery set. In this study, we propose a novel bidirectional framework for person re-identification which is called cascade-iterative ranking. The framework consists of iterative ranking and cascade strategy. The iterative ranking adjusts the rank order of candidates repeatedly by sorting with the bidirectional distance we propose. This distance exploits the bidirectional information of rank order hidden in both sets to get more robust result than the one-way methods. And the multiple features are integrated by a cascade strategy. This strategy can relieve the case that the effect of features offsets for each other. Experimental results on VIPeR and ETHZ datasets verify the effectiveness of our method.

Keywords: Person re-identification, bidirectional distance, iterative ranking, cascade strategy.

1 Introduction

Person re-identification can be defined as the task of assigning the same identifier to all the instances (images and videos) of the same person [1]. There are usually two image sets for matching, the probe image set and the gallery image set. The images in both sets are usually captured in distributed locations at different times. Each image in the probe set is matched to a set of candidates in the gallery set [2]. The aim of person re-identification is to associate the images of the same person and discard the irrelevant ones. It is one of the most challenging issues in video processing due to a series of aspects, such as changes of illumination, variations of person pose and camera viewpoint, and occlusion.

State-of-the-art methods on person identification can be classified into two main groups, the feature-based group and the learning-based group. The first group focuses on investigating the discriminative features and exploiting them to represent a pedestrian. In [3], Farenzena et al. proposed the Symmetry-Driven Accumulation of Local Features (SDALF), where they exploited the symmetry

S. Li et al. (Eds.): CCPR 2014, Part I, CCIS 483, pp. 335–344, 2014.

property of different body parts to extract the powerful features and showed good robustness to pose and viewpoint variation. The precise model proposed in [4, 5] can obtain more reliable appearance features. And different features show different ability for matching individuals in person re-identification [6, 7]. The second group concentrated on the learning method and distance metric. Many learning methods, such as large margin nearest neighbor (LMNN), Adaboost, RankSVM, are used in [7–11] to make re-identification more robust. A series of distance metrics were proposed for matching in [12–14], which can measure the similarity between images more precisely.

As far as we know, all the existing works on person re-identification treat the re-identification as a one-way process, that is, only the probe set matches against the gallery set without the reversed matching process. We can generate the neighbor list of the probe by sorting the gallery images with the absolute distance (e. g., L2 or Bhattacharyya distance between extracted re-identification features). Generally, the correct corresponding image of probe ranks highly but not the first in the neighbor list. This matching error results from the limited re-identification information of the gallery set. Since images of the same person appear in both of the probe and gallery sets, the two sets can be exchanged. Then the image in gallery set can match against with the probe images. By applying this reversed re-identification process, we can collect more information in both sets to obtain reliable and robust result.

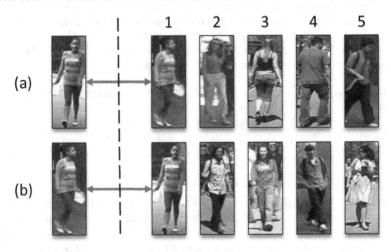

Fig. 1. Example of two images from the same person. In the left, (a) and (b) are the images from the same person. In the right, they are the neighbor lists of the left images. The images from the same individual are more likely to have high rank order in the neighbor list mutually.

Thus, we propose a novel bidirectional framework, cascade-iterative ranking, for person re-identification. This framework consists of two parts, iterative ranking and cascade strategy. In iterative ranking, the core is the new distance we propose which is called the bidirectional rank order distance. This distance is inspired by an interesting observation which is shown in Figure 1. The probe and gallery images from the same individual are more likely to have high rank order in the neighbor list mutually. The neighbor list of each image in both sets can be generated by sorting this new distance repeatedly. The bidirectional rank order information is exploited in iterative ranking rather than only the one-way information. Besides, traditional methods integrate multiple features by combining the absolute distance of features linearly. The matching ability of one feature may weaken that of another one in this combination strategy. We exploit the cascade strategy to add a different feature after the iterative ranking of both sets. The distinction of features for person re-identification can be reserved in this method.

The contributions of this paper are as follows. (i) We propose a novel bidirectional framework, cascade-iterative ranking, for person re-identification. The framework combined the bidirectional information of ranking and the discriminative ability of features. (ii) We propose a new similarity distance, the bidirectional rank order distance, which investigates the stabilization of the nearest neighbor ranking.

2 Cascade-Iterative Ranking

In this section, we introduce the two parts of our framework, iterative ranking and cascade strategy. The part of iterative ranking obtains stable neighbor list of each image by sorting candidate images with bidirectional rank order distance iteratively. The cascade strategy improves the result of re-identification gradually by combining different features in each step.

2.1 Bidirectional Rank Order Distance

We introduce a new distance, bidirectional rank order distance, to measure the similarity of two images of the same person. This distance is inspired by an interesting observation that two images of the same person tend to rank highly in the neighbor list of each other. If the images are from different persons, they usually have low rank order in at least one of the neighbor list.

Formally, given the two image sets to be re-identified, we first generate the order list of each image in the two sets by sorting the absolute distance of features. Next, we defined the bidirectional distance $BD(a, b)$ between image a and b as

$$BD(a, b) = O_{a \to b}(a, b) + O_{b \to a}(a, b) \tag{1}$$

where $O_{a \to b}(a, b)$ is the rank order of image b in the neighbor list of image a and $O_{b \to a}(a, b)$ is the rank order of image a in the neighbor list of image b. For example, a and b are the images to be matched which are shown in Figure 2 and they are from different cameras. The summation of the rank order $O_{a \to b}(a, b)$ and $O_{b \to a}(a, b)$ is the bidirectional distance $BD(a, b)$ between image a and b. It

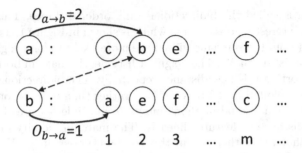

Fig. 2. Example of bidirectional rank order distance. The images in the upper row are a and its neighbor list. And the images in the bottom row are b and its neighbor list. The bidirectional rank order distance between a and b is the summation of rank order from a to a via b.

is obvious that the distance is symmetric: $BD(a, b)$ is equal to $BD(a, b)$. If the images a and b are similar, they have a smaller bidirectional distance.

Furthermore, we exploit the weight to balance the bidirectional distance and the absolute distance. The weighted bidirectional distance is defined as

$$WBD(a,b) = \omega_{a \to b}(a,b) \cdot O_{a \to b}(a,b)$$
$$+ \omega_{b \to a}(a,b) \cdot O_{b \to a}(a,b) \qquad (2)$$

where $\omega_{a \to b}(a, b)$ is the weight of the order of b in the neighbor list of a, $\omega_{b \to a}(a, b)$ is the weight of the order of a in the list of b. The weight respects the similarity

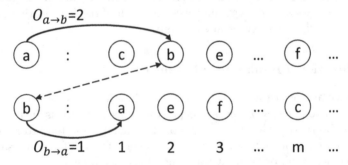

Fig. 3. Example of the weighted bidirectional rank order distance. The distance between a and $b1$ is equal to that between a and $b2$ measured by bidirectional distance. However, the distance between a and $b1$ is shorter than that between a and $b2$ measured by weighted bidirectional distance.

between a and b and it is generated by normalizing the absolute distance. There was a positive correlation between the weight and the absolute distance. Notice that the weight $\omega_{a \to b}(a, b)$ is not equal to $\omega_{b \to a}(a, b)$ due to the normalization. Example in Figure 3 shows that the distance with weights is more robust than the one without weights.

2.2   Iterative Ranking

In person re-identification, we usually use the nearest neighbor image in the neighbor list as the re-identification result. When using the absolute distance, the neighbor lists are fixed after the first sorting. However, the neighbor lists may be changed for each time by sorting the weighted bidirectional rank order distance. In order to obtain more stable and reliable result, we repeat the sorting process and obtain the final neighbor lists.

Since images of the same person appear in both of the probe and gallery sets, the two sets can be exchanged. For each probe image, we can calculate its neighbor list by sorting the gallery images with the absolute distance. Similarly, the neighbor list of each gallery image could also be generated by sorting the probe images. Then in the neighbor list of probe image, we can adjust the rank order of each gallery image by sorting in the weighted bidirectional rank order distance. And the neighbor list of gallery image can also be adjusted in the same way. We treat the two adjustment as one ranking round and proceed with the round repeatedly. For the two image sets to be re-identified, the neighbor lists would be adjusted iteratively by repeating the ranking round. The mutual ranking adjustment in an iterative way is called iterative ranking.

In order to describe the iterative step clearly, we use the bidirectional distance as the example, the case of weighted bidirectional rank order distance is similar. Suppose that there were two images $B1$ and $B2$ in the neighbor list of probe image A. The rank order of $B1$ is higher than that of $B2$, that is, $O_{A \to B1}(A, B1) < O_{A \to B2}(A, B2)$. As the definition, we have the bidirectional rank order distance between A and $B1$

$$BD(A, B1) = O_{A \to B1}(A, B1) + O_{B1 \to A}(A, B1) \qquad (3)$$

and the bidirectional rank order distance between A and $B2$

$$BD(A, B2) = O_{A \to B2}(A, B2) + O_{B2 \to A}(A, B2). \qquad (4)$$

Only when $BD(A, B2)$ is smaller than $BD(A, B1)$, the rank order of $B2$ would be adjusted higher than that of $B1$. If $B1$ is much similar to A than $B2$, the order of A in neighbor list of $B1$ is usually higher than that of $B2$, i.e. $O_{B1 \to A}(A, B1) < O_{B2 \to A}(A, B2)$. Accordingly, the $BD(A, B1)$ is shorter than the $BD(A, B2)$, the rank order of $B1$ and $B2$ would not be changed. If $B2$ is much similar to A than $B1$, the order of image A in $B1$'s neighbor list is usually not sorted at the top position, but the order of image A in $B2$'s neighbor list is usually high. It's possible for $B2$ to adjust its rank order in this case. Hence, the rank order would be modulated when $O_{A \to B2}(A, B2) - O_{A \to B1}(A, B1) < O_{B1 \to A}(A, B1) - O_{B2 \to A}(A, B2)$, that is, $BD(A, B2) < BD(A, B1)$. Once the rank order is adjusted, the neighbor list would be modulated iteratively until getting the reliable result.

2.3   Cascade Strategy

In this section, we show how the cascade strategy combines with iterative ranking to enhance the accuracy of re-identification. The cascade structure makes use

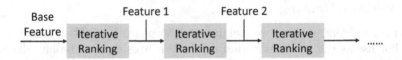

Fig. 4. The cascade strategy for person re-identification. At each iterative ranking step, a different feature is added to adjust neighbor lists.

of all the information collected from the output of the last iterative ranking step and the additional information of a feature extracted by current step. This multistage strategy can be combined with most of informative features extracted for re-identification.

Generally, traditional method use linear combination to integrate the absolute distance of different features. However, this combination may lead to the situation that features weakens the re-identification ability of each other. So we exploit the cascade strategy instead of the linear combination method. In each step, we only need the weights and neighbor lists to process iterative ranking. The output of each step is the adjusted neighbor lists. As showed in Figure 4, at the first iterative ranking, we use the base feature to compute the absolute distance and generate the weights and neighbor lists. Then we proceed the iterative ranking to compute the new neighbor lists. At the second step, we calculate the absolute distance of a different feature and add it to the first absolute distance. Then, we could get the new weights for the new weights for the second step by the updated absolute distance. The initial neighbor lists of the second iterative ranking is the output neighbor list of the first step. Therefore, the second iterative ranking can generate a new neighbor list for the next step. As long as we add a different feature to the re-identification processing, we can cascade an iterative ranking step to the whole process. The detailed description of the algorithm is shown in Algorithm 1. Given that each feature has different ability of

---

Algorithm 1. Cascade-iterative ranking

Input: Two image sets for re-identification, the probe set A and gallery set B
Output: The person identification of each image, the images from the same person has the same identification
1: **Initialize** the original neighbor lists L and weights W by base feature.
2: **repeat**
3:    Use the neighbor lists L and weights W to proceed iterative ranking and obtain the new neighbor lists L'.
4:    **Update** the neighbor list L with L'.
5:    Add a different feature to the previous features to compute the weight W'.
6:    **Update** the weights W with W'.
7: **until** no feature is added.
8: **return** the person identification of each image. For each image, the nearest neighbor in its list has the same identification.

---

re-identification, if we just use the feature itself to compute the new weight rather than the combination of features, the ranking result would fluctuate frequently. Moreover, We usually put the color-based feature in the head and put the other features (texture-based feature and feature points) in the following part.

3   Experimental Results

In this section the evaluation of our approach is presented. Two publicly available person re-identification datasets, VIPeR [15] and ETHZ [16], were used for evaluation. These two datasets are most widely used for evaluation and reflect most challenges in the real word.

VIPeR Dataset. The VIPeR dataset consists of 632 image pairs, each pair is two images of the same person with different viewpoints. The data were collected in an outdoor academic environment. The dataset is challenging due to viewpoint, pose, illumination variation, low resolution and background clutter. The total 1264 images can be divided into 2 sets, camera A and camera B.

We use the Cumulative Matching Characteristic (CMC) curve [17] to measure our method. The CMC curve represents the expectation of finding the correct match in the top n neighbors. For fair comparing, the splitting assignment of the SDALF is used in our experiments. We randomly sample half of the dataset, that is, 316 image pairs, to be matched. The features we used in our cascade-iterative ranking are the same with the SDALF approach. They are weighted HSV histograms [3] (wHSV), Maximally Stable Color Regions [18] (MSCR) and Recurrent High-Structured Patches [3] (RHSP) respectively. The whole procedure is repeated for 10 times, and the average result is reported.

Figure 5 show the comparison result and the IR and the CIR are our methods. The IR stands for the iterative ranking based on the absolute distance which is the linear combination of these 3 features' Bhattacharyya distance. And the CIR represents the case that we add the 3 features step-by-step in cascade strategy with iterative ranking. We can see that IR consistently outperforms the SDALF: the rank 1 matching rate of IR is 23.67% while that of SDALF is 19.08%. The rank 10 matching rate for IR is 56.90% while that of SDALF is 51.43%. The rank 1 matching rate of CIR is 17.12% which is less than SDALF. Overall, the matching rate of CIR is about the same with SDALF. On one hand, the improvement of IR can be explained as: exploiting the bidirectional information can improve the rank order of the correct image. As the whole information of features was collected in the absolute distance, the rank 1 matching rate is higher than that of SDALF. On the other hand, the CIR collect the distinction of features gradually. The limited discriminative ability of base feature has an influence on the rank 1 matching rate. In addition, the features we used in experiments could be replaced with the others extracted for re-identification.

ETHZ Dataset. The ETHZ dataset contains three video sequences of crowded street scenes captured by two moving cameras. There were multiple images of the same individual with a range of variations in appearances. The images in this

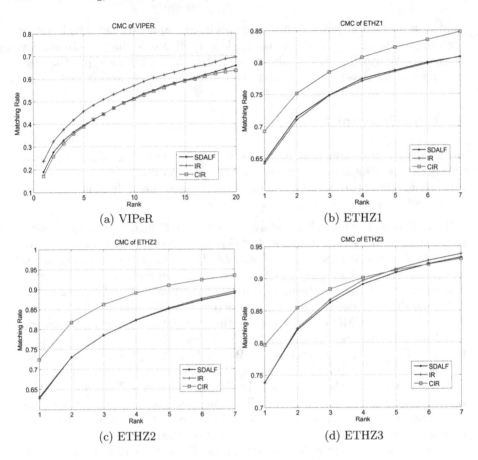

Fig. 5. Performances comparison using CMC curves on VIPeR dataset and ETHZ dataset

dataset has not the uniform scale as that in VIPeR dataset. The dataset consists of: SEQ. #1 includes 4,857 images of 83 pedestrians, SEQ. #21,961 images of 35 pedestrians, and SEQ. #31,762 images of 28 pedestrians.

The same settings of experiments in [3] are reproduced to make fair comparisons. In [3], a single shot evaluation strategy was used. For each person, one image was randomly selected to form the gallery set and the probe set was composed of the rest images. When the image in probe set is correctly matched with the image in the gallery, we can get the rank order. Our methods require the sizes of the probe and the gallery are about the same, and it is perfect in the case of VIPeR dataset. But in the ETHZ dataset, the size of the probe and gallery sets are extremely unbalanced. In order to make our framework work well for both one shot case and multiple shots case, we need to do some adjustment to deal with this condition. The adjustment is just concentrated in the part of iterative ranking. As the size of gallery set is much smaller than that of probe set, the neighbor list is just generated by the probe set and the neighbor list of gallery set is replaced with it. Then the iterative ranking can be processed. 10 trials of evaluation are repeated to achieve stable statistics, and the average result is plotted in Figure 5.

As shown in Figure 5, we can see that IR and CIR consistently outperforms SDALF on all the 3 sequences. The rank 1 matching rates of CIR have visible increase than that of the SDALF. The IR result is almost the same as the SDALF approach. The results could be explained as: the unbalanced size of the probe and gallery sets makes the bidirectional information unbalanced. The adjustment information for neighbor lists of probe set is limited. Besides, the base feature performs well in the ETHZ dataset and the rank 1 matching rate increases visibly.

4   Conclusion

This paper proposed a novel bidirectional framework called cascade-iterative ranking for person re-identification. Our framework exploited the bidirectional information of both image sets and reserved the distinction information carried by different features. Experimental results show that our cascade-iterative ranking approach improve the performance of person re-identification effectively. There are several aspects to be further studied in the future, especially the combination between cascade-iterative ranking and the salience of features.

References

1. Vezzani, R., Baltieri, D., Cucchiara, R.: People Reidentification in Surveillance and Forensics: A Survey. ACM Comput. Surv. 46, 1–37 (2013)
2. Loy, C.C., Liu, C., Gong, S.: Person re-identification by manifold ranking. In: 20th IEEE International Conference on Image Processing, pp. 3567–3571. IEEE, Melbourne (2013)
3. Farenzena, M., Bazzani, L., Perina, A., Murino, V., Cristani, M.: Person re-identification by symmetry-driven accumulation of local features. In: IEEE Conference on Computer Vision and Pattern Recognition, pp. 2360–2367. IEEE, San Francisco (2010)
4. Bak, S., Corvee, E., Brémond, F., Thonnat, M.: Person re-identification using spatial covariance regions of human body parts. In: 7th IEEE International Conference on Advanced Video and Signal Based Surveillance, pp. 435–440. IEEE, Boston (2010)
5. Cheng, D.S., Cristani, M., Stoppa, M., Bazzani, L., Murino, V.: Custom pictorial structures for re-identification. In: British Machine Vision Conference, pp. 1–11. BMVA Press, Dundee (2011)
6. Liu, C., Gong, S., Loy, C.C., Lin, X.: Person re-identification: What features are important? In: Fusiello, A., Murino, V., Cucchiara, R. (eds.) ECCV 2012 Ws/Demos, Part I. LNCS, vol. 7583, pp. 391–401. Springer, Heidelberg (2012)
7. Zhao, R., Ouyang, W., Wang, X.: Unsupervised salience learning for person re-identification. In: IEEE Conference on Computer Vision and Pattern Recognition, pp. 3586–3593. IEEE, Portland (2013)

8. Weinberger, K.Q., Saul, L.K.: Distance metric learning for large margin nearest neighbor classification. The Journal of Machine Learning Research 10, 207–244 (2009)
9. Dikmen, M., Akbas, E., Huang, T.S., Ahuja, N.: Pedestrian recognition with a learned metric. In: Kimmel, R., Klette, R., Sugimoto, A. (eds.) ACCV 2010, Part IV. LNCS, vol. 6495, pp. 501–512. Springer, Heidelberg (2011)
10. Gray, D., Tao, H.: Viewpoint invariant pedestrian recognition with an ensemble of localized features. In: Forsyth, D., Torr, P., Zisserman, A. (eds.) ECCV 2008, Part I. LNCS, vol. 5302, pp. 262–275. Springer, Heidelberg (2008)
11. Prosser, B., Zheng, W., Gong, S., Xiang, T.: Person re-identification by support vector ranking. In: British Machine Vision Conference, pp. 1–11. BMVA Press, Aberystwyth (2010)
12. Kostinger, M., Hirzer, M., Wohlhart, P., Roth, P.M., Bischof, H.: Large scale metric learning from equivalence constraints. In: IEEE Conference on Computer Vision and Pattern Recognition, pp. 2288–2295. IEEE, Providence (2012)
13. Li, W., Wu, Y., Mukunoki, M., Minoh, M.: Common-near-neighbor analysis for person re-identification. In: 19th IEEE International Conference on Image Processing, pp. 1621–1624. IEEE, Orlando (2012)
14. Zhu, C., Wen, F., Sun, J.: A rank-order distance based clustering algorithm for face tagging. In: IEEE Conference on Computer Vision and Pattern Recognition, pp. 481–488. IEEE, Providence (2011)
15. Gray, D., Brennan, S., Tao, H.: Evaluating appearance models for recognition, reacquisition, and tracking. In: 10th IEEE International Workshop on Performance Evaluation of Tracking and Surveillance (2007)
16. Schwartz, W.R., Davis, L.S.: Learning discriminative appearance-based models using partial least squares. In: Brazilian Symposium on Computer Graphics and Image Processing, pp. 322–329. IEEE, Rio de Janiero (2009)
17. Moon, H., Phillips, P.J.: Computational and performance aspects of pca-based face-recognition algorithms. Perception-London, 303–322 (2001)
18. Forssén, P.-E.: Maximally stable colour regions for recognition and matching. In: IEEE Conference on Computer Vision and Pattern Recognition, pp. 1–8. IEEE, Minneapolis (2007)

Stereo Camera Based Real-Time Local Path-Planning for Mobile Robots

Huanqing Yang, Jianhua Zhang, and Shenyong Chen

Department of Computer Vision, Zhejiang University of Technology, China
yhqairqq@gmail.com
{zjh,sy}@ieee.org

Abstract. This paper presents a framework of local path-planning technique for stereo camera-equipped mobile robot with real-time local free road detection in unknown indoor environments. The aim of the proposed framework is to produce an optimized local path using 3D point cloud data, from which a global optimized trajectory can be generated in unknown indoor scene by finding series of sub-goal-points to start point. The framework is constructed with free road detection, variant rapidly-exploring random tree for a path planning and reactive obstacle avoidance behaviors. The information of free road and obstacles computed by 3D point cloud is prepared for path-planning and quick obstacle avoidance. We can make use of the precise relative position obtained by the sensor to efficiently solve the navigation problem, without building a global map. The result of the whole experiments shows that the framework proposed in the paper has a satisfactory performance of local navigation and path-planning.

Keywords: Mobile robot, navigation, path-planning, stereo camera.

1 Introduction

Path-planning is one of the most essential problems in robotics research, which solves the problem of how to find a safe path from the initial position to the target position without obstacle collision. For global path-planning, most of the proposed methods are based on global map-build or known environment [1, 2, 3], [11, 12, 13]. The existing methods are difficult to estimate a globally optimized path from local information directly. Most approaches build a global map by extracting information from surroundings with sensors to update the map-building or the prior global map, and then find a collision-free path between the current position and the destination [3, 4]. For local path planning, the issues are simplified as the tasks that only find a local path in partially-known environment, partially-map or by online environment perception. Mobile robot's local path planner, without being given the prior environment information, can use various sensors to detect the unknown obstacles and regulate the robot's velocity and pose to avoid the obstacles in real time correspondingly. Local path planner can provide on-the-fly obstacle avoidance in known environment effectively

S. Li et al. (Eds.): CCPR 2014, Part I, CCIS 483, pp. 345–354, 2014.

and reliably, but it is difficult to keep the path's global optimization in practical applications and relies heavily on the accuracy of local observation [5, 6].

As is known to us, mobile robot can sense surrounding by various sensors (e.g. sonar, ultrasonic, laser range finder, vision). According to different ways of information acquisition, proposed method can be divided into two categories: single modality data [2, 3] based and hybrid modality data based. Obviously each kind of sensor has its advantage. Some sensor can measure large region. But they have respective limitation. In order to overcome the problem, we make full use of advantage of each sensor and mix them so that mobile robot can sense the environment better than one.

In our research, we focus on how to predict a next-best searching path, which relies on local path generated by local path planner with online environment perception. Using portable sensors (e.g. Kinect) as a pathway of online environment perception, the capability of environment perception and the detection of obstacles are greatly improved by generating 3D point cloud of space. Thus the capability of subsequence structure of environment prediction and local path-planning in the range of vision can be enhanced. We can predict a most likely local path, which can be constructed as a searching path to build the possible pathways. In order to enhance adaptability of approach and be easier for the implementation of path planning in complex indoor environments, our strategy consists of two stages. In the first stage, we find the most likely local path. In the second stage, mobile robot moves along a waypoint path while executing collision detection that ensures the mobile robot safe. A set of experimental results of local path planning for finding the most possible pathways is given to test the effectiveness and robustness of our method in the practical scene.

The remainder of this paper is organized as follows. Section 2 briefly introduces relative work about acquisition of spatial information and information process including extraction of free road and obstacle position. Section 3 mainly presents kinematic model of nonholonomic mobile robot and selects the proper controlling speed. In section 4 proposes a solution to the idea, which contains design and implementation of variant rapidly-exploring random trees, selection of most likely sub-goal and strategy of obstacle avoidance. In Section 5, experiments conducts in complex indoor environment with a real robot as shown in Figure 6. Conclusions are given in Section 6.

2   Data Preprocessing

2.1   Acquisition of Spatial Information

Autonomous robot operation in complex real-world environments requires powerful perception capabilities. 3D structure perception has a considerable progress recently. Here, we focus on two aspects, extraction of spatial structure information including free road and obstacle from 3D data and obstacle avoidance in real time. We can acquire precise special information generated by Xtion. The 3D point cloud of the scene in real time is shown in Figure 1, which reduces computing errors in the subsequence work.

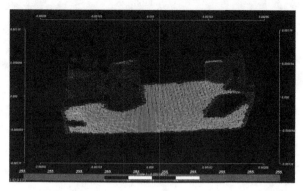

Fig. 1. Display a scene of 3D point cloud

2.2   Information Process

The relation between free road and obstacle extraction from a scene is a complementary set for each other.   Thus we only extract a set of them. Obviously, free road is more suitable and easier implementation to find a reasonable path from the start position of mobile robot to in current scene. Extraction of free road is the main task. Meanwhile there has been exiting many methods such as [7]. Spatial normal based method is used in our solution to segment free road with high precision as shown in Figure 1. Region of free road is covered with orange. Then we extract edge of free road with edge detector [8] as shown Figure 2 corresponding to the result of Figure 1.

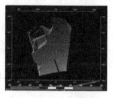

Fig. 2. An example for edge extraction of free road. The three columns contain robot perspective with a set of edge extraction from result of free road, third perspectivescene, 3D point cloud corresponding to robot perspective.

3   Control of Mobile Robot

3.1   Controller of Mobile Robot

Kinematic model of nonholonomic of mobile robot for controller of mobile robot is designed by Fierro et al. [9]. We implement necessary parts of this framework for controlling our mobile robot.

A typical example of nonholonomic mobile robot is shown in Figure 3, where is a front wheel that drives mobile robot with axisymmetrical and nonholonomic constraints. The robot's position in global coordinate is (x_r, y_r); the angle between X direction and X_r direction is θ_r; and the pose of nonholonomic mobile robot q can be described as $[x, y, \theta]^T$.

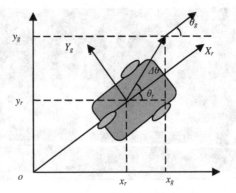

Fig. 3. The kinematics model of nonholonomic mobile robot

The kinematics model of nonholonomic mobile robot is

$$\begin{bmatrix} \dot{x}_r \\ \dot{y}_r \\ \dot{\theta}_r \end{bmatrix} = \begin{bmatrix} \cos\theta_r & 0 \\ \sin\theta_r & 0 \\ 0 & 1 \end{bmatrix} \begin{bmatrix} v \\ \omega \end{bmatrix} \tag{1}$$

where v is the linear velocity and ω is the angular velocity. Assuming there is only rolling operation but sliding operation between the wheels and ground, the nonholonomic constraint equation is

$$\dot{x}_r \sin\theta_r - \dot{y}_r \cos\theta_r = 0. \tag{2}$$

The pose of the final position is $[x_r, y_r, \theta_r]$, thus the steering angle of robot's motion is

$$\Delta\theta_g = \arctan(\frac{y_g - y_r}{x_g - x_r}) - \theta_r \tag{3}$$

3.2 Control of Speed

According to the size of the free road region where the robot moves, different control laws of linear velocity are employed in the planning, so that mobile robot can select the appropriate speed rate to adapt to various scenes. The control law is defined as

$$v = \begin{cases} v_{\max} \times \dfrac{1}{n}\sum\limits_{i=1}^{n} \dfrac{w_r}{d_{p_i}} & \dfrac{1}{n}\sum\limits_{i=1}^{n} \dfrac{w_r}{d_{p_i}} > 0.6, n = N/2 \\[4mm] v_{\max} & \dfrac{1}{n}\sum\limits_{i=1}^{n} \dfrac{w_r}{d_{p_i}} <= 0.4, n = N/2 \end{cases} \tag{4}$$

where N denotes the number of waypoints constructed by local path programming in section IV, w_r is the width of mobile robot, d_{pi} shown in Figure 4 denotes the width of a pathway.

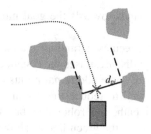

Fig. 4. An example of simulation in a scene

4   Local Path-Planning and Obstacle Avoidance

4.1   Variant Rapidly-Exploring Random Trees

Rapidly-exploring random trees (RRTs) for path planning is proposed by the LaValle et al. in [1]. With its advantages of low computational cost and state-of-the-art performance, it is extensively used for path planning [1] [10]. We propose an algorithm based on rapidly-exploring random trees, which is named as variant rapidly-exploring random trees (VRRTs). Comparing RRTs with VRRTs, VRRTs can substantially reduce the computational cost, while obtains a more appropriate local path planning.

Our VRRTs algorithm requires the following four domain-specific function primitives:

- Function AddNode(trees, node$_{new}$, node$_{father}$)
- Function InCollision_Node(node$_{new}$, boundaryNodes$_{obstacle}$): state
- Function InCollision_Edge(boundaryNodes$_{obstacle}$, node$_{new}$, node$_{nearest}$): state
- Function randomRegion(node$_{neearest}$, randRadius): node
- Function SmoothPath(rrt_path): rrt_path

First the AddNode function adds a valid new node into trees before a new state that can be reached from target state given a previous stage of path planning. InCollision_Node function checks whether the new node nodenew, which is generated at random constraints by size of random region (collision-free with obstacle), is valid. InCollision_Edge function checks if there are obstacles between the nearest node in rrt_tree and the nodenew. Function randomRegion is to randomize a new node in region of given radius and the nearest   node of the rrt-tree. This function is the key point improving the basic algorithm RRTs. Finally SmoothPath function is to smooth the final path. After obtaining a path from current position to the target, a mobile robot can move along with this path. The distance that the mobile robot moved is computed by the function Distance where the Euclidean distance is computed with meter used as unit. Table I shows the complete VRRTs planner with its local limited stochastic decision between the following two search options:

- with probability *p*, it expands towards the goal minimizing the objective function *Distance*,
- with probability 1-p, it executes a random exploration by generating a RandomState.The function findNearest uses the distance function to find the nearest point in the tree to prepare some additional points outside of tree. The function SmoothPath is implemented to reduce the distance of a path by smoothing it. Through this smoothed path, the robot can be controlled more easily. The smoothed path is covered by the green line as shown in Figure 5, where the red line is the original path. Thus our proposed VRRTs has a lower computational cost than basic RRTs. But the method has limitations that the process of local region will lose global information. Thus this method is only used in special situation. As is shown in Figure 2, we can find that the goal of path always locates the top of the image.

4.2   Most Likely Sub-goal

In this part, we introduce how to select sub-goal. For path planning of stochastic decision, the sub-goal is also a stochastic result so that we cannot manually decide a sub-goal. Then we design a strategy of local path planning to determine the position of sub-goal which should be the most acceptable one. The strategy can be formulated as:

$$S = \{p_i, i <= N\}, \tag{5}$$

$$d_{max} = \max\{\|p_{oi}\|, i <= N\}, \tag{6}$$

where S is a set of free road extracted in section II, N is the capacity of S, p_i is a vector $[x_i, y_i, z_i]^T$, d_{max} denotes the max distance between all points of the set and the original point. According to the distance from the original point to the boundary of S, the position of the sub-goal is determined by the criterion as follows,

$$g = \begin{cases} d_{max} & \dfrac{d_{max}}{measure_{max}} >= 0.7 \\[2ex] 0 & \dfrac{d_{max}}{measure_{max}} < 0.7 \end{cases} \tag{7}$$

where $measure_{max}$ is the largest value of measures with sensor.

Table 1. The VRRT planner stochastically region constraints based expands its search tree to the goal or to a random state

```
Function VRRTPlan(env:environment,initial:state,goal:state):path-planning
        var    nearest;
    var tree:rrt-tree;
            randRadius= env :width
            nearest : = initial;
            rrt-tree : = initial;
            furthest : = initial;
            while(iter < env:maxiters)
                    node_new=randomRegion(furthest,randRadius);
                    col=InCollision_Node(node_new,env. boundaryNodes_obstacle);
                    if col=false;
                        continue;
                    nearest=findNearest(rrt-tree, node_new);
                    col=Incollision_Edge(env. boundaryNodes_obstacle, node_new,nearest);
                    if col=false
                        continue;
                AddNode(rrt-tree, nodenew,nearest);
                if Distance(nodenew,goal)<env.threshold
                        path=findPath(rrt-tree, nodenew);
                path=smoothPath(path);
            return path;

Function findNearest(rrt-tree, node_new):state
            var nearest:state;
            nearest : = EmptySate;
            foreach states in rrt-tree
                    if Distance(s,node_new)<Distance(nearest,node_new)
                        nearest : s;
        return nearest;
```

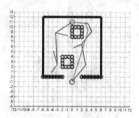

Fig. 5. An example of simulation for path planning

4.3   Obstacle Avoidance

Obstacle avoidance is as a kind of error complementation for moving robot. In real experiments, robot comes to some unexpected errors, for example robot may not move along the path line accurately, even though we have obtained a local path with high accuracy. To assure that the security of robot and collision-free, we define a strategy as shown in Figure 2. We estimate a safe region covered with red, when mobile robot finds a local path and moves along the path line. The system enter obstacle avoidance mode. Mobile robot modifies the current position and pose, if there are obstacles in the safe region detected. More details are in Section V.

5   Experiment Result

In our experiment, we use AS-R mobile robot along Asus Xtion pro live (shown in Figure 6), which is mid-sized and powerful robot platform. In our experiment, we only use Xtion to acquire enough information from indoor environment. The data is processed on a workstation, which are connected to the mobile robot by a local network.

Fig. 6. Xtion, workstation, AS-R mobile robot

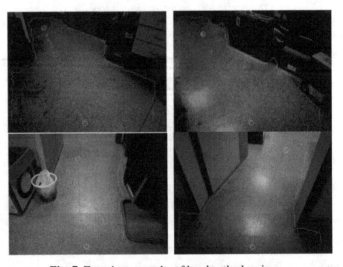

Fig. 7. Experiment results of local path planning

Fig. 8. Experiment results of obstacle detection

Local path planning experiments without any prior environmental information are conducted firstly to test validity and practicability of our local path planner. We can observe the image from sensor to evaluate the performance of our framework. Especially, we test the performance of local path planning. A set of pictures shown in Figure 7 are extracted from the experiment results of local path planning displayed in online supervisor console interface simultaneously.

Mobile robot can accomplish local path planning and obstacle avoidance effectively, as shown in Figure 7 and Figure 8, respectively, by using the method proposed in this paper until mobile robot cannot find a local path. According to the experimental results, the angle information is easy to lose. That's why we add a stage of collision detection to correct the trajectory of mobile robot and assure the operation is safe. We can see the experiment results in Figure 8 that first picture on the left side shows that mobile robot detect obstacle occupying the safe region on the right front of the mobile robot. Mobile robot turns steering to left in order to correct current moving direction.

6   Conclusion

In this paper we proposed a framework that is concentrated on how to autonomously work out mobile robot path planning in unknown indoor environments of practical application. We have improved Kinematic model of nonholonomic of mobile robot, as well as the speed control. More importantly, the proposed VRRT can improve the performance of local path planning. By integrating these improvements, our proposed framework is self-adaptive and practical, as proved by experimental results.

Acknowledgment. This work is supported by the national Nature Science Foundation of China, No 61305021, the distinguished Young Scholars of   NSFC, No. R1110679.

References

1. LaValle, S.M.: Rapidly-Exploring Random Trees A new Tool for Path Planning (1998)
2. Wang, L.C., Lim, S.Y., Ang, V.: Hybrid of global path planning and local navigation implemented on a mobile robot in indoor environment. In: Proceedings of the 2002 IEEE International Symposium on Intelligent Control, pp. 821–826. IEEE (2002)
3. Fujimori, A., Murakoshi, T., Ogawa, Y.: Navigation and path-planning of mobile robots with real-time map-building. In: 2002 IEEE International Conference on Industrial Technology, IEEE ICIT 2002, vol. 1, pp. 7–12. IEEE (2002)

4. Podsedkowski, L., Nowakowski, J., Idzikowski, M., Vizvary, I.: A new solution for path planning in partially known or unknown environment for nonholonomic mobile robots. Robotics and Autonomous Systems 34(2), 145–152 (2001)
5. Minguez, J., Montano, L.: Nearness diagram (ND) navigation: Collision avoidance in troublesome scenarios. IEEE Transactions on Robotics and Automation 20(1), 45–59 (2004)
6. Borenstein, J., Koren, Y.: The vector field histogram-fast obstacle avoidance for mobile robots. IEEE Transactions on Robotics and Automation 7(3), 278–288 (1991)
7. Holz, D., Holzer, S., Rusu, R.B., Behnke, S.: Real-time plane segmentation using RGB-D cameras. In: Röfer, T., Mayer, N.M., Savage, J., Saranlı, U. (eds.) RoboCup 2011. LNCS, vol. 7416, pp. 306–317. Springer, Heidelberg (2012)
8. Canny, J.: A computational approach to edge detection. IEEE Transactions on Pattern Analysis and Machine Intelligence (6), 679–698 (1986)
9. Fierro, R., Lewis, F.L.: Control of a nonholonomic mobile robot: backstepping kinematics into dynamics. In: Proceedings of the 34th IEEE Conference on Decision and Control, vol. 4, pp. 3805–3810. IEEE (1995)
10. Kuffner, J.J., LaValle, S.M.: RRT-connect: An efficient approach to single-query path planning. In: Proceedings of the IEEE International Conference on Robotics and Automation, ICRA 2000, vol. 2, pp. 995–1001. IEEE (2000)
11. Kavraki, L.E., Svestka, P., Latombe, J.-C., Overmars, M.H.: Probabilistic roadmaps for path planning in high-dimensional configuration spaces. IEEE Transactions on Robotics and Automation 12(4), 566–580 (1996)
12. Kavraki, E., Kolountzakis, M.N., Latombe, J.-C.: Analysis of probabilistic roadmaps for path planning. IEEE Transactions on Robotics and Automation 14(1), 166–171 (1998)
13. Ge, S.S., Cui, Y.J.: New potential functions for mobile robot path planning. IEEE Transactions on Robotics and Automation 16(5), 615–620 (2000)

A Tracking Method with Structural Local Mean and Local Standard Deviation Appearance Model

Dawei Yang[1,2], Yang Cong[1], Yandong Tang[1,*], and Yulian Li[3]

[1] State Key Laboratory of Robotic, Shenyang Institute of Automation,
Chinese Academy of Sciences, Shenyang, China
{dwyang,congyang,ytang}@sia.cn, yulian-lee@163.com
[2] University of Chinese Academy of Science, Beijing, China
[3] Shenyang Metrology Testing Institution, Shenyang, China

Abstract. Aiming at the problem of illumination variation and partial occlusion in the object tracking, a structural local mean and local standard deviation appearance model is proposed. The object image is divided into some blocks. In each block, the local mean and local standard deviation are calculated, then, a feature vector is composed. In order to weaken the effect of the partial occlusion, an adaptive weighted value is set to each feature component. The Native Bayesian theory is applied to track the object in affine transform space. The experimental results demonstrate that the proposed tracking method performs favorably against several state-of-the-art methods.

Keywords: object tracking, local mean, local standard deviation, structural appearance model, the Native Bayesian.

1   Introduction

Object tracking has been widely studied in computer vision because it is very important in many applications, especially for automated surveillance, traffic monitoring and human computer interface, etc [1]. Numerous tracking algorithms have been proposed during the past decades. However, it is still a very challenging problem to design a robust tracking method due to some factors, such as illumination changes, partial occlusions, pose changes, background clutter and scale variable [1,2].

The current tracking algorithms can be categorized into generative [2,3,4] or discriminative [6,7,8,9,10,11,12] approaches. Generative tracking methods typically learn a model to represent the target object and then use it to search for the image region that is most similar to the target model. Black et al. [4] learned a subspace appearance model offline, which is difficult to adapt the appearance variations. Then some online models have been proposed such as the IVT method [3]. These generative models do not take into account background information [11].

---

[*] Corresponding author.

S. Li et al. (Eds.): CCPR 2014, Part I, CCIS 483, pp. 355–362, 2014.
© Springer-Verlag Berlin Heidelberg 2014

The discriminative methods formulate tracking as a classification problem which aims to distinguish the target from the background. Avidan [12] extends the optical flow approach with a support vector machine classifier for object tracking. Collins et al. [13] demonstrates that the most discriminative features can be learned online to separate the target object from the background. Grabner et al. [7,8] proposed an boosting algorithm to track oject. Babenko et al. [9] introduce multiple instance learning into online tracking where samples are considered within positive and negative bags or sets. In 2010, a semi-supervised learning approach [10] is developed in which positive and negative samples are selected via an online classifier with structural constraints.

Recently, several tracking methods based on sparse representation have been proposed [5],[14,15]. Mei et al. [5],[15] adopt the holistic representation of an object as the appearance model and then track the object by solving the ℓ1 minimization problem. Liu et al. [14] proposed a tracking algorithm based on local sparse model which employs histograms of sparse coefficients and the mean-shift algorithm for object tracking.

In this paper, we propose an adaptive weighted structural appearance model based on local mean (LM) and local standard deviation (LSD). The proposed appearance model divides the target image into some blocks with spatial structure, LM and LSD of each block are calculated. The appearance feature is formed with these LMs and LSDs with adaptive weighted values. To cope with partial occlusion, for each feature component, an adaptive weighted value is set. The Native Bayesian theory is applied to track the object in the affine transform space.

2   Structural LM and LSD Appearance Model

Given the current frame image I and the candidate target image $T \in I$. We sample $m \times n$ local image blocks inside T with a spatial layout B

$$
B = \begin{bmatrix} B_{11} & \cdots & B_{1n} \\ \vdots & \ddots & \vdots \\ B_{m1} & \cdots & B_{mn} \end{bmatrix}
\tag{1}
$$

Where, B_{ij} represents one fixed part in the target region defined as a $s \times t$ window.

Let f_{xy} denote the gray value of the pixel locating in (x, y), and (i, j) denote the center of a local region with size $s \times t$. The LM and LSD are calculated as:

$$
m_{ij} = \frac{1}{s \times t} \sum_{x=i-\frac{s}{2}}^{i+\frac{s}{2}} \sum_{y=j-\frac{t}{2}}^{j+\frac{t}{2}} f_{xy} \qquad d_{ij} = sqrt(\frac{1}{s \times t} \sum_{x=i-\frac{s}{2}}^{i+\frac{s}{2}} \sum_{y=j-\frac{t}{2}}^{j+\frac{t}{2}} (f_{xy} - m_{ij})^2)
\tag{2}
$$

The LM and LSD are calculated for each block, then composing them into a vector, $LMD = [m_1, m_2, ..., m_N, d_1, d_2, ..., d_N]^T$.

The features of intensity and texture often have different importance in different video sequences. Adaptive weighted values are set for LM and LSD according to the features of positive samples and negative samples.

$$w_m = \frac{|\bar{m}_p - \bar{m}_n|}{|\bar{d}_p - \bar{d}_n| + |\bar{m}_p - \bar{m}_n|} \qquad w_d = \frac{|\bar{d}_p - \bar{d}_n|}{|\bar{d}_p - \bar{d}_n| + |\bar{m}_p - \bar{m}_n|} \qquad (3)$$

Where, w_m and w_d represents the weight value of LM and LSD of the feature vector respectively. $\bar{d}_n = \frac{1}{N_n}\sum_{i=1}^{N_n} d_i^n$ and $\bar{d}_p = \frac{1}{N_p}\sum_{i=1}^{N_p} d_i^p$ are the mean values of LSD of negative and positive samples, $\bar{m}_n = \frac{1}{N_n}\sum_{i=1}^{N_n} m_i^n$ and $\bar{m}_p = \frac{1}{N_p}\sum_{i=1}^{N_p} m_i^p$ are the mean values of the responding LM. N_p and N_n are the number of positive samples and negative samples respectively. The feature vector can be represented as:

$$wLMD = [w_m M, w_d D]^T \qquad (4)$$

Where $M = [m_1, m_2, ... m_N]$ and $D = [d_1, d_2, ..., d_N]$.

When there is partial occlusion in the tracking, each block in different position will not play a same role. A weighted value is set to each block to represent their different roles in tracking. Let $v = [v_1, v_2, ..., v_N]^T$, v_i represents the feature of the i-th block of a target image, N is the number of the blocks. An adaptive weighted value w_i is set to v_i

$$w_i = \frac{\bar{w}_i}{\sum_{i=1}^{N} \bar{w}_i} \qquad i = 1, ..., N, \bar{w}_i = \exp(-\frac{|v_i^t - v_i^{t-1}|}{\sum_{i=1}^{N} |v_i^t - v_i^{t-1}|}) \qquad (5)$$

Where, v_i^t and v_i^{t-1} denote the i-th feature component of the adjacent frames. Then, the proposed appearance model can be formulated as:

$$WLMD = \{w_m w_i m_i, w_d w_i d_i\}_{i=1}^{N} \qquad (6)$$

3   Proposed Tracking Method

Let $p_t(x) = [p_1, ..., p_6] \in R^6$ denote the affine transform parameter of sample x at the t-th frame. Then, n scalable affine transform parameters of positive samples x^p can be predicted using random function. That is formulated as

$$p_t(x^p) = p_t(x) + randn(6, n) \qquad (7)$$

Let $l(x) = [cx, cy]$ denote the center location of sample x. The center location of negative samples x^n can be gotten using the following formulation:

$$X = \{l(x^n) \mid max(w, h) < \| l(x^n) - l(x) \| < sum(w + h)\} \qquad (8)$$

Where, X denotes the set of the center coordinates of the negative samples image.

The proposed tracking method is carried out within the Native Bayesian [6] inference framework. The main steps of the proposed tracking method are summarized as following:

Input: t-th video frame
1. Computing affine transform parameters of candidate object images using formula (7), then, clipping the candidate object images.
2. Getting the feature vector of each candidate object image using formula (6).
3. Using the Native Bayesian classifier to find the tracking location.
4. Updating the weighted value of each feature component as formula (5).
5. Sampling the negative sample images using formula (8) and computing their feature vectors.
6. Updating the weighted value with formula (3).
7. Updating the parameters of the classifier.

Output: The affine transform parameter of the tracking result and the parameters of the classifier.

4   Experiments and Discussion

The proposed tracking method is implemented in MATLAB 2010b on an Intel (R) 2.99 GHz Dual Core PC with 2GB memory. The tracked object image is resized to 32×32 pixels and is divided into 8×8 local blocks. The initial values of weighted value are set to be equal respectively. We tested our tracking method on several typical video sequences and compared it with CT tracker [6], MIL tracker [9], L1 tracker [15] and ASLSAM tracker [16].

4.1   Quantitative Comparison

We evaluate the above mentioned algorithms using the center location error as well as tracking time. Table 1 shows the tracking time, the best and second best results are in red and blue fonts. Figure 1 shows the center location errors of the evaluated algorithms on some test sequences.

Table 1. Average tracking time (in second)

	ASLSAM	L1	CT	MIL	Ours
car4	0.11	1.20	0.19	0.32	0.05
car11	0.14	1.38	0.09	0.28	0.05
Davidin300	0.16	0.44	0.08	0.29	0.05
Singer1	0.19	1.49	0.16	0.30	0.05
Woman_sequence	0.11	1.27	0.10	0.27	0.05
Threepastshop2cor	0.16	1.35	0.12	0.29	0.05
Faceocc2	0.09	1.48	0.08	0.28	0.05
dudek	0.11	1.21	0.19	0.31	0.05
girl	0.20	1.33	0.08	0.28	0.05
Board	0.19	1.41	0.19	0.31	0.08

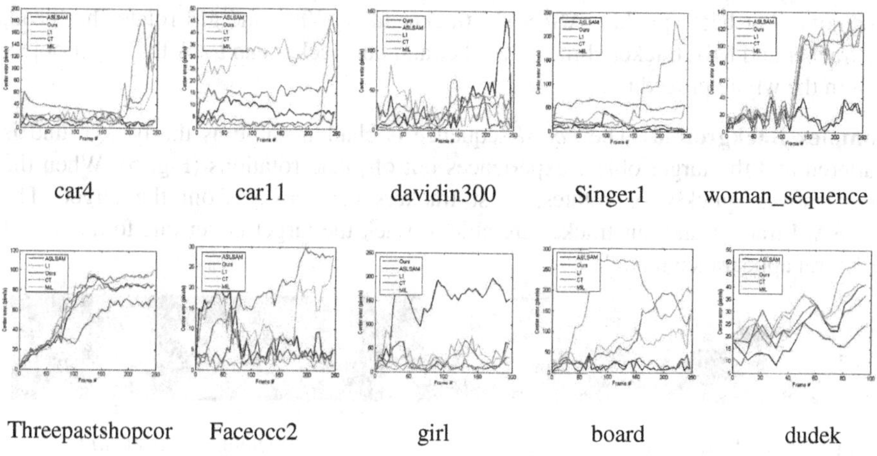

car4   car11   davidin300   Singer1   woman_sequence

Threepastshopcor   Faceocc2   girl   board   dudek

Fig. 1. Quantitative evaluation in term of center location error(pixels)

4.2   Qualitative Comparison

Illumination Variation: Tracking result is heavily affected by illumination variation, especially for the trackers using the intensity as the features. Some representative tracking results on sequences with illumination variations are shown in figure 2. In the *car4* sequence (Fig. 2(a)), there is significant illumination change when the car passes beneath the overpass. In the *car11* sequence (Fig. 2(b)), the contrast between the target object and the background is low and the ambient light changes significantly. In the *singer1* sequence (Fig. 2(c)), the stage light changes drastically. In the *davidin300* sequence (Fig. 2(d)), the target object undergoes large pose and illumination change. ASLSAM tracker can track the target due to its structural appearance model and tracking method based on sparse representation. The appearance model of our tracker is consisted of intensity and texture with different weighted value, which can weaken the effect of illumination variation, so it can track the target accurately and robustly. The other trackers, such as CT tracker, MIL tracker and L1 tracker are affected heavily by illumination variation.

Partial Occlusion: Partial occlusion is one of the most general yet crucial problems in object tracking. In the *woman* sequence (Fig. 3(a)), the target object undergoes pose variation together with long-time partial occlusion. In the *threepastshop2cor* sequence (Fig. 3(b)), the target is occluded by two people at times and one of them is similar in color and shape to the target. In the *faceocc2* (Fig. 3(c)) and *dudek* (Fig. 3(d)) sequences, the target object undergoes partial occlusion. Our tracker and ASLSAM tracker can track the target accurately due to the structural appearance model, while there are some shifts in other trackers.

Rotation: In the *girl* sequence, the target object undergoes out-of-plane rotations, pose change and scale variation. Some tracking results are shown in Fig. 4. When the girl moves her head quickly, ASLSAM tracker fails. When the girl rotates her head, CT tracker and MIL tracker shift. L1 tracker and our tracker can track the target object well in the whole procedure.

Complex Background: The *board* sequence is challengeable as the background is cluttered and the target object experiences out-of-plane rotations (Fig. 5). When the target moves quickly or rotates, most trackers drift away from the target. The ASLSAM tracker and our tracker are able to track the target better due to the use of structural appearance models.

(a)Tracking results of *car4*   (b)Tracking results of *car11*

(c)Tracking results of *singer1*   (d)Tracking results of *davidin300*

—— Ours —— ASLSAM —— L1   CT —— MIL

Fig. 2. Tracking results on sequences with illumination variation

(a)Tracking results of *woman_sequence*   (b)Tracking results of *threepastshop2cor*

(c)Tracking results of *faceocc2*   (d)Tracking results of *dudek*

Fig. 3. Tracking results on sequences with partial occlusion

Fig. 4. Tracking results on sequence *girl*   **Fig. 5.** Tracking results on sequence *board*

5   Conclusions

In this paper, we proposed a structural local mean and local standard deviation appearance model with adaptive weighted value and a simple but robust tracking method to illumination variant and partial occlusion.

Experimental results compared with several state-of-the-art methods on some sequences demonstrate the effectiveness and robustness of our proposed method.

Acknowledgments. This work was supported by the National Science Foundation of China under Grant No. 61105013 and 61333019.

References

1. Alper, Y., Omar, J., Mubarak, S.: Object tracking: A survey. ACM Computing Surveys 38, 4 (2006)
2. Amit, A., Ehud, R., Ilan, S.: Robust fragments-based tracking using the integral histogram. In: Proceedings of IEEE Conference on Computer Vision and Pattern Recognition (CVPR 2006), New York, USA, June 17-22, pp. 793–805 (2006)
3. David, A.R., Jongwoo, L., Ruei, S.L., Ming, H.Y.: Incremental Learning for Robust Visual Tracking. International Journal of Computer Vision 77, 125–141 (2008)

4. Black, M., Jepson, A.: Eigentracking: Robust matching and tracking of articulated objects using a view-based representation. International Journal of Computer Vision 26(1), 63–84 (1998)
5. Mei, X., Ling, H.: Robust visual tracking using l1 minimization. In: Proceedings of International Conference on Computer Vision, Kyoto, Japan, pp. 1436–1443 (2009)
6. Zhang, K., Zhang, L., Yang, M.-H.: Real-time compressive tracking. In: Fitzgibbon, A., Lazebnik, S., Perona, P., Sato, Y., Schmid, C. (eds.) ECCV 2012, Part III. LNCS, vol. 7574, pp. 864–877. Springer, Heidelberg (2012)
7. Grabner, H., Grabner, M., Bischof, H.: Real-time tracking via online boosting. In: British Machine Vision Conference, Edinburgh, pp. 47–56 (2006)
8. Grabner, H., Leistner, C., Bischof, H.: Semi-supervised on-line boosting for robust tracking. In: Forsyth, D., Torr, P., Zisserman, A. (eds.) ECCV 2008, Part I. LNCS, vol. 5302, pp. 234–247. Springer, Heidelberg (2008)
9. Babenko, B., Yang, M., Belongie, S.: Robust object tracking with online multiple instance learning. IEEE Transactions on Pattern Analysis and Machine Intelligence 33(8), 1619–1632 (2011)
10. Kalal, Z., Matas, J., Mikolajczyk, K.: P-N learning: Bootstrapping binary classifiers by structural constraints. In: IEEE Conference on Computer Vision and Pattern Recognition, San Francisco, CA, USA, pp. 49–56 (2010)
11. Wang, Q., Chen, F., Xu, W., Yang, M.: An experimental comparison of online object tracking algorithms. In: Proceedings of SPIE Optical Engineering Applications, San Diego, California, USA (2011)
12. Avidan, S.: Support vector tracking. IEEE Transactions on Pattern Analysis and Machine Intelligence 26(8), 1061–1072 (2004)
13. Robert, T.C., Liu, Y., Leordeanu, M.: Online selection of discriminative tracking features. IEEE Transactions on Pattern Analysis and Machine Intelligence 27(10), 1631–1644 (2005)
14. Liu, B., Huang, J., Yang, L., Kulikowski, C.A.: Robust tracking using local sparse appearance model and k-selection. In: Conference on Computer Vision and Pattern Recognition, Crowne Plaza, Colorado Springs, Colombia, pp. 1313–1321 (2011)
15. Mei, X., Ling, H.: Robust Visual tracking and vehicle classification via sparse representation. IEEE Transactions on Pattern Analysis and Machine Intelligence 33(11), 2259–2272 (2011)
16. Jia, X., Lu, H., Yang, M.: Visual tracking via adaptive structural local sparse appearance model. In: Conference on Computer Vision and Pattern Recognition, Providence, Rhode Island, June 16-21, pp. 1822–1829 (2012)

Hough-RANSAC: A Fast and Robust Method for Rejecting Mismatches

Hongxia Gao[1,2], Jianhe Xie[1,2], Yueming Hu[1,2], and Ze Yang[1,2]

[1] School of Automation Science and Engineering,
South China University of Technology, Guangzhou, 510641, China
[2] Engineering Research Center for Precision Electronic Manufacturing Equipment
of Ministry of Education, Guangzhou, 510640, China
{hxgao,auymhu}@scut.edu.cn, xiejianhe_2006@163.com,
yangze007@foxmail.com

Abstract. This paper proposed a novel method - Hough-RANSAC for rejecting mismatches in image registration. Many well-known algorithms for rejecting mismatches, such as the Least Median of Square regression algorithm (LMedS) and the Random Sample Consensus algorithm (RANSAC), perform poorly when the percent of mismatches is more than 50%. Compared with the two well-known algorithms, the Hough-RANSAC algorithm can guarantee both time performance and accuracy, even if the percent of correct matches fell much below 20%.

Keywords: Rejecting mismatches, LMedS, RANSAC, Hough-RANSAC.

1   Introduction

In image registration, there are mismatches after matching the points detected in two images. To get the correct matches is very important for many algorithms which are based on image registration, for example, image stitching, object recognition, object tracking, model reconstruction, etc. [1]

SIFT (Scale Invariant Feature Transform) [2][3] and SURF (Speeded Up Robust Features) [4], are now commonly used descriptors for detecting key points in two images in registration. The correspondence of points in the two images is usually established by matching the descriptors of them with KNN (K Nearest Neighbor) method. However, a large amount of corresponding points are mismatches due to the similar region, viewpoint changes, blur and light changes.

The well-known algorithms for rejecting mismatches are LMedS (Least Median of Square regression algorithm) [5] and RANSAC (Random Sample Consensus) [6]. LMedS is invalid when the percent of mismatches is more than 50%. And RANSAC costs too much time when the percent of correct matches falls much below 50%. The Hough-RANSAC algorithm proposed by this paper for rejecting mismatches, described in section 3, is compared to the two well-known algorithms. The experiments show that the proposed Hough-RASANC algorithm can reject mismatches effectively even if the percent of mismatches is 80%.

S. Li et al. (Eds.): CCPR 2014, Part I, CCIS 483, pp. 363–370, 2014.
© Springer-Verlag Berlin Heidelberg 2014

2   SIFT or SURF Features and Initial Matching

SIFT and SURF are widely used in image registration for extracting distinctive invariant features. In addition, there are several improved algorithms of SIFT and SURF, i.e. ASIFT (Affine-SIFT) [7], FAIR-SURF (Fully Affine Invariant SURF) [8], which can be used for images registration under large angle of view changes. In the paper, only plain image registration is discussed. The features generated by them are invariant to image scale, location and rotation, and provide robust matching. To generate the set of image features, scale-space detection, keypoint localization, orientation assignment and keypoint descriptor are used. Finally, the features are described by a set of vectors. To get the matches, the feature vectors from one image have to be compared with them from another image. Then, the distances between one feature vector from one image and the nearest and second nearest feature vectors in the other are found. If the ratio of the two distances is within a certain threshold (which is the ratio between the nearest and second nearest feature vectors, so set it to 2), the feature vector and its nearest one are matched. However, the mismatches are also generated, because they are not conformed to the real projection transformation between the images.

3   Rejecting Mismatches

The homography matrix H can be estimated with the initial matches. For one match (a_i, a_i'), if the error $dv = d(a_i', Ha_i)$ is smaller than the threshold, the match is inlier. Otherwise, the match is outlier. In this section, the two well-known algorithms for rejecting mismatches are introduced, and Hough-RANSAC algorithm is proposed.

3.1   LMedS

The LMedS method estimates the parameters by solving the nonlinear minimization problem:

$$min(med_i r_i^2) \tag{1}$$

LMedS performs well if there are less than 50% mismatches [9]. One of the LMedS's advantages is that there is no requirement of setting threshold. The time that used by LMedS is hardly influenced by the percent of mismatches. The major disadvantage of LMedS is that it would be invalid with more than 50% mismatches. For the set of matches $\{X_i | X_i = \{(x_i, y_i), (x_i', y_i')\}, i = 1,2, \dots, N\}$, LMedS records the median of squared residuals computed for the entire matches set with homography matrix H estimated by random subsamples.

$$r_S^2 = median_{i=1,2,\dots N}(||(x_i', y_i') - H(x_i, y_i)||^2) \tag{2}$$

Then, LMedS gets the minimum of r_S^2, $r_{jLMedS}^2 = min(r_{Si}^2), i = 1,2, \dots, m$. The final homography matrix H is the homography corresponding r_{jLMedS}^2.

3.2   RANSAC

RANSAC is a robust iterative method for fitting parameters of a homography matrix in the presence of many mismatches. Because of its robust performance, RANSAC is used most commonly. RANSAC could reject mismatches successfully when the percent of mismatches is very high, but its time performance would be very poorly.

Firstly, RANSAC estimates the homography matrix H using the 4 matches selected randomly from the given set of matches I. Then, RANSAC computes the homography m times. The final homography H is the one which has the highest number of correct matches. Only the 4 selected matches are all correct matches, the homography is estimated correctly. To make sure that, we have to set a suitable iteration number m. To get at least choosing 4 correct matches with the probability p, the iteration number should satisfies [10]

$$N = \log(1 - p)/\log(1 - (1 - \varepsilon)^4) \tag{3}$$

where ε is the percentage of mismatches. When ε is unknown, ε and N can be estimated dynamically.

The percent of mismatches deeply influences the iteration number of RANSAC. When the percent of mismatches is above 50%, the time performance of RANSAC would drop down quickly.

3.3   Hough-RANSAC

When the percent of mismatches is high, neither of LMedS or RANSAC works well. So, we propose a novel algorithm, Hough-RANSAC. Hough-RANSAC has its initial rejecting mismatches with Hough algorithm. This can make the algorithm work quickly. After the initial rejecting, the matches are dealt with RANSAC algorithm, and this can guarantee the accuracy.

Hough transform is widely used in image analysis and computer vision. The essence of Hough transform is a voting procedure [11][12]. This voting procedure is carried out in a parameter space. After voting, the parameter subspace getting the highest number of votes is found. The main attributes of the matches are used as the Hough parameter in Hough-RANSAC algorithm. We need to access each matches only once, and vote on the parameter space. Then matches in the subspace getting the highest number of votes are the result of initial rejecting. The steps of Hough-RANSAC are as follows:

1. Generating parameter space: The keypoint a_i in image one is matched to the keypoint a_i' in image two. The localization, scale and orientation of keypoint a_i are (x_i, y_i), s_i, θ_i. And (x_i', y_i'), s_i', θ_i' are for keypoint a_i'. The translation between two keypoints is $(dx, dy) = (x_i' - x_i, y_i' - y_i)$. The scale change between two keypoints is $ds = s_i'/s_i$. The rotation between two features is $d\theta = \theta_i' - \theta_i$. So, $(dx, dy, ds, d\theta)$ is set as Hough parameter space.
2. Setting bin sizes: If the bin sizes are too broad, the error would be large. However, if the bin sizes are too small, the algorithm would be sensitive to noise and cost

much time and memory. Therefore, the bin sizes are set as 30 degrees for orientation, 2 for scale, and a quarter of the training image's width and height for translation.

3. Voting on the Hough parameter space: $(dx, dy, ds, d\theta)$ is computed for each match and the matching keypoint pair votes on the Hough space. To avoid boundary effects, the matching keypoint pair votes on the 2 closest bins in each dimension. So, each matching keypoint pair votes on 16 subspaces. The Hough parameter space can be realized with suitable hash function and one-dimensional hash table.

4. Choosing the subspace: The subspace getting the highest number of votes is found. The matches in this subspace would be used in step 5. By now the initial rejecting has been finished.

5. Using RANSAC to get the homography H with the matches gotten by step 4. Due to Hough transform may ignore some correct matches, all matches including rejected matches by Hough transform should be judged by RANSAC after the homography H is obtained.

Hough-RANSAC algorithm can guarantee both time performance and accuracy.

3.4   The Proposed Hough-RANSAC and Related Works

The RANSAC algorithm was put forward by Fischler et al. in 1981. After years of developments, there are many improved algorithms, including LO-RANSAC (Locally Optimized RANSAC) [13], LO+-RANSAC (Locally Optimized plus RANSAC) [14], PROSAC (Progressive Sample Consensus) [15], etc. Unlike Hough-RANSAC, in order to accelerate the algorithm and improve the accuracy, LO-RANSAC uses an optimization for solving homography H of random sampling matches, especially when the actual running time of the RANSAC algorithm for low proportion inliers is much larger than theoretical calculation. But when the percentage of correct matches is high, LO-RANSAC's efficiency is poor. So LO+-RANSAC was proposed to improve the running speed of LO-RANSAC with the high percentage of correct matches. The proposed Hough-RANSAC uses Hough transform to initially reject mismatches, then uses RANSAC algorithm to obtain homography H and rejects outliers again. Thus Hough-RANSAC doesn't affect the use of other improved RANSAC algorithms. And Hough-RANSAC can combine other improved algorithms, such as PROSAC, to improve the efficiency and quality of image registration further.

4   Experiments and Discussions

In this section, we compare the performance of LMedS, RANSAC and Hough-RANSAC on image registration. In our experiments, the keypoint matches are computed by SIFT descriptors with KNN method (where k is set to be 2). The time and accuracy performance (the ratio of recognizing inliers) are analyzed under the percent of mismatches changing, with the total number of matches being 500, 1000, 1500, 2000. To obtain the accurate number of matches, images with a large amount of matches are selected, in which inliers and outliers were selected after judged by a known or computed homography H of other algorithm.

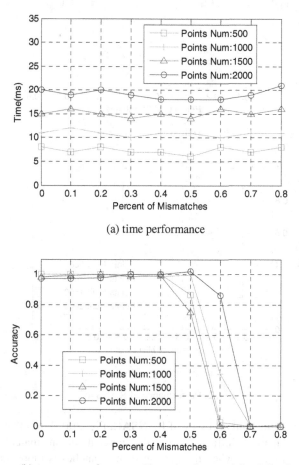

(a) time performance

(b) accuracy performance (the ratio of recognizing inliers)

Fig. 1. Performance of LMedS

The time and accuracy of LMedS are shown as Fig. 1. Fig. 1(a) shows that the time used to finish the rejecting is almost independent with the percent of mismatches. The time performance is mainly influenced by the number of total matches. Fig. 1(b) shows that LMedS can work well if the percent of mismatches is less than 50%. But LMedS breaks down when there are more than 50% mismatches.

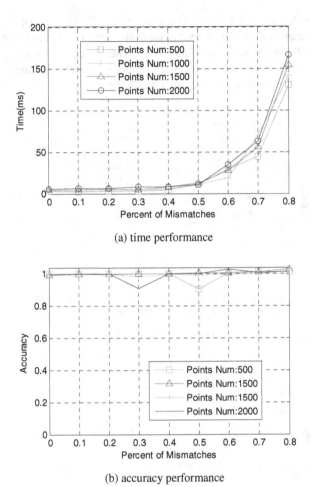

(a) time performance

(b) accuracy performance

Fig. 2. Performance of RANSAC

Fig. 2 shows the time and accuracy of RANSAC. Fig. 2(a) shows that the time cost by RANSAC is mainly influenced by the percent of mismatches. The time performance drops quickly when the percent of mismatches is more than 50%. Fig. 2(b) shows that RANSAC has excellent robust performance. The accuracy is near 100% even initial 80% mismatches.

The time and accuracy of Hough-RANSAC are shown as Fig. 3. Fig. 3(a) shows that the time cost by Hough-RANSAC is mainly influenced by the number of matches when there are less than 60% mismatches. The time increases a little as the percent of mismatches rising. Comparing to 166ms by RANSAC, the time cost by Hough-RANSAC is only 37ms when the percent of mismatches is 80% under the number of matches being 2000. At the same time, Hough-RANSAC has almost the same accuracy performance with RANSAC as Fig. 3(b) shown. So it is perfectly robust.

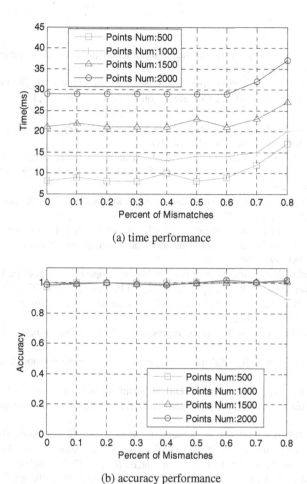

(a) time performance

(b) accuracy performance

Fig. 3. Performance of Hough-RANSAC

5   Conclusions

In this paper, we propose a novel Hough-RANSAC algorithm for rejecting mismatches. Hough-RANSAC algorithm has its initial rejecting with Hough algorithm, and finishes the mismatch rejecting with RANSAC. The experiment results indicate that Hough-RANSAC's performance is much better than LMedS, and comparing to RANSAC, Hough-RANSAC has almost the same robust performance and a faster speed.

Acknowledgements. This work is supported by Natural Science Foundation of China (No. 61403146) and National High-tech R&D Program (863 Program) (No. 2012AA041312).

References

1. Brown, L.G.: A survey of image registration techniques. ACM Computing Surveys (CSUR) 24(4), 325–376 (1992)
2. Lowe, D.G.: Object recognition from local scale-invariant features. In: The Proceedings of the Seventh IEEE International Conference on Computer Vision, vol. 2, pp. 1150–1157. IEEE (1999)
3. Lowe, D.G.: Distinctive image features from scale-invariant keypoints. International Journal of Computer Vision 60(2), 91–110 (2004)
4. Bay, H., Tuytelaars, T., Van Gool, L.: SURF: Speeded up robust features. In: Leonardis, A., Bischof, H., Pinz, A. (eds.) ECCV 2006, Part I. LNCS, vol. 3951, pp. 404–417. Springer, Heidelberg (2006)
5. Rousseeuw, P.J.: Least median of squares regression. Journal of the American Statistical Association 79(388), 871–880 (1984)
6. Fischler, M.A., Bolles, R.C.: Random sample consensus: A paradigm for model fitting with applications to image analysis and automated cartography. Communications of the ACM 24(6), 381–395 (1981)
7. Yu, G., Morel, J.-M.: A fully affine invariant image comparison method. In: IEEE International Conference on Acoustics, Speech and Signal Processing, pp. 1597–1600 (2009)
8. Pang, Y., Li, W., Yuan, Y., Pan, J.: Fully affine invariant SURF for image matching. Neurocomputing 85, 6–10 (2012)
9. Rousseeuw, P.J., Leroy, A.M.: Robust regression and outlier detection, vol. 589. John Wiley & Sons (2005)
10. Hartley, R., Zisserman, A.: Multiple view geometry in computer vision. Cambridge university press (2003)
11. Grimson, W.E.L., Huttenlocher, D.P.: On the sensitivity of the Hough transform for object recognition. IEEE Transactions on Pattern Analysis and Machine Intelligence 12(3), 255–274 (1990)
12. Achtert, E., Böhm, C., David, J., Kröger, P., Zimek, A.: Global correlation clustering based on the Hough transform. Statistical Analysis and Data Mining 1(3), 111–127 (2008)
13. Chum, O., Matas, J., Kittler, J.: Locally optimized RANSAC. In: Michaelis, B., Krell, G. (eds.) DAGM 2003. LNCS, vol. 2781, pp. 236–243. Springer, Heidelberg (2003)
14. Lebeda, K., Matas, J., Chum, O.: Fixing the Locally Optimized RANSAC. Research Report CTU-CMP-2012-17, Center for Machine Perception, Czech Technical University, Prague, Czech Republic (2012)
15. Chum, O., Matas, J.: Matching with PROSAC – progressive sample consensus. In: Proc. of the Conf. on CVPR, pp. 220–226 (2005)

Partial Static Objects Based Scan Registration on the Campus

Chongyang Wei[1], Shuangyin Shang[2], Tao Wu[1], and Hao Fu[1]

[1] College of Mechatronic Engineering and Automation,
National University of Defense Technology, Hunan, P.R. China
{cyzq3566,fuhao927}@gmail.com, wt.cs@163.com
[2] CSR Zhuzhou Electric CO.,LTD.
ssyin@ustc.edu.cn

Abstract. Scan registration has a critical role in mapping and localization for Autonomous Ground Vehicle (AGV). This paper addresses the problem of alignment with only exploiting the common static objects instead of the whole point clouds or entire patches on campus environments. Particularly, we wish to use instances of classes including trees, street lamps and poles amongst the whole scene. The distinct advantage lies in it can cut the number of pairwise points down to a quite low level. A binary trained Support Vector Machine (SVM) is used to classify the segmented patches as foreground or background according to the extracted features at object level. The Iterative Closest Point (ICP) approach is adopted only in the foreground objects given an initial guesses with GPS. Experiments show our method is real-time and robust even when the the signal of GPS suddenly shifts or invalid in the sheltered environment.

Keywords: scan registration, object level, binary classification, autonomous ground vehicle.

1 Introduction

Scan Registration of 3D point clouds is an essential part of several data processing techniques in autonomous driving, e.g, object recognition, scene understanding and common Simultaneous Localization And Mapping (SLAM). The algorithms of alignment rely on the overlapping geometry to optimize the relative rigid transformation between the two scans. Our community's aspiration is to obtain the fast and precise transformation parameters for AGV.

Besides the basic precise demand, 3D scan registration for AGV has another distinct real-time characteristic. They are two main differences in the implementation of scan matching between self-driving vehicle and other robotic platforms. Despite the AGV has these two rigorous demands, it also provides a convenience with GPS-aided Inertial Navigation System (INS) being loaded onto it. The integrated unit usually can provide a good initial value which can be regarded as a crude fitting. However, there exists a shortcoming that the signal of GPS could

S. Li et al. (Eds.): CCPR 2014, Part I, CCIS 483, pp. 371–380, 2014.

suddenly shift or invalid when sheltered from big trees or high buildings. This paper investigates the issue of how to fast and robustly register scans with the initial guesses given by the integrated unit.

Our AGV is equipped with a Velodyne HD-LIDAR with 64 beams scanner, which can be seen in Fig. 1. The HD-LIDAR unit spins at 10 HZ and provides over 1.3 million 3D points per second. The scan registration with so vast quantity of data will inevitablely bring high computing burden. Our idea is that there is no need to exploit the entire point clouds of the scene to match and the alignment at object level will have stronger distinguishing power than at point-to-point level. So, we only exploit the points from those persistent and static objects instead of the whole point clouds or entire patches to estimate the matching on campus environments. In particular, we wish to use prior instances of classes consisting of trees, street lamps and poles and thus favor for a relatively narrow recognition problem. Except for the distinct advantage of reducing the calculation complexity greatly owing to cutting the pairwise points number down to a low level, another benefit lies in it can remove disturbance of dynamic objects due to considering only static segments in the scene. To simplify the problem, a binary SVM classifier is used to classify the segmented patches according to the extracted features for every object. Compared to common algorithms of multiple classes recognition, the binary classification can accomplish a high accuracy. Experiments show our method is fast and robust even when the signal of GPS suddenly shifts or invalid in the sheltered environment.

Fig. 1. Our autonomous vehicle, equipped (on top) with a Velodyne HD-LIDAR 64-beam scanner

The rest of the paper is organized as follows. In the next section, a survey of related works are summarized. After that, the shape features at object level are described in Section 3. The binary patch classification algorithm is presented in Section 4. Experimental results are reported in Section 5. We conclude this paper in Section 6.

2   Related Works

In the context of 3D rigid registration, scan alignment algorithms could be classified into the ones of points based, object level based and global according to the basic processing cell of alignment. If the extracted feature only exploits the fashion of point-to-point, the registration between two input scans could be regarded as points based, so do others. The most famous points based method is ICP [9], [10] which attempts to optimize transformation parameters at the point level such that the Euclidean distance between nearest neighbor points is minimized. The distinct drawback of ICP is the costly nearest neighbor search which is generally computationally expensive, especially for the Velodyne 64-beam sensor with abundant of points. Considering the shortcoming of ICP, three-Dimensional Normal Distributions Transform (3D-NDT) was proposed [11] and later expanded [12] from point-to-distribution to distribution-to-distribution. The benefit of this method lies in it does not require to estimate the nearest neighbor associations because it models the scan as a set of Gaussian distributions instead of as individual points. The points based algorithms can be adopted as the refinement with given good initial parameters estimation, while the main bottleneck lies in the real-time application when existing vast points.

Data alignment at the object level derives from the idea that the segmented objects (*patches*) represent the semantic meanings which have more strong expressive power. Recently presented segmentation methods [13],[14] make the objects based registration possible and meanwhile the separations compose the input of alignment. The common flowchart of object level matching includes: scan segmentation, feature description extraction of each patch, matching between pair patches, refinement of point level. For every segmented object only one feature vector, such as common Spin Image [1], Fast Point Feature Histogram (FPFH) [2], Shape Context descriptor [16], is extracted. In [15], an algorithm for pairwise 3D alignment which solves data correspondence by matching stable scan separations between scans was proposed. Every segmented patch in the current scan is given a set of proximities to all ones from last scan according to shape similarity between corresponding patches. The distance matrix consisting of proximities is optimized using Hungarian algorithm to form potential pairs and these pairs could be further refined to stable ones using geometric constant of position. The advantage of the object level matching lies in that it is robust to recover large displacements and reduce the computational cost, while the shortcoming lies in that it deals with the whole point clouds, not cutting down the number of processed points, which is not enough for real-time self driving.

Global representations of 3D point clouds are desirable because they can capture characteristics which encode invariance and allow for direct comparisons for alignment and recognition tasks. The Spectral Registration with Multilayer Resampling algorithm [17] is the global feature-less approach which resamples the spectral magnitude of 3D fast fourier transform calculated on discrete cartesian grids of the 3D scans. By this means, the 3D rotation of alignment parameters is separated from 3D translation and the alignment problem could be solved with the cross correlation technique. The algorithm is demonstrated validity only within giving a precise estimation of roll and pitch offset between point clouds. A algorithm [18] which is based on spherical entropy images (SEI) and the generalized convolution theorem was recently proposed . The 3D rotation is calculated by the Generalized Convolution Theorem based on Spherical Fourier Transform of the SEI. Then, the Phase Only Matched Filtering is adopted for translation recovery.

In summary, the 3D alignment algorithms need to integrate the matching of object level or global level with the one of point level in order to obtain precise transformation parameters. The former two techniques are a coarse fitting which is used to estimate an initial guesses, so, they are usually adopted as a pre-processing step for refined point level alignment.

3   Shape Feature Extraction

For each segmented patch which is here given in [14], a fixed-dimensional feature vector is constructed by concatenating four sets of common invariant descriptors. The descriptors consist of 66-dimensional global Spin Images [1] of the shape computed at the centroid and about the central axis perpendicular to the ground, 45-dimensional hierarchical descriptor [3] using a context-dependent typical vertical extrusion model, 33-dimensional FPFH [2] using the angular variations between normals at point pairs in the neighbor of the centroid and the three dimensions of the bounding box [6] along PCA directions. These give rise to a 147-dimensional feature vector for each segmented object.

3.1   Global Spin Images Descriptor

The Spin Images feature is a local descriptor which is commonly used for scan registration, object recognition in 3D point clouds. It was initially presented in[1], and lately has been widely applied in robotic community [4], [5], [6]. Given a oriented 3D point p (*surface mesh vertical*) and the estimated surface normal n, the Spin Images of point p is calculated by rotating a grid around the reference normal n, where the gird is restricted in the search radius r of point p. For a 3D point $x \in N_p^r$, the projection in the 2D Spin Image S_o with index (i, j) is represented by the non-negative distance α between the point p and its foot of a perpendicular in the tangent plane P defined by the pair (p, n), and the signed β defined by the distance between x and its foot. In this way, each oriented 3D point x of segmented object can be translated into a 2D (α, β) through the basis pair (p, n) as follows:

$$S_o : \mathbb{R}^3 \to \mathbb{R}^2.$$
$$S_o(x) \to (\alpha, \beta) = (\sqrt{||x - p||^2 - (n \cdot (x - p))^2}, n \cdot (x - p)) .$$

(1)

The fashion that 2D points (α, β) are accumulated into discrete bins with index (i, j) can be seen:

$$i = [\frac{\beta + r}{2\rho}].$$
$$j = [\frac{\alpha}{\rho}].$$

(2)

where r denotes the radius of neighbor, $\rho = \frac{r}{b}$ represents the grid resolution of the Spin Image, b is the width (height) of the Spin Image.

For the feature extraction of the whole object with large support neighbor, this descriptor can be almost global [7]. So, in our experiment, each segmented object only extracts one Spin Image descriptor computed at the centroid and about the central axis perpendicular to the ground.

3.2 Hierarchy Descriptor

The Hierarchy or K_i descriptor [3] has the specificity of being represented as a set of horizontal sub-structured patterns organized vertically. It exploits the fact that objects in a structured campus environment mostly have a distinctive vertical profile. The object-centeric global Spin Image descriptor cannot be built in fine shape detail on account of the low density of points, while the Hierarchy feature using a context dependent representation captures the information contained in the typical appearance of an object sitting on the ground, thereby it can be well regarded as a compensate for object-centeric descriptor.

In our experiments, the vertical direction of each segment, ranging from 0 to 3 meters due to only considering the persistent trunk (the crown changes with season and has a variety of shapes), pole and street lamp, is divided into 15 levels with resolution set to 0.2m. Each level is a data structure which consists of two variables (length, width) calculated by first fitting a 2D horizontal rectangle to the points falling in the corresponding level and the ratio of points of this level to the whole segment points. In this way, each segment can generate a hierarchy descriptor with 45 dimensions. With respect to rotation, the descriptor only obtains independence around the vertical axis. As mentioned above, the fact that the objects for AGV in campus environment mostly sit on the ground suggests that a partial independent only about Z axis is sufficient.

3.3 FPFH Feature

The FPFH descriptor [2] is a robust multi-dimensional feature which describes the geometry around a point p in point clouds. The computation of it needs the definition of new 3D coordinates and relative surface normals. For each point p, first select all of p's neighbors enclosed in the sphere with a given radius r (k-neighborhood), pick randomly out a pair of points p_i and p_j ($i \neq j$) in the k-neighborhood and their corresponding estimated normals n_i and n_j (p_i being the point with a smaller angle between its associated normal and the line connecting *the point pair*), then, define a Darboux *uvw* frame($u=n_i$, $v=(p_j\text{-}p_i)\times u$, $w=u\times v$) and calculate the angular variables as follows:

$$\begin{aligned}
\alpha &= v \cdot n_j. \\
\phi &= (u \cdot (p_j - p_i))/\|p_j - p_i\|. \\
\theta &= \arctan(w \cdot n_j, u \cdot n_j).
\end{aligned} \qquad (3)$$

To simplify the histogram computation, fast point feature histogram of p can be calculated by considering the relationships of k neighbors:

$$FPFH(p) = SPF(p) + \frac{1}{k} \sum_{i=1}^{k} \frac{1}{w_k} \cdot SPF(p_k). \qquad (4)$$

By this means, each patch can generate a 33-dimensional descriptor of angular variations in the whole point cloud.

4   Patch Classification

In our implementation, the immobile foreground classes simply consist of the union of the trunk, pole and street lamp. We employ SVM classifier with the non-linear Radial Basis Function (RBF) kernel in the patch classification stage to produce a clean binary segmentation of the campus scene. The cross-validation procedure is employed to prevent over-fitting problem. We first divide the labeled training set into five equal size fold subsets. Sequentially one subset which is selected randomly is tested using the classifier trained on the remaining four subsets. In this scheme, each instance of the whole training set is predicted only once.

There are two unknown parameters for an RBF kernel: C and γ to be evaluated to obtain the best performance for a given classification problem. We employ a grid-search on various pairs of (C, γ) using cross-validation to pick up the one with the best performance. Trying exponentially growing sequences of pairs of (C, γ) has been proved to be a practical method to identify good parameters [8]. We employ a coarse-finer grid search strategy to reduce the burden on computing. First, we loose a grid search on $C=2^{-5}$, 2^{-3}, ..., 2^{15} and $\gamma=2^{-15}$, 2^{-13}, ..., 2^3, next, trying a finer one on the neighborhood of a better pair($C=2^7,\gamma=2^{-5}$). After the best pair (C, γ) is found, the whole labeled training set is trained again to generate the final SVM classifier.

5   Experiments

In order to evaluate the performance of our algorithm, more than 6 thousands scans are acquired using the Velodyne HD-LIDAR 64 beam sensor on campus environment. The experiment scene contains not only large numbers of static trees, poles, buildings et. al but also dynamic objects such as cars, pedestrians, bicyclists which are strong disturbances for scan alignments.

5.1   The Classification Performance

We hand-labelled 50 randomly chosen scans to train the binary SVM classifiers with RBF kernel. The classes of interest which are used to match scans are regarded as foreground while the left segments as background. More than eight hundreds segmented patches are labeled, of which about sixty percentage are regarded as the foreground. The parameters are optimized using five-fold cross validation as described in section 4. Fig. 2 shows the result of one of the frames by distinguishing the segmented patches with trained binary SVM classifier.

Fig. 2. The classification performance. The rectangular coordinate system denotes the position of our test platform with green axis representing the orientation of the head of the vehicle (*the following figures with the same meaning*). The red point clouds denote the determined foreground which may be trunks, street lamps or poles. The classes of remaining colors represent the background which consists of pedestrians (*static with ID 41 or moving with ID 1*), bicyclist (*with ID 3*), dynamic vehicles (*with ID 19 and 46*) and buildings et.al. This figure is best viewed in color.

Our trained classifier can well distinguish the interested foreground classes used as scan alignment from background clutter as shown in the Fig. 2. Sometimes, missing one of the foreground is inevitable such as the ID 12 which is mistook as the background. However, there is no impact on the accuracy of alignment considering so many remaining foreground objects still can be adopted.

5.2   The Matching Performance

The initial estimation of ICP algorithm is given by a NovAtel SPAN-CPT GPS-aided INS system equipped on our self-driving vehicle which can provide a good guesses in most cases. However, when the GPS signal is invalid, the registration of point clouds only exploiting the integrated unit would generate a large

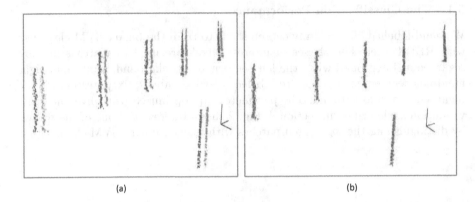

(a)   (b)

Fig. 3. The alignment performance. Fig. 3(a) shows the registration result of a part foreground objects just with the given initial value by GPS and INS. The red point clouds denote the classified patches of last scan while the green ones represents the segments of current frame which have been transformed to the coordinate system of last frame through the transformation parameters. The result of our registration approach is shown in Fig. 3(b). This figure is best viewed in color.

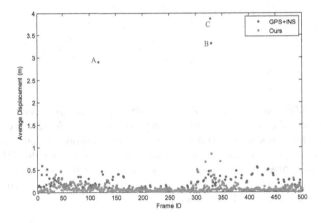

Fig. 4. The average displacement. This figure is best viewed in color.

displacement while the work here presented can well deal with this situation through the further refinement with a part of static foreground objects as shown in Fig. 3.

Just as shown in Fig. 3, the alignment represents the displacement of a few meters because of a bad original value given by GPS and INS. The displacement can be well eliminated using our approach. We also calculate the average displacement of matched classes of interest in the whole data set, which can be seen in Fig. 4 (to visualize clearly, only the result of five hundreds frames are shown).

In Fig. 4, unexpected shifting of the signal results in the displacement of several meters as shown in points A, B and C. These few points would be capable of generating crucial impact on the subsequent processing such as the establishing of global map or the precise localization. These special situations can be well solved with our approach. Meanwhile, we also calculate the error of the whole data set to estimate the quantitative quality. The average displacement of using initial guesses is about 0.14 meter while our approach can cut it down to 0.08 meter.

The runtime of scan registration is crucial for self-driving vehicle. Each frame with a Velodyne HD-LIDAR 64E sensor can obtain over one hundred thirty thousands points. So, exploiting a suitable strategy to reduce the number of point associations is a finer selection for saving the computation time. In [15], the number of points in different sets can be reduced to about sixty thousands by processing at object level with the geometry constraint and the average computation time is about 7.3 seconds. The work here presented only adopts some static foreground classes to register between two scans, the number of pairwise point associations is about forty hundreds which is no less than one order of magnitude comparing with the method in [15]. The average runtime, tested by vast experiments, is about 30 milliseconds which is suitable for real-time applications.

6 Conclusion and Future Work

This paper addresses the problem of alignment with only exploiting the common and static objects instead of the whole point clouds or entire patches to match on campus environments. In particular, we only use instances of classes consisting of trees, street lamps and poles in the whole scene. The advantage result in it can reduce the number of pairwise points to a quite low level. For the specific prior classes, a binary trained SVM is used instead of multiple classes recognition to classify the segmented patches according to the extracted features at object level. The ICP approach is only adopted in the foreground objects given an initial guesses with GPS. Experiments show the proposed method is real-time and robust when the the signal of GPS suddenly shifts or invalid in the sheltered environment.

In the near future work, firstly, we would like to focus on the more complicated environments and selecting more classes of segmented objects in this scene. This will be helpful to solve the problem that the number of current used foreground objects is not enough or not existing in certain scene. Secondly, more information, the normals of overlapped points and the surface orientations of the objects, should be taken into account in the refinement algorithm.

References

1. Johnson, A.E., Hebert, M.: Using spin images for efficient object recognition in cluttered 3D scenes. Pattern Analysis and Machine Intelligence 21(5), 433–449 (2002)

2. Rusu, R.B., Blodow, N., Beetz, M.: Fast Point Feature Histograms (FPFH) for 3D Registration. In: IEEE International Conference on Robotics and Automation (2009)
3. Douillard, B.: Laser and vision based classification in urban environments. Ph.D. dissertation, The University of Sydney (2009)
4. Aleksey, G., Vladimir, G.K., Thomas, F.: Shaped-based Recognition of 3D Point Clouds in Urban Environments. In: IEEE International Conference on Computer Vision (2009)
5. Xiong, X.H., Daniel, M., Bagnell, J.A., Martial, H.: 3D Scenes Analysis Via Sequenced Predictions Over Points and Regions. In: International Conference on Robotics and Automation (2011)
6. Dominic, Z.W., Ingmar, P., Paul, N.: What could move? Finding Cars, Pedestrians and Bicyclists in 3D Laser Data. In: International Conference on Robotics and Automation (2012)
7. Douillard, D., Quadros, A., Morton, P., Deuge, M.D.: A 3d classifier trained without field samples. Automatic Control 50(4), 511–515 (2012)
8. Chih, W.H., Chih, C.C., Chih, J.L.: A Practical Guide to Support Vector Classification (2013)
9. Besl, P., McKay, N.: A method for registration of 3-D shapes. IEEE Transactions on Pattern Analysis and Machine Intelligence 14(2), 239–256 (1992)
10. Pomerleau, F., Colas, F., Siegwart, R., Magnenat, S.: Comparing ICP variants on real-world data sets. Autonomous Robots 34(3), 133–148 (2013)
11. Magnusson, M., Lilienthal, A., Duckett, T.: Scan registration for autonomous mining vehicles using 3D-NDT. Journal of Field Robotics 24(10), 803–827 (2007)
12. Stoyanov, T., Magnusson, M., Lilienthal, A.: Point set registration through minimization of the L2 distance between 3D-NDT models. In: IEEE International Conference on Robotics and Automation (2012)
13. Frank, M., Pink, O., Stiller, C.: Segmentation of 3D Lidar Data in non-flat Urban Environments using a Local Convexity Criterion. In: IEEE Intelligent Vehicles Symposium (2009)
14. Chen, T.T., Dai, B., Wang, R., Liu, D.: Gaussian-process-based Real-time Ground Segmentation for Autonomous Land Vehicles. Journal of Intelligent and Robotic Systems (2013)
15. Douillard, B., Quadros, A., Morton, P., Underwood, J.P.: Scan Segments Matching for Pairwise 3D Alignment. In: International Conference on Robotics and Automation (2013)
16. Frome, A., Huber, D., Kolluri, R., Bülow, T., Malik, J.: Recognizing objects in range data using regional point descriptors. In: Pajdla, T., Matas, J(G.) (eds.) ECCV 2004. LNCS, vol. 3023, pp. 224–237. Springer, Heidelberg (2004)
17. Blow, H., Birk, A.: Spectral 6 DOF registration of noisy 3D range data with partial overlap. Pattern Analysis and Machine Intelligence 35(4) (2013)
18. Sun, B., Kong, W.W., Xiao, J.H., Zhang, J.W.: A Global Feature-less Scan Registration Strategy Based on Spherical Entropy Images. Intelligent Robots and Systems (2014)

Quasi-Orthorectified Panorama Generation Based on Affine Model from Terrain UAV Images

Yuchong Li

National Laboratory of Pattern Recognition,
Institute of Automation, Chinese Academy of Sciences, Beijing, P.R.China
yuchong.li@nlpr.ia.ac.cn

Abstract. In this paper we present a new panorama generation method based on affine model. The images used for panorama generation are captured by an Unmanned Aerial Vehicle (UAV). We focus our research on terrain data, which contains few high buildings. In our method a Best-First Affine Model is used to generate panorama, with the affine parameters solved by a locally optimized RANSAC. The process of our image stitching method is fully automatic. Compared with existing methods, the panorama generated by ours is a quasi-orthorectified one and free from visible distortions.

Keywords: Panorama, UAV, Affine Model.

1 Introduction

Panorama generation from multiple overlapping images of the same scene has long been studied. Many important methods have been proposed and the results are quite impressive.

In our research we generate a panorama from hundreds of terrain airborne images captured by an Unmanned Aerial Vehicle (UAV). Traditionally UAV is used in military fields. More recently UAV finds its applications in various civilian domains as image capturing platforms.

UAV images are different from traditional aerial photos. At first, UAV flies much lower than fixed-wing planes, which means when the terrain has topographically complex ground, the scene captured in an UAV image cannot be regarded as a planar one. Second, the flying attitude is more changeable than traditional planes, which could possibly make the airborne images contain obviously tilted viewing angles.

Fig.1 shows some images with topographically complex ground and tilted viewing angle in one of our UAV image datasets. These two factors will inevitably cause visible distortions in the panorama generated from UAV images by existing image stitching methods, hence how to generate a panorama from UAV images, which is free from visible distortions, is a problem worthy exploring.

In the field of remote sensing, researchers have proposed numerous methods to generate ortho-mosaic of airborne images which could effectively solve the

S. Li et al. (Eds.): CCPR 2014, Part I, CCIS 483, pp. 381–390, 2014.

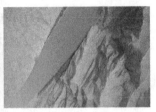

Fig. 1. UAV images with topographically complex ground or tilted viewing angle

problem of distortion in the final panorama. However, these methods rely on precise digital elevation model (DEM) and ground control points (GCP), which are not available in our experiments. In this paper, we present a new method to generate quasi-orthorectified panorama from UAV images based on affine model without DEM or GCP.

The main contribution of our work is that we use affine model based on a Best-First strategy to generate panorama, with the affine parameters solved by a locally optimized RANSAC. The Best-First Affine Model ensures the image stitching result to be a quasi-orthorectified panorama without visible distortions. Our algorithm can effectively handle poorly textured regions in the process of image stitching. Details of the algorithm are discussed in Section 5.

2   Related Work

Panorama generation has long been studied in various research fields such as computer vision, image processing and remote sensing. Much work has been done and many impressive algorithms have been proposed.

Direct (pixel-based) alignment which aims to estimate the parameters of motion model is applied in image stitching. C. D. Kuglin[1], L. G. Brown[2], I. Matthews et al.[3] have proposed representative methods in this field. While I. Zoghlami et al.[4], A. Zisserman et al.[5], P. F. McLauchlan et al.[6], D. Lowe et al.[7] proposed feature-based registration methods which could also be used in panorama generation.

In order to find a globally consistent set of alignment parameters which minimizes the mis-registration between all pairs of images [8], researchers, for example R. Szeliski et al.[9], proposed some global registration methods.

The goal of existing image stitching methods mainly focuses on minimizing the mis-registration between images, and preventing visible seams, blur or ghosting in the final panorama [10,11]. However, distortion removal is not considered in the existing methods.

Some researchers in remote sensing field have proposed methods to generate ortho-mosaic of airborne images [12,13]. These methods are similar, which all need precise digital elevation model (DEM) and ground control points (GCP) to orthorectify the airborne images. However precise DEM and GCP are not available in many applications, including ours.

So in this paper, we propose a new method to generate quasi-orthorectified panorama based on affine model.

3   Algorithm Overview

Fig.2 shows the flowchart of our algorithm.

Fig. 2. Flowchart of our algorithm

4   Data Preparation

Before we create panorama, a 3D point cloud needs to be generated using UAV images and adjusted by the GPS data from UAV.

4.1   3D Point Cloud Generation

Using all the UAV images as input, the Structure from Motion (SFM) [14] is used to compute accurate camera parameters and create a 3D sparse point cloud. Then it is followed by the Patch-based Multi-View Stereo (PMVS) [15] to generate a dense 3D point cloud of the scene.

Points in the 3D dense point cloud are used as the feature points in our algorithm. Thousands of feature points are detected in each image, and every pair of overlapping airborne images are globally registered.

4.2   Coordinate System Transformation

The GPS module on UAV provides optical center positions of the airborne images. The GPS data gives approximate 3 dimensional coordinate values for every optical center in the real world. Meanwhile, the optical centers are restored in the process of SFM as well.

Using the optical center positions as point pairs, the similarity transformation from the point cloud coordinate system to the real world coordinate system is determined. Then the 3D dense point cloud is transformed to the real world system.

5   Panorama Generation

In this section we introduce our Best-First Affine Model for Panorama Generation. Affine parameters for local regions are solved by a locally optimized RANSAC (Section 5.2). A Best-First Strategy for texture mapping is implemented (Section 5.2). Our algorithm can well handle the poorly textured regions (Section 5.2). Since we don't have precise DEM or GCP (Section 2), our final result can not be regraded as an ortho-mosaic strictly, however it can be regarded as a quasi-orthorectified panorama and it is free from visible distortions.

5.1 Choosing Stitching Surface

The real world coordinate system has three mutually orthogonal coordinate axes represented as x, y and z. The x axis is heading east and the y axis is heading north, while the z axis is heading vertically above.

In our algorithm we choose the x-y coordinate plane as the stitching surface. All the 3D points are projected onto this surface. A 2D feature point set, denoted as E, represents the projection of all 3D points. We use the smallest bounding rectangle of E whose sides are parallel to the x and y axes to represent the maximum potential region of the final panorama. We denote this rectangle area as the Mosaic Area.

5.2 Best-First Affine Model

We divide the Mosaic Area into M×N non-overlapping grids. Each grid is a square region with the size of k×k pixels. We count the number of 2D feature points, which are projected 3D feature points, contained in each grid, and all grids can be classified into two category groups denoted as $C_{texture}$ and $C_{untexture}$. A grid in $C_{texture}$ contains non-zero number of 2D feature points, while a grid in $C_{untexture}$ contains zero 2D feature points.

Solution for Affine Parameters. A grid in $C_{texture}$ can be regarded as a k×k pixels square patch. We denote the patch as P_{patch}. Because of the overlapping of UAV images, a P_{patch} must have its registered regions in at least one UAV image.

If P_{patch} has its registered regions in N UAV images (N⩾1), in order to determine which registered region we should choose for P_{patch}, we sort all the N images according to the number of feature points contained within each one. Then the image containing the highest number of feature points is chosen for the registered region, and the region is denoted as R_{region}.

In our experiments parameter k is set to 50 pixels, and both P_{patch} and R_{region} can be regarded as planar. Inspired by J. M. Morel[16] we use affine model to describe the transform between them. The next section will discuss the determination for value of parameter k.

Assume the number of 2D feature points contained in P_{patch} is q, we denote a feature point set in P_{patch} as $\{P_i\}_{i=1}^q$. For R_{region}, it has a point set registered to the set $\{P_i\}_{i=1}^q$, denoted as $\{p_i\}_{i=1}^q$.

The affine transform is written as $p_i = AP_i$, where A is an unknown 2D affine matrix,

$$p_i = \begin{bmatrix} a_{00} & a_{01} & a_{02} \\ a_{10} & a_{11} & a_{12} \\ 0 & 0 & 1 \end{bmatrix} P_i \tag{1}$$

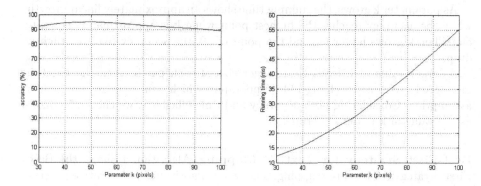

Fig. 3. (a)Left is the accuracy, (b)Right is the average running time

Using $\{P_i\}_{i=1}^{q}$ and $\{p_i\}_{i=1}^{q}$ as pairs of points, the parameters for affine transform are solved by a locally optimized RACSAC, which is an enhanced RANSAC similar to LO-RANSAC[17].

We define an error metric function F_{error} to evaluate the accuracy of this affine transform between P_{patch} and R_{region}.

$$F_{error} = 1/q \sum_{i=1}^{q} (p_i - AP_i)^T (p_i - AP_i) \qquad (2)$$

For each point pair $\{p_k, P_k\}$, the metric function f_{error} is used to evaluate its accuracy.

$$f_{error} = (p_k - AP_k)^T (p_k - AP_k) \qquad (3)$$

Determination for Value of Parameter k. The size of each airborne image in our UAV datasets is 1024×683, for F_{error} we define a threshold which is set to 5 pixels in our experiments. When choosing different values of parameter k, we calculate F_{error} of each patch (grid) in $C_{texture}$ and record the percentage of patches whose F_{error} is smaller than the threshold, which is defined as the accuracy in Fig.3(a). We also record the average running time for solving affine parameters between one patch and its registered region in Fig.3(b). The statistical results are shown in Table 1.

Table 1. Statistical results of accuracy and running time for different values of k

Parameter k(pixels)	30	40	50	60	70	80	90	100
Accuracy(%)	92.3	94.6	95.1	94.2	92.9	91.6	90.8	89.2
Running time(ms)	12.3	15.6	20.5	25.6	32.5	39.6	47.2	55.3

As parameter k grows, the running time shows an approximately linear growth, while the accuracy reaches the highest point when k is approximately equal to 50. When k grows larger beyond the point of 50, the accuracy tends to slightly drop.

A larger value of k leads to a bigger size of each patch, then the patch is more likely to contain changeable topography which could violate our planar assumption. Considering both accuracy and time efficiency, we choose 50 pixels as the value of k in our experiments.

Best-First Strategy for Texture Mapping Algorithm 1 shows the Best-First Strategy for texture mapping. The whole algorithm is an iterative process. We define a set G to represent all the patches (grids) classified in $C_{texture}$.

Algorithm 1. Best-First Strategy for Texture Mapping

While ($G \neq \{\phi\}$) {
    Choose patch containing the most feature points as P_{patch};
    Solve affine parameters between P_{patch} and R_{region};
    Calculate F_{error} between P_{patch} and R_{region};
    If (F_{error} is larger than a pre-defined threshold) {
        Find $P_k \subseteq P_{patch}$ whose f_{error} is maximum among $\{P_i\}_{i=1}^q$ (Section 5.2);
        Create a new patch P_{patch_new} whose center is P_k, with the size of k×k;
        Add P_{patch_new} to G;
    }
    Do texture mapping of the grid represented by P_{patch};
    If (part of the grid was textured in a previous iteration) {
        Assume patch in that iteration is $P_{patch\_previous}$;
        If ($F_{error} < F_{error\_previous}$)
            Update the overlapping region texture;
        Else
            Maintain the texture of the overlapping region;
    }
    Remove P_{patch} from G;
}

If F_{error} is larger than a threshold (set to 5 pixels in our experiments), it means the scene covered by P_{patch} is not a planar, it may contain complex topography. To deal with this problem we create a new patch P_{patch_new} with the size of k×k. P_{patch_new} is added to the set G. In the process of texture mapping, bilinear interpolation inspired by P. S. Heckbert[18] is implemented using affine model between P_{patch} and R_{region}.

At the end of each iteration, the current P_{patch} is removed from G. When the set G is empty, the whole algorithm is done.

Process of Poorly Textured Regions. We detect every grid in $C_{untexture}$ which contains no feature point. If a grid in $C_{untexture}$ is surrounded by textured grids already, then we regard it as part of the panorama. However, the regions in UAV images corresponding to such grids are poorly textured, hence no feature point is detected in Section 4.1.

For the poorly textured regions, we use a dense matching method similar to E. Tola et al.[19] to detect feature points. Then the same process is implemented as mentioned earlier in Section 5.2 to accomplish the panorama generation.

5.3 Color Balancing

We use a gradient domain blending method similar to H. Hoppe et al.[20] to minimize visible seams and color difference between different parts of the panorama, which is caused by differences in exposure and lighting conditions between UAV images.

6 Experimental Results

In this section, we report our experimental results on two terrain airborne image datasets collected by UAV. The meta-information of each dataset is shown in Table 2.

Table 2. Meta-information of each dataset

Dataset name	UAV image number	Airborne image size
D-Valley	145	1024×683
D-Village	501	1024×683

We compare our experimental results with panorama generated by Microsoft Image Composite Editor (ICE) in terms of visual effects, region of panorama and time performance. ICE is an advanced panoramic image stitching software provided by Microsoft Research.

The computer hardware used in our experiments is: Intel(R) Core(TM) i5-2400 CPU @ 3.10GHz, 4.00 GB RAM and 64 bits operating system.

6.1 Panorama Generated by Our Method and ICE

Fig.4 is the panorama of D-Valley and Fig.5 is the panorama of D-Village.

6.2 Comparison

In both datasets our method shows good visual effect of quasi-orthorectification, the panorama generated by our method does not suffer from visible distortions.

The left and right part of Fig.4(b) has visible distortions, while distortions are not found in the corresponding areas in Fig.4(a). Fig.6 shows the comparison of a pair of corresponding local regions in Fig.4(a) and Fig.4(b).

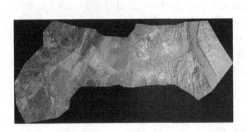 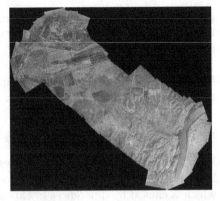

Fig. 4. (a)Left is by our method (8192×3748),(b)Right is by ICE (7257×6419)

 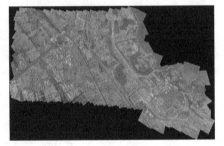

Fig. 5. (a)Left is by our method (8192×4836),(b)Right is by ICE (14253×9047)

Fig.7 shows the comparison of a pair of corresponding local regions in Fig.5(a) and Fig.5(b).

The region of panorama is almost the same in both datasets between our results and those generated by ICE.

For time load, ICE is better than ours, which is shown in Table 3. Our time efficiency is not as good as ICE because our method calculates an affine model for each local region, which will take some time.

Table 3. Comparison of our algorithm and ICE

Method	Visual effect	Region of panorama	Time D-Valley	Time D-Village
Ours	Better: Good effect of quasi-orthorectification	Same	17min	26min
ICE	Worse: Visible distortions	Same	9min	14min

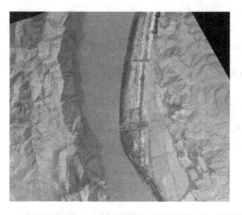 

Fig. 6. (a)Left is our result, (b)Right is by ICE. Distortion is visible in (b) and stitching error occurs in the red box region.

Fig. 7. (a)Left is our result,(b)Right is by ICE. The structure in the red box should be round as shown in (a), however it appears elliptic in (b) because of distortion.

7   Conclusion and Future Work

In this paper we present a new image stitching method which is used to process UAV images. In our method the panorama is generated by a Best-First Affine Model, with the parameters solved by a locally optimized RANSAC. The algorithm is fully automatic and can handle poorly textured regions in the process of panorama generation. The experimental results show good effect of quasi-orthorectification, which ensures the panorama generated by our method contain no visible distortions.

Looking into the future, we will focus on improving the time efficiency. The other research direction we will pursue is to extend the application of our method to UAV images which contains high-rise buildings. Usually high-rise buildings are in urban areas which are fundamentally different from terrain areas, and we hope to continue our research on panorama generation of urban UAV images.

References

1. Kuglin, C.D.: The phase correlation image alignment method. In: Proc. Int. Conf. on Cybernetics and Society (1975)
2. Brown, L.G.: A survey of image registration techniques. ACM Computing Surveys (CSUR) 24(4), 325–376 (1992)
3. Baker, S., Matthews, I.: Lucas-kanade 20 years on: A unifying framework. International Journal of Computer Vision 56(3), 221–255 (2004)
4. Zoghlami, I., Faugeras, O., Deriche, R.: Using geometric corners to build a 2D mosaic from a set of images. In: Computer Vision and Pattern Recognition, pp. 420–425. IEEE (1997)
5. Capel, D., Zisserman, A.: Automated mosaicing with super-resolution zoom. In: Computer Vision and Pattern Recognition, pp. 885–891. IEEE Press, Santa Barbara (1998)
6. McLauchlan, P.F., Jaenicke, A.: Image mosaicing using sequential bundle adjustment. Image and Vision Computing 20(9), 751–759 (2002)
7. Brown, M., Lowe, D.: Recognizing panoramas. In: International Conference on Computer Vision (ICCV), pp. 1218–1225. IEEE Press, Nice (2003)
8. Szeliski, R.: Image alignment and stitching: A tutorial. Foundations and Trends in Computer Graphics and Vision 2(1), 1–104 (2006)
9. Shum, H.Y., Szeliski, R.: Systems and experiment paper: Construction of panoramic image mosaics with global and local alignment. International Journal of Computer Vision 36(2), 101–130 (2000)
10. Agarwala, A., Dontcheva, M., Agrawala, M., et al.: Interactive digital photomontage. ACM Transactions on Graphics (TOG) 23(3), 294–302 (2004)
11. Uyttendaele, M., Eden, A., Skeliski, R.: Eliminating ghosting and exposure artifacts in image mosaics. In: Computer Vision and Pattern Recognition, vol. 2, pp. 509–516. IEEE (2001)
12. Turner, D., Lucieer, A., Watson, C.: An automated technique for generating georectified mosaics from ultra-high resolution unmanned aerial vehicle (UAV) imagery, based on structure from motion (SfM) point clouds. Remote Sensing 4(5), 1392–1410 (2012)
13. d'Oleire-Oltmanns, S., Marzolff, I., Peter, K.D., et al.: Unmanned Aerial Vehicle (UAV) for monitoring soil erosion in Morocco. Remote Sensing 4(11), 3390–3416 (2012)
14. Agarwal, S., Snavely, N., Seitz, S.M., Szeliski, R.: Bundle adjustment in the large. In: Daniilidis, K., Maragos, P., Paragios, N. (eds.) ECCV 2010, Part II. LNCS, vol. 6312, pp. 29–42. Springer, Heidelberg (2010)
15. Furukawa, Y., Ponce, J.: Accurate, dense, and robust multiview stereopsis. IEEE Transactions on Pattern Analysis and Machine Intelligence 32(8), 1362–1376 (2010)
16. Morel, J.M., Yu, G.: ASIFT: A new framework for fully affine invariant image comparison. SIAM Journal on Imaging Sciences 2(2), 438–469 (2009)
17. Chum, O., Matas, J., Kittler, J.: Locally optimized RANSAC. In: Michaelis, B., Krell, G. (eds.) DAGM 2003. LNCS, vol. 2781, pp. 236–243. Springer, Heidelberg (2003)
18. Heckbert, P.S.: Survey of texture mapping. Computer Graphics and Applications 6(11), 56–67 (1986)
19. Tola, E., Lepetit, V., Fua, P.: Daisy: An efficient dense descriptor applied to wide-baseline stereo. Pattern Analysis and Machine Intelligence 32(5), 815–830 (2010)
20. Kazhdan, M., Hoppe, H.: Streaming multigrid for gradient-domain operations on large images. ACM Transactions on Graphics (TOG) 27(3), 21 (2008)

Shape Recognition by Combining Contour and Skeleton into a Mid-Level Representation

Wei Shen[1], Xinggang Wang[2], Cong Yao[2], and Xiang Bai[2]

[1] School of Communication and Information Engineering, Shanghai University,
149 Yanchang Road, Shanghai 200072, P.R. China
[2] Dept. of Electronics and Information Engineering, Huazhong University of Science
and Technology, 1037 Luoyu Road, Wuhan, Hubei Province 430074, P.R. China

Abstract. Contour and skeleton are two main stream representations for shape recognition in the literature. It has been shown that such two representations convey complementary information, however combining them in a nature way is nontrivial, as they are generally abstracted by different structures (closed string *vs* graph), respectively. This paper aims at addressing the shape recognition problem by combining contour and skeleton into a mid-level of shape representation. To form a mid-level representation for shape contours, a recent work named **B**ag of **C**ontour **F**ragments (BCF) is adopted; While for skeleton, a new mid-level representation named **B**ag of **S**keleton **P**aths (BSP) is proposed, which is formed by pooling the skeleton codes by encoding the skeleton paths connecting pairs of end points in the skeleton. Finally, a compact shape feature vector is formed by concatenating BCF with BSP and fed into a linear SVM classifier to recognize the shape. Although such a concatenation is simple, the SVM classifier can automatically learn the weights of contour and skeleton features to offer discriminative power. The encouraging experimental results demonstrate that the proposed new shape representation is effective for shape classification and achieves the state-of-the-art performances on several standard shape benchmarks.

Keywords: Shape Recognition, Mid-level Shape Representation, Bag of Contour Fragments, Bag of Skeleton Paths.

1 Introduction

Shape plays an important role in human perception for object recognition. The objects shown in Fig. 1 have lost their brightness, color and texture information and are only represented by their silhouettes, however it's not intractable for human to recognize their categories. This simple demonstration indicates that shape is stable to the variations in object color and texture and light conditions. Due to such advantages, recognizing objects by their shapes has been a long standing problem in the literature. Shape recognition is usually considered as a classification problem that is given a testing shape, to determine its category label based on a set of training shapes as well as their category label. The main challenges in shape recognition are the large intra-class variations induced

S. Li et al. (Eds.): CCPR 2014, Part I, CCIS 483, pp. 391–400, 2014.
© Springer-Verlag Berlin Heidelberg 2014

Fig. 1. Human biological vision system is able to recognize these object without any appearance information (brightness, color and texture)

by deformation, articulation and occlusion. Therefore, the main focus of the research efforts have been made in the last decade [5,12,17,18,3,4] is how to form a informative and discriminative shape representation.

Generally, the existing main stream shape representations can be classified into two classes: contour based [5,12,9] and skeleton based [1,2,16,14]. The former one delivers the information that how the spatial distribution of the boundary points varies along the object contour. Therefore, it captures more informative shape information and is stable to affine transformation. However, it is sensitive to non-ridge deformation and articulation; On the contrary, the latter one provides the information that how thickness of the object changes along the skeleton. Therefore, it is invariant to non-ridge deformation and articulation, although it only carries more rough geometric features of the object. Consequently, such two representations are complementary. Nevertheless, very few works have tried combining these two representations for shape recognition. The reason might be that combining the data of different structures is not trivial, as the contour is always abstracted by a closed string while the skeleton is abstracted either by a graph or a tree. So far as we know, ICS [3] is the only work to explicitly discuss how to combine contour and skeleton to improve the performance of shape recognition. However, the combination proposed in this work is just a weighted sum of the outputs of two generative models trained individually on contour features and skeleton features respectively. Therefore, how to combine contour and skeleton into a shape representation in a principled way is still an open problem.

In this paper, our goal is to address the above combination issue to explore the complementary between contour and skeleton to improve the performance of shape recognition. The main obstacle of the combination is how to transform the data of different structures into a common form. Recently, a contour based shape representation named **B**ag of **C**ontour **F**ragments (BCF) [20] was proposed, which is inspired by the well-known Bag of Features framework. In BCF, a contour is decomposed into a set of contour fragments, which will be then encoded and pooled to form a feature vector to represent the contour. BCF sheds lights onto the issue of the combination of contour and skeleton: Since a contour can be represented by a feature vector in BCF, a straightforward way to combine the contour and its skeleton is converting its skeleton to a feature vector as well followed by concatenating the two feature vectors. Toward this end, we propose a skeleton based representation named **B**ag of **S**keleton **P**aths (BSP) inspired by the framework of BCF.

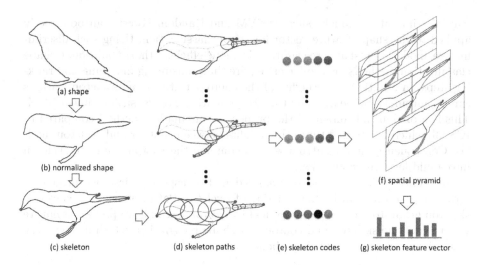

Fig. 2. The pipeline of building skeleton based shape representation by Bag of Skeleton Paths. (a) A shape. (b) The normalized shape obtained by aligned its major axis with the horizontal line. (c) Some examples of skeleton paths in green color. (d) The skeleton codes encoded from the skeleton paths. (e) $2^l \times 2^l (l = 0, 1, 2)$ subregions are used in SPM for max pooling. (e) The formed skeleton based shape representation.

Fig. 2 shows the pipeline of building skeleton based shape representation by Bag of Skeleton Paths. Given a shape, firstly a normalization step is performed to align the shape according to its major axis, as the spatial pyramid matching (SPM) [11] step shown in Fig. 2(f) is not rotation invariant. Then, the skeleton of the shape is extracted and decomposed into a set of skeleton paths. The skeleton paths, shown by the green curves in Fig. 2(d), are the shortest paths between pairs of end points of the skeleton. According to [2], a skeleton path is represented by a sequence of the radii of the maximal discs centered at skeleton points, as shown by the red circles in Fig. 2(d). Next, each skeleton path is encoded into a skeleton code. Finally, the skeleton codes are pooled into a compact skeleton feature vector by SPM. To encode skeleton paths, we adopt local-constrained linear coding (LLC) [19] scheme, as it has been proved to be efficient and effective for image classification. SPM provides additional spatial layout information and has been widely used in feature learning framework to boost the performance of image classification. It partitions the image into increasingly finer spatial subregions and computes histograms of local features from each sub-region. However, skeleton paths are different from the popular image features computed on rectangular image patches, such as SIFT [13] and HOG [7]. To perform SPM, we determine which sub-region a skeleton paths falls in by the location of the end point from which it emanate. The proposed BSP provides a effective way to convert a skeleton graph to a vector, a conventional form that can be dealt with by general classification models.

By concatenating the contour feature vector obtained by BCF with the skeleton feature vector obtained by BSP, a final shape feature vector is formed.

Any discriminative models, such as SVM and Random Forest, can be directly applied to the shape feature vector for shape classification. Using such discriminative models for shape recognition is more efficient than traditional shape classification methods, as the latter require time consuming matching and ranking steps. In addition, the weights of the contour features and skeleton features can be automatically learned by the discriminative models, such as linear SVM. This is a obvious advantage of the proposed combination method compared to ICS [3], which has to fine tunes the weights between contour and skeleton models. Consequently, it's a natrual way to combine the contour and the skeleton into a mid-level representation.

Our contributions can be summarized in two aspects. First, we propose a novel shape representation named Bag of Skeleton Paths, which can convert a skeleton graph to a compact single feature vector. Second, we provide a nature way to combine skeleton and contour for shape recognition, which achieves the state-of-the-arts on several shape benchmarks.

2 Related Work

There have been a rich body of works concerning shape recognition in recent years [5,12,17,18]. In the early age, the exemplar-based strategy has been widely used, such as [5,12]. Generally, there are two key steps in this strategy. The first one is extracting informative and robust shape descriptors. For example, Belongie et al. [5] introduce a shape descriptor named shape context (SC) which describes the relative spatial distribution (distance and orientation) of landmark points sampled on the object contour around feature points. Lin and Jacobs [12] use inner distance to extend shape context to capture articulation. As for skeleton based shape descriptors, the shock graph and its variants [16,14] are most popular, which are abstracted from skeletons by designed shape grammar. The second one is finding the correspondences between two sets of the shape descriptors by matching algorithms such as Hungarian, thin plate spline (TPS) and dynamic programming (DP). A testing shape is classified into the class of its nearest neighbor ranked by the matching costs. The exemplar-based strategy requires a large number of training data to capture the large intra-class variances of shapes. However, when the size of training set become quite large, it's intractable to search the nearest neighbor due to the high time cost caused by pairwise matching.

Generative models are also used for shape recognition. Sun and Super [17] propose a Bayesian model, which use the normalized contour fragments as the input features for shape classification. Wang et al. [18] model shapes of one class by a skeletal prototype tree learned by skeleton graph matching. Then a Bayesian inference is used to compute the similarity between a testing skeleton and each skeletal prototype tree. Bai et al. [3] propose to integrate contour and skeleton by a Gaussian mixture model, in which contour fragments and skeleton paths are used as the input features. Unlike their method, ours combine contour and skeleton into the mid-level of shape representation, and learn the weights between contour features and skeleton features automatically.

Recently, researchers begin to apply the powerful discriminative models to shape classification. Daliri and Torre [8] transform the contour into a string based representation according to a certain order of the corresponding contour points found during contour matching. Then they apply SVM to the kernel space built from the pairwise distances between strings to obtain classification results. Wang et al. [20] utilize LLC strategy to extract the mid-level representation BCF from contour fragments and they use linear SVM for classification. The proposed BSP is a extension of BCF for skeleton based mid-level representation.

3   Methodology

In this section, we will introduce our method for shape recognition, including the steps of shape normalization, BSP representation and shape classification by the combination of contour and skeleton.

3.1   Shape Normalization

As the SPM strategy assumes that the parts of shapes falls in the same sub-region are similar, it is not rotation invariant. To apply SPM to shape classification, a normalization step is required to align shapes roughly. One straight forward solution is to align each shape with its major axis. Here, we use principal component analysis (PCA) to compute the orientation of the major axis of each shape. Formally, given a shape $F \subset \mathbb{R}^2$, we apply PCA to the point set $\{p_i = (x_i, y_i) | p_i \in F\}_{i=1}^N$. First, the $N \times N$ covariance matrix Σ is computed by $\Sigma = \frac{1}{N-1} \sum_{i=1}^N (x_i - \overline{x_i})(y_i - \overline{y_i})$, where $\overline{x_i} = \sum_{i=1}^N x_i / N$ and $\overline{y_i} = \sum_{i=1}^N y_i / N$. Then, the two eigenvectors $\mathbf{v}_1$ and $\mathbf{v}_2$ of Σ form the columns of the $N \times N$ matrix V, and the two eigenvalues of Σ is $(\lambda_1, \lambda_2)^\mathrm{T} = \mathbf{diag}(V^\mathrm{T} \Sigma V)$. The orientation of the major axis of the shape F is the orientation of the eigenvector whose corresponding eigenvalue is bigger. All shapes are rotated to ensure their estimated major axes are aligned with the horizontal line, such as the example given in Fig. 2(b).

3.2   Bag of Skeleton Paths

In this section, we show how to build a BSP shape representation for a give shape F step by step.

Skeleton Paths Given a shape F, we obtain its skeleton $S(F)$ by the method introduced in [15], which does not require parameter tuning for skeleton computation. An end point in a skeleton is a skeleton point only have one adjacent skeleton point, such as the red points in Fig. 2(d). The shortest path between two end points, such as the green curves in Fig. 2(d), is called skeleton path, which is a informative skeleton descriptor and has been successfully used for skeleton matching [2]. Suppose there are m end points $\{e_i\}_{i=1}^m$ in the skeleton

$S(F)$. Let $h_{i,j}$ denote the skeleton path between e_i and e_j, then the set of the skeleton paths of $S(F)$ are

$$S(S(F)) = \{h_{i,j} | i \neq j, i, j = 1 \ldots m\}. \tag{1}$$

Note that, the skeleton paths $h_{i,j}$ and $h_{j,i}$ are two different skeleton paths. To represent a skeleton path $h_{i,j}$, a sequence of T skeleton points on it are sampled equally. Thus, the skeleton path $h_{i,j}$ is represented by $\mathbf{r}_{ij} = (\frac{R_t}{\bar{R}}; t = 1 \ldots T)^T$, where R_t is the radius of the maximal disc centered at the t-th sampled skeleton points and $\bar{R}$ is the mean value of the radii of all the skeleton points of $S(F)$. $\bar{R}$ is a normalization factor to ensure $\mathbf{r}_{ij}$ is scale invariant. The radius of the maximal disc centered at a skeleton point p is computed by the value of the distance transform of p w.r.t the object contour. In the following steps, we describe a skeleton path $h_{i,j}$ by its radii sequence descriptor $\mathbf{r}_{ij} \in \mathbb{R}^T$ for notation simplification.

Skeleton Paths Encoding. Encoding a skeleton path $\mathbf{r} \in \mathbb{R}^T$ is transforming it into a new space $\mathcal{B}$ by a given codebook with K entries, $\mathbf{B} = (\mathbf{b_1}, \mathbf{b_2}, \ldots, \mathbf{b_K}) \in \mathbb{R}^{T \times K}$. In the new space, the skeleton path $\mathbf{r}$ is represented by a skeleton code $\mathbf{c} \in \mathbb{R}^K$.

Codebook construction is usually achieved by unsupervised learning, such as k-means. Given a set of skeleton paths randomly sampled from all the skeletons in a dataset, we apply k-means algorithm to cluster them into K clusters and construct a codebook $\mathbf{B} = (\mathbf{b_1}, \mathbf{b_2}, \ldots, \mathbf{b_K})$. Each cluster center forms a entry of the codebook $\mathbf{b_i}$.

To encode a skeleton path $\mathbf{r}$, we adopt LLC scheme [19], as it has been proved to be effective for image classification. Encoding is usually achieved by minimizing the reconstruction error. LLC additionally incorporates locality constraint, which solves the following constrained least square fitting problem:

$$\min_{\mathbf{c}_{\pi_k}} \|\mathbf{r} - \mathbf{B}_{\pi_k} \mathbf{c}_{\pi_k}\|, \quad \text{s.t.} \quad \mathbf{1}^T \mathbf{c}_{\pi_k} = 1, \tag{2}$$

where $\mathbf{B}_{\pi_k}$ is the local bases formed by the k nearest neighbors of $\mathbf{r}$ and $\mathbf{c}_{\pi_k} \in \mathbb{R}^k$ is the reconstruction coefficients. Such a locality constrain leads to several favorable properties such as local smooth sparsity and better reconstruction. The code of $\mathbf{r}$ encoded by the codebook $\mathbf{B}$, i.e. $\mathbf{c} \in \mathbb{R}^K$, can be easily converted from $\mathbf{c}_{\pi_k}$ by setting the corresponding entries of $\mathbf{c}$ are equal to $\mathbf{c}_{\pi_k}$'s and others are zero.

Skeleton Code Pooling. Given a skeleton S, its skeleton paths are encoded into skeleton codes $\{c_i\}_{i=1}^n$, where n is the number of the skeleton paths in S. Now we describe how to obtain a compact skeleton based shape representation by pooling the skeleton codes. SPM is usually used to incorporate spatial layout information when pooling the image codes. It usually divide a image into $2^l \times 2^l (l = 0, 1, 2)$ subregions and then the features in each subregion are pooled respectively. While skeleton paths are quite different from the image features computed on rectangular image patches. We find that skeleton paths emanate from one end point to others describe how the thickness of the object varies from the near to the distant (seeing the three skeleton paths emanate from one end point shown in Fig. 2(d)). For the aligned shapes belong to one category, the skeleton paths emanate from the end points falls in the same subregions should be similar. Therefore, we determine which subregion a skeleton path belong to by the location of the end point from which it emanates. More specifically, we divide a shape F into $2^l \times 2^l (l = 0, 1, 2)$ subregions, i.e. 21 subregions totally. Let $\mathbf{c}^e \in \mathbb{R}^K$ denote the skeleton code of a skeleton path emanate from a end point e, to obtain a skeleton based shape representation $\mathbf{g}(S(F))$, for each subregion $SR_i, i \in (1, 2, \ldots, 21)$, we perform max pooling as follow:

$$\mathbf{g}_i(S(F)) = \max(\mathbf{c}^e | e \in SR_i), \tag{3}$$

where the "max" function is performed in an element-wise manner, i.e. for each codeword, we take the max value of all skeleton codes in a subregion. Max pooling is robust to noise and has been successfully applied to image classification. Thus, $\mathbf{g}(S(F))_i$ is a K dimensional feature vector of the subregion SR_i. The skeleton based shape representation $\mathbf{g}(S(F))$ is a concatenation of the feature vectors of all subregions:

$$\mathbf{g}(S(F)) = (\mathbf{g}_1^T(S(F)), \mathbf{g}_2^T(S(F)), \ldots, \mathbf{g}_{21}^T(S(F)))^T. \tag{4}$$

Finally, $\mathbf{g}(S(F))$ is normalized by its ℓ_2 norm: $\mathbf{g}(S(F)) = \mathbf{g}(S(F))/\|\mathbf{g}(S(F))\|_2$.

3.3   Shape Classification by Combining Contour and Skeleton

For a given shape F, to combine its contour $C(F)$ and skeleton $S(F)$ to classify it, we simply concatenate its BCF representation $\mathbf{f}(C(F))$ with its BSP representation $\mathbf{g}(S(F))$ to form a shape feature vector: $\mathbf{x}(F) = (\mathbf{f}^T(C(F)), \mathbf{g}^T(S(F)))^T$. Given a training set $\{(\mathbf{x}_i, y_i)\}_{i=1}^M$ consists of M shapes from L classes, where $\mathbf{x}_i$ and $y_i \in \{1, 2, \ldots, L\}$ are the concatenated shape feature vector and the class label of i-th shapes respectively, we train a multi-class linear SVM [6] as the classifier:

$$\min_{\mathbf{w}_1, \ldots, \mathbf{w}_L} \sum_{j=1}^M \|\mathbf{w}_j\|^2 + \alpha \sum_i \max(0, 1 + \mathbf{w}_{l_i}^T \mathbf{x}_i - \mathbf{w}_{y_i}^T \mathbf{x}_i), \tag{5}$$

where $l_i = \arg\max_{l \in \{1,2,\ldots,L\}, l \neq y_i} \mathbf{w}_l^T \mathbf{x}_i$ and α is a parameter to balance the weight between the regularization term (left part) and the multi-class hinge-loss term (right part). For a testing shape vector $\mathbf{x}$, its class label is given by

$$\widehat{y} = \arg\max_{l \in \{1,2,\ldots,L\}} \mathbf{w}_l^T \mathbf{x}. \tag{6}$$

4   Experimental Results

In this section, we evaluate our method on two shape benchmarks and give the comparisons with the state-of-the-arts.

dog   duck

Fig. 3. Two classes with large intra-class variations inthe Animal dataset [3]

4.1 Experimental Setup

The parameters introduced in our method are set as follow: the number of sampled points on a skeleton paths $T = 50$, the codebook size $K = 1000$, the number of the nearest neighbors used for skeleton paths encoding $k = 5$ and the weight between the the regularization term and the multi-class hinge-loss term in the multi-class linear SVM formulation $\alpha = 10$. We adopt the default parameter settings reported in [20] and [15] to extract BCF shape representation and skeletons, respectively.

For all the shape benchmarks, we randomly select half of the shapes in each class as the training samples and use the rest half for testing. To avoid the basis caused by randomness, such a procedure is repeated 10 times. Average classification accuracy and standard derivation are reported to evaluate the performance of different shape classification methods.

4.2 Animal Dataset

We first test our method on the Animal Dataset [3], which contains 2,000 animal shapes from 20 classes, such as bird, cat and dog. This dataset is the most challenging shape dataset, as each class has 100 shape images with large intra-class variations caused by view point change and significant deformation, such as the shapes shown in Fig. 3. The performances of the proposed method as well as other competing methods are depicted in Table 1. Our method achieves the best performance which outperforms BCF [20] by over 2%. This result proves that the skeleton based mid-level representation is complementary to contour based. Note that, our method is significantly superior to ICS [3], which proves that the proposed combination approach for contour and skeleton is more effective.

Table 1. Classification accuracy comparison on Animal dataset [3]

	Contour Segments [17]	IDSC [12]	ICS [3]	BCF [20]	Ours
Accuracy	69.7%	73.6%	78.4%	$83.40 \pm 1.30\%$	$\mathbf{85.50 \pm 0.88\%}$

4.3 Mpeg7 Dataset

Mpeg7 dataset [10] is the most well-know shape dataset, which contains 1,400 shapes, including animals, artificial objects and symbols. It has 70 classes, in each of which there are 20 different shapes. Table 2 demonstrates the classification accuracies obtained by competing methods. Our method also outperforms others on this dataset, which shows its generality.

The performance gain achieved by the proposed method compared to ICS [3] are mainly due to two reasons: (1) Skeleton is sensitive to contour noise, however max pooling provides the robustness to noise for BSP. Therefore, the combination of BCF and BSP does not induce additional noise; (2) The adopted multi-class linear SVM automatically learns the weights of contour and skeleton features and offers discriminative power, further increasing the accuracy.

Table 2. Classification accuracy comparison on Mpeg7 dataset [10]

	Contour Segments [17]	ICS [3]	BCF [20]	Ours
Accuracy	90.9%	96.6%	$97.16 \pm 0.79\%$	$\mathbf{98.35 \pm 0.63\%}$

5   Conclusion

We have proposed a principled way to explore the complementary nature between contour and skeleton for shape recognition. A contour is represented by Bag of Contour Fragments; While for a skeleton, a novel skeleton based mid-level representation named Bag of Skeleton Paths has been proposed, for the purpose of capturing the geometric features along skeleton paths. Concatenating such two mid-level representations into one provides a compact and informative shape feature vector, which can be well handled by discriminative classifiers, such as multi-class linear SVM. The experimental results obtained on standard benchmarks verify the effectiveness of the proposed combination methods and demonstrate that it consistently outperforms the current stat-of-the-arts.

Acknowledgements. This work was supported in part by the National Natural Science Foundation of China under Grant 61303095 and Grant 61222308, in part by Innovation Program of Shanghai Municipal Education Commission under Grant 14YZ018, in part by Research Fund for the Doctoral Program of Higher Education of China under Grant 20133108120017 and in part by the Excellent Ph.D. Thesis Funding in Huazhong University of Science and Technology and Microsoft Research Asia Fellow 2012.

References

1. Aslan, C., Erdem, A., Erdem, E., Tari, S.: Disconnected skeleton: shape at its absolute scale. IEEE Trans. Pattern Analysis and Machine Intelligence 30(12), 2188–2203 (2008)
2. Bai, X., Latecki, L.: Path similarity skeleton graph matching. IEEE Trans. Pattern Analysis and Machine Intelligence 30(7), 1282–1292 (2008)

3. Bai, X., Liu, W., Tu, Z.: Integrating contour and skeleton for shape classification. In: ICCV Workshops, pp. 360–367 (2009)
4. Bai, X., Rao, C., Wang, X.: Shape vocabulary: A robust and efficient shape representation for shape matching. IEEE Trans. Image Processing 23(9) (2014)
5. Belongie, S., Malik, J., Puzicha, J.: Shape matching and object recognition using shape contexts. IEEE Trans. Pattern Analysis and Machine Intelligence 24(4), 509–522 (2002)
6. Crammer, K., Singer, Y.: On the algorithmic implementation of multiclass kernel-based vector machines. Journal of Machine Learning Research 2, 265–292 (2001)
7. Dalal, N., Triggs, B.: Histograms of oriented gradients for human detection. In: CVPR, pp. 886–893 (2005)
8. Daliri, M.R., Torre, V.: Robust symbolic representation for shape recognition and retrieval. Pattern Recognition 41(5), 1782–1798 (2008)
9. Felzenszwalb, P.F., Schwartz, J.: Hierarchical matching of deformable shapes. In: CVPR (2007)
10. Latecki, L.J., Lakämper, R., Eckhardt, U.: Shape descriptors for non-rigid shapes with a single closed contour. In: CVPR, pp. 1424–1429 (2000)
11. Lazebnik, S., Schmid, C., Ponce, J.: Beyond bags of features: Spatial pyramid matching for recognizing natural scene categories. In: CVPR, pp. 2169–2178 (2006)
12. Lin, H., Jacobs, D.W.: Shape classification using the inner-distance. IEEE Trans. Pattern Analysis and Machine Intelligence 29(2), 286–299 (2007)
13. Lowe, D.G.: Distinctive image features from scale-invariant keypoints. International Journal of Computer Vision 60(2), 91–110 (2004)
14. Sebastian, T., Klein, P., Kimia, B.: Recognition of shapes by editing their shock graphs. IEEE Trans. Pattern Analysis and Machine Intelligence 26(5), 550–571 (2004)
15. Shen, W., Bai, X., Yang, X., Latecki, L.J.: Skeleton pruning as trade-off between skeleton simplicity and reconstruction error. Science China Information Sciences 56(4), 1–14 (2013)
16. Siddiqi, K., Shokoufandeh, A., Dickinson, S., Zucker, S.: Shock graphs and shape matching. Int'l J. Computer Vision 35(1), 13–32 (1999)
17. Sun, K.B., Super, B.J.: Classification of contour shapes using class segment sets. In: CVPR, pp. 727–733 (2005)
18. Wang, B., Shen, W., Liu, W., You, X., Bai, X.: Shape classification using tree -unions. In: ICPR, pp. 983–986 (2010)
19. Wang, J., Yang, J., Yu, K., Lv, F., Huang, T.S., Gong, Y.: Locality-constrained linear coding for image classification. In: CVPR, pp. 3360–3367 (2010)
20. Wang, X., Feng, B., Bai, X., Liu, W., Latecki, L.J.: Bag of contour fragments for robust shape classification. Pattern Recognition 47(6), 2116–2125 (2014)

Visual Texture Perception with Feature Learning Models and Deep Architectures

Yuchen Zheng, Guoqiang Zhong, Jun Liu, Xiaoxu Cai, and Junyu Dong*

Department of Computer Science and Technology, Ocean University of China,
238 Songling Road, Qingdao, China 266100
zhengyuchen@live.shop.edu.cn,
{gqzhong,juneliu,dongjunyu}@ouc.edu.cn, caixiaoxu90@163.com

Abstract. Texture is an important property of images, and a key component for human visual perception. In this work, based on several feature learning models and deep architectures, we study the visual texture perception problem, which is helpful for understanding both the impact of texture itself and the basic mechanisms of human visual systems. Through a series of psychophysical experiments, we find that 12 perceptual features are significant to describe the texture images with regard to the human perceptions. Hence, we represent each texture image with a 12-dimensional vector, corresponding to the values of the 12 perceptual features. To improve the learnablity of existing feature learning models, we propose a set of deep architectures to learn compact representations of the texture perceptual features. Extensive experiments on texture images classification demonstrate the effectiveness of both the feature learning models and the deep architectures. In particular, the advantage of deep architectures over existing feature learning models is shown.

Keywords: Texture visual perception, feature learning, deep architectures.

1 Introduction

Texture is a fundamental property of images, which is generally used to describe a variety of surface characteristics. For example, a textured region might be "like brick", "horizontally oriented", or "rough". Fig. 1 shows some texture images from 20 categories. The appearance of texture allows the observer to determine whether or not two textured images show the same object, and whether or not the objects to be made of the same material. If two adjacent image regions have different textures, this may be helpful for the detection of an intervening border. Image segmentation and shape identification applications may benefit from such texture-defined boundaries. Moreover, nowadays, texture synthesis technologies are used to generate large-scale and colorful scenes in films and games, which can bring dramatic effect for visualization.

---

* To whom correspondence should be addressed.

S. Li et al. (Eds.): CCPR 2014, Part I, CCIS 483, pp. 401–410, 2014.

Fig. 1. Texture images from 20 categories

Visual texture perception is among the most important problems studied in several related areas, including image processing, computer vision, computer graphics, and virtual reality. The study of visual texture perception is helpful for understanding both the impact of texture itself, and the basic mechanisms of human visual systems [10]. In the literature, many papers on texture representation have been published [3, 4, 15, 19]. Particularly, Rao and Lohse found that three dimensions appeared to suffice for sets of natural textures [15], while Gurnsey and Fleet showed that three dimensional representations were sufficient for artificial ones as well [3]. Additionally, few psychophysical tests on statistical characterizations of texture were carried out [2,8]. Kurtosis and density were found to be the most sensitive to the observers, respectively. However, on the one hand, very few texture images were provided to the observers in the estimation of the perceptual features (e.g., only 56 texture images were used in the psychophysical test organized by Rao and Lohse [15]), and on the other hand, rare work has exploited the semantic structure underlying the perceptual features.

In order to address the above two issues, we have conducted a series of psychophysical tests and numerical experiments. 450 texture images were generated using 23 process texture models, while 81 observers were invited to estimate the texture perceptual features. We found that 12 perceptual features were significant to describe the texture images with regard to the observers' perceptions. They are contrast, repetitiveness, granularity, randomness, roughness, density, direction, structural complexity, coarseness, regularity, orientation and uniformity. Hence, in this work, we represent each texture image with a 12-dimensional vector, corresponding to the values of the 12 perceptual features. For the detail settings of our psychophysical experiments, please refer to Section 4.1. To learn the semantic structure underlying the perceptual representations of textures, we implemented 8 feature learning models, and compared their performance. In order to further improve the learnablity of the feature learning models, we propose a set of deep architectures. The performance of these deep architectures was tested on the texture perceptual features as well.

The rest of this paper is organized as follows: In Section 2, we introduce the feature learning models used in our experiments. In Section 3, we present the proposed deep architectures in detail. The experimental settings and results are reported in section 4, while Section 5 concludes this paper with remarks and future work.

2   Feature Learning Models

Feature learning models are often used to compress high-dimensional data to avoid the curse of dimensionality and mitigate undesired properties of high-dimensional spaces [13]. Since some decades ago, many feature learning models have been proposed [5, 7, 13, 21–24]. In this work, to learn the semantic structure of the texture perceptual features, we have tested 8 feature learning models, and compared their performance. They are principal components analysis (PCA) [7], Sammon mapping (Sammon) [17], stochastic neighbor embedding (SNE) [5], probabilistic principal components analysis (PPCA) [18], multidimensional scaling (MDS) [9], local tangent space alignment (LTSA) [21], linear local tangent space alignment (LLTSA) [20] and Gaussian process latent variable models(GPLVM) [11].

The feature learning problem is generally formulated as follow. Given n data, $\{\mathbf{x}_1, \ldots, \mathbf{x}_n\} \in \Re^D$, where D is the dimensionality of the data space, we seeks the compact representations of these data, i.e. $\{\mathbf{y}_1, \ldots, \mathbf{y}_n\} \in \Re^d$, where d is the dimensionality of the low dimensional embeddings. Due to space limitation, in the following, we only introduce principal components analysis (PCA) [7], linear local tangent space alignment (LLTSA) [20] and stochastic neighbor embedding (SNE), that related to the proposed deep architectures in Section 3. For other models, please refer to the corresponding reference papers.

2.1   Principal Components Analysis (PCA)

PCA [7] is a linear feature learning model. Assume that the data is zero mean. The data covariance matrix can be defined as

$$\mathbf{C} = \frac{1}{n} \sum_{i=1}^{n} \mathbf{x}_i \mathbf{x}_i^T. \tag{1}$$

Since C is a positive semi-definite matrix, it can be diagonalized as

$$\mathbf{C} = \mathbf{B} \Lambda \mathbf{B}^T, \tag{2}$$

where $\Lambda = diag(\lambda_1, \lambda_2, \cdots, \lambda_n)$, and $\mathbf{BB}^T = \mathbf{I}$ ($\mathbf{I}$ is an identity matrix). We choose the eigenvectors corresponding to the d largest eigenvalues to form the projection matrix.

2.2   Linear Local Tangent Space Alignment (LLTSA)

LLTSA [20] is a linear version of local tangent space alignment (LTSA) [21]. Its objective function has the following form:

$$\underset{\mathbf{A}}{\operatorname{argmin}} \ \operatorname{tr}(\mathbf{A}^T \mathbf{X} \mathbf{H}_N \mathbf{B} \mathbf{H}_N \mathbf{X}^T \mathbf{A})$$

$$s.t. \ \mathbf{A}^T \mathbf{X} \mathbf{H}_N \mathbf{X}^T \mathbf{A} = \mathbf{I}_d, \tag{3}$$

where $\mathbf{A}$ is the projection matrix, $\mathbf{B}$ is a matrix encoding the local information of the given data, $\mathbf{H}_N = \mathbf{I} - \mathbf{ee}^T/N$ is the centering matrix and $\mathbf{I}_d$ is an identity matrix of size $d \times d$. Problem (3) can be easily solved using a generalized eigenvalue decomposition method.

2.3   Stochastic Neighbor Embedding (SNE)

SNE [5] minimizes the Kullback-Leibler divergences:

$$C = \sum_i \sum_j p_{ij} \log \frac{p_{ij}}{q_{ij}} = \sum_i KL(P_i \parallel Q_i), \tag{4}$$

where

$$p_{ij} = \frac{\exp(- \parallel \mathbf{x}_i - \mathbf{x}_j \parallel^2 /2\sigma_i^2)}{\sum_{k \neq i} \exp(- \parallel \mathbf{x}_i - \mathbf{x}_k \parallel^2 /2\sigma_i^2)}, \tag{5}$$

and

$$q_{ij} = \frac{\exp(- \parallel \mathbf{y}_i - \mathbf{y}_j \parallel^2)}{\sum_{k \neq i} \exp(- \parallel \mathbf{y}_i - \mathbf{y}_k \parallel^2)}. \tag{6}$$

It is aimed at preserving the neighborhood relationship between data in the low dimensional space. The optimization of SNE is based on a gradient descent procedure.

3   Deep Architectures

In order to improve existing feature learning models for visual texture perception, we exploit deep architectures. However, since the data sets collected for texture perception is generally not large, and the dimensionality of perceptual features is low, previous deep learning methods, such as deep autoencoders [6] and deep Boltzmann machines (RBM) [16], might not perform well. Hence, here, we propose a set of novel deep architectures.

Assume that the dimensionality of the original data is D, and the dimensionality of the low dimensional embeddings is d. The mapping of data by our deep architectures can be described as

$$D \Longrightarrow D_1 \Longrightarrow \cdots \Longrightarrow D_i \Longrightarrow \cdots \Longrightarrow D_{p-1} \Longrightarrow d, \qquad (7)$$

where D_i represents the dimensionality of the i-th intermediate representation space, and p is the total steps of mappings. In our work, $D = 12$ and d is set to $\{3, 4, 5, 6\}$, respectively. Here, the range of d is estimated using the technique of [13]. It indicates that, the intrinsic dimensionality of the perceptual features is among $\{3, 4, 5, 6\}$. In the following, we introduce the proposed deep architectures in detail.

3.1 Data Mapping

To simplify the learning of the deep architectures, we design them with 3 to 6 hidden layers. If the dimensionality of the target embedding space is 6, we first project the original data to a 10 dimensional space using PCA, then we use LLTSA map the 10 dimensional meta-data to a 8 dimensional space. Finally, we use LLTSA again map the 8 dimensional meta-data to the 6 dimensional space. This process can be described as

$$12D \xrightarrow{PCA} 10D \xrightarrow{LLTSA} 8D \xrightarrow{LLTSA} 6D. \qquad (8)$$

Similarly, if the dimensionality of the target embedding space is 5, we map the perceptual features as follows:

$$12D \xrightarrow{PCA} 10D \xrightarrow{LLTSA} 8D \xrightarrow{LLTSA} 6D \xrightarrow{LLTSA} 5D. \qquad (9)$$

If the dimensionality of the target embedding space is 4, the following mapping process is used:

$$12D \xrightarrow{PCA} 10D \xrightarrow{PCA} 8D \xrightarrow{LLTSA} 6D \xrightarrow{LLTSA} 5D \xrightarrow{LLTSA} 4D. \qquad (10)$$

If the dimensionality of the target embedding space is 3, we map the data using the following architecture:

$$12D \xrightarrow{SNE} 10D \xrightarrow{SNE} 8D \xrightarrow{SNE} 6D \xrightarrow{SNE} 5D \xrightarrow{SNE} 4D \xrightarrow{SNE} 3D \qquad (11)$$

Note that, here, SNE instead of PCA and LLTSA is used.

In the above deep architectures, we mainly use PCA, LLTSA and SNE for mapping the high dimensional data to low dimensional spaces. The reason is that PCA and LLTSA can be used to find a linear subspace that preserves global (PCA) or local (LLTSA) geometrical information of data, while SNE is a nonlinear feature learning model, which preserves the similarity between nearby data.

4   Experimental Results

4.1   Psychophysical Experiments

To conduct the psychophysical experiments for visual texture perception, we generated 450 texture images using 23 process texture models (23 categories) [12]. Fig. 1 shows some example images randomly selected from this data set. 81 observers (graduate students in computer science major) were invited to estimate the perceptual features. The score was between 1 and 9. A '1' meant that the perceptual feature was very weak, while a '9' very strong. For each perceptual feature of a texture image, we used the mean of the scores given by the observers as the final score. The perceptual features are designed based on previous work on texture perception [3, 15]. Through a thorough analysis to the psychophysical test results, we found that 12 perceptual features are significant to describe the texture images with regard to the observers' perceptions. They are contrast, repetitiveness, granularity, randomness, roughness, density, direction, structural complexity, coarseness, regularity, orientation and uniformity. Hence, to further explore the visual texture perceptions using pattern analysis approaches, we represent each texture image with a 12-dimensional vector, corresponding to the values of the 12 perceptual features.

4.2   Visualization

To visualize the 12-dimensional perceptual features in 2D and 3D spaces, we used SNE to learn the low dimensional embeddings of the original data. Fig. 2 shows the learned results. We can easily see that, in the original data space, different classes are heavily overlapped with each other, and it's very challenging to distinguish the classes from each others.

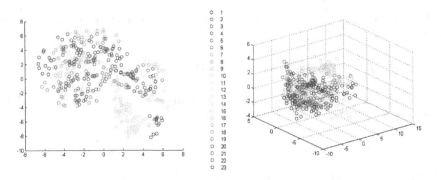

Fig. 2. 2D and 3D embeddings of the original data. Here, different colors represent different classes.

Fig. 3 shows two texture images of two different categories. However, the appearance of these two images are very similar. The psychophysical test results show that the 12 perceptual features of the left image are (5.3, 6.05, 4.8, 3.35, 4.75,

5, 5.25, 3.65, 5, 5.3, 5.6, 6.7), and that of the right image are (5.65, 6.7, 4.75, 2.9, 4.3, 5.15, 4.65, 3.85, 4.4, 6.05, 5.35, 6.75). Even human are very difficult to distinguish them from each other. Due to this fact, we considered to combine data belonging to different classes but with similar appearance together. In this case, we obtained a 13-class problem. Fig. 4 shows the 2D and 3D embeddings of the combined data.

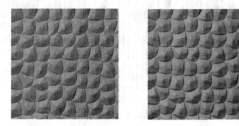

Fig. 3. Tow texture images belong to different categories, but are with very similar appearance

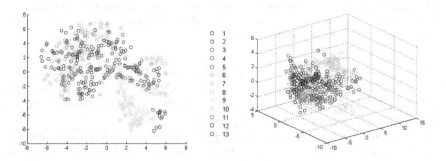

Fig. 4. 2D and 3D embeddings of the combined data

4.3   Classification

To evaluate the feature learning models and the proposed deep architectures for visual texture perceptions, we compared them on both the original and the combined perceptual data. Support vector machine (SVM) with radial basis function (RBF) kernel [1] was used as classifier. The average classification results based on 5-fold cross validation were reported. As mentioned above, we tested the compared methods on different settings with respect to the dimensionality of the low dimensional embeddings. Concretely, the dimensionality of the low dimensional embeddings was set to 3, 4, 5, 6, respectively. For linear feature learning models, we used the learned projection matrix to map the test data into the low-dimensional subspace, whilst for nonlinear feature learning models, we found 3 nearest neighbors of a test datum in the training data first, and then, used their low dimensional embeddings to estimate the low dimensional representation of the test datum. For the proposed deep architecture, we mapped

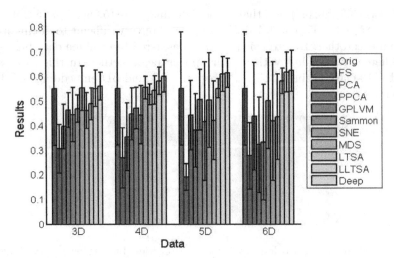

Fig. 5. Classification accuracy and standard deviation obtained by the compared methods on the original data. Here, 'Orig' means that the classification results were obtained in the original data space, 'FS' means that the classification results were obtained by feature selection approaches, and 'Deep' means that the classification results were obtained by the proposed deep architectures.

the test data layer by layer to seek their low dimensional representations. For the code of GPLVM, we directly used that provided by van der Maaten [13]. For SNE, LTSA and LLTSA, we set the number of nearest neighbors, k, for the adjacency graph construction, to 'adaptive' [14].

To facilitate the comparison, we also presented the classification results obtained in the original space (Orig) and that by feature selection (FS) approaches. Here, the feature selection approaches were based on the significance of the perceptual features: for the 3-dimensional space, we used the perceptual features corresponding to *regularity*, *direction* and *density*; for the 4-dimensional space, we added the perceptual features corresponding to *contrast*; for the 5-dimensional space, we added the perceptual features corresponding to roughness further; finally, for the 6-dimensional space, we added the perceptual features corresponding to *structural complexity*.

Fig. 5 shows the classification results obtained by the compared methods. We can see that, firstly, feature learning methods consistently perform better than feature selection approaches; secondly, both the feature learning models and the proposed deep architectures are effective for the visual texture perception problem; thirdly, deep architectures perform better than or at least comparable with the compared feature learning models, and they are very robust in each scenarios.

One more interesting point we can see from Fig. 5 is that, the obtained results are basically consistent with the theories of Rao and Lohse [15], and Gurnsey and Fleet [3], that three dimensional representations are sufficient for texture images. However, we emphasize that the three dimensional representations are indeed learned from the perceptual features, but not (carefully) selected from them. In

Table 1. Classification accuracy obtained by the compared methods on the combined data. The best two results for each scenario are highlighted in bold face.

Method	3D	4D	5D	6D
Orig(12D)	**0.8212**	**0.8212**	**0.8212**	0.8212
FS	0.4291	0.6738	0.6866	0.7278
PCA	0.6657	0.7356	0.7703	**0.8352**
PPCA	0.6513	0.7043	0.7531	0.7961
GPLVM	0.6748	0.7067	0.7313	0.6171
Sammon	0.7014	0.7284	0.7400	0.7544
SNE	0.7211	0.7450	0.7534	0.7472
MDS	0.6832	0.7060	0.7313	0.7441
LTSA	0.6555	0.6720	0.7088	0.6796
LLTSA	0.6746	0.7563	0.7766	0.8063
Deep	**0.7381**	**0.7689**	**0.7916**	**0.8234**

our experiments, we carefully selected the features based on their significance to observers' perceptions. However, it is easy to see that, the feature selection method performed worst in each scenario, compared with the feature learning models and deep architectures. Hence, the "three dimensional representations" should be the intrinsic representations of the texture perceptual features.

Table 1 shows the classification results obtained by the compared methods on the combined data. It is easy to see that, deep architectures could slightly improve the compared feature learning models for most of the scenarios. Since the number of texture images was small and the dimensionality of perceptual features was low, deep architectures didn't deliver significant improvement over all the existing feature learning models. However, the improvement still shows the advantage of the deep architectures for visual texture perception problems.

From Table 1, it is easy to see that, there is an obvious gap between the results obtained in the three-dimensional representation space and that in the six-dimensional representation space, for most of the compared methods. This indicates that, for **complex** texture images, three-dimensional representations is not enough to represent the intrinsic characteristics of the images. We may need to learn higher dimensional representations for the textural images.

5   Conclusion

In this paper, based on 8 feature learning models and a set of the proposed deep architectures, we exploit the visual texture perception problem. Extensive experiments on texture image classification demonstrate the effectiveness of both the feature learning models and the proposed deep architectures. Particularly, the advantage of the deep architectures is shown. In future work, we plan to design and test more deep architectures (either with or without pre-training, either using or not using back propagation fine-tuning, etc) for visual texture perceptions. Furthermore, we plan to construct a large scale visual texture perception data set, and use it to evaluate deep learning models, such as that of [6] [16], for the texture perception and recognition problems.

References

1. Chang, C.C., Lin, C.J.: Libsvm: A library for support vector machines. ACM Transactions on Intelligent Systems and Technology (TIST) 2(3), 27 (2011)
2. Durgin, F.: Texture contrast aftereffects are monocular, texture density aftereffects are binocular. Vision Research 41, 2619–2630 (2001)
3. Gurnsey, R., Fleet, D.: Texture space. Vision Research 41, 745–757 (2001)
4. Heeger, D., Bergen, J.: Pyramid-based Texture Analysis/Synthesis. In: SIGGRAPH, pp. 229–238. ACM (1995)
5. Hinton, G., Roweis, S.: Stochastic Neighbor Embedding. In: NIPS, vol. 2, pp. 833–840 (2002)
6. Hinton, G., Salakhutdinov, R.: Reducing the Dimensionality of Data with Neural Networks. Science 313(5786), 504–507 (2006)
7. Jolliffe, I.: Principal Component Analysis, 2nd edn. Springer (October 2002)
8. Kingdom, F., Hayes, A., Field, D.: Sensitivity to contrast histogram differences in synthetic wavelet-textures. Vision Research 41, 585–598 (2001)
9. Kruskal, J., Wish, M.: Multidimensional Scaling, vol. 11. Sage (1978)
10. Landy, M., Graham, N.: Visual Perception of Texture. In: The Visual Neurosciences, pp. 1106–1118. MIT Press (2004)
11. Lawrence, N.: Gaussian Process Latent Variable Models for Visualisation of High Dimensional Data. In: NIPS, vol. 2, p. 5 (2003)
12. Liu, J., Dong, J., Qi, L., Chantler, M.: Identifying perceptual features of procedural textures. In: ECVP (2013)
13. van der Maaten, L.: An Introduction to Dimensionality Reduction Using MATLAB. Report 1201(07-07), 62 (2007)
14. Mekuz, N., Tsotsos, J.K.: Parameterless isomap with adaptive neighborhood selection. In: Franke, K., Müller, K.-R., Nickolay, B., Schäfer, R. (eds.) DAGM 2006. LNCS, vol. 4174, pp. 364–373. Springer, Heidelberg (2006)
15. Rao, A., Lohse, G.: Towards a Texture Naming System: Identifying Relevant Dimensions of Texture. Vision Research 36, 1649–1669 (1996)
16. Salakhutdinov, R., Hinton, G.: Deep Boltzmann Machines. In: AISTATS, pp. 448–455 (2009)
17. Sammon, J.: A Nonlinear Mapping for Data Structure Analysis. IEEE Transactions on Computers 18(5), 401–409 (1969)
18. Tipping, M., Bishop, C.: Probabilistic Principal Component Analysis. Journal of the Royal Statistical Society: Series B (Statistical Methodology) 61(3), 611–622 (1999)
19. Wolfson, S., Landy, M.: Examining Edge- and Region-based Texture Mechanisms. Vision Research 38(3), 439–446 (1998)
20. Zhang, T., Yang, J., Zhao, D., Ge, X.: Linear Local Tangent Space Alignment and Application to Face Recognition. Neurocomputing 70(7), 1547–1553 (2007)
21. Zhang, Z., Zha, H.: Principal Manifolds and Nonlinear Dimensionality Reduction via Tangent Space Alignment. SIAM J. Scientific Computing 26(1), 313–338 (2004)
22. Zhong, G., Cheriet, M.: Large Margin Low Rank Tensor Analysis. Neural Computation 26(4), 761–780 (2014)
23. Zhong, G., Li, W.J., Yeung, D.Y., Hou, X., Liu, C.L.: Gaussian Process Latent Random Field. In: AAAI (2010)
24. Zhong, G., Liu, C.L.: Error-Correcting Output Codes Based Ensemble Feature Extraction. Pattern Recognition 46(4), 1091–1100 (2013)

Objects Detection Method by Learning Lifted Wavelet Filters[*]

Aireti Abulikemu, Aliya Yushan,
Turghunjan Abdukirim Turki[**], and Abdurusul Osman

School of Mathematical Sciences, Xinjiang Normal University, Urumqi, China
tabdukirim@sina.com, thj@xjnu.edu.cn

Abstract. A fast objects detection method is proposed, which is based on the variance-maximization learning of lifting dyadic wavelet filters. First, we derive a difference equation from two kinds of lifting high-pass components of a target image. The difference equation is an approximation of an inverse problem of an elliptic equation, which includes free parameters of the lifting filter. Since this discrete inverse problem is ill-conditioned, the free parameters are learned by using the least square method and a regularization method. Objects detection is done by applying the learned lifting filter to a query image.

Keywords: Lifting wavelet filter, Difference equation, Inverse problem, Regularization, Learning, Objects detection.

1 Introduction

So far, many pattern recognition techniques have been developed: template matching method, graph matching method [2], principle component analysis [3], self-organizing map[4], support vector machine [5] and etc. However, many problems still remain to be resolved. For example, we have a problem of robustness for noise, illumination, scale and so on. The speed of recognition is also an important problem. The accuracy of recognition is required for practical applications.

In this paper, we propose a method for recognizing a target image by using lifting wavelet filters, which were introduced by Sweldens [6]. Our method is based on the learning of lifting filters adaptive to training images. We first compute low-pass components and two kinds of high-pass components in vertical and horizontal directions, respectively, by applying lifting wavelet transform to a target image. These high-pass components include free parameters to be learned. Next, we derive a difference scheme from the condition that the sum of both high-pass components vanishes. The difference scheme is just an equation for solving approximately the inverse problem of an elliptic equation. Since this discrete inverse problem is ill-conditioned, we identify the free parameters by employing the least square method and a regularization method. This identification gives a learning process of lifting wavelet filters. Thus, a lifting filter

---

[*] Foundation item: Supported by the National Natural Science Foundation of china under Grant Nos. 11261061, 61362039, 10661010; The National Natural Science Foundation of Xinjiang Province of china under Grant No.200721104.

[**] Corresponding authors.

S. Li et al. (Eds.): CCPR 2014, Part I, CCIS 483, pp. 411–417, 2014.

with the learned free parameters is constructed. Applying the lifting filter to a query image, we extract images similar to the target image. The extracted images are recognized as the target image.

2   Lifting Wavelet Filters

In this section, we use Sweldens lifting scheme for constructing a new bi-orthogonal wavelet filter from an initial bi-orthogonal wavelet filter [1]. We consider a set of wavelet filters $\left\{ h_n, g_n, \tilde{h}_n, \tilde{g}_n \right\}$ in which h_n and g_n are called low-pass and high-pass analysis filters, respectively, and $\tilde{h}_n$ and $\tilde{g}_n$ are low-pass and high-pass synthesis filters, respectively. The filters $\left\{ h_n, g_n, \tilde{h}_n, \tilde{g}_n \right\}$ are called bi-orthogonal wavelet filters if they satisfy the bi-orthogonal condition:

$$\sum_m h_{m-2k}\tilde{h}_{m-2k'} = \delta_{k,k'}, \quad \sum_m h_{m-2k}\tilde{g}_{m-2l} = 0$$

$$\sum_m g_{m-2l}\tilde{h}_{m-2k'} = 0, \quad \sum_m g_{m-2l}\tilde{g}_{m-2l'} = \delta_{l,l'} \quad (1)$$

with Kronecker's delta symbol $\delta_{k,k'}$. Let $\left\{ h_n^o, g_n^o, \tilde{h}_n^o, \tilde{g}_n^o \right\}$ satisfy (1). Sweldens lifting scheme is written as

$$h_n = h_n^o,$$
$$g_n = g_n^o - \sum_k \lambda_k h_{n-2k}^o,$$
$$\tilde{h}_n = \tilde{h}_n^o + \sum_k \lambda_{-k}\tilde{g}_{n-2k}^o,$$
$$\tilde{g}_n = \tilde{g}_n^o \quad (2)$$

where λ_k are free parameters. Sweldens proved that the lifting filters $\left\{ h_n, g_n, \tilde{h}_n, \tilde{g}_n \right\}$ satisfy the bi-orthogonal condition (1). In this paper, we propose the design of an adaptive filter by learning free parameters λ_k in the lifting filter (2) for detecting objects in an image. And we recognize the objects by applying the learned filter to a query image.

3   Wavelet Decomposition

Let $A_{i,j}^1$ denote an image. Applying the lifting wavelet filters h_n and g_n to the image $A_{i,j}^1$, we can decompose $A_{i,j}^1$ into the following four components:

$$A_{m,k}^o = \sum_{i,j} h_{i-2m}h_{j-2k}A_{i,j}^1 \quad (3)$$

$$D^o_{m,k} = \sum_{i,j} h_{i-2m} g_{j-2k} A^1_{i,j} \tag{4}$$

$$E^o_{m,k} = \sum_{i,j} g_{i-2m} h_{j-2k} A^1_{i,j} \tag{5}$$

$$F^o_{m,k} = \sum_{i,j} g_{i-2m} g_{j-2k} A^1_{i,j} \tag{6}$$

Here $A^o_{m,k}$, $D^o_{m,k}$, $E^o_{m,k}$, and $F^o_{m,k}$ indicate the low frequency components, the high frequency components in the y-direction, in the x-direction, and in the xy-direction, respectively. We call (3), (4), (5) and (6) wavelet decomposition formulas. Figure 1 shows an example of wavelet decomposition.

Conversely, by virtue of the bi-orthogonality (1), we can reconstruct the original image $A^1_{i,j}$ from $A^o_{m,k}$, $D^o_{m,k}$, $E^o_{m,k}$, and $F^o_{m,k}$ by the formula:

$$A^1_{i,j} = \sum_{m,k} \left(\tilde{h}_{m-2i}\tilde{h}_{k-2j}A^0_{m,k} + \tilde{h}_{m-2i}\tilde{g}_{k-2j}D^0_{m,k} + \tilde{g}_{m-2i}\tilde{h}_{k-2j}E^0_{m,k} + \tilde{g}_{m-2i}\tilde{g}_{k-2j}F^0_{m,k} \right) \tag{7}$$

We call (7) a wavelet reconstruction formula.

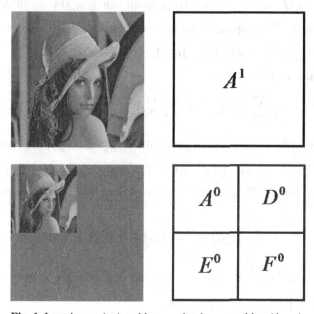

Fig. 1. Lena image (up) and its wavelet decomposition (down)

4   Learning of Free Parameters

In this section, we denote a sub-image again by $u_{i,j}$. Applying the low-pass analysis filter h^o_n in vertical direction to the image $u_{i,j}$, and the lifting filter (2) in horizontal direction to the resulting components, we obtain

$$D_{m,k} = D_{m,k}^o - \sum_{l=-L}^{L} \lambda_l^d A_{m+l,k}^o, \tag{8}$$

Here λ_l^d's denote free parameters in horizontal direction and

$$A_{m,k}^o = \sum_{i,j} h_{i-2m}^o h_{j-2k}^o u_{i,j}, \quad D_{m,k}^o = \sum_{i,j} g_{i-2m}^o h_{j-2k}^o u_{i,j}.$$

Next, we apply the low-pass analysis filter h_n^o in horizontal direction to the image $u_{i,j}$ j, and the lifting filter (2) in vertical direction to the resulting components to get

$$E_{m,k} = E_{m,k}^o - \sum_{l=-L}^{L} \lambda_l^e A_{m,k+l}^o, \tag{9}$$

Here λ_l^e's denote free parameters in vertical direction and

$$E_{m,k}^o = \sum_{j,i} g_{j-2m}^o h_{i-2k}^o u_{i,j}.$$

We denote by Ω a set of positions (m,k) such that $(2m,2k)$ are in the domain of the target image $u_{i,j}$. We impose on the free parameters λ_l^d land λ_l^e _the condition

$$D_{m,k} + E_{m,k} = 0, \ (m,k) \in \Omega$$

which is equivalent to

$$D_{m,k}^o + E_{m,k}^o - \left(\sum_{l=-L}^{L} \lambda_l^d A_{m+l,k}^o + \sum_{l=-L}^{L} \lambda_l^e A_{m,k+l}^o \right) = 0, \ (m,k) \in \Omega \tag{10}$$

We choose the initial high-pass filter g_n^o as $g_{-1}^o = g_1^o = 0.25\sqrt{2}$, $g_0^o = -0.5\sqrt{2}$ and $g_n^o = 0 \ (n \neq -1,0,1)$. Actually, there exist such bi-orthogonal wavelet filters. Then, (10) gives a difference scheme that approximates the elliptic equation

$$\frac{\partial^2}{\partial x^2}(I_y u) + \frac{\partial^2}{\partial y^2}(I_x u) - I(\lambda^d, \lambda^e)u = 0, \tag{11}$$

Here $I_x u, I_y u$ and $I(\lambda^d, \lambda^e)$)indicate the following integral operators

$$I_x u(x,y) = \int h^o(s) u(x+s, y) ds,$$

$$I_y u(x,y) = \int h^o(t) u(x, y+t) dt,$$

$$I(\lambda^d, \lambda^e)u(x,y) = \int \int h^o(s) h^o(t) \left(\sum_{l=-L}^{L} \lambda_l^d u(x+s+2l, y+l) + \sum_{l=-L}^{L} \lambda_l^e u(x+s, y+t+2l) \right) ds dt,$$

respectively, $\lambda^d = (\lambda_{-L}^d, \cdots, \lambda_L^d)$ and $\lambda^e = (\lambda_{-L}^e, \cdots, \lambda_L^e)$.

The problem of determining λ^d and λ^e from (11) is an inverse problem, and (10) can be regarded as an approximation of the inverse problem. It is well-known that the inverse problem (11) is ill-conditioned. So, the difference scheme (10) is also an ill-conditioned equation, and it must be solved by utilizing some regularization methods.

We present a method for determining free parameters λ^d and λ^e appearing in (10) adaptive to a target image. From now on, we call the target image positive data, and another image negative data. Using these data, we solve (10) by combining the least square method with a regularization method. Practically, the solution can be described as

$$
\begin{aligned}
&\sum_{(m,k)\in\Omega} \left(\sum_{l=-L}^{L} \lambda_l^d A_{m+l,k}^o + \sum_{l=-L}^{L} \lambda_l^e A_{m,k+l}^o - w_{m,k} \right)^2 \\
&-K \sum_{(m,k)\notin\Omega} \left(\sum_{l=-L}^{L} \lambda_l^d A_{m+l,k}^o + \sum_{l=-L}^{L} \lambda_l^e A_{m,k+l}^o - w_{m,k} \right)^2 \to \min..
\end{aligned} \tag{12}
$$

Here $w_{m,k}$ represents

$$
w_{m,k} = D_{m,k}^o + E_{m,k}^o,
$$

and K is a positive constant.

5   Extraction Algorithm

The second term on the left-hand side is added for separating positive and negative data. In simulation, we see that it also plays the role of regularization. The solution of the minimization problem (12) can be obtained by solving a linear system of simultaneous equations, which are derived by differentiating the functional on the left-hand side of (12), with respect to the free parameters λ_l^d and λ_l^e. The size of coefficient matrix of the linear system depends on the number of the free parameters. Usually, it is small. Therefore, we can solve the linear system fast by employing Gauss elimination method. Thus, we can construct a lifting filter (2) with the learned free parameters λ^d and λ^e.

Pattern recognition is done by exploiting the learned lifting filter. The process of pattern recognition includes the following steps:

1. Compute the low frequency components $A_{m,k}^o$ and the high frequency components $D_{m,k}^o$ and $E_{m,k}^o$;kby applying the initial analysis filters h_n^o and g_n^o to a query image.

2. Compute the new high frequency components $D_{m,k}$ and $E_{m,k}$ defined by (8) and (9), where the free parameters λ^d and λ^e are learned for the target image.

3. Find the positions (m, k) where $D_{m,k}$ and $E_{m,k}$ are less than a threshold.

4. Extract the block with the same size as the target image, in which the searched positions $(m, k))$ concentrate.

5. Recognize an image in the extracted block as the target image.

Our recognition algorithm is very fast, because only two kinds of learned filters are applied to a query image for searching similar images to the target image.

6   Experimental Results

We carry out simulations of face recognition. "Smile" and "angry" images are prepared for learning a lifting filter, which are shown in Figure 2.

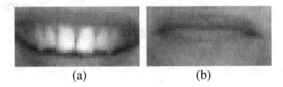

(a)   (b)

Fig. 2. (a) Smile image, (b) Angry image

Considering the smile image as positive data, and the angry image as negative data, we learn a lifting filter. The penalty constant K in (12) is chosen as $K = 1$. Applying the initial filters listed in Table 1 [1] to these images, we compute low-pass components and two kinds of high-pass components.

Table 1. Bi-orthogonal wavelet filter

n	$g_n^o / \sqrt{2}$	$h_n^o / \sqrt{2}$
-3		0.028615978889
-2		-0.057231957778
-1	0.25	-0.120372564768
0	-0.5	0.297977087314
1	0.25	0.702022912686
2		0.297977087314
3		-0.120372564768
4		-0.057231957778
5		0.028615978889

First, large high-pass components are extracted from both images, which are plotted in Figure 3. Figure 4 shows the positions detected from both images using the learned filter. The number of extracted positions in the smile image is much more than in the angry image.

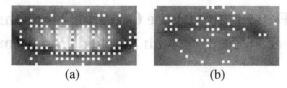

(a)   (b)

Fig. 3. (a) Large high-pass components of the smile image, (b) Large high-pass components of the angry image

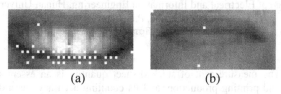

(a)   (b)

Fig. 4. (a) Extracted positions in the smile image, (b) Extracted positions in the angry image

7   Conclusions

We have proposed a fast and robust method capable of detecting objects in an image. The method is based on the variance-maximization learning of free parameters in a lifting dyadic wavelet filter. Our learning and detecting algorithms are very fast, because only one set of free parameters is learned and only one lifting filter with the learned parameters is applied to a query image for finding objects similar to the target object.

References

1. Abdukirim Turki, T., Niijima, K., Takano, S.: Design of bi-orthogonal wavelet filters using dyadic lifting scheme. Bulletin of Informatics and Cybernetics 37(1), 123–136 (2005)
2. Wiskott, L., Fellous, J.M., Krfiger, N., vonder Malsburg, C.: Face recognition by elastic bunch graph matching. IEEE Transaction on PAMI 19(7), 775–779 (1997)
3. Turk, M., Pentland, A.: Eigen faces for recognition. Journal of Congnitive Neuroscience 3(1), 71–86 (1991)
4. Burel, G., Carel, D.: Detection and localization of faces on digital images. Pattern Recognition Letters 15(10), 963–967 (1994)
5. Osuna, E., Freund, R., Girosi, F.: Training support vector machines: An application to face detection. In: Proceedings of the IEEE International Conference on Computer Vision and Pattern Recognition, pp. 130–136 (1997)
6. Sweldens, W.: The lifting scheme: A custom-design construction of biorthogonal wavelets. Appl. Comput. Harmon. Anal. 3(2), 186–200 (1996)
7. Abdukirim Turki, T., Hussain, M., Niijima, K., Takano, S.: The dyadic lifting schemes and the de-noising of digital image. International Journal of Wavelets, Multi-resolution and Information Processing 6(3), 331–351 (2008)
8. Abdukirim Turki, T.: Lifting Dyadic Wavelet Theory and Design of Filters for Image Processing. Ph.D Thesis, Kyushu University (February 2005)

A Fast Straight-Line Growing Algorithm for Sheet-Counting with Stacked-Paper Images

ZhenXiao Gang, Yang Shuo, and Changyan Xiao

College of Electrical and Information Engineering, Hunan University
Changsha, P.R. China
zl199124@gmail.com

Abstract. The measurement of stacked-sheet quantity is an essential step in packaging and printing production, and its counting accuracy has a direct impact on economic efficiency of related companies. With its noncontact, nondestructivity and real-time measurement merits, the machine vision method has been widely applied to quality control for high-end printing products. In this paper, we aim to circumvent the fringe detection problem in stacked-sheet images by introducing a level line guided line-segment growing algorithm. Then, a high-accuracy measurement of stack quantity can be realized with the improvement of precision and completeness on fringe identification.Our work mainly consists of three parts: 1) A unidirectional gradient operator is adopted to eliminate multiple responses on a single fringe. 2) The gradient magnitude and level-line direction are combined to improve the growth of line support regions in noisy environment. 3) To completely identify each sheet fringe, a connected component analysis algorithm is integrated to remedy the local gap in line detection. The performance of our algorithm has been verified in experiments using various kinds of printed-papers with a large number. It is shown that the long-term measurement error is less than 0.75‰ and is sufficient to meet the requirement of factory applications.

Keywords: Machine vision, Stacked sheet counting, Line segment detection LSD.

1 Introduction

In printing and packaging industry, accurate statistics on number of high-end printing paper products has very important significance. If the count is inaccurate and which will cause a direct economic loss to enterprises. Traditional altitude measurement and weighing measurement may cause large errors and lower efficiency of defects. With the rapid development of computer technology,machine vision method has been widely used in the production practice.However,there is a wide variety of stacked sheets in processing workshops, various kinds of cross section in stacked sheet imaging effect can make a big difference, such as large color and thickness difference, uneven illumination,disarranged, tilt etc, these has brought great difficulties in giving an accurate count.

Stacked sheet counting apparatus in foreign literature mostly present with patents [1-2], Lack of detailed algorithm and the technical describes. In recent years, There are

S. Li et al. (Eds.): CCPR 2014, Part I, CCIS 483, pp. 418–425, 2014.
© Springer-Verlag Berlin Heidelberg 2014

many domestic scholars in the related field of study. MiaoLiang etc [3]proposed the pixel projection algorithm based on image tilt correction and the difference of statistical algorithm based on statistical point of view. require accuracy of tilt correction, higher requirements for image quality. Qin Shuwei etc[4] used paper counting method based on mathematical morphology, through the binary morphological opening and closing and expansion operation fills the hole in the stacked sheet texture, while these need to select the appropriate structural elements. Yao Jianlong etc[5] is based on the hole feature image board counting method,but non-uniform surface will produce large errors. Zhang Mingyang etc[6] proposed probability and contour statistics methods, image acquisition needs cross section in stacked sheet stacked neatly, is not conducive to practical application. The traditional Hough line detection method exists excessive response[7-8], the Canny operator [9] edge detection accuracy is largely affected by the threshold. Direct combination of these two methods will produce a large stack of spurious edges,this is not conducive to the number of statistics,in fact, the precision of stacked sheet quantity measurement mainly depends on accurate identification of each stacked sheet transverse stripe. Traditional methods often fail to fully consider the global linear features [10] and local gray level difference, processing the actual complex image will inevitably produce a variety of deviation.

Aiming at the linear transverse stripe in detection problem of stacked sheet image, this paper adopt and improve a horizontal line (Level line) direction growth line segment extraction algorithm, in order to improve the identification precision of the stacked sheet,the basic idea is: On the base of Von Gioi et al line segmentation operator straight segmentation algorithm(LSD algorithm for short below),using similar linear gradient direction support regional gradient direction,introduction of unidirectional gradient operator,to eliminate the same stripe problem of multiple response,combination of gradient amplitude and horizontal direction information,based on regional growth and probability of error control steps,support regional growth and improve line, combining with Bresenham algorithm[11] on the fracture line to connect local abnormal fracture, and fill the partial gap, the accuracy has been greatly improved. This paper is organized as follows next: Section 1 introduces the stacked sheet counting imaging device; section 2 describes the counting algorithm, section 3 introduce the experiment and analysis,section 4 as a summary.

2   System Architecture

The design of stacked sheet counting imaging device is as shown in figure 1: (a) schematic diagram of the imaging device, describes the part of the whole apparatus and frame structure, (b) shows the physical photo. The device is mainly composed of industrial PC, CMOS cameras, lenses, strip light, chassis parts, etc. The image acquisition process is accomplished by real-time dynamic scanning at the front of glass window of chassis, to obtain high resolution image, using program of image processing to counting on the industrial PC, and total number of stacked sheet results will displayed in real time. Below the support platform is equipped with a light sensor, when paper stacked on the platform, the photosensitive sensor automatically send signals to the internal light source controller, control and open the LED light; When moved away the stacked sheet, light controller receives the photosensitive sensor signal, then the control strip light automatically shut down.Such measures both save energy and avoid the strong light of direct illuminate to operators.

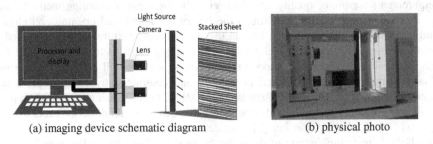

(a) imaging device schematic diagram   (b) physical photo

Fig. 1. schematic imaging device

3   Sheet Counting Algorithm

The obtained stacked sheet from the imaging device have the characteristics of light stripe and dark stripe alternately. The core problem of stacked sheet counting is how to accurate positioning, and identify a single stripe of cross section.However, due to the thickness, color, light reflection characteristics, such as the surface roughness attribute differences, Elastic deformation, compression inequality and cross section factors may cause imaging distortion, The actual performance of laminated paper image rarely ideal, uniform linear streaks. The traditional edge detection methods are difficult to meet the requirements of such complex line extraction. In addition, as a real-time measuring instrument, the counting algorithm is high efficiency requirements. LSD algorithm is an efficient line segment segmentation method based on pixel, and can get subpixel accuracy level in linear time. However, direct use of the original LSD algorithm processing laminated paper image will generate too many false response, frequent stripe fracture phenomenon, and lead to ultimately unable to get the number of accurate measurement. Combined with the specific application paper image, this paper to prevent multiple response, such as improve integrity line detection point of view, The original LSD algorithm is improved and specific algorithm is as follows:

3.1   Unidirectional Edge Direction Field

Image gradient field reflects the image intensity between the adjacent pixels in size and direction of change, in the area of gray level change obviously, the size of the gradient and direction will have great changes, in this paper we defined a unit vector level line based on the gradient field description, and the level line field amplitude sets as the unit of length, what's more,the level line direction is perpendicular to the gradient direction; As is shown in the figure below:

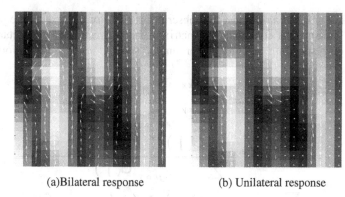

(a)Bilateral response   (b) Unilateral response

Fig. 2. level line field

Figure 2 (a) shows level bilateral response describes level line field. According to the gradient and the level we set the image on the edge of the line Angle, which can appear from white to black and converting from black to white, but the transition process is different, they are on the difference of 180 °,the ilateral response has carried on the limits as shown in figure2(b).Unilateral stripe edge response corresponding to an edge of stacked sheet,what is more conducive to paper counting.

3.2   Region Growing

By traverse the entire image with stacked sheet, gradient value is divided into 1024 levels (bins), the 1024 gradient level covers the range from 0 to 255, and the seed point bin began to search from the top of the gradient value,then turn down until all points are marked as USED. Level line field is divided into several connected area, named as line support region, every time when increase a point, the direction of the detection of each pixel point range is within theτ, ifτ is in the line support area,then added it, and called it sub pixel alignment points, until there is no any pixels can be added to the rectangle,we set the angle error ofτis 22.5 ° by default, statistical minimum circumscribed rectangle all pixels within the number of pixels and its alignment points and the method of probability and statistics can judge whether a straight line [12]. Line support regional spindle used to represent the main direction of rectangle, spindle direction is determined according to the principle of moment of inertia, and the spindle direction Angle is theta.

The center of the rectangle can use formula expressed as:

$$Cx = \frac{\sum_{j \in Re\,gi\,on} G(j) * x(j)}{\sum_{j \in Re\,gi\,on} G(j)} \qquad (1)$$

$$Cy = \frac{\sum_{j \in Re\,gi\,on} G(j) * y(j)}{\sum_{j \in Re\,gi\,on} G(j)} \qquad (2)$$

G(j) is pixel gradient amplitude, the subscript j is used for traverse all the pixel rectangle area. the smallest eigenvalue of matrix in main direction of the rectangular is set to the corresponding feature vector angle, specific expressed in formula as follows:

$$M = \begin{pmatrix} m^{xx} & m^{xy} \\ m^{xy} & m^{yy} \end{pmatrix} \tag{3}$$

$$m^{xx} = \frac{\sum_{j \in \mathrm{Region}} G(j) * (x(j) - Cx)^2}{\sum_{j \in \mathrm{Region}} G(j)} \tag{4}$$

$$m^{yy} = \frac{\sum_{j \in \mathrm{Region}} G(j) * (y(j) - Cy)^2}{\sum_{j \in \mathrm{Region}} G(j)} \tag{5}$$

$$m^{xy} = \frac{\sum_{j \in \mathrm{Region}} G(j) * (x(j) - Cx)(y(j) - Cy)}{\sum_{j \in \mathrm{Region}} G(j)} \tag{6}$$

Figure 3 (a)shows local grayscale stacked sheet, figure 3 (b) is the local gradient field after image magnification, from gray level we can see regional gradient has great changes. Figure 3 (c) shows region growing figure after limiting the edge direction, growth only on the side edges of the stripe is responsive, each one corresponding to one side of the stack sheet ridge.And the limitation on the left edge or right edge, according to the demand of the actual situation. In this way, after the region growing, segmentation can be obtained corresponding to the stripe.

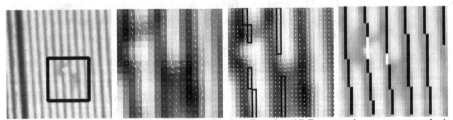

(a)stacked sheet (b) Unilateral response (c) Region Growing (d)Connected component analysis

Fig. 3. Algorithm process description

3.3   Connected Component Analysis

However, due to the cross section have scratches, spots,rupture,as shown black marking line in figure 3(d), according to the characteristics of the straight line segmentation, combined with Bresenham algorithm,connect the broken lines, fill the local interval, using white mark to fill fracture line. Bresenham algorithm is used to describe is decided by two points line algorithm, the advantage of the proposed algorithm can use incremental calculation, makes for each column, as long as the symbol, check for an error term can determine the desires of the column of pixels. connection results is as shown in figure 3(d) of the white line, after the connection analysis of stripe images we can see clearly that marked stripes obviously.

3.4   Counting

Finally, by using stacked sheet stripe image segmentation to count the number of sheets for single pixel lines, in order to accurate statistics number of element,we proposed a method that could calculate the nonzero number of each line and defined with N_i, $1 \leq i \leq Row$. Get a set of array of N_i, which appears most frequently in statistical array in N_i is the nonzero frequency N_{mode}, so N_{mode} is the final number of stacked sheet.

4   Experiments

In this section, we selected the stacked sheet which is difficult to measure in experiment. As shown in figure 4, comparised with the improved Canny algorithm [13]and morphological method. Canny algorithm is a kind of classical edge detection method, in this paper, the Canny algorithm of gradient direction is improved, and the detected edge only response one side edge. Mathematical morphology method is by denoising open and close corrosion expansion and connection broken stripes processing to extract image stripes.Figure4(a) is uneven illumination, respectively, from top to bottom we can see the disarranged, tilt and fainter three types of stacked sheet original image, figure 4 (b) is Canny algorithm to calculate the three types of the figure, white mark line shows line rupture or leak problem, because the Canny algorithm with double threshold method, when facing with different brightness and exposure images, threshold limits will cause leakage inspection, and fracture stripes will affect the accuracy of the count. Figure4(c) is the result of morphological method, morphological method

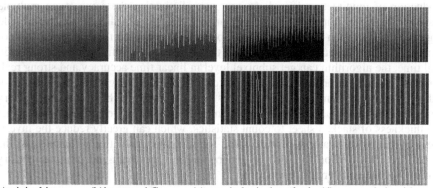

(a)original image   (b)improved Canny   (c)morphological method   (d)proposed algorithm

Fig. 4. Stacked sheet image algorithm performance comparison (from top to bottom, uneven illumination, respectively, are arranged not neat, tilting three types)

has great influence on the selection of structure elements, the figure shows the residual and adhesion problems, which needs to choose the appropriate structure elements and parameters, and this method is time-consuming.Figure4(d) is the proposed method, this algorithm overcomes the uneven illumination disarranged,tilt,fainter, etc.Through the comparison of several kinds of algorithm performance, the proposed method can accurately segment the basic stacked sheet stripes, suitable for the number of accurate statistics.In experiment, each time we can measure about 500 lists of stacked sheets.Table1 is 1000 list a stacked sheet images repeated experiments, several algorithms and calculate the average accuracy error of the result.Compared with the improved Canny algorithm and mathematical morphology method, the proposed algorithm has a greater increase in accuracy.

Figure 4 Stacked sheet image algorithm performance comparison (from top to bottom, uneven illumination, respectively, are arranged not neat, tilting three types).

Table 1. comparison algorithm accuracy

Algorithm name	Error rate
Improved Canny algorithm	$\leqslant 3.05‰$
Morphological method	$\leqslant 5.25‰$
The proposed algorithm	$\leqslant 0.75‰$

5   Discussion and Conclusions

The counting accuracy of stacked sheet is relevant to the light source and wether alignment or not, this paper proposed a straight line extraction algorithm based on horizontal direction guide growth, compared with the improved Canny algorithm and mathematical morphology method, which has better accuracy and reliability, the introduction of unidirectional gradient operator, eliminating the same stripe multiple response problem; Improved linear support regional growth direction, which could improve the operation efficiency; This paper is also proposed the connected component analysis procedure,and make up for the local abnormal fracture effectively. In real time, the algorithm can get subpixel level in linear time accuracy,and strong real-time performance. Through a lot of different types of printing paper test, the algorithm in this paper and the apparatus has been successfully bring into the factory workshop inspection applications, and for more than ten kinds of different colors and the thickness of stacked sheet to count statistics, which can greatly reduce the investment of manpower material resources,and improve the production efficiency. At the same time, this method can also be generalized to other high-end printing industry statistics of the number of applications.

References

1. Otsuka,T.: Compiler: US, 7980394 (2011)
2. Phillips, C.A.P.: Compiler: US, 4255651 (1981)
3. Miao, L., Ping, X.: Algorithm of Paper Counting Based on Texture Feature. Institute of Information Engineering, Information Engineering University (2006)
4. Qin, S., Wong, G.: Image Processing and Recognizing of Chip Shape Based on Mathematical Morphological. Journal of SooChow University (2006)
5. Yao, J., Chen, J.: Research on Cardboard Counting Method Based on Pore Characteristics Image. Industrial Control Computer (2013)
6. Zhang, M., Chen, Z., Wang, X.: Paper counting algorithm based on image texture. Optical Technique (2013)
7. Von Gioi, R.G., Jakubowicz, J., et al.: LSD: A line segment detector. Image Processing OnLine (2012)
8. Jošth, R., Dubská, M., Herout, A., Havel, J.: Real-time line detection using accelerated high-resolution Hough transform. In: Heyden, A., Kahl, F., et al. (eds.) SCIA 2011. LNCS, vol. 6688, pp. 784–793. Springer, Heidelberg (2011)
9. John, C.: A computational approach to edge detection. IEEE Transactions on Pattern Analysis and Machine Intelligence (1986)
10. Akinlar, C., Topal, C.: EDLines: A real-time line segment detector with a false detection control. Pattern Recognition Letters (2011)
11. Bresenham, J.E.: Algorithm for computer control of a digital plotter. IBM Systems Journal (1965)
12. Desolneux, A., Moisan, L., et al.: From gestalt theory to image analysis: A probabilistic approach. Springer, France (2007)
13. Haibin, Z., Xiao, C., Gao, J., et al.: An apparatus and method for stacked sheet counting with camera array. In: Chinese Automation Congress, CAC. IEEE (2013)

Automatic Labanotation Generation Based on Human Motion Capture Data

Hao Guo[1], Zhenjiang Miao[1], Feiyue Zhu[2], Gang Zhang[2], and Song Li[2]

[1] School of Computer and Information Technology, Beijing Jiaotong University,
Beijing, China
{12120339,zjmiao}@bjtu.edu.cn
[2] Center for Ethnic and Folk Literature and Art Development,
Ministry of Culture, Beijing, China
zhufeiyue@aliyun.com,13801240583@139.com,13051270916@163.com

Abstract. As a kind of dance notation, Labanotation has been adopted extensively as an analysis and record system for performing dances. This article aims to generate Labanotation automatically from human motion capture data stored in BVH (Bio-vision Hierarchy) files. First, we convert motion capture data into position format. Then we analyze motions separately according to whether the motion belongs to supporting motion or not. Using the obtained Primary Motion Segments, a sequence of coded description of Labanotation - the Labanotation Data (LND) - is built. And finally, Labanotation is drawn and stored correctly on the basis of LND.

Keywords: motion capture data, Labanotation, motion segment, motion analysis, BVH.

1 Introduction

Labanotation is to dance what musical notation is to music. It is a vivid, scientific and logical analysis and record system for human body motion. And it plays an important role in the intercultural communication for dance arts. But drawing of it is time-consuming and inconvenient because of high degree of freedom of human body joints and dependencies of different body parts.

The automatic generation of Labanotation will simplify the drawing process in order to promote the communication of dance arts. It can also be used to preserve folk dance arts that are in danger of dying out. Besides, Labanotation sequences generated from motion capture data may serve as a kind of motion feature for motion retrieval.

Calvert et al. [1] introduced several applications that assist in drawing Labanotation. Laban Writer [2] is the most commonly used application. There are also similar applications such as Laban Editor [3]. Hachimura and Nakamura [4] proposed the spatial relationship between notation characters and body parts movements. But it was limited to recognition of motions of arms and ignored legs supporting motions. Chen et al.[5] presented a system which transfers motion

S. Li et al. (Eds.): CCPR 2014, Part I, CCIS 483, pp. 426–435, 2014.
© Springer-Verlag Berlin Heidelberg 2014

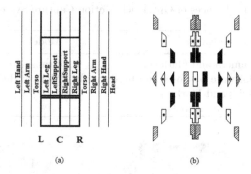

Fig. 1. Staff and the characters of Labanotation: (a) columns for Labanotation (b) 27 notation characters: place, forward, left forward, right forward, left, right, left back, right back and back. Each in the levels of low (black), middle (dot) and high (slash).

capture data to Labanotation. Shen, Li, Yu, Geng and Zhang [6],[7],[8] explored the transformation from motion capture data to Labanotation and motion retrial with Labanotation. However, their generating results are distinct with actual Labanotation.

This article aims to generate Labanotation automatically and correctly from motion capture data. With instruction of Professor Luo Bingyu, an expert on Labanotation, we gave full consideration in rules of Labanotation when carrying on our research. We parse BVH file and analyze human motions. Then the Primary Motion Segment (PMS) defined as basic unit for composing each of human action can be extracted. The LND is produced by these processes. The output results are both pictures of Labanotation and LW4 files [9].

2   Labanotation and Motion Capture

Labanotation. Rudolf Laban created Labanotation in early 20th century. According to comprehensive interpretations in [10] and [11], it is a kind of vertical structure written and read from the bottom up. The staff is a format of 3 lines with 11 columns. The middle line represents spine of human body as shown in Fig.1(a). Laban divided human body motion into gaits and poses. Gaits in supporting columns represent motions of gravity center of human body. Poses in non-supporting columns express motions of body parts.

There are 27 primary characters of Labanotation expressing 27 orientations: 9 directions and 3 levels. The prototype of each notation character is a rectangle, which means the place orientation. And the other characters derive from it by cutting right parts of it, as shown in Fig.1(b). Details refer to [11], an authoritative masterpiece.

Motion Capture. We used two kinds of optical motion capture system to obtain motion capture data, BVH file. The one with markers is for indoor use

Table 1. Devices of OptiTrack Motion Capture System

OptiTrack	Device Name	Model	Count
Hardware	Camera and platform	Prime 41	8
Software	Software platform and hardware key	Motive: Body	1
Accessories	Suits and Markers		1
	Calibration tools		1

Fig. 2. (a) Motion capture system with markers: cameras on top (b) Environment for motion capture without markers

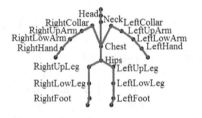

Fig. 3. Skeleton structure for motion data

only. And the one without markers is used under various circumstances. But motion capture system with markers is more precise.

We were offered with OptiTrack, the motion capture system with markers, as Fig.2(a) shows. It mainly contains devices in Table 1. And the motion capture without markers is designed and implemented by other members of our team [12], [13], [14]. It contains 8 cameras and 1 workstation, Fig.2(b).

A BVH file, motion data, is divided into 2 sections. A keyword *HIERARCHY* in the first line signifies the skeleton definition. The other section, saving motion data, starts with *MOTION*. Motion data is a matrix, of which each row is a frame of data recording a posture of human body at the moment of capturing.

The hierarchy, a depth-first tree structure, defined in BVH file specifies the mean-ing of each data in motion section. The basic unit in the hierarchy is a *joint*, a braced block with attributes of *offset*, *channels* and *children joints*. 23 joints make up the hierarchy of BVH file in this article shown in Fig.3.

Table 2. Two data structures

PMS		LND	
Duration	start frame	start time	Duration
	end frame	end time	
Orientation	direction	direction	Orientation
	level	level	
Body Part		Laban Column	

3   Motion Analysis

We defined two data structures: PMS as basic motion unit for motion data and LND. Shown in Table 2.

3.1   Data Converting

The meanings of joints in hierarchy are identified by the structure rather than the names of them. Joints in hierarchy should be calibrated with the human body part. According to Fig.3, we devised the calibrating method.

1. Traverse from ROOT depth-first. Find the first joint, R, with 3 children joints, J_1, J_2 and J_3. R is the joint of hips. And J_1, J_2 and J_3 represent the start of left leg, right leg and torso.
2. Compute each depth and joint count of branches that start with J_1, J_2 and J_3. Considering the symmetry of human body, 2 branches, starting with joints A and B, share the same depth and joint count. The third joint, C, is the start joint of chest branch.
3. Contrast initial offset of joint A and B. As the skeleton structure in BVH faces to the direction of positive z-axis in Cartesian coordinates. The joint with initial $Offset.x < 0$ is the start joint of right leg. And the joint with $Offset.x > 0$ is the start joint of left leg.
4. Traverse from C. Find a second joint with 3 children joints. Identify the start joints of left arm, right arm and head with the same processes in 2 and 3.

The motion data in BVH files records human body motion with Euler Angle [15]. To facilitate motion analysis, we convert Euler Angle to position data. Assume a joint, P, and its child joint J with (x_0, y_0, z_0) as initial relative offset to P. Its relative offset changes to (x_1, y_1, z_1) after P rotating. Suppose the rotation matrix of P is M. Then the new relative offset after rotation is

$$Offset(x_1, y_1, z_1) = M \cdot Offset(x_0, y_0, z_0) \tag{1}$$

Considering all ancestor joints of J, offset of J (to P) in world coordinate system is computed. Assume $M_i (i = 1, ..., A)$ represent the rotation matrix of ith parent joint of J from bottom up.

$$Offset_{new} = M_A \cdot ... \cdot [M_2 \cdot (M_1 \cdot Offset_{initial})] \tag{2}$$

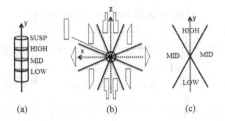

Fig. 4. The partition of space (a) four height space (b) 9 horizontal space corresponding with 9 Labanotation directions (c)3 vertical space corresponding with 3 Labanotation levels

3.2 Supporting Analysis

Supporting analysis is designed for analyzing gaits of human body. Notation characters in supporting columns of Labanotation describe the tendency of each primary motion rather than the posture after the motion.

Extraction of Support-Durations

When human body is moving, it is either supported or unsupported. Suppose the frame number of motion data is N. We defined the supporting state, $SS_i(i = 1, ..., N)$. It signifies which part (or parts) of the body is (or are) supporting. A threshold is used to determine whether a body part supports body or not. Empirically, when a foot is higher than 3.4 inches from the ground, this foot is off the ground and does not support the body. Each state lasts a period of time. So we integrate consecutive identical supporting states into a support-duration, $SD_i(i = 1, ..., M)$. Suppose M is the number of support-durations.

Extraction of Motion-Durations: Direction Obtained

Motion data is a high-dimension time series. The variation between adjacent frames represents the change of body posture. Thus, the velocity $v_i(i = 1, ..., N)$, which is the adjacent frame difference, can be used to express the tendency of human body motion. We classified velocities into 9 directions by analyzing the horizontal pointing of velocity vectors as Fig.4(b) shows. The circle in Fig.4(b) means $PLACE$ direction that occurs when the angle between velocity and y-axis is among $[0, 20) \cup (160, 180]$.

This yields horizontal directions of orientations in PMS between every pair of adjacent frames. Similar with the extraction of support-durations, consecutive identical directions are merged into motion-durations $MD_i(i = 1, ..., K)$.

Isolating Primary Motion Segments: Duration Obtained

The way to isolate PMS from motion-durations and support-durations is shown in Fig.5. Duration of each PMS is supplied by this.

Respective Analysis: Levels and Moving Part Obtained

We generalize 3 types of supporting motion based on the motion mode. They have different features. The respective analysis completes each PMS.

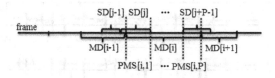

Fig. 5. Isolating PMS from MD and SD

Fig. 6. Relationship between movements of foot and whole human body

Vertical up and down - This type of motion is recorded with the notation character *PLACE*. The height that human body at is the basis for level judgment as shown in Fig.4(a). According to our observation, the level is in *MID* level when difference between the height human body at and its initial height locates in $(-1, 1)$ inch. Lower is in *LOW* level. And higher but no more than 3.4 inches is in *HIGH* level. Besides, the moving part in vertical up and down is the body part supporting the body. This is determined according to *SD* above.

Stepping - The level of PMS is determined by the method shown in Fig.4(c). Moving part of PMS is the foot which results in this primary motion. The moving direction of human body is the same with direction of this foot. As Fig.6 shows, when human body moves to right forward, in one case, the right foot stays still while left foot moves the same direction. Thus, it is the left foot lead to human bodys motion.

Leaping - The level of this motion is determined with the same way as stepping motion. We distinguish the foot that drives this leaping motion with the supporting state of previous frame. And this supporting foot is the moving part of PMS.

3.3   Non-supporting Analysis

Non-supporting analysis includes analyzing poses of five active branches: head, two arms and two legs. As each part is analyzed separately, the moving part in PMS needs no judgment. Duration is obtained from motion segmenting. Orientation derives from orientation determining.

Motion Segmenting

Motion segmenting is aim to segment the motion data sequence at the border between different motions. Barbič et al. [16] proposed 3 approaches, PCA, PPCA and an approach based on GMM, to segment motion capture data into distinct behaviors. In this article, we use PCA method which is easy to implement with certain accuracy.

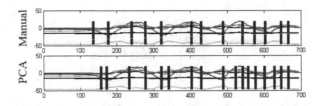

Fig. 7. Comparison of manual segmenting and PCA segmenting

Suppose a branch with m joints. Then each frame of data, $x_i (i = 1, ..., N)$, is a point in the space of $M = m \times 3$ dimensions. We can get a diagonal matrix Σ with the Singular Value Decomposition (SVD). Suppose the diagonal elements are $\sigma_i (i = 1, ..., M)$. Project x_i to the specified r-dimension space and define projection error.

$$e = \Sigma_{i=1}^{N} \|x_i - x'\|^2 = \Sigma_{j=r+1}^{M} \sigma_j^2 \tag{3}$$

$$R = 1 - e/(\Sigma_{j=1}^{M} \sigma_j^2) \tag{4}$$

Set a threshold, $\tau = 0.95$, compute the minimum r to make $R > \tau$. Assume e_i represents the projection error for first i frames of motion capture data. e_i will remain almost unchanged if the motion data describe a singular primary motion; but it changes rapidly at a frame between adjacent different primary motions. This frame is the border of different motions. Fig.7 shows the comparison of PCA segmenting and manual segmenting.

Orientation Determining

There are *Initial Joint* and *Terminal Joint* for each branch. For example, the initial joint of left arm is the joint of *LeftUpArm*. And the terminal joint of left arm is the joint of *LeftHand*. It is the relative position of Initial Joint and Terminal Joint that is used to determine the orientation of PMS. As shown in Fig.4(b) and (c), the Initial Joint locates at the center. Then we inspect the position of Terminal Joint. It must locate in one of the 27 space regions. Thus, the orientation in each PMS is obtained.

3.4   Build LND

Just as the definition of PMS and LND, they share the same structure. But there is still a problem that is the redundancy of LND. It is not absolutely precise because of the deviations in processing, like errors of segmenting in Fig.7. So we merge LND sequence under some rules.

Progressive motions. A singular continuous primary motion with different orientations in its moving may be determined as two primary motions, in Fig.8(a).

Sustaining motions. A continuous primary motion is divided into two because of deviation of segmenting, in Fig.8(b).

Nonexistent motions. Noises in motion capture data may result in nonexistent motions, meaningless and too short to express a primary motion, in Fig.8 (c).

Cracked motions. Noises may also lead to a singular primary motion cracked, in Fig.8(d).

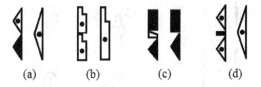

(a)   (b)   (c)   (d)

Fig. 8. Four merged situations: unmerged left and after merged right

Fig. 9. Method of drawing Labanotation characters

4   Generating Results

This project was developed on Microsoft Visual Studio 2008 with C++ program language and OpenCV library under Windows system. It reads a piece of BVH file. With some musical parameters, the project generates Labanotation after parsing BVH file and analyzing human motion performed in it. We use MFC tools to draw and display Labanotation. The character of *PLACE* is the prototype of all other characters, shown in Fig.9.

Fig.10 shows two examples of generated Labanotation. The left piece describes a period of walk motion. And the right one describes motions of some times of leaping with arms swing. To verify the usability of this project, we compare generated Labanotation with its original motions in Fig.11. This piece of Labanotation is the left part of Fig.10. It records a period of walking which lasting 693

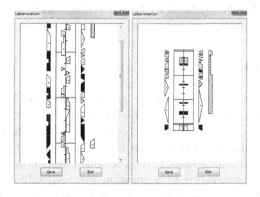

Fig. 10. Two examples of Labanotation, generated automatically

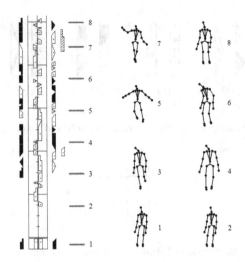

Fig. 11. Comparison between Labanotation and original motions

frames with 60 FPS. In this motion duration, the human body walks forward and strides sometimes.

As Fig.11 shows, 8 actions in Labanotation (left) and 8 original postures (right) are obtained by picking one about every 100 frames. Action 1 is the initial state of human body. Compare it with Posture 1. Both legs support the human body. The right arm towards right while left arm biases front. This makes up an action just like Action 1 expressing. Similarly, Action 3, 4, 5, 6, 7 and 8 can be compared separately with Posture 3, 4, 5, 6, 7 and 8. We can find each pair of them matches well. Specially, it is move-less between Action 1 and 2. So Posture 2 is the same with Posture 1.

According to the result of comparisons, the generated Labanotation can express motions recorded in motion capture data correctly. Then we can save the generated Labanotation. Besides the picture displayed Fig.10 and Fig.11, it can also be saved in LW4 file, defined by Laban Writer 4.0. It is a kind of text file encoded in ASCII format.

5   Conclusions

The generating results indicate that we are able to generate Labanotation from motion capture data correctly. We first used two types of motion capture system to capture human body motion. Then the motion capture data in BVH files is processed. After analysis of both supporting and non-supporting motion, we get PMS as basic motion unit. Hence, LND, the coded description of Labanotation, is built. And finally, generating Labanotation automatically is implemented.

The next step of our work is to make the generating more accurate and develop our own file format to save Labanotation with reader software for it.

Acknowledgments. Our work is supported by National Key Technology R&D Program of China 2012BAH01F03. We thank Professor Luo Bingyu for instruction on Labanotation.

References

1. Calvert, T., Wilke, W., Ryman, R., Fox, I.: Applications of computers to dance. IEEE Computer Graphics and Applications 25(2), 6–12 (2005)
2. Venable, L., Sutherland, S., Ross, L., Tinsley, M.: Laban Writer 2.0. The Ohio State University, Department of Dance (1989)
3. Kojima, K., Hachimura, K., Nakamura, M.: Labaneditor: Graphical editor for dance notation. In: Proceedings of the 11th IEEE International Workshop on Robot and Human Interactive Communication, pp. 59–64. IEEE (2002)
4. Hachimura, K., Nakamura, M.: Method of generating coded description of human body motion from motion-captured data. In: Proceedings of the 10th IEEE International Workshop on Robot and Human Interactive Communication, pp. 122–127. IEEE (2001)
5. Chen, H., Qian, G., James, J.: An Autonomous Dance Scoring System Using Marker-based Motion Capture. In: 2005 IEEE 7th Workshop on Multimedia Signal Processing, pp. 1–4. IEEE (October 2005)
6. Shen, X., Li, Q., Yu, T., Geng, W., Lau, N.: Mocap data editing via movement notations. In: Ninth International Conference on Computer Aided Design and Computer Graphics, p. 6. IEEE (December 2005)
7. Yu, T., Shen, X., Li, Q., Geng, W.: Motion retrieval based on movement notation language. Computer Animation and Virtual Worlds 16(3-4), 273–282 (2005)
8. Zhang, S., Li, Q., Yu, T., Shen, X., Geng, W., Wang, P.: Implementation of a notation-based motion choreography system. In: Zha, H., Pan, Z., Thwaites, H., Addison, A.C., Forte, M. (eds.) VSMM 2006. LNCS, vol. 4270, pp. 495–503. Springer, Heidelberg (2006)
9. LabanWriter 4 file format, http://dance.osu.edu/labanwriter/resources/labanwriter-4-file-format
10. Xiang, B.: The scientific notation of movement: The principle of science and function of labanotation. Master's thesis, Shanghai Normal University (2008)
11. Guest, A.H.: Labanotation: The system of analyzing and recording movement. Psychology Press (2005)
12. Wan, C.: Research on human body motion capture and pose estimation. Dissertation. Beijing Jiaotong University (2009)
13. Sun, Y.: Research on Touch-free Human Body Motion Capture Under Multiple Viewpoints. Dissertation. Beijing Jiaotong University (2006)
14. Li, J.: Research on Multiview 3D Human Motion Capture. Dissertation. Beijing Jiaotong University (2013)
15. Dunn, F., Parberry, I.: 3D math primer for graphics and game development. CRC Press (2011)
16. Barbič, J., Safonova, A., Pan, J.Y., Faloutsos, C., Hodgins, J.K., Pollard, N.S.: Segmenting motion capture data into distinct behaviors. In: Proceedings of the 2004 Graphics Interface Conference, pp. 185–194. Canadian Human-Computer Communications Society (May 2004)

Self-organizing Map-Based Object Tracking
with Saliency Map and K-Means Segmentation

Yuanping Zhang[1,2], Yuanyan Tang[1,3], Bin Fang[1], Zhaowei Shang[1], and C.Y. Suen[4]

[1] College of Computer Science, Chongqing University, Chongqing, China
[2] College of Computer and Information Science,
Southwest University, Chongqing, China
[3] Faculty of Science and Technology,
University of Macau, Macau, China
[4] Centre for Pattern Recognition and Machine Intelligence,
Concordia University, Montreal, Canada
zlvilla@swu.edu.cn, yytang@umac.mo,
fb@cqu.edu.cn, szw@cqu.edu.cn,
suen@cse.concordia.ca

Abstract. In this paper, a new method is presented for long-term object tracking in surveillance videos. The developed method combines surrounding image sampling, saliency map, self-organizing map neural network, k-Means segmentation and similarity measurement. Saliency map can provide valuable information to reduce over-segmentation. The surrounding image sampling always extracts the regions which are close to the centroid of the latest tracked target. The self-organizing map quantizes the image samples into a topological space, it compresses information while preserving the most important topological and metric relationships of the primary features. The k-Means algorithm will generate segmentation based on the output of the self-organizing map. Then, according to the segmentation results of the new frame and the first frame, a similarity measurement is used to get the most similar image sample to the specified object in the first frame and thus object position in new frame is found. We apply the developed method to track objects in the real-world environment of surveillance videos, computer simulations indicate that the proposed approach presents better results than those obtained by a direct method approach.

Keywords: object tracking, self-organizing map, saliency map, k-Means segmentation, similarity measurement.

1 Introduction

Object tracking is one of the most crucial component in computer vision applications such as surveillance, driver assistance systems, remote sensing, defense systems and perceptual user interface. It is even more difficult when the objects change their scale, pose, or illumination. Traditional feature-based methods, such as those based on color [1] or motion blobs [2,3], perform tracking by maintaining a model of the target and

S. Li et al. (Eds.): CCPR 2014, Part I, CCIS 483, pp. 436–444, 2014.
© Springer-Verlag Berlin Heidelberg 2014

adapting such a model over time, but these may fail when the object model deviate from its original one over time. In recent years, neural networks-based tracking methods [4] have been used to overcome these limitations.

In this paper, we present a hybrid object tracking method with self-organizing map (SOM) network, saliency map and k-Means segmentation for real-time tracking in surveillance videos. The pixel features of prespecified region in the first frame are trained with SOM after a pre-processing step in which RGB color space is transformed into $L*u*v*$ color space, the intensity and saliency map are integrated to form input patterns of SOM. Once the training is finished, the output prototype vectors of SOM are segmented by k-Means algorithm and the segmentation results will be the reference target. When a new frame arrive, we extract surrounding rectangles of image according the centroid of the previous tracked object. These rectangles of image will be converted into $L*u*v*$ color space image and sent to the trained SOM, with intensity and saliency map. K-Means algorithm is adopted to segment the outputs of SOM to generate candidate targets. The last work is to compute similarity between each of these candidate targets and the reference target. Then we will regard the most similar rectangle of image to the reference target as the matched object and return it as a tracking result if the distance is close enough. We measured performance of our method with TLD dataset [5].

The remainder of this paper is organized as follows: the related work of our method are described in sections 2. The tracking algorithm and preliminaries are presented in Section 3. We present and discuss experimental results in section 4 and section 5 presents analysis and limitations of our approach.

2   Related Work

2.1   Saliency Map

In many cases, an image is always over-segmented. Salient objects are crucial for further image retrieval or scene understanding, and it may provide valuable information to improve the segmentation performance. Itti et al. introduced their bottom-up visual attention model [6] inspired by the behavior and the neuronal architecture of the early primate visual system. The saliency maps produced by Itti's approach have been used by other researchers for applications like adapting images on small devices and unsupervised object segmentation [12]. In the Itti model, an input color image is computed by three human different early vision features, such as intensity, color, and orientation. This leads to a multi-feature representation of the scene, the saliency map S can be computed as follows:

$$S = \frac{1}{3}(N(\overline{I}) + N(\overline{C}) + N(\overline{O}))$$ (1)

where operator N means the normalization. $\overline{I}, \overline{C}$ and $\overline{O}$ is the conspicuity map of feature intensity, color, and orientation, respectively.

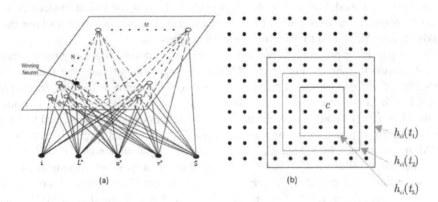

Fig. 1. (a)Two-layered SOM Network with Rectangular Topology. (b) Neighborhood function which starts as $h_{ci}(t_1)$ and reduces in size to $h_{ci}(t_3)$ over time.

2.2   The Self-Organizing Map

The SOM, first put forward by T. Kohonen [7], is a kind of widely used unsupervised artificial neural network. The typical features of SOM are topology visualization of the input patterns and representation of a large number of input patterns. SOM in our method defines a mapping from an input space R^5 onto a topologically ordered set of nodes. Our used two-dimensional SOM is shown in Fig.1. Nodes in SOM are updated according to:

$$m_i(t + 1) = m_i(t) + h_{ci}(t)[x(t) - m_i(t)] \qquad (2)$$

where t is the time and the $h_{ci}(t)$ the neighbourhood function, the neighbourhood function is:

$$h_{ci} = \alpha(t)\exp\left(-\frac{|l_c - l_i|^2}{2\sigma^2(t)}\right) \qquad (3)$$

where $\alpha(t)$ is the learning rate and l_c is the node with the closest weight vector to the input sample and l_i ranges over all nodes, $\sigma(t)$ defines the width of the kernel.

2.3   K-Means Segmentation and Cluster Evaluation

After the large quantities of pixel data are projected to a 2-dimension space to become a member in a group of nodes, a typical k-means method is adopted to segment the prototype vectors. Segmenting the SOM prototype vectors instead of directly segmenting the data is a computationally effective approach [8].

Being a typical segmenting method, k-means method assigns each point to the cluster with the nearest center. The main advantages of k-means algorithm are its simplicity. Its disadvantages are heavy computation if the amount of data is large.

Because the number of prototype vectors is very small, the computation cost is not a problem in our method. With the standard k-means algorithm, the prototype vectors are clustered from 2 clusters to $\sqrt{n}$(n is the number of SOM nodes) clusters, respectively, and image segmentation results with 2 clusters to $\sqrt{n}$ clusters are obtained.

The results of image segmentation can be evaluated directly with an image segmentation evaluation index named quantitative-based index [9] in which a lower quantitative value leads to better segmentations. The Q index of quantitative image evaluation method is defined as below:

$$Q(I) = \frac{1}{10000(N \times M)} \sqrt{R} \times \sum_{i=1}^{R} \left[\frac{e_i^2}{1 + \log A_i} + \left(\frac{R(A_i)}{A_i} \right)^2 \right] \tag{4}$$

where $N \times M$ is the size of image I, R is the number of regions of the segmented image, A_i is the area (measured by the number of pixels) of the ith region, and e_i is the sum of the Euclidean distance between the $L*u*v*$ color vectors of the pixels of region i and the color vector attributed to region i in the segmented image. The $R(A_i)$ represents the number of regions having an area equal to A_i. The Q index was declared to be an effective guide in tuning segmentation algorithms [9].

2.4   Similarity Measure

In our object tracking method, the segmentation results of the new frame need to be compared with the segmentation result of the reference image to obtain the similarity value. William Rand proposed a similarity measure function that converted the problem of comparing two segmentation results with possibly differing number of classes into a problem of computing pairwise label relationships [10].

Consider two segmentation results R and R' which contain the label assignments of reference target and one of the candidate targets from a new frame respectively. The two images have same pixels. So they can be denote $X = \{x_1, x_2, \ldots, x_N\}$ and $X' = \{x_1', x_2', \ldots, x_N'\}$ respectively. Segmentation result $R = \{r_1, r_2, \ldots, r_{k1}\}$ and $R' = \{r_1', r_2', \ldots, r_{k2}'\}$, we define

$$S(R, R') = \frac{1}{\binom{N}{2}} \sum_{i<j} \left[I(l_i = l_j \wedge l_i' = l_j') + I(l_i \neq l_j \wedge l_i' \neq l_j') \right] \tag{5}$$

where I is the identity function, l_i and l_i' are the labels contained in R and R' respectively, and the denominator $\binom{N}{2}$ is the number of possible unique pairs among N data points.

There is another computational form for S. Given a pair of segmentation results R and R' of the same N pixels, arbitrarily number of the clusters in each segmentation and let n_{ij} be the number of pixels simultaneously in the ith cluster of R and the jth cluster of R'. Then the similarity function between R and R' is:

$$S(R, R') = \frac{\left[\binom{N}{2} - \left[\frac{1}{2} \{ \sum_i (\sum_j n_{ij})^2 + \sum_j (\sum_i n_{ij})^2 \} - \sum \sum n_{ij}^2 \right] \right]}{\binom{N}{2}} \tag{6}$$

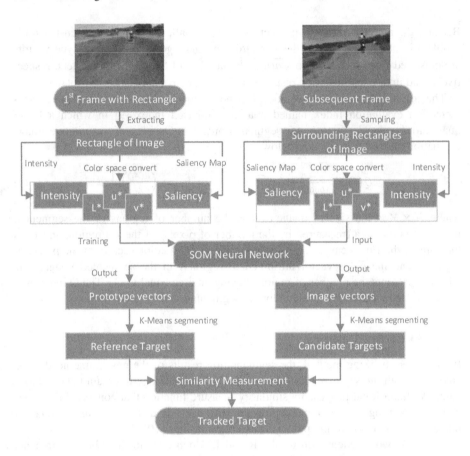

Fig. 2. Flowchart of our method

3   Proposed Method

In our proposed method, the rectangle of RGB color space image from the first frame is converted into $L*u*v*$ color space image. With the intensity and saliency map, the converted image is used to train the SOM neural network. The output prototypes are filtered with hits map, blank nodes (not hit by any pixels) will be deleted. The k-Means method is applied to further segment the prototypes. During the process of segmentation, a best segmentation result (best cluster number) is acquired according to the guidance of a quantitative image evaluation index.

When a new frame arrives, a surrounding sampling algorithm is used to get ROI patches. The sampled patches are applied to the SOM neural networks and thus transformed into the multi-dimensional feature vectors at the output of the neural network, just as the way in which human retina senses objects [12]. The multi-dimensional feature vectors are segmented as the candidate targets, and each of the candidate targets and the reference target would be used to compute the similarity as (6), then the patch with the largest similarity would be regarded as the tracked object image if the largest similarity is larger than the threshold. Otherwise, the largest similarity is too small, it means that the occlusion occurs or the target disappeared. To handle occlusion in object tracking, a sequence of information nodes is adopted. When a new frame is processed, a corresponding information node is created and added into the sequence. Each information node includes: Value of similarity, Centroid and Occluded, where centroid is the central point of tracked object, or it is the corresponding value of previous node when the value of similarity is smaller than 0.25, and if there is a failure of object tracking, information "Occluded" would be "1". When the object appears in one of the sequent frames, at the time when the value of similarity of object in the frame is larger than 0.25. And when occlusion occurs, we will extend the search range by enlarge the radius in our surrounding sub-image extracting algorithm. Once the object appears, we set the radius to the original value, half of the minimum one of width and height of the sub-image. The detailed flowchart of our proposed method is shown in Fig. 2.

SOM adopted in our method is described in section 2.2, it is trained in unsupervised manner. We define SOM network: the input size is 5 and the output size is 9x9, the weight vector $w_i^{(0)}$ of the ith neuron is randomly initialized. Rectangular topology for ANN and Gaussian neighborhood function is used in this paper. Neighborhood radius $r = 17$, and learning rate $\alpha = 0.05$. The image intensities and colors of the prespecified region in the first frame are iteratively used to train the network for few times. During the training, each point is cyclically chosen from the data set, and presented to all neurons on the map simultaneously. Once training of SOM is finished, a typical k-Means method is adopted to segment the prototype vectors to generate the reference target represented with segmentation results. When a new frame arrives, we use a surrounding sampling algorithm to extract sub-images from around the centroid of the latest tracked object and send each of the sub-images into the SOM with the saliency map. The mentioned surrounding sampling algorithm is based midpoint circle algorithm and described as Fig.3.

Fig. 3. An Illustration of Surrounding Sub-image Extracting Based Midpoint Circle Algorithm

The segmentation results will be used to evaluate the similarity to the reference target. A highest quantitative value leads to the most similar sub-image which means it is the expected position where specified object now lies. The similarity measurement we proposed is described in section 2.4.

4   Experimental Results

Through our experiment, we evaluate the performance of our proposed method on a challenging benchmark, the TLD dataset [5]. It is an appropriate dataset to evaluate performance for tracking task since each video sequence has various challenges such as occlusion, scale, pose and illumination changes. Each video contains only one target which is specified with a rectangle in the first frame and corresponding ground-truth. Performances are measured by the F-measure $F = \frac{1}{\alpha\frac{1}{P}+(1-\alpha)\frac{1}{R}}$, where the weight $\alpha \in [0,1]$. When $\alpha = 1/2$, F-measure can be written as $F = 2PR/(P + R)$. In our evaluation, detection is classified as positive if the overlapped area between bounding boxes from prediction and ground-truth is greater than 25. We compare our method to five trackers: 1) OnlineBoost[12], 2) MIL [13], and 3) CoGD [14]. Binaries for trackers 1) are available on the Internet. Trackers 2), 3) were kindly evaluated directly by their authors. The abbreviated name of our method is SOM_SK. The tracking performance is measured and presented in table 1.

Table 1. Tracking performace Measured by Precision/Recall/F-Measure

Sequence	Frames	OnlineBoost[12]	MIL[13]	CoGD[14]	SOM_SK
David	761	0.41 / 0.29 / 0.34	0.15 / 0.15 / 0.15	1.00 / 1.00 / 1.00	0.98/0.84/0.91
Jumping	313	0.47 / 0.05 / 0.09	1.00 / 1.00 / 1.00	1.00 / 0.99 / 1.00	0.94/0.93/0.93
Pedestrian1	140	0.61 / 0.14 / 0.23	0.69 / 0.69 / 0.69	1.00 / 1.00 / 1.00	1.00/1.00/1.00
Pedestrian2	338	0.77 / 0.12 / 0.21	0.10 / 0.12 / 0.11	0.72 / 0.92 / 0.81	0.92/0.73/0.81
Pedestrian3	184	1.00 / 0.33 / 0.49	0.69 / 0.81 / 0.75	0.85 / 1.00 / 0.92	0.92/0.75/0.83
Car	945	0.94 / 0.59 / 0.73	0.23 / 0.25 / 0.24	0.95 / 0.96 / 0.96	0.86/0.72/0.78
Motocross	2665	0.33 / 0.00 / 0.01	0.05 / 0.02 / 0.03	0.93 / 0.30 / 0.45	0.99/0.70/0.82
Volkswagen	8576	0.39 / 0.02 / 0.04	0.42 / 0.04 / 0.07	0.79 / 0.06 / 0.11	0.97/0.70/0.81
Carchase	9928	0.79 / 0.03 / 0.06	0.62 / 0.04 / 0.07	0.95 / 0.04 / 0.08	0.84/0.72/0.77
Panda	3000	0.95 / 0.35 / 0.51	0.36 / 0.40 / 0.38	0.12 / 0.12 / 0.12	0.81/0.70/0.75
Mean	2685	0.62 / 0.09 / 0.13	0.44 / 0.11 / 0.13	0.80 / 0.18 / 0.22	0.92/0.78/0.84

5   Conclusion

In this paper, a hybrid object tracking method is represented that was based on saliency map, SOM and k-Means algorithm. For improving segmentation quality, images are converted into modified $L*u*v*$ color space. A two SOM layers network with square topology is trained and used to reduce features which are composed of intensity, $L*u*v*$ and saliency map. Output of the SOM is segmented with k-Mean segmentation algorithm. The segmentation results of prespecified object is regarded as reference target and a similarity measurement is adopted to compute the similarity value between each candidate targets produced from surrounding images and the reference target. The position of the specified object in the new frame is found in the best similar surrounding images. Experimental results show that using saliency map and SOM with unsupervised leaning can yield satisfactory features reduction and k-Mean algorithm may generate a perfect object tracking result. Using our proposed method can produce near-optimal object tracking.

In future works, we plan to improve this method by introducing an interactive feedback process when the object prespecifying. That means we can specify the reference target exactly and distinguish background patches in the first step. Thus, better segmentation results and tracking results are expected.

Acknowledgment. The authors would like to thank the anonymous reviewers for their constructive comments. This work was supported by the Fundamental Research Funds for the Central Universities under grant no. XDJK2011C059.

References

1. Dundar, A., Jin, J., Culurciello, E.: Visual tracking with similarity matching ratio, arXiv preprint arXiv:1209.2696 (2012)
2. Zhang, T., Ghanem, B., Liu, S., Ahuja, N.: Robust visual tracking via multi-task sparse learning. In: 2012 IEEE Conference on Computer Vision and Pattern Recognition (CVPR), June 16-21, pp. 2042–2049 (2012)
3. Jin, J., Dundar, A., Bates, J., Farabet, C., Culurciello, E.: Tracking with deep neural networks. In: 2013 47th Annual Conference on Information Sciences and Systems (CISS), March 20-22, pp. 1–5 (2013)
4. Angelova, D., Mihaylova, L., Petrov, N., Gning, A.: Extended object tracking with convolution particle filtering. In: 2012 6th IEEE International Conference on Intelligent Systems (IS), September 6-8, pp. 96–101 (2012)
5. Avidan, S.: Ensemble tracking. IEEE Trans. Pattern Anal. Mach. Intell. 29(2), 261–271 (2007)
6. Itti, L., Koch, C., Niebur, E.: A model of saliency-based visual attention for rapid scene analysis. IEEE Transactions on Pattern Analysis and Machine Intelligence 20(11), 1254–1259 (1998)
7. Kohonen, T.: Self-Organize maps, Berlin, 3rd edn. Springer, Germany (2000)
8. Vesanto, J., Alhoniemi, E.: Clustering of the self-organizing map. IEEE Transactions on Neural Networks 11(3), 586–600 (2000)
9. Borsotti, M., Campadelli, P., Schettini, R.: Quantitative evaluation of color image segmentation results. Pattern Recognition Letters 19(8), 741–747 (1998)
10. Hunt, R.W.G., Pointer, M.R.: Measuring color, 4th edn. Wiley & Sons, Chichester (2011)

11. Ko, B.C., Nam, J.-Y.: Object-of-interest image segmentation based on human attention and semantic region clustering. Journal of Optical Society of America A 23(10), 2462–2470 (2006)
12. Grabner, H., Bischof, H.: On-Line Boosting and Vision. In: Proc. IEEE CS Conf. Computer Vision and Pattern Recognition (2006)
13. Babenko, B., Yang, M.-H., Belongie, S.: Visual Tracking with Online Multiple Instance Learning. In: Proc. IEEE Conf. Computer Vision and Pattern Recognition (2009)
14. Yu, Q., Dinh, T.B., Medioni, G.: Online Tracking and Reacquisition Using Co-Trained Generative and Discriminative Trackers. In: Forsyth, D., Torr, P., Zisserman, A. (eds.) ECCV 2008, Part II. LNCS, vol. 5303, pp. 678–691. Springer, Heidelberg (2008)

Superpixel-Based Global Optimization Method for Stereo Disparity Estimation

Haiqiang Jin, Sheng Liu, Shaobo Zhang, and Gaoxuan Ying

College of Computer Science and Technology, Zhejiang University of Technology
Hangzhou, 310023, Zhejiang, P.R. China
edliu@zjut.edu.cn

Abstract. We proposed a novel global optimization method based on superpixel for stereo matching in this paper. Comparing with the pixel-based global optimization methods, the matching accuracy of our method is significantly improved. For improving the initial matching cost's accuracy, we developed an adaptive matching window integrated with shape and size information to build the data term. To ensure the soft constraints of planar disparity distribution, a superpixel-based plane fitting method is introduced to obtain the initial disparity plane. We present a global optimization framework with data term and pixel-based smooth term to refine the disparity results. The experimental results on the Middlebury Stereo Datasets show that our method outperforms some state-of-the-art pixel-based global optimization approaches both quantitatively and qualitatively.

Keywords: global optimization, stereo disparity estimation, superpixel, stereo matching.

1 Introduction

Global matching algorithms usually model the stereo matching process to the energy minimization problems. The energy functions are built in those global optimization frameworks, and then solved by certain global optimization solver. Through minimization of the energy function, the optimal matching results were achieved. The Markov Random Field, Bayesian and relevant derivative models are popular in machine vision problems currently, usual MRF-based optimization methods such as Graph Cut(GC)[1] and Belief Propagation(BP)[2] are the most widely used global optimization method. We take GC as our global optimization solver in this paper, but focus on building the optimization energy function. In MiddleBury Stereo Benchmark[4], stereo matching methods based on global optimization framework tend to achieve higher accuracy, consequently these methods are always top ranked. Bleyer[5] proposed a method based on scene treated by plane fitting, they improved matching accuracy by scene classification, expansion and spline fitting. Hirschmuller[6] adopted a sub-global stereo matching algorithm, they handled with the relative merits of local method and global method preferably.

S. Li et al. (Eds.): CCPR 2014, Part I, CCIS 483, pp. 445–454, 2014.

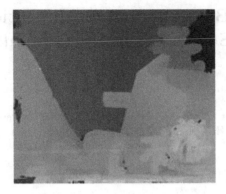

Fig. 1. Disparity of Teddy generated by method based on pixel[24]. A large error region exists in the top-right corner of the picture obviously, it is difficult to solve the problems like this by improving or adding the energy term simply.

In real scene, the regions with no texture or weak texture, as well as occlusion will cause difficulty for matching. Occlusion is often located on the boundary between the objects and the disparity discontinuous regions. Nevertheless, the superpixels performs well to clarifying these areas. Therefore, the stereo matching algorithms based on superpixels accessed to high achievement[8–10]. These methods fitted the disparity planes with superpixels to solve the problem of noise while keeping the boundary contour information. Ladick et al[11] presented a stereo matching method based on superpixel and achieved good results by using the higher-order Markov model to model and calculate the optimal solutions.

From the tested results we can clearly see that although the global pixel-based methods[24] have obtained outstanding performances, there are still some obvious errors in local regions as shown in Fig.1. So we proposed a new global superpixel-based optimization method to solve these errors. Rather than previous pixel-based methods which set single pixel in the image as node of the graph, we define each superpixel as the node of the graph. Therefore, we build the global matching algorithm based on superpixel and the corresponding particular energy terms related to superpixels in the paper.

2   Proposed Global Method Based on Superpixel

2.1   Algorithm Overview

The input of the proposed algorithm is a pair of epipolar-rectified images, which are preprocessed by over-segmentation algorithm to generate superpixels and local stereo matching window to get the matching cost. In this paper, we use mean-shift color segmentation algorithm[23] to separate the image into superpixels (shown as many uniform color regions). According to "Winner takes all" principle, the reliable pixels are determined by Cross-Checking on basis of obtained energy cost. Then on each piece of the superpixel, initial disparity and

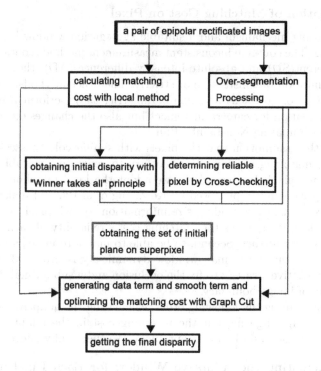

Fig. 2. Algorithm flow chart, it shows the procedure of our method from inputting image to generate final disparity

reliable pixels are used to plane fitting to get the set of initial planes. Not only the data term but also the smooth term is constructed to optimize the matching cost with Graph cut to get the final disparity. The whole procedure of our algorithm is illustrated in Fig.2.

2.2 Over-Segmentation Processing

In the first step, the input images are separated as color or gray uniform regions. We assume here, the disparity's value of these regions transit smoothly and the discontinuity of disparity only appear on the edges of these regions. The reason to choose superpixel is that it's suitable for the assumption in real scene. So we adopt the mean-shift color segmentation algorithm[7] proposed by Comaniciu and Meer, it's successfully applicated in graph cut recently. Originally defined as a gradient rising search strategy, mean shift analysis is in order to maximize a density function defined on a high-dimensional feature space. In process of analysis, a high-dimensional space coordinate in the feature space is defined, and all the involving relevant attributes are associated with each dimension of the high-dimensional space. It's one of the biggest advantages to mean shift method that combine the boundary information.

2.3   Calculation of Matching Cost on Pixel

Defining a scoring mechanism and a suitable aggregation window is needed for local matching. The common inconsistent measurement methods contain squared intensity different(SD) and absolute intensity differences(AD), they all comply with the assumption of constant color strictly. The other methods, such as the measuring based on gradient and non-parametric, they perform robustly not only in compensation for camera increment but also the changes on the surface of the low discriminating Non-Lambertian.

Accepting the assumption that the pixels with similar color possesses similar disparity in a matching window, it's necessary to generate a suitable adaptive window for each pixel. In this article, we adopt the local matching algorithm based on adaptive window proposed by Ke Zhang et al[12], and make improvements in three areas. First, adding size information to each pixel in a adaptive matching window, it increases the matching cost's reliability of each pixel with consistent disparity further. Second, to be able to match robustly, a mechanism that increased in the most small window dynamically is proposed. Third, we present an alternative strategy to fix the occlusion and a suboptimal strategy to solve the issue of image boundary.

The method runs as the following order, calculating the adaptive window for each pixel in image, figuring out the matching cost in the adaptive window, dealing with occlusion and boundary problem. We specifically addressed below.

Step 1. Calculating the Adaptive Window for Each Pixel in Image. Obtain an adaptive cross for each pixel using the method of Ke Zhang[12], make integral operation in the region respectively along the vertical and horizontal directions, then the adaptive matching window on two separating directions are obtained. It is necessary to calculate the adaptive matching window for each pixel in both stereo images.

Step 2. Figuring out the Matching Cost in the Adaptive Window. We suppose p as the pixel in the left image and p' as the corresponding pixel in the right image. To obtain the set of reliable matching cost, the adaptive window $U(p)$ of pixel p and $U'(p')$ of pixel p' are calculated respectively. The formula of matching cost between p and p' show as below

$$C_d(p) = \frac{1}{\|U_d(p)\|} \sum_{t \ni U_d(p)} e_d(t) * (\log \Theta + 1) \tag{1}$$

Where $U_d(p) = \{(x,y)|(x,y) \in U(p), (x-d,y) \in U'(p')\}$ and $\Theta = \frac{\|U(p)\|}{\|U_d(p)\|}$, $e_d(t)$ denote the rough matching cost of pixel t with disparity d, it is defined as

$$e_d(t) = \min(\sum_{c \in \{R,G,B\}} |I_c(t) - I'_c(t')|, T) \tag{2}$$

Here T is the truncation limit of matching cost, $I(t)$ means the value of color component c in pixel t, and $I'_c(t')$ is a value retrieved from c one of three color channels$\{R, G, B\}$ in pixel t'.

Step 3. Dealing with Occlusion and Boundary Problem. Based on five occlusive region approach[12] proposed by Geoffrey Egnal et al, we adopt an alternative strategy dealing with occlusive region, replace the matching cost of occlusion with the cost of the adjacent pixels.

To image boundary, we neither assess the two disparity map with the left and right consistency check[13, 14], nor a simple boundary inference, but a suboptimal strategy instead. $C_{d^\wedge}(p)$ is the suboptimal matching cost of pixel p, $d^\wedge$ is defined as below

$$d^\wedge = \arg \min_{d\in[d_{min},d_{max}],(x_p-d)>0,d\neq d^*} C_d(p) \tag{3}$$

It denote the needed suboptimal label, d^* means optimal label, given as follows

$$d^* = \arg \min_{d\in[d_{min},d_{max}],(x_p-d)>0} C_d(p) \tag{4}$$

Finally, when $(x_p - d(p)) < 1$, we use $C_{d^\wedge}(p)$ as the matching cost of boundary pixel p.

2.4   Determine the Set of Initial Plane

In this article, a set of two-dimensional disparity plane is used to simulate the structure of real scene. Parameters a, b, c represent the disparity plane, they determine the disparity $d = ax + by + c$ of a pixel in image. So we adopt triples $\{a, b, c\}$ as the disparity plane.

As we know, the value of disparity is discrete artificial integer, and its quantity is limited. Therefore they can be traversed when searching. But the plane $\{a, b, c\}$ is continuous, and it can't be set artificially. The amount of computation will tend to be infinity if traverse the entire planes. In case of this, a set of initial planes is needed in advance to reduce the quantity, and the plane set can represent the whole structure of scene.

We regard the result of plane fitting on each superpixel's initial disparity as our initial plane set. The method relies on the reliable pixels in superpixel to plane fitting, so the reliable pixels of each superpixel are required, and we use Cross-Checking to get them. After plane fitting, some disparity planes with obvious error should be deleted, such as $\{0, 0, 0\}$. To represent the whole structure of the scene using the least quantity of planes, the disparity planes set will convergence constantly to be the most reasonable set of planes through iterative optimization.

Though the disparity planes are generated by plane fitting on the reliable pixels of each superpixel, wrong points may still exist among reliable pixels. The method least squares system is used to determine the parameters of disparity plane directly. As all know, this system is very sensitive to these wrong points.

In this part, a robust solution is generated by a decomposition method to solve each of the parameters. First of all, we calculate the horizontal tilt rate by a disparity set of reliable pixels located on the same level. Import all the derivative $\delta d/\delta x$ into a list, obtain a robust horizontal tilt rate by sorting and making gaussian convolution in the list. In a similar manner, get the vertical tilt rate using the reliable pixels in a vertical line. At last, we acquire a robust disparity in center of the superpixel by those tilt rate.

2.5   Global Optimization Framework

Proposed Energy Function. Our defined energy function is consisted of data term and smooth term. Unlike the global matching algorithm based on pixel that each node of undirected graph corresponds to a pixel in Markov random field, each node corresponds to a piece of superpixel here. The value of pixel is a set of discrete artificial integers, but the value of superpixel is a set of calculated disparity planes. Therefore, there is a big difference for the used graph cut algorithm between them. And the label f changes from mapping of pixel to disparity into mapping of superpixel to disparity plane. We come up with the definition of the minimized energy function of label f as below

$$E(f) = E_{data}(f) + E_{smooth}(f) \tag{5}$$

Data Term. In the first, obtain matching cost of superpixel using the matching cost based on pixel. The matching cost of pixel means $C_d(p)$ when pixel $p(x, y)$ has disparity d, and the matching cost of superpixel points to $C_s(p)$ when superpixel S gets disparity plane $P\{a, b, c\}$. Here, make a reliable judgment to each superpixel, if the disparity plane generated by plane fitting is wrong, we predicate the superpixel is unreliable. And on the contrary, we confident it reliable. When the superpixel is reliable, its form of matching cost as below

$$C_s(p) = \sum_{p \in \{S-O\}} C_{(ax+by+c)}(p) \tag{6}$$

O here means the set of occluded pixels in superpixel S. And when the superpixel is unreliable, the cost expresses as

$$C_s(p) = \sum_{p \in \{S-O+U\}} C_{(ax+by+c)}(p) \tag{7}$$

Where U represents the set of restored pixels. Data term $E_{data}(f)$ is a set of matching cost based on superpixel, the form as show

$$E_{data}(f) = \sum_{S \in R} C_S(f(S)) \tag{8}$$

The ultimate goal is to get the unique joint labeling f that each superpixel $S \in R$ corresponds to a disparity plane $f(S) \in D$. The R points to the set of superpixels in input images, D means disparity planes.

Smooth Term. We consider three factors of adjacent superpixels to generate smooth term here. (1)The length of the common border between adjacent superpixels. (2)The difference of disparity planes between adjacent superpixels.

Fig. 3. Each row is corresponding to a different instance, named Venus, Tsukuba, Teddy, Cones, Aloe and Plastic respectively. Each column represents a different budget. First col: Original image. Second col: Results obtained by using global method based on pixel[24]. Third col: Disparity by global method based on superpixel. Fourth col: Ground Truth. Just judging from the results directly, the difference between the two methods is unconspicuous, so we need quantitative analysis to compare advantages and disadvantages of them.

(3)The difference of color information between adjacent superpixels. For simplicity here, we adopt the mean value of all pixels in the superpixel to represent the color information. The form of smooth term will be

$$E_{smooth}(f) = \sum_{\substack{\forall(S_i,S_j)\in \\ S_N|f(S_i)\neq f(S_j)}} ColorD(S_i,S_j)*PlaneD(S_i,S_j)*CommonB(S_i,S_j) \quad (9)$$

Among them, the S_N is the set of all the adjacent superpixels in input images, $ColorD(S_i,S_j)$ refers to the difference of color information, its value is the euclidean distance in RGB color space between adjacent superpixels. $PlaneD(S_i,S_j)$ is mean of the difference between disparity planes, the value is the euclidean distance between adjacent superpixels in disparity plane $\{a,b,c\}$. $CommonB(S_i,S_j)$ is the length of the common border between adjacent superpixels.

3   Experiments and Results

3.1   Experimental Conditions and Data Sets

We used Visual Studio 2008 of Win 8 operating system in an Intel quad-core (2.90GHz) machine with 8GB memory to test our algorithm on data sets[16–19].

3.2   Comparison of the Results

Although the pixel-level global matching algorithm has achieved a high accuracy, it still exists quite serious errors in some regions of the graph. For instance, there is an entire mismatching region in the right corner of Teddy (Fig.3 the second image of the third row). To solve this problem, we propose a global matching algorithm based on superpixel, this will further improve the matching accuracy.

3.3   Comparison with Other Methods

We test our method (global matching algorithm based on superpixel) and other three stereo matching method on the same standard test data (Tsukuba, Venus, Teddy, and Cones in Middlebury data sets). The error rate of each method is shown in Table.1.

Table 1. Quality assessment results of different method based on data sets Tsukuba, Venus, Teddy and Cones, here the error threshold is 2. As we can see, our algorithm is more substantial upgrade compare to others.

Algorithm	Tsukuba	Venus	Teddy	Cones	Average error rate
Our method	1.47	0.37	6.53	8.61	4.24
ESAW[20]	2.13	1.15	8.48	9.98	5.43
VarMSOH[21]	3.60	0.49	10.10	8.20	5.60
Method on pixel[24]	2.03	0.89	10.40	10.30	5.91
CSBP[22]	3.84	2.52	17.30	14.20	9.47

4   Summary

This paper proposed a new global matching algorithm based on superpixel. Unlike the method based on pixel, each of our node in graph is corresponding to a superpixel in Markov random field model. We introduce the whole algorithm generally, illustrate over-segmentation processing which used to generate superpixel simply. And then calculate the matching cost to obtain initial disparity, plane fitting on the set of superpixel to get initial disparity planes. Finally, generate energy function, it includes data term and smooth term, obtain the final disparity with the minimum solved by optimization algorithm to the entire energy function. In future work, we plan to focus on improving our method based on different energy term or other ways to make our system more comprehensive.

References

1. Boykov, Y., Veksler, O., Zabih, R.: Fast approximate energy minimization via graph cuts. IEEE Transactions on Pattern Analysis and Machine Intelligence 23(11), 1222–1239 (2001)
2. Felzenszwalb, P.F., Huttenlocher, D.P.: Efficient belief propagation for early vision. International Journal of Computer Vision 70(1), 41–54 (2006)
3. Tappen, M.F., Freeman, W.T.: Comparison of graph cuts with belief propagation for stereo using identical MRF parameters. In: Ninth IEEE International Conference on Computer Vision, pp. 900–907 (2003)
4. Scharstein, D., Szeliski, R.: Middlebury Stereo Vision Research Page (2011), http://vision.middlebury.edu/stereo/eval/
5. Bleyer, M., Rother, C., Kohli, P., Scharstein, D., Sinha, S.: Object stereo-joint stereo matching and object segmentation. In: IEEE Conference on Computer Vision and Pattern Recognition, pp. 3081–3088. IEEE Computer Press, Washington (2011)
6. Hirschmuller, H.: Accurate and efficient stereo processing by semi-global matching and mutual information. IEEE Transactions on Pattern Analysis and Machine Intelligence 30(2), 328–341 (2008)
7. Comaniciu, D., Meer, P.: Mean shift: A robust approach toward feature space analysis. IEEE Transactions on Pattern Analysis and Machine Intelligence 24(5), 603–619 (2002)
8. Yang, Q.X., Wang, L., Yang, R.G., Stewenius, H., Nister, D.: Stereo Matching with Color-Weighted Correlation, Hierarchical Belief Propagation, and Occlusion Handling. IEEE Transactions on Pattern Analysis and Machine Intelligence 31(3), 492–504 (2009)
9. Bleyer, M., Gelautz, M.: A layered stereo algorithm using image segmentation and global visibility constraints. In: International Conference on Image Processing, pp. 2997–3000 (2004)
10. Zitnick, C., Kang, S.B.: Stereo for image-based rendering using image over-segmentation. International Journal of Computer Vision 75(1), 49–65 (2007)
11. Ladick, L., Sturgess, P., Russell, C., Sengupta, S., Bastanlar, Y., Clocksin, W., Torr, P.: Joint Optimization for Object Class Segmentation and Dense Stereo Reconstruction. International Journal of Computer Vision, 1–12 (2011)

12. Zhang, K., Lu, J.B., Lafruit, G.: Cross-Based Local Stereo Matching Using Orthogonal Integral Images. Circuits and Systems for Video Technology 19(7), 1073–1079 (2009)
13. Geoffrey, E., Richard, P.W.: Detecting Binocular Half-Occlusions: Empirical Comparisons of Five Approaches. Pattern Analysis and Machine Intelligence 24(8), 1127–1133 (2002)
14. Yoon, K.J., Kweon, S.: Adaptive support-weight approach for correspondence search. Pattern Analysis and Machine Intelligence 28(4), 650–656 (2006)
15. Tombari, F., Mattoccia, S., Di Stefano, L.: Segmentation-based adaptive support for accurate stereo correspondence. In: Mery, D., Rueda, L. (eds.) PSIVT 2007. LNCS, vol. 4872, pp. 427–438. Springer, Heidelberg (2007)
16. Scharstein, D., Szeliski, R.: High-accuracy stereo depth maps using structured light. In: Computer Vision and Pattern Recognition, pp. 195–202 (2003)
17. Scharstein, D., Szeliski, R.: A taxonomy and evaluation of dense two frame stereo correspondence algorithms. In: IEEE Workshop on Stereo and Multi-Baseline Vision, pp. 131–140 (2001)
18. Scharstein, D., Pal, C.: Learning conditional random fields for stereo. In: Computer Vision and Pattern Recognition, pp. 1–8 (2007)
19. Hirschm'ller, H., Scharstein, D.: Evaluation of cost functions for stereo matching. In: Computer Vision and Pattern Recognition, pp. 1–8 (2007)
20. Yu, W., Chen, T., Franchetti, F.: High performance stereo vision designed for massively data parallel platforms. Circuits and System for Video Technology 20(11), 1509–1519 (2010)
21. Ben-Ari, R., Sochen, N.: Stereo matching with Mumford-Shah regularization and occlusion handling. Pattern Analysis and Machine Intelligence 32(11), 2071–2084 (2010)
22. Yang, Q., Wang, L., Ahuja, N.: A constant-space belief propagation algorithm for stereo matching. In: Computer Vision and Pattern Recognition, pp. 1458–1465 (2010)
23. Comaniciu, D., Meer, P.: Robust Analysis of Feature Spaces: Color Image Segmentation. In: Proc. IEEE Conf. Computer Vision and Pattern Recognition, pp. 750–755 (1997)
24. Jin, H., Liu, S.: Self-adaptive matching in local windows for depth estimation. In: Proc. of the 27th European Conference on Modelling and Simulation, pp. 831–837. European Council for Modeling and Simulation, Aalesund (2013)

Two-Stage Saliency Detection
Based on Continuous CRF and Sparse Coding

Qiyang Zhao[1], Weibo Li[2], Fan Wang[1], and Baolin Yin[1]

[1] NLSDE, School of Computer Science and Engineering
Beihang University, Beijing, China
[2] Beijing Youth Politics College, Beijing, China

Abstract. In the state-of-the-art saliency detection methods based on contrast priors, little attention is paid on the region smoothness constraints. The paper proposes a two-stage saliency detection method in which a smoothness prior is explicitly involved in a continuous Conditional Random Field (CRF). In stage one, we construct a continuous CRF based on the sparse codes of perceptual features on all locations, and minimize the energy of CRF to obtain discrimination maps. In stage two, we train a discriminative machine and learn the saliency maps from discrimination maps, aiming to take the human attention priors into consideration. Our experiments on MSRA-1000 show that the new method is effective against the state-of-the-art methods.

Keywords: saliency, continuous CRF, sparse coding.

1 Introduction

In recent years, saliency detection is an emerging problem in object recognition and image understanding. Generally, there are two parallel directions of saliency detection researches: bottom-up detection [1]-[12] and top-down detection [13]. The two directions differ from each other in both their targets and adopted features. The top-down detection uses high-level concepts to localize objects of particular categories, while the bottom-up detection uses only low-level cues to highlight informative regions of any categories. Here we focus on the bottom-up detection.

Earlier methods focus on the analysis on human eye fixation data, so to extract the human attention prior and predict the most salient regions [1][2]. Recent literatures pay more attention on contrast priors of perceptual differences between salient regions and background regions, such as mutual information [6], incremental coding length [3], and center-versus-surround perceptual discrepancy [7]-[9]. Other methods predict the saliency on the global scale, including boolean map [4]hypergraph modeling [5], geodesic saliency [10], saliency filters [11], low-rank decomposition [12].

However, beyond the contrast priors and attention priors, it is empirically shown that salient locations are spatially clustered, in other word, the saliency of adjacent pixels are coherent. This observation has already been exploited in

S. Li et al. (Eds.): CCPR 2014, Part I, CCIS 483, pp. 455–463, 2014.

recent top-down saliency detection method [13] in the form of smoothness priors, but only focusing on a small set of semantic labels and incapable of dealing with unknown categories. Smoothness priors have played key roles in other fields such as interactive segmentation and image editing. However in existing bottom-up saliency detection methods, it is only involved implicitly in the center-versus-surround priors [7]-[9], but seldom explicitly posed.

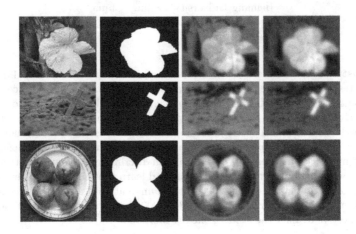

Fig. 1. Examples of our method on MSRA-1000. From left to right: images, groundtruths, discrimination maps and saliency maps.

In this paper, we aim to provide a new method for bottom-up saliency detection, to fulfill contrast priors and attention priors simultaneously. We introduce a continuous Conditional Random Field (CRF) model to impose the smoothness constraint on the saliency of adjacent pixels. Compared with [13], our model focus on low-level cues instead of high-level concepts, and pay much more attention to the pixel-level precisions. Our method is more suitable for genetic saliency detection rather than for specific categories. The method includes two stages: (1) estimate a discrimination map to make a rough saliency proposal. This discrimination map is produced by optimizing a continuous CRF with spectral methods; (2) construct a discriminative machine involving the human attention priors, and learn the saliency map from the discrimination maps obtained in stage one.

2   The Proposed Method

The method consists of two stages: discrimination-map stage and saliency-map stage, as depicted in Fig.2. In stage one, we focus on contrast priors and smoothness priors which are integrated in a CRF model. In stage two, we focus on the human attention prior, which is encoded in a trained Multi-Layer Perceptrons (MLP).

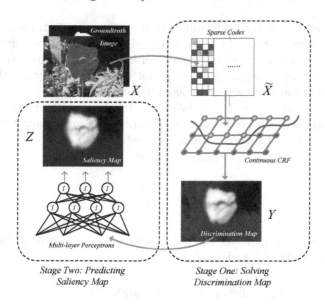

Fig. 2. The flow chart of our method

2.1 Continuous CRF Based on Sparse Codes

In the first stage, we aim to produce a discrimination map, which indicates the saliency discriminations between locations rather than the saliency itself. The discrete CRF models are widely used in interactive segmentation methods to impose smoothness constraints [15][16]. Given an image $X = \{x_i\}(i = 1, 2, \cdots, n)$, the goal in discrete CRFs is to obtain the optimum label configuration $Y = \{y_i\}$ by minimizing the energy function

$$E_{discrete} = \sum_i \phi(i, y_i) + \lambda \cdot \sum_{(i,j) \in N} \psi(i,j) \cdot [y_i \neq y_j]. \tag{1}$$

Here $y_i \in \{0, 1\}$ indicates whether i belongs to the *foreground* or not. The smoothness prior ψ encourages adjacent pixels belonging to the same region. λ is a tunable coefficient.

However in saliency detection tasks, the saliency map is of real values in $[0, 1]$. Therefore we relax y_i in (1) to be in $[0, 1]$ (1 stands for the highest saliency and 0 negative. Its inverse also works). Now the discrete model in (1) are rewritten as a continuous CRF which is proposed in [17]:

$$E_{continuous} = \sum_i \phi(i, y_i) + \lambda \cdot \sum_{(i,j) \in N} \psi(i,j) \cdot f(y_i, y_j). \tag{2}$$

where $f(y_i, y_j) = y_i(1-y_j) + y_j(1-y_i)$. On ϕ we follow the well-adopted likelihood term in [15] and [16], but in the continuous forms again:

$$\phi(i, y_i) = -y_i \cdot \ln p^+(i) - (1 - y_i) \cdot \ln p^-(i) \tag{3}$$

where p^+ and p^- are the probabilities of the perceptual features occurring in salient/non-salient regions. In order to model the perceptual features comprehensively, we adopt sparse coding instead of hand-tuned features. We calculate the sparse code $\widetilde{x}_i = [\widetilde{x}_{i,1}, \widetilde{x}_{i,2}, \cdots, \widetilde{x}_{i,K}]$ for each pixel i following the way in [18]. The sizes of dictionaries constructed in sparse coding are set to be 75, and all local blocks are of size 5×5, following [18]. In order to make the sparse coding manipulations feasible for corner locations, we make mirror replications on image borders. All sparsity level K's are set to be 3. Finally we calculate its composing vector $\alpha_i = [\alpha_{i,1}, \alpha_{i,2}, \cdots, \alpha_{i,K}]$ as

$$\alpha_{i,k} = \frac{|\widetilde{x}_{i,k}|}{\sum_j |\widetilde{x}_{i,j}|} \tag{4}$$

Roughly to say, $\alpha_{i,k}$ indicates the portions to which i consists of the patterns corresponding to the kth codeword. Let

$$n_{i,k}^+ = y_i \alpha_{i,k}, \ n_{i,k}^- = (1 - y_i)\alpha_{i,k},$$
$$n_k^+ = \sum_i n_{i,k}^+, \ n_k^- = \sum_i n_{i,k}^-, \ n_k = \sum_i \alpha_{i,k},$$
$$n^+ = \sum_k n_k^+, \ n^- = \sum_k n_k^-. \tag{5}$$

Intuitively, n_k^+ and n_k^- are the portions of the kth pattern in two regions. We have $n_k = n_k^+ + n_k^-$ for all k's. The two densities are written as *polynomial distributions*

$$p^+(i) = \prod_k (\frac{n_k^+}{n^+})^{(n_{i,k}^+)}, p^-(i) = \prod_k (\frac{n_k^-}{n^-})^{(n_{i,k}^-)}, \tag{6}$$

and we rewrite ϕ as

$$\phi(i, y_i) = - n_{i,k}^+ \sum_k \left(\ln \frac{n_k^+}{n^+} \right) - n_{i,k}^- \sum_k \left(\ln \frac{n_k^-}{n^-} \right) \tag{7}$$

Apparently ϕ stands for the entropy of describing i given the perceptual feature distributions from the salient/non-salient region. Hereafter our goal is to optimize the energy E in (2) under the constraints on y_i's:

$$\min E_{continuous}, \text{s.t. } 0 \leq y_i \leq 1, \ \forall i \tag{8}$$

Unfortunately it is harder to tackle than (1) in interactive segmentation tasks, because we have to optimize p^+, p^- and Y jointly. Furthermore, logarithm functions in ϕ magnify the hardness and complexity in our settings. To address this, we present a new approximate way in the next section.

2.2 Obtaining Discrimination Map by Optimizing Continuous CRF

Following (7), we have

$$\sum_i \phi(i, y_i) = \left[n \cdot \left(\frac{n^+}{n} \ln \frac{n^+}{n} + \frac{n^-}{n} \ln \frac{n^-}{n} \right) + n \ln n \right]$$
$$- \sum_k \left[n_k \cdot \left(\frac{n_k^+}{n_k} \ln \frac{n_k^+}{n_k} + \frac{n_k^-}{n_k} \ln \frac{n_k^-}{n_k} \right) + n_k \ln n_k \right] \tag{9}$$

The first step is to tackle these logarithm terms to make them easier to handle. Notice that all logarithm terms are of the form $(\mu \ln \mu + \nu \ln \nu)$ where $(\mu + \nu = 1)$. We can get the asymptotic form with the help of its *Taylor expansion*:

$$-\frac{5}{2} \cdot \mu\nu + O\left(\mu^3\nu\right) + O\left(\nu^3\mu\right). \tag{10}$$

All high order terms can be neglected in following calculations because μ, ν are both less than 1. After replacing all related terms in (9) with the first term in (10), and eliminating all constant terms, we find it is equivalently minimizing the following E^* when working on (8):

$$E^* = -\frac{5}{2n} n^+ \cdot n^- + \sum_k \left(\frac{5}{2n_k} n_k^+ \cdot n_k^- \right) - \frac{1}{2} \cdot \lambda \sum_{(i,j) \in N} \psi(i, j) \cdot (\tilde{y}_i \cdot \tilde{y}_j). \tag{11}$$

where $\tilde{y}_i = 2y_i - 1$. Although the convexity of $E_{continuous}$ is hard to determine, it is easily to infer that E^* is convex with respect to each $\tilde{y}_i$, given all other $\tilde{y}_j$ fixed($i \neq j$). Based on this observation, our target is equivalent to

$$\min E^*, \text{s.t. } \tilde{y}_i \in \{-1, +1\}, \forall i. \tag{12}$$

However this is a quadric binary optimization problem of NP-hardness. Our solution to this is relaxing the constraint $\tilde{y}_i^2 = 1(i = 1, 2, \cdots, n)$ to be $||\tilde{Y}||^2 = n$. After that, our problem can be dealt with spectral analysis, as shown in below.

First we construct a $n \times n$ matrix W, in which the entry $w_{i,j}$ is the sum of the following three terms

$$w_{i,j}^{(1)} = -\frac{5}{2n}, w_{i,j}^{(2)} = \frac{5}{2} \cdot \sum_k \frac{\alpha_{i,k}\alpha_{j,k}}{n_k}$$
$$w_{i,j}^{(3)} = \begin{cases} -\frac{1}{2} \cdot \lambda \cdot \psi(i, j), & \text{if } (i, j) \in N, \\ 0, & \text{otherwise.} \end{cases} \tag{13}$$

It is easy to prove that $E^* = \frac{1}{2}\left(S_W - \tilde{Y}^T W \tilde{Y}\right)$, here S_W denotes the sum of all entries of W. So it is equivalent to

$$\max \tilde{Y}^T W \tilde{Y},$$
$$\text{s.t. } \sum_i \tilde{y}_i^2 = n \tag{14}$$

Apparently the optimum solution is the largest eigenvector of W [20],where we can draw support from reduced eigensystems to improve the computational efficiency [14]. Finally, we map $\widetilde{Y}$ back into $[0,1]^n$ to get Y:

$$y_i = \frac{\widetilde{y}_i - \min_j \widetilde{y}_j}{\max_j \widetilde{y}_j - \min_j \widetilde{y}_j} \tag{15}$$

2.3   Predicting Saliency from Discrimination Map

In order to accommodate images of diverse sizes, all training and prediction are done on regular sizes: first, we resize the discrimination maps to be of regular sizes, and predict saliency values on them; at last, we cast the saliency maps back to original sizes by interpolation. Currently, the regular image size is set to be 128×128.

Given an image X and the human-labeled saliency map $Z = \{z_i\}$ where $z_i \in \{0,1\}$, our aim is to learn the saliency predicting function F:

$$F(y_1, y_2, \cdots, y_n) = (z_1, z_2, \cdots, z_n). \tag{16}$$

Here we adopt Multi-layer Perceptrons (MLP) to fulfill F. The training data are constructed in the following way. Given an image X and human-labeled saliency map Z, we calculate its discrimination map $Y = \{y_i\}$ as described in Sec.2.2. Then we resize Y and Z to be of regular sizes. After that, we get two training samples, Y and its inverse $(1 - Y)$, both with the same saliency label Z (recall that we are not sure which one of Y or $(1 - Y)$ would be obtained in stage one). We repeat this procedure on each image and establish the complete training set.

The training procedure are implemented by the popular gradient descending method. After the training is finished, we predict the saliency map for each new image with the trained MLP instead of the underlying true function F.

Notice that the location information are encoded in the indices of y_i, to say, spatial relations are involved in the saliency prediction. As its consequence, the human attention priors are implicitly encoded in the structure of MLP.

3   Experiments

We evaluate our method on the widely-used MSRA-1000 dataset [19]. This dataset includes 1,000 images with accurate human labels of salient regions. The partitioning ratio of train/validation/test image amounts is 3:3:4. The performance measures include precision, recall and F-measure. Here the F-measure is calculated as

$$F_\beta = \frac{(1 + \beta^2) \cdot precision \cdot recall}{\beta^2 \cdot precision + recall}, \tag{17}$$

where $\beta^2 = 0.3$ as suggested in [19].

In the smoothness prior, we choose ψ as the learned gaussian function in [16], but plus 1 to emphasize smoothness everywhere. The coefficient λ varies from

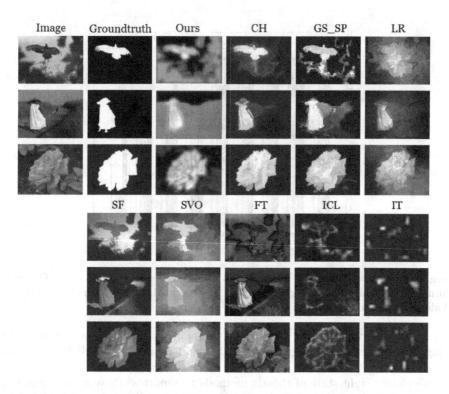

Fig. 3. Salient region examples from all nine methods on MSRA-1000. Notice our saliency values are slightly more continuous due to our optimization method, but the salient regions can be distinguished easily also.

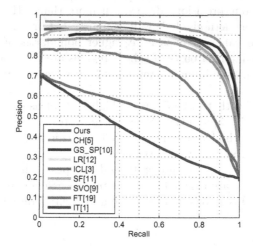

Fig. 4. Quantitive *PR* performance of all nine methods on MSRA-1000. Our method obtain a competitive *PR* performance in all methods. Values are reproduced from [5].

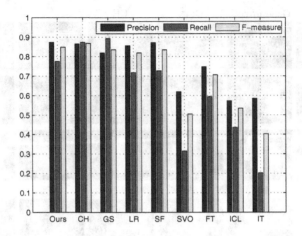

Fig. 5. Quantitive *F*-measure performance of all methods on MSRA-1000. Our performance is slightly worse only than CH in [5], but clearly better than other methods. Values are reproduced from [5].

0.1 to 10 with the stepsize 0.1, and we find 4.6 is of the best performance. In stage two, there is one hidden layer of 1000 hidden units in the MLP of saliency prediction.

We choose eight state-of-the-art methods to report as the counterparts: CH [5], GS_SP [10], LR [12], ICL [3], SF [11], SVO [9], FT [19], and IT [1]. The *PR* curves and *F*-measures are shown in fig.4-5. It could be concluded that our method is rather competitive among all methods, except that its precisions are slightly lower than CH [5] and GS_SP [10] on high recalls. When the recalls are approaching 1, our precisions drop down more than CH and GS_SP, but are higher than other methods. It is well demonstrated in fig.3: compared with CH and GS_SP, our saliency maps have vaguer boundaries of salient regions. Roughly to say, the internal parts of salient regions are paid more attention in our method, following the human attention schemes learned by MLPs in stage two.

Furthermore, notice that in fig.5, on the highest *F*-measures, our precision is higher than that of CH [5] and GS_SP [10]. It indicates that precisions are more emphasized in our method, which is suitable to specific high-level tasks such as simultaneous object recognition and segmentation.

Our time consumptions are moderate and acceptable in real applications. After the sparse codes are calculated in the preprocessing stage, the time consumption MSRA-100 is 11.32s in average on a i5 2.2GHz Intel CPU.

4 Conclusions

The paper presents a two-stage salient region detection method. Our experiments on MSRA-1000 show it is competitive in *PR* performance and feasible in time consumptions. Contrast priors and attention priors are integrated well in our framework to obtain the final saliency maps. Future works lie in potential improvements on the optimization task in stage one, and the robustness of precisions under changing recalls in a large range.

Acknowledgement. This work is supported by the State Key Laboratory of Software Development Environment (No.SKLSDE-2013ZX-29, SKLSDE-2013ZX-34).

References

1. Itti, L., Koch, C., Niebur, E.: A model of saliency-based visual attention for rapid scene analysis. IEEE Trans. PAMI 20(11), 1254–1259 (1998)
2. Bruce, N., Tsotsos, J.: Saliency based on information maximization. In: NIPS, vol. 18, p. 155 (2005)
3. Hou, X., Zhang, L.: Dynamic visual attention: Searching for coding length increments. In: NIPS, vol. 5, p. 7 (2008)
4. Zhang, J., Sclaroff, S.: Saliency detection: A boolean map approach. In: ICCV (2013)
5. Li, X., Li, Y., Shen, C., et al.: Contextual Hypergraph Modeling for salient object detection. In: ICCV (2013)
6. Gao, D., Mahadevan, V., Vasconcelos, N.: The discrimininant center-surround hypothesis for bottom-up saliency. In: NIPS (2007)
7. Feng, J., Wei, Y., Tao, L., et al.: Salient object detection by composition. In: ICCV (2011)
8. Klein, D., Frintrop, S.: Center-surround diverfence of feature statistics for salient object detection. In: ICCV (2011)
9. Chang, K., Liu, T., Chen, H., et al.: Fusing generic objectness and visual saliency for salient object detection. In: ICCV (2011)
10. Wei, Y., Wen, F., Zhu, W., Sun, J.: Geodesic saliency using background priors. In: Fitzgibbon, A., Lazebnik, S., Perona, P., Sato, Y., Schmid, C. (eds.) ECCV 2012, Part III. LNCS, vol. 7574, pp. 29–42. Springer, Heidelberg (2012)
11. Perazzi, F., Krahenbuhl, P., Ferrari, Y., et al.: Saliency filters: Contrast based filtering for salient region detection. In: CVPR (2012)
12. Shen, X., Wu, Y.: A unified approach to salient object detection via low rank matrix recovery. In: CVPR (2012)
13. Yang, J., Yang, M.: Top-down visual saliency via joint CRF and dictionary learning. In: CVPR (2012)
14. Taylor, C.: Towards Fast and Accurate Segmentation. In: CVPR (2013)
15. Vicente, S., Kolmogorov, V., Rother, C.: Joint optimization of segmentation and appearance models. In: ICCV (2009)
16. Rother, C., Kolmogorov, V., Blake, A.: Grabcut: interactive foreground extraction using iterated graph cuts. In: SIGGRAPH (2004)
17. Qin, T., Liu, T., Zhang, X., et al.: Global ranking using continuous conditional random fields. In: NIPS (2008)
18. Ren, X., Bo, L.: Discriminatively trained sparse code gradients for contour detection. In: NIPS (2012)
19. Achanta, R., Smith, K., et al.: Frequency-tuned salient region detection. In: CVPR (2009)
20. Golub, G., Van Loan, C.: Matrix Computations. John Hopkins Press (1996)

Continuous Energy Minimization
Based Multi-target Tracking

Zhe Shi, Songhao Zhu, Wei Sun, and Baoyun Wang

School of Automatic, Nanjing University of Post and Telecommunications,
Nanjing, 210046, China
njuptzsl@yeah.net

Abstract. This paper proposes a novel method to deal with the issue of multi-target tracking by taking into account the information of continuous energy minimization and discriminative appearance models simultaneously. Specifically, the information of observation model, appearance model, exclusion model, dynamic model, trajectory persistence model and trajectory regulation model are first adopted to construct an objective function of each tracking trajectory; then, the gradient descent method is here adopted to obtain an approximate minimum of the constructed objective function at every moment, and to obtain the number of and the status of tracking targets; finally, continuous energy minimization based intelligent extrapolation method is here utilized to achieve the final continuous and smooth tracking trajectories. Experimental results on PETS 2009/2010 benchmark and TUD-Stadtmitte video database demonstrate the effectiveness and efficiency of the proposed scheme.

1   Introduction

Multi-target tracking has emerged as an active research topic in the past two decades due to its widespread applications in many areas, including intelligent surveillance, smart rooms, visual human computer interfaces, autonomous robotics, augmented reality and video compression. The aim of multi-target tracking is to locate the location of targets, obtain the number of targets, infer the trajectories of targets, and keep the tracking of targets. With the performance improvement of target detection algorithms in recent years, detection-based multi-target tracking methods are receiving more and more attention worldwide. For these detection-based multi-target tracking methods, several features including appearance feature, displacement feature, and speed feature are integrated into an object function to measure the similarity between detection responses.

Detecting and Tracking multi targets simultaneously is a highly complex and challenging problem, especially in crowded environment where targets with similar appearance and frequently occluding each other. To solve the problem of false alarms caused by frequent mutual occlusion between targets, [1] proposes a target detection method based on the continuous energy minimum. Specifically, the information of targets is first adopted to construct an energy function. The, the optimal solution of the energy function is utilized to achieve the accurate association between different detection responses, rather than implementing target tracking by checking the association between all targets. Therefore, tiny tracelets are gradually connected to form a longer tracking trajectory, and smooth trajectories are achieved.

S. Li et al. (Eds.): CCPR 2014, Part I, CCIS 483, pp. 464–473, 2014.

Appearance features, such as color histograms [2], templates [3], and gradients histogram [4], are utilized to determinate the location of each target. The association between targets is utilized to help to solve the false alarm problem caused by mutual occlusion between targets. Therefore, there are reasons for believing that appearance features and data association are two important factors that affect the tracking performance. Although there are many data association techniques have been proposed in recent years, relatively less previous works have been focused on the improved appearance contour model.

To get satisfactory tracking results, this paper proposes a novel approach based on the continuous energy minimization and discriminative appearance models, namely an objective function is constructed using appearance features and motion features. Specifically, observation model, appearance model and dynamic model are adopted to get the state information of each target; then, exclusive model, trajectory keep model and trajectory correction model are utilized to reduce the false alarm rate, missed alarm rate and identity interchange rate; finally, the gradient descent method is utilized to solve the energy function constructed using these six models to achieve the approximate minimum energy of each target, and to achieve the total number of targets and the accurate state information of each target. Note that the energy function constructed here is a non-convex function, and therefore there may be two or more peaks in the process of global tracking. Therefore, a series of jumping motion is introduced to change the dimension of the current state and the direction of the search space. In this case, the iteration process is done along the direction of energy decrease to obtain the minimum energy.

The rest of the paper is organized as follows. Related work is discussed in section 2. The detail of the proposed approach is presented in section 3. The experimental are shown in section 4. The conclusions are given in section 5.

2   Related Works

It can be seen form the discussed above, appearance feature and data association are two important factors that affect the tracking performance significantly. Therefore, a lot of efforts have been done to perform a global optimization to build correct data associations, such as Multi-Hypothesis Tracking (MHT) [5], Joint Probabilistic Data Association Filters [6]. The performance of these recursive methods is strictly affected by computational resources, and these recursive methods are usually not applicable for long time data association since the size of search space grows exponentially with the number of video frames. Therefore, many non-recursive methods are proposed to obtain a global optimization of the data association within a long time interval, such as Hungarian algorithm based tracking [7], hierarchical association based tracking [8], network flow based tracking [9], maximum weight-independent set based tracking [10], and flow linear programs based tracking [11].

The aim of these recursive or non-recursive methods is to achieve local or global optimization. In the present work, the question of whether the restriction to a finite state space is really necessary in multi-target tracking is investigated. It turns out that a well-designed local optimization scheme in a continuous state space can achieve good solutions, in terms of visual quality and tracking precision.

The performance of multi-target tracking is also affected by the selected appearance contour models, and there are many technologies that have been proposed to collect training samples online from tracking tracklets to learn appearance contour models. In [12], the positive samples are collected from the same tracklets within a few neighboring frames, and the collected positive samples are always deficient in diversity. Therefore, in case of illumination changes or pose changes, tracklets from the same target within a long time interval may have different appearance information. On the contrary, the entry/exit points are here utilized to obtain correct associations between tracklets, and the diversity of the positive samples collected from tracklets with long gaps are high.

3   Multi-target Tracking

3.1   Energy Minimization

Recently, continuous or offline energy minimization method is widely utilized in multiple-target tracking to achieve the association between targets. Energy minimization method is developed on the basis of linear programming, and the goal of which is to track interested targets robustly throughout the whole video sequence. That is, for the whole video sequence, every tracking target or tracking trajectory needs to be assigned a unique label, and this assigned label needs to be as close as possible to the true target or true motion trajectory.

There are two major problems needed to be solved when designing an energy function: (1) Noise is more often found in input data, which requires training and learning a robust classifier; (2) It is difficult to detect and track interested targets from surveillance video sequences in real-time case. Furthermore, the constructed energy function is usually a non-convex function, which makes it hard to get the optimal association.

Based on the above discussion, the optimal association can be obtained by implementing the following two steps: (1) A global optimal energy function is defined and the optimization of the energy function is implemented; (2) The gradient descent method is adopted to obtain the optimal solution of the optimized energy function throughout the whole video sequence. The energy function is here defined as:

$$E(X) = \alpha E_{app}(X) + \beta E_{vis}(X) + \gamma E_{dyn}(X) + \kappa E_{exc} + \lambda E_{mat}(X) + \mu E_{cor}(X) \quad (1)$$

where $\alpha, \beta, \kappa, \gamma, \lambda, \mu$ are the different model weights. E_{app} is the energy of appearance model, and E_{det} denotes the energy of visibility model and helps to eliminate the association between targets. E_{exc}, E_{dyn} and E_{per} denote the energy of exclusion model, dynamic model, trajectory persistence model respectively, which help to optimize the tracking results. E_{cor} denotes the energy of trajectory correction model, which helps to prevent the over-fitting in the process of iterating to a certain extent.

The optimal tracking trajectory $X*$ is the optimal solution of the following equation:

$$X^* = \arg\min_{X \in R} E(X) \quad (2)$$

where $E(X^*)$ is consecutive minimum energy in the search space R. The value of $E(X^*)$ depends on the length of video sequences and the number of tracking target, and generally between 10^3 and 10^4. Next, the six components in equation (1) will be detailed one by one.

3.1.1 Appearance Model

The appearance model is here adopted to compare the detected tracking trajectory with initialized tracking trajectory to ensure that the iteration process is done along the direction of energy decrease. That is, it can be said that the current energy is the minimum energy when the location in each direction exactly matches each initialized value. To achieve the exact location of each tracking target, the smoothing technology is here adopted to increase the distance between the location of the ith tracking target X_i^t and the given position d_{gt}^t.

The energy function of the appearance model can be formulated as follows:

$$E_{det}(X) = \sum_{t=1}^{F} \sum_{i=1}^{N} (\phi + \sum_{g=1}^{D(t)} \omega_{gt}^j \frac{-s^2}{\left\| X_i^t - d_{gt}^t \right\|^2 + s^2}) \tag{3}$$

where F and N are the number of video frames and tracking respectively, and $D(t)$ is the number of detected peaks in the tth frame. φ, a punishment coefficient, is utilized to punish those video frames with no interested targets and is 0.05 in all experiments. ω_{pl}^i is the weight of each tracking target, and s is the size of each tracking target.

3.1.2 Visibility Model

The appearance information will be incomplete as there exists mutual occlusion between two targets, and therefore the visibility information between two targets is here adopted to lessen the impact of mutual occlusion on the tracking performance:

$$AC(X_i^t) = \sqrt{v(X_i^t).v(X_i^{t+1})}.(1 - C(X_i^t)) \tag{4}$$

where $v(X_i^t)$ is the visibility information of the ith tracking target in the tth frame, and $C(x_i^t)$ is the texture information computed using the following formula:

$$\begin{cases} C(X_i^t) = \frac{1}{n-1} \sum_{k=1}^{n} (z_k - \mu)(z_k - \mu)^T \\ z_k = [\frac{\partial I}{\partial x}, \frac{\partial I}{\partial y}, \frac{\partial^2 I}{\partial x^2}, \frac{\partial^2 I}{\partial y^2}, \frac{\partial^2 I}{\partial x \partial y}]^T \end{cases} \tag{5}$$

where n is the number of pixels.

The energy function of model is here defined as the nonlinear sigmoid function:

$$E_{app}(X) = \sum_{i=1}^{N} \sum_{t=s_i}^{e_i-1} \frac{1}{1 + \exp(\alpha_1 - \alpha_2 * AC(X_i^t))} \tag{6}$$

where α_1 and α_2 are 7.2 and 33.7 respectively according to the experimental results.

3.1.3   Exclusive Model

The exclusive model is here proposed to deal with the mutual occlusion problem, and the corresponding energy function is formulated as follows:

$$E_{exc}(X) = \sum_{t=1}^{F} \sum_{j \neq i}^{N(t)} \frac{s}{\left\| X_i^t - X_j^t \right\|^2} \tag{7}$$

where the scale factor s is set to be 45cm as the same in equation (3).

3.1.4   Dynamic Model

According to the daily experience that the movement speeds of each tracking target is lower than the change speed of the content within each frame. Therefore, the movement information of a tracking target is relatively limited and can be obtained using a dynamic model as shown in the following equation:

$$E_{dyn}(X) = \sum_{t=1}^{F-2} \sum_{i=1}^{N} \left\| X_i^t - 2X_i^{t+1} + X_i^{t+1} \right\|^2 \tag{8}$$

Equation (8) shows the distance between consecutive velocity vectors can be minimized by a dynamic model

3.1.5   Trajectory Maintenance Model

Missed alarm of a target will lead to the corresponding tracking process being terminated, and it is important that tracking trajectories should be smoothed when targets move out of the monitored area. Therefore, a trajectory maintenance model, namely a modified sigmoid function, is here introduced to integrate the missed alarm information into the energy function as shown in equation (1) to generate more precise tracking trajectories:

$$E_{per}(X) = \sum_{t=1}^{F} \sum_{i=1}^{N} \left(\frac{1}{1 + \exp(1 - q \cdot d(X_i^t))} \right) \tag{9}$$

where $d(x_i^t)$ represents the distance between the ith tracking trajectory and the nearest tracking trajectory. q is the entry margin and set to be $1/s$ with s=45cm the target size as shown in equation (6).

3.1.6   Trajectory Correction Model

The aim of trajectory correction model is to avoid label confusion of tracking trajectories and obtain longer tracking trajectories. That is, trajectory correction model as shown in the following equation is here utilized to restrict the number of tracking trajectories and optimize the length of tracking trajectories:

$$E_{cor}(X) = N + \sum_{i=1}^{N} \frac{1}{F(i)} \tag{10}$$

where $F(i)$ represents the length of the ith tracking trajectory in a video sequence. It should be noted that the length of a video sequence can be seen as an important cue for adjusting the length of tracking trajectories.

3.2   Multi-target Tracking

The energy function constructed as shown in equation (1) is a non-convex function, and there may be two or more peaks in the global optimization procedure. Therefore, a series of jump motions are first introduced to change the dimension of the current tracking state X_{curr}; then, the searching of minimum energy is performed in different regions; finally, the minimum energy is achieved iteratively along the direction where energy declines.

As an example shown in the following figure (2), a new tracking tracklet is added and an unreasonable tracking tracklet is deleted after the operation of moving and relating along the direction where energy declines. Meanwhile, the deleted tracking tracklet is added into the existing trajectory to achieve longer tracking trajectory.

Intelligent deduction is here utilized to achieve the minimum energy of equation (1), which consists of the following three types of strategies: (1) Lengthening and shorting strategies; (2) Merging and splitting strategies; (3) Adding and deleting strategies. Next, these three types of strategies will be detailed as below.

●**Lengthening and Shorting Strategies:** The aims of the lengthening strategy are to recover those undetected targets, and the aim of the shorting strategy is to delete those falsely detected as new targets. That is, the current tracking trajectory will be shorted if the optimization tracking location can not be detected in the next iteration step; on the contrary, the current tracking trajectory will be lengthened if the iteration process is implemented along the direction where the energy declines.

●**Adding and Deleting Strategies:** The aim of the adding and deleting strategies is to distinguish occluded targets from each other. That is, a unified appearance model is adopted to track occluded targets with manually annotated labels continuously; then, new tracklet will be captured at the locations with the strongest energy, and the newly captured tracklet is not assigned to any current trajectory; next, the energies of the newly captured tracklet within three consecutive frames are computed; finally, the newly captured tracklet will be added into one existing trajectory if the computed energies within three consecutive frames reduce gradually, and otherwise the newly captured tracklet will be deleted.

●**Merging and Splitting Strategies:** The aims of the merging and splitting strategies are to eliminate the issue of label switching between occluded targets. That is, one trajectory can be split if the energy reduces after the splitting operation, and the split trajectory can be integrated into an reasonable trajectory; several   trajectories can be merged into one trajectory if the energy are less than before and the movement direction is reasonable.

Different from the Reversible Jump Markov Chain Monte Carlo method, the proposed intelligent deduction method is deterministic: (1) Gradient descent is adopted to perform the iteration operation along the direction where the energy declines, and perform the association operation between adjacent targets; (2) The jumping will be not be ended as long as the iteration process is performed along the direction where the gradient energy declines.

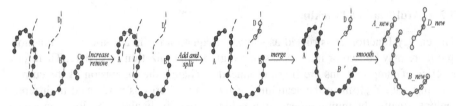

Fig. 1. The true trajectories in crowed scenes even with a poor initial configuration can also be recovered using the proposed energy function, where the information of jumping and standard conjugate gradient helps to achieve longer and smoother trajectories

4   Experiments

4.1   Experimental Setting

The performance of the proposed method is evaluated on PETS 2009 and TUD-Stadtmitte datasets. It should be noted that the above common database with different resolutions, density and velocity; however each parameter in the experiments is set to be the same value. It is known to all that the detection results will have an important effect on the final tracking performance, and to be fair the detected results of all video sequences are the same results.

There are six parameters needed to be set in the proposed tracking algorithm: α, β, κ, γ, λ, and μ. To solve the over-fitting problem in the process of manual optimization, a method where only one parameter is variable while other parameters are fixed is here utilized to test the effect of each parameter on tracking performance, and the optimum value of this variable parameter is selected as the proposed tracking algorithm achieves its best performance. After the experimental comparisons of tracking performance, the five optimum parameters β, κ, γ, λ, and μ for video sequences without occlusion are set to be 1, 0.05, 1, 0.5, and 0.25 respectively. These five optimum parameters for video sequences S2L1 and S3MF1 are set to be 1, 0.05, 1, 2, 0.5 respectively, and are 1, 0.1, 1, 0.5, 0.5 respectively for others video sequences with occlusion.

Feature selection is an open problem and might have a great impact on final tracking results. The feature vector here simply consists of color histogram, gradient histogram and correlation coefficient since the tracking performance comparison is here the focus issue.

A series of experiments are performed to compare the tracking performance using the following three methods: energy minimization-based method (EM)[1] formulates the multi-target tracking issue as a minimization of a continuous energy function issue; appearance model-based method (AM)[13] deals with the multi-target tracking issue by online learning of non-linear motion patterns and robust appearance models; the proposed method handles the multi-target tracking issue by minimizing a continuous energy function with discriminative appearance models.

The chosen metrics are adopted to evaluate the performance of both target detection and target tracking, including the following metrics: (1) Recall: The number of targets correctly detected divided by the number of ground truth targets; (2) Precision: The number of targets correctly detected divided by the number of targets detected using one method; (3) False Alarms Per Frame (FAF): The number of targets detected falsely in each frame; (4) Mostly Tracked Trajectories (MT): The number of trajectories which are successfully tracked for more than 80%; (5) Fragments (Frag): The number of interruptions for the same trajectory during the tracking process; (6) Id Switch (IDS): The number of trajectories whose labels change with other.

4.2   Performance Comparison

The performance comparison result of different target tracking methods is shown in table 1. It can be seen from table 1 that the proposed method achieves the best tracking performance in comparison with the other two methods.

Table 1. The performance comparison result of three different target tracking methods

Database	Recall	Precision	FAF	MT	PT	Frag	IDs
EM [1]	74.1	87.4	0.62	84.2	10.5	75	56
AM [13]	80.4	86.1	0.99	76.1	19.3	37	31
Ours	93.5	90.8	0.55	94.7	5.3	35	25

4.2.1   Examples of Experimental Comparison

The tracking results of PETS2009S3MF1-c1 video sequence using the appearance model-based method, the minimum energy method, and the proposed method are illustrated in figure 3 respectively. It can be seen from the 43th frame in figure 3 (a) and the 45th frame in (b) that the target in red clothing is not detected immediately whereas the target in black clothing entering after her is detected, which means that some targets are here undetected. Three targets entering into the tracking region successively are detected and tracked correctly until the 49th frame as shown in figure 3 (a) and (b). The above tracking results demonstrate that the mutual occlusion between targets can lead to the phenomenon of missed alarm for the appearance model-based method and the energy minimization-based method.

The target annotated with No.1 changes his movement direction in the 64th frame in figure 3 (a) and (b), which then leads to the failure detection in the following 65th and 66th frames. From the 67th frame, the original target annotated with No.1 is detected and tracked with a new label No.7. The tracking results show that the change of motion direction can lead to the phenomenon of false alarm for the appearance model-based method and the energy minimization-based method.

It can be seen from the 45th frames in figure 3 (c), the target in red clothing is not detected immediately and other two targets entering after her are not detected immediately either. From the 51th frame in figure 3 (c), these three targets are all correctly detected and tracked in order.

(a) Tracking results using appearance model-based method.

(b) Tracking results using the minimum energy-based method.

(c) Tracking results using the proposed method.

Fig. 2. Tracking results conducted on the tested PETS2009S2L1 video sequence

5   Conclusions

This paper proposes a novel method to deal with the multi-target tracking problem with continuous energy minimization and discriminative appearance models. Firstly, observation model, appearance model, exclusion model, dynamic model, trajectory persistence model and trajectory regulation model are adopted to construct an objective function of each tracking trajectory; then, the gradient descent method is adopted to obtain the number of and the status of each tracking target; finally, continuous energy minimization based intelligent extrapolation method is utilized to achieve the final continuous and smooth tracking trajectories. Experimental results on PETS 2009/2010 benchmark and TUD-Stadtmitte video database demonstrate that effectiveness and efficiency of the proposed method.

Acknowledgments. This work is supported by Postdoctoral Foundation of China under No. 2014M550297, Postdoctoral Foundation of Jiangsu Province under No. 1302087B, China Natural Science Fund under No. 61271232, Graduate Education Reform Research and Practice Program of Jiangsu Province under No. JGZZ13_041, Graduate Bilingual Teaching-Learning Pilot Program of Pattern Recognition and Intelligent Systems of Jiangsu Province.

References

[1] Andriyenko, A., Schindler, K.: Multi-Target Tracking by Continuous Energy Minimization. In: IEEE Conference on Computer Vision and Pattern Recognition, pp. 1265–1272 (2011)

[2] Zhao, T., Nevatia, R., Wu, B.: Segmentation and Tracking of Multiple Humans in Crowded Environments. IEEE Transactions on Pattern Analysis and Machine Intelligence 30(7), 1198–1211 (2008)

[3] Yang, J., Vela, P., Shi, Z., Teizer, J.: Probabilistic Multiple People Tracking Through Complex Situations. In: IEEE International Workshop on Performance Evaluation of Tracking and Surveillance, pp. 79–86 (2009)

[4] Dalal, N., Triggs, B.: Histogram of Oriented Gradients for Human Detection. In: IEEE Conference on Computer Vision and Pattern Recognition, pp. 886–893 (2005)

[5] Reid, D.: An Algorithm for Tracking Multiple Targets. IEEE Transactions on Automatic Control 24(6), 843–854 (1979)

[6] Shalom, Y., Fortmann, T., Scheffe, M.: Joint Probabilistic Data Association for Multiple Targets in Clutter. In: IEEE Conference on Information Sciences and Systems, pp. 25–35 (1980)

[7] Perera, A., Srinivas, C., Hoogs, A., et al.: Multi-Object Tracking Through Simultaneous Long Occlusions and Split-Merge Conditions. In: IEEE Conference on Computer Vision and Pattern Recognition, pp. 666–673 (2006)

[8] Huang, C., Wu, B., Nevatia, R.: Robust Object Tracking By Hierarchical Association of Detection Responses. In: Forsyth, D., Torr, P., Zisserman, A. (eds.) ECCV 2008, Part II. LNCS, vol. 5303, pp. 788–801. Springer, Heidelberg (2008)

[9] Zhang, L., Li, Y., Nevatia, R.: Global data Association for Multi-Object Tracking using Network Flows. In: IEEE Conference on Computer Vision and Pattern Recognition, pp. 1–8 (2008)

[10] Brendel, W., Amer, M., Todorovic, S.: Multiobject Tracking as Maximum-Weight Independent set. In: IEEE Conference on Computer Vision and Pattern Recognition, pp. 1273–1280 (2011)

[11] Berclaz, J., Fleuret, F., Fua, P.: Multiple object Tracking using Flow Linear Programming. In: IEEE International Workshop on Performance Evaluation of Tracking and Surveillance, pp. 1–8 (2009)

[12] Kuo, C., Nevatia, R.: How does person identity recognition help multi-person tracking? In: IEEE Conference on Computer Vision and Pattern Recognition, pp. 1217–1224 (2011)

[13] Yang, B., Nevatia, R.: Multi-Target Tracking by Online Learning of Non-Linear Motion Patterns and Robust Appearance Models. In: IEEE Conference on Computer Vision and Pattern Recognition, pp. 1918–1925 (1925)

Author Index